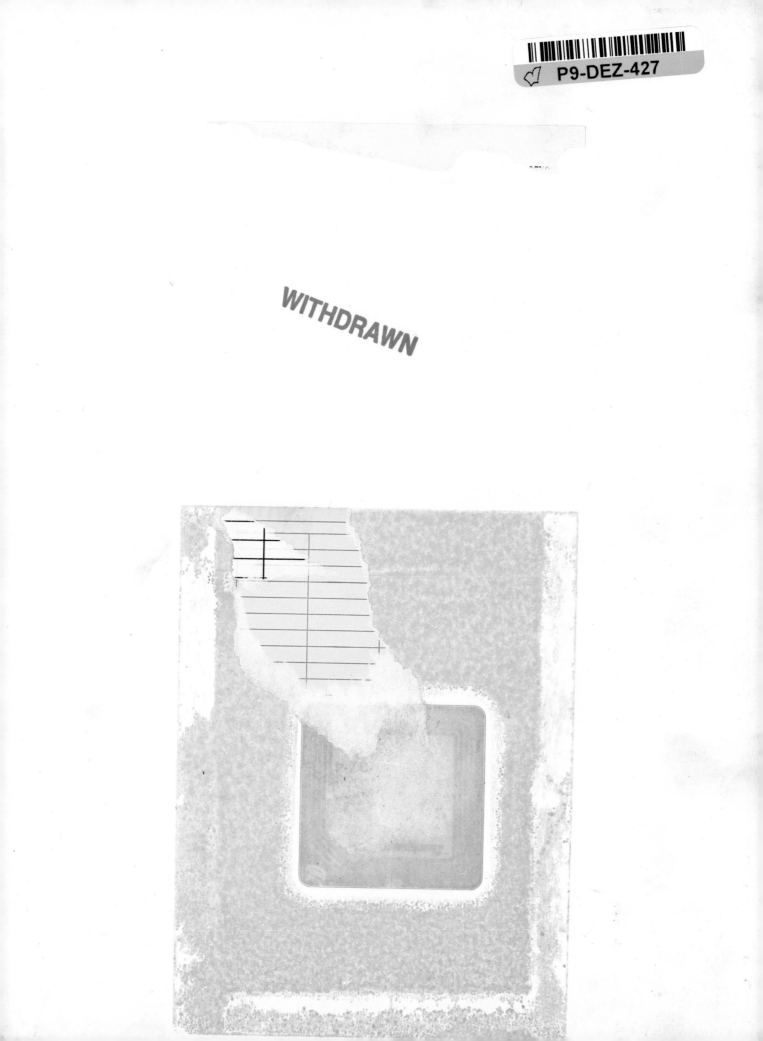

THE
CIVIL WAR
AND
RECONSTRUCTION

AN EYEWITNESS HISTORY

THE
CIVIL WAR
AND
RECONSTRUCTION

AN EYEWITNESS HISTORY

JOE H. KIRCHBERGER

■ Facts On File
New York • Oxford

The Civil War and Reconstruction: An Eyewitness History

Copyright © 1991 by Joe H. Kirchberger

Facts On File, Inc.
460 Park Avenue South
New York NY 10016
USA

Facts On File Limited
Collins Street
Oxford OX4 1XJ
United Kingdom

Library of Congress Cataloging-in-Publication Data
Kirchberger, Joe H.
  The Civil War and reconstruction : an eyewitness history / Joe Kirchberger.
     p. cm.—(The Eyewitness history series)
  Includes bibliographical references and index.
  Summary: Portrays the American Civil War and its aftermath through such primary sources as memoirs, diaries, letters, contemporary journalism, and official documents.
  ISBN 0-8160-2171-6
  1. United States—History—Civil War, 1861–1865—Personal narratives. 2. United States—History—Civil War, 1861–1865——Chronology. 3. United States—History—Civil War, 1861–1865——Sources. 4. Reconstruction—Sources. 5. Reconstruction——Chronology. [1. United States—History—Civil War, 1861–1865——Sources.]
E601.K569 1991   90-40852
973.7'02'02—dc20   CIP
                                      AC

A British CIP catalogue record for this book is available from the British Library.

Facts On File books are available at special discounts when purchased in bulk quantities for businesses, associations, institutions or sales promotions. Please call our Special Sales Department in New York at 212/683-2244 (dial 800/322-8755 except in NY, AK or HI) or in Oxford at 865/728399.

Jacket design by Keith Lovell
Composition by Maple-Vail Book Manufacturing Group
Manufactured by the Maple-Vail Book Manufacturing Group
Printed in the United States of America

10 9 8 7 6 5 4 3 2 1

This book is printed on acid-free paper.

Contents

The Eyewitness History Series

Historians have long recognized that to truly understand the past we must relive it. We can only see past eras and events clearly when we free our minds from the knowledge of what unfolded between then and now and permit ourselves to experience events with the fresh vision of a contemporary participant or observer.

To stimulate our powers of historical imagination we must begin by immersing ourselves in the documents of the period, so that we can view events as eyewitnesses. THE EYEWITNESS HISTORY SERIES offers readers and students the opportunity to exercise their historical imaginations by providing in a single volume a large collection of excerpts from what historians call "primary sources," the memoirs, diaries, letters, journalism and official documents of the period.

To give these historical raw materials a framework, each chapter begins with a brief summary of the "Historical Context" followed by a detailed "Chronicle of Events." However, the bulk of each chapter consists of a large selection of quotations from eyewitness accounts of the events of the time. These have been selected to give the reader the widest range of views possible. Each has a specific source in the Bibliography to facilitate further study. To further stimulate the reader's historical imagination, a selection of contemporary illustrations is included in each chapter. Modern maps have been included in an appendix for the convenience of readers.

Rather than interrupt the main text with lengthy official documents, we have included them in an appendix. Another appendix includes brief biographies of the major personalities referred to in the text.

EYEWITNESS HISTORIES are intended to encourage students and readers to discover the powers and the pleasures of historical imagination, while also providing them with comprehensive and self-contained works of reference to significant historical periods.

Preface

ITS PLACE IN AMERICAN HISTORY

The American Civil War has left a deeper impression on the American mind than any other event in history, with the possible exception of two much more recent ones, the world wars of the 20th century. It has been said that for every day since it ended, at least one book or article has been published about the Civil War, making it the most discussed episode in American history by a large margin. Every year, parades of blue and gray uniforms take place and speeches are made commemorating events of the Civil War, although five generations have passed. Many sayings, songs and images from this period are still alive today. For most Americans, men like Abraham Lincoln, Robert E. Lee, Ulysses S. Grant, Jefferson Davis, William Tecumseh Sherman, "Stonewall" Jackson, Philip Henry Sheridan and many others are more than just names.

The reasons for this are clear. Not only were the years between 1860 and 1865 the most dramatic of the whole century for America, they also showed the only real danger the United States has ever faced: the first, and last tension test of a comparatively young nation that, unlike most European nations, had organized itself only a short "four score and seven years ago." The war spread over the whole country and was fought not only along the Eastern seacoast, but in Pennsylvania, Kentucky, Tennessee, along the Mississippi River and even in the far Western desert. It left no man or woman unaffected. There were Union sympathizers in the South and Confederacy sympathizers in the North, but no one could remain indifferent. The war occupied everyone's mind for four long years, arousing emotions, enthusiasm and loyalty as well as hatred to an unprecedented pitch.

By comparison, in the war of the American Revolution, the colonies were not as fully committed to the cause of the war against Great Britain. It has been estimated that only about one-third of the colonists were in favor of independence, while the rest of the population was either loyal to the crown or just indifferent. Similarly, in the War of 1812, neither side displayed much enthusiasm. The Mexican War of 1846–47 and the Spanish–American War of 1898 were fought against an enemy considered inferior and, therefore, did not leave much of an impression. In World War I, American intervention certainly played a decisive role but came only during the last few months of a struggle that had already gone on for almost four years. Only World War II has brought forth a similar level of response in general interest and literature; yet it was fought in faraway places, and the United States was but one of several major participants. The subsequent wars in Korea and Vietnam were neither popular nor particularly successful.

In contrast, the Civil War was all-American, and perhaps its most significant characteristic is that the losses on both sides were staggering. More than 600,000 soldiers died on the battlefield or of disease.- These losses were greater than sustained in all other American wars combined, from the War of Independence to the Korean War, including both World Wars. The Civil War battle of Antietam, in September of 1862, incurred four times as many casualties as the landing on Normandy beaches on June 6, 1944. And while all previous wars had left American cities and the countryside more or less untouched, except for the burning of Washington, D.C. by the British in 1812, the Civil War devastated whole regions of the Southern states, particularly in Virginia and Georgia. The defeated South needed many years to rise again, and some of the damage done to its economy have been repaired only recently.

CHARACTERISTICS AND NOVELTIES

The conflict that started on April 12, 1861 with the bombardment of Fort Sumter and ended exactly four years later at Appomattox was quite different from any war fought before in Europe or America. Gunpowder and firearms had been introduced into warfare in the 14th century, and very little change had taken place in the use of arms for hundreds of years since. It has been observed that a soldier of the 15th or 16th century could have appeared during the Napoleonic wars and not have found any weapon he could not understand or operate. Weapons changed radically in the 1840s when the fruits of the Industrial Revolution were beginning to be applied to warfare. For instance, the effective range of firearms had been greatly extended. One explanation of the horrifying casualties of the Civil War is that generals, who belonged to an older generation, were using old military tactics of attack, although the range of rifles and artillery had greatly increased, rendering the attacking forces much more vulnerable than they had been before.

Even more important, railroads had been built and were used widely in the vast areas affected by the war. In 1850, only 9,000 miles of railway had existed in the United States, but by 1860 there were 30,620 miles, most of them in the North. The South had only 8,450 miles. Ohio had 2,900 miles of railway; Illinois, 2,867; New York, about 2,700. Virginia, the best equipped of the Southern states, had 1,770 miles, but the South had many roundabout rail connections. Many battles and skirmishes were fought for the control of vital railway connections, and some mass transports of troops were brilliantly accomplished by railroad.

For the first time in war, the telegraph was in full use, particularly in the North, where 15,000 miles of communication lines were established. The South was handicapped by a shortage of equipment and operators.

The great rivers also played an important role in the war. The North not only gained control of the Mississippi through elaborate attacks but also the great rivers in Virginia: the Potomac, Rappahannock, York and James, as well as the Cumberland, the Tennessee and many other rivers—all of which saw considerable military action. Even the Red River, west of the Mississippi, became the scene of a major campaign. Unprecedented use of gunboats and other military vessels was made, and, though ironclads had been built before by Britain and France, the first battle between them took place in the famous encounter of the *Monitor* and the *Merrimac/Virginia* outside of Norfolk Harbor in March 1862.

The great blockade of the Southern coastline organized by the Northern navy was not the first large-scale blockade—that was introduced by Napoleon against the British—but the first one executed by a navy. Observation balloons were used, though not very effectively, for the first time; also, to some extent, trenches and wire entanglements.

Cavalry was still used in the Civil War but was on the decline. It had been important in the Crimean War of 1854–55 (the charge of the Light Brigade) and was still to play a role in the Franco–Prussian War of 1870–71, but the greater accuracy and range of the infantry weapons made its use much more precarious. In the beginning of the Civil War, Union foot soldiers were saying derisively that they had never seen a dead cavalry man—because the cavalry was usually withdrawn before fighting began in earnest. But that changed in the course of the war, when Southern cavalry raids, especially under Jeb Stuart, Nathan Bedford Forrest and others, became extremely annoying and dangerous for the Northern armies.

In many ways, the Civil War stands on the border between old and modern warfare. In spite of all the new weaponry and technology introduced, it was still fought with chivalry on both sides and produced romantic heroes like Robert E. Lee, "Stonewall" Jackson and "Unconditional Surrender" Grant as well as an innumerable number of folksy and nostalgic songs on both sides. Although the war was much more horrible and bloodier than anyone had foreseen, it should not be forgotten that many of the generals opposing each other had fought side by side in the Mexican War, only 15 years before and that former Confederate generals wore Federal blue in the Spanish–American War. At Grant's funeral, several former Confederate generals attended, and joint reunions of Union and Confederate veterans occurred well into the 20th century, notably at Gettysburg.

EVALUATION

All those affected by the war, and that meant almost the entire population of the United States and its territories, were convinced that right, and God, were on their side and that their opponents were either irresponsible rebels or brutal conquerors and tyrants. This explains why the war, even long after its cessation, was seen in entirely different lights, not only by the average citizen from North or South, but also by professional historians striving for objectivity. For a long time, it was even called by many different names: in the North, the War of Rebellion, or the War of Secession; in the South, the War Between the States, or the War of Southern Independence.

It is instructive to take a short look at the way historians have dealt with the questions of the causes of the war, its evaluation and the guilt on either side, over the years after 1865.

During the first period, lasting about to the turn of the century, history was written by men who had seen the war with their own eyes. They all subscribed to what Howard K. Beale has called the "devil theory" of history and saw the cause of the war in a conspiracy of wicked or selfish men. Southerners described an aggressive North bent on destroying the South and its time-honored institutions. They pointed at the constant propaganda of the abolitionists, their acts of violence and attempts to stir up slave insurrections and to help fugitive slaves. Violence on the side of the South was excused as mere reaction against the antislavery societies, the speeches and writings of antislavery leaders like John Quincy Adams, Joshua Giddings, Charles Sumner and William Lloyd Garrison. The Southern apologists emphasized the activities of the New England Emigrant Society, John Brown's violence in Kansas and at Harper's Ferry, the boycott of the stricter Fugitive

Law enacted in 1850, the North's refusal to admit Kansas under the so-called Lecompton, proslavery constitution, the North's rejection of the Dred Scott decision, the unfairness of the picture that Harriet Beecher Stowe's book *Uncle Tom's Cabin* painted of the slavery practiced in the South and many other circumstances, which all culminated in the program of the Republican Party and Lincoln's election as president. They portrayed the South as a peace- and Union-loving entity that only wanted to be left alone under a Constitution repeatedly violated by the North, in particular by the "black" Republicans.

The Northern school of this period depicted a conspiracy of slaveholders aiming to rule the North and force the nation to accept slavery and protect it not only in the old states of the South but also in newly acquired territories. They pointed at the "gag" rule by which Congress for more than seven years refused to hear antislavery petitions, at the attempts to censure former President John Quincy Adams because of his courageous antislavery speeches, at the suppression of discussions of slavery in the South, at the Southern plot to add Texas and even tropical possessions such as Cuba to the United States in order to extend slavery, at the undermining of the Missouri Compromise by Douglas's Kansas–Nebraska Act and at Southern violence in Kansas. They explained the Dred Scott decision of the Supreme Court as a conspiracy instigated by the slaveholders and President Buchanan and accused Southern leaders of violence in Congress and of making heroes of the chief brutal perpetrators such as Preston Smith Brooks, and emphasized the "slavocracy's" determination to rule or ruin, to secede rather than compromise. As late as 1886, Theodore Roosevelt mentioned the "reckless ambition" of the Southern leaders and compared Jefferson Davis to Benedict Arnold, in fact, calling him a traitor as late as 1904.

The second generation of historians was less partisan and tried to see the story of both sides, though they still had a better understanding of what their own parents had stood for than of their enemies. The expressions "rebel" and "black Republican" were dropped. The war was no longer seen as a conspiracy and was no longer called "War Between the States" or "War of the Rebellion." Northerners began to appreciate the personalities of Robert E. Lee, Jefferson Davis and Alexander Hamilton Stephens and the South acknowledged the stature of Abraham Lincoln. The great majority of historians of the third generation, writing after World War I, no longer blamed the outbreak of the war on one side or the other and sought other approaches to explain the catastrophe. Relapses occurred however. Frank L. Owsley described the Northern attacks on slavery as worse than Goebbels's or Stalin's propaganda—in 1941.

The first generation of Southern writers had usually played down the part the controversy over slavery played in the outbreak of the conflict. Both Alexander H. Stephens and Jefferson Davis had denied that slavery was the real cause of the war but had explained it as a contest over two kinds of government: The Republicans wanted a centralized regime and violated constitutional guarantees to achieve their goal, while the Southerners saw in the states' rights the governing principle of the Constitution. Northern writers emphasized the moral issue of slavery to explain the sectional clash, seeing the war as the "irrepressible conflict" between the principle of freedom and equality as expressed not only in the Constitution but also in the Declaration of Independence. The abolitionists were shown as noble crusaders, and John W. Burgess undertook an elaborate refutation of Davis's and Stephens's constitutional theories. Historians writing after World War I saw the slavery controversy as a rivalry of political systems, of political philosophy or as a clash of economic interest and rival labor systems. They also declared that westward expansion played a decisive role by rendering a balance between the free and the slave states impossible, some even stating that the conflict started as early as the first westward expansion through the Louisiana Purchase of 1803 and that all later agreements between North and South such as the Missouri Compromise of 1820, the Compromise of 1850 and the Kansas–Nebraska Act of 1854 could at best delay, but not avoid, the ultimate conflict.

In addition, many single factors about the origins of the war were now brought into the debate: Calhoun's uncompromising attitude, Douglas's ambitious schemes, Buchanan's ineptitude and Lincoln's thesis of the "house divided"—which actually had not differed so much from what Calhoun had said much earlier, even though with the opposite outcome in mind (that in the long run, the Union would have to be either all free or all slave). While Southern insistence on the continuation of slavery is sometimes explained as necessitated by its economic structure and social system, other writers think that fear of a general slave revolt was the main underlying motive, and, more generally, the inability to deal with four million freed slaves. Secession was the only way to keep the black population "in the proper place." It was a brave attempt to attain the freedom that would have been denied the Southern states within the Union. Other writers have stated that the conflict arose out of the Southern dilemma that slavery had no other place to go, since none of the territories acquired in the 1840s, except for Texas, was suited for slavery. The earlier alliance between Southern and Northwestern farmers had come to nought when the latter were won over to the Republican camp by promises of free land.

Post-World War I history writers also speculated that the war might have been prevented if Lincoln could have entered the White House right after his election, instead of four months later, by which time seven states had already seceded. Most historians answered this question with "No," and, in fact, the reputation of the "inept" incumbent president during this time, Buchanan, has recently risen again, as has that of Calhoun, who, long regarded by Northern writers as a one-sided fanatic, is now widely recognized as a true patriot who tried to save the Union by protecting the Southern minority. Douglas, too, has been defended against accusations of excessive personal ambition and is credited with great foresight that took into consideration not just the North–South antagonism but also the future role of the West.

Racism, too, had its day in explaining the war but not in the antiblack sense. As early as 1861, George Fitzhugh claimed that the hostility between North and South was not so much abolitionism, but the fact that the Cavaliers, Huguenots and Jacobites had settled in the South; thus Southerners were the sons of the ancient Romans and the noble Normans. The North, in contrast, had been settled by Puritans, descendants of inferior Saxon serfs. In 1923, Hamilton J. Eckenrode saw the war as "a struggle between that part of the Nordic race which was prepared to renounce its tradition of mastery for equality, modernism and material comfort, and that part of the race [the South] which was resolved, despite modernity, to remain true to its ruling instincts." Others have linked the Northern attitude to the British Tories, or the large influx of foreign immigrants into the North, while defenders of the North have characterized the Southern attitude as too sensitive to criticism, of feeling insecure, inferior, and jealous.

A question that has come up time and time again is why the Southern states wanted to withdraw from the Union and why they thought they could succeed. One explanation that has been offered is that they believed the North would be unwilling to fight or be weak in warfare, particularly since Northern manpower would be hamstrung by military personnel requirements, while in the South, the blacks did all the work, leaving the white men free to fight. Also, they expected aid from Europe, which depended on Southern cotton. Others argue that the South was merely bluffing to get concessions and that their bluff was called in 1860.

At any rate, war had not broken out when Abraham Lincoln became president. Most writers agree that what made open hostilities inevitable was the Southern attack on Fort Sumter (April 12, 1861). Could Lincoln have avoided this attack and was his plan to provision the fort a deliberate provocation of the Southern states—forcing them to attack and thus causing public opinion in the North to swing behind the government? Or was his policy to attempt to prevent hostilities?

PROBLEMS OF CAUSES AND INEVITABILITY

This leads to the general question about the causes of the war. Practically all historians who doubt its inevitability wrote only after World War I, possibly because of the feeling of futility and disillusionment that followed that war. Historians like Avery O. Craven and James G. Randall, taking into account all the vast economic, social, cultural and moral differences between North and South, nevertheless concluded that psychological factors, not actual issues, were responsible for the outbreak of hostilities. Mutual misunderstanding and a lack of proper intercommunication as well as the activity of fanatics on both sides created an overheated atmosphere. Slavery was used as a point of attack and defense, covering up for many other vital disagreements. But slavery, a cumbersome and wasteful system, would, according to this view, have disappeared within a generation without "one of the most cruel and needless of wars." That is why historians like James G. Randall distinguish between the causes of conflict and the causes of war, with one not necessarily leading to the other, and speak of the "blundering generation," similar to the way Lloyd George and others blamed the political leaders of 1914 for the outbreak of World War I. Since World War II, on the other hand, the outbreak of which is clearly connected with the leading personalities of its time, the tendency to analyze the role of leadership in bringing about the Civil War has grown again.

A simple, unequivocal answer to the question of what caused the conflict is obviously not possible. After 130 years of research and analysis, we can only say that none of the earlier attempts to find a clear-cut answer has lead to satisfactory results: Not the moral issue of slavery, nor the conflict of constitutional principles, or the contrast between the agrarian, aristocratic society of the South and the increasingly industrialized democratic structure of the North, or any of the other proposed reasons, let alone any individuals of the period are solely responsible, although most of them certainly contributed to the outbreak of hostilities.

Equally futile is the question about the inevitability of the war. While at first glance, most of the events and developments of the preceding years seem to lead surely to the ultimate conflict, one could just as well, as Howard K. Beale has suggested, compile an equally impressive list of likenesses between North and South and reasons why war could not possibly occur between them. The law of cause and effect applies to history only in a very limited way: Issues, developments and events will never be more than potential causes for a certain effect, which will only come to pass when they and many other circumstances coincide at a certain time. Nothing in history is inevitable—until it happens. When it does happen, it is impossible for us to imagine it undone. The Civil War broke out. To ask whether it would not have happened had there been leaders other than Lincoln and Seward, Davis and Douglas at the time, if Fort Sumter had been sufficiently provisioned, etc., is, unfortunately, futile. It is, as Kenneth Stampp has said, a metaphysical, not a historical, question.

EFFECT ON THE NATION

To define the effect the great upheaval had on the nation may be a little easier. Although the South experienced a great amount of despair, hatred and bitterness caused not only by the defeat but also by the subsequent suppression and exploitation by Northerners during the Reconstruction era, it is safe to say that, in the long run, the terrifying, lasting experience of the war unified the country and made one nation out of it. The "Union" had been constantly referred to in pre-war days, but it was more an idea or ideal than a reality. Some decades after the war, the word was hardly used any more because the union was taken for granted and no longer under discussion. The war had removed the one great obstacle between the states, slavery, and opened the way to the Pacific. Manpower, energies and capital released by the outcome of the war flowed into the new frontier in the West. The first transcontinental railroad was completed in 1868 and introduced a new age of prosperity and rapid growth. While resentment and impoverishment continued in the South, the results of the defeat were accepted implicity, and no serious attempt was ever made to reverse the outcome.

Only the people for whom, to a large degree, the war had been fought, the blacks, did not profit from it in the manner they could expect. After a brief period in Reconstruction days, when they acquired some political power and representation in Congress, white supremacy reestablished itself in the South. The blacks were free—but they remained second-class citizens for a long time to come.

1. The Developing Conflict: From the Missouri Compromise to Lincoln's Election: 1820–1860

THE HISTORICAL CONTEXT

The history of the United States in its first few decades of existence was tied up, to a large extent, with European history, in particular the history of England and France and their relation to one another.

The conflict between these two powers encompasses a period of no less than 60 years, starting with their first confrontation in 1755 over their respective possessions on the American continent and ending only with Napoleon's defeat in 1815. During this time, the American colonies had achieved, with French help, their independence from Britain, had acquired from France the huge territory west of the Mississippi and fought a second war with Britain, which ended almost simultaneously with the Napoleonic Wars.

From this time on, and throughout the whole 19th century, outside pressure, which would serve to hold the states together, did not exist. There was no conceivable foreign enemy from whom an invasion of the North American continent could have been forthcoming; the relations with Britain, victorious in Europe, became friendly, and the mere existence of the British navy guaranteed the security of the United States.

An era of peaceful coexistence within the Union and of expansion into the Western lands followed. A new national bank and the U. S. Patent

Office were established in 1816, the Erie Canal built from 1817–25 and the tenure of President James Monroe became known as one of "good feeling." With the acquisition of Florida from Spain in 1819, the entire Eastern and Southern coast up to the Sabine River, separating Louisiana from Texas, now belonged to the U. S. New states were added to the Union in rapid succession: Indiana in 1816; Mississippi in 1817; Illinois in 1818; Maine in 1820; and Missouri in 1821. The Monroe Doctrine of 1823, which declared that the American continents were henceforth not to be considered as subjects for colonization by any European power, fortified the feeling of independence and security in the U. S.

Monroe was the last president belonging to the Revolutionary generation. With its passing, the differences and dissensions within the nation became more and more apparent. Major controversies developed around the following questions and, in most of the controversies, the Northern states were on one side, the Southern states on the other:

1.   **Federal versus State Authority:** Could the president or a majority in Congress force a state to accept laws that went against its interest, thereby threatening the traditional independence of the individual states? The doctrine that the states were independent of one another and of the federal government, which had been pronounced by Kentucky and Virginia as early as 1798, was, since the 1820s, strongly supported by all Southern states, as a protection against too much power in the hands of the central government. Its most forceful and eloquent promoter was John C. Calhoun of South Carolina, while Daniel Webster of Massachusetts became the prominent spokesman for the supremacy of the union; he expressed the opinion of most Northerners. This controversy about state sovereignty, which played a decisive role in all political problems in which North and South had diverging viewpoints, surfaced again when the state of Georgia, contrary to the treaties concluded by the United States, expelled Creek and Cherokee Indians from its territory.

2.   **Protective Tariff:** The South, mostly agrarian, depended on inexpensive machinery imported from Europe, while in the North the young agrarian industry wished to be protected from European, in particular British, competition. The tariffs, introduced in 1824, were fiercely opposed by the Southern states, which were, however, outvoted in Congress. When the tariffs were further extended and increased in 1828 (the so-called tariff of abomination), the state of South Carolina declared that the tariffs had become too oppressive to be borne, and a state conven-

tion in November of 1832 passed an ordinance pronouncing the tariffs null and void for its territory and threatening to withdraw from the Union should the Union try to enforce the tariffs. This threat of "nullification" was immediately met by President Andrew Jackson, who announced that in case of resistance, the whole force of the Union would be used against South Carolina. An open break was finally avoided when Henry Clay, leader of the protectionists, introduced a compromise with a modified tariff that was accepted by the South. Here, as well in the case of Georgia versus the Creek and Cherokee Indians, the doctrine of state sovereignty was not put to the final test. In the case of Georgia, the state finally won out, partly because President Jackson, who had been fighting Indians all his life, did not have great sympathies for them.

3. **The Problem of a United States Bank versus State Banks:** Again, most Southerners preferred their local banks, and here they had the support of Andrew Jackson. As the champion of the common people against privileged interests, Jackson felt the United States Bank, chartered in 1816, had become too powerful and had interfered with local banks. He managed to break it up in 1836. As a result, state banks began to flourish everywhere, particularly in the Mississippi Valley, and a fluctuating paper currency ensued that favored Southwestern and Northwestern farmers, who were often in debt for their land and equipment, and worked against the Eastern seaboard establishment.

4. **The Question of Whether Congress Should Engage in Building National Roads to Help Settlements in the West:** Jackson and his followers held that the central government had no constitutional right to engage in any kind of business—contrary to the ideas of Thomas Jefferson, in all other respects the great paragon of the Jacksonians. Federal action for internal improvement thus diminished in Jacksonian times but became vigorous again when railroads proved to be a success and the first plans for a transcontinental railway were discussed with two routes under consideration where, again, North stood against South.

5. **The Problem of Free Land in the West versus Its Sale for Revenue Purposes:** The policy of Congress had been to sell the land of the Western territories to settlers in small lots—or in large lots to speculators—first for $2.00, then for $1.25 per acre. This provided a substantial revenue for the federal treasury. Modest as this price seems to us now, many poor farmers or city workers who wanted to settle in the West found raising such sums difficult. Voices asking for a sharp reduction of the price and finally in favor of giving land away free in lots of 160 acres grew louder. Planters of the South opposed this movement, fearing that it would establish a supremacy of the slave-free states, par-

ticularly as more land was available in the Northwest than in the Southwest. The question was only settled in the midst of the Civil War, since President Buchanan had vetoed a Homestead Bill in 1860.

The great political parties of the time, the Democrats and the Whigs, were not entirely clear on any of the above issues. The old parties, the Federalists (Alexander Hamilton, John Adams) and the Democratic Republicans (Jefferson, James Madison, Monroe) had been reshaped by the personality of Andrew Jackson, the first non-Europe oriented, frontier-type president who introduced the "spoils system" and stood for the rights of the common man versus big capital and also against interference by the government. From this time on, the Democrats stood, more or less, for a narrow interpretation of the Constitution as far as dealings of the federal government with the states and with individuals were concerned. The other new party, the Whigs, grew from the National–Republican party, a coalition of John Quincy Adams and Henry Clay against Andrew Jackson. They began as a loose combination of Jackson opponents, and while they were represented by many great statesmen and orators, such as Daniel Webster, Henry Clay and Edward Everett, they managed to win the presidency only twice between 1828 and 1860, with the Harrison–Tyler and Taylor–Fillmore administrations. They were united in the opposition to Jackson's high-handed, "dictatorial" methods, and generally stood for wider activity of the federal government, even in matters not specifically mentioned in the Constitution.

On the main problem of the decades preceding the Civil War, that of slavery, they were as divided as the Democrats.

Slavery had existed in the American colonies since the first blacks were brought to Virginia in 1619. By 1770, about one-sixth of the entire population of the colonies consisted of blacks. But in the North, climate, soil and the kind of agriculture made large-scale slavery rather unprofitable. At the end of the colonial era at least 90% of the people lived on the land, with the North producing wheat and corn; the South, tobacco, rice, sugar, indigo and, a little later, vast quantities of cotton. The South depended more and more on slave labor—around 1783, no less than two-thirds of the inhabitants of South Carolina were blacks. Still, 10 of the original 13 states forbade the importation of slaves in their constitutions—the exceptions were South Carolina, North Carolina and Georgia. At the time of the first U. S. census, in 1790, the nine Northern states showed only 67,000 blacks—of which 27,000 were free—out of a population of 1,968,000. The eight Southern

Henry Clay.

states had 657,000 slaves (and 32,450 free blacks) out of a total of 1,961,000 people.

The Northwest Ordinance of 1787 forbade slavery in the Northwest territory recently ceded by Britain—north of the Ohio River and east of the Mississippi. The U. S. Constitution prohibited slave trade after January 1, 1808, and slavery began to die out in the North and to dwindle slowly in the South.

Yet, with the introduction of the cotton gin, invented by Eli Whitney in 1793, the South geared into large-scale cotton production and required an ever-increasing number of slaves, particularly since now Southern lands had become available all the way to the Mississippi and the Sabine River.

The balance between North and South in regard to slavery that existed at the time of the Constitution continued to exist, at least on the surface, until 1820. Of the 22 states in the Union in 1819, 11 were slave states and 11 committed to freedom. But now the Missouri territory had gained sufficient population to be admitted into the Union as a state. As her settlers had mostly come from the South, Missouri was expected to become a slave state, as had happened in Alabama in 1819. Congress was sharply divided on this issue and a long, bitter debate followed, until a compromise was achieved: Missouri was admitted as a slave state, but Maine, certainly a free one, was to be admitted also, preserving the balance and with the proviso that in the future the territory acquired through the Louisiana Purchase (west of the Mississippi), slavery north of the southern boundary of Missouri (latitude 36°, 30') would be prohibited. This formula, for which Henry Clay, speaker of the House, was given most of the credit (while actually Senator Jesse B. Thomas of Illinois was far more responsible for it) held until 1854, in spite of the growing imbalance between slave and free states.

The number of slaves increased constantly, and, by 1830, more than two million were in the United States, almost all of them in the South.

The population difference between North and South had also changed drastically during this time. While the South stayed with large plantation-type agriculture, the North industrialized and expanded rapidly into the Western territories. By 1830, one million more lived in the free states than in the slave states, and by 1840 the difference was almost two million. The South had reason to be worried: The tariff legislation had shown that the North could outvote the South in the House of Representatives; internationally the institution of slavery was disappearing fast. The new states of South America, which had fought for their independence against Spain in the 1820s, abolished slavery immediately—Mexico, the last one, in 1829. In the British empire, slavery was finally stopped by the Abolition Act of 1833, and in the United States, propaganda against the institution on moral grounds, which had existed almost from the beginning, became stronger and louder.

Some antislavery sentiment already existed during the American Revolution. The Quakers, for example, had always opposed any kind of slavery or servitude. Now, the appearance of the abolitionist movement—William Lloyd Garrison, whose *Liberator* began to appear in 1831, Lydia Maria Child and many others who condemned slavery as inhuman and unworthy of a genuine democracy—made the Southern slaveowners, whose existence depended on slave labor, feel threatened from within and without.

The abolitionists met with violent resistance, both in the North and in the South. But they were never silenced, and the prosecutions suffered by Garrison, Elijah Parish Lovejoy and others actually created martyrs and furthered their cause. In 1836, the House of Representatives was deluged by thousands of antislavery petitions, which in particular demanded the abolition of slavery in the District of Columbia. Consequently, Southerners, with the help of Northern Democrats, passed a "gag rule," preventing debate on antislavery proposals in

William Lloyd Garrison, influential abolitionist.

House. Former President John Quincy Adams, now a representative from Massachusetts, fought vigorously against these rules, which were repealed in 1844.

All in all, in spite of constant friction, the balance between North and South was preserved in the late 1830s and early 1840s. When, in 1836, Arkansas was admitted to the Union as a slave state, Michigan followed the next year as a free one, and the same process took place when slaveholding Florida became a state in 1845, with free Iowa following in 1846. One constant source of mutual irritation, however, was the situation of fugitive slaves. The Constitution had given slaveholders the right to recover slaves if they escaped to another, presumably Northern, state. But the activity of the abolitionists and the increasing hostility of the people in the North made such recovery more and more difficult. When, in 1842, the U. S. Supreme Court declared a Pennsylvania state law that forbade the seizure of fugitive slaves unconstitutional, there was indignation in the North. The enforcement of these laws remained lax, however, and a regular "underground railroad" system was developed by white and free black abolitionists in the North to help fugitives escape into safe Northern states or Canada. Many Northern statesmen, such as William H. Seward of New York and Charles Sumner of Massachusetts, argued eloquently that slavery was morally wrong and ought to be abolished.

Meanwhile, the general attitude of Southerners had also stiffened. While most of the early statesmen from Virginia, like Washington and Jefferson, had deplored the system, people now accepted it as right and desirable. The inferiority of the black race was derived from the Bible (the "graceless sons of Ham"). As the number of blacks increased, the fear of uprisings, such as had been attempted by Nat Turner and others, grew and, with it, the resentment of the support and sympathy the slaves received in the Northern states. More and more, the Southerners, accepting Calhoun's doctrine, saw themselves as one social unit, and, with him, insisted that the property of slave-owners was protected by the Constitution throughout the Union.

In spite of the cotton boom, slavery was not enriching the South. The slaves were kept ignorant and received no reward for their labor, and therefore, quite naturally, worked as little as they could, having nothing to gain by industry. There was waste everywhere, and the economy, which was concentrated in cotton, rice, tobacco and sugar had become stagnant. Meanwhile, the Northern states engaged in a great variety of enterprises and expanded rapidly, both in population and in territory. The North also found a great market for its goods in the Southern states, so the industry bosses and prominent bankers were interested in maintaining peace and the status quo.

The only way that the Southern slave states could hope to keep abreast with the Northwestern expansion of the free states was to make Texas a part of the United States and reintroduce slavery there. Texas was part of Mexico and had abolished slavery, but since the 1830s at least 20,000 American farmers, planters and traders lived there.

Presidents John Quincy Adams and Andrew Jackson had attempted to buy Texas from Mexico, but Mexico refused to sell. Then, in 1835, when Mexico tried to stem the tide of American emigration, the Americans, under General Sam Houston, declared their independence from Mexico, and Houston's forces defeated the Mexican General Santa Ana. Texas was now an independent country and applied for admission to the United States, but President Jackson and his successor, Martin Van Buren, stalled, and the Whigs, under Webster and Clay, opposed the annexation because it meant war with Mexico and a great strengthening of the slave states. President Tyler, who had split with the Whig party, concluded a treaty of annexation with Texas, only to see it rejected by the Senate. Democrat James Knox Polk, who favored annexation, defeated Henry Clay in the presidential campaign of 1844, and thereafter Texas was annexed by resolution of Congress. War with Mexico became inevitable and broke out in 1846 and soon extended into the huge possessions Mexico held in the West up to the Pacific Ocean. U. S. General Zachary Taylor moved against Monterey, and General Winfield Scott marched from Vera Cruz up to Mexico City, which surrendered in September of 1846. Simultaneously, Colonel Kearney led an expedition into New Mexico to Santa Fe and took possession of the country, declaring it a territory of the Union. Also, Captain John C. Frémont, who was on an exploring expedition in California in anticipation of any British moves in this territory, expelled the Mexican soldiers and took Monterey, California. A movement for an independent California, with a bear flag, came to a quick end when Frémont and Commodore John Sloat raised the U. S. flag over Monterey and proclaimed the annexation of California by the U. S. Californians held a convention in 1849, drafting a constitution that prohibited slavery and demanded statehood. Its population had swelled in the meantime through the influx of about 100,000 immigrants because of the discovery of gold in the Sacramento Valley.

With the huge territories acquired by the Union within a few years, the question of how to settle the slavery question became crucial. Texas was to be a slave state, California a free one, and the new Oregon territories were never seriously considered for slavery. But a bitter controversy developed over the question of what should be arranged for the other territories acquired from Mexico. The Wilmot Proviso of 1846–47 (named for a Democratic congressman from Pennsylvania), which would have prohibited any slavery in the lands acquired in the Mexican War, crystallized the conflict between North and South. After a heated debate it was defeated in Congress. In the 1848 presidential election, the Proviso was ignored by both the Democratic and the Whig parties, but it was adopted by a new party, the Free-Soilers, led by former President Martin Van Buren. In the election, the considerable Free-Soil vote helped to elect Whig candidate Zachary Taylor, hero of the Mexican War, but the slavery question remained unsolved.

Once again, a compromise was proposed and carried through by Henry Clay, who at the age of 73 came out of retirement to help overcome the controversy that threatened to split the Union. President Taylor favored admission of California and New Mexico as free states and was strongly supported by Senator William Seward of New York. John C. Calhoun and many other Southerners, in particular Jefferson Davis of Mississippi, insisted that the South should be given guarantees of equal position in the territories, protection against the abolitionists and the proper execution of the fugitive laws. The omnibus bill proposed by Clay and supported by Stephen A. Douglas of Illinois provided: the admission of California as a free state; the organization of New Mexico and the Utah territories without any mention of slavery (in that the territories themselves were supposed to determine

John C. Calhoun of South Carolina.

their status by the time they were ready to be admitted as states—a formula that became known as the principle of "Popular Sovereignty"); the prohibition of slave trade in the district of Columbia; a more stringent fugitive law; and the settlement of the contested Texas boundaries. The plan was bitterly opposed by fanatics on both sides. But Daniel Webster's speech of March 7, 1850—which made him a traitor to the antislavery cause in the eyes of many of his followers—and the death of President Taylor, who was followed by the more conservative Millard Fillmore, helped finally pass the bill in September of 1850. The passage was hailed by many as the ultimate solution to the slavery question and did provide a relative calm for about three and one-half years.

But the truce was to be of short duration. Shortly after it had been concluded, its two moderate authors, Clay and Webster, died in 1852. Calhoun had also died, but his successors in the representation of the South were no less radical and unbending. For a long time the slavery issue had been discussed mainly in Congress and in the hundreds of newspapers that appeared all over the country. It was now, all of a sudden, debated in thousands of households, in the North as well as in the South, because of one book that, shortly after its appearance in 1851, was more widely read throughout the world than any other: Harriet Beecher Stowe's *Uncle Tom's Cabin.* Although hardly a literary masterpiece, the book vividly described the conditions of slavery in the South, the misery of the slaves and the cruelty of the slaveowners.

Stephen Douglas, the "little giant."

Read by hundreds of thousands of Americans, it did more to arouse sympathies for the enslaved than any other single factor. In the South, the book was decried as unfair, one-sided and essentially incorrect. In the North, the image of the villain Simon Legree became the prototype of the typical Southern slavemaster. The South began to see a wild abolitionist in every Northerner.

Still, the peace achieved by the 1850 compromise could have continued under the Democrats after the victory of their presidential candidate, Franklin Pierce, in the 1852 election. In retrospect, it seems that the issue of slavery in the new territories may have subsided slowly had it been left alone. But Stephen A. Douglas, Democratic senator from Illinois, proposed a new settlement for the Northwest territories, which has been called the most fateful legislation in all American history, the so-called Kansas–Nebraska Act, by which all questions of slavery were to be left to the residents of the new territory as it had been arranged for New Mexico and Utah. By this expansion of the principle of Popular Sovereignty (or "squatter sovereignty," as it was called by its opponents), Douglas hoped to reunite the badly split Southern and Northern wings of the Democratic Party and open the way for a transcontinental railway through the Northern territories. But the acceptance of the Act in 1854 had a number of unforeseen results. Since the territory involved lay north of latitude 36° 30', the old Missouri Compromise of 1820 was thereby definitely repealed—though some claimed that this had been done already by the Compromise of 1850. It destroyed the three-year truce, split the Democratic Party worse than ever, meant practically the end of the Whig Party, started a new political party and instigated what amounted to a civil war in Kansas. The chances of avoiding a civil war had been fair before Kansas–Nebraska; after it was enacted, they were slim indeed.

The irony of it was that Douglas, while indifferent to the moral question of slavery, was a great believer in national unity. In effect, his initiative split the nation wide open. The people of the North at once began organizing companies of immigrants in order to create a solid antislavery majority in the territories, and from the western borders of Missouri great numbers of armed men moved into Kansas, intimidated the voters and voted down the free-state men. They secured the removal of the territorial governor, moved the capital to Lecompton and, after an election in which the voters were given a choice only between limited and unlimited slavery, adopted a proslavery constitution. In retaliation, the antislavery settlers set up a rival government at Topeka. By the end of 1855, the territory had turned into "bleeding Kansas." Armed groups, called "border-ruffians" raided Lawrence in May of 1856, and a few days later abolitionist leader John Brown murdered five proslavery men at Pottawatomie Creek. Although the validity of the "Lecompton Constitution" seemed more than doubtful, President Buchanan recommended it for acceptance, but Congress returned it for another territorial vote. Finally, in 1859, the antislavery so-called Wyandotte Constitution was accepted by Congress, and Kansas became a free state after the Civil War had broken out.

The long, bloody conflict in Kansas had embittered both sides, but efforts to avoid an open conflict between North and South continued. New men appeared on the national scene destined to lead the country during the years to come. Beside Douglas, Jefferson Davis and Abraham Lincoln had become national figures. Although fated to stand on opposite sides during the coming great conflict, they had much in common. Both were born in Kentucky, less than a year apart. Both were essentially moderate men, ready to compromise in order to find peaceful solutions. Both had rather indecisive fathers, both their families moved out of Kentucky soon after they were born and both participated in the so-called Black Hawk War of 1832 against the Sac and Fox Indians, but neither saw military action. Kentucky, though a slave state, was more Western than Southern in character. There were few large plantations, but mostly small farms, where tobacco, hemp and horses, not cotton, were produced. It had been the core of the new West, and most immigrations into Ohio, Missouri, Illinois, Indiana and western Virginia had started from there. A strong prounion sentiment prevailed in the state and left its mark on both men. But their ways soon parted: The Davis family moved south to Mississippi; Jefferson, born a Baptist, attended a Catholic seminary back in Kentucky, in 1824 went on to West Point and then became a plantation owner in Mississippi. He enjoyed a much better education than Lincoln, whose family moved into the grim frontier wilderness of southern Indiana.

Abraham, born in a log cabin, had less than one year in school but educated himself by reading. After the family moved to Illinois, Lincoln worked in a village store, managed a mill and undertook two trips to New Orleans. After his service in the Black Hawk War, he became partner in a grocery store that failed, leaving him heavily in debt. He then worked as a surveyor, postmaster, even rail splitter, but acquired on the side a good knowledge of the law and was elected into the state legislature, where the served from 1834–41. Thereafter, he established himself as an attorney in Springfield, Illinois. He then served one term in the U. S. Congress, 1847–49, but remained obscure and made himself unpopular because, like his idol Henry Clay, he opposed the Mexican War. After the election of Zachary Taylor to the presidency, he retired from politics, and only his opposition to Douglas's Kansas–Nebraska Act brought him back into national politics.

Jefferson Davis had a more successful career. He was elected to the House of Representatives in 1845, fought as a regimental commander in the Mexican War and, in 1847, returned to Washington as a senator. President Pierce appointed him secretary of war in 1853. In this position, he proved to be very effective, promoting an expansionist policy including a plan to acquire Cuba, supporting the Gadsden Purchase from Spain in order to promote the Southern Transcontinental Rail-

Abraham Lincoln, in 1859, and in 1864, visibly aged by the Civil War.

road route, introducing the new minie-ball rifle and enlarging the regular army considerably. He even experimented with Arabian camels in the Southwest desert.

In the meantime, the political picture in Washington had changed radically. The once powerful Whig Party had lost its prominent leaders. In the 1852 election, the party was torn wide open by sectional interests and fell completely apart after the poor showing of its candidate Winfield Scott against Pierce.

Other parties profited from its disintegration. An antiforeign party, first named the American Republican, then the American Party, but better known under their nickname, "Know-Nothings," gained national prominence in the 1854 election but split when it tried to expand to the South, over the slavery question, as had the Whigs. The antislavery men joined the new party that had come into being—the Republican Party. It originated among Midwestern farmers, and Jackson, Michigan has been called its birthplace in July of 1854. It was founded by men who opposed the Kansas–Nebraska Act and was the first party to take a clear stand against any expansion of slavery into the new territories. Soon it was joined by disenchanted antislavery men like William Seward and Thurlow Weed, by elements of the Know-Nothing Party, Free-Soilers, abolitionists, European immigrants who were seeking freedom after the failure of the 1848–49 revolution and anti-Nebraska Democrats. Lincoln joined the party in 1856, and, as a moderate acceptable to most, he was mentioned as a vice-presidential candidate in the same year. The party nominated John Charles Frémont of California fame to run against Democrat James Buchanan, and, in the following election, it made a credible showing, with a popular vote of 1.4 million against 1.9 million for the victorious Buchanan, though, obviously, few people from the South voted Republican.

The new party was regarded by the South with both hatred and fear. Several circumstances had again increased the tension. In May of 1856, Charles Sumner, abolitionist and senator from Massachusetts, attacked Andrew P. Butler of South Carolina vehemently in a speech and a few days later was bodily assaulted with a cane by a relative of Butler, Congressman Preston Brooks. Sumner could not return to the Senate until December 1859. Much more far-reaching was the so-called Dred Scott decision of the Supreme Court in 1857, which declared the Missouri Compromise unconstitutional and stated that Congress had no power to prohibit slavery in the territories. This verdict struck many Northerners as preposterous and further inflamed the sectional controversy. Horace Greeley, the highly influential founder of the *New York Tribune*, remarked that a ruling from a Washington barroom would demand more respect, and poet William Cullen Bryant exclaimed, "Paint the flag black, with whip and fetters!" There was much talk in the North of a "slave-power conspiracy," since seven of the nine judges had been Democrats and five were Southerners. President Buchanan was rumored to have pressured the court and lost much of his popularity in the North. Many Democrats felt they would have been better off nominating Douglas in 1856. Jefferson Davis, on the other hand, hailed the Dred Scott decision. His position was that freedom belonged only to those capable of mastering it—by which he meant the whites. He had become a disciple of Calhoun and traced the right of the South to secede when necessary back to the views of Thomas Jefferson. Apparently he believed in the eventual emancipation of the slaves but thought it should occur only after the blacks had been properly instructed. Of course, they had been deliberately kept illiterate in the South, and no measures were ever taken to educate them.

During the 1850s, the nation had made great strides economically. Railways had been built all over the East, a rail connection was established between New York and Chicago in 1853. Telegraph services were installed. Copper was discovered in Michigan, oil in Pennsylvania and coal in the Appalachian mountains. Steamboats ran on the great rivers and new technologies were used in farming. There was a lively trade between North and South, as Northern products were bought by Southern farmers. But the South remained essentially static, its products remained the same. In the early 1850s, the slave population in the deep South almost equaled that of the whites, and the feeling that slavery no longer had a place in the world became widespread—and not only in the North.

All these problems came to the surface in 1858 when Douglas and Lincoln ran for the Senate seat of Illinois and agreed to engage in seven debates in various towns. In accepting the nomination, Lincoln had given a ringing declaration in support of the Union: "A house divided against itself cannot stand!" In the debates, of which the one in Freeport was the most important, he stated that slavery was an injustice and an evil. He denied that he strove for complete racial equality but emphasized that the black man had a right to life, liberty and the pursuit of happiness, same as the white man. There were many hackneyed accusations. Douglas called the "house divided" speech demagogic, called Lincoln an abolitionist and claimed that the fathers of the Constitution had embraced slavery wholeheartedly, which was probably no more correct than Lincoln's retort that they had been certain about its ultimate extinction. Lincoln's strategy was to show the rift caused by the Democratic acceptance of the Dred Scott decision with Buchanan on the one side and Douglas's doctrine on the other. His decisive question to Douglas, "Can the people of a U. S. territory, in any lawful way . . . exclude slavery from its limits prior to formation

Caricature of the Lincoln-Douglas debates in 1858.

of a state constitution?" (in Freeport, August 27, 1858)—could not be answered satisfactorily by Douglas without losing him many constituents both in the North and the South. In the ensuing election, the Republicans drew 125,000 votes, the Democrats, 121,000. But, as the Republicans were underrepresented in the northern districts of the state, Douglas was elected while Lincoln disclaimed any future political ambition; yet Lincoln had become a national figure and had made Douglas unacceptable in the South. He declared that all he wanted was another try for the Senate in 1864, and the *Chicago Tribune* and other organizations began to work on his behalf.

Douglas's Democratic rival, Jefferson Davis, had expressed his sincere convictions all over the North and by his unyielding attitude hastened the break between North and South. Speaking at Boston's Faneuil Hall in October 1858, Davis declared that many Irish immigrants in Boston lived in worse slums than the Southern slaves. This may have been so, but the Irish had hopes while the blacks had none. Strangely, he entertained a close friendship with William Seward of New York whose views differed so widely from his. He spoke vividly against Seward's doctrine of "higher laws than the Constitution,"—the laws of humanity that would justify antislavery crusades—and even suggested lynching of these "higher law" advocates. Still, his Northern speeches were considered too conciliatory in the South. Back in the South, Davis vowed, as Calhoun had done, that secession would be better than submission, should the Republicans win a national victory.

The year 1859 was a prosperous one for the country. A financial panic of 1857 had been overcome, Minnesota and Oregon had been admitted to the Union and, within the Republican Party, the moderates seemed to be gaining everywhere. But in October of that year, John Brown, the radical abolitionist from Kansas, attempted to liberate the slaves through armed intervention, by establishing a stronghold to which slaves and free blacks could flee and from where further insurrections could be stirred up. He rented a farm near Harper's Ferry, Virginia and, on October 16, crossed the Potomac with 21 followers, black and white. He captured the arsenal against little resistance, imprisoned the inhabitants and took possession of the little town. The local militia blocked his escape, and, during the following night, a company of U. S. marines, commanded by Colonel Robert E. Lee, arrived and assaulted the armory in the morning. Ten of Brown's men were killed, he himself was wounded and taken prisoner. He was tried by the state of Virginia, sentenced and hanged at Charlestown on December 2, 1859. His raid aroused wild fears in the South and caused shock and surprise in the North. Yet, his dignified and calm defense during the trial won him much sympathy in the North, and he was regarded as a martyr by many, while most responsible leaders, including Lincoln, firmly endorsed his punishment. At any rate, the emotional impact of his deed dealt a fatal blow to the moderates on both sides. Jefferson Davis stated that the Republican Party had been Brown's accomplice, and throughout the South Brown became the typical representative of the rapacious, violent North, similar to the fictional Simon Legree, who had become the typical slavemaster in the eyes of the North.

In February of 1860, Jefferson Davis pronounced his Southern Manifesto, in which, following Calhoun, he demanded legal protection for the Southern slaveholders in all territories, asserting that the federal government could not prohibit slavery there. By this, Davis wanted to commit his party against Douglas and his principle of popular sovereignty. He actually played into the hands of the Southern radicals and prevented the nomination of a Democratic presidential candidate who could count on the support of all Democrats.

A few weeks later, Lincoln, in his first appearance in the East, spoke at Cooper Union in New York, declaring that the fathers of the Constitution had prevented slavery wherever they could, that George Washington had called for restriction of slavery and that slavery, as a necessary evil, must be contained. He claimed that the South was asking the North to agree that slavery was right. "Let us have faith that right makes right."

For the Democratic party, it was probably a mistake to have its convention in Charleston, South Carolina, where the radical partisans filled the galleries to overflowing. Stephen A. Douglas was the great frontrunner among the candidates, but President Buchanan, as well as all Southern diehards, were dead set against him, and thought he was at risk of losing the election to William H. Seward, considered to be the future Republican candidate. Although Douglas was the only man who could unite the party, the slave states, effectively organized by William L. Yancey of Alabama, stood by Calhoun's principles and resisted the Northern Democrats' program: popular sovereignty, free homesteads, a Pacific Railroad. When the Northern platform, which repeated the program of the 1856 convention, was reaffirmed, the Southern delegates announced their withdrawal. The remaining "rump" convention could not muster the required two-thirds majority for Douglas and decided to reconvene in Baltimore in June, while the radicals planned to meet again in Richmond.

Before this happened, the Constitutional Union Party, consisting mostly of former Whigs and Know-Nothings had been founded and had convened. At their Baltimore meeting, they adopted a platform that did not even mention slavery but simply vowed to uphold the Constitution, the Union and law enforcement. Their candidate, John Bell of Tennessee, had no chance of getting elected, but he threatened to divide the Northern vote.

When the Republicans met in Chicago, the atmosphere of the city again influenced the proceedings. Chicago had been a raw frontier town only 10 years before but had grown since from 30,000 to 100,000 inhabitants. Chicago took pride in her favorite son, Abraham Lincoln, a dark horse, who was ably represented by his friend and long-time associate, the lawyer David Davis.

More than 25,000 visitors had come to the city, and its 42 hotels were jammed. For the first time, the press gallery was provided with telegraph instruments. More than 900 press reporters applied for the 60 available seats.

The platform called for a condemnation of the Buchanan administration and any attempts to carry slavery automatically into the territories and came out for a homestead act, a protective tariff and a railroad to the Pacific. When it was adopted, the general enthusiasm rose so high that, had the nomination taken place right then, the frontrunner Seward might very well have been nominated. But the tally sheets were not ready, the voting was postponed, and, in the meantime, Seward's opponents acted. They pointed out that Seward could not carry the critical states of Pennsylvania, Indiana and Illinois, that he had many enemies among the former Know-Nothings and Free-Soilers. Other candidates were rejected for various reasons: Salmon P. Chase as an extremist, Judge Bates of St. Louis as a former Know-Nothing. That left Lincoln who had fewer enemies than anyone. It seems that against

Lincoln's express wishes, Davis made a deal with another rival, Simon Cameron, boss of Pennsylvania who promised his votes if he would become secretary of the Treasury. The Lincoln people also managed to fill the galleries with their men and keep out the Seward supporters from New York. On the first ballot, Seward led with 173½ votes against Lincoln's 102, Cameron's 50½ and Bates's 48 votes. On the second ballot, Pennsylvania went over to Lincoln who now pulled 181 against Seward's 184½ votes. On the third ballot, Seward lost votes in New England and Ohio. Lincoln, with 231½ votes, needed only one and a half more votes for victory, which he immediately received from Ohio.

To balance their ticket, the convention then nominated Hannibal Hamlin of Maine, a moderate and friend of Seward, for vice president, against Cassius Marcellus Clay, a radical Kentucky Republican.

Shortly after the Democrats reconvened at Baltimore, Douglas wrote letters to his floor manager and other Democratic leaders asking that his name be withdrawn for the sake of unity, but the recipients ignored them. After the majority report had been accepted, the delegates from Virginia, Carolina and Tennessee, as well as some other delegates withdrew. Douglas then received 173 out of 190½ votes cast and was unanimously declared the nominee. Herschel V. Johnson of Georgia was nominated as Douglas's running mate.

The anti-Douglas Northerners and all Southerners then convened and quickly put together a radical proslavery platform, also recommending the acquisition of Cuba. They then proceeded to nominate John C. Breckinridge, the current vice president, on the first ballot, with Joseph Lane, former territorial governor of Oregon, as his running mate.

So the stage was set for the election campaign that was run much more on emotions than on logic. Few people foresaw a civil war in case of a Republican victory, and most Republicans did not take the Southern threat of secession seriously. The Lincoln people organized semimilitary groups that paraded in gaudy uniforms for the "railsplitter," carrying long rails with lamps or flags on top. Douglas was ridiculed and denounced as a Catholic, and, in the South, he was hated even more as a renegade and turncoat. Yet he was the only candidate who tried to run a campaign on the issues. Breckinridge was extremely careful not to commit himself unduly, and Lincoln remained silent, asserting that he had already said all he had to say on the issues before the voters. At one point, Jefferson Davis even suggested that all three candidates opposing Lincoln withdraw, so that the South could concentrate on one candidate capable of beating the Republicans; but obviously, it was too late for that. Most governors of the Southern states were reluctant to come right out for secession, feeling that their people were not yet ready for it, except for South Carolina whose governor, William H. Gist, announced that his state would go it alone, if necessary. None of the candidates had come out for secession, and this possibility received little serious discussion.

When the results of the election and the Republican victory became known, there was, of course, great jubilation in Springfield, Illinois—with Lincoln appearing to be the least elated man in the celebrating crowd. But, strangely, there was also great elation in Charleston, South Carolina, where not a single vote for Lincoln had been cast. Here the overwhelming Republican triumph gave people a sense of relief and the feeling that a new nation had been born in the South. The local paper, the *Mercury*, announced: "The tea has been thrown overboard; the revolution of 1860 has been initiated."

CHRONICLE OF EVENTS

1808:
January: Importation of slaves into the United States is legally ended, as called for by the Constitution. Buying and selling of slaves within the U.S. continues.

1814/1815:
December–January: Secret meetings of some prominent New Englanders opposed to the war against England, during which secession from the Union is considered.

1816/1817:
In Washington, D.C., the American Colonization Society is founded to aid in the settling of freed slaves in Africa. Eventually, it helps to move 11,000 blacks to the new African state of Liberia, but is not supported by abolitionists nor by the great majority of black Americans.

1820:
Congress passes the "Missouri Compromise": Missouri is admitted to the Union as a slave-holding state, Maine as a free state. Slavery is forbidden forever in the territory ceded by France to the United States (Louisiana), lying north of latitude 36° 30' except for Missouri.

1822:
May: Around Charleston, S.C., an attempted slave revolt led by Denmark Vesey, a former slave, is betrayed and suppressed. Vesey and 34 blacks are hanged.

1824:
May: A protective Tariff Law is passed by Congress which arouses Southerners who feel discriminated against.

1827:
The last vestiges of slavery in New York state are eradicated.

1828:
A new Tariff Law, introducing high duties, is called "tariff of abominations" by the South and leads to demands to separate from the Union, in particular in South Carolina (John C. Calhoun) and Georgia.

1830:
Southern senators against Northern senators in the debate on land sales in the West.
January: In a great Senate debate with Robert Young Hayne from South Carolina, in which all political differences between North and South are discussed, Daniel Webster emphasizes that the Union is superior to the States.

The population of the free states now exceeds that of the Southern states by one million.

1831:
January: William Lloyd Garrison, Boston abolitionist, starts publication of his *Liberator*, which advocates unconditional emancipation of all slaves.
August: Uprising of slaves in Southampton County, Virginia, under Nat Turner. Soldiers put down the rebellion. About 100 blacks are killed, Turner and 12 of his followers are executed.

1832:
The U.S. Supreme Court rules that the state of Georgia has no jurisdiction over the Cherokee Indians, but President Jackson does not support this decision.

1833:
Slavery within the British Empire is abolished.

Oberlin College opens its doors to blacks as well as to women.

Compromise on the tariff bills is arranged by Henry Clay of Virginia, calling for a gradual cutback, and avoiding a North-South confrontation.

Arthur and Lewis Tappan found the American Anti-Slavery Society.

1835:

October: The abolitionist William Lloyd Garrison is paraded through the streets of Boston with a rope around his neck.

1836:

May: Southern members of the House introduce the "gag" resolution, which suppresses any discussion on the slavery issue.

1839:

August: The Spanish slave-ship *Amistad* is taken over in a mutiny of the slaves led by Cinque and taken to a Connecticut port. Despite Spain's demand to return the slaves, the U.S. Supreme Court rules that they be freed.

1842:

January: In *Prigg vs. Commonwealth of Pennsylvania,* the U.S. Supreme Court decides that a Pennsylvania law forbidding the seizure of fugitive slaves is unconstitutional and that the enforcement of fugitive slave laws is a federal responsibility.

1844:

June: A treaty on the annexation of Texas, negotiated by Secretary of State Calhoun, is rejected by the Senate because of the implications on the slavery question.

1845:

After the election of James K. Polk as president, the annexation of Texas is passed by Congress.

1846/47:

A bill proposed by David Wilmot of Pennsylvania forbids any territory acquired in the Mexican War to be open to slavery. The bill passes the House, but is defeated in the Senate in the following year. The Wilmot Proviso is adopted by the Free-Soil Party in the 1848 election.

1847:

December: Senator Lewis Cass of Michigan proposes the doctrine that the decision on slavery should be left to the territorial government ("popular sovereignty doctrine").

1848:

February: In the Peace Treaty with Mexico, the United States acquires more than 500,000 square miles, including the future states of California, Nevada, Utah, New Mexico and Arizona, also parts of Wyoming and Colorado. Texas is also ceded to the States.

1849:

California adopts a constitution forbidding slavery and asks for admission into the Union. Southerners object and talk again of secession. President Taylor threatens to crush any secession.

1850:

January–September: Senator Henry Clay suggests a compromise that would admit California as a free state, leave the question of slavery in the other territories gained from Mexico undecided and introduce a stricter fugitive law. He is opposed by William Seward of New York on the one side, and John Calhoun on the other, but supported by Daniel Webster who emphasizes that the preservation of the Union is the most important issue. Clay's compromise is finally accepted and signed by President Fillmore.

November: In a Southern convention at Nashville, the extremists have a majority and propose to stress the South's right to secede, but at a state convention in Georgia the desire to remain in the Union, if the North abides by the rules of the new compromise, is expressed.

1851:

June: Uncle Tom's Cabin by Harriet Beecher Stowe is beginning to appear in the *National*

Uncle Tom's Cabin, *by Harriet Beecher Stowe, published in 1852.*

Era. It will sell more than a million copies within a year.

1852:

November: Franklin Pierce, Democrat, defeats General Winfield Scott, hero of the Mexican War, for the presidency. The Democratic platform supports the 1850 compromise.

1854:

January: Senator Stephen A. Douglas of Illinois proposes to organize the Great Plains region west of the Missouri River as Kansas and Nebraska territories, the slavery question to be decided by "popular sovereignty." This would repeal the Missouri Compromise of 1820 because both territories lie above latitude 36° 30'.

April: In Massachusetts, the Emigrant Aid Society is founded to support antislavery settlers in Kansas.

May: Douglas's Kansas–Nebraska Act is approved by Congress and signed by President Pierce. But Northerners threaten to boycott the Fugitive Law of 1850.

July: In Michigan, antislavery men found the Republican Party and demand the repeal of the Kansas–Nebraska Act and the Fugitive Slave Law.

Fighting between pro- and antislavery settlers begins in Kansas, the former being supported by "border-ruffians" crossing over from Missouri.

1855:

July: The Kansas Legislature adopts extreme proslavery laws and expels antislavery legislators.

December: The Free-Soil people of Kansas adopt the Topeka Constitution, which outlaws slavery and bans all blacks from the territory.

1856:

May: Senator Charles Sumner of Massachusetts, after an outspoken antislavery speech, is attacked at his desk by South Carolina Representative Preston Brooks and severely wounded.

In a retaliatory raid, an abolitionist group led by John Brown kills five proslavery men at Pottawotamie Creek, Kansas.

July: Kansas's Topeka Constitution is approved by the House of Representatives, but rejected by the Senate.

November: Democrat James Buchanan defeats the Republican candidate John Frémont for the presidency.

1857:

March: In the Dred Scott decision, the U.S. Supreme Court, under Chief Justice Roger Taney, declares the Missouri Compromise to be unconstitutional, that a slave taken out of slave territory never ceases to be a slave and that

James Buchanan, President of the United States.

Congress has no power to deprive a citizen of his property, such as slaves. Northerners protest this decision.

December: A proslavery Constitution is adopted by Kansas at Lecompton.

1858:

January–April: While the majority of the Kansas populace reject the Lecompton Constitution, President Buchanan recommends admitting Kansas as a state under this constitution. Finally, a bill is passed in Congress to allow another popular vote on the constitution.

June: The Republican Party nominates Abraham Lincoln to challenge Stephen A. Douglas for the Senate seat of Illinois. In his acceptance speech, Lincoln emphasizes that the government cannot permanently endure half slave and half free.

August–October: Lincoln and Douglas meet in seven debates across Illinois. Douglas tries very hard to avoid any rift within his party, emphasizing the right of Americans to vote their preference, while Lincoln condemns slavery on moral and political grounds and opposes any extension of it. Douglas wins by a close margin, but Lincoln emerges as a national figure.

1859:

March: In *Ableman vs. Booth,* the Supreme Court rules that state courts cannot free federal prisoners and confirms the constitutionality of the Fugitive Slave Act of 1850. The Wisconsin legislature protests this decision, but Booth, who had freed a fugitive slave, is rearrested.

May: The Annual Southern Commercial Convention recommends reopening the African slave trade.

October: Abolitionist John Brown leads an armed group of 12 white and five black men to seize the Federal Arsenal at Harper's Ferry, Virginia. Within a day he and four survivors are taken prisoner by a U. S. marine force under Colonel Robert E. Lee. Brown is tried for conspiracy and treason, convicted and hanged on December 2.

Kansans vote in favor of an antislavery constitution.

1860:

February: Jefferson Davis, senator from Mississippi, proposes resolutions affirming that the federal government cannot prohibit slavery in the territories, but must protect the slaveowners there. Davis is trying to unite the Democratic Party against Douglas's principle of popular sovereignty.

Lincoln's first appearance in the East, at Cooper Union, New York.

April–May: At the Democratic convention in Charleston, South Carolina, a proslavery-platform is rejected; delegates from eight Southern states leave. The remaining delegates cannot agree on a candidate, and the convention is adjourned.

May: At the Republican convention in Chicago, the favorite candidate, Senator William H. Seward, fails to get the nomination because of his extreme position on slavery. On the third ballot, the more moderate Abraham Lincoln is nominated.

June: The Democratic Party reconvenes in Baltimore, Senator Douglas's opponents walk out and Douglas is nominated by the Northern Democrats. Later, the Southern Democrats nominate Vice President John C. Breckenridge on a proslavery platform.

November 6: Abraham Lincoln is elected 16th president of the United States. Hannibal Hamlin of Maine is his vice president. The Republican ticket received 1,866,452 votes and 180 electoral votes in 17 of the 33 states, as against 1,376,957 votes, and only 12 electoral votes for the Northern Democratic ticket of Stephen A. Douglas and Herschel V. Johnson of Georgia. On the Southern Democratic ticket, John C. Breckinridge of Kentucky and Joseph Lane of Oregon received 849,781 votes and 72 electoral votes from 11 of the 15 slave states. The Constitutional Unionists John Bell of Tennessee and Edward Everett of Massachusetts received 588,879 votes and 39 electoral votes.

Eyewitness Testimony

That the slave population will, at some certain period cause the most horrible catastrophe, cannot be doubted; those who possess them act defensively in behalf of all that is nearest and dearest to them, when they endeavor to acquire all the strength and influence to meet that period which they can; and hence the political and civil opposition of these to the restriction which is proposed to be laid on Missouri . . . It is easy to use severe terms against the practice of slavery; but let us first tell the Southern people what they can safely do to abolish it, before we condemn them wholesale.

Niles Register, *Baltimore, December 23, 1820.*

Is it worth while to continue this union of states, where the North demands to be our masters and we are required to be their tributaries?

Thomas Cooper, president of South Carolina College, in May of 1824, protesting against the new tariff laws.

The President's [Jackson] toast at the late Jeffersonian banquet was, "The Federal Union—it must be preserved!" To this we respond, amen. But how preserved? There is but one mode, and that is by inducing the majority to respect the rights and feelings of the minority, or, in other words, by inducing the North and East to repeal or modify the iniquitous measures by which the South is impoverished and enslaved. And that the President alludes to this mode is too evident we think, to admit a shadow of a doubt.

Charleston Mercury, chief organ of the South Carolina Nullificationists, April 24, 1830. Actually, Jackson's speech was a direct defiance of the Nullifiers.

I shall strenuously contend for the immediate enfranchisement of our slave population . . . On this subject, I do not wish to think, or speak, or write, with moderation. No! No! Tell a man whose house is on fire, to give a moderate alarm; tell him to moderately rescue his wife from the hands of the ravisher; tell the mother to gradually extricate her babe from the fire into which it has fallen;—but urge me not to use moderation in a cause like the present. I am in earnest—I will not equivocate—I will not excuse—I will not retreat a single inch—and I WILL BE HEARD.

William Lloyd Garrison, in Liberator, *Boston, on January 1, 1831.*

Can there be a doubt of the purpose of the Nullifiers to carry it to a civil war? Why the recent language of their leading partizans? Why do we hear of pledges of life, fortune and sacred honor . . . Why has Governor Hamilton been so assiduously courting and drilling the militia? Why has he recently . . . procured himself to be elevated to the military rank of a brigadier-general? What is all that but preparation for war? What does Hamilton mean, but to be the military hero of Nullification . . . This, then, is Nullification: It is *Civil War and Disunion!*

Washington Globe, *November 29, 1832.*

Should a civil war break out in consequence of resistance to the revenue laws, we have no doubt it will first begin among the citizens of South Carolina. Any feeling of jealousy, animosity or indignation with which the people of the two portions of the Union may regard each other is complacency itself to that which subsists between the two parties of South Carolina.

New York Evening Post, *December 21, 1832.*

Champion of those who groan beneath/ Oppression's iron hand,/ In view of penury, hate and death,/ I see thee fearless stand./ Still bearing up thy lofty brow/ In the steadfast strength of truth,/ In manhood sealing well the vow/ And promise of thy youth.

John Greenleaf Whittier: "To William Lloyd Garrison" (1833).

An extraordinary colloquy took place in the United States Senate some short time since between Mr. Rives and Mr. Calhoun, in which the latter Senator maintained with much vehemence that slavery is not an evil, but "a good, a great good", and reproached Mr. Rives, in sharp terms, for admitting the contrary . . . we do hold from the bottom of our soul that slavery is an evil, a deep, detestable, damnable evil . . . Slavery is such an evil that it withers what it touches. Where it is once securely established, the land becomes desolate, as the tree inevitably perishes which the sea-hawk chooses for its nest . . . If anyone desired an illustration . . . let him look at the two sister States of Kentucky and Ohio. Alike in soil and climate . . . how different are they in all respects

over which man has control! On the one hand, the air is vocal with the mingled tumult of a vast and properous population . . . Let us turn to Kentucky, and note the opposite influences of slavery. A narrow and unfrequented path through the close and sultry canebrake conducts us to a wretched hovel . . .
New York Plaindealer, February 25, 1837.

What we would have done by legislation with regard to lands may be summed up as follows: 1. Let the Public Lands, whether of the Union or of any state, be disposed of to actual settlers only. 2. Let each man who needs land be permitted to take without price so much land as he actually needs. 3. Let no man be authorized to acquire . . . more than a fixed of arable land, say 160,320 feet, or 540 acres. 4. Take from no man that which is lawfully his. 5. Let the Homestead of a family, to the extent of forty acres, not including more than one dwelling, be rendered inalienable by mortgage, execution or otherwise than by voluntary deed . . . That the idea will encounter vehement hostility and misrepresentation was inevitable from the outset, but the day for its triumph "Is coming yet for a'that".
Horace Greeley. New York Tribune, *March 6, 1847. (The Homestead act became law in 1862.)*

The contest against slavery will not cease or be relaxed until slavery itself shall be extinguished . . . Is General Taylor identified with the slave power? If not, will he identify himself with it? These are questions which will agitate the free States during the coming Presidential campaign. He is known to be a slaveholder; how does he stand as to the power which slavery gives . . . ?
Springfield Republican, December 29, 1847.

So far is slavery from being naturally opposed to all progress and improvement in rural and mechanical arts, in internal trade and foreign commerce, in public education and moral instruction, that it can easily be made auxiliary to all these important ends. It is the perfection of human wisdom to make the best possible use of all the means which a good Providence has placed at our disposal.
Augusta (Georgia) Sentinel, May 1849.

Mr. Webster stands before the public as a man under circumstances which force upon him the imputation of a sordid motive, deserted it when its apostasy was desired by the Administration, and immediately after an office had been conferred upon his son.
New York Evening Post, March 8, 1850, after Webster had opposed a measure to prohibit slavery in the territories.

The Union is the source of our greatness and strength; its dismemberment will probably be of our impotence and ruin, whilst all the world will look on, with amazement, upon a dissolution of a fabric so fair . . . Thus we should feel and think. Yet, there must be an end, somewhere, of concessions. If not a voluntary end, a necessary one, when everything to be conceded is gone. It becomes the South to determine how far its safety will admit of concession . . . None can mistake the anti-slavery growth—The cry is onward! . . . Every concession made to it will induce a more imperious tone . . . There is a voice higher than the Constitution! . . . Slavery will go by the board in the District of Columbia—in the forts and navy yards. The trade between the states will be prohibited. The final act is not yet, but soon. There is a precedent in the British Parliament and the West Indies. They will use the precedent. We know the rest . . .
De Bow's Review, New Orleans, July 1850.

. . . "Uncle Tom" over whose fate every reader will drip the scalding tear, and for whose character the highest reverence will be felt . . . Towards his merciless oppressors he cherishes no animosity, and breathes nothing of retaliation. Like his Lord and Master, he was "willing to be led as a lamb to the slaughter", returning blessing for cursing . . . His character is sketched with great power and rare religious perception. It triumphantly exemplifies the nature, tendency and results of Christian nonresistance.
William Lloyd Garrison in The Liberator, *March 26, 1852, reviewing Harriet Beecher Stowe's* Uncle Tom's Cabin.

It is useless for us to tell the benevolent ladies and gentlemen who have undertaken to instruct us in our catechism of humanity that they are entirely ignorant of the condition of the negro. "Uncle Tom's Cabin" tells them differently. It is useless for us to tell them that our slaves are not "interdicted education in the truths of the gospel and the ordinances of Christianity"; it is useless for us to repeat that

their family and social affections are respected and indulged in a greater degree than those of any laboring class in the world. "Uncle Tom's Cabin" says differently . . .
De Bow's Review, New Orleans, March
1853.

Did the country, did Congress, did Mr. Douglas, understand when the Adjustment of 1850 was under consideration, that its success would repeal the Missouri Compromise and open the Territories . . . to the introduction of human slavery? . . . In view of the notorious, acknowledged, unbroken silence in 1850 of all parties upon this point, is not this fundamental assumption of Douglas & Co. not only a fraud, but one of the most impudent, shameless, audacious . . . ?
Horace Greeley, New York Tribune, *February 15, 1854.*

We are in the midst of a revolution, is our response to the proceedings at Washington on the Nebraska bill. The attempted passage of this measure is the first great effort of slavery to take American freedom directly by the throat. Hitherto it has but asked to be allowed to grow and expand side by side with that freedom, until now, at what is believed a favorable moment, it springs from its lair and clutches at the life of its political associate in the government. It engages in a coup d'etat, and by the aid of Northern traitors to liberty attempts the most intolerable usurpation.
New York Tribune, *May 18, 1854.*

The first duty of Whigs is to unite with some organization of our countrymen to defeat and dissolve the new geographical party calling itself Republican . . . If the Republican party accomplishes its object and gives the government to the North, I turn my eyes from the consequences. To the fifteen states of the South that government will appear an alien government . . . It will appear a hostile government. It will represent to their eye a vast region of states organized upon anti-slavery, flushed by triumph, cheered onward by the voice of the pulpit, tribune and press; its mission, to inaugurate freedom and put down the oligarchy; its constitution, the glittering and sounding generalities of natural right which make up the Declaration of Independence. . . . Practically the contest, in my judgment, is be-

tween Mr. Buchanan and Colonel Frémont. In these circumstances, I vote for Mr. Buchanan.
Rufus Choate, New England Whig lawyer and politician, in 1854, quoted by N. W. Stephenson in Abraham Lincoln and the Union, *(1918).*

. . . the effect of the Know-Nothing policy would be such that in a few years the community would be divided into two distinct and aristocratic classes or privileged patricians and disfranchised plebeians. The native would be haughty and overbearing . . . The foreignborn population, detached and dissociated from the community; exasperated by consciousness of wrong and degradation; bound by no interest to the state; driven into compact array by the blows of oppression, and animated by exclusive sympathies and hopes, would indeed be an alien people in a foreign country . . . But the Democratic Party denies that the foreign population is a pest . . .
Richmond Enquirer, *April 1855.*

Kansas is to be saved to freedom by a steady, persevering emigration thither from the free states. What we need now is time to get a foothold. We require a great mass of free emigrants there—too great to be outvoted by a few thousand ruffians from Missouri, who at a given signal intend to rush in and extemporize a state constitution, as they have extemporized a Legislature. Give us the masses there before slavery shall be allowed to affix its black seal to the fundamental law of the State. Kansas without slavery is our motto.
Horace Greeley in the New York Tribune,
April 18, 1855.

Divine Providence, for its own high and inscrutable purposes, has rescued more than three millions of human beings from the hardships of a savage state, and placed them in a condition of greater comfort than any other laboring class in the world; it has delivered them from the barbarous idolatries of Africa, and brought them within the blessings covenanted to believers in Christ. At the same time it has provided the whites of the Anglo-Norman race in the Southern states with the necessary means of unexampled prosperity, with that slave labor without which, as a general rule, no colonization in a new country has ever or ever will thrive and grow rapidly; it has given them a distinct and inferior race to fill a position equal to their highest capacity, which in less

fortunate countries is occupied by the whites themselves.
De Bow's Review, July 1855, expressing John C. Calhoun's opinion on the subject of slavery.

[the career of the typical Southern planter]—from the cradle to the grave is one of unbridled lust, of filthy amalgamation, of haughty domination, of swaggering braggadocio, of cowardly ruffianism, of boundless dissipation, of matchless insolence, of infinite self-conceit, of unequalled oppression, of more than savage cruelty.
William Lloyd Garrison, abolitionist, as quoted by Robert Penn Warren in The Legacy of the Civil War *(1961).*

What are the facts respecting Kansas? Briefly these: "squatter sovereignty" has turned out to be repeated invasions of the Territory by armed bandits from Missouri, who have successfully made it a conquered province, manufactured a Territorial Government, enacted a code of laws worthy of pandemonium, and trampled the civil and political rights of the bona-fide settlers under their feet; and for one sole subject—to make Kansas a slave state.
William Lloyd Garrison, The Liberator, *April 4, 1856.*

The friends of slavery in Washington are attempting to silence the members of Congress from the free States by the same modes of discipline which make the slaves unite on their plantations. Two ruffians from the House of Representatives, named Brooks and Keith, both from South Carolina, made the Senate Chamber the scene of their cowardly brutality . . . Has it come to this that we must speak with bated breath in the presence of our Southern masters; that even their follies are too sacred a subject for ridicule; that we must not deny the consistency of their principles or the accuracy of their statements? If we venture to laugh at them or question their logic, or dispute their facts, are we to be chastised as they chastise their slaves? Are we, too, slaves, slaves for life, a target for their brutal blows, when we do not comport ourselves to please them?
William Cullen Bryant in the New York Evening Post, *May 23, 1856, after the assault on Senator Sumner in the Senate Chamber.*

What would commerce be without cotton, sugar, tobacco, rice, and naval stores? All these are the products of slave labor . . . It has been said that one free laborer is equal to five slaves. If this be so, why has not free labor been employed in the production of the above staples? It has been attempted and in every case in which it has been introduced has failed . . .
Richmond Dispatch, May 1856.

The wild and irrational ravings of the abolition press proper were supposed to be confined to a few fanatics, small in number and despicable in character, and by no means representing the opinions of the Northern people in the aggregate. Most unfortunately, different impressions begin to prevail. We cannot beguile ourselves any longer with such delusive hopes.
New Orleans Bulletin, August 1856.

The real abstract question between the two parties is, whether Congress shall control the destinies of the Territories, and dedicate them as of old to freedom, of whether they shall be left for bitter and bloody struggles between the settlers, like those which in Kansas now shock the moral sense of civilization everywhere . . . Of the two contestants, the Republicans can alone afford to be beaten. With the Democracy, defeat is destruction. The party is only held together by its alliance with the national treasury and the slaveholder. Separated from one, it becomes useless to the other, and its power is gone.
Springfield Republican, November 4, 1856, before the Buchanan–Frémont election.

Some of the journalists who support the cause of the Administration are pleasing themsleves with the fancy that the decision of the Supreme bench of the United States in the Dred Scott case will put an end to the agitation of the slavery question. They will soon find their mistake. The feeling in favor of liberty is not so easily smothered; discussion is not so readily silenced . . . The more our Presidents have meddled with the matter, the more the majority in Congress have sought to stifle the discussion, the more force has been employed on the side of slavery—whether under the pretext of legal authority, as when Mr. Pierce called out the New Jersey troops to enforce the pretended laws of Kansas, or without that pretext, as when armed men crossed the border of that territory to make laws for the inhabitants—the more determined is the zeal by which the rights of freemen

are asserted and upheld against the oligarchy. It will not cool the fiery temper of this zeal to know that slavery has enlisted the bench on its side . . .
William Cullen Bryant in the New York Evening Post, *March 9, 1857.*

We shall reorganize the Court and thus reform its political sentiments and practices.
William Seward, after the Dred Scott decision of the U. S. Supreme Court in 1857.

. . . the first and ruling consideration of every American is business. Walk up Broadway and listen to the conversation of the people whom you pass—ninety nine out of a hundred are talking of dollars, percentages and premiums . . . Wherever two or three Americans are gathered together there you may be sure that business and dollars are on the tapis . . . They are too busy to sin . . . An English merchant works seven hours a day . . . A Frenchman . . . dines at five after which he may be seen at an opera or in a ballroom. An American begins work before he is dressed in the morning and never stops till he goes to bed.
George W. Curtis in Harper's Weekly, *February 27, 1858.*

I am not, nor ever have been, in favor of bringing about in any way the social and political equality of the white and black races.
Abraham Lincoln in Charleston, Ill., in 1858, as quoted by Robert Penn Warren in The Legacy of the Civil War.

He [John Brown] has been known to vow vengeance against the whole class of slaveholders for the outrages perpetrated by their representatives in Kansas, and this insurrection, if he is at the head of it, is the manner in which he gluts his resentments . . . They [the slaveholders] must remember that they accustomed men . . . to the idea of using arms against their political opponents, that by their crimes and outrages they drove hundreds to madness, and that the feelings of bitterness and revenge thus generated have since rankled in the heart. Brown has made himself an organ of these in a fearfully significant way.
New York Evening Post, *October 18, 1859.*

This scene [of John Brown's trial] shows the wonderful impression made by Brown upon those about him. It is this great sincerity and heroic self-sacrifice to what he believed to be right that gave him such influence over the men who enlisted in his scheme, and that so impressed the Virginians with respect, from Governor Wise down, and that will make it a difficult thing to hang him.
Springfield Republican, *November 4, 1859.*

How the conquerors wore their laurels, how they hastened on the trial;/ How Old Brown was placed, half dying, on the Charleston court-house floor;/ How he spoke his grand oration, in the scorn of all denial;/ What the brave old Madman told them, These are known the country o'er./ "Hang Old Brown,/ Osawatomie Brown,"/ Said the judge, "and all such rebels", with his most judicious frown—
Edmund Clarence Stedman, "How Old Brown took Harper's Ferry" (November 1859).

I, John Brown, am now quite certain that the crimes of this guilty land will never be purged away but with blood.
John Brown, last words, when facing the scaffold, December 2, 1859.

John Brown still lives. The great State of Virginia has hung his venerable body upon the ignominious gallows, and released John Brown himself to join the "noble army of martyrs." There need be no tears for him. Few men died so happily, so satisfied with time, place and circumstance, as did he . . . A Christian man, hung by Christians for acting upon his convictions of duty—a brave man hung for a chivalrous and self-sacrificing deed of humanity—philanthropist hung for seeking the liberty of oppressed men. No outcry about violated law can cover up the essential enormity of a deed like this.
Springfield Republican, *December 3, 1859.*

I tell you, gentlemen of the South, in all candor, I do not believe a Democratic candidate can ever carry any one Democratic state of the North on the platform that it is the duty of the Federal government to force the people of a territory to have slavery if they do not want it.
Stephen A. Douglas, in the Senate, around December 1859.

There is no necessity for legislation; no grievances to be remedied; no evil to be avoided; no action is necessary; and yet the peace of the country, the integrity of the Democratic party, is to be threatened by abstract resolutions, when there is confessedly no necessity for action.

Douglas in Congress, February 1860, speaking against Jefferson Davis's proposed resolutions.

The question recurs, what will satisfy them [the Southerners]? Simply this; We must not only let them alone, but we must somehow convince them that we do let them alone. This, we know by experience, is no easy task.

Lincoln at Cooper Union, February 27, 1860.

It [slavery] has the violence of robbery, the blood and cruelty of piracy, it has the offensive and brutal lusts of polygamy, all combined and concentrated in itself.

Owen Lovejoy, abolitionist, brother of the murdered Elijah, in Congress April 5, 1860.

Ours is the property invaded. Ours are the institutions which are at stake; ours is the peace that is to be destroyed; ours is the property that is to be destroyed; ours is the honor at stake—the honor of children, the honor of families, the lives, perhaps, of all—all of which rests upon what your course may ultimately make a great heaving volanco of passion and crime, if you are enabled to consummate your designs. Bear with us then, if we stand sternly here upon what is yet that dormant volcano, and say we yield no position here until we are convinced we are wrong.

William L. Yancey, at the Democratic convention at Charleston, April 27, 1860.

. . . there was no swagger, no bluster. There were no threats, no denunciations. The language employed by the representatives of these seven sovereignties was as dignified as it was feeling, and as courteous as it was either. As one followed another in quick succession, one could see the entire crowd quiver as under a heavy blow. Every man seemed to look anxiously at his neighbor as if inquiring what is going to happen next. Down many a manly cheek did I see flow tears of heartfelt sorrow.

The Richmond Dispatch, after the walkout of the Southern representatives at Charleston, on April 30, 1860.

Mark me, when I repeat that in less than twelve months we shall be in the midst of a bloody war. What is to become of us then God only knows. The Union will certainly be disrupted; and what will make it so disastrous is the way in which it will be done.

Alexander Hamilton Stephens, after the deadlock at Charleston. Quoted by Bruce Catton in The Coming Fury *(1961).*

The power of resistance consists, in no small degree, in meeting the enemy at the outer gate. I can speak for myself—having no right to speak for others—and do say that if I belonged to a party organized on the basis on making war on any section or interest in the United States, if I know myself, I would instantly quit it. We of the South have made no war upon the North. We have asked no discrimination in our favor. We claim but to have the Constitution fairly and equally administered.

Jefferson Davis in the Senate, May 7, 1860.

While I can never sacrifice the principle, even to attain the Presidency, I will cheerfully and joyfully sacrifice myself to maintain the principle. If, therefore, you and my other friends, who have stood by me with such heroic firmness at Charleston and Baltimore, shall be of the opinion that the principle can be preserved and the unity and the ascendancy of the Democratic party maintained and the country saved from the perils of Northern abolitionism and Southern disunion by withdrawing my name and uniting upon some other non-intervention and Union-loving Democrat, I beseech you to pursue that course.

Douglas, letter to his floor manager, W. A. Richardson, during the Baltimore convention, June 1860.

It has been my purpose, since I have been placed in my present position, to make no speeches . . . I appear upon the ground here at this time only for the purpose of affording for myself the best opportunity of seeing you and enabling you to see me . . . You will kindly let me be silent.

Lincoln, during a Republican rally at Springfield, Illinois, August 8, 1860. Quoted by Bruce Catton in The Coming Fury.

Look at the history of the last two administrations in which the slave interest has had undisputed sway. This sway, the most disgraceful and shameless of anything in the history of the government, must now be thrown off or else the Union will be dissolved. Let's try it! Are we forever to be governed by a slave-holding minority? Will the passage of four years more

of misrule make it any easier for the majority to assume its functions?
Springfield Republican, *August 25, 1860.*

For ten, aye twenty years, these threats have been renewed in the same language and in the same form, about the first day of November every four years, when it happened to come before the day of the presidential election. I do not doubt but that these Southern statesmen and politicians think that they are going to dissolve the Union, but I think they are going to do no such thing.
William H. Seward, during the election campaign at New York, September 1860. Quoted by Bruce Catton in The Coming Fury.

From my knowledge of our Southern population it is my solemn conviction that there is some danger of an early act of rashness preliminary to secession, viz, the seizure of some or all of the following posts: . . . In my opinion, all these works should be immediately so garrisoned as to make any attempt to take any of them, by surprise or coup de main, ridiculous. With the army faithful to its allegiance, and the navy probably equally so . . . there is good reason to hope that the danger of secession may be made to pass away . . .
Winfield Scott, commander in chief of the army, to President Buchanan, October 29, 1860.

As to the threats of Revolution so freely indulged in, we do not care whether they are sham or in earnest. We believe them to be mere bravado—empty gasconading, intended merely to alarm, but that is no matter. They are equally disgraceful whether made for political effect or otherwise; and the people of the North will be false to their rights if they fail to rebuke them.
Pittsburgh Gazette, *during the presidential election campaign, October 1860. Quoted by Bruce Catton in* The Coming Fury.

Immediate danger will be brought to slavery in all the frontier States. When a party is enthroned at Washington, in the executive and legislative departments of the government, whose creed is to repeal the fugitive slave law, the underground railroad will become an overground railroad. The tenure of slave property will be felt to be weakened . . . If in our present position of power and unitedness we have the raid of John Brown, and twenty towns burnt down in Texas in one year by abolitionists, what will be the measures of insurrection and incendiarism which must follow our notorious and abject prostration to abolition rule in Washington, with all the patronage of the Federal government and a Union organization in the South to support its Secret conspiracy and its attendant horrors, with rumors of more horrors, will hover over every portion of the South; while in the language of the Black Republican patriarch, Giddings, they will "laugh at our calamities, and mock when our fear cometh."
Charleston Courier, *November 1860.*

2. From the Beginning of Secession to the First Battle of Bull Run: December 1860–July 1861

THE HISTORICAL CONTEXT

Four months passed between the time the Republican Party and Abraham Lincoln won their election victory and the day the new administration was to take over. During that period, seven states of the deep South seceded from the Union, organized themselves as the Confederate States of America, drafted a Constitution and established their capital in Montgomery, Alabama.

Few people had foreseen such a swift development. In the North, most voters were convinced the Southern threats of secession were a bluff. But even in the South, a strong Union minority existed in many states and also the widespread opinion that one should wait and see what the attitude of the new regime would be before acting. Jefferson Davis seems to have thought that at a convention of the slave states a motion to secede would probably fail.

James Buchanan, the outgoing president, saw the imminent danger of dissolution of the Union. His views were diametrically opposed to Lincoln's, but both agreed on one point, that state sovereignty was not superior to national sovereignty, as the Southern radicals claimed, and that therefore no state had the right to leave the Union. But Buchanan also stressed that the federal government had no power to coerce a state into submission, which caused William H. Seward to remark sarcastically that the president "had demonstrated that no state had the right to secede unless it wishes to." Buchanan's annual message to

Congress stated all the difficulties of the present situation but offered no solution. His cabinet was hopelessly divided between Northerners and Southerners and he was little inclined to make bold decisions by himself. But the Republicans could not agree on any solution either, and some advised to let the Cotton States go in peace if they really wanted to leave the Union. In December of 1860, Lincoln did not give the impression that he knew what to do, and, at any rate, he had no power to act.

From their point of view, the fire eaters of South Carolina were probably right in acting by themselves and quickly. They had reason to fear that an administration hostile to slavery would slowly but surely erode the position of the slaveholders in the deep South. After all, the vast majority of whites in the South were not slave-owners and might be persuaded one day that their interests did not necessarily coincide with those of the slaveholders. By declaring the secession and the dissolution of the Union before the end of the year, the state of South Carolina established a *fait accompli* and triggered a chain reaction in all the states of the deep South: By February 1, 1861, six more states had declared their secession in this order: Mississippi, Florida, Alabama, Georgia, Louisiana and Texas. Only a few days later, delegates of all seven states met in Montgomery to organize a Confederacy. By this time, most Southern sympathizers had left Buchanan's cabinet as well as the Senate and the House of Representatives.

The new situation created problems that called for an immediate solution. Custom duties collected at Confederate ports—did they belong to the Union or the Confederacy? Buchanan avoided any action that could have been interpreted as coercion. The North claimed that the enforcement of existing and approved laws was not coercion and could not be interpreted as a hostile act while the South made no such distinction and declared any such attempt to be a foreign invasion.

Even if Buchanan had taken a more aggressive position, he would have been poorly equipped to follow through. The regular army of the Union consisted of about 16,000 men, and they were spread over a frontier more than 2,000 miles long. Most of the U.S. Navy's ships were in distant waters. The strongest armed forces within the United States were the militias of the seceded or seceding states, and from January 1861 on, Southern state militias began to take over U.S. arsenals and forts in their areas. One of these strong points was of major interest for both sides: Fort Sumter in Charleston Harbor, on which the newly elected governor of South Carolina, Francis W. Pickens, had his eye from the very beginning. Right after his inauguration he had sent an emissary to Washington demanding the surrender of the fort.

The bombardment of Fort Sumter, April 12–13, 1861 (Currier & Ives).

Even Buchanan could not accede to such a demand at this point, but the instructions given by the governments in Washington to Major Robert Anderson, the commanding officer at the fort, continued to be vague. Nevertheless, Anderson succeeded in concentrating manpower and equipment at Sumter partly by moving troops and equipment from the nearby untenable Fort Moultrie to Sumter on December 26, 1860. When this discreetly executed maneuver was discovered in Charleston, it was considered a hostile act. Under these circumstances, the last attempts in Washington to find a compromise solution had to fail. The "Crittenden Compromise," which tried to revive the old Missouri Compromise, as well as William Seward's suggestion for constitutional amendments came to nothing. When General-in-Chief Winfield Scott sent badly needed supplies and about 200 soldiers to Fort Sumter on the unarmed *Star of the West*, it was fired upon by South Carolina shore batteries and turned back. Lacking instructions from Washington, Anderson did not participate in the firing. While emotions ran high on both sides, no blood had yet been shed, and nothing changed until the new administration took over.

Lincoln's journey to Washington had not been without incident. After a 12-day, zig-zagging trip from Springfield, Illinois, he reached Harrisburg, Pennsylvania. There, he was informed by several people, including the private detective Allan Pinkerton, that a conspiracy existed to murder him, probably during his stay in Baltimore. Both General Winfield Scott and William H. Seward believed in the reality of the plot, and Lincoln, slightly disguised, slipped quietly out of town and got safely through Philadelphia and Baltimore to Washington. It has never been decided whether there had been a plan to assassinate him then. Pinkerton, apparently, had a very vivid imagination.

Lincoln's inaugural address was intended to buy time and cool passions on both sides. But on the next day, a report from Major Anderson informed Lincoln that he was running short of supplies. By now, not only General Scott and the majority of the new cabinet were for evacuation, it also turned out that Seward, the new secretary of state, had assured Southerners behind Lincoln's back that the fort would be abandoned.

Seward, a very capable but overambitious man, had done more than this to secure for himself the leading position in the new administration. He proposed to Lincoln that he demand explanations from France and Spain for interfering in Mexico and Santo Domingo and that he declare war on both powers should their answers be unsatisfactory. Such a war would reunite the country against a common foe. Lincoln made it clear that he disapproved of any such course and that any change of policy would have to come from him. He also informed Governor Pickens that a peaceful attempt to get supplies into Fort Sumter would be made. This put the Southern fanatics in a difficult position because they did not want to appear to be the aggressors in view of the still undecided attitude of the states of the "upper South": Virginia, North Carolina, Tennessee and Arkansas.

But Jefferson Davis, the president of the Confederacy, decided that he had to act now. Although warned by his own secretary of state, Robert Toombs, a dyed-in-the-wool secessionist, that an attack on Fort Sumter would result in a terrible civil war that would be fatal for the South, orders were sent to the commanding general in the Charleston area, Pierre G. T. Beauregard, to demand, and, if necessary, enforce a surrender. By this time, Anderson had only five days of supplies left. He would not submit to unconditional surrender, so the firing began, killing all hope for reinforcement by sea and for a peaceful solution. The fort, which surrendered after heavy bombardment, proved to be a strong fortress. Properly supplied and reinforced by the Confederates, it withstood innumerable heavy attacks by Union troops in the course of the war. The only consolation for the North was that Federal troops had occupied Fort Pickens, Florida, at the same time, without meeting serious opposition.

Lincoln took the attack on Sumter to be a declaration of war. For the time being, he could act by himself, since he had called for Congress to convene in July only. In his decision to go to war, he had not only the Republicans, but also the Northern Democrats, at least for some time, on his side. Stephen A. Douglas had met him and endorsed his forthcoming proclamation of an insurrection and a call for arms, though he advised him to call out 200,000 men rather than 75,000. The proclamation evoked a tremendous response in all the Northern states, but at the same time it pushed the vital state of Virginia, which had

Confederate General Pierre G.T. Beauregard.

been wavering up to this point, definitely into the Southern camp. In Richmond, the government's call to provide three Virginia regiments for the Union army was considered an insult and an attempt at brutal coercion. While the state convention had shown a Unionist majority before, it now voted for secession 88 to 55, with most of the Unionist votes coming from the western part of the state, which was to separate and turn independent (West Virginia) during the coming year. One day after Virginia's secession, Colonel Robert E. Lee, who had been serving in Texas, rejected General Scott's invitation to stay in the Union army and followed the course of his native state, a decision that, during the following years, turned out to be a great blow for the North. The other border states, North Carolina, Tennessee, Arkansas and Missouri, rejected Lincoln's call for troops in the same manner. All of them, except for Missouri, would soon join the Confederacy.

The secession of Virginia necessitated the abandonment of the federal arsenal at Harper's Ferry [now in West Virginia], which had become untenable. The Union officer in charge, Lieutenant Roger Jones, was a cousin of Robert E. Lee. More important yet, it significantly exposed the Union capital to attacks from the South. The transport of Union troops sent to protect the capital was seriously handicapped by sabotage in Maryland, which had a strong prosecession minority, and President Lincoln spent some troublesome days in Washington before the first Union troops arrived.

The secession of the four states of the upper South had not yet established the front lines completely. The four border states, Maryland,

Kentucky, Missouri and Delaware, had yet to decide on which side they stood. All four were slave states, though the proportion of slaves and slaveowners was less than half that of the already seceded states. The outcome was by no means a foregone conclusion, except for Delaware where a Southern request for secession had been immediately rejected. Much was at stake, because these four states would have added 45% to the white population and manpower of the Confederacy, as well as a considerable increase in industrial output and military supplies. Kentucky would be of great strategic value in case of an invasion from the North, and Maryland was even more crucial, as it enclosed Washington on three sides. But all four states wound up in the Union camp eventually.

Strong pro-Confederacy sentiment in Maryland surfaced when, right after Lincoln's proclamation, a Massachusetts regiment passing through on the way to the capital was attacked by a mob in Baltimore. In the wake of this, the mayor and chief of police of the city ordered the destruction of railroad bridges and telephone lines, thereby cutting off the capital for several days. But the legislature that Governor Thomas Hicks called into session decided against secession and declared the state "neutral," a position that was impossible to maintain under the circumstances. Unionism asserted itself more and more, although a sharp controversy arose over the prosecution of a violent secessionist, John Merryman, resulting in a clash between Supreme Court Justice Taney and the president. Secessionism flared up again after the first Battle of Bull Run, causing Lincoln to seal off Frederick where the legislature was meeting and arrest prosecession members and the mayor of Baltimore. When a new legislature was elected in November of 1861, the Union Party won an overwhelming victory, and this decided the position of the state for the rest of the war.

In Missouri, a long and violent struggle developed between the pro-secessionists led by Governor Claiborne Fox Jackson, a former "border ruffian" leader, and pro-Union Congressman Francis P. Blair, brother of Lincoln's postmaster general. The state was a blend of South and Middle West and included large numbers of German immigrants who settled mostly around St. Louis and had little use for Southern traditions and slavery. A state convention had rejected secession, but the governor asked for help from the distant Jefferson Davis in seizing the St. Louis U. S. arsenal, the largest in the slave states. But Captain Nathaniel Lyon, commander of the Union troops, was able to easily overwhelm the governor's militia with the help of German Americans. When the Confederate prisoners were led through the streets of St. Louis, a riot ensued that left 28 civilians and two soldiers dead. When Jackson appointed Sterling Price, a veteran of the Mexican War, to command the secessionist troops, civil war seemed to be at hand. Lyon's forces drove Price out of Jefferson City and Boonville. Now the Union controlled the greater part of the state, although confederate and Unionist guerilla bands kept on tearing the country apart.

In Kentucky, the Northern and Southern sympathies were more evenly divided. The state was surrounded by three slave and three free states, was the birthplace of both Abraham Lincoln and Jefferson Davis and prided itself on being the mediator between North and South in the tradition of Henry Clay. The legislature declared the state to be neutral, which, in practice, came close to secession because neutrality was based on the doctrine of state sovereignty. Although great amounts of goods passed through the state into the secession states, Lincoln refrained from exerting any pressure on Kentucky, a policy that paid off in the end. In the June and August 1861 elections, the Unionists won easy victories. When Confederate troops under Leonidas Polk invaded the state in order to seize strategically important Columbus, Kentucky, the neutrality came to an end. Three grandsons of Henry Clay fought for the Union, four others for the Confederacy, and all four brothers of Lincoln's wife fought for the South. The southwest corner of Kentucky remained in Confederate hands throughout the war, the rest was controlled by the Federals.

During the first months of the war, no large scale military activity took place near either capital because neither side had any army to speak of, let alone adequate weapons and equipment. The South had 15,000 men in the field, and had started to organize and equip an army of 100,000 men. About one-third of the North's officers joined the South; most of the high-ranking officers remaining in the North were veterans of the War of 1812, including General-in-Chief Winfield Scott. The new Secretary of War Cameron, political boss of Pennsylvania, had a reputation for corruption since his participation in dealings with the Winnebago Indians in the 1830s. Most of the arms in the U.S. arsenals, including those seized by the Confederates, were antiquated, the muskets being old smooth-bores or even flintlocks.

Both sides took out large war loans and called great numbers of men to arms. But many months would pass before they were assembled and could be trained; there was no adequate officers' corps to train them. Consequently, no attempt was made to seize each other's capitals, although Washington and Richmond were close to the borderline and hardly 100 miles apart. Instead, Winfield Scott developed a grand strategy that he believed would require a minimum of bloodshed, would avoid the devastation of large areas and would not have to rely on the newly recruited troops, which he considered worthless: He proposed to envelop the South by a blockade of the East Coast and a move down the Mississippi River, thus sealing off the secession states from both sides.

Lincoln, a Westerner who appreciated the strategic value of the Mississippi Valley, apparently was not averse to the plan. Actually, what developed later, after many vain frontal assaults by the Union armies, was not so different from what Scott had suggested in May of 1861. But Scott himself foresaw that the realization of his plan would take years, and that public opinion in the North simply would not tolerate the slow build-up of forces for the envelopment. This is exactly what happened. The cry "On to Richmond" grew louder day by day all over the North—and similarly, the South shouted "On to Washington." Scott's plan was ridiculed as the "Anaconda" plan by Republicans; he even was suspected of having Southern sympathies, since he had been born and raised in Virginia. There was also a practical reason that spoke for immediate action. Many of the volunteers had signed up for three months only, and it seemed reasonable to use them in action before their time was up.

One part of Scott's plans had been put into action by Lincoln a few days after the fall of Fort Sumter—a blockade against Confederate ports. At first, this amounted to no more than a nuisance to the South, for the Union was not equipped to control the long coastline from Virginia to Texas. But practically all the shipbuilding capacity in the country was in the North, and in Secretary of the Navy Gideon Welles and his assistant Gustavus V. Fox, Lincoln had two able organizers who within weeks had chartered or bought many merchants' ships, which were added to the few available Union warships. The South had almost no navy, but did have Secretary of the Navy Stephen R. Mallory, an ingenious organizer who converted various types of available commercial ships into gunboats, developed mines (called "torpedoes") that were planted at the entrances of harbors and rivers and even activated the first combat submarine, the C.S.S. *Hunley*. Building on British and French experiments with ironclads, he had the half-destroyed *Merrimack* rebuilt and sent his assistant James D. Bulloch to England to have some commerce raiders built there.

In their war against Northern merchant shipping, the Southern states depended at first on privateers, private craft armed by the government, which began to hunt down Northern merchants' ships. These privateers had been used with great success against the British in the wars of independence and of 1812. Lincoln had immediately announced that captured privateers would be treated as pirates, and, in response, Jefferson Davis threatened to execute one Union prisoner of war for every privateer hanged. Neither threat was actually carried out, as Lincoln gave in just in time. His position had been hardly tenable because, by imposing a blockade, he had acknowledged that the conflict was a war, not an internal insurrection, which made the privateers prisoners of war.

Although both sides avoided getting the problem of slavery into the conflict, the question was brought into the foreground when Benjamin F. Butler, Federal commander of Fort Monroe, declared some fugitive slaves, whom he was expected to return to their rightful owner, as "contraband of war" who could be held and used by the Union, the same as any other confiscated rebel property. Secretary of War Cameron agreed to this interpretation but forbade Union troops to give any encouragement to slaves to run away. This was all the more remarkable because at this time the Washington government did not legally recognize secession, so that the fugitive laws should still have been applied—the first indication that the war was certain to turn into a war against slavery eventually.

Before the main forces of the North and the South clashed in the Eastern theater, an important campaign was fought in western Virginia. When Virginia seceded, Southern troops cut off the vital Baltimore and Ohio railroad line connecting Washington with the Midwest. Appeals for help from western Virginia, where a strong pro-Union sentiment prevailed, found no response in Washington, where Scott and Irvin McDowell, his Northeastern commander, were more concerned with the defense of the capital. But William Dennison, governor of the neighboring state of Ohio, where more regiments of volunteers had been raised than had been called for by Lincoln's proclamation, immediately sent help. Under the command of Major General George B. McClellan, some Ohio and Indiana regiments crossed the Ohio River and joined up with two Unionist Virginia regiments, the B. & O. Railroad was reopened, and Southern troops under Brigadier General Robert S. Garnett were defeated by McClellan and Brigadier General William Starke Rosecrans's Union troops at Rich Mountain and Corrick's Ford. McClellan took all the credit for these successes and was hailed as "The Young Napoleon." Indeed, his proclamations to his troops were beginning to sound more and more like those of Napoleon in 1796.

The Northeastern Commander McDowell had, meanwhile, developed his own plan to advance against Manassas Junction, where Beauregard had amassed an army of about 25,000 men. His aim was to attack Beauregard and at the same time have General Robert Patterson keep Southern General J. E. Johnston busy. Johnston, in the Shenandoah

Jefferson Davis and his cabinet, with Robert E. Lee center.

Valley, threatened to move down to join up with Beauregard. McDowell's advance was extremely slow because of a shortage of supply wagons and his inexperienced troops were unaccustomed to long marches. Also, Union General Patterson was duped by Confederate General J. E. Johnston, who disengaged his troops, joined Beauregard and took the overall command in the first large scale battle of the war, the First Battle of Bull Run (Manassas Junction).

Both sides fought under severe handicaps. Their troops had very little training: Most of them had never been trained on more than company level so that coordinated larger-scale attacks soon became confused. Neither side managed to get all troops into battle. The flag used by the Confederates was often indistinguishable from the Union flag, and much confusion surrounded the uniforms, as in each army some troops wore blue and some gray. Both Northern and Southern soldiers, tired and hungry after long hours of marching, frequently broke ranks and went into the fields to eat blackberries. McDowell's grand strategy, a huge flanking movement in order to get behind the Confederate's left flank, got as far as Sudley Springs but then developed an attack by driblets only and was halted after Johnston and Beauregard recognized McDowell's plan and reorganized their troops. The fighting then concentrated on Henry House Hill where McDowell, on July 21 at noon, amassed about 10,000 of the 18,000 men who had crossed Bull Run. He himself got to the top of the hill where the 84-year-old mistress of Henry House had been killed by shellfire. Then strong Confederate counterattacks, led by Beauregard and Colonel Jubal Early, drove the Union army back, over-ran many of its batteries and managed to disorganize the Union units completely. The officers got separated from their men, who began to scramble for safety in ever-increasing numbers. The picture on the Confederate side was not much better, however. Jefferson Davis, who had come up from Richmond, had the impression that his armies were in a state of dissolution and tried personally to get the men back into the fight. But Brigadier General Thomas Jonathan ("Stonewall") Jackson, whose brigade had withstood all attacks on the hills, was correct in stating that by then the Union troops were no longer an army, but a panic-stricken mass of individuals scrambling to safety in the direction of Washington. He asked—in vain—for 5,000 fresh troops—which would suffice to take the capital.

In all, it is safe to say that at the time of the Battle of Bull Run very few Americans had realized what war in earnest was all about. Many officers were not up to their tasks, most of the troops had been used beyond their capacity and civilians in Washington were naive enough to consider the battle as a pleasant spectacle to be observed for entertainment from a safe distance. The fact that July 21 was a Sunday and that thousands of spectators, including some members of Congress, had come close to the battlefield added to the disaster that followed. Civilians got entangled with retreating stragglers and fleeing soldiers; the huge human jam that resulted was increased by Confederate cannon fire and overthrown civilian carriages. McDowell tried in vain to make a stand at Centreville, but there was no way of halting the panic-stricken masses until they had reached the Potomac. Jefferson Davis intended at first to order an immediate pursuit but was then persuaded that his army, too, was utterly exhausted. Later, he was blamed for having wasted a glorious chance for a complete victory and an early end of the war. More likely, however, such an attempt would have failed because sufficient fresh Union troops that had never been ordered into the battle remained to defend the capital.

The First Battle of Bull Run was by far not the largest fought in the war, nor were the casualties on either side excessive, compared with later figures. But the unexpected, thorough defeat of the Union troops had a devastating effect all over the country and also abroad. One forgot that the number of troops engaged by both sides had been almost equal, that the Union troops had done all the attacking and had come close to victory. They were ridiculed at home and abroad. The German-American Carl Schurz, an ardent Republican and at that time U. S. minister to Spain, reported that the standing joke in the coffeehouses of Madrid was that the battle should have been called "patassas" (feet) instead of "Manassas" (hands). Walt Whitman furiously attacked the Union officers who had gathered at Willard's Hotel in Washington for telling each other their version of the battle instead of standing by their men.

The battle put an end to McDowell's career and postponed for eight months any Union efforts to invade the heartland of Virginia. But the defense of Washington was secured and, in the long run, the impact on the North was renewed determination, not defeatism.

CHRONICLE OF EVENTS

1860:

November 10: South Carolina passes a law for a convention to meet on December 17 to discuss the question of secession. The two Senators from South Carolina resign from the U.S. Senate.

November 12: Heavy selling in the New York financial market and a sharp drop in prices.

November 13: The South Carolina legislature decides to raise 10,000 volunteers.

November 18: The Georgia legislature votes a million dollars for arming the state.

November 20: Attorney General Jeremiah Sullivan Black advises President Buchanan that it is his duty to protect public property despite resistance, but that he could not take action with troops against elements that opposed the government with words only. Also, that the government could repel aggression, but could not wage an offensive war against a state and that law enforcement must be enacted through the courts.

December 1: The legislature of Florida convenes in special session to consider the issues of the hour.

December 3: The second session of the 36th Congress of the United States convenes in Washington.

December 4: President Buchanan's message on the state of the Union, blaming the free states for the secession.

December 5: President-elect Lincoln expresses disagreement with Buchanan's statement.

December 8: Howell Cobb of Georgia, secretary of the treasury, resigns, since he has convinced himself that the election of a Republican justified secession. He is succeeded by Philip F. Thomas of Maryland—for about one month.

December 12: Lewis Cass of Michigan, secretary of state, resigns because President Buchanan refuses to reinforce the Charleston forts, in order to avoid a confrontation.

December 13: Seven senators and 23 representatives from the South issue a manifesto urging secession.

December 17: The South Carolina Secession Convention meets.

President Buchanan appoints Attorney General Jeremiah S. Black as secretary of state to succeed Lewis Cass.

December 18: In Washington, Senator John J. Crittenden proposes his "Crittenden Compromise," which prohibits all slavery north of latitude 36° 30', the old Missouri Compromise line.

December 20: South Carolina formally secedes from the Union.

President Buchanan appoints Democratic leader Edwin M. Stanton as attorney general to replace J. S. Black.

December 24: South Carolina Governor Pickens issues a proclamation declaring the state separate, independent, free and sovereign.

In Washington, Senator William H. Seward proposes an amendment to the Constitution that Congress should never interfere with slaves in the states, that jury trial be given fugitive slaves and that state constitutions with personal liberty laws in opposition to the federal Constitution be revised.

December 26: Outside of Charleston Harbor, Major Robert Anderson completes the transfer of the small garrison from Fort Moultrie to Fort Sumter. South Carolina and other Southern areas are outraged, and Secretary of War Floyd opposes the move. The president had been surprised by it and regretted it.

December 28: Buchanan sees commissioners of the state of South Carolina as "private gentlemen."

December 29: Resignation of Secretary of War Floyd. Buchanan had requested his resignation on December 23 when Floyd proposed the removal of federal troops from Charleston.

December 30: South Carolina troops seize the

Federal Arsenal at Charleston and complete the occupation of all federal property in the area except Fort Sumter.

December 31: Postmaster General Joseph Holt is named acting Secretary of War replacing Floyd. The president orders the War and Navy departments to send ships with troops and supplies to Fort Sumter.

The Senate Committee of Thirteen reports that it is not able to agree on any plan for adjustment or compromise, including the Crittenden proposal.

1861:

January 3: Former Secretary of War Floyd's order to transfer guns from Pittsburgh to Southern forts is cancelled by the War Department.

The State Convention of Florida assembles at Tallahassee.

Georgia state troops occupy Fort Pulaski, at the mouth of the Savannah River, manned only by an ordnance sergeant and a civilian.

January 4: Alabama takes over the U.S. Arsenal at Mount Vernon, Alabama.

January 5: The *Star of the West,* a merchant vessel, leaves New York for Fort Sumter with supplies and 250 troops.

January 5: State troops of Alabama occupy Forts Morgan and Gaines at the entrance to Mobile Bay.

January 6: The Apalachicola Arsenal is taken over by the state of Florida.

January 7: Fort Marion at St. Augustine is occupied by Florida troops.

The Mississippi and Alabama State Conventions begin deliberating.

The House of Representatives in Washington approves Major Anderson's troops transfer from Fort Moultrie to Fort Sumter.

January 8: The last Southerner in the Cabinet, Secretary of the Interior Jacob Thompson, resigns. He telegraphs Charleston that the *Star of the West* is coming.

In a special message to Congress, Buchanan advocates the Crittenden Compromise.

January 9: The Mississippi State Convention at Jackson votes to secede, 84 to 15.

Outside of Charleston Harbor, the *Star of the West* is fired upon and returns to New York undamaged. Major Anderson protests the firing to Governor Pickens, but takes no action to support the *Star of the West.*

January 10: The Florida State Convention votes 62 to 7 to secede.

The Federal garrison at Pensacola, Florida is transferred to Fort Pickens on Santa Rosa Island.

Louisiana state troops seize the U.S. Arsenals at Baton Rouge, Fort Jackson and St. Philip.

William H. Seward accepts the post of secretary of state.

January 11: Alabama votes to secede, 61 to 39.

South Carolina again demands the surrender of Fort Sumter and is refused by Major Anderson.

January 12: Mississippi representatives withdraw from the House.

Florida state troops occupy Fort Barrancas, Fort McCree and the Pensacola Navy Yard. Surrender of Fort Pickens is demanded and refused.

January 14: The House Committee of Thirty-Three is unable to agree on any compromise proposal. But Chairman Thomas Corwin proposes another compromise in the form of a Constitutional amendment protecting slavery, which is passed by Congress but never ratified by the states.

Louisiana troops seize Fort Pike, near New Orleans, while federal troops garrison Fort Taylor at Key West, Florida.

January 18: Postmaster Joseph Holt of Kentucky is appointed secretary of war.

Federal troops garrison Fort Jefferson, off Key West, which will become famous as a prison for political prisoners during the Civil War.

January 19: The Georgia State Convention at Midgeville votes 208 to 89 in favor of secession. There remains, however, a strong moderate group led by Alexander H. Stephens, Herschel V. Johnson and Benjamin H. Hill.

January 20: Forces of the state of Mississippi take Fort Massachusetts in the Gulf of Mississippi.

January 21: Five Southern Senators, including Jefferson Davis of Mississippi, leave the senate chamber in a dramatic scene.

January 24: The U.S. Arsenal at Augusta, Georgia is taken over by Georgia state troops.

January 26: At Baton Rouge, the Louisiana State Convention votes for secession, 113 to 17; it is the 6th state to secede.

The Oglethorpe Barracks and Fort Jackson at Savannah, are occupied by Georgia state troops.

January 28: Louisiana state troops take Fort Macomb, near New Orleans.

January 29: Kansas is admitted to the Union as the 34th state. Its constitution (Wyandotte Constitution) prohibits slavery.

The U.S. revenue cutter *Robert McClelland* surrenders to Louisiana state authorities in New Orleans, despite orders from Washington to defend the vessel.

January 30: At Mobile, Alabama, the U.S. revenue cutter *Lewis Cass* surrenders to state officers.

January 31: The U.S. Branch Mint and Custom House at New Orleans and the revenue schooner *Washington* are taken over by the state of Louisiana.

February 1: At Austin, the Texas State Convention voters for secession, 166 to 7.

February 4: A convention of the seven seceded states meets in Montgomery, Alabama. Louisiana Senators Benjamin and Slidell withdraw from the U.S. Congress.

The Peace Convention called by Virginia convenes in Washington. One hundred and thirty-one members represent 21 states, but none of the seceded states participates. Former President John Tyler presides.

February 5: The South Carolina Commissioner

is advised by the Buchanan administration that Fort Sumter will not be surrendered under any circumstances.

February 7: The Choctaw Indian Nation declares its adherence to the Southern states.

February 8: At Montgomery, Alabama the Provisional Constitution of the Confederate States is adopted unanimously. It is mainly based on the Constitution of the United States, but mentions explicitly the right to own slaves; the importation of slaves is prohibited. Slavery in any territories of the Confederacy is protected, and the fugitive slave law is strengthened.

Arkansas state troops seize the U.S. Arsenal at Little Rock.

President Buchanan approves a loan of $25,000,000 for current expenses and redemption of treasury notes.

February 9: Jefferson Davis is elected Provisional President and Alexander Stephens Provisional Vice-President of the Confederacy. Davis is considered a moderate. His aim had actually been a high military command in the Confederacy. Other candidates for the presidency were William Lowndes Yancey, Howell Cobb, Robert Toombs and Robert Barnwell Rhett.

In Tennessee, a proposal to call a convention to consider secession is rejected by the voters, 68,282 to 59,449.

February 11: President-elect Lincoln leaves Springfield, Illinois for his inauguration in Washington.

Jefferson Davis leaves his plantation in Brierfield, Warren County, Mississippi, for his inauguration at Montgomery, Alabama.

February 18: Jefferson Davis is inaugurated as president of the Confederacy.

February 23: Lincoln arrives in Washington.

February 26: Camp Colorado in Texas is evacuated by federal authorities.

February 27: Confederate President Davis names three Confederate commissioners to attempt negotiations in Washington.

The Peace Convention in Washington recommends six constitutional amendments that, however, have no chance to be passed by Congress.

February 28: The Confederate Congress authorizes a domestic loan of $15,000,000.

The U.S. territory of Colorado is formed.

The House of Representatives passes the amendment of Thomas Corwin, proposed by The Committee of Thirty-three and approved by Lincoln, declaring that slavery would not be interfered with where it already existed.

March 1: At Fort Sumter, Major Anderson advises Washington that further delay on the decision to evacuate or to reinforce the fort is impossible.

March 2: The Confederate Congress provides for the admission of Texas to the Confederacy.

President Buchanan approves two new territories, Nevada and Dakota (later to be divided into North Dakota and South Dakota).

The Senate rejects the Peace Convention's resolutions, against the advice of John J. Crittenden of Kentucky.

March 3: President-elect Lincoln gives a dinner for his newly appointed cabinet and visits the Senate.

Brigadier General Pierre Gustave Toutant Beauregard assumes command of the Confederate troops around Charleston Harbor.

March 4: Abraham Lincoln is inaugurated as 16th president of the United States, with Hannibal Hamlin of Maine as his vice-president. Chief Justice Roger B. Taney administers the oath of office. Three members of the new Cabinet, William H. Seward, secretary of state; Salmon P. Chase, secretary of the treasury and Attorney General Edward Bates had been leading contenders for the Republican nomination.

March 5: Major Anderson's recent message that reinforcements could probably not reach Fort Sumter before its supplies ran out and that it would take at least 20,000 men to hold the fort is discussed at Lincoln's first cabinet meeting. Lieutenant General Winfield Scott agrees with Major Anderson.

March 7: Ringgold Barracks and Camp Verde in Texas are evacuated by federal forces.

The Missouri Convention shows strong pro-Union sentiment and considers the Crittenden Compromise as a possibility to avoid a conflict.

March 11: The Confederate Congress unanimously adopts the Constitution of the Confederacy. Seven states will ratify it by the end of April.

March 12: Fort McIntosh, Texas, is evacuated by federal troops.

March 15: In a Cabinet meeting, Lincoln asks all members for their written opinion on whether or not to send provisions to Fort Sumter. Most members voice opposition to an attempt to relieve the fort.

March 17: Camp Hudson, Texas, is evacuated by federal troops.

March 18: Governor Sam Houston of Texas refuses to take the oath of allegiance to the Confederacy and retires from public life.

March 19: In Texas, Forts Clark, Inge and Lancaster are abandoned by federal troops.

March 20: Fort Brown and Fort Duncan in Texas are given up.

March 29: Lincoln finally decides to send an expedition by sea to reinforce Fort Sumter, to sail not later than April 6.

March 30: Lincoln orders a relief expedition for Fort Pickens, Florida. The majority of his Cabinet is in favor of such expeditions—but not Secretary of State Seward.

Fort Bliss, Texas, is abandoned by the federals.

April 6: Lincoln informs Governor Pickens of South Carolina that an attempt will be made to supply Fort Sumter with provisions and, if there is no resistance, no reinforcements would be sent.

April 11: General Beauregard, upon instructions from his secretary of war, demands of Major Anderson that he evacuate the fort. Anderson refuses but adds that he would be starved out in a few days anyway. Confederate Secretary of War Walker instructs Beauregard not to bombard if Anderson will state the time of evacuation.

The three Confederate commissioners leave Washington, feeling they have been misled by Seward and the federal government.

April 12: Shortly after midnight, Beauregard's messengers ask Anderson again about the time of evacuation. Anderson replies he would evacuate on the 15th at noon, unless he receives additional supplies or further orders from his government. He is told that Confederate batteries would open fire within one hour.

The bombardment begins at 4:30 A.M. The fort's 48 guns, manned by only 85 officers and men and some women employed in the fort, answer by 7:00 A.M. They face 4,000 Confederate troops and about 70 guns.

Federal troops are landed at Fort Pickens, Florida, at the entrance to Pensacola Bay. The Confederates cannot prevent the landings.

April 13: After 34 hours of bombardment, Fort Sumter is forced to surrender. Several federal ships have arrived, but cannot complete their mission because the firing had started. Food supplies at the fort are exhausted, and few artillery cartridges are left. Fires have become unextinguishable, and the powder magazine is threatened. The fort is surrendered at 2:30 in the afternoon. Some 4,000 shells had been fired at it, but no one was killed.

April 14: At the formal surrender, two men are killed and four wounded by an accidental explosion. Great celebrations in Charleston.

The cabinet in Washington approves Lincoln's call for 75,000 militia, and a special session of Congress to meet only on July 4.

April 15–16: President Lincoln's proclamation declaring that an insurrection has taken place is welcomed in the Northern states, but his call for troops is rejected in Kentucky, North Carolina and Virginia.

Forts Caswell and Johnston are seized by North Carolina state troops.

April 17: The Virginia State Convention votes in favor of secession.

Confederate soldiers at the outbreak of the war.

Large secessionist meeting in Baltimore.

Missouri and Tennessee refuse to furnish their quota of militia.

April 18: The first five companies of Pennsylvania troops arrive in Washington.

The Sixth Massachusetts marches triumphantly through New York.

The U.S. Armory at Harper's Ferry, Virginia is abandoned and burned by its garrison.

A secessionist flag is raised on Federal Hills in Baltimore, Maryland.

The U.S. Customs House and Post Office in Richmond, Virginia are taken over by state troops.

April 19: President Lincoln declares a blockade of the ports of the seven seceded states.

Riots in Baltimore, as the Sixth Massachusetts passes through on its way to Washington.

Colonel Robert E. Lee resigns his commission in the U.S. Army.

Several railroad bridges are burnt to prevent

passage of Union troops from Baltimore to Washington.

The Federal Gosport Navy Yard near Norfolk, Virginia is evacuated and partially burned on orders of Commandant Charles S. McCauley, perhaps prematurely.

April 22: The steamer *Boston* brings the Seventh New York to Annapolis, Maryland.

Illinois troops arrive at Cairo, Illinois.

Robert E. Lee is nominated as commander of the forces of Virginia.

April 23: Arkansas troops seize Fort Smith. President Davis in Montgomery promises aid to the governor of Missouri, if Missouri secessionists would attack the St. Louis Arsenal.

April 25: The Seventh New York and the Eighth Massachusetts regiments reach Washington. The capital was temporarily isolated because of the hostilities in Maryland, and they had to go by water to Annapolis and then rebuild the railroad as they went.

April 26: Governor Joseph Brown of Georgia issues an order for repudiation by citizens of all debts owed to Northerners.

Major General Joseph E. Johnston is assigned to command state forces in and around Richmond, Virginia.

April 29: The Maryland House of Delegates votes against secession, 53 to 13.

April 30: Following orders of the federal government to evacuate garrisons in Indian territory, Fort Washita near the Texas border is abandoned by Colonel William H. Emory. This leaves the Cherokees, Choctaws, Chickasaws, Creeks and Seminoles open to pressure from the Confederates.

May 1: Major General Robert E. Lee orders out further volunteer troops, with a concentration at Harper's Ferry.

Troops continue to pour into Washington, including the New York Fire Zouaves under Colonel Elmer E. Ellsworth.

The mouth of the James River is placed under strict blockade by the federal Navy.

May 3: President Lincoln calls for 42,034 volunteers to serve for a maximum of three years, plus ten additional regiments for the regular army, and 18,000 seamen.

General Winfield Scott reveals to General McClellan his "Anaconda Plan," which was to envelop the insurgent states by blockading the East coast and moving down the Mississippi all the way to its mouth.

May 6: The legislatures of Arkansas and Tennessee pass secession ordinances.

President Davis in Montgomery approves a bill of the Confederate Congress declaring that the Confederacy recognizes a state of war between the USA and the CSA.

May 7: The Tennessee legislature votes to join the Confederacy.

Riot between pro-Union and pro-Secessionist elements in Knoxville, Tenn.

May 9: Pro-Confederate units leave Maryland as this state swings toward the Union.

U.S.S. *Constitution* and U.S. steamer *Baltic* arrive at Newport, Rhode Island to set up the Naval Academy dispossessed from Annapolis for the duration.

May 10: Riots in St. Louis, Missouri between pro-Union regular army troops and the German population on the one hand, and the pro-secession militia. About 29 people are killed.

Off Charleston, the U.S.S. *Niagara* begins a blockade patrol.

President Davis calls for the purchase of six warships, arms and stores, while his secretary of the navy urges the building of ironclads.

May 13: Union troops under Brigadier General Benjamin F. Butler occupy Baltimore.

May 17: President Davis authorizes a loan to the Confederacy of $50,000,000, and the issuance of treasury notes.

May 18: Arkansas is officially accepted to the Confederacy. The mouth of the Rappahannock River in Virginia is blockaded by the Federal Navy.

May 20: North Carolina, the 11th and last state to leave the Union, joins the Confederacy.

The governor of Kentucky issues a proclamation of neutrality.

The Provisional Congress of the Confederacy

votes to move the capital from Montgomery to Richmond, Virginia.

May 23: The citizens of Virginia vote in favor of secession, three to one. In western Virginia, the vote is overwhelmingly against secession.

May 24: Federal troops enter Virginia and take Alexandria. Elmer Ellsworth, leader of the First Fire Zouave team is shot while removing a secession flag from the Marshall House and becomes the first martyr for the federal cause.

May 29: Three Federal vessels bombard enemy batteries for three days at Aquia Creek, Virginia.

May 30: Federal troops occupy Grafton, in western Virginia, in order to guard the Baltimore and Ohio Railroad.

May 31: Federal troops occupy Fort Leavenworth, Kansas, after abandoning posts in the Indian territory.

June 2: General Beauregard takes command of the Confederate forces in northern Virginia.

June 3: Stephen A. Douglas dies in Chicago, only 48 years old.

Federal troops launch a surprise attack on a Confederate detachment at Philippi, in western Virginia ("Philippi Races"). The Southerners, under Colonel G. A. Porterfield, make no defense and flee, hotly pursued by the federals under General T. A. Morris.

June 8: Tennessee voters approve secession by a large majority.

June 10: Several Federal regiments, about 2,500 men, unsuccessfully attack a Confederate position at Big Bethel, Virginia.

In St. Louis, Missouri, clash between General Nathaniel Lyon, Commander of the Federals, with the pro-Confederate Governor Claiborne Jackson, who calls for 50,000 state militia to protect citizens against the threats from the federal troops.

June 15: The pro-Confederates under Governor Jackson evacuate the Missouri state capital. Federal raid on Romney in western Virginia causes Confederate troops under Joseph E. Johnston to evacuate Harper's Ferry.

June 17: Federal troops under General Lyon move up in the Missouri River and occupy Boonville, Missouri after a short fight. Governor Jackson retires to the southwestern part of the state.

June 29: The Eleventh Massachusetts Infantry and the Twelfth New York enter Washington.

June 30: The Confederate C.S.S. *Sumter* under Raphael Semmes, runs the blockade near New Orleans and starts on a career as a commerce raider.

July 3: Federal troops under Brigadier General Robert Patterson cross the Potomac, march into the Shenandoah Valley and advance to Martinsburg. Confederate troops under General Joseph E. Johnston fall back toward Winchester, Virginia.

July 4: Special session of the 37th Congress. Lincoln asks for ratification of special measures necessitated by the war, for at least 400,000 men and $4 million.

July 5: Federal troops, mostly Germans, under Colonel Franz Sigel, attack the poorly equipped and greatly outnumbered force of Governor Jackson near Carthage, Missouri, but are repulsed.

July 7: Skirmishes at Bellington and Laurel Hill, western Virginia, and at Great Falls, Maryland.

July 11: Brigadier General William Starke Rosecrans, under McClellan, defeats Confederate troops at Rich Mountain in western Virginia.

July 12: A treaty between the Confederates and the Chocktaw and Chickasaw Indians is signed.

July 13: Confederate troops under General Robert S. Garnett are defeated at Corrick's Ford in western Virginia.

July 14: Blockade of Wilmington, North Carolina is set up by the U.S.S. *Daylight*.

July 16: General Irvin McDowell begins to move his army in direction of Centreville and Manassas, Virginia.

July 17: Confederate troops under General J. E. Johnston disengage themselves from the enemy in the Shenandoah Valley and cross the mountains to aid General Beauregard.

July 18: A Federal reconnaissance force sent by McDowell against the Confederate positions at Bull Run is repulsed at Blackburn's Ford, Virginia, by General Longstreet's troops.

July 20: General Johnston joins Beauregard at Manassas and takes over supreme command.

In a message to his Congress, President Davis announces that Arkansas, North Carolina, Tennessee and Virginia are joining the Confederacy and that the capital is transferred to Richmond, Virginia.

July 21: The Battle of First Bull Run (or Manassas). About 35,000 Union troops, of which only 18,500 are actually engaged, face approximately 32,000 Confederates some of whose reinforcements arrive only during the battle and of which only 18,000 are engaged. Both sides plan an attack on their right flank. There is much confusion on either side. After initial successes, the Federal army is frustrated by Confederate cavalry attacks under Colonel J. E. B. Stuart and halted by General "Stonewall" Jackson at Henry House Hill. With the help of Colonel Jubal A. Early's brigade, the Confederates counterattack while the Union troops flee in great disorder toward Washington, running into civilian crowds from the city who had come to watch the engagement. The Confederates are too weak to follow up with an assault on Washington, but capture great amounts of arms and equipment. The Federals lose about 3,000 troops killed, wounded or missing, the Confederates about 2,000.

July 22: Young Major General George McClellan who had been victorious in western Virginia is named successor to the defeated McDowell.

EYEWITNESS TESTIMONY

I could say nothing which I have not already said and which is in print and open for the inspection of all. To press a repetition of this upon those who have listened, is useless; to press it upon those who have refused to listen, and still refuse, would be wanting in self-respect, and would have an appearance of sycophancy and timidity . . .

Lincoln, November 10, 1860, in Springfield, Illinois.

Good governments can never be built up or sustained by the impulse of passion . . . Let the fanatics of the North break the Constitution, if such is their fell purpose.

Alexander H. Stephens, Congressman from Georgia, at the legislature in Milledgeville, November 14, 1860.

Let there be no compromise on the question of extending slavery. If there be, all our labor is lost, and, ere long, must be done again . . . The tug has to come and better now, than any time thereafter.

President-elect Lincoln to Senator Lyman Turnbull, December 10, 1860.

It is no less than our fixed determination to throw off a government to which we have been accustomed, and to provide new safeguards for our future security. If anything has been decided by the elections which sent us here, it is, that South Carolina must dissolve her connection with the (Federal) Confederacy as speedily as possible . . . Let us no longer be duped by paper securities. Written Constitutions are worthless, unless they are written, at the same time, in the hearts, and founded on the interests of the people; and as there is no common bond of sympathy or interest between the North and the South, all efforts to preserve this Union will not only be fruitless, but fatal to the less numerous section.

D. F. Jamison, president of the Convention of the People of South Carolina, at the Baptist Church of Columbia, South Carolina, December 17, 1860.

The South would be in no more danger in this respect [the interference with slavery by the federal government], than it was in the days of Washington. I suppose, however, that this does not meet the case.

You think slavery is right and ought to be extended; we think it is wrong and ought to be restricted. That I suppose is the rub.

Lincoln to Alexander H. Stephens, congressman from Georgia, December 22, 1860.

You are pressing me too importunately, you don't give me time to consider; you don't give me time to say my prayers; I always say my prayers when required to act upon any great state affair.

President Buchanan to two South Carolina commissioners, during their conference on December 27/28, 1860. Quoted by N. W. Stephenson in Abraham Lincoln and the Union *(1918).*

It may have been treason . . . but he awaits sentence at the bar of history in a very respectable company, including . . . Oliver Cromwell, Sir Henry Vane and George Washington . . .

Charles Francis Adams, on Lee's decision to fight for the South, quoted by Robert Penn Warren, The Legacy of the Civil War *(1961).*

If the cotton states shall decide that they can do better out of the Union than in it, we shall insist on letting them go in peace . . . We hope never to live in a republic where one section is pinned to the residue by bayonets.

Horace Greeley, in the New York Tribune, *end of 1860.*

These gentlemen claim to be ambassadors. It is preposterous! They cannot be ambassadors; they are lawbreakers, traitors. They should be arrested. You cannot negotiate with them; and yet it seems by this paper that you have been led into doing that very same thing. With all respect to you, Mr. President, I must say that the Attorney General, under his oath of office, dares not to be cognizant of the pending proceedings. Your reply to these so-called ambassadors . . . is wholly unlawful, and improper . . . and to send it as an official document will bring the President to the verge of usurpation.

Attorney General Stanton to Buchanan, December 29, 1860.

You have resolved to hold by force what you have obtained through our misplaced confidence, and by refusing to disavow the action of Major Anderson, have converted his violation of orders into a legitimate act of your executive authorities . . . If you choose to force the issue upon us, the State of South Carolina will accept it.

Commissioners of South Carolina to President Buchanan, letter of January 2, 1861. The President declined to receive it officially.

Let the people, therefore, speak. Of the five millions of voters in the United States, it is within bounds to say that four million three hundred thousand are conservative in sentiment and prepared to concede to the South their reasonable demands. A constituent convention of the Southern States is already impending. The effervescence which has resulted in mob rule, violence, the seizure of national fortresses . . . is generally disapproved of, even in slaveholding communities.

James Gordon Bennett's Herald, *New York, January 5, 1861.*

Senators, we are rapidly drifting into a position in which this is to become a Government of the Army and Navy, in which the authority of the United States is to be maintained, not by law, not by constitutional agreement between the States, but by physical force; and you will stand still and see this policy consummated?

Senator Jefferson Davis, in the Senate on January 10, 1861.

I concur in the action of the people of Mississippi, believing it to be necessary and proper, and should have been bound by their action if my belief had been otherwise . . . I am sure I feel no hostility to you, Senators of the North. I am sure there is not one of you, whatever sharp discussion there may have been between us, to whom I cannot now say, in the presence of my God, I wish you well . . .

Jefferson Davis, farewell address in the Senate, January 21, 1861.

You're a traitor convicted, you know very well!/ Jefferson D., Jefferson D.!/ You thought it a capital thing to rebel, / Jefferson D.!/ But there's one thing I'll say;/ You'll discover some day,/ When you see a stout cotton cord hang from a tree,/ There's an accident happened you didn't foresee,/ Jefferson D.!

H. S. Cornwell, Jefferson D. *(1861).*

Whilst in Washington, we passed our time principally in the Senate, where we always found a seat in the diplomatic loges. We heard Seward, Douglas . . . speak, and heard one of Douglas' most able debates. Nothing ever interested me so much, although I was astonished to see the apathy with which the Senators generally listened and wrote or read their papers whilst such vital subjects were discussed and integrity of the United States (so great a nation) hung upon their vote . . . The Senators from the Eastern states seemed to have no other idea than that they were the victors (in the election) and that the slavery and the South should suffer. Senator Crittenden from Kentucky seemed the only patriot except Thomson (Senator from New Jersey) and Douglas in the house.

Maria L. Daly, January 31, 1861, Diary of a Union Lady *(1962).*

We went to one of the President's levees. I never saw so incapable a face as Buchanan's. Surely no woman would have been crazy enough, had he been in the profession of medicine, to entrust him with the health of her poodle. And that was the poor, almost imbecilic looking man who was President of the United States and possessed more power than any constitutional monarch in Europe . . . Indeed, when I looked over the two houses [of Congress] I was struck with want of statesmanlike looking men in both.

Maria L. Daly, January 31, 1861, Diary.

The separation is perfect, complete and perpetual. The great duty is now imposed upon us of providing for these States a government for their future security and protection.

Howell Cobb, president of the Convention of Seceded States in Montgomery, Alabama, February 4, 1861.

I have not maintained silence from any want of real anxiety. It is a good thing there is no more than anxiety, for there is nothing going wrong. It is consoling circumstance that when we look out there is nothing that hurts anybody. We entertain different views upon political questions, but nobody is suffering anything.

Lincoln in a speech at Columbus, Ohio, on his trip to Washington, on February 13, 1861. His remarks puzzled many of his listeners.

The time for compromise has now passed, and the South is determined to maintain her position, and make all who oppose her smell Southern powder

and feel Southern steel if coercion is persisted in . . . It may be that our career will be ushered in the midst of a storm; it may be that, as this morning opened with clouds, rain and mist, we shall have to encounter inconveniences at the beginning; but, as the sun rose and lifted the mist, it dispersed the clouds and left us the pure sunshine of heaven. So will progress the Southern Confederacy, and carry us safe into the harbor of constitutional liberty and political equality.
Jefferson Davis in Montgomery, February 16, 1861.

Upon my weary heart was showered smiles, plaudits and flowers; but, beyond them, I saw troubles and thorns innumerable. We are without machinery, without means, and threatened by a powerful opposition; but I do not despond, and will not shrink from the task imposed upon me.
Jefferson Davis, letter to his wife after his inauguration on February 18, 1861.

I never had a feeling politically that did not spring from the sentiments embodied in the Declaration of Independence. It was that which gave promise that in due time the weights should be lifted from the shoulders of all men, and that all men should have an equal chance.
Lincoln, speech at the Washington's birthday celebration at Independence Hall in Philadelphia, February 22, 1861.

The more we see and hear of his outgivings on his way to Washington, the more we are forced to the conclusion that he is not even a man of ordinary capacity. He assumes to be insensible of the difficulties before him—treats the most startling political questions with childish simplicity, and manifests much of the disposition of the mad fanatic who meets his fate—not in the spirit of respectful Christian resignation, but with the insane smile of derision upon his lips, as if unconscious of the destiny that awaits him. We may readily anticipate that such a man will be the pliant tool of ambitious demagogues, and that his administration will be used to subserve their wicked purposes.
Montgomery Post *on Lincoln February 22, 1861.*

They say if we had been left out in the cold alone, we might have sulked a while, but back we would have had to go . . . We needed a little wholesome neglect. Anderson has blocked that game, but now our Sister states have joined us and we are strong . . .
Mrs. Mary Boykin Chesnut, The situation at Fort Sumter, February 1861. A Diary from Dixie *(1929).*

It would have been almost as instructive if President Lincoln had contented himself with telling his audience yesterday a funny story and let them go. His inaugural is but a paraphrase of the vague generalities contained in his pilgrimage speeches, and shows clearly either that he has not made up his mind respecting his future course, or . . . that he desires, for the present, to keep his intentions to himself.
New York Herald, *March 5, 1861.*

Other press reactions to Lincoln's Inaugural Speech:
If declaring the Union perpetual mean coercion, then Lincoln's Inaugural means war!
The Arkansas True Democrat.

War. War, and nothing less than war will satisfy the Abolition chief.
The Weekly Adviser, *Montgomery.*

A more lamentable display of feeble inability to grasp the circumstances of this momentous emergency could scarcely be exhibited.
The Charleston Mercury.

Every word of it has the ring of true metal.
The New York Tribune.

The atmosphere was thick with treason. Party spirit and old party differences prevailed, however, amidst these accumulated dangers. Secession was considered by most persons as a political party question, not as a rebellion. Democrats to a large extent sympathized with the Rebels more than with the Administration . . . not that they wished Secession to be successful and the Union divided, but they hoped that President Lincoln and the Republicans would, overwhelmed by obstacles and embarrassments, prove failures. The Republicans, on the other hand, were scarcely less partisan and unreasonable.
Gideon Welles, about the time preceding the fall of Fort Sumter, April of 1861, quoted by N. W. Stephenson in Abraham Lincoln and the Union *(1918).*

I am ordered by the Government of the Confederate States to demand the evacuation of Fort Sumter . . . All proper facilities will be afforded for the removal of yourself and command, together with company arms and property, and all private property to any post in the United States which you may select. The flag you have upheld so long and with so much fortitude, under the most trying circumstances, may be saluted by you on taking it down.
General Beauregard, message to Major Anderson, April 11, 1861.

General, I have the honor to acknowledge the receipt of your communication demanding the evacuation of this fort, and to say, in reply hereto, that it is a demand with which I regret that my sense of honor, and of my obligation to my government, prevent my compliance. Thanking you for the fair, manly and courteous terms proposed, and for the high compliment paid me, I am, general, very respectfully, your obedient servant . . .
Major Anderson's reply to General Beauregard, April 11, 1861.

I was (now) awakened by someone groping about my room in the dark and calling out my name. It proved to be Anderson who came to announce to me that he had just received a dispatch from Beauregard . . . to the effect that he should open fire upon us in an hour. Finding it was determined not to return the fire until after breakfast, I remained in bed. As we had no lights, we could in fact do nothing before that time.
Abner Doubleday, second-in-command at Sumter, in Reminiscences *(1876).*

. . . shot and shell went screaming over Sumter as if an Army of devils were sweeping around it. As a rule, the guns were aimed too high, but all the mortar practice was good. In a few minutes the novelty disappeared in a realizing sense of danger, and the watchers retired to the bomb-proofs, where they discussed probabilities until reveille . . . No serious damage was being done to the fort.
James Chester, member of the Sumter garrison, quoted in R. Wheeler's Voices of the Civil War *(1976).*

In aiming the first gun fired against the rebellion I had no feeling of self-reproach, for I fully believed that the contest was inevitable and was not our

seeking . . . Our firing now became regular and was answered from the rebel guns which encircled us on four sides of the pentagon . . . When the immense mortar shells, after sailing high in the air, came down in a vertical direction and buried themselves in the parade ground, their explosion shook the fort like an earthquake.
Abner Doubleday, April 12, 1861, in Reminiscences.

The Disunion conspiracy which has for the last twenty years been gnawing at the heart-strings of the great American republic, has at last culminated in open war upon its glittering and resplendent flag. For the first time in the history of the United States, an organized attempt is made to destroy, by force of arms, the government which the American people have formed for themselves—to overthrow the glorious Constitution which has made us the envy of the world. The history of the world does not show so causeless an outrage . . . The South has chosen war, and it must have all the war it wants.
New York Times, *April 13, 1861, after the bombardment of Fort Sumter had begun.*

Anderson has not yet silenced any of our guns . . . But the sound of those guns make regular meals impossible . . . Not by one word or look can we detect any change in the demeanor of these Negro servants. Lawrence sits at our door, sleepy and respectful, and profoundly indifferent. So are they all, but they carry it too far. You could not tell that they even heard the awful roar going on in the bay . . . People talk before them as if they were chairs and tables. They make no sign. Are they stolidly stupid? Or wiser than we are; silent and strong, biding their time?
Mary Boykin Chesnut, April 13, 1861, A Diary from Dixie.

The scene at this time was really terrific. The roaring and crackling of the flames, the dense masses of whirling smoke, the bursting of the enemy's shells and our own which were exploding in the burning rooms, the crashing of the shot, and the sound of masonry falling in every direction, made the fort a pandemonium.
Abner Doubleday, April 13, 1861, Reminiscences.

Major Anderson, his officers and men were blackened by smoke and cinders, and showed signs of fatigue and exhaustion . . . It was soon discovered, that it was a bloodless battle. Not a man had been killed or wounded on either side . . . Congratulations were exchanged on so happy a result.

Stephen Lee, Confederate delegate at the surrender of Fort Sumter. Quoted by R. Wheeler's Voices of the Civil War.

I told him (Anderson) that I should prefer to leave the fort with the flag flying . . . and the drums beating "Yankee Doodle," and he authorized me to do so. As soon as our tattered flag came down . . . and the silken banner made by the ladies of Charleston was run up, tremendous shouts of applause were heard from the vast multitude of spectators; and all the vessels and steamers (scattered about the harbour) with one accord made for the fort.

Abner Doubleday, April 14, 1861, Reminiscences.

Comments to the surrender of Fort Sumter, April 14, 1861:
We have met them and we have conquered.
Governor Pickens of South Carolina.

Our Southern brethren have done grievously wrong, they have rebelled and have attacked their father's house and their loyal brothers. They must be punished and brought back, but this necessity breaks my heart.
Major Anderson.

The next day, April 14, was Sunday. The pulpits thundered with denunciations of the rebellion . . . Some of the ministers counselled war . . . Better that the land should be drenched with fraternal blood than that any further concessions should be made to the slaveocracy . . . The same vigorous speech was heard on the streets through which surged hosts of excited men. . . . Monday dawned, April 15. Who that saw that day will ever forget it! For now . . . there rang out the voice of Abraham Lincoln calling for seventy-five thousand volunteers . . . This proclamation was like the first peal of a surcharged thunder-cloud, clearing the murky air. The . . . whole North rose as one man . . . As they [the volunteers] marched from the railroad station, they were escorted by crowds cheering vociferously. Merchants and clerks rushed out from stores, bareheaded, saluting them as they passed. Windows were flung up and women

leaned out into the rain, waving flags . . . As the men filed into Faneuil Hall, in solid columns, the enthusiasm knew no bounds.
Mary Ashton Livermore, My Story of the War *(1889).*

Fort Sumter has been fired upon! . . . There was great rejoicing over this inglorious victory of 7,000 men over 160 . . . The attack upon Fort Sumter has united all the North as one man against the South. Party is forgotten. Alı feel that our very nationality is at stake, and to save the country from anarchy (learning what South America and Mexico are) that every man must do his best to sustain the government, whoever and whatever the President may be. It is a sublime spectacle.
Maria L. Daly, April 1861, Diary.

Spread, spread the tidings far and wide,/ Ye winds take up the cry,/ "Our soil's redeemed from hateful yoke,/ We'll keep it pure or die!"
Banner, Columbia, South Carolina, *April 1861, after the fall of Fort Sumter.*

I was detained . . . over Sunday in Auburn, New York. The war spirit was rampant there, as everywhere . . . The sermon . . . was a radical discourse, and recognized slavery as the underlying cause of the outbreak . . . The choir sang patriotic odes, the audience joining with one voice in the exultant refrain: "It is sweet, it is sweet, for one's country to die!" . . . In Chicago, there was more stir and excitement than I had seen elsewhere . . .
Mary A. Livermore, April 1861. My Story of the War.

In reply to this communication, I have only to say that the militia of Virginia will not be furnished to the powers at Washington for any such use or purpose as they have in view. Your object is to subjugate the Southern States, and a requisition made upon me for such an object—an object, in my judgment, not within the purview of the Constitution . . .— will not be complied with. You have chosen to inaugurate civil war, and having done so we will meet it in a spirit as determined as the Administration has exhibited toward the South.
Governor Letcher of Virginia, in reply to Lincoln's request for militia, April 16, 1861.

I cannot begin to give you a just conception of the excitement created, not only here, but throughout the whole Southern country, by the proclamation [Lincoln's calling for volunteers] . . . The Union party and the Union feeling has been almost entirely swept out of existence. You cannot meet with one man in a thousand who is not influenced with a passion for war.

John Minor Botts, a Virginian Unionist, letter to Washington on April 19, 1861, as quoted in R. Wheeler's Voices of the Civil War.

You can scarcely conceive the struggle it had cost Robert to resign to contend against the flag he has so long honored disapproving, as we both do, the course of the North & South, yet our fate is now linked with the latter & may the prayers of the faithful for the restoration of peace be heard . . . We shall remain quietly at home as long as possible.

Mrs. Lee to Mrs. G. W. Peter, letter written apparently in April 1861, quoted by Bruce Catton in The Coming Fury *(1961).*

I found Mobile, like the rest of the Confederacy, in a great state of excitement. It was boiling over with enthusiasm. The young merchants had dropped their day-books and ledgers, and were forming and drilling companies by night and day, while the older ones were discussing the question of the Confederate Treasury, to see how it could be supported . . .

Raphael Semmes, Confederate naval officer, around April 20, 1861, quoted by R. Wheeler in Voices of the Civil War.

You express great horror of bloodshed, and yet would not lay a straw in the way of those who are organizing in Virginia and elsewhere to capture this city . . . Keep your rowdies in Baltimore, and there will be no bloodshed.

Lincoln on April 22, 1861, to a peace seeking committee from the Baltimore YMCA.

From the mountain-tops and valleys to the shores of the sea, there is one shout of fierce resolve to capture Washington City . . . That filthy cage of unclean birds must and will assuredly be purified by fire . . . It is not to be endured that this flight of abolition harpies shall come down from the black North for their roost in the heart of the South, to defile and brutalize the land . . . The fanatical yell for the immediate subjugation of the whole South is going up hourly from the united voices of all the North . . . they have determined to hold Washing-ton City as the point hence to carry on their brutal warfare. Our people can take it—they will take it.

The Examiner, Richmond, April 23, 1861.

But once, on the afternoon of the 23rd [of April, 1861], the business of the day being over, the Executive office being deserted, after walking the floor alone in silent thought for nearly half an hour, he stopped and gazed long and wistfully out of the window down the Potomac in the direction of the expected ships; and, unconscious of the other presence in the room, at length broke out with irrepressible anguish in the repeated exclamation: "Why don't they come! Why don't they come!"

Lincoln's secretary, his report quoted by N. W. Stephenson in Abraham Lincoln and the Union.

Civil war was an evil we had never contemplated. Besides, we had been taught so long to regard it as a political bugbear, a mere party menace, that we looked upon it with little or no alarm. More than this, the people had been told so long by unscrupulous politicians that the South dare not fight, that at the first call to arms the slaves would rush into insurrection—that it really believed at the first show of determination the South would decline the contest. The people of the South had been beguiled in the same manner by their leaders. They had been assured over and over again that the money-loving North would never go to war with a source of their wealth—a "race of shop-keepers" would never fight for a sentiment; and if they attempted it, would be crushed at the onset by the chivalrous, war-like South.

Joel Tyler Hedley, Northern historian in The Great Rebellion *(1863–66).*

Washington is the weak point with our enemies—their fears and their preparations prove that they feel and know it. It is to Washington that the Northern rabble is summoned. Cannot Virginians and other Southerners reach Washington before this multitudinous and disorderly rabble arrives? . . . If companies, and regiments, and individuals, from Richmond and Petersburg . . . and from the counties between the James River and the Blue Ridge and Potomac, will hurry on to Alexandria, they will soon be joined by large forces from the Southern Confederacy. Soon, very soon, Davis and Beauregard, and Lee of Virginia will be there to lead them on . . .

Richmond Examiner, April 28, 1861.

We feel that our cause is just and holy; we protest in the face of mankind that we desire peace at any sacrifice save that of honor and independence; we seek no conquest, no aggrandizement, no concession of any kind from the States with which we were lately confederated; all we ask is to be let alone; let those who never held power over us shall not now attempt our subjugation by arms.

Jefferson Davis, at the Provisional Congress of the Confederacy at Montgomery, on April 29, 1861.

The business of war was such a novelty that McDowell's army accumulated an extraordinary number of camp-followers and non-combatants. The vigilant newspapers of the chief cities sent a cloud of correspondents . . . The volunteer regiments carried with them companionships unknown to regular armies . . . Senators and representatives . . . in several instances joined in what many rashly assumed would be a mere triumphal parade.

John G. Nicolay, private secretary to Lincoln, in The Outbreak of the Rebellion, Vol. 1 *(1881).*

Sir, Having served for fifteen years in the regular army, including four years at West Point, and feeling it the duty of every one who has been educated at the government expense to offer their services for the support of the the government, I have the honor very respectfully to tender my services until the close of the war, in such capacity as may be offered. I would say in view of my present age and length of service, I feel myself competent to command a regiment . . .

Ulysses S. Grant, letter to the authorities in Washington, May 24, 1861. Reprinted in his Personal Memoirs *(1885–86).*

Next to Charleston, there is no city in the rebel States whose occupancy by the Union forces would strike more dread to the hearts of the traitors, and so encourage the loyal citizens of the South, and so elate the masses of the loyal States, as that of Richmond. For years it has been the den of conspirators, plotting the destruction of the Republic. . . . Mr. Jeff. Davis has summoned his Congress of Confederate rebels to meet in Richmond on some day in July. Ere that time, we trust its capital will be the headquarters of the commander-in-chief of the Federal forces.

New York Tribune, *June 3, 1861.*

A reckless and unprincipled tyrant has invaded your soil. Abraham Lincoln, regardless of all moral, legal and constitutional restraints, has thrown his abolition hosts among you, who are murdering and imprisoning your citizens, confiscating and destroying your property and committing other acts of violence and outrage too shocking and revolting to humanity to be enumerated.

Confederate general P. G. T. Beauregard, proclamation at Manassas, Virginia, on June 5, 1861.

Lincoln, though a man of little practical ability, seems to be straightforward and honest, but Charles (Mrs. D's husband) seems to think that Seward, the Secretary of State, is not the man for the occasion; he is too wrapped up in himself. So long as you will listen whilst he preaches, well, but he cannot believe in anyone else nor see any wisdom in those who differ from him.

Maria L. Daly, June 10, 1861, Diary.

Who says the Constitution must come in, in bar of our action? It is the advocates of rebellion, of rebels who have sought to overthrow the Constitution and trample it in the dust—who repudiate the Constitution . . . I deny that they have the right to invoke this Constitution . . . I deny that they can be permitted to come here and tell us we must be loyal to the Constitution.

Thaddeus Stevens in Congress, on the question of slavery in the Southern districts occupied by the North, July 1861.

Whether this war shall last one, or three, or five years is a problem they leave to be solved by the enemy alone; it will last till the enemy shall have withdrawn from their borders—till their political rights, their altars and their homes are freed from invasion. Then, and only then, will they rest from this struggle . . .

Jefferson Davis in the Congress of the Confederate States, July 1861.

. . . war is a science which is not learned in a day. I have studied it all my life. It requires three things:— time, money and patience, sir. And sir, the President has promised that I shall have all three.

General Winfield Scott, as quoted in Maria L. Daly's Diary, July 15, 1861.

Soldiers of the Army of the West! . . . You have annihilated two armies . . . You have taken five

guns, twelve colors . . . one thousand prisoners . . . Soldiers! I have confidence in you, and I trust you have learned to confide in me.
General George McClellan, victory proclamation
to his army on July 16, 1861.

Near Cub Run we saw carriages and barouches which contained civilians who had driven from Washington to witness the operations. A Connecticut boy said: "There's our Senator!" and some of our men recognized . . . other members of Congress . . . We thought it wasn't a bad idea to have the great men from Washington come out to see us thrash the Rebs.
James Tinkham, volunteer from Massachusetts,
on the beginning of the first battle of Bull Run,
July 21, 1861, as quoted in R. Wheeler's
Voices of the Civil War.

The spirit of the soldiery was magnificent . . . There was glowing rivalry between the men of different states. "Old Massachusetts will not be ashamed of us tonight". "Wait till the Ohio boys get at them". "We'll fight for New York today", and a hundred similar utterances were shouted from the different ranks.
Edmund Clarence Stedman, of the New York
World *on Bull Run, July 21, 1861.*

Men fall . . . They are bleeding, torn and mangled . . . The trees are splintered, crushed and broken, as if smitten by thunderbolts . . . There is smoke, dust, wild talking, shouting; hissings, howlings, explosions. It is a new, strange, unanticipated experience to the soldiers of both armies, far different from what they thought it would be.
Charles Coffin, correspondent for the Boston
Journal *on Bull Run.*

I could see the gleam of arms and the twinkling of bayonets. On the hillside beside me there was a crowd of civilians on horseback and in all sorts of vehicles, with a few of the fairer, if not gentler sex . . . The spectators were all excited and a lady with an opera glass who was near me was quite beside herself when an unusually heavy discharge roused the current of her blood: "That is splendid! Oh, my! Is not that first-rate? I guess we will be in Richmond this time tomorrow."
William Howard Russell of the London
Times, *on Bull Run, July 1861.*

The next thing I remember was the order to advance which we did under scattering fire . . . The boys were saying constantly, in great glee: "We've whipped them." "We'll hang Jeff Davis to a sour apple tree." "They are running." "The war is over."
James Tinkham, volunteer from Massachusetts,
after the battle of Bull Run, as quoted by R.
Wheeler in Voices of the Civil War.

This estimable lady [widow Henry at the Henry House] who had spent here a long life . . . was now bed-ridden. There she lay amid the horrid din, and no less than three of the missiles of death that scoured through her chamber inflicted their wounds upon her. It seems a strange dispensation of Providence that one whose life had been so gentle and secluded should have her end amid such a storm of human passion.
The Richmond Enquirer *about the fighting at*
Henry House Hill, July 21, 1861.

General Bee wheeled his horse and galloped back to his command . . . In the storm which followed . . . he was soon on foot, his horse shot from under him. With the fury of despair he strode among his men . . . and tried to rally and to hold them . . . finally, in a voice which rivalled the roar of the battle, he cried out, "Oh, men, there are Jackson and his Virginians standing behind you like a stone wall!" . . . It was Bee who gave Jackson the name of "Stonewall," but it was his own Virginians who made that name immortal.
Henry Kyd Douglas, one of Jackson's men, in I
Rode with Stonewall *(1940).*

The fight was just then hot enough to make him (Jackson) feel well. His eyes fairly blazed. He had a way of throwing up his left hand with the open palm toward the person he was addressing. And as he told me to go, he made this gesture. The air was full of flying missiles, and . . . he jerked down his hand, and I saw that blood was streaming from it. I exclaimed "General, are you wounded?" He replied, as he drew a handkerchief from his breast-pocket and began to bind it up: "Only a scratch—a mere scratch" and galloped away along his line.
John Imboden, Southern battery commander,
quoted in R. Wheeler's Voices of the Civil
War.

They [General Jubal Early's troops] threw themselves in the woods on our right, and toward the rear of our right, and opened a fire of musketry on our men, which caused them to break and retire down the hillside. This soon degenerated into disorder for which there was no remedy. Every effort was made to rally them . . . but in vain.

Union General McDowell, quoted in R. Wheeler's Voices of the Civil War.

All sense of manhood seemed to be forgotten . . . Even the sentiment of shame had gone . . . Every impediment to flight was cast aside. Rifles, bayonets, pistols, haversacks, cartridge-boxes, blankets, belts and overcoats lined the road.

New York Tribune, *about the Union defeat at Bull Run, July 21, 1861*

The larger part of the men are a confused mob, entirely demoralized. It was the opinion of all the commanders that no stand could be made this side of the Potomac . . . many of the volunteers did not wait for authority to proceed to the Potomac but left on their own decision.

McDowell's report to Washington on the defeat of Bull Run, July 21, 1861.

The further they ran, the more frightened they grew. We called to them, tried to tell them there was no danger, implored them to stand. We called them cowards, denounced them in the most offensive terms, put out our heavy revolvers, and threatened to shoot them, but all in vain; a cruel, hazy, mad, hopeless panic possessed them, and communicated to everybody about in front and read . . . their mouths gaped, their lips cracked and blackened with the powder of the cartridges they had bitten off in the battle, their eyes starting in frenzy; no mortal ever saw such a mass of ghastly wretches.

Congressman Albert Riddle, one of the Washington spectators, on the Union retreat after the battle of Bull Run, July 21, 1861, quoted by James M. McPherson in Battle Cry of Freedom *(1988).*

Both these Congressmen bravely stood their ground till the last moment . . . But what a scene! . . . For three miles, hosts of Federal troops . . . were fleeing along the road . . . Army wagons . . . and private carriages choked the passage, tumbling against each other amid clouds of dust and sickening sights and sounds. Hacks containing unlucky spectators of the late affray were smashed like glass, and the occupants were lost sight of in the debris.

E. C. Stedman of the New York World, *on the Union troops beaten at Bull Run.*

The loyal people in Washington were rejoicing over a victory, steadily reported during the greater part of the day, when suddenly, at about five o'clock, came the startling telegram: "General McDowell's army in full retreat through Centreville. The day is lost . . ." By midnight, officers and civilians who were lucky enough to have retained horses began to arrive, and the apparent proportions of the defeat to increase. Next day . . . through this rain the disbanded soldiers began to pour into Washington City, fagged out, hungry and dejected and having literally nowhere to turn their or lay their head. History owes a page of honorable mention to the Federal capital . . . on this occasion. The rich and poor, the high and low of her loyal people . . . opened their doors and dealt out food and refreshments to the footsore, haggard and half-starved men, . . . so unexpectedly reduced to tramps and fugitives.

John Nicolay, The Outbreak of the Rebellion *(1881).*

There you are, shoulder-straps! But where are your companies? Where are your men? Incompetents! Never tell of chances of battle, of getting strayed, and the like. I think this is your work, this retreat, after all. Sneak, blow, put on airs, there in Willard's sumptuous parlors and barrooms, or anywhere—no explanation will save you. Bull Run is your work; had you been half or one-tenth of your men, this would never have happened.

Walt Whitman, accusing the Union officers after the first battle of Bull Run, as quoted by Bruce Catton, The Coming Fury *(1961).*

The great blunder of Sunday lay in fighting the battle which ended so disastrously. Under no circumstances is it ever justifiable, in a military sense, for an inferior force to attack a superior when the latter has his own choice of position and is strongly entrenched. The chances are fifty to one against success. In this instance General McDowell was perfectly aware that the rebel forces either outnumbered his own, or could easily be made to do so by reinforcements.

New York Times, *July 25, 1861, after the first battle of Bull Run.*

The breakdown of the Yankee race, their unfitness for empire, forces dominion on the South. We are compelled to take the sceptre of power. We must adapt ourselves to our new destiny.

Richmond Whig, *after the first battle of Bull Run, as quoted by James M. McPherson in* Battle Cry of Freedom.

Yankee Doodle, near Bull Run,/ Met his adversary,/ First he thought the fight he'd won,/ Fact proved quite contrary./ Panic-struck he fled, with speed/ Of lightning glib with unction,/ Of slippery grease, in full stampede/ From famed Manassas Junction.

Unknown, July 1861.

3. The West Up to the Battle of Shiloh: April 1862

The Historical Context

Four days after the battle of Bull Run, John C. Frémont, major general and commander of the Western Department, arrived in St. Louis. Frémont was the first Republican presidential candidate in 1856 and had long military experience. He enjoyed a great reputation as the "Pathfinder" in the untracked West, but he lacked the administrative and diplomatic qualities required for the delicate situation in politically divided Missouri. His main goal was to build up a large army and navy force to sweep down the Mississippi Valley, but he failed to support Commander Nathaniel Lyon who had become his subordinate when the latter was threatened by the reinforced General Sterling Price and 5,000 Confederate troops under General Ben McCulloch. In spite of his poor position, Lyon decided to attack before the enemy could attack him. But at Wilson's Creek, the Union attack under Brigadier General Franz Sigel's German troops failed, Lyon was killed and the Union army had to retreat to Springfield. Each side had lost about 1,300 men, a much higher percentage than at Bull Run.

Frémont's reputation suffered badly, and his political backers, the influential Blair family, withdrew their support. Still, by his bold, suicidal action, Lyon had gained enough time for the pro-Unionist forces to rally at the State Convention in Jefferson City where the Unionists remained in complete control. Frémont, in the meantime, declared martial law throughout the state, confiscated all rebel property and freed all the slaves of Confederate activists. This was an ill-considered, partly politically motivated move that contributed much to the expansion of the war and the mutual hatred on both sides. Lincoln, who had not been consulted or notified, could not possibly have approved this action, as it was bound to alienate Union sympathizers in the South as well as in the doubtful states. When Frémont ignored his "request" to modify part of the proclamation, Lincoln revoked the emancipation order and removed Frémont from his command. The visit of

John C. Frémont, explorer and Union general.

Frémont's wife Jessie on his behalf at the White House did not help his cause, as she met with a very cool reception from the president. By overruling Frémont, Lincoln alienated the Republican fanatics in the North, but his main concern was Kentucky, lying between the two battlegrounds of Virginia and Missouri, which was trying hard to stay out of the war. Indeed, Kentucky could have developed into a major obstacle for any concentrated Union effort to drive down the Mississippi Valley from Cairo, Illinois, the southernmost city of the free states, where Union forces were stationed under the command of Admiral Andrew Hull Foote, who had assembled a substantial fleet of improvised vessels, and army Commander Ulysses S. Grant. When, in early September 1861, a Confederate army crossed over from Tennessee and occupied the Kentucky towns of Hickman and Columbus, Grant moved also and took the small Kentucky town of Paducah. This ended the neutrality of Kentucky, which thereafter was split into two camps.

Several efforts were made by Union forces to invade Tennessee and come to the help of loyalists there. But William Tecumseh Sherman, Union commander in Kentucky, called off a planned invasion after he received exaggerated estimates of a Confederate build-up in Tennessee. When Sherman's successor General Don Carlos Buell authorized the invasion, Union General Thomas's force was attacked by a Confederate force of equal size under General Felix Kirk Zollicoffer. In the Battle of Mill Springs (Logan's Crossroads), the Confederates were beaten and Zollicoffer killed, but in the severe winter Thomas could advance no further, and the loyal Unionists in Tennessee, who had waited in vain for military support from the North, suffered.

The Confederate forces in the Western area were under the overall command of Albert Sidney Johnston, a man who enjoyed the complete confidence of Jefferson Davis. The Eastern command, after Frémont's departure, was split between Henry W. Halleck, commander of Missouri, a military theorist and good administrator, and, east of the Cumberland River, Don Carlos Buell, an able organizer also and successor to the then very indecisive William T. Sherman. Unfortunately, Buell and Halleck did not cooperate. Also, Grant and Foote had a difficult time getting Halleck's approval for a joint move against the Confederate forts on the Tennessee and Cumberland Rivers, which were less heavily fortified than those on the Mississippi.

In the meantime, western Virginia had been won for the Federal side. Union troops under Rosecrans had been successful at Carnifix Ferry, and Robert E. Lee's first major campaign at Cheat Mountain, undertaken with an army handicapped by lack of proper food, disease and exhaustion, had failed. Thereafter, the people of western Virginia voted overwhelmingly to form a separate state (West Virginia) to join the Union side. Similarly, Sterling Price's success at Lexington, Missouri, against James A. Mulligan's "Irish Brigade" did not suffice to secure the state for the Confederates.

Grant's first step in his Mississippi campaign was to move down on the western shore to attack the Confederate camp at Belmont, Missouri, the heavily fortified Confederate "Southern Gibraltar." This attack, however, accomplished little, as Confederate General Leonidas Polk, a former bishop, ferried troops across the river to repulse Grant's attack. Foote's and Grant's main move against the Confederate forts started on February 1, 1862. Fifteen thousand Union troops were landed on the Tennessee River just below Fort Henry, which General Albert Sidney Johnston, apparently believing the main attack would be directed against Columbus, had not fortified sufficiently. Foote's fleet of gunboats and three ironclads exchanged heavy artillery fire, but when Grant's army came up through heavy rain (which had caused the river to flood the fort's lower level), the fort's commander sent the 2,500 men garrison cross-country to reinforce the stronger Fort Donelson on the Cumberland River. Fort Henry was surrendered and Foote's fleet moved down the Tennessee again, but Johnston still could not know whether the next attack would be on Columbus in the West or on Fort Donelson. He decided to make a stand at Donelson but sent part of his forces up the Cumberland to defend Nashville.

Grant's troops surrounded Donelson on three sides, but Foote's navy was badly crippled by Confederate guns. While Grant was conferring downstream with Foote, the Confederates counterattacked with some success, but their three commanders, Floyd, Pillow and Buckner, could not agree on how to continue the fight. Only Buckner remained at the fort, and his request to discuss surrender terms was met with Grant's famous "No terms except an unconditional and immediate surrender can be accepted. I propose to move immediately on your works." Buckner—who had done Grant some personal favors in 1854 when the latter resigned his captaincy amid rumors of heavy drinking—had no choice and surrendered his 12,000 men. This victory was celebrated all over the North, Grant became a celebrity, a popular hero and major general overnight. Columbus, Kentucky, and Nashville, Tennessee had to be evacuated, and all of Kentucky as well as most of Tennessee came under Union control.

While between December 1861 and March 1862, the Confederates had gained victories in minor clashes at Chustenahlah in Indian Territory and also in New Mexico, the next major decision was bound to fall around Corinth, Mississippi. Halleck, who had taken the credit for the victories at Forts Henry and Donelson and had been made supreme union commander of the West, prepared a two-pronged attack on this Southern depot and major stronghold. He sent Grant up the Tennessee River with 40,000 men and Buell via Nashville and Columbia, Tennessee, with another 35,000 men. They were to meet and act jointly at Pittsburgh Landing on the Tennessee River, north of Corinth. Halleck then intended to lead in person the onslaught on Corinth. But General A. S. Johnston, undaunted after his setbacks at Forts Henry and Donelson and unmoved by the criticism that followed, had his own plans. Reinforced by Beauregard from the south and by Braxton Bragg, commander at Mobile, Alabama, he set out to attack Grant before Buell's forces could arrive. His troops were green and his staff officers, for the most part, inexperienced, but he was determined to drive the Yankees back all the way to the Ohio River.

His initial move was to push the Union army out of Missouri where General Samuel R. Curtis had recently succeeded in driving Price's troops all the way south to the Arkansas border. Earl Van Dorn was appointed to command this campaign, and under him the two Confederate generals, Price and McCulloch, who had never been able to agree on a common strategy, began to cooperate. Van Dorn also enlisted the help of Brigadier General Albert Pike, a specialist in Indian affairs who managed to persuade many Creeks, Chickasaws, Choctaws, Cherokees and Seminoles to fight for the Confederacy. The clash occurred at Pea Ridge, at the Arkansas–Missouri border. The attack had been well-prepared by Van Dorn, but here, as in all his later en-

Ulysses S. Grant.

terprises, he was unlucky. Although this was one of the few battles where the Confederates had the advantage in numbers, the Union troops under General Samuel Ryan Curtis were not caught by surprise, the German divisions under General Franz Sigel fended off the first assault and, in the subsequent heavy fighting, the Indian troops panicked under Union artillery fire. McCulloch was killed, and though Van Dorn had come close to victory on the first day, the Union counterattacked on March 7, 1862, and the Confederates retreated in disorder. All Southern designs on regaining Missouri had been frustrated.

Johnston's main counterattack, however, was to be launched east of the Mississippi. He had managed to raise the spirit of his troops and they were eager to fight. He was also helped by Halleck's extreme caution, which prevented Grant from advancing toward Corinth immediately and thereby missed the chance of taking it in the first assault. At any rate, both Grant and his subcommander Sherman were overconfident after Buell's force arrived in the vicinity and discounted indications that the woods near Shiloh church were full of Confederate soldiers. So Johnston achieved an almost complete surprise when he attacked in the morning of April 6, with all of his six divisions. Buell's troops were stationed too far away, so that his men could not be brought into battle on the first day. General Lew Wallace (who later wrote *Ben Hur*) received contradictory orders and also arrived too late with his division, so that Grant's five divisions had to bear the brunt of the fighting. Many of the inexperienced Union soldiers panicked and cowered under the bluffs of Pittsburgh Landing. Many of the Southern soldiers acted in the same way. Both sides suffered staggering losses. Grant and Sherman did everything possible to inspire their troops. The latter, anxious to restore his damaged reputation, was wounded twice and had three horses shot under him. Johnston, trying to make his right wing renew its attack in the afternoon, was shot in the leg and bled to death.

Grant's retreat to the Tennessee River was greatly helped by the stubborn stand of Benjamin M. Prentiss's division. With barely 4,000 men, Prentiss repulsed the attacks of 18,000 Confederates long enough to enable Grant to reorganize his troops along the Pittsburgh Landing ridge. By this time, Wallace's division had arrived, and Buell's troops were crossing the river. Beauregard, now in charge, refused to order a final twilight attack. Still unaware of all the Union reinforcements, he expected to perform a simple mop-up operation the next day. The scouts of his cavalry commander, Nathan Bedford Forrest, had observed Buell's troops in transit, but he could not contact Beauregard to warn him.

The soldiers of both armies, 95,000 in all, spent a miserable night amid the dead and wounded in pouring rain. In the morning, Beauregard was surprised by Buell's and Grant's counterattack, which rolled back the disorganized Confederates until their lines stiffened by mid-morning. By the afternoon, however, the Confederates had been pushed back to their original positions. By this time, both armies were completely exhausted and Beauregard ordered retreat. Sherman's pursuit of the enemy with two brigades, on April 8, did not achieve much, except that Confederate cavalry General Nathan Bedford Forrest was wounded.

Although it is not as well-remembered as the first Battle of Bull Run, Shiloh, or Pittsburg Landing, fought on a much larger scale, was the first battle encounter that resulted in the mass slaughter typical of the great battles to follow during the next three years. About 20,000 soldiers were killed or wounded—about 10,000 on each side—more than at Bull Run, Fort Donelson, Wilson's Creek and Pea Ridge combined. Although the Confederate counterattack had failed, the outcome of this massacre was a draw and certainly served to dispel any Northern hopes for an early collapse of the Confederate positions in the West.

But simultaneously, a combined Union army-navy attack had overrun the Southern stronghold on Island #10 on the Mississippi, 50 miles below Columbus, Kentucky. Admiral Foote's fleet now included seven ironclads and 10 heavy-mortar boats and cooperated closely with army units under General Pope. The Confederate garrison, surrounded and heavily bombarded, surrendered on April 7. Pope suffered very few casualties and became a new Northern hero—for a while.

CHRONICLE OF EVENTS

1861:

July 22: The State Convention in Jefferson City, Missouri, affirms the loyalty of the state and moves the capital to St. Louis. The pro-Confederate government under Claiborne Jackson also claims to represent the sate.

July 26: Federal troops under Major I. Lynde abandon Fort Fillmore, New Mexico, and surrender to Confederate troops at San Augustine Springs without a fight. Major Lynde is discharged, but later reinstated.

July 31: In Missouri, Governor Isaac Jackson is replaced by pro-Union Hamilton R. Gamble.

August 1: Skirmish between Confederates (so-called buffalo-hunters) under John R. Baylor and pro-Unionists in New Mexico Territory.

August 10: Battle of Wilson's Creek, Missouri. General Nathaniel Lyon, though greatly outnumbered, attacks a Confederate force under General Benjamin McCulloch. The Union attack under German–American general Franz Sigel fails, Lyon is killed, his troops withdraw and leave the Springfield area to the Confederates.

August 14: Martial law is declared in St. Louis by Major General John Charles Frémont.

August 15: Brigadier General Robert Anderson, former commander of Fort Sumter, is named commander of the Department of the Cumberland, which consists of Tennessee and Kentucky.

August 30: Major General John Charles Frémont issues an unauthorized emancipation declaration for Missouri and announces martial law throughout the state. President Lincoln calls the order "dictatorial."

September 2: President Lincoln asks Frémont to "modify" his proclamation of August 30, because it would alarm our Southern Union friends.

September 3: Confederate forces under Gideon Pillow enter Kentucky from Tennessee, thus ending the "neutrality" of Kentucky.

September 6: A small Federal force sent from Cairo by General U. S. Grant takes Paducah Kentucky, preventing a Southern takeover of the state. Its governor is prosecession, the legislature pro-Union.

September 10: Federal units under General Rosecrans attack Confederates at Carnifix Ferry in western Virginia. Confederate General John B. Floyd withdraws.

General Albert Sidney Johnston becomes commander of the Western armies of the Confederacy.

September 11: General Lee attacks separate Union forces under J. J. Reynolds at Cheat Mountain Summit and Elkwater in western Virginia, but fails. Western Virginia is now secured for the Union.

September 12: Lincoln sends an emissary to St. Louis to make Frémont modify his slave emancipation order.

A small Federal force under Colonel J. Mulligan is besieged in Lexington, Missouri by Confederate troops under General Sterling Price.

September 18: Confederate forces occupy Bowling Green, Kentucky.

September 20: After a stubborn defense, the 3,600 Federal troops at Lexington, surrender to General Price's Confederate force of 18,000 men, since the expected help from General Frémont in St. Louis was not forthcoming.

September 23: Engagements in Romney, Mechanicsburg Gap and Hanging Rock Pass in western Virginia, also in Albany, Kentucky.

October 7: General Frémont moves from St. Louis against Confederate General Price, who withdraws from Lexington.

October 8: Brigadier General William T. Sherman supersedes General Robert Anderson in command of the Cumberland forces. Anderson suffered from nervous exhaustion and never returned to active service.

October 11: General Rosecrans assumes command of the Union troops in western Virginia.

October 12: The new Confederate ironclad *Manassas* heads down the Mississippi and rams

William S. Rosecrans, Union general.

U.S.S. *Richmond* and *Vincennes* near the mouth of the river.

October 16: Union troops enter Lexington, Missouri.

October 19: Inconclusive engagement between U.S.S. *Massachusetts* and C.S.S. *Florida* off the Mississippi shore.

October 24: The people of western Virginia vote overwhelmingly in favor of forming a new state.

October 25: A cavalry unit of Frémont defeats a small Confederate force and occupies Springfield, Missouri.

October 31: A remnant of the Missouri legislature at Neosho votes Missouri into the Confederacy; the state now belongs to both nations.

November 2: Major General John C. Frémont is notified that he has been relieved of his duties and temporarily replaced by Major General David Hunter.

November 7: A Federal flotilla under Ulysses S. Grant sails down the Mississippi from Cairo,

Illinois and captures Belmont, opposite Columbus, Ohio. After a counterattack led by Leonidas Polk, it withdraws north.

November 9: Major General Henry Wager Halleck is put in charge of the Union forces in Missouri, Arkansas, Illinois and western Kentucky. Brigadier Don Carlos Buell replaces W. T. Sherman as commander of the Department of the Ohio which also includes Indiana, Michigan, Tennessee and eastern Kentucky.

November 18: Like Missouri, Kentucky now has governments representing both the Union and the Confederacy.

November 28: The Congress in Richmond officially admits Missouri to the Confederacy.

December 10: The Confederate Congress admits the state of Kentucky to the Confederacy (the 13th state).

December 13: Clash between Federal and Confederate troops at Cheat Mountain in western Virginia. After heavy fighting, both armies retreat.

December 26: Engagement at Chustenahlah, Indian Territory, between Confederate and pro-Union Creek Indians. The latter have to flee to Kansas.

1862:

January 10: In Cairo, Illinois General Grant prepares a move toward Columbus, Kentucky.

Federal troops evaluate Romney in western Virginia in the face of Stonewall Jackson's advance.

January 19: Battle of Mill Springs, or Logan's Crossroads, Kentucky. About 4,000 men on either side clash on the North bank of the Cumberland River. After some initial successes, the Confederates are defeated and withdraw across the Cumberland, their commander Zollicoffer is killed. The Federal cause in Kentucky and eastern Tennessee is boosted.

January 22: Federal gunboats shell Fort Henry on the Tennessee River.

February 1: At Cairo, Grant starts on a campaign to take Fort Henry on the Tennessee.

February 6: Confederate Brigadier General

Union Ironclads at Fort Donelson.

Lloyd Tilghman sends the bulk of his troops to Fort Donelson and surrenders Fort Henry after a brief fight.

February 7: Various detachments of Confederate troops are ordered to move to threatened Fort Donelson on the Cumberland.

February 13: Fort Donelson is besieged and attacked.

February 14: Four ironclads and two wooden gunboats bombard Fort Donelson from the Cumberland river. After heavy fighting, they are forced to withdraw.

February 15: A Confederate division at the fort under Gideon Pillow attacks and breaks through the Federal lines, but then withdraws into the fortress.

February 16: Confederate generals Floyd and Pillow leave the fort and General Buckner asks Grant for surrender terms. Grant insists on "unconditional and immediate surrender." Approximately 12,000 Confederates are taken prisoner. The fall of Fort Henry and Fort Donelson loses Kentucky for the South and leaves Tennessee wide open. Grant becomes a popular hero in the North.

February 19: Federal forces occupy Clarksville, Tennessee.

February 21: In New Mexico Territory, Confederates under Brigadier General H. H. Sibley defeat a Federal force under Colonel E. R. S. Canby and move toward Santa Fe.

February 23: As Federal troops and gunboats approach Nashville, Tennessee, soldiers and citizens evacuate the city. Lincoln names Andrew Johnson as military governor of Tennessee.

February 25: Troops under General Don Carlos Buell move into Nashville, which becomes a vital base for the Union for the remainder of the war.

February 28: Federal troops under General John Pope move south along the west shore of the Mississippi toward New Madrid, Missouri.

March 1: General Halleck orders Grant to proceed up the Tennessee River toward Eastport, Mississippi. A field battery at Pittsburgh Landing, Tennessee is silenced by Federal gunboats.

March 2: Columbus, Kentucky is abandoned by the Confederates.

March 3: The Mississippi Federals under Pope begin the siege of New Madrid, Missouri.

Federals occupy Martinsburg, western Virginia and Amelia Island, Florida.

March 4: Santa Fe in New Mexico Territory is occupied by Confederate troops.

General Halleck orders Grant to stay at Fort Henry while C. F. Smith is put in charge of the Federal advance up the Tennessee. Halleck had accused Grant of insufficient reporting and other misconduct.

March 5: A large Federal force under C. F. Smith arrives northeast of Corinth, Tennessee.

March 6: Confederate general Earl Van Dorn

passes around the flank of Federal General Samuel Curtis's troops at Pea Ridge, Arkansas and attacks. After several days of heavy fighting the Confederates retreat.

March 8: Chattanooga and Knoxville, Tennessee are occupied by Confederate forces.

March 11: Confederate President Davis relieves generals Floyd and Pillow, who had fled from Fort Donelson, of their commands.

March 14: New Madrid, Missouri, falls to U.S. General John Pope.

March 15: General Grant is exonerated by Halleck and resumes his command of the U.S. forces in Tennessee.

March 26: Engagement of Confederate forces and a Federal column of Colorado volunteers at Apache Canyon, New Mexico. After severe fighting, the Federals fall back.

March 28: Major fight at Pigeon's Ranch near Santa Fe, New Mexico. The outnumbered Federals retreat, but manage to take possession of the enemy's supply depot, forcing Confederate Colonel Scurry to retreat to Santa Fe.

March 30: Union City, Tennessee is occupied by the Federals.

April 3: A contemplated attack by General A. S. Johnston's troops on Grant's army near Pittsburgh Landing, Tennessee is delayed.

April 4: A. S. Johnston's army marches from Corinth, Mississippi, toward Pittsburgh Landing, but is delayed by heavy rain.

April 6–7: Battle of Shiloh, or Pittsburgh Landing, Tennessee. General A. S. Johnston attacks Grant with 40,000 Confederate troops. After

John Pope, Union general.

furious fighting, Grant's unprepared army is partially beaten, but Johnston is killed. On the second day, Grant is reinforced by Buell's troops and counterattacks. Confederate commander Beauregard finally withdraws. Heavy losses on both sides: The Confederates suffer about 10,700 dead, wounded or missing, the Federals more than 13,000.

Island No. 10 in the Mississippi in Missouri falls to a combined naval and land attack by Federal forces under General Pope and Commodore Foote.

Eyewitness Testimony

I have found this command in disorder, nearly every county in an insurrectionary condition, and the enemy advancing in force by different points of the Southern frontier . . . I am sorely pressed for want of arms . . . Our troops have not been paid, and some regiments are in a state of mutiny, and the men whose terms of service is expired generally refuse to enlist.

General John Charles Frémont, letter to Lincoln, July 30, 1861.

From all that I have yet learned, from spies and loyally disposed citizens, I am led to believe there is no force within 30 miles of us that entertains the least idea of attacking this position . . . It is fortunate, too, for many of the officers seem to have so little command over their men, and military duty seems to be done so loosely, that I fear at present that our resistance would be in reverse ratio to the number of troops to resist with. Spies are said to be seen every day within a few miles of our camp; marauding parties are infesting the country, pillaging Union men, within 10 miles of here. At present, I can spare no force; in fact, have no suitable troops to drive these guerillas out . . . Artillery and cavalry are much needed, and the quartermaster's department is yet quite deficient . . .

Brigadier-General Grant, first report to General Frémont as commander of the southeastern district of Missouri, August 8, 1861. Quoted in General James Marshall Cornwall, Grant as Military Commander *(1970).*

The victory in Missouri is gloriously confirmed . . . The brave sons of Louisiana were there and foremost in the fight, as at Manassas. There was a panic, it seems, of the untried and probably half-armed troops of Missouri, but the steady discipline and dashing courage of the Arkansas and Louisiana regiments retrieved the day . . . The flying enemy, interrupted by Hardee, have laid down their arms and the day of the deliverance of Missouri is nigh.

New Orleans Picayune, *August 17, 1861, after the battle of Wilson's Creek.*

Thy error, Frémont, simply was to act/ A brave man's part, without the statesman's tact,/ And, taking counsel but from common sense,/ To strike at cause as well as consequence./ Oh, never since Roland wound his horn/ At Roncesvalles, has a blast been blown/ Far heard, wide-echoed, startling as thine own,/ Heard from the van of freedom's shape forlorn!

John Greenleaf Whittier, "To John Frémont" (August 31, 1861).

It is a happy stroke of genius that can overstep the bounds of tradition or conventional rule, and show a clear path in a direction supposed to be beset with insuperable difficulties. Such is the service rendered the nation by General Frémont's proclamation, placing Missouri under martial law . . . It has long been the boast of the South . . . that its whole white population could be made available for the war, for the reason that all its industries were carried on by the slaves, in peace as well as war; While those of the North rested upon those very men who, in case of hostilities, must be sent into the field. For the North, consequently, to fight, would be the destruction of all its material interests; for the South, only a pleasant pasttime for hundreds of thousands of men, who without war would have no occupation . . . In this crisis General Frémont has sounded the keynote of the campaign . . . He has declared that every slave who may be employed or permitted by his master to aid in the rebellion against the United States, shall be free . . . It is very clear, that Frémont's proclamation is, up to this time, by far the most important event of the war.

New York Times, *September 2, 1861. Frémont's proclamation was disapproved by Lincoln.*

Credit will not do at this place longer. I understand that the credit of the Government has been already used to the extent of some hundred thousand dollars, and no money ever paid out. This causes much murmuring among the citizens, and unless the paymaster is soon sent to pay off the troops, the same may be expected from the soldiers.

Grant, report to Frémont, September 29, 1861.

The condition of this command is bad in every particular except discipline. In this latter I think they will compare favorably with almost any volunteers. There is great deficiency in transportation. I have no ambulances. The clothing received has been almost universally of an inferior quality and deficient in quantity. The arms in the hands of the men are mostly the old flintlock repaired . . . and others of still more inferior quality. My cavalry force are none of them properly armed . . . Eight companies are entirely without arms . . .

Grant, report to his new commander, General Halleck, November 21, 1861.

The leave [to go to St. Louis] was granted, but not graciously. I had known General Halleck but very slightly in the old army, not having met him either at West Point or during the Mexican War. I was received with so little cordiality that I perhaps stated the object of my visit with less clearness than I might have done, and I had not uttered many sentences before I was cut short as if my plan was preposterous. I returned to Cairo very much crestfallen.

Grant about his visit with General Halleck to discuss the invasion of Tennessee, January 6, 1862 in his Personal Memoirs *(1885–86).*

The plan of the enemy seems to be to attack us at many points simultaneously and thus preventing our sending aid to any given point, they outnumbering us at every point of attack. If they now fail, they can hardly make another such effort—But will they fail? of if they partially succeed now, what is to be the effect? It is vain to disguise the fact that we are in imminent peril . . . a few days may decide our fate. God be with us and help us.

Southern Attorney General Thomas Bragg, diary entry of January 21, 1862.

One of these regiments passed before me down the slope of the river-bank, and the men as a body seemed to be healthy. Very many were drunk, and all were mud-clogged up to their shoulders and very caps. It must be understood that these soldiers, the volunteers, had never been made subject to any discipline as to cleanliness. They wore their hair long. Their hats or caps, though all made in some military form and with some military appendance, were various and ill-assorted. They all were covered with loose, thick, blue-grey great-coats, which no doubt were warm and wholesome, but which from their looseness and colour seemed to be peculiarly susceptible of receiving and showing a very large amount of mud. Their boots were always good; but each man was shod as he liked.

Anthony Trollope, on Grant's embarkation at Cairo for the expedition against Fort Henry, about February 2, 1862, in North America *(1862).*

From the first his silence was remarkable. He knew how to keep his temper. In battle, as in camp, he went about quietly, speaking in a conversational tone; yet he appeared to see everything that went on, and was always intent on business. He had a faithful assistant adjutant-general, and appreciated him; he preferred, however, his own eyes, word and hand. His aides were little more than messengers. In dress he was plain, even negligent; in partial amendment of that, his horse was always a good one and well kept.

Lew Wallace about his chief Grant at Fort Donelson, February 1862 in Battles and Leaders of the Civil War *(1865).*

I have had no communication with General Grant for more than a week. He left his command without my authority and went to Nashville. His army seems to be as much demoralized by the victory of Fort Donelson as was that of the Potomac by the defeat of Bull Run. It is hard to censure a successful general after a victory, but I think he richly deserves it . . . Satisfied with his victory, he sits down and enjoys it without any regard to the future. I am worn out and tired with his neglect and inefficiency.

Halleck to McClellan, on March 1, 1862, as quoted by General J. Marshall-Cornwall, Grant as Military Commander.

Your dispatch of yesterday is just received. Troops will be sent under command of Major-General Smith as directed . . . I am not aware of ever having disobeyed any order from headquarters—certainly never intended such a thing. I have reported almost daily the condition of my command and reported every position occupied . . .

Grant, to Halleck, after the latter had replaced him with General C. F. Smith as head of the Tennessee expedition, March 5, 1862. Reported in Grant's Personal Memoirs.

It has been reported that soon after the battle of Fort Donelson, Brigadier-General Grant left his command without leave. By direction of the President, the Secretary of War desires you to ascertain and report whether General Grant left his command at any time without proper authority, and if so, for how long; whether he has made to you proper reports and returns of his force; whether he has committed any acts which were unauthorized or not in accordance with military subordination and propriety, and if so, what.

Adjutant-general at Washington to Halleck, letter; Halleck gave in and reinstated Grant on March 13, 1862.

Soldiers of the Army of the Mississippi: I have put you in motion to offer battle to the invaders of your country . . . You can but march to a decisive victory over . . . mercenaries sent to subjugate and despoil you of your liberties, property, and honor. Remember the precious stake involved; remember the dependence of your mothers, your wives, your sisters and your children on the result; remember the fair, broad, abounding lands, the happy homes that will be desolated by your defeat. The eyes and hopes of eight million people rest upon you.

General Albert Sidney Johnston, general order to his Confederate troops before the battle of Shiloh, April 3, 1862.

At four o'clock in the morning, we rose from our damp bivouac . . . Next to me . . . was a boy of seventeen, Henry Parker . . . While we stood at easy, he drew my attention to some violets at his feet and said: "It would be a good idea to put a few into my cap. Perhaps the Yankees won't shoot me if they see me wearing such flowers, for they are a sign of peace." "Capital" said I "I will do the same."

Henry Morton Stanley, later to become a famous journalist and explorer, the dawn of the battle of Shiloh, April 4, 1862, in his Autobiography (1909).

Three of the five divisions engaged on Sunday were entirely raw, and many of the men had only received their arms on the way from the States to the field. Many of them had arrived by a day or two before, and were hardly able to load their muskets according to the manual. Their officers were equally ignorant of their duties. Under these circumstances it is not astonishing that many of the regiments broke at the first fire.

Grant on the battle of Shiloh, April 6, 1862, in his Personal Memoirs.

No one has sympathized with you in the troubles with which you are surrounded more sincerely than myself. I have watched your every movement, and know the difficulties . . . I need not urge you, when your army is united, to deal a blow at the enemy in your front, if possible before his rear gets up from Nashville. You have him divided, keep him so if you can.

Lee to General A. S. Johnston, before the battle of Shiloh, April 6, 1862.

How unconscious of danger lay the army of the Union that night! . . . At midnight, stepping from my tent, . . . I listened . . . but all was still save the measured tread of the sentinel and the gentle whispers of the genial night breeze. No sound came from the distant wood . . . Quietness reigned . . . throughout the rebel camps.

Colonel Wills de Hass of the Union Army, occupying a tent nearest the Confederate army before the battle of Shiloh, as quoted in R. Wheeler's Voices of the Civil War (1976).

As the firing continued . . . wild birds in great numbers, rabbits in commotion, and numerous squirrels came flocking toward the Union lines as though they were being driven from the woods . . . An officer said: "The rebels must be attacking our outposts." The words were scarcely spoken when a struggling squad of men came running by in great excitement, their officers in vain trying to keep them in order. They shouted the news that the Confederates were making an attack on the picket line . . . By this time the bugles had sounded . . . The long roll was beaten among the infantry regiments in every direction. The men were just at breakfast, and many of them had to spring into ranks, without waiting to drink their coffee or eat their hardtack.

Jesse Bowman Young, the Confederate attack at Shiloh, April 6, 1862, in Young's What a Boy Saw in the Army (1894).

There was a good deal of a panic at the beginning of the battle. The roads were filled with all manner of fugitives . . . Army wagons, some empty and others full of rations and camp stores and baggage were being driven toward the landing [on the Tennessee River], and other wagons with ammunition were trying to get to the front. Colored servants . . . were scampering out of reach of the rebel bullets . . . Officers were in vain attempting to quiet the alarm and organize the wild, surging, frantic mob that was pressing toward the place where the transports were tied up. Word was quickly sent down to the landing to have the steamers anchor in the middle of the stream and to let no one come on board.

Jesse Bowman Young on the battle of Shiloh, April 6, 1862 in What a Boy Saw in the Army.

Men glared at each other as at wild beasts; and when a shell burst with fatal effect among a crowd of the advancing foe, and arms, legs and heads were torn off, a grim smile of pleasure lighted up the smoke-begrimed faces of the transformed beings who witnessed the catastrophe . . . Men with knitted brows and flushed cheeks fought madly over ridges, along ravines, and up steep ascents, with blood and perspiration streaming down their faces . . . Everywhere was mad excitement; everywhere was horror.

Junius Henry Browne, correspondent of the New York Tribune, *on the battle of Shiloh, in* Browne's Four Years in Secessia *(1865).*

It was a case of Southern dash against Northern pluck and endurance . . . In moving along the line, however, I never deemed it important to stay long with Sherman . . . He inspired a confidence in officers and men that enabled them to render services . . . worthy of the best of veterans . . . A casualty to Sherman that would have taken him from the field that day would have been a sad one for the troops engaged at Shiloh. And how near we came to this! . . . Sherman was shot twice, once in the hand, once in the shoulder, and a third ball passed through his hat. In addition to this, he had several horses shot during the day. The nature of this battle was such that cavalry could not be used in front. I therefore formed ours into line in rear, to stop stragglers . . . When there would be enough of them to make a show, and after they had recovered from their fright, they would be sent to reinforce some part of the line.

General U. S. Grant on the Battle of Shiloh Personal Memoirs.

The sabbath closed upon a scene which had no parallel on the Western Continent . . . Night fell upon and spread its funeral pall over a field of blood where death held unrestrained carnival! Soon after dark the rain descended in torrents . . . The groans of the dying, and the solemn thunder of the gunboats (as they drew their heavy missiles toward the Con-

federate lines) came swelling at intervals high above the peltings of the pitiless storm.

Colonel Wills de Hass, on the night of April 6/7 at Shiloh, quoted in R. Wheeler's Voices of the Civil War *(1976).*

With the exception of a few thousand disciplined troops . . . the whole [Southern] army degenerated into bands of roving plunderers, intoxicated with victory, and scattered in a shameful hunt for the rich spoils of the battle-field . . . Hundreds were intoxicated with wines and liquors found; and . . . scenes of disorder and shouts of revelry rose around the large fires which had been kindled, and mingled with the groans of the wounded.

Edward Pollard, Southern historian, the Shiloh battlefield, The Lost Cause *(1866).*

The underbrush had been literally mowed off by the bullets, and great trees had been shattered by the artillery fire . . . All the bodies had been stripped of their valuables, and scarcely a pair of shoes or boots could be found upon the feet of the dead . . . Further on, I passed . . . the corpse of a beautiful boy in gray who lay with his blond curls scattered about his face and his hands folded peacefully across his breast. He was clad in a bright and neat uniform, well garnished with gold, which seemed to tell the story of a loving mother and sisters who had sent their household pet to the field of war . . . He was about my age . . . It was no uncommon thing to see the bodies of Federal and Confederate lying side by side as though they has bled to death while trying to aid each other . . .

John A. Cockerill, regimental musician, 16 years old, about the Shiloh battlefield, as quoted in R. Wheeler's Voices of the Civil War.

In the sudden start we made, Major Hawkins lost his hat. He did not stop to pick it up. When we arrived at a perfectly safe position, we halted to take an account of damages. McPherson's horse was panting as if ready to drop . . . A ball had struck the metal scabbard of my sword, just below the belt, and broken it nearly off . . . There were three of us: One had lost a horse . . . one a hat and one a sword-scabbard. All were thankful that it was no worse.

Grant about the Shiloh battle of April 7, 1862 in Personal Memoirs.

. . . Step by step, from tree to tree, position to position, the rebel lines went back . . . infantry, horses and artillery. The firing was grand and terrific . . . To and fro, now in my front, then in Sherman's rode General Beauregard, inciting his troops and fighting for his fading prestige of invincibility.

Union General Lew Wallace who later became a famous fiction writer (Ben Hur) *about the Federal counterattack at Shiloh, April 7, 1862, quoted in R. Wheeler's* Voices of the Civil War *(1976).*

I wanted to pursue, but had not the heart to order the men who had fought desperately for two days, lying in the mud and rain whenever not fighting, and I did not feel disposed to positively order Buell, or any part of his command to pursue. Although the senior in rank at the time, I had been so only a few weeks.

Grant about the aftermath of the Battle of Shiloh, April 7, 1862, Personal Memoirs.

The camps were regained. The rebels were repulsed. Their attack had failed. We stood where we began . . . and so ended the battle . . .

Whitelaw Reid, correspondent of the Cincinnati Gazette, *about the two-day battle of Shiloh.*

Our trust is in thee, Beauregard!/ In thy hand the God of Hosts/ hath placed the sword;/And the glory of thy fame/Has set the world aflame,/ Hearts kindle at thy name, Beauregard!

Mrs. C. A. Warfield, Beauregard. *After the battle of Shiloh (April 6, 1862).*

. . . I saw more of human tragedy and woe than I trust I will ever be called on to witness. The retreating host wound along a narrow and almost impassable road . . . Here was a long line of wagons loaded with wounded piled in like bags of grain, groaning and cursing, while the mules plunged on in mud and water . . . Next came a struggling regiment of infantry, pressing on past the train of waggons, then a stretcher borne upon the shoulders of four men, carrying a wounded officer; then soldiers staggering along, with an arm broken and hanging down, or other fearful wounds. . . . A cold, drizzling rain commenced about nightfall, and soon came harder and harder, then turned to pitiless, blinding hail . . . I passed long wagon trains filled with wounded and dying soldiers, without even a blanket to shield them . . .

Confederate Lieutenant William G. Stevenson, about the retreat to Corinth, April 7, 1862 quoted in R. Wheeler's Voices of the Civil War.

It was an awful thing to hear not intermission in firing and hear the clatter of small arms and the whizzing minny balls and rifle shots and the sing of grape shot, the hum of cannon balls and the roaring of the bomb shell and explosion of the same seeming to be a thousand every minute . . . O God, forever keep me out of such another fight. I was not scared, I was just in danger . . .

W. A. Howard, 33rd Tennessee, letter to Mrs. Howard, April 11, 1862, after the battle of Shiloh.

4. The East Up to the Battle of Antietam: September 1862

The Historical Context

In the Eastern theater, the months following the first battle of Bull Run were characterized by relative military inactivity. The Confederate troops entrenched themselves within sight of Washington but made no serious attempt to attack the capital. Congress, meanwhile, enacted important legislative and organizational changes almost immediately. Congress passed the so-called Crittenden–Johnson resolution disavowing antislavery aims of the Union. This was in line with Lincoln's policy (as demonstrated in his revocation of Frémont's emancipation order), but it antagonized the Republican radicals and abolitionists who pointed out that slavery was the South's real strength, with more than half of its labor force consisting of slaves, and that fighting against slaveholders without fighting against slavery was a halfhearted business. Congress also passed the first income tax in the United States (which, however, was never put into effect in that form) and tariffs to finance the war. Several newspapers in the Union states were suppressed for pro-Confederate leanings, among them the *Brooklyn Eagle* and the *New York Daily News*. New volunteers were called in, and the first, limited mutinies flared up in New York, where volunteers of the 79th Regiment were denied furloughs. The entire unit had to be placed under armed guard.

The losers at Bull Run were replaced: General Patterson by General Nathaniel Banks in the Shenandoah Valley, and, more importantly, McDowell by the rising star from West Virginia, General George B. McClellan, who immediately went to work reorganizing the defeated army and lifting its morale. McClellan took good care of his men, instilled discipline and pride in them and became, for his soldiers, the most popular general of the Union. After he assumed power of the newly organized Army of the Potomac, everyone, including Lincoln, expected him to begin the great move toward Richmond.

79

*"All Quiet on the Potomac,"
cartoon on the situation after
the first battle at Bull Run.*

Lincoln also pushed the blockade of Southern ports as much as possible. The building of new ironclads was authorized, commercial intercourse between Northern and Southern states forbidden and Southern Forts Clark and Hatteras on the North Carolina coast, which had served as a haven for blockade runners, were forced to surrender. Here, as well as in the assault on the strongly fortified Port Royal, South Carolina, which was bombarded on November 7, the navy did practically the whole job alone.

Before this second action, the Union army had tried to reoccupy Leesburg, Virginia, 40 miles upriver from Washington, which the Confederates had taken in summer. The Union commander was Colonel Edward Baker, an Illinois politician and personal friend of Lincoln who had no combat experience. Baker's troops were badly beaten and driven into the Potomac by the Confederates, and Baker was killed. A Congressional committee investigated the humiliating defeat and put the blame on Baker's superior, General Charles P. Stone, who had acquired a proslavery reputation and was accused of conspiracy with Confederate officers. Stone was imprisoned and his career ruined, though no formal charges were brought against him. The whole action was politically inspired and probably instigated by radical Republicans against Stone's superior, McClellan, who was suspect as a Democrat and known to be indifferent to the slavery issue. McClellan managed to stay clear of the controversy but did nothing to help the probably innocent Stone.

McClellan, after pushing old General Winfield Scott out and becoming commander-in-chief, had already gotten himself into trouble by early spring of 1862. After repeatedly promising a great push against Richmond, he always found new reasons to postpone an attack. He consistently overestimated his enemy's strength and was always inclined to

believe the estimates supplied to him by Allan Pinkerton's private detective agency. Pinkerton and his men were quite successful in tracing
down and arresting Confederate agents in Union territory, but their
estimates of Confederate troop strength were greatly exaggerated. In
October of 1861, McClellan had about 120,000 men around Manassas,
while Beauregard and J. E. Johnston had about 45,000. Yet McClellan
believed the enemy had 150,000 men at his disposal and was preparing to attack him. He despised all Republican leaders including Lincoln, whom he called "the original gorilla," and idiot behind his back,
Seward and Stanton, the new secretary of war. In fact most people
agree he had no high opinion of anybody but himself. When the
Army of the Potomac went into winter quarters without having dis-
lodged the enemy and McClellan contracted typhoid fever, Lincoln
was near despair, as he got no action out of his newly appointed
Western generals, Buell and Halleck, either.

Jefferson Davis also had troubles with his generals. When he named
five officers to the rank of full general, Joseph E. Johnston was ranked
only fourth and complained bitterly. Beauregard, too, caused trouble
in his report on the Manassas battle, which implied that Davis had unduly delayed Johnston's reinforcement of Beauregard. Davis's answer
was to send Beauregard west to help Albert Sidney Johnston in the
western theater of operations.

Before the Army of the Potomac started moving, the navies on both
sides had acted again: On February 8, an amphibious force led by
Brig. General Ambrose E. Burnside attacked Roanoke Island and
quickly overwhelmed its 2,675 Confederate defenders. This established
another base for the blockade fleet of the North and left only two important Atlantic harbors in the heads of the South, Charleston and
Wilmington.

Even more important was the conquest of New Orleans, the largest
city of the Confederacy. Because most army units had been moved
North to assist the Confederates at the battle of Shiloh, the city's defense rested on Forts Jackson and Philip. Flag-Officer David Glasgow
Farragut, the Union navy commander, decided to run the gauntlet
with his fleet and on April 24 managed to get past both forts without
suffering much damage. He also silenced the river batteries below the
city and entered the city without encountering further resistance. The
streets were filled with burning cotton and cursing mobs, and Union
General Benjamin Butler, who entered two days later, had to establish
a harsh rule to control the occupied city. The occupation forces were
exposed to vile insults by the civilians, and, in May of 1862, Butler
outraged the whole South and public opinion in England by decreeing

that any woman who persisted in insulting Northern soldiers would be "regarded and held liable to be treated as a woman of the town plying her avocation." British Prime Minister Palmerston's indignant condemnation of this decree caused a temporary estrangement between him and Union ambassador Charles Francis Adams.

The South had begun its own seafare program. The powerful steam frigate *Merrimack*, scuttled by the Union forces at Norfolk Navy Yard when the war began, was raised and equipped with heavy armor. This huge ironclad, renamed *Virginia*, was very slow and quite unmaneuverable and could not operate in shallow water nor venture onto the open sea but was, on the other hand, practically invulnerable. Commanded by Franklin Buchanan, she sailed into Hampton Roads and rammed two large wooden Union vessels, the *Cumberland* and the *Congress*. Now the whole Union fleet at Hampton Roads, the Union's primary blockade base, was threatened, and there was panic in Washington.

The North started later on an ironclad building program but, once started, took advantage of its better shipbuilding facilities. The eminent marine engineer John Ericsson had designed a boat looking like a flat raft, with less than two feet of freeboard and a revolving turret containing two 11-inch guns. This "cheese-box on a a raft" was subcontracted, built under Ericsson's supervision in record time, named *Monitor* and launched in Brooklyn, New York on January 30, 1862. In spite of some dire predictions, she survived a storm on the way to Hampton Roads and, under the command of Lieutenant John L. Worden, attacked the much larger *Virginia*. The two ships battled for four hours, each trying in vain to pierce the other one's armor or to ram her. The fight ended in a draw, but the Union fleet at Hampton Roads was saved. For the next two months, neither boat attacked the other, as there were no other ironclads in reserve as yet. When Norfolk was taken by McClellan's army in May, 1862, the *Virginia* was blown up by her crew because she was not seaworthy enough to go through open water and too deep-drafted to go up the James River. The *Monitor* did not survive much longer. While being towed south for a blockade assignment, she sank in a gale in December of 1862.

Although both ships had shown great vulnerability, both sides continued to build ironclads—the South about 20, the North about 60. They were all designed for river and bay combat rather than the open sea. Many of them never saw action, and deep-water wooden warships remained the North's chief weapon for the blockade.

In February of 1862, McClellan submitted to Lincoln his new plan for a spring offensive. He proposed not to attack Joseph E. Johnston's army

The battle between the Monitor *and the* Merrimac *in Hampton Roads.*

around Manassas directly but to transport his army by water through Chesapeake Bay to the mouth of the Rappahannock River, thus placing the Northern forces between General Johnston and Richmond and forcing him to retreat to defend his capital. Lincoln did not care for this plan because it would leave Washington exposed to Johnston. The plan came to nought anyway because Johnston had decided to abandon his Manassas position and retreat south behind the Rappahannock River. This unexpected move angered President Davis who considered the retreat unnecessary and was furious about the destruction of large supplies that could not be moved along. Lincoln was equally angry when he discovered that the Confederate defenses at Manassas had not been nearly as strong as McClellan had led him to believe. Here, as before near Washington, the Confederates had fooled their enemy with "Quaker guns," faked cannons made of painted wood.

McClellan now proposed to move his army to Fort Monroe, at the tip of the peninsula formed by the James and York Rivers in Virginia, thus avoiding the long overland invasion Lincoln had in mind. Lincoln consented but demoted McClellan from general-in-chief to commander of the Army of the Potomac. He also withheld some divisions from McClellan's army because he felt that the defense of the capital had been weakened too much. He was all the more concerned because Stonewall Jackson had attacked Banks's troops at Kernstown near Winchester in the Shenandoah Valley. Although Banks was much stronger than Jackson assumed and the Confederates were thrown back, Lincoln found it necessary to keep Banks's army in the Shenandoah Valley. He also kept McDowell's large army in northern Virginia, so that McClellan, after a successful transport of his huge army to the peninsula, had only 100,000 men at his disposal instead of the 150,000 he had counted on. Again he overestimated the strength of Southern defenses at Yorktown, fooled by maneuvers of Confederate General John B. Magruder, and, instead of attacking, besieged it. This gave Johnston a chance to bring his troops to the Peninsula, but when McClellan brought up his siege guns, Johnston decided to retreat up the Peninsula, much against Jefferson Davis and Robert E. Lee's wishes. The latter had been called in from Savannah as Davis was beginning to lose confidence in Johnston. The Confederates kept on retreating, and the Union army followed slowly, delayed by rain and a rearguard fight near Williamsburg, almost half-way up to Richmond. Union gunboats moved up all the way to Drewry's Bluff, just seven miles below Richmond, but were stopped there by Southern shore batteries. The *Monitor,* still in action, could not raise her guns sufficiently to shoot at the batteries.

The fate of the South seemed to hang in the balance. President Davis had a general conscription enacted—the first in American history—and came under heavy attack in the Southern Congress and in the press. Governors opposed the conscription laws; and, since hiring of substitutes and other exemptions were permitted, the saying spread that this was "a rich man's war but a poor man's fight." Still, during 1862, the strength of the Confederate armies rose from about 250,000 to 450,000. But martial law had to be declared in Richmond and several other districts, and Davis was enpowered by his Congress to suspend the writ of habeas corpus—the guaranty against unlawful imprisonment—for a period of 16 months. Lincoln, incidentally, had suspended the writ as early as October 1861; by February 1862, more than 200 political prisoners were detained in the North.

The battle for Richmond continued, at first 100 miles northwest of the city, in the Shenandoah Valley. Here Stonewall Jackson's troops, reinforced by a division under Richard B. Ewell, managed to move between the Union troops under Frémont, Banks and James Shield, defeating them separately three times and marching almost to Harper's Ferry. They then escaped through forced marches, wedged in between enemy troops, and reached the only undamaged bridge over the Shenandoah River, at Port Republic. In this five-week campaign, Jackson's division had marched over 350 miles. He had diverted 60,000 Union soldiers from other assignments, had frustrated Frémont's campaign in eastern Tennessee and prevented McDowell from joining up with McClellan before Richmond. Jackson's reputation in the South rose to almost mythical proportions after this feat.

The decisive battle for Richmond began on May 31 when Johnston, urged by President Davis, attacked the Union's left wing, which was separated from the rest of the army by the rain-swollen Chickahominy

River. The attack was poorly organized and dissolved in a number of small engagements. Johnston was wounded and replaced by Lee, who did not yet enjoy a great reputation. Lee at first withdrew, and the battle of Seven Pines, or Fair Oaks, ended with an advantage for the Union side. Then he sent his cavalry commander "Jeb" Stuart on a daring reconnaissance ride around McClellan's right wing, which won for Stuart all the acclaim he had desired and gave Lee the information he needed. Still, when Lee attacked on June 26 at Mechanicsville, his General A. P. Hill was repulsed because Jackson failed to show up form the Shenandoah Valley, probably because he and his troops were finally overcome by fatigue. Yet McClellan felt he was not ready to counterattack and gave Lee a new chance to attack his right flank. This time Jackson joined in, and Magruder on the south side of the Chickahominy again acted so threatening that McClellan did not dare to bring up his 69,000 troops to help his North wing. Lee won, though only after suffering extremely heavy casualties, and McClellan reported that he had been attacked by superior forces on both sides of the river. He began to retreat to the James River. Lee's various schemes to cut off his retreat failed because his subcommanders were slow in executing his orders, and because of stubborn Union resistance. On the last day of the fighting, at Malvern Hill, the attacking Confederates were smashed by Union artillery. Although urged by his subcommanders to attack again, McClellan insisted on retreating to Harrison's Landing at the James River. In this "Seven Days" battle the South had liberated the besieged Southern capital but had suffered very heavy losses, and Lee found it necessary to reorganize his command structure completely. It has never been explained sufficiently why Jackson had failed him in these days.

About 30,000 men had been killed or wounded in this battle, even more than at Shiloh. The battle became a pattern for the extremely costly fighting that became typical for the war in Virginia. Richmond was turned into one large hospital for the many thousands of Southern wounded, and hundreds of women volunteered as nurses. Slaves were organized as gravediggers.

Lee, who was very dissatisfied with the results of the great battle, became nevertheless the hero of the South. Lincoln recognized that the cessation of the recruiting he had ordered in April had been a mistake and called for 300,000 new volunteers. General Halleck became commander-in-chief; he ordered McClellan to move the Army of the Potomac from the Peninsula to Aquia Creek on the Potomac, about 40 miles south of Washington.

After the failure of the great Peninsula campaign, the North adopted a harsher policy in conducting the war. The Confiscation Act signed by

Lincoln on July 17 provided freedom for slaves coming into Federal jurisdiction from outside the Union, and General John Pope, commander of the newly organized Army of Virginia authorized his officers to seize rebel property without compensation, to shoot captured guerrillas and to expel civilians who refused the oath of allegiance. More and more slaves had come over to the Union side and were "confiscated" as "contraband" and put to work. While McClellan and many Democrats still advocated a more conciliatory policy and opposed any confiscation of property and any forcible abolition of slavery, Lincoln had come to the conclusion that a proclamation of freedom for all slaves had become a military necessity and would strike at the heart of the rebellion. However, he went along with Secretary Seward who approved of such a proclamation but would have it postponed until some military success had been achieved. Consideration of the sentiments in the Army of the Potomac, which still idolized McClellan, may have also played a role in his decision to delay.

By the end of July, Lincoln and Halleck had decided to unite the Army of the Potomac with Pope's force at the Rappahannock River in Virginia. Union General Nathaniel P. Banks, believing he would be reinforced soon, attacked the Confederates under Jackson and A. P. Hill at Cedar Mountain but had to withdraw after a counterattack of superior Confederate forces. A few days later, Pope, who had proudly declared that in the West where he had been fighting Union troops had never retreated, was pushed back to the North bank of the Rappahannock into the old battleground of Bull Run.

Jackson, who had found back his old energy and determination, marched his whole corps of 24,000 men to Manassas, covering 50 miles in two days. The large Union supply depot was unprotected, and the underfed and underclothed Confederates plundered the depot to their hearts' content before they set fire to what was left. Then the corps disappeared to a wooded ridge west of the old battlefield. The corps of McClellan and his friend Fitz-John Porter, urged on by Halleck, did not come to Pope's rescue because both commanders bore a grudge against Pope. Jackson, on the other hand, was in close touch with both Longstreet's and Lee's detachments who had followed him. When Pope found Jackson, he attacked. After one day's fighting on August 29, Pope sent a victory dispatch to Washington, but when he set out to pursue on the following day, his units were attacked by Jackson's and Longstreet's troops and driven back to Henry House Hill, scene of the heaviest fighting 13 months ago. On September 1, the defeated Union soldiers retreated to the Washington defenses, after suffering 16,000 casualties, and once more a panic gripped the capital. Lincoln's cabinet wanted McClellan removed, and Lincoln himself thought that McClellan had wanted Pope to fail; but he decided, in view of McClellan's great popularity with the soldiers, to put him in charge of Washington's defense.

Although his armies were exhausted and hungry, Lee decided to use the psychological moment to attack the Union capital and crossed the Potomac 35 miles above Washington on September 4. When they entered Maryland, they received a less enthusiastic welcome than they had expected, and when McClellan, who had restored the spirit of his troops, advanced to intercept Lee, he had an unusual stroke of luck: Union soldiers found a copy of Lee's orders to his subcommanders, which revealed to McClellan that Lee had taken the risk of splitting his forces. Still believing his forces to be outnumbered, McClellan moved too slowly; and even before the Union commander started moving, Lee was warned through a Southern sympathizer that his plans were known to the enemy. As the whole Union army was moving toward South Mountain, having fought its way through Crampton's Gap after heavy fighting, there seemed to be only one way out for Lee: Retreat to the Shenandoah Valley. However, when Lee learned that Jackson was moving on Harper's Ferry, Lee decided to give battle and concentrated around Sharpsburg, Maryland. Harper's Ferry, poorly defended, fell to Jackson without much of a fight on September 15. Again, before Jackson could join Lee, McClellan, who had arrived at Antietam Creek the same day, had his chance to attack the outnumbered Lee—who in fact had only 25,000 to 30,000 men against McClellan's 60,000. When the latter attacked on the 17th, he and Burnside did not coordinate their attacks, and through Lee's skillful maneuvering and the bravery of his ragged soldiers, the Confederates held. The battle of Sharpsburg, or Antietam, raged all day and resulted in a dreadful slaughter. Five Union and five Confederate divisions were decimated so badly that they had to back out of the fight. After five hours of fierce fighting, the rebel center known as "bloody lane" was overrun by the Federals. When Lee's right seemed to be crushed, troops from Harper's Ferry joined in the fight and threw back Burnside's regiments. When night fell, many Southern brigade commanders had suffered casualties of 50 percent or more. Lee held his position on the following day, and McClellan, though reinforced by two fresh divisions, refused to give battle once more. During the night of September 18 and 19, Lee withdrew and ordered his forces back to Virginia, only feebly pursued by Federal units.

The battle of Antietam was a strategic Union success. Lee's invasion of Maryland had been beaten back, almost one-third of his troops had become casualties. Lincoln, though disappointed that the enemy had not been destroyed, had his victory and the opportune moment to proclaim the emancipation.

CHRONICLE OF EVENTS

1861:

July 22: The House of Representatives declares that the war is waged to defend and maintain the supremacy of the Constitution and to preserve the Union, and not to interfere with slavery (Crittenden Resolution).

July 25: In the U. S. Senate, Andrew Johnson of Tennessee moves to adopt the Crittenden Resolution (30 are for, five against it).

In the Shenandoah Valley, Major General Banks succeeds Patterson who had failed to contain Johnston's forces and thus contributed to the defeat at Bull Run.

July 29: Horace Greeley of the *New York Tribune,* who had consistently called for a march against Richmond, now writes to the president suggesting peace negotiations.

August 2: The Federal Congress passes the first national income tax measure: 3% on incomes over $800 (revised in 1862).

August 5: The departing 34th Federal Congress authorizes the president to enlist seamen for the entire length of the war, tariff increases, more taxes, and the issuance of more bonds. It also approves all acts and orders of the president since his inauguration.

August 7: Federal authorities order the construction of seven ironclad gunboats to be used in western waters.

August 14: New York volunteers start a mutiny and are put under guard.

August 16: President Lincoln proclaims that commercial intercourse between loyal and rebellious states is, with some exceptions, unlawful.

August 20: Major General George McClellan assumes command of the newly organized Army of the Potomac.

August 28–29: A Federal army and navy expedition attacks and occupies Fort Clark and Fort Hatteras on the North Carolina coast, sealing off an important blockade-running route.

September 25: Continued disputes between President Davis and General J. E. Johnston over reinforcements, strategy and general policies.

September 27: Heated discussion between Lincoln and General McClellan, with the president pressing for increased action in Virginia.

October 4: Lincoln approves a contract for more ironclad warships (including the *Monitor*).

The Confederate government signs treaties with the Shawnee and Seneca Indians and then with the Cherokees.

October 14: Lincoln authorizes General Winfield Scott to suspend, if necessary, the privilege of *habeas corpus* (guarantee against unlawful imprisonment) anywhere between Bangor, Maine and Washington.

October 21: Battle of Ball's Buff, or Leesburg, Virginia. Federal troops under General Charles P. Stone and Colonel Edward D. Baker shuttle across the Potomac and advance toward Leesburg, but are defeated by Confederates under General Nathan G. Evans. Baker is killed and many Federal soldiers drown. Stone is indicted and imprisoned, probably unjustly.

October 24: Western Union completes the transcontinental telegraph system.

October 29: A large land and sea expedition under Brigadier General Thomas W. Sherman sails from Hampton Roads, Virginia, for the Carolina coast and Port Royal, off Savannah, Georgia, but runs into heavy gales.

November 1: General-in--hief Winfield Scott retires in favor of Major General George Brinton McClellan.

November 4: General "Stonewall" Jackson assumes command of the Shenandoah Valley district.

November 5: General Robert E. Lee is named commander of the new Department of South Carolina, Georgia and East Florida.

November 6: Jefferson Davis is chosen without opposition and confirmed by the voters as permanent president of the Confederacy.

November 7: A strong Federal naval squadron forces a landing at Port Royal, on the Georgia coast, between Savannah and Charleston; 12,000 troops under Thomas W. Sherman occupy the area.

November 9: Federal troops at the newly established base of Port Royal capture the city of Beaufort, South Carolina.

November 18: A convention at Hatteras, North Carolina, repudiates the secession and affirms loyalty to the Union.

November 22–23: Bombardment of Confederate installations at Pensacola, Florida, from Fort Pickens and two Union warships.

November 24: Union forces land at Tybee Island, Georgia, which controls the entrance to the Savannah River.

November 29: Many farmers along the South Atlantic coast near Savannah and Charleston burn their cotton to prevent it from falling into Union hands.

December 1: U. S. gunboat *Penguin* captures the blockade-runner *Albion* off Charleston.

December 5: Petitions and bills calling for the abolition of slavery are introduced in the Federal Congress.

December 9: The U. S. Senate establishes the Joint Committee on the Conduct of the War.

December 11: A disastrous fire sweeps through Charleston, South Carolina.

December 15: Two more Confederate blockade-runners are captured near Cape Fear and off Cape Hatteras.

December 17: After a skirmish, Confederate troops evacuate Rockville, South Carolina, which is threatened by the Federal beachhead at Port Royal and Hilton Head Island.

December 20: Sixteen old whaling boats are sunk in the main ship channel of Charleston to stop blockade-runners.

1862:

January 1: Stonewall Jackson begins to move his troops north, in order to break up the Baltimore and Ohio Railroad and to destroy dams on the Chesapeake and Ohio Canal.

January 6: Lincoln confers with General Mc-Clellan, who is recovering from an attack of typhoid fever.

January 11: A fleet of about 100 vessels under Union Brigadier Ambrose E. Burnside sails from Hampton Roads, Virginia to the North Carolina coast, carrying about 15,000 men.

Lincoln accepts the resignation of Secretary of War Simon Cameron, who is appointed Minister to Russia.

January 13: In a war council, General McClellan refuses to discuss his plan of operations with the president or the other generals.

January 15: The U. S. Senate confirms the appointment of Edwin M. Stanton as secretary of war.

January 27: Lincoln issues his War Order #1, declaring that on February 22 a general movement of the Union land and naval forces against the insurgents must begin.

January 30: A revolutionary ironclad ship, the U.S.S. *Monitor*, designed by John Ericsson, is launched at Greenpoint, Long Island.

February 7: General Ambrose E. Burnside's Federal expedition lands on Roanoke Island, North Carolina. Federal troops also occupy Romney in western Virginia.

February 8: Burnside's 7,500 men quickly overwhelm the 2,000 Confederates under Colonel H. M. Shaw, who surrenders. This gives the Union a first-rate base for operations against North Carolina.

February 14: In Washington, the president grants an amnesty to all political prisoners who consent to take an oath not to aid the rebellion.

February 20: Lincoln's son Willie dies of typhoid.

February 22: Jefferson Davis is inaugurated as regularly elected president of the Confederate States of America.

February 26: President Lincoln signs the Loan and Treasury Bill, which creates a national currency of United States notes and provides for sale of stock to finance the currency.

February 27: President Davis is given the authority to suspend the privilege of *habeas cor-*

pus. He orders martial law for Norfolk and Portsmouth, Virginia.

February 28: General McClellan informs Lincoln that no operations could be instituted at Harper's Ferry because the boats sent to form a pontoon bridge over the Potomac are too large for the locks.

March 1: Martial law is declared in Richmond.

March 6: McClellan's Army of the Potomac finally starts moving toward Manassas. Federal General Joseph E. Johnston retreats south toward Fredericksburg, Virginia.

Outside of Norfolk Harbor, the C.S.S. *Virginia (Merrimack)* defeats three of four older Federal warships. Federal Commander Buchanan is wounded.

Federal forces take Leesburg, Virginia.

March 9: The iron-constructed U.S.S. *Monitor* arrives from New York and battles the C.S.S. *Virginia (Merrimack).* Neither vessel is seriously damaged, but the *Merrimack* is in no position to threaten the U. S. fleet in Washington and New York.

McClellan's army returns to Alexandria without having encountered the enemy. General Joseph E. Johnston withdraws from northern Virginia and concentrates his troops at the Rappahannock River.

March 11: In War Order # 3 Lincoln relieves Major General George McClellan as general-in-chief, but he retains his command of the Army of the Potomac. No new general-in-chief is named, and all generals report directly to the secretary of war.

March 12: Federal troops march into Winchester, Virginia and also temporarily occupy Jacksonville, Florida.

March 13: At a war conference at Fairfax Court House, Virginia, McClellan develops his Peninsular Campaign Plan to move the Army of the Potomac by boat up the York and James Rivers toward Richmond.

March 14: Burnside's troops occupy New Berne, North Carolina, after heavy fighting.

March 20: Stonewall Jackson drives Federal troops back from Strasburg, Virginia, toward Winchester.

March 21: Burnside's Federals capture Washington, North Carolina.

March 23: Beginning of Jackson's Shenandoah Valley Campaign. He attacks the superior forces under General James Shields at Kernstown, Virginia, south of Winchester. Although Jackson has to withdraw eventually, Washington is forced to take forces from the front to protect the capital.

April 3: Lincoln discovers that McClellan, against orders, left fewer than 20,000 troops for the defense of the capital. Lincoln recalls one of his corps and orders McClellan to commence forward movement at once. The U. S. Senate votes 29 to 14 in favor of abolishing slavery in the District of Columbia.

April 5: McClellan begins the siege of Yorktown, Virginia, opposed by 15,000 Confederates under J. E. Johnston. Another Confederate army is approaching.

April 9: The Confederate Senate passes a bill calling for the conscription of troops.

April 10: A joint resolution of the U. S. Congress calling for the gradual emancipation of the slaves by the states is approved by Lincoln.

From Tybee Island, Union General Quincy Adams bombards Fort Pulaski at the entrance to the Savannah harbor.

April 11: After further bombardment, Fort Pulaski surrenders to Union General Quincy Adams Gillmore.

April 12: General Magruder, defending Yorktown, is being reinforced from Joseph E. Johnston's troops, but is still outnumbered 100,000 to 30,000 by McClellan.

April 16: President Lincoln signs a bill ending slavery in the District of Columbia.

April 18: Forts Jackson and St. Philip on the Mississippi, below New Orleans, are bombarded by U. S. mortar boats, with little success.

April 24: A large fleet under Admiral Farragut

David Farragut, Union admiral.

rushes past the Confederate forts and, suffering few losses from the Confederate shore guns and vessels, anchors at the undefended city of New Orleans the following day. The waterfront is set afire by the hostile population.

After a month-long siege of Fort Macon Beaufort, North Carolina surrenders to Federal troops under John G. Parke.

April 27: Four small forts protecting New Orleans surrender to the Federals. Forts Jackson and St. Philip follow the next day.

May 3: General Joseph E. Johnston withdraws his 55,000 men from besieged Yorktown before MacClellan begins his major bombardment and moves through Williamsburg toward Richmond.

May 5: Battle of Williamsburg, Virginia. Advance units of McClellan's army clash with rearguard divisions of Johnston's army. After heavy fighting, the Federals suffer about 2,200 losses, the Confederates about 1,700. The Confederate troops continue their retreat.

Union forces occupy Williamsburg. Stonewall Jackson's troops arrive at Staunton in the Shenandoah Valley and start pushing back the Federals under Banks up to Strasburg. Beginning of Jackson's Valley Campaign.

May 7: President Lincoln visits U.S.S. *Monitor* near Fort Monroe.

May 8: Battle of McDowell, Virginia. Stonewall Jackson defeats 6,000 troops of Frémont's army and then proceeds north in the Shenandoah Valley.

May 9: Norfolk, Virginia is evacuated by the Confederates; this leaves the C.S.S. *Merrimack* without a port.

At Hilton Head Island, South Carolina, U. S. Major General David Hunter orders the emancipation of slaves in Florida, Georgia, and South Carolina and authorizes arming of all able-bodied blacks in these states. Lincoln disavows this order 10 days later.

May 11: The C.S.S. *Merrimack (Virginia)* is scuttled by the Confederates.

May 15: Battle of Drewry's Bluff, Virginia. Five

Joseph E. Johnston, Confederate general.

Union vessels, including the *Monitor*, move up the James River toward Richmond, but are stopped eight miles below the capital by Confederate shore batteries. After four hours of fighting, they have to withdraw.

May 18: Jackson's Confederates press forward in the Shenandoah Valley and Union troops fall back along the north fork of the valley.

May 20: Lincoln signs the Homestead Act, granting a free plot of 160 acres to actual settlers on land in the public domain.

Jackson, pressing on in the Shenandoah, is reinforced by Major General Richard Ewell's troops and now has 16,000 men at his disposal.

May 23: Jackson enters Front Royal in the Shenandoah, defeating a small Federal force.

May 24: After several skirmishes in the Shenandoah, Jackson attempts to cut off Banks's retreat, but most Federals get away.

Lincoln orders Frémont in western Virginia and McDowell near Fredericksburg to move to the Shenandoah Valley in order to cut off and capture the forces of Jackson and Ewell. This gives McClellan another excuse to delay action against Richmond.

May 25: Battle of Winchester, Virginia. Jackson attacks and defeats Banks's retreating forces. Banks suffers more than 2,000 casualties.

Lincoln again urges McClellan to attack Richmond.

May 27: Banks crosses the Potomac, Jackson pushes toward Harper's Ferry. Minor fighting around Richmond.

May 31: Battle of Seven Pines, or Fair Oaks, Virginia. General Joseph E. Johnston attacks the two corps McClellan has sent south of the Chickahominy. The attack fails after some inroads had been made, Johnston is wounded and replaced by Robert E. Lee on June 1.

Stonewall Jackson withdraws to avoid a trap and squeezes through the converging armies of McDowell and Frémont.

June 1: At Seven Pines, after a new attack of the Confederates under General James Longstreet, Lee orders withdrawal to the original

Robert E. Lee, Confederate commander.

positions. The casualties of the Confederates are higher than those of the Union.

June 8: At Port Republic, Virginia, Stonewall Jackson and Ewell face two Federal forces under Frémont and James Shields. Ewell forces Frémont to withdraw after considerable losses. On the following day, both Southern commanders drive back Frémont's forces, commanded by E. B. Tyler. This ends Jackson's Shenandoah Campaign which made him a war hero in the South.

June 12–15: Confederate Brigadier General James Ewell Brown (Jeb) Stuart and his 1,200 cavalrymen undertake a successful ride around McClellan's entire army.

June 16: Engagement of Secessionville, South Carolina. Against orders, Federal Brigadier General H. W. Benham assaults Confederate works at Secessionville on James Island near Charleston, but fails completely and is later relieved of his command.

June 17: Jackson's men have left Shenandoah

Valley and are being shipped toward Richmond.

June 19: President Lincoln signs a law prohibiting slavery in U. S. territories.

June 21: Skirmishes along the battle lines on the Chickahominy River near Richmond.

June 25: Beginning of the Seven Days Battle. Only secondary engagements on the first day.

June 26: Confederate troops under General D. H. Hill attack at Mechanicsville. Federal Commander Porter falls back to Beaver Dam Creek, and Hill's frontal attack fails as Jackson does not come to his aid. Porter withdraws further and McClellan orders his supplies to be sent to the James River.

June 27: Lee attacks again, and Porter's line is broken, but the disorganized Confederates do not fully exploit their advantage. Nevertheless, McClellan retreats to the James River.

June 28: At Richmond, both armies reorganize. In a telegram to the president, McClellan complains that he lost the battle because his force was too small.

June 29: Confederate forces cross the Chickahominy River and attack McClellan's retreating troops. McClellan withdraws safely but must leave 2,500 sick and wounded behind. Jackson again fails to join in the battle.

June 30: In a series of confused engagements, McClellan effectively halts the Confederate advance and prevents Lee from cutting his army in two.

July 1: On the last day of the Seven Days Battle the Federal army takes a strong defensive position at Malvern Hill, north of the James River. Confederate attacks fail. Richmond is saved, but Lee has failed to cripple McClellan's army. Of the Federal army of 115,000 men, 83,000 were engaged in battle and 8,000 became casualties, not counting the missing. The Confederates with 88,000 men lost about the same number.

President Lincoln raises the federal income tax.

July 4: Tension increases between McClellan and the president. In a letter, McClellan ad-

vises Lincoln that military operations should not interfere with slavery.

July 11: Major General Henry W. Halleck becomes general-in-chief of all Federal land forces.

July 13: Lincoln asks Congress for an act to compensate any state that may wish to abolish slavery.

July 17: Lincoln signs the Second Confiscation Act, providing that slaves of rebels who came within Union control would be free and allowing for confiscation of various kinds of property.

Federal troops under Pope capture Gordonsville, Virginia.

July 22: At a cabinet meeting, Lincoln reads his first draft of the Emancipation Proclamation, but then follows Seward's advice to delay such announcement until the army had achieved a victory.

July 23: Federal cavalry units from Fredericksburg conduct a raid on Confederate cavalry and supplies near Carmel Church, Virginia.

General Halleck, as commander-in-chief, confers with McClellan on the joint campaign of McClellan and Pope against Lee.

August 2: Union troops reoccupy Malvern Hill, Virginia.

August 3: Over McClellan's protests, Halleck orders him to move his Army of the Potomac from the Peninsula to Aquia Landing, near Fredericksburg, Virginia, to aid in the defense of Washington.

August 4: Lincoln orders a draft of 300,000 militia to serve for nine months. The president also advises Western delegates that he is not yet prepared to enlist blacks as soldiers.

August 9: Battle of Cedar Mountain, or Slaughter Mountain, Virginia. Pope's Federal Army of Virginia advances to Culpeper. One of his corps under Banks attacks two of Stonewall Jackson's division at Cedar Mountain. With the help of a third division under A. P. Hill, the Confederates counterattack. The Confederates, superior in numbers, suffer fewer casualties.

August 10: The Confederate steamer *General Lee*

is captured near Fort Pulaski, Georgia.

August 13: The Federal steamers *George Peabody* and *West Point* collide in the Potomac, with the loss of 73 lives.

August 16: McClellan's Army of the Potomac has evacuated Harrison's Landing and moved to Aquia Creek and Alexandria.

August 18: The Army of Virginia under Pope is pushed back by Lee's forces and retreats to the north bank of the Rappahannock River.

In the second session of the Confederate Congress, President Davis protests against the atrocities of the Yankees, particularly of Butler in New Orleans.

August 22: Skirmishes between Lee's and Pope's armies along the Rappahannock River. Jeb Stuart captures Pope's baggage train on Catlett's Station, Virginia.

August 24: A new cruiser of the Confederate navy, the C.S.S. *Alabama,* is commissioned near the Azores in the Atlantic.

August 25: Secretary of War Edwin M. Stanton authorizes the commander of the Southern Department to take black soldiers up to five thousand in number in to service of the United States. Stonewall Jackson's forces approach the Rappahannock, and Longstreet's corps follows.

August 26: Confederate cavalry captures Manassas Junction, seizing large amounts of supplies.

August 27: Both sides move additional forces to Manassas. About half of the Confederate army is now between Pope's army and Washington.

August 28: Jackson withdraws from Manassas. Pope concentrates his troops around Centerville. Heavy fighting near Groveton. Lee and Longstreet arrive at Thoroughfare Gap.

August 29: Second battle of Bull Run, or Manassas: Pope attacks Jackson near Groveton, but his and Major General Porter's attacks fail. McClellan, ordered by Halleck to help, is slow to respond.

August 30: Jackson and Longstreet repulse Pope's and Porter's attacks. The defeated Federals hold on to the Henry House Hill, then retreat toward Washington.

In this second battle of Bull Run, the Federals fielded about 75,000 troops and suffered 16,000 casualties, including generals Isaac Stevens and Philip Kearney. The Confederates sustained 9,200 casualties out of about 48,500 troops. Washington is again threatened by the Confederates.

September 1: Lee sends Jackson's corps around the right of the retreating Union army. Federal units opposing Jackson are forced to withdraw. The Confederate advance is then halted.

September 2: Lincoln, against Secretaries Stanton's and Chase's advice, restores McClellan to full command in Virginia, leaving Pope without a command. Winchester, in the Shenandoah Valley, is evacuated by the Federals.

September 3: Lee finds it impossible to attack Washington and turns toward Leesburg, Virginia. Winchester is occupied and skirmishes occur around Falls Church, Bunker Hill, Harper's Ferry and other places.

September 4–7: On their way to Maryland Lee's army crosses the Potomac in the Leesburg area. Pope delivers a report to Halleck, charging Porter with disobeying orders and McClellan with failing to support him.

September 6: Stonewall Jackson's troops occupy Frederick, Maryland, but are not welcomed by the population. The Union evacuates Aquia Creek, near Fredericksburg.

September 8: Major General N. P. Banks assumes command of the defenses of Washington.

September 9: Lee issues orders to Jackson to march on Harper's Ferry and to other commanders to advance in Maryland.

September 11: Confederate forces take Hagerstown, Maryland.

September 12: The Army of the Potomac begins to move into Frederick as the Confederates move out. The Federal Army of Virginia is incorporated into the Army of the Potomac.

Archives and treasures of the state of Pennsylvania are moved from Harrisburg and Philadelphia to New York.

September 13: By accident, two Union soldiers

A Maryland battery at Antietam, sketch by A.R. Waud.

find a copy of Lee's orders for the Maryland campaign. It is rushed to McClellan who starts moving accordingly.

September 14: Battle of Crampton's Gap and South Mountain (Boonsborough). Union Major General William B. Franklin, trying to relieve the threatened garrison at Harper's Ferry, advances against the Confederates at Crampton's Gap. At South Mountain, Federal cavalry and infantry forces engage D. H. Hill's Confederates in a fierce battle. Major General Jesse L. Reno is killed, the Federals suffer about 2,300 casualties, the Confederates about 2,700. They withdraw in the evening, but Union troops cannot prevent Jackson's troops from besieging the garrison at the Ferry.

September 15: The Federal garrison at Harper's Ferry surrenders to Stonewall Jackson, about 12,000 prisoners are taken. At South Mountain, the Confederates fall back to Sharpsburg.

September 16: Lee gathers his forces along Antietam Creek in Maryland.

September 17: Battle of Antietam, or Sharpsburg. McClellan attacks the great outnumbered Lee, and one of the bloodiest battles of the War develops. The Confederates hold their positions in spite of five main Federal drives. Of the 75,000 Federal troops participating, about 12,500 become casualties; of the 40,000 Confederates, about 13,700 are casualties.

September 18: Lee begins his withdrawal across the Potomac at Blackford's Ford. McClellan refrains from attacking him although he has received large reinforcements of fresh troops.

September 19: McClellan's cavalry pursuing Lee's troops is stopped by Confederate batteries.

September 20: Two of McClellan's divisions sent across the Potomac are halted by A. P. Hill's troops.

EYEWITNESS TESTIMONY

I find myself in a new and strange position here: President, cabinet, General Scott and all deferring to me . . . By some strange operation of magic I seem to have become the power of the land. I almost think that was I to win one whole success now I could become dictator or anything else that might please me—but nothing of the kind please me—therefore I won't be Dictator. Admirable self denial!

General McClellan, letter to his wife after his visit in Washington, July 27, 1861.

I shall carry this thing on *en grand* and crush the Rebels in one campaign. I flatter myself that Beauregard has gained his last victory . . . Gen. Scott has been trying to work a traverse to have Emory made Inspector General of *my* army and of *the* army. I respectfully declined the favor and perhaps disgusted the old man . . . He cannot long retain command I think—when he is retires I am sure to succeed him, unless in the meantime I lose a battle—which I do not expect to do.

General McClellan, letter to his wife, August 2, 1861.

When I . . . found those old men flocking around me; when I afterwards stood in the library, looking over the Capitol of our great nation, and saw the crowd gathering around staring at me, I began to feel how great a task committed to me . . . Who would have thought, when we were married [May of 1860], that I should so soon be called upon to save my country?

General George B. McClellan, letter to his wife, August 1861, as quoted in R. Wheeler's Voices of the Civil War *(1976).*

I am here in a terrible place—the enemy have from 3 to 4 times my force—the Pres't is an idiot, the old General is in his dotage—they cannot or will not see the true state of affairs . . . They sit on the verge of the precipice and cannot realize what they see. Their reply to everything is: "Impossible! Impossible!" They think nothing possible which is against their wishes.

General McClellan, letter to his wife, August 16, 1861.

What does the entrance of the Yankees into our waters amount to? It amounts to this: The whole of the Eastern part of the State is now exposed to the ravages of the merciless vandals. New Berne, Washington, Plymouth, Edenton . . . are all now exposed, beside the whole adjacent country . . .

Petersburg, Va., Express, dispatch from Raleigh, August 30, 1861, after the occupation of Forts Clark and Hatteras.

The secesh women, in order to show their contempt for the yankee mud sills, had a fashion of pasting miniature rebel flags, made of paper, on the hydrants at night, and looking through the blinds at the aggravation of the soldiers on discovering them in the morning . . .

Alfred Bellard, September 1861, Gone for a Soldier, *with the Fifth N.J. Infantry in Alexandria, Virginia (1975).*

The enemy must be made to feel the war. They must be made to understand that there is a God that punishes the wicked, and that the Southern army is His instrument.

Richmond Examiner, September 24, 1861.

One . . . morning I rode to Bailey's Cross-Roads, which is about a mile from Munson's Hill. Looking across a cornfield, I could see the Rebels behind their breastworks. Their battle-flags were waving gaily . . . A group of officers had gathered on the summit of the hill. With my field-glass, I could see what they were doing. They examined maps, looking toward Washington and pointed out the position of the Union fortifications. There were ladies present who looked earnestly toward the city and chatted merrily with the officers . . . The summer passed away . . . The troops were organized into brigades and divisions. They drilled daily . . . At sunset each regiment had a dress parade . . . In the evening, there were no military duties to be performed, and the soldiers told stories around the campfires, or sang songs, for in each company there was usually one who could play the violin.

Charles C. Coffin, September, 1861, My Days and Nights on the Battle-Field *(1863).*

I am sorry, as you say, that the movements of the armies cannot keep pace with the expectations of the editors of papers. I know they can regulate matters satisfactorily to themselves on paper. I wish they could do so in the field. No one wishes them more success than I do and would be happy to see them have full swing.

Robert E. Lee, letter to his wife, September 1861, after his failure at Cheat Mountain Summit in Western Virginia had been criticized in the Southern press.

I have just received and read your letter of the 12th instant. Its language is, as you say, unusual; its arguments and statements utterly one-sided, and its insinuations as unfounded as they are unbecoming.

Jefferson Davis, letter of September 1861 to General Joseph E. Johnston, who had complained about being outranked by three other generals.

Charles [her husband] and I have invested all our spare money in the government loan. I feel quite proud to do even that little. Indeed I will do anything so long as I not be called to give up my dear ones for soldiers. I wish I had more courage, but I cannot do that. Thank Heaven Charles will be forty-five on the 31st of the month and beyond the age of service!

Maria L. Daly, October 8, 1861, Diary of a Union Lady (1962).

I will not consent to one other man being detached from this army for that expedition. I need far more than I have now to save this country and cannot spare any disciplined regiment. Instead of diminishing this army, true policy would dictate its immediate increase to a large extent. It is the task of the Army of the Potomac to decide the question at issue. No outside expedition can effect the result. . . .

General McClellan, letter to Assistant Secretary of War Scott, October 17, 1861, refusing to contribute troops for General Thomas West Sherman's expedition against Port Royal.

His hands were clasped upon his heart; he walked with a shuffling, tottering gait, reeling as if beneath a staggering blow. He did not fall, but passed down the street, carrying not only the burden of the nation but a load of private grief which, with the swiftness of the lightning's flash, had been hurled upon him.

Charles Coffin of the Boston Journal, *about Lincoln, as he learned of the death of Colonel Edward D. Baker, a personal friend at Ball's Bluff, on October 21, 1861.*

This is a humiliation I had hoped I should never be subjected to. I thought there was one calumny that could not be brought against me . . . the gov-

ernment has not a more faithful soldier; of poor capacity, it is true, but a more faithful soldier this government has not had . . .

General Charles P. Stone, after the battle of Ball's Bluff, October 21, 1861.

If we fail to get into battle here now all is lost, and up to this time a fight is scarcely contemplated. Washington is safe now, and that seems to be all they care for . . . If the South had one tenth our resources Jeff Davis would be today in Philadelphia and before a month in Boston.

Senator Zachariah Chandler of Michigan, letter to his wife, October 27, 1861.

General Scott has retired from the service. His resignation must have been one of the most touching and dignified ceremonies ever witnessed. His letter to the President was most admirable—faultless, indeed—and the President's reply was infinitely the best thing he has ever done. Dear old General—may McClellan show himself worthy of the trust placed in him!

Maria L. Daly, November 4, 1861, Diary.

Mrs. Captain Dodge . . . says that there is a great discontent among the regulars, that civilians are placed and ranked over them. She intimated that the officers generally were in favor of a limited monarchy. Perhaps a despotism would develop our country more advantageously than the present system, which brings the worst of the population only to its surface.

Maria L. Daly, November 4, 1861, Diary.

I am becoming daily more disgusted with this imbecile administration . . . Seward is the meanest of them all—a meddlesome, officious, incompetent little puppy . . . Welles is a garrulous old woman . . . The Presdt. is nothing more than a well meaning baboon . . . 'the original gorilla' . . . It is sickening in the extreme . . .

McClellan to his wife, in letters between October 2 and November 17, 1861.

There cannot be much bloody work where a Lee is opposed by a Sherman . . . These generals are true scions of West Point, and both will take time before they go into action . . . The effect of these grand demonstrations of the Yankees at various points will be admirable upon the Southern people, government, army and generals. All had grown over-confident and had consequently relapsed into listlessness and inactivity. The enemy are curing all this for us.

Richmond Examiner, *November 23, 1861,* *after the capture of Port Royal.*

Paid a visit to Mrs. Lieber and encountered the Doctor [Francis L., editor of the Encyclopedia Americana]. He told me that he had always said and wished that it might be published as history that the causes of this war were first Satanic Pride and Whiskey. Whilst living in Columbia, he said he noticed that when the legislature of South Carolina was in session there was a constant stream of men, like a body of ants, down the courthouse steps to the different drinking houses. And at election time, certain friends of the principal candidates would have what some used to call pews where they could keep men in a constant state of intoxication, sometimes for three days, and then take them up tipsy to the polls to drop in their vote . . .

Maria L. Daly, November 25, 1861, Diary.

Those who make war against the Government justly forfeit all rights of property . . . It is as clearly a right of the Government to arm slaves, when it may become necessary, as it is to use gunpowder taken from the enemy.

Secretary of War Simon Cameron, in his annual report released to the press, against Lincoln's wishes, on December 1, 1861.

The Union must be preserved, and hence, all indispensable means must be employed. We should not be in haste to determine that radical and extreme measures, which may reach the loyal as well as the disloyal, are indispensable, . . . The insurrection is largely, if not exclusively, a war upon the first principle of popular government—the rights of the people . . . Labor is prior to, and independent of, capital. Capital is only the fruit of labor, and could never have existed if labor had not first existed . . . Capital has its rights which are as worthy of protection as any other rights.

Lincoln's State of the Union message of December 3, 1861.

The war continues. In considering the policy to be adopted for suppressing the insurrection, I have been anxious and most careful that the inevitable conflict for this purpose shall not degenerate into a violent and remorseless struggle. I have therefore, in every case, thought it proper to keep the integrity of the Union prominent as the primary object of the contest on our part, leaving all questions which are not of vital military importance to the more deliberate action of the legislature.

Lincoln, message to the Congress, December 3, 1861.

Charles returned yesterday and is full of anecdotes of the celebrities of Washington . . . Evidently Chase, he says, is the greatest man in the administration, and a very great man, he thinks . . . Charles says that there was a deputation from Indians in the South in Washington who came to see for themselves whether Uncle Sam was dead, as the Southern Confederacy wished them to believe . . . Lincoln is mentally what he is physically, long and loose in the joints. He cannot gather himself up easily for an effort, but all agree (he) is a conscientious, honest fellow, most unfit for the high position, not realizing the peril of the country, content to be President and have Mrs. Lincoln dress herself up and hold levees. Mrs. Lincoln behaves in the most undignified manner possible . . . she is not a young woman by any means, and dresses like one and rather bullies her husband, which they say accounts for his meekness.

Maria L. Daly, December 19, 1861, Diary.

All this [the inactivity of the army] is hanging upon one man who keeps his counsels entirely to himself. If he was an old veteran who had fought a hundred battles, or we knew him as well as Bonaparte or Wellington was known, then we could repose upon him with confidence. But how can this nation abide the secret counsels that one man carries in his head, when we have no evidence that he is the wisest man in the world?

Senator Ben Wade, radical Republican, about McClellan, end of December 1861.

The new year [1862] opened with comparative quiet around Washington, and indeed all along the great line of defense that crossed half the continent. Even at Richmond, the rebel capital, more than usual gaiety prevailed . . .

John Tyler Headley, The Great Rebellion (1863–66).

Do? I intend to accomplish three things. I will make Abe Lincoln President of the United States. I will force this man McClellan to fight or throw up; and last but not least I will pick up Lorenzo Thomas [the adjutant general] up with a pair of tongs and drop him from the nearest window.

Edwin M. Stanton, newly appointed secretary of war, to journalist Donn Piatt, January 1862.

I take it for granted, general, that what has heretofore been done has been the result of political policy rather than military strategy, and that the want of success on our part is attributable to the politicians rather than to the generals.

General Halleck, letter to General McClellan on January 20, 1862.

Although Seward has been prophesying like Jonah continually, yet thirty days and Nineveh will be destroyed, still the rebel army of the Potomac threatens Washington, and still hopes to take it, whilst our three hundred thousand soldiers lie opposite them, idle and well-fed, with full pay, their families supported by public charity, their officers spending their time in reveling, flirting and drinking . . . In these days, Washington is the scene of continual gaiety. No one seems to feel the danger in which we stand, or to realize that we are a bankrupt and ruined nation, should this continue longer. McClellan, they now say, is incapable and is striving after the Presidency, instigated by his wife.

Maria L. Daly, January 29, 1862, Diary.

The North Carolina troops had not been paid, clothed or drilled, and they had no teams or tolls or materials for constructing works of defense, and they were badly commanded and led, and, except a few companies, they did not fight.

Confederate General Henry A. Wise, letter to President Davis after Burnside had occupied Roanoke Island, North Carolina, on February 8, 1862.

. . . We freely commented upon the assurance of a wife of a second-rate Illinois lawyer being obliged to choose her company and selecting five hundred elite to entertain at the White House—and then to have affectation to put on court mourning out of respect to Queen Victoria's recent loss [of her husband, prince consort Albert]! It is too comical; it is too sad to see such extravagance and folly in the White House with the country bankrupt and a civil war raging.

Maria L. Daly, February 18, 1862, Diary.

The tyranny of an unbridled majority, the most odious and least responsible form of despotism, has denied us both the right and the remedy. Therefore we are in arms to renew such sacrifices as our fathers made to the holy cause of continual liberty . . . Civil War there cannot be between States held together by their volition only.

Jefferson Davis in his inauguration address at Richmond, February 22, 1862.

Late in February [1862] a Negro woman who resided in Norfolk came to the Navy Department and desired a private interview with me. She and others had closely watched the work upon the *Merrimac,* and she, by their request, had come to report that the ship was nearly finished, had come out of the dock and was about receiving her armament. The woman had passed through the lines, at great risk to herself, to bring me the information; and, in confirmation of her statement, she took from the bosom of her dress a letter from a Union man (i.e., sympathizer), a mechanic in the Navy Yard, giving briefly the facts as stated by her. This news, of course, put an end to the plan . . . of destroying the *Merrimac* in the dry-dock; but made us not less anxious for the speedy completion of the battery.

Gideon Welles, secretary of the Union navy, quoted in R. Wheeler's Voices of the Civil War.

Recent disasters have depressed the weak, and are depriving us of the aid of the wavering. Traitors show the tendencies heretofore concealed, and the selfish grow clamorous for local and personal interests. At such an hour, the wisdom of the trained, and the steadiness of the brave, possess a double value.

Jefferson Davis to General Joseph E. Johnston, in a letter of February 28, 1862.

We left New York in tow of the tug-boat *Seth Low* at 11 a.m. of Thursday, the 6th of March. On the following day a moderate breeze was encountered, and it was at once evident that the *Monitor* was unfit as a sea-going craft . . . The berth-deck hatch leaked in spite of all we could do, and the water came down under the turret like a waterfall . . . The waves also broke over the blower-pipes, and the water came down through them in such quantities that the belts of the blower-engines slipped and the engines consequently stopped . . . The fires (coal being the fuel) could not get air for combustion.

. . . During the greater part of the night we were constantly engaged in fighting the leaks, until we reached smooth water again just before daylight.

Lieutenant S. Dana Greene, second-in-command, on the initial trip of the Monitor *from New York to Hampton Roads, quoted in R. Wheeler's* Voices of the Civil War.

As she [the *Merrimac/Virginia*] came ploughing through the water . . . she looked like a huge, half-submerged crocodile. Her sides seems of solid iron, except where the guns pointed from the narrow ports . . . At her prow I could see the iron ram projecting straight forward, somewhat above the water's edge . . . Still she came on, the balls pounding upon her mailed sides like India-rubber, apparently making not the least impression, except to cut off her flagstaff and thus bring down the Confederate colors . . . We had probably fired six or eight broad-sides when a shot was received from one of her guns which killed five of our marines. It was impossible for our vessel to get out of her way, and the *Merrimac* soon crushed her iron horn, or ram, into the *Cumberland* . . . knocking a hole in the side . . . and driving the vessel back upon her anchors with great force. The water came rushing into the hold.

A. B. Smith, pilot of the U.S.S. Cumberland, *anchored at Newport News, Virginia on the* Merrimac's *attack, March 8, 1862, as quoted in R. Wheeler's* Voices of the Civil War.

The scene around the [Federal] *Congress* is represented as heart-sickening. The officers of the [confederate] *Beaufort* . . . who boarded her for the purpose of removing the wounded . . . represented the deck of the vessel as literally covered with the dead and dying. One of them assured us that as he went from fore to aft his shoes were well-nigh buried in blood and brains. Arms, legs and heads were found scattered in every direction . . .

Norfolk Day-Book, *report on the battle of Hampton Roads, March 8, 1862.*

The day . . . closed most dismally for our side, and with the most gloomy apprehensions of what would occur the next day. The [federal] *Minnesota* was at the mercy of the *Merrimac,* and there appeared no reason why the iron monster might not clear the roads of our fleet, destroy all the stores and warehouses on the beach, drive our troops into the Fortress [Monroe], and command Hampton roads against

any number of wooden vessels the Government might send there . . .

The correspondent of Baltimore's American *about Hampton Roads on March 8, 1862.*

She [the *Merrimac*] had already in a single half-day one of the most remarkable triumphs ever made on the water . . . The *Cumberland* went into action with 387 men. When the survivors were mustered there were only 255 . . . The crew of the *Congress* were 434 officers and men; of these, 298 got to shore . . .

Edward Pollard, Richmond historian The Lost Cause *(1866).*

Mr. Stanton, impulsive and always a sensationalist . . . walked the room in great agitation . . . "The *Merrimac*" said Stanton . . . "will change the whole character of the war; she will destroy, *seriatim,* every naval vessel; she will lay all the cities on the seaboard under contribution . . . Port Royal [South Carolina] must be abandoned . . ." He had no doubt, he said, that the monster was at this moment on her way to Washington; and, looking out of the window, which commanded a view of the Potomac for many miles, (he said it was "not unlikely that we shall have a shell or cannon-ball from one of her guns before we leave this room." Most of Stanton's complaints were directed to me . . . I had little to impart, except my faith in the untried *Monitor* experiment . . . "How many guns does she carry?" When I replied two, he turned away with a look of mingled amazement, contempt and distress that was painfully ludicrous.

Gideon Welles, secretary of the navy, about the Cabinet meeting on March 9, 1862, quoted in R. Wheeler's Voices of the Civil War.

My place was in the turret, to work and to fight the guns. With me were Stodder and Stimers and sixteen brawny men, eight to each gun . . . the physical condition of officers and men of the two ships at this time was in striking contrast. The *Merrimac* had passed the night quietly near Sewell's Point, her people enjoying rest and sleep . . . The *Monitor* had barely escaped shipwreck twice within the last thirty-six hours, and since Friday morning, forty-eight hours before, few if any of those on board had closed their eyes in sleep or had anything to eat but hard bread, as cooking was impossible. She was surrounded by wreck and disaster, and her efficiency in action had yet to be proved. Worden [the *Monitor*'s

commander] lost no time in bringing it to a test . . .
He steered directly for the enemy's vessels . . .

Lieutenant Dana S. Greene, second-in-com-
mand at the Monitor, *March 9, 1862 as quoted*
in R. Wheeler's Voices of the Civil War.

For nearly an hour we manoeuvered for a position
. . . At last an opportunity offered [to ram the *Mon-*
itor] . . . But before the ship gathered headway the
Monitor turned, and our disabled ram only gave a
glancing blow, effecting nothing. Again she came up
on our quarter, her bow against our side, and at this
distance fired twice. Both shots struck about half-
way up the shield . . . and the impact forced the
side in bodily two or three inches. All the crews of
the guns were knocked over by the concussion, and
bled from nose or ears. Another shot at the same
place would have penetrated . . . Although there is
no doubt that the *Monitor* first retired . . . the battle
was a drawn one, so far as the two vessels engaged
were concerned. But in its general results the advantage was with the *Monitor.*

Jon Taylor Wood of the Merrimac, *about the*
battle of March 9, 1862, quoted in R. Wheeler's
Voices of the Civil War.

The fight continued . . . as fast as the guns could
be served, and at very short range . . . Worden
skillfully manoeuvered his quick-turning vessel, trying
to find some vulnerable point in his adversary. Once
he made a dash at her stern, hoping to disable her
screw, which he thinks he missed by not more than
two feet. Our shots ripped the iron of the *Merrimac,*
while the reverberation of the shots against the tower
caused anything but a pleasant sensation. . . . It was
difficult to start [the turret] revolving, or, when once
started, to stop it, on account of the imperfections of
the novel machinery

Dana S. Greene, of the Monitor, *quoted in R.*
Wheeler's Voices of the Civil War.

I told at length what had occurred . . . Mr. [Jef-
ferson] Davis made many inquiries . . . During the
evening the flag of the *Congress* was brought in, and
to our surprise, in unfolding it, we found it in some
places saturated with blood. On this discovery it was
quickly rolled up and sent to the Navy Department.

John Taylor Wood, reporting to President Davis
on the naval battle of March 9, 1862, quoted in
R. Wheeler's Voices of the Civil War.

The *Monitor* fought. In grim amaze/The *Merrimac*
upon it gaze,/Cowering 'neath the iron hail/Crashing
into their coat of mail;/They swore "this devil's craft,/
Looked like a cheese-box on a raft."

Hurrah! Little giant of '62!/Bold Worden with his
gallant crew/Forces the fight; the day is won;/Back to
his den the monster's gone,/With crippled claws and
broken jaws/Defeated in a reckless cause.

George Henry Boker, "The Cruise of the Monitor*" (March 9, 1862).*

We had a great fright on Sunday on hearing of the
attack of the *Merrimac* on our vessels. Now they are
fretting lest she should get out again, despite the
Monitor, but I have great faith that God means the
utter overthrow of the Confederates, for it was a
revolt of the few, the gentlemen in broadcloth, against
the good of the many in frieze.

Maria L. Daly, March 11, 1862, Diary.

It is the unalterable determination of the people of
the Confederate States, in humble reliance upon Almighty God, to suffer all the calamities of the most
protracted war, but they never, on any terms, politically affiliate with a people who are guilty of the
invasion of their soil and the butchery of their citizens.

Confederate Congress, resolution of March 11,
1862.

I think you had better break the enemies' line . . .
at once. By delay the enemy will relatively gain upon
you . . . It is indispensable that *you* strike a blow
. . . The country will not fail to note—is now not-
ing—that the present hesitation to move upon an
entrenched enemy, is but the story of Manassas
repeated . . . I have never written you . . . in greater
kindness of feeling than now, nor with a fuller purpose to sustain you . . . *But you must act.*

Lincoln to McClellan, April 6 and 9, 1862.

. . . The philanthropic ladies who went down to
instruct Mrs. Stowe's ideal Negro find him a very
different article in reality, and . . . two of the ladies
. . . thought it injudicious to emancipate them as
yet, that they must have masters and be made to
obey them or help themselves . . . "What can be
done with them?" . . . I think they should be billeted
upon the abolitionists. I wish the Democrats would

refuse to assist them, and then they will be obliged to emigrate.
Maria L. Daly, April 20, 1862, Diary.

On the 21st [of April, 1862] we had orders to move, and as it had been raining all day the roads were simply horrible. Before leaving camp, some of the boys had made an effigy of Jeff Davis, by getting together some old clothes and stuffing them with straw. This after being duly labeled was hung on the limb of a tree and left behind.
Alfred Bellard, during the Peninsular campaign in Gone for a Soldier.

The rebels had again planted some of their infernal machines through which 3 or 4 men lost their lives. Torpedos [mines] were planted in any place that was likely to be visited by our men, on the walks by the forts and between the graves where rebel soldiers had been buried. Wherever a torpedo had been buried, a short stick or branch was standing up and woe be to the man or animal who tread on it or kicked it. On the main road to Williamsburg they were planted in the middle of the road . . .
Alfred Bellard, in Yorktown, evacuated by the Confederates, early May 1862, in Gone for a Soldier.

Giving one of their blood curdling yells the rebels came on. The celebrated Louisiana Tigers carrying the stars and stripes to prevent our firing upon them. This ruse however did not succeed, and buck and ball was poured into them so thick from the 6th, 7th and 8th who were immediately in their front that they were well satisfied to get back as quick as their legs could carry them . . . In the afternoon the battle had become furious and the rebels making their third and last charge, captured a battery of the regulars (the gunners having run away from their pieces) and immediately turned the guns on our Regt.
Alfred Bellard on the battle of Williamsburg, May 5, 1862. in Gone for a Soldier.
(It is doubtful whether the ''Louisiana Tigers'' actually carried the stars and stripes in this battle).

In the fallen timber a reb was found who had one hand in the pockets of a Union soldier and had been shot while leaning over a log and rifling the pockets of his enemy. In a ravine . . . the dead rebels were piled one on the other. They were buried where they

fell by throwing dirt from the top of the hill on top of them and so covering them up.
Alfred Bellard on the battle of Williamsburg in Gone for a Soldier.

I found everybody discouraged . . . our troops in wrong positions . . . no system, no cooperation, no orders given, roads blocked up. As soon as I came upon the field, the men cheered like fiends and I saw at once that I could save the day. I immediately reinforced Hancock and arranged to support Hooker, advanced the whole line . . . The result was that the enemy saw that he was gone if he remained in his position, and scampered during the night.
General George B. McClellan, letter to his wife about the battle of Williamsburg, May 5, 1862.

I do not think you over much rejoiced at the results I gained. I really thought that you would appreciate a great result gained by fine skill & little cost more than you seem to. It would have been easy for me to have sacrificed 10,000 lives in taking Yorktown, & I presume the world would have thought it was brilliant . . . I am very sorry that you do not exactly sympathize with me in the matter.
McClellan, letter to his wife after he had occupied Yorktown, early May 1862.

I regret that my presence with the army at this particular time is of such vast importance that I cannot leave to confer with the President or yourself.
McClellan, letter from Williamsburg to Secretary Stanton at Fort Monroe, May 7, 1862. (The distance between the two places is only 30 miles.)

. . . an explosion took place which made the earth and water tremble for miles around. In the midst of the bright flame which shot up . . . The timbers and iron from the monster steamer could be seen flying through the air. No doubt was entertained that the *Merrimac* had ceased to exist.
Union report from Fort Monroe on the scuttling of Merrimac, *May 11, 1862, quoted in R. Wheeler's* Voices of the Civil War.

What splendid news! Norfolk taken, Portsmouth captured, the Navy Yard saved, the *Merrimac* ours, President Lincoln with the army before Norfolk! . . . Now there may be truth in what Mrs. McClellan told

George B. McClellan, Union general.

us yesterday, that the war would be over by the Fourth of July.
Maria L. Daly, May 11, 1862, Diary.

Battle after battle—disaster after disaster . . . How could I sleep? The power they are bringing to bear against our country is tremendous . . . Every morning's paper enough to kill a well woman [or] age a strong and hearty one . . . New Orleans gone—and with it the Confederacy. Are we not cut in two? . . . I have nothing to chronicle but disasters . . . The reality is hideous.
Mary Boykin Chesnut, April and May 1862, A Diary from Dixie (1929).

The panic here has subsided and with increasing confidence there has arisen a desire to see the city destroyed rather than surrendered . . . The great temporal object is to secure our independence and

they who engage in strife for personal or party aggrandisement, deserve contemptuous forgetfulness.
Jefferson Davis, letter from Richmond to his wife, May 16, 1862, after the Confederate success at Drewry's Bluff.

I shall go twice a week to the Park Barracks and give one day to working at the Central Relief Association in Cooper Institute. I've collected together some 40 shirts, and some dozen sheets, vests, drawers, quilts, etc. I have sent a donation to the Central Relief Association.
Maria L. Daly, May 18, 1862, Diary.

Those hounds in Washington are after me again. Stanton is without exception the vilest man I ever knew or heard of.
McClellan to his wife, letter of May 18, 1862.

You can not, if you would, be blind to the signs of the times. I beg of you a calm and enlarged consideration of them, ranging, if it may be, far above personal and partisan politics. This proposal makes common cause for a common object, casting no reproaches on any. It acts not the Pharisee. The change it contemplates would come gently as the dews of heaven, not rending nor wrecking anything. Will you not embrace it?
Lincoln, on May 19, 1862, after denouncing Hunter's proclamation of emancipation, appealing at the same time to the slaveholders.

Judge P. says the President is rising above all exterior influence and learning to depend on himself and taking his own judgment, that Seward, even, has little influence on him now. "He is greater than he seems. His manners are so against him, but he is great from being so good, so conscientious. His having been no politician and having little experience has been a providential circumstance instead of being a misfortune."
Maria L. Daly, May 22, 1862, Diary.

The investment of the line of the Chickahominy [River] brought the two armies face to face . . . For nearly a year an immense labor had been expended upon the fortifications of Richmond. Earthworks . . . swept all the roads, crowned every hillock; and mounds of red earth could be seen in striking contrast with the rich green of the landscape . . . Beyond, through the open and cultivated country . . . stretched the camp of the enemy . . . There were alarm and excitement in the mixed and restless population of Richmond; and the popular feeling found but little assurance in the visible tremour of the authorities. The Confederate Congress had adjourned in such a haste as to show that the members were anxious to provide for their own personal safety. President Davis sent his family to North Carolina . . . At the railroad depots were piles of baggage awaiting transportation, and the trains were crowded with women and children . . .

Edward Pollard, in the Richmond Examiner, *about McClellan's army before Richmond, May 1862.*

I think the time is near when you must either attack Richmond or give up the job and come to the defense of Washington.

Lincoln, message to McClellan, May 25, 1862.

The South seems to be desperate, and horrible atrocities are committed. Stragglers from our army are found tied by their feet to the trees with their throats cut, and it seems that what they said of their barbarities at Manassas after the battle of Bull Run was only too true, that they did boil the flesh and carry away the bones of our poor soldiers as trophies, their boasted chivalry rivalling the Indians, exceeding them even in barbarity.

Maria L. Daly, May 30, 1862, Diary.

There is at present the most serious apprehension that the Grand Army of the Potomac is on the eve of a terrible and disgraceful defeat, not from the rebels, but from rum. An order has been . . . carried into execution to issue each morning to every officer and soldier of the army half a gill [one-eighth of a pint] of whiskey. Gen. McClellan is said to be the author of this monstrous wrong, both to soldier and country . . . All this . . . under profession of kindness to the soldier, a medicine . . . to prevent him from getting sick! . . . Never did I feel so tempted and pressed to relinquish the chaplain service and yield all to the control of Satan.

Reverend A. M. Stewart: on the situation at the Army of the Potomac before Richmond, May 26, 1862, in March and Battlefield *(1865).*

Saturday morning, the 31st, was dull and wet. The storm had ceased; but the roads were flooded, the woods were weeping and a gray pale mist hung over . . . the long belt of forest on the opposite of the river . . . The dark turbulent waters of the Chickahominy were rushing and surging through the meadow, filled with wreckwood from the bridges . . . At ten o'clock the mysterious movement of a column of the enemy . . . was reported. At fifteen minutes of one o'clock our whole camp was startled by the sudden, crashing sound of infantry, and the deep roar of cannon. It seemed that twenty thousand infantry had discharged simultaneously . . . in such rapid succession that it were impossible to count the volleys . . . Then we heard the long roll beating on the opposite hills. "As I thought" said General Franklin, who had been nearly washed out of his tent during the night . . .: "they have attacked us in our weakest point." In another minute it was all bustle and motion at General McClellan's headquarters . . . Bugles sounded along the line, cavalry began saddling up . . . all with a spirit and quickness that proved how anxious they were to proceed (across the river, if the surviving bridges permitted) to the relief of their comrades now engaged in the terrible struggle.

F. Colburn Adams, Union cavalry officer, on the battle of Fair Oaks, May 31, 1862, The Story of a Trooper *(1865).*

I was left alone on horseback, with my men dropping rapidly around me. My soldiers declared that they distinctly heard the command from the Union lines, "Shoot that man on horseback." In both armies it was thought that the surest way to demoralize troops was to shoot down the officers . . . Still I . . . marvellously escaped, with only my clothing pierced. As I rode up and down the line, encouraging the men forward, I passed my young brother, only nineteen years old but captain of one of the companies. He was lying with a number of dead companions near him. He had been shot through the lungs and was bleeding profusely. I did not stop. I could not stop; nor would he permit me to stop. There was no time for that—no time for anything except to move on and fire on . . . My field officers and adjutant were all dead. Every horse ridden into the fight, my own among them, was dead . . . In water knee- to hip-deep, the men were fighting and falling, while a detail propped up the wounded against stumps or trees to prevent their drowning.

John B. Gordon, Confederate colonel on the battle of Fair Oaks, May 31, 1862 in Reminiscences of the Civil War.

When we had arrived within a mile of the fight, we met a stream of stragglers and wounded men, all making their way to the rear, as fast as shank's mare could carry them. They were so thick in one place on the road that our Regt. being the advance, had to force their way with the bayonette. The report from the front that we got from these men was not very encouraging. One of them, an officer from the Red Legged ZouZou's, gave us the pleasing information that he was the only one left out of the Regt. while another of the same Regt. said he was capt., col., cook, and all hands.

Alfred Bellard on the battle of Fair Oaks, May 31, 1862 in Gone for a Soldier.

. . . we advanced over a wheat field to the music of the rebel bullets that had begun to fly pretty sharp. In marching over this field I experienced for the first time a sensation of fear. I got so sick at the stomach that I thought I should have to fall out of the ranks to relieve myself, but we had no sooner got under fire, then it all vanished and I was myself again.

Alfred Bellard at Fair Oaks, May 31, 1862, in Gone for a Soldier.

In the afternoon, Genl. McClellan rode by our Regt. and was loudly cheered by the boys. Taking off his cap he said, Boys, we've licked them, right, left and centre, and we're going into Richmond. This sounded well and put the boys in good humor. At the head of our Regt. he dismounted and had a long chat with our Col. who was a West Pointer, having been 25 years in the regular service.

Bellard at the battle of Fair Oaks, May 31, 1862 in Gone for a Soldier.

The only exhibition of brutal passion that came under my notice was at this fight [of the 8th Alabama Regiment]. One of the wounded rebs who was lying in the woods got rather too independent for a man in his position, and he riled one of our men so much that he raised his musket for the purpose of dashing out his brains, when he was stopped by one of our officers . . .

Bellard at Fair Oaks, May 31, 1862, in Gone for a Soldier.

No pen can describe the agonies of that battlefield during this fearful night . . . The dead of both armies mingled promiscuously . . . The groans and cries of the dying are heard in every clump of trees . . .

Nourishment is not to be had. Medical attendance is not a tithe of what it should be . . .

F. Colburn Adams on the battle of Fair Oaks in The Story of a Trooper.

The whole town [Richmond] was on the street. Ambulances, litters, carts, every vehicle that the city could produce, went and came with a ghastly burden . . . Women with pallid faces flitted bareheaded through the streets searching for the dead or wounded. The churches were thrown open . . . for prayer. . . . Men too old or infirm to fight went on horseback or afoot to meet the returning ambulances, and in some served as escort to their own dying sons. By afternoon of the day following the battle, the streets were one vast hospital . . .

Constance Cary Harrison of Richmond, as quoted in R. Wheeler's Voices of the Civil War.

It is hard to see incompetence losing opportunity and wasting hard-gotten means, but harder still to bear is the knowledge that there is no available remedy.

Jefferson Davis, letter to his wife June 2, 1862, after the battle of Seven Pines.

Since that order, no man or woman has insulted a soldier of mine in New Orleans. And from the first hour of our landing, no woman has complained of the conduct of my soldiers toward her, nor had there been a single cause for complaint.

Benjamin Butler, letter to C. C. Garner in New York, June 10, 1862, defending his order of May 15.

It is a pity that the abolition female saints and the Charleston female patriots could not meet in a fair fight and mutually annihilate each other. It seems to me that the Southern women are turned into furies. The truth is that the South is jealous of the North, and hates us for our wealth and enlightenment.

Maria L. Daly, June 11, 1862, Diary.

. . . [Dempsey] looked upon the South as the best portion of the people, but his opinion has changed by living among them. Such a set of ignorant, foul-mouthed wretches he had never met, to use his own words.

Maria L. Daly, June 19, 1862, Diary

Two armies—the largest ever marshalled on the Western continent, stood now confronting each other in such close proximity that the advance pickets of the contending forces could converse together, and all felt that a mighty struggle was close at hand. And yet an amazing amount of good feeling, and even jollity cropped up between these opposed pickets at times. A brisk trade in newspapers was kept up almost continually. The exchange of coffee for tobacco was a very usual thing.—Among the facetious things of these perilous posts was the conference between the Reb who called out: "Hello, Yank! What regiment do you belong to?" "To the Ninety-ninth Rhode Island." . . . "Good heavens!" cried the astonished questioner. "How many regiments must New York have if Rhode Island has ninty-nine?"

John W. Urban, Union soldier on the battle of Seven Days, June 1862, as quoted in R. Wheeler's Voices of the Civil War.

I shall have to contend against vastly superior odds if these reports were true; but this army will do all in the power of men to hold their position and repulse any attack. I regret my great inferiority in numbers, but feel that I am in no way responsible for it . . . if the result of the action, which will probably occur tomorrow . . . is disaster, the responsibility cannot be thrown on my shoulders; it must rest where it belongs.

McClellan, telegram to Secretary Stanton on the eve of the battle of Seven Days, June 24, 1862.

. . . a part of the ground was low and swampy, making it almost impossible for troops to cross. Into this a part of the rebel column charged, and a scene of most indescribable horror, confusion and tumult ensued. Hundreds of horses and men sank into the mire and were shot down by the deadly rifles of the first brigade.

John W. Urban on the first day of the battle of Seven Days, June 25, 1862, as quoted in R. Wheeler's Voices of the Civil War.

Some of the dead had their heads broken in by blows from butts of rifles, and others lay dead with bayonets thrust through them, the weapon having been left sticking in their bodies. Some of the wounded begged piteously to be helped to the rear . . .

John W. Urban on the battle of Seven Days, as quoted in R. Wheeler's Voices of the Civil War

Had I twenty thousand or even ten thousand fresh troops to use tomorrow, I could take Richmond; but I have not a man in reserve, and shall be glad to cover my retreat and save the material and personnel of the army.

McClellan, telegraphic report to Washington, at 12:20 A.M., June 28, 1862.

I have lost this battle because my force was too small . . . If I save this army now, I will tell you plainly that I owe no thanks to you or to any other persons in Washington. You have done your best to sacrifice this army.

General McClellan's telegram to Lincoln during the battle of Seven Days, on June 28, 1862. Only the first part of the telegram was passed on to Lincoln.

While we were lying idle all day on the 28th, unable to cross the Chickahominy, the clouds of smoke from the burning stores in the Federal camps, and the frequent explosions of magazines indicated a retreat; but General W. H. C. Whiting kept insisting . . . that all this was but a ruse de guerre of McClellan preparatory to a march upon Richmond.

Confederate General D. H. Hill, June 28, 1862, quoted in R. Wheeler's Voices of the Civil War.

I saw Jackson helping with his own hands to push [Captain James] Reilly's North Carolina battery farther forwards. It was soon disabled, the woods around us being filled with shrieking and exploding shells. I noticed an artillery man seated comfortably behind a very large tree, and apparently feeling very secure. A moment later a shell passed through the huge tree and took off the man's head.

Confederate General D. H. Hill, about the attack on Malvern Hill, July 1, 1862, quoted in R. Wheeler's Voices of the Civil War.

At the foot of the last steep ascent . . . I found that McClellan's guns (because of the elevation of their muzzles) were firing over us; as any further advance by this unsupported brigade would have been . . . foolhardy, I halted my men . . . In vain I looked behind us for the promised support . . . As a retreat in daylight promised to be almost or quite as deadly as had been the charge, my desire for . . . darkness . . . can be well imagined. In this state of extreme anxiety, a darkness which was unexpected and terrible came to me alone. A great shell fell, buried itself in the ground and exploded near where I stood. It heaved dirt over me, filling my face and ears and eyes with sand. I was literally blinded . . . Thoughts never ran more swiftly through a perplexed mortal brain. Blind! Blind in battle! . . . What was I to do . . . The blindness, however, was of short duration . . .

Confederate Colonel John B. Gordon, on the fight on Malvern Hill, July 1, 1862, Reminiscences of the Civil War.

The effect of these repeated repulses [on Malvern Hill] can hardly be conceived . . . The demoralization was great, and the evidences of it palpable everywhere. The roads and forests were full of stragglers. Commands were inextricably confused, some, for a time, having actually disappeared. Those who retained sufficient self-respect and sense of responsibility to think of the future were filled with the deepest apprehension. I know this was the state of mind of some of our strongest and best officers.

Robert Stiles, Four Years under Marse Robert *(1903).*

It was difficult to wake General (Stonewall) Jackson, as he was exhausted and very sound asleep. I tried it myself, and, after many efforts, partly succeeded. When he was made to understand what was wanted, he said: "McClellan and his army will be gone by daylight," and went to sleep again.

Dr. Hunter McGuire, Jackson's medical director, as quoted in R. Wheeler's Voices of the Civil War. *(Jackson was right: McClellan retreated.)*

At the foot of the hill, at Malvern Hills Tavern, the artillery, baggage wagons and infantry were in a disorganized mass, all jumbled together without regularity or purpose and everyone for himself. The artillery was driven along the road as fast as the horses could pull it, and the infantry had to keep their eyes open, and get out of the way to avoid being run over or crushed to death between two guns. The mud in some places was over our boots . . .

A. Bellard on the battle at Malvern Hill, July 1, 1862 in Gone for a Soldier.

Nothing occurred during the whole war so much to give new life, spirit, energy and courage to the Confederate army and people as this untoward retreat of McClellan from the Peninsula . . .

John Minor Botts, Union sympathizer in Richmond, The Great Rebellion *(1866).*

We are coming, Father Abraham, three hundred thousand more,/From Mississippi's winding stream, and from New England's shore;/We leave our ploughs and workshops, our wives and children dear,/With hearts too full for utterance, but with a silent tear./We dare not look behind us, but steadfastly before:/We are coming, Father Abraham, three hundred thousand more.

New York Tribune, July 3, 1862, after Lincoln's call for 300,000 more men.

King Log [Lincoln] is honest, certainly, but that is but a scanty endowment of virtue and talent for President of the United States. We are paying the penalty for our venality. We are giving offices to the highest bidder, and the South has placed authority in the hands of brigands. Some change must soon take place. Why the President cannot be made to cease his interference with military matters, I cannot conceive. Nor why it is necessary to be so forbearing to such malignant foes.

Maria L. Daly, July 3, 1862, Diary.

Thus the idea of sending you fifty thousand, or any considerable force promptly, is simply absurd. If in your frequent mention of responsibility you have the impression that I blame you for not doing more than you can, please be relieved of such impression. I only beg that in like manner you will not ask impossibilities of me. If you think you are not strong enough to take Richmond just now, I do not ask you to try . . . Save the Army, material and personal, and I will strengthen you for the offensive as fast as I can. The Governors of 18 states offer me a new levy of three hundred thousand, which I accept.

Lincoln to McClellan, July 1862.

He [Judge Pierrepont, cabinet officer and diplomat] says that poor Stanton has to be bear the blame of the foolish acts of President Lincoln who, since the taking of Norfolk, thinks himself a general, and goes about with his compass in his pocket. He is thinking about being reelected. Can our countrymen be so blind, so stupid, as to again place such a clod . . . in the presidential chair? . . . Would that God would raise us up a deliverer.

Maria L. Daly, July 13, 1862, Diary.

[General John] Pope was credited with . . . expressions such as that he . . . hoped in Virginia to see the faces of the rebels, as in the West he had been able to see only their backs. When General Lee heard of these strange utterances, his estimate of Pope was considerably lessened . . . For centuries there has been among soldiers a maxim: "Don't despise your enemy." General Pope's words seem to indicate great contempt for his enemy.

Confederate General James Longstreet referring to Pope's proclamation of July 14, 1862, as quoted in R. Wheeler's Voices of the Civil War.

No wonder that those who cling with love, which is often the highest form of reason, to the old framework of our society, shudder at the thought of a Lowell on the Appomattox or a Manchester in the Piedmont region.

De Bow's Review, *May–August 1862, about the dangers of increasing industrialization on account of the war.*

Instead of finding our women at the piano or on the fashionable promenade, we find them busy at their looms, busy at their wheels, busy making soldiers' uniforms, busy making bandages, busy in hospitals, busy girding up their sons, their husbands and their fathers for the battlefield.

Southern Field and Fireside, *Confederate periodical, August 1861.*

The way to make war is to destroy slavery. The way to secure peace after war is to destroy slavery. If any have scruples about interfering with Southern rights, their scruples are too late. We have already done it. War is supreme interference. We have violated State sovereignty as much as it can be done. What state sovereignty is there under an imposed military governor intruded upon New Orleans, Nashville and Newbern? The only question is whether we will use that lawful intrusion for the ends of health and peace, or whether we will go on with a timid and fatuous policy . . .

Henry Ward Beecher, in The Independent, *August 14, 1862.*

He [Reverend W. Rodman] is a mad abolitionist and said that unless emancipation was the policy of the government, he would discourage every man from going to keep or help to foster the fetters on the Negro. He thought the Negro had a right to rise and, he intimated, recover his freedom even by the murder of his master. He does not go to the war, nor none of his kind, but seeks every flimsy excuse

. . . to escape. Their fine, patriotic, virtuous philanthropic principles stand them in lieu of great patriotic action. How one despises such creatures!

Maria L. Daly, August 20, 1862, Diary.

I learn that the rulers more than ever dread doing anything with you since the Army of the Potomac began to arrive at Alexandria. I find that many of the general officers are expressing themselves very strongly in favor of your having moved on Richmond instead of coming here . . . all of which tends to increase the fears of Lincoln and his coadjustors, and this is the only point to hope from now.

Allan Pinkerton, report to McClellan from Washington, August 25, 1862.

Upon Manassas Junction, we met a [Federal] brigade, the First New Jersey . . . they were fools enough to send a flag demanding our surrender at once. Of course, we scattered the brigade, killing and wounding many . . . At the Junction was a large depot of stores . . . T'was a curious sight to see our ragged and famished men helping themselves to every imaginable article of luxury and necessity, whether of clothing, food or what not. For my part, I got a toothbrush, a box of candles, a quantity of lobster salad, a barrel of coffee . . .

Confederate Lieutenant John Hampden Chamberlayne on the beginning of the second battle of Bull Run, August 26, 1862, quoted in R. Wheeler's Voices of the Civil War.

. . . on the 28th [of August] Pope did not know, practically, where his own forces were, or those of the enemy who had so manoeuvered as to mislead, elude and confuse him. His divisions, scattered by contradictory and confusing orders, were held so loosely in hand, and were so isolated from each other, that so far as exercising control over them was concerned, it would almost been as well for him to have been in the West, where he came from, as in Virginia.

Warren Lee Goss, on the second battle of Bull Run, in Recollections of a Private *(1890).*

The command was as unlike my own as it was possible to conceive. Such a congress of nations only the Cosmopolitan Crescent City [New Orleans] could have sent forth, and the tongues of Babel seemed resurrected in its speech. English, German, French and Spanish, all were represented, to say nothing of Doric brogue and local "gumbo." There was, more-

over, a vehemence of utterance and gesture curiously at variance with the reticence of our Virginians.
Allen C. Redwood, Confederate soldier at Bull Run, who had accidentally stumbled into a battalion of Louisianans, as quoted in R. Wheeler's Voices of the Civil War.

[Many of the Federals] . . . came upon the rusty remains of guns, bayonets, weather-beaten fragments of gun carriages and equipments, and the bleaching skulls and bones of their comrades who had perished on the field the year before—the first sacrifices to the blunders of the war.
Warren Lee Goss in Recollections of a Private.

On our left . . . the enemy was repulsed, and those who had pressed us back . . . now hesitated and commenced to yield. We pressed them, in our turn. They broke and fell back in disorder. I recollect that as they did so, they left a mule which, notwithstanding all the turmoil, was quietly cropping a green blade, here and there, in the bloodstained grass around him . . . We could hear the enemy advancing, and had not a round with which to greet them, but must wait the onslaught with only our bayonets . . . they had nearly reached the railroad . . . when a shout behind us paralyzed us with dread. Was this . . . an unseen movement to our rear? Terror stricken, we turned; when lo!, there were our friends, coming to our assistance . . . with a wild Confederate yell they rushed upon [federal general Issac I.] Stevens as he was in the confusion of crossing the railroad to our attack. The Federals halted, turned and fled . . .
Confederate officer Edward McGrady, of General Gregg's South Carolina brigade, on the fighting at Bull Run, quoted in R. Wheeler's Voices of the Civil War.

. . . as soon as the fighting ceased, many sought without orders to rescue comrades lying wounded between the opposing lines. There seemed to be a mutual understanding between the men of both armies that such parties would not be disturbed in their mission of mercy . . . Blankets attached to poles and muskets often served as stretchers . . . The condition of Pope's army on Saturday, August 30, was such that a more cautious general would have hesitated before giving battle. His men were exhausted by incessant marching and fighting; thousands had straggled from their commands; the men had had but little to eat for two days previous . . .

But Pope believed . . . that the enemy were demoralized, while in fact their lines held the rail road embankment as a fortress . . .
Warren Lee Goss, on the second battle of Bull Run in Recollections of a Private.

It was late in the evening, and . . . from all directions came the warring sound of cannon and musketry . . . How hot it was! The clothes damp with perspiration, the canteens empty, throats parched with thirst, faces blackened with powder, the men mad with excitement.
Alexander Hunter on the Union retreat at Bull Run in Johnny Reb and Billy Yank *(1904).*

The ambulances, too few for the occasion, were supplemented by hacks and carriages of every description, brought from Washington. The tender hand of woman was there to alleviate distress; and the picture of misery was qualified by the heroic grit of those who suffered.
Warren Goss on the Union defeat at Bull Run in Recollections of a Private.

Men show themselves in a thousand ways incompetent, yet still they receive the support of the Government . . . The battle comes; there is no head on the field; the men are handed over to be butchered . . . The army finds that nothing has been learned. New preparations are made, with all the old errors retained. New battles are prepared for, to end in new disasters. Alas, my poor country!
Captain William T. Lusk of New York summarizing the Union disaster in the second battle of Bull Run in War Letters *(1911).*

Two days after our second defeat at Bull Run, while yet the roads were crowded with stragglers and despondency overshadowed all, McClellan resumed command of the army. It was the morning of September 2d, 1862, and reorganization began at once. . . . In no direction was the ability of McClellan so conspicuous as in organizing. Even before the soldiers knew he was again in command, they began to detect a new influence around them.
Warren Lee Goss, Recollections of a Private.

Again I have been called upon to save the country . . . I still hope for success . . . It makes my heart bleed to see the poor, shattered remnants of my noble Army of the Potomac . . . and to see how they love

me even now. I hear them calling out to me as I ride among them: "George, don't leave us again!"
McClellan, letter to his wife, early September 1862.

We are stronger today than we ever have been, while our enemy is weaker. As our people have become firmly bound together for this war, those of the North have become discontended, and discord is now prominent in their counsels. Lincoln's cabinet dread a defeat, and hence their armies are everywhere retreating . . . If we should defeat Pope decidedly, the backbone of the war will be over; for the opposition to the abolition party would shear it of its strength.
Confederate Secretary of the Navy Stephen R. Mallory, letter to his wife on August 31, 1862.

The thing I complain of is a criminal tardiness, a fatuous apathy, a captious, bickering rivalry among our commanders who seem so taken up with their quick made dignity that they overlook the lives of their people and the necessities of their country. They, in grotesque egotism, have so much reputation to take care of that they dare not risk it.
Federal Attorney General Edward Bates, letter to Francis Leiber of September 2, 1862, alluding in particular to the rivalry between McClellan and Pope.

The Marylanders in the corps imparted much of their enthusiasm to the other troops; but we were not long in finding out that if the General had hopes that the decimated regiments of his army would be filled by the sons of Maryland, he was doomed to a speedy and unqualified disappointment. However . . . one enthusiastic citizen presented Jackson with a gigantic gray mare . . . Yet the present proved almost a Trojan horse to him, for the next morning when he mounted his new steed and touched her with his spur, the . . . undisciplined beast reared straight into the air and . . . threw herself backward, horse and rider rolling upon the ground. The general was stunned and severely bruised . . .
Henry Kyd Douglas, Lee invades Maryland, September 5, 1862, in I Rode with Stonewall (1940).

Since I have been in the city, we have been deeply humiliated, Stonewall Jackson having forced our splendid army and over-prudent civilian generals across the Potomac, threatening Washington and invading Pennsylvania whilst the pothouse administra-

tion in Washington seems as sanguine as ever . . . To think that we should be conquered by the bare feet and rags of the South, fed from our wagons, supplied from our caissons!
Maria L. Daly, September 11, 1862, after the second battle of Bull Run in Diary.

Baron Gerolt [the Prussian minister to the United States] tells us that fifteen hundred men were lying for five days, still alive, on the battlefield, and that thousands died from mere starvation, no one going to their succour. The wretched heads of departments know nothing of their duties, and the honest fool at their head is content playing President. God forgive the authors of all these horrors and enlighten the mind of the poor creature who dared to take upon himself the high office of President in such a time with no ability to fill the office! Better a dishonest but clever man!
Maria L. Daly, September 11, 1862, Diary.

On the march that day . . . we entered each village before the inhabitants knew of our coming. In Middletown two very pretty girls, with ribbons of white, red and blue floating from their hair, and small Union flags in their hands, rushed out of the house as we passed, came to the curbstone, and with much laughter waved their flags defiantly in the face of the general [Jackson]. He bowed and raised his hat, and turning with a quiet smile to his staff, said: "We evidently have no friends in this town."
Henry Kyd Douglas on Jackson in Maryland, September 1862, in I Rode with Stonewall.

There seems to be a panic at the North at Jackson's success. As far as I am concerned, I would as willingly be ruled by Jefferson Davis as by poor Lincoln, and I suppose many feel the same . . . An aide-de-camp of McDowell says that whenever it is possible, McDowell keeps out of danger, and so do most of our generals . . . McClellan, after all, has most greatness of mind of all. To the thousands of attacks made upon him he returns no answer, but keeps a dignified silence.
Maria L. Daly September 12, 1862, Diary.

Here is a paper with which, if I cannot whip Bobbie Lee, I will be willing to go home.
General McClellan, after Lee's orders for the Maryland campaign had fallen into his hands September 13, 1862. Quoted in R. Wheeler's Voices of the Civil War.

The luxury and refinements of peace contrasted sharply with the privations and squalor of war . . . well appointed carriages rolled along those charming drives, bearing fair women in cool and fresh costumes; and by their side the ragged, dusty, sunburnt regiments from the Peninsula trudged along . . . The carriages returned to their stables, the fair ladies returned to the enjoyment of every pleasure that Washington could confer; but the Army of the Potomac moved steadily northward, to bivouac under the stars, and to march again in its tatters . . .
Francis W. Palfrey, Antietam and Fredericksburg *(1882).*

. . . while the artillery of both armies thundered, McClellan's compact columns of infantry fell upon the left of Lee's lines . . . with the crushing weight of a landslide . . . Pressed back . . . the Southern troops enthused by Lee's presence, re-formed their lines and, with a shout as piercing as the blast of a thousand bugles, rushed in countercharge upon the exulted Federals [and] hurled them back in confusion . . . Again and again . . . by charges and counter-counter-charges, this portion of the field was lost and recovered, until the green corn that grew upon it looked as if it had been struck by a storm of bloody hail . . . From sheer exhaustion, both sides, like battered and bleeding athletes, seemed willing to rest. General Lee took advantage of the respite and rode along the lines . . .
John B. Gordon on the battle of Antietam, September 17, 1862.

The first volley sent a ball . . . through the calf of my right leg. On the right and left my men were falling . . . like trees in a hurricane . . . Higher up in the same leg I was again shot; but still no bone was broken . . . I could not consent to leave them in such a crisis . . . I had a vigorous constitution, and this was doing me good service . . . A fourth ball ripped through my shoulder . . . I could still stand and walk, although the shocks and loss of blood had left but little of my normal strength. I remembered the pledge to the commander that we would stay there till the battle ended or night came. I looked at the sun. It . . . seemed to stand still . . . I then attempted to go myself, although I was bloody and faint, . . . I had gone but a short distance when I was shot down by a fifth ball which struck me squarely in the face . . . I fell forward and lay unconscious with my face in the cap; and it would seem that I might have been smothered by the blood running into my cap . . . but for the act of some Yankee who . . . shot a hole through the cap, which let the blood out. I was borne on a litter to the rear.
John B. Gordon on the battle of Antietam in Reminiscences.

Many were found so covered with dust, torn, crushed and trampled that they resembled clods of earth and you were obliged to look twice before recognizing them as human beings.
David H. Strother about the Antietam battlefield in Harper's Magazine, *February 1868.*

. . . McClellan estimated Lee's troops at nearly double their actual numbers . . . I do not doubt that most of his subordinates discouraged the resumption of the attack, for the rooted belief in Lee's preponderance of numbers had been chronic in the army during the whole year. That belief was based on the inconceivably mistaken reports of the secret service organization . . . The result was that Lee retreated unmolested on the night of the 18th, and that what might have been a real and decisive success was a drawn battle in which our chief claim to victory was the possession of the field.
Union General Jacob D. Cox, Atlanta (1882).

The spectacle yesterday was the grandest I could conceive of; nothing could be more sublime. Those in whose judgment I rely tell me that I fought the battle splendidly and that it was a masterpiece of art.
McClellan, letter to his wife September 18, 1862, after the battle of Antietam.

5. Life in Wartime

THE HISTORICAL CONTEXT

Neither side was prepared for war, and certainly neither side expected a long war. The military forces that grew out of this situation were quite different from any the world had seen before or was to see again.

At the outbreak of the war, the regular army had a poor reputation and played a minor role in the country, except for the officers. Many of them were veterans of the Mexican War and maintained a loyalty to one another, even though they now fought on different sides. Many families were split, with brothers fighting on both sides, and many officers had to face an agonizing decision because their loyalties were split: Robert E. Lee, who was offered a top command in the Union army but decided to fight for the South, is the best known example. The majority of the trained officers decided to stay with the Union. Of about 1,100 regular army officers, only 286 resigned and joined the South. Union Commander-in-Chief Winfield Scott himself was a Virginian by birth.

On both sides, the volunteers were the best soldiers. In the first enthusiasm, many more enlisted than were needed, and many lied about their age to get into the army. A well-known trick of the young country boys was to put a piece of paper in their shoe with the number 18 written on it, and then to declare with a clear conscience: "I am over 18." A great many mere boys served in both armies: In the North, 127 boys were only 13; 320 were 14; almost 800 were 15; 2,758 were 16; and almost 6,500 were 17 years of age. The largest contingent were farm boys, about 48%, 24% were mechanics and 16% were laborers. The unspoiled country boys made the best soldiers. Many of them had never seen underwear before they were recruited. The equipment issued to them was unlikely to spoil them: Often the right and left shoes were identical. There were no professional army cooks, and the kitchens were often of very poor quality. Basic rations on the march were salt pork, bacon and "hard tack" (crackers). Coffee was supplied in whole bean, because the army was afraid that suppliers would mix inferior ingredients into the powder. So the soldiers ground their beans with rifle butts. The tents in camp were floorless.

113

Many volunteers were soon disillusioned. If they had enlisted for only three months, they were likely to see no action at all. Still, many of those who were in for three years reenlisted in the spring of 1864: 30,000 in the Army of the Potomac alone. Later, it became a great honor to belong to such a "Veteran Volunteer Regiment." Many also volunteered when victory for the North was in sight—to be in on the kill.

The volunteers were trained locally: State governors had to provide quota and relied on prominent or popular citizens for forming units and training them. These citizens received a commission but, of course, knew no more about training or fighting than their men did. Also, the discipline was quite loose. The newly created officers went easy on their men because they needed their votes after the war when they would run for political office.

It was the practice on both sides to keep newly formed units together, rather than mixing them in with more experienced outfits. This boosted the local pride and esprit de corps of the newcomers but robbed many units of badly needed fighting experience and expertise.

Most of the volunteers, in the North and the South, were brave, even heroic, in combat, but many fell back after the battle, feeling they had done enough. Frequently during long marches, as many as 50% were stragglers. During the first months, most soldiers were so unused to marching that military movements took two or three times longer than the generals had anticipated. Looting was a general habit, even in friendly territory. In battle, soldiers who helped their wounded comrades to get back often failed to return to the front. Later, they were often stopped by cavalry pickets behind the front who shouted at the retreating soldiers: "Show blood!" Many drafted goldbricks and dead-beats faked rheumatism to get a dismissal because doctors had difficulty checking for rheumatism. Finally no more discharges on account of rheumatism were granted.

Desertion plagued both sides—in the beginning less in the South than in the North, where the average was 7,300 men per month. Later on, masses of Southern boys deserted to help their struggling families. Many escaped from state hospitals where they had been sent; the local authorities had been in no hurry to return them because they had put the convalescents to work. A great number did not return from furlough or returned late. In the North, a reward was given for arresting a deserter, but the amount was soon reduced from $30 to $5, and a lot of red tape was involved, so few people bothered. During Sherman's march through Georgia and South Carolina, straggling got totally out of control.

Union Troops, drawing by R.F. Zogbaum in Harper's Weekly.

The inexperience of many soldiers staggers the imagination. At the battle of Shiloh, many recruits did not know how to load and fire a rifle, and as late as after the battle of Gettysburg, Meade's ordinance officers collected 37,000 abandoned rifles, one-third of them loaded. The soldiers had not learned to put the percussion cap under the hammer. Sometimes there were six loads in a rifle, and if the cap had been used at this point, it would have blown into the recruit's face.

Of the more than 600,000 dead of the war, more than half died of camp diseases, in particular, typhoid, pneumonia, dysentery, chicken pox and malaria, the cause of which was not then known. It was almost the rule on both sides that half of the men in a regiment were lost before they saw any action. Medical care was extremely poor: At Fredericksburg, in December of 1862, the Army of the Potomac was camped only 50 miles from Washington and was greatly plagued by scurvy. The warehouses of the capital had plenty of fresh food, but the army was too poorly organized to retrieve the supplies.

Captured prisoners could be released on parole, if they promised not to take up arms again until formally exchanged. Both governments trusted each other, and both kept "parole camps." But when released, the prisoners were often reluctant to return to their armies. This system was discontinued by Grant in 1864 because there were many more Confederate than Federal prisoners. By then, prison camps had become so overcrowded that thousands of prisoners died. The camp at Andersonville, Georgia, was notorious; more than 10,000 Union soldiers died there, and its commander, Henry Wirz, was executed after the war. The Union camp at Elmira, New York, was almost as bad. The mortality rate in Northern prisons was about 12%, in Southern ones, 15%. Generally, the personnel in charge were not at fault, since neither government paid much attention to the camps.

After about two years of war, the number of volunteers had dwindled so much that both sides had to resort to the draft. The South, which suffered from a lack of manpower and undermanned factories and railroads, started earlier and developed a better draft law. In the North, a drafted man could buy himself free for $300—about a year's income for an unskilled laborer—or could hire a substitute. There were at least 75,000 of the latter. In districts where the volunteer quota had been reached, no draft was imposed. To avoid the necessity of a draft, "bounties" were offered to volunteers by towns, counties, even states, and, in the cities, substitute brokers went into business. A new type of soldier developed, the "bounty jumper" who deserted and enlisted again, sometimes six to eight times! In the South, it became a practice to hire deserters for factory work, but this was stopped in 1864.

In the North, the opposition to the draft laws resulted in riots, the worst one occurring in New York on July 13, 1863, when a mob of more than 50,000 people, many of them Irish working men, set fire to the New York draft office, killed its superintendent and then went on to kill and loot. The violence was directed mostly against blacks, and when Federal troops back from Gettysburg were brought in and subdued the mob, more than 1,000 people lay dead—the worst race riot in American history. Boston, Troy and other towns experienced similar riots. In Pennsylvania, coal miners rioted because many unionized miners had been drafted first. Lincoln settled that by rearranging the districts so that draft in the critical areas could be suspended.

Black soldiers were enlisted in the Union only late in 1862, so that their three-year term did not expire before the end of the war. Before that time, some blacks in Northern cities had tried to volunteer for the Union army, but the War Department had rejected them on the principle that this was a white man's war. On the other hand, the Union navy had always accepted blacks, who served as firemen, cooks, coal carriers and even as a gun crew on the U.S.S. *Minnesota* as early as August 1861.

Black spokesmen like Frederick Douglass had long advocated black enlistment, but Lincoln hesitated to use them as frontline soldiers even at the time of the Emancipation Proclamation, fearing that this would turn "50,000 bayonets against us that were for us." Black military service, however, could no longer be stopped. Regiments of free and "contraband" blacks formed in Kansas, Louisiana and other places as early as July 1863. Black units fought well at Vicksburg and at Charles-

Frederick Douglass, escaped slave and abolitionist.

ton, where the black Massachusetts 54th Infantry Regiment was assigned a frontal assault against Fort Wagner, suffered almost 50% casualties but gained Wagner's parapet. It's leader, Colonel Shaw, was killed and became a war hero—just a few days after hundreds of blacks had been lynched during the draft riots in New York. Much resistance to the use of black troops in the Union army remained. General Godfrey Weitzel first rejected them, but in December of 1864 was put in charge of the only all-black corps in the American army, the 25th, and in this capacity he commanded the troops that, in April 1865, first entered the Confederate capital. For the South, of course, the idea of armed black soldiers was a nightmare and its response was ferocious. Beauregard recommended the execution of "abolition prisoners" by the garrote, and in several instances the summary execution of captured black soldiers was sanctioned by Secretary of War Seddon and President Davis. The South's refusal to treat black soldiers as legitimate prisoners also contributed to the breakdown of the prisoner of war exchanges. Just how many black prisoners were massacred by the Confederates is hard to establish. Few records were kept since they were not regarded as legitimate prisoners, but it is certain that hundreds were murdered at Fort Pillow, at Milliken's Bend above Vicksburg and other places. Some captured freedmen were sold as slaves. Of the 180,000 blacks in the Union army, almost 30,000 died of diseases.

In addition to the black units, the Union army was composed of many different elements. Of the approximately two million Federal soldiers, about 500,000 were foreign born. About 175,000 of these were German;

150,000 Irish; 50,000 were English or came from Canada. Of the native Americans, the Westerners considered themselves hardier than the "pale-faced" Easterners, but it seems that the latter were less susceptible to diseases.

As in most prolonged wars, fraternization between the opposing armies occurred time and again. When camped closely together, the troops often exchanged for example, coffee for tobacco. At the Rapidan River, Federals used the same outpost at night that Confederates used during the day and shared the same firewood. Occasionally, even boxing matches and joint dances were arranged. At the Rappahannock, in February 1863, a Northern band played Northern songs, and then a Southern one across the river brought up their own, and, finally all joined in singing "Home, Sweet Home" and choked up doing it.

When the war broke out, it must have been obvious to the Southern leaders that the North had a tremendous advantage in manpower and industrial capacity. In 1860, almost 20 million people lived in the North, while only nine million lived in the South (of which almost four million were slaves) and three million in the border states: Delaware, Kentucky, Maryland, Missouri and in the New Mexico Territory. The largest cities in the United States were: New York with 800,000; Philadelphia with 562,000; Brooklyn with 266,000; Baltimore with 212,000; Boston with 177,000; New Orleans with 168,000; Cincinnati with 161,000; St. Louis with 160,000 and Chicago with 109,000 inhabitants—all except New Orleans located in the North. The other large Southern cities were Charleston with 40,000; Richmond with 37,900; Montgomery with 35,000; Mobile with 30,000; and Memphis and Savannah with 22,000 inhabitants each. The Southern white male potential for the armed service was around one million, for the rest of the nation it was four and one half million. Actually, the Federal enlistment consisted of two and one half million whites, about 179,000 blacks and 3,500 Indians (these figures include some men who enlisted twice). In the South, about 750,000 enlisted. The Southern figures are not entirely reliable, and one has to take into consideration that by the beginning of 1865, about 33% of the North's enlistment were absentees, in the South more than 50%.

The North also had much greater industrial capacity—New York state alone had more than 22,000 industrial establishment, Pennsylvania more than 20,000 and Ohio, 10,000, while the most industrialized Southern state, Virginia, had about 4,000. As a result, the South was short of almost everything: guns, gunpowder, uniforms. Throughout the war Southern soldiers were undernourished, poorly clad and frequently barefoot. When hostilities began, the Confederacy immediately

Trading between the lines.

began to purchase goods of all kinds from Europe, but the blockade made this more and more difficult. However, trade between North and South went on all the time, despite all legislation and this probably prolonged the war. The North needed cotton, sugar, tobacco and rice; the South, machinery, manufactured goods, leather, medicine, corn, salt (to preserve the meat) and many other items. Two months after Union troops occupied Nashville, a lively trade had developed. The price for cotton, around $40 per bale before the war, went up to $100. At Memphis, General Sherman tried in vain to stop goods coming from Cincinnati and remarked that Cincinnati furnished more contraband goods than Charleston and did more to prolong the war than all of South Carolina. At New Orleans, occupied by the Union since April 1862, a merchant could buy a sack of salt for $1.25, smuggle it across Lake Pontchartrain into the Confederacy and sell it for $60 to $100. He could then buy cotton for 10 to 20 cents a pound and sell it in the city for 60 cents or $1.00. Even if he managed to get only one of five cargos through, this profit was enormous. To some extent, both governments tacitly consented to this trading, while publicly insisting on suppressing it. But in 1864, a Congressional committee in Washington stated that occupied New Orleans was helping the Confederacy more than any other Southern port except Wilmington, Delaware.

The economic superiority of the North was evident in agriculture as well as in business. In 1860, the North possessed 163,000 acres of improved farmland; the South, 57,000. The North had almost three times as many horses and more than twice as many cows as the South and produced more corn, wood, potatoes, even tobacco than the South. Only in cotton, rice and sweet potatoes was the South more productive. Of the 30,626 miles of railroad lines, only 8,451 were in the seceded states, and many of these were feeder lines that could not be interconnected. There were many roundabout connections: In order to go from Richmond to the Mississippi River, one had to travel via Chattanooga, Tennessee. The North, on the other hand, could make excel-

Confederate currency.

lent use of its existing railroad lines, as did, for instance, McClellan in 1863, moving his army from Virginia to Chattanooga.

The South was also handicapped in the use of the telegraph because it lacked trained operators and equipment, while in the North the telegraph was in full use.

The Confederates had but one reconnoitering balloon—in front of Richmond—because they lacked silk to manufacture more, while Union troops used them repeatedly in the Peninsular campaign. The confederate government had great difficulty finding a machine shop capable of making a heavy propeller for a gunboat needed for the defense of New Orleans. In fact, Farragut succeeded in taking the city mainly because the two Southern ironclads, which could have stopped his fleet, had been left incomplete.

To cover the enormous expenditures both sides went heavily into debt as the war went on. It is estimated that the North spent about $2,500,000 per day during 1863. Its total land operations cost about $2,713,000,000; the naval operations, $314,000,000—not counting pensions, interest paid, etc. There was a great deal of inflation, much worse in the South than in the North. In Richmond, one gold dollar was worth $3 at the end of 1862; $7 to $8 in 1863; $20 to $50 in 1864; and $60 to $70 by March of 1865. In Washington, the gold dollar cost

$1.32 at the end of 1862; $2.59 in July–August 1864; and then dropped to $1.46 in April of 1865.

In spite of these difficulties, life in the Northern areas not directly affected by the war went on close to normal. The majority of the population belonged to the war party and willingly curtailed their luxuries, while contributing heavily to the war effort. But the considerable anti-war minority tried to go on with business as usual. Many businessmen took advantage of the war emergency and supplied the army with inferior merchandise, shoddy uniforms, sometimes even uniforms showing the wrong color, so that Union soldiers shot at their comrades. Speculators in Cincinnati forced the price of iron up when the government needed it most. The war stimulated industry. In the war's third year, the North managed to show more production and higher profits than in 1860. True, Northern cotton cloth manufacturers had to close shop, but they were not as badly off as the English cotton laborers, particularly in the Manchester area. In the Union, many jobless joined the army or went West, where the Homestead Act of 1862 provided them with 160 acres of free land, after cultivating it for five years. Wages increased during the war by about 60%, and prices increased by an estimated 100%. Agricultural production also went up in wartime: In 1859, the whole country had produced 173 million bushels of wheat, but in 1862, the North alone produced 177 million. Immigration into the Union decreased only during the first years of war. In 1860, 153,000 immigrants had entered the country, in both 1861 and 1862 about 91,000. By 1863, the number had risen again to 176,000 and continued to climb thereafter.

Internal politics were by no means subdued during the war, but there was a significant difference between the Northern and the Southern way. The South had only one political party, the Democrats. The remnants of the old Whig Party, which had been briefly revived as the Constitutional Party in 1860, no longer played an active role. But opposition within the Democratic Party to the Davis administration was strong and outspoken, particularly when the war seemed to take a turn for the worse. In the 1863 elections, after the battle of Gettysburg, the Davis administration preserved only a small majority in the Southern Congress, and several former Whigs won governorships. The opposition was particularly strong in Georgia where Vice President Alexander Stephens, his brother Linton, former General Robert Toombs and Governor Joseph Brown spoke out and worked against Davis's conscription laws, his suspension of the writ of habeas corpus and accused Davis of aiming at absolute power. Other opponents called "Reconstructionists" or "Tories" called the war a failure and advocated peace negotiations. This group was particularly strong in North Caro-

Bread riots in Richmond.

lina where it was represented by former Whig William W. Holden and, for a while, by Governor Zebulon N. Vance. Davis's position was further weakened by his constant feuds with his generals, especially General Joseph E. Johnston. In the spring of 1863, there were also a number of bread riots in the South, the most serious on April 2 in Richmond. It was dispersed without bloodshed by the courageous and firm move of President Davis who placed himself in the middle of the crowd and told the rioters to leave because within five minutes the militia would shoot. Newspapers were ordered not to mention the riot in order "not to embarrass our cause or to encourage our enemies." The government then distributed some rice to the needy.

In the North, the opposition party was divided into war and peace Democrats, but they were united in their fight against emancipation. They aroused the white workers with the picture of two-to-three million "semi-savages" overrunning the North and competing with white laborers. Even Lincoln was toying with the idea of colonizing the blacks in Central America after emancipation, but most black spokesmen ridiculed these proposals. In the Congressional elections of 1862, the Democrats made considerable gains, particularly in New York, New Jersey, Illinois and Wisconsin. Democrat Horatio Seymour became governor of New York. He opposed the draft and the Emancipation Proclamation but did his best to fight the draft riots and sup-

Salmon P. Chase, Union secretary of the treasury.

ported the war effort. Republic victories in the border states, New England and Michigan helped the Lincoln administration to maintain control of the House of Representatives. But the peace faction of the Democratic Party, the so-called Copperheads, grew stronger with each defeat of the Federal armies. Its unofficial leader was Clement Laird Vallandigham who, when campaigning for the nomination for the Ohio Democratic governorship, attacked the administration so ferociously that General Burnside, commander of the Department of the Ohio, had him arrested in May 1863. He was convicted by a military court, and Lincoln commuted his imprisonment to expulsion to the Confederate lines. But the South distrusted him also, and he had to find a home in Canada.

For the presidential election in 1864, Lincoln's nomination was by no means assured. There was a tradition against it: No incumbent president had been nominated since 1840, and none had been reelected since Andrew Jackson in 1832. But more important, Lincoln had some strong rivals. One was Salmon Portland Chase, secretary of the treasury, who had been Lincoln's competitor already in 1860. Chase had so high an opinion of himself that his friend, Senator Benjamin F. Wade from Ohio, remarked that "his theology was unsound; he thinks there is a fourth person in the Trinity." Chase's attempt to condemn

"Copperheads" (Peace Demo-crats), cartoon.

Lincoln's financial policies backfired when Postmaster Montgomery Blair, leading the conservative faction, delivered a fierce anti-Chase speech after which most Republicans got on the Lincoln bandwagon. Other candidates, like Grant and Butler, were mentioned, but the only serious contender was John Charles Frémont who had been waiting in the wings since he had refused to serve under the command of his old adversary, General Pope. However, he permitted himself to be exploited by the prospect of a third party, which turned out to be a Democratic trick to divert some Republican votes. After that, most radical Republicans decided that there was no alternative to Lincoln after all.

His opponent was George McClellan, the most popular Democrat, who, after being deposed as commander of the Army of the Potomac, continued to be the idol of the army and became a magnet for many high-ranking officials who were dissatisfied with Lincoln's way of handling the war. His main problem was reconciling the war and peace Democrats. Nominated on a peace platform and with a running mate who was a close friend of Vallandigham, McClellan ran his campaign on "peace first" plank, but it is doubtful if he was completely committed to it. Still, there was so much discontent with the administration that in August of 1864 Lincoln was convinced he was going to lose the election. The news that Sherman had taken Atlanta, however, changed all that. McClellan, in a letter of September 8, repudiated the peace at any price platform, explaining that he could not look into the faces of his former comrades and tell them that their sacrifice had been in vain. Sheridan's successes in the Shenandoah Valley helped the Republicans too, and on November 8, 1864, Lincoln, who had chosen Tennessee war-Governor Andrew Johnson as his running mate, won 55% of the votes, and all the states except Kentucky, Delaware and New Jersey. All governorships also went Republican except for these three. The Republicans had a Congressional majority of three-fourths in the next Congress.

In spite of all the infighting, the U.S. Congress worked extremely well in the war years and especially in the second session of the 37th Congress, 1861–62, which was one of the most constructive in its history. That session took the first steps toward the abolition of slavery, completely reorganized the nation's monetary and tax structures, arranged for the disposition of public land, created a Department of Agriculture and organized the future of higher education and the building of the first transcontinental railroad. This legislation—the Homestead Act, the Legal Tender Act, the Internal Revenue Act, the National Banking Act, the Pacific Railroad Act, etc.—changed the whole course of national life. Their passage was only possible because of the absence of Southern delegates, and the result was what Charles and Mary Beard have called the "Second American Revolution," in which the industrialists, bankers, workers and farmers of the North and the West pushed the plantation aristocracy of the South out of power in the national government and laid the foundation for the America of big business and tremendous industrial output that in the 1880s would surpass Britain and make the United States the world's leading economic power.

EYEWITNESS TESTIMONY

They stopped every moment to pick blackberries or get water; they would not keep in ranks, order as much as you pleased. When they came where the water was fresh, they would pour the old water out of their canteens and fill them with fresh water. They were not used to denying themselves much; they were not used to journeys on foot.

General McDowell on the new volunteers, June 1861, quoted in R. Wheeler's Voices of the Civil War *(1976).*

One of our men who seemed to be very anxious to be off for a soldier, had his ardor suddenly dampened by the appearance of his wife who told the captain that her husband was nothing but a drunkard, did not support his family as he ought . . . and in order to enforce the argument she pitched him right and left to the great amusement of the boys who soon saw that she was the better man of the two. As this Amazonian display was retarding the movements of the company, Captain Sewell ordered him out of the room, and Uncle Sam lost one would be recruit.

Alfred Bellard on enlisting on August 19, 1861 in Gone for a Soldier *(1975).*

Military punishments were various according to the offence committed or the whim of the officers. The buck and the gag being the favorite. When a man was very drunk and abusive, a bayonette or a piece of wood was placed in his mouth and a string tied behind his ears kept it in position, seating him on the ground with his knees drawn up to his body. A piece of wood is run through his legs, and placing his arms under the stick on each side of his knees, his hands are then tied in front, and he is as secure as a trapped rat. For light offences, the culprits are made to stand all day on the head of a pork barrel or on the edge of it with the head knocked out, while sometimes an extra barrel is furnished with a hole cut out of the top for his head, and one on each side for the hands. After putting on this coat, he is mounted on the head of another and there he has to stand. For sentences of courtmartial a 24-pound ball is attached to his leg by a chain, and this ornament he has to carry with him on all duty.

Alfred Bellard on the Union army in Washington, November 1861, in Gone for a Soldier.

The South is seceding from the North because the two are not homogeneous. They have different instincts, different appetites, different morals, and a different culture. It is well for one man to say that slavery has caused the separation; and for another to say that slavery has not caused it. Each in so saying speaks the truth. Slavery has caused it, seeing that slavery is the great point on which the two have agreed to differ. But slavery has not caused it, seeing that other points of difference are to be found in every circumstance and feature of the two people.

Anthony Trollope, North America *(1862).*

The winter was a severe one, and the men suffered greatly—not only for want of sufficient preparation, but because those from farther south were unaccustomed to so cold a climate. There was much sickness in camp. It is amazing to see the number of country boys who had never had the measles. Indeed, it seemed to me that they ran through the whole catalogue of complaints to which boyhood and even babyhood are subjected. They had everything almost except teething, nettle-rash and whooping-cough. I rather think some of them were afflicted with this latter disease.

John B. Gordon, Reminiscences of the Civil War *(1904).*

Although the whipping post had been abolished for soldiers, it would seem that for citizens it was a matter of taste. The orders at this time were that no liquor should be sold to soldiers . . . Two men from Washington however . . . took it into their heads that they would make a few surplus stamps for themselves by ignoring the order . . . The Regt's court martial was convened and the prisoners tried. They were each found guilty and sentenced to receive 20 lashes on their bare back and to be set adrift in the Potomac in an open boat without oars . . .

Alfred Bellard in Washington in January 1862 in Gone for a Soldier.

I advise that the commissary general be authorized to contract for bacon and salt, and the quartermaster general for blankets and shoes, payable in cotton, delivered under these contract to pass our lines.

Confederate Secretary of War George W. Randolph, to President Davis, spring of 1862.

The objection to this is the proposed shipment to a port in possession of the enemy. If the supplies

Punishments in the ranks.

can be obtained free from this objection it should be done . . . At a last resort we might be justified in departing from the declared policy in regard to exports, but the necessity should be absolute.

President Davis's reply to Secretary of War
Randolph, spring of 1862.

It was wonderful, the attraction and reverence and admiration that the sight of a woman created in the wilderness . . . The soldiers, hungry to see a woman's face and form, stood about the hospitals and transports, waiting by scores until one of the female nurses appeared. Then they would crowd up with grateful and respectful attentions and beg permission simply to shake hands.

Jesse Bowman Young, What a Boy Saw in
the Army, *April 1862 (1894).*

On the march from Yorktown, I had on a pair of tight boots, and by the time we encamped they had become so tight from being wet, that I could not pull them off, and as sand had got into them in some way, I was hardly able to walk. As there was no way of pulling them off, some of the men cut them off with knives, and when they did come off at last, some of the skin went with them. There being no clothing with the army, I had to get a pair of dead men's shoes from the battle field, and at last succeeded in getting a pair of 12, which I wore until we were close to Richmond, causing considerable amusements and remarks, by the slip slop manner in which I had to march.

Alfred Bellard, advancing with McClellan's
army, May 1862, in Gone for a Soldier.

Went this morning . . . to the Dark Barracks to see the wounded and sick soldiers brought on by the *Ocean Queen* from Yorktown . . . The soldiers seemed mostly to suffer from exhaustion . . . Some of them looked grey with pallor and weakness . . . Another poor fellow of about 50 was dying of consumption from a kick on the breast by a drunken lieutenant. "Oh" said he, "had I died from a blow from the enemy, I could have borne it better. I was not to blame, and I had my pistol in hand, I should have shot him. But I remembered I am a Christian . . ." He spoke with tears rolling down his face of the scenes he had witnessed of young fellows dying, moaning for one look at their mothers and sisters or someone still dearer.

Maria L. Daly, May 14, 1862, Diary of a
Union Lady *(1962).*

Considerable foraging was done, on the sly, about the neighboring plantations . . . There was much tobacco raised in the section of the country, and we found the barns filled with the best quality of tobacco in leaf. This we appropriated . . . All the trades were represented in our ranks, that of cigar-maker was included, and the army rioted in cigars without enriching the sutlers.

Warren Lee Goss, about the Union army in May 1862 before Richmond, in Recollections of a Private *(1890).*

. . . on the 25th we moved to Poplar Hill, 14 miles from the city of Richmond. Tents were pitched and woods were perfectly covered with fruit bearing trees and shrubs of different [sic] kinds . . . We also found plenty of reptiles such as snakes, newts, sand lizards and frogs, but were not much bothered by them, except one man who was bitten by a snake one night, and his leg swelled up to an enormous size . . .

Alfred Bellard with McClellan before Richmond, May 1862 in Gone for a Soldier.

All of the horses killed at this battle, and there were quite a number of them, some batteries having lost them all, were covered over with brush and fence rails and burnt. Our stomachs being so strong by this time that we cooked our coffee over their ribs.

A. Bellard, after the battle of Fair Oaks in Gone for a Soldier.

. . . Captain Kirker and two returned Union prisoners arrived, one of whom was Lieutenant Dempsey of the 69th [New York regiment, the so-called Irish Brigade]. Dempsey said that nothing we had heard of their treatment in Richmond was in the least exaggerated. The Southerners would walk in and say that though they did not look comfortable, Northerners were used to such things—they were nothing but laborers and used to being shut up in shops. For a free Southern gentleman, imprisonment was a much greater hardship.

Maria L. Daly, June 19, 1862, Diary.

In Baltimore, he [Baron Gerolt, the Prussian minister to the United States] says, it is the fashion to look upon those who are Unionists as low people. They think, he says, in this way to keep on the safe side in case the secessionists succeed, feeling assured that the government will not resent their conduct. In the paper this morning, there is an incendiary

appeal of the women of New Orleans to the Southern soldiers, the burden of which is that they would rather be buried beneath the ruins of their homes than be left to the mercy of the barbarous Yankees—these barbarous creatures who have done nothing but feed their hungry and clothe their naked since they took their pestilent city. I suppose it was suggested by some Southern politician whose neck is in danger.

Maria L. Daly, June 26, 1862, Diary.

. . . the main thing that struck us was the immense quantity of abandoned stores and equipment, indicating how abundant had been the supply of the Federal forces, and how great the demoralization of their retreat. Near Savage Station there must have been acres covered by stacks of burning boxes of bacon, crackers and desiccated vegetables—"desecrated vegetables", as our boys called them. To us poorly equipped and half-starved rebels it was a revelation. Here and elsewhere we picked up a few rations and a few choice equipments, . . . but had really neither time nor taste for plunder. There were other mementoes of their stay and of their hasty departure . . . not quite so attractive or appetizing—the ghastly leavings of numerous field hospitals; pale, naked corpses and grotesque piles of arms and legs.

Robert Stiles, Confederate artillery man, June 29, 1862, Four Years under Marse Robert *(1903).*

Augt, 2nd our Division was ordered out in light marching order but returned to camp in about 3 hours, having taken the wrong road, through the incompetancy [sic] of the guide. On the 3rd we were again on picket, but had no opportunity of picking berries this time, as our company was stationed on what they were pleased to term the telegraph picket, that is a line of posts consisting of three men each extending from the pickets in the woods to our camp. The idea was, to give an alarm in the shortest possible time of any attack on the outposts in front.

A. Bellard, after the Seven Days campaign, August 1862, in Gone for a Soldier.

After the rebels retreated on the 5th, Genl. [F. E.] Patterson was driven up to our lines in an ambulance having been taken sick or incapacitated in some way, and this after his speech on the night of the 4th did not look very well.

On the 8th a little excitement was created in our Regt. by Co. "A" having lost their captain by resignation the company was ordered to be disbanded and the men distributed amongst the rest of the companys. Upon enforcing this order, a mutiny was the consequence. The men refusing to obey were placed under arrest. The mutineers were ordered to walk up and down on the rifle works with a log of wood on their shoulder as punishment, and Co. "C" was detailed as a guard to see that they kept on the go. Sticking it out as long as they could, they had to give in, and were distributed through the Regt. This consolidation was condemned by the rest of the Regt., but orders were orders and had to be obeyed or take the consequence.

A. Bellard, retreating with McClellan, August 1862, in Gone for a Soldier.

As foraging was strictly forbidden in general orders, we could not do much of that but still managed to get a little on the sly. I know one day we passed a corn field, when some of the men went after some. As they were busy filling their haversacks the old farmer came across his farm with a gun and big dog, to frighten us off, I suppose, but when he saw we were armed and not disposed to go, he took the hint and went himself.

A. Bellard, at Harrison's Landing, August 1862, in Gone for a Soldier.

The balloon was used as a means of finding out what the rebels were doing, how many troops they had, and what kind of fortifications they had ready for us. The rebels fired at it on several occasions but did not succeed in hitting it. When the balloon was in the air, it was held by men holding on to the ropes so that it could be moved from one place to the other. I do not know that it did us much good, although it might. The gas used in the balloon was made on the field by machines the balloonist carried with him.

A. Bellard, at Harrison's Landing, August 1862, in Gone for a Soldier.

. . . we passed through the fortifications of Yorktown . . . the works had been turned since we left them, the guns now pointing towards Williamsburgh instead of Fortress Monroe. The 8th N.Y. Volls. and a Regt. called the Lost Children were doing the guard duty and a lost looking lot they were. Desertions were going on every day but when you take into consideration that they were the dregs of New York City, it need not be wondered at.

A. Bellard, August 19, 1862, on the way to come to General Pope's assistance, in Gone for a Soldier.

Upon reaching the city [Alexandria], the Regt. disembarked and marched to the outskirts of the city and encamped on a square. We had been away from any city for so long that the boys very naturally had an inclination to enjoy themselves, and in a short time nearly half of the Regt. was reeling round the streets drunk. The Col. in order to stop it had double guards put on to keep the boys in camp, but it was no use, for as fast as one came in, two would slip out between the guards . . . The next morning soldiers could be seen laying on the stoops with the pocket cut clean out of their pants, and the money gone of course.

A. Bellard in Alexandria, August 19–20, 1862, in Gone for a Soldier.

In fording Bull Run creek, just before going into battle, some of Pope's officers were waiting there on horseback, thinking perhaps that we were not crossing quick enough to suit them or were shirking our duty, told us that if we did not cross they would shoot us, at the same time pulling out a revolver. One of our men who had got over told the officer, that if he shot anyone he would be shot himself, at the same time bringing his piece down for action, informing them . . . that we belonged to the Army of the Potomac, and were not used to running away or be shot down either. This had the desired effect . . .

A. Bellard, on the second battle of Bull Run, August 29, 1862, in Gone for a Soldier.

Leaving camp after breakfast, we marched about 20 miles and camped at Fort Lyons near Alexandria . . . pretty well tired out and ragged. Our uniforms at this time would have disgraced a beggar. Our pants were worn away so much that they hardly reached the knee, and the bottoms were in tatters. Our overcoats were not much better being burnt here and there in the skirts, by laying too near a fire. The whole uniform being pretty well stained up with mud and ashes. The shirt I had on had seen service for some 3 or 4 weeks . . .

A. Bellard, retreating from Bull Run, end of August, 1862, in Gone for a Soldier.

These insects [body lice] which in camp parlance were called "graybacks," first made their appearance in the winter of 1861. At first the soldier was mortified and felt almost disgraced at discovering one of these insects on his person . . . At first the soldier used to steal out companionless . . . once hid from the eyes of men, he would pursue and murder the crawling insects with a vengeful pleasure . . . On his stealthy way back he would be sure to run into a dozen solitary individuals, who tried to look unconcerned, as if indeed they were in the habit of retiring in the dim recesses of the forest for private meditation. The satisfaction he felt would not last long. In a day or two his body would be infested again . . . It was simply impossible to exterminate them . . . Once lodged in the seams of the clothing, they remained until time mouldered the garments . . . On this march, when the troops had no change of clean clothes for weeks, the soldiers were literally infested with them. Many used to place their underraiment in the bottom of a stream, and put a large stone to keep them down . . .

Unnamed private in the Confederate army, on Lee's Maryland campaign, quoted in R. Wheeler's Voices of the Civil War.

I wish, my dearest Minnie, you could have witnessed the transit of the Rebel army through our streets [of Frederick, Maryland] . . . Their coming was unheralded by any pomp and pageant whatever . . . Was this body of men, moving . . . along with no order . . . no two dresses alike, their officers hardly distinguishable from the privates—were these, I asked myself in amazement, were these dirty, lank, ugly specimens of humanity, with shocks of hair sticking through the holes in their hats, and the dust thick on their dirty faces, the men that had coped and encountered successfully and driven back again and again our splendid legions . . . ? I must confess, Minnie, that I felt humiliated at the thought that this horde of ragamuffins could set our grand army of the Union at defiance . . .

Unionist woman of Frederick, Maryland (only her first name, "Kate," is known), letter to a friend in Baltimore, on Lee's entry into Frederick (September 6, 1862); quoted in R. Wheeler's Voices of the Civil War.

. . . I wish you could see how they behaved. A crowd of boys on a holiday don't seem happier. They are on the broad grin all the time . . . There is not a scarecrow in the cornfields that would not scorn to exchange clothes with them . . . I saw some strikingly handsome faces though, or rather they would have been so if they could have had a good scrubbing. They were very polite, I must confess. . . . Many of them were barefooted. Indeed, I felt sorry for the poor misguided wretches, for some of them limped along so painfully, trying hard to keep up with their comrades.

"Kate" from the same letter.

In truth, Northern men are educated to act individually and are unwilling to submit to discipline of any kind. This begins in the family, thence to the private soldier who dissents from his captain, the captain from his colonel, the colonel from his general, the general from the commander-in-chief and the generals are all rivals—whilst at the South, Jefferson Davis is the head; Lee's and Jackson's orders are obeyed.

Maria L. Daly, September 12, 1862, Diary.

None had any under-clothing. My costume consisted of a ragged pair of trousers, a stained, dirty jacket; an old slouch hat, the brim pinned up with a thorn; a begrimed blanket over my shoulder, a grease-smeared cotton haversack full of apples and corn, a cartridge box full, and a musket. I was barefooted and had a stone bruise on each foot . . . There was none there who would not have been "run in" by the police had he appeared on the streets of any populous city.

J. R. Boulware, assistant surgeon, 6th South Carolina, at the time of the battle of Antietam, diary, September 1862.

The operating surgeons [in an emergency hospital in Kedysville, near Sharpsburg] were in their shirtsleeves . . . leaving their bare arms exposed and covered with blood, giving them the appearance of a bevy of butchers in a Chicago abbatoir . . . Pretty soon a young surgeon came up, and, grabbing me by the shoulder, said: . . . "Shoulder smashed?" A sickening feeling came over me and I replied that it certainly would be [now] if it were not [before] . . . A glass of whisky . . . did not seem to affect me any more than would so much water, the pain was so intense. Then the young surgeon thrust his finger into the hole where the bullet had entered, and with his other forefinger plunged into the place of its exit he rummaged around for broken bones, splinters etc., until I swooned away . . .

H. A. Nickerson, Union lieutenant, on the battle of Antietam, quoted in R. Wheeler's Voices of the Civil War.

He [Judge Pierrepont, cabinet officer] gave us a most discouraging account of the conduct of our men in the field, 200 only being the average of those who fight in a regiment. It is incredible, he says, how many slink to the rear pretending want of ammunition etc. Some pretend to fall and are carried off by half a dozen other friends and all kinds of excuses are found. So our material is not quite as good as the papers make out!

Maria L. Daly, October 4, 1862, Diary.

Mrs. Dix told me that a saddler's wife went to Tiffany's and Young's yesterday and ordered the greatest quantity of pearls and diamond and plate. Before the war began, her husband could scarcely get his bread . . . Would God these wretches could be exposed! You see magnificent equipages in the street, and you look at those who are seated in them, they look like the commonest kind of humanity. Old women who might be apple-sellers or fruit-carriers are dressed in velvet and satins.

Maria L. Daly, October 24, 1862, Diary.

There were stringent orders against plundering; but . . . the soldiers appropriated to their own use whatever pleased their fancy. They cooked bacon and eggs, made hotcakes in the kitchen, eating them with sugar and molasses. They carried mattresses and beds into the streets, spreading them upon the sidewalks for a luxurious night's repose . . .

Charles Coffin, Federal newsman on the Union troops in Fredericksburg, December 1862 in My Days and Nights on the Battlefield *(1863).*

All the surrounding forests had disappeared, built into huts, with chimneys of sticks and mud, or [cut for burning] in the stone fireplaces constructed by the soldiers, who also built mud ovens and baked their beans and bread. The winter was severe, the snow deep. The soldiers were discouraged . . . Homesickness set in and became a disease.

Charles C. Coffin on the army of the Potomac in winter quarters near Fredericksburg in My Days and Nights on the Battlefield.

. . . Entire brigades lined up against each other for the fight [with snowballs]. And not the masses of men only, but the organized military bodies—the line and field officers, the bands and the banners, the generals and their staffs, mounted as for genuine battle. There was the formal demand for surrender . . . and the refusal, the charge and the repulse; . . . sometimes limbs were broken and eyes, at least temporarily, put out; and the camp equipment of the vanquished was regarded as fair booty to the victors.

One would have supposed these veteran troops had seen too much of the real thing to seek amusement in playing at battle.

Robert Stiles on the Confederate soldiers in winter quarters 1862–63 in Four Years Under Marse Robert.

A Confederate officer of pickets . . . asked a Union lieutenant [on the opposite shore of the Rappahannock] if he would not come over after dark and go with him to a farmhouse near the lines, where certain Confederates had invited the country girls to a dance. The Union officer hesitated, but the Confederate insisted and promised to call for him in a boat after dark and to lend him a suit of citizen's clothes, and pledged his honor as a soldier to see him safely back to his own side . . . the invitation was accepted, and at the appointed hour the Confederate's boat glided silently to the place of meeting on the opposite bank. The citizen's suit was a ludicrous fit, but it served its purpose. The Union soldier was introduced to the country girls as a new recruit just arrived in camp. He enjoyed the dance and, returning with his Confederate escort, was safely landed in his own lines before daylight.

John B. Gordon, winter of 1862/63 at the Rappahannock, Reminiscences of the Civil War.

During our march from Bristoe to Manassas, we passed Genl. Sickles with the two other brigades or our division going to the front as we supposed. His own brigade [Excelsior] were so drunk that nothing could be done with them and they returned to camp. While they were marching past, our boys struck up "Johnny stole a ham, and Sickles killed a man" but no notice was taken of it.

A. Bellard, November of 1862, in Gone for a Soldier. *(Before the war, Sickles had shot down his wife's lover, but was acquitted).*

On the 22nd a first squad of "cullud gemmens" [colored gentlemen] arrived bringing with them a good stock of fresh bread and provisions. As it happened, our own grub had not arrived, so the darkeys had to suffer. While one man would offer his services to help them carry the bread . . . two more would act together, and before the one who was carrying the bread got half the way to the tent, it was knocked out of his arms and vanished in a moment. When the darkies found out the dodge they carried it themselves . . . The stealing did not end there . . .

A. Bellard, near Alexandria, end of November 1862 in Gone for a Soldier.

During the day a secesh gentleman came into the camp looking for his cow that he believed had been shot by one of our men . . . The captain turned to the men who were standing round and told them in the presence of old Virginia that he would shoot the first man whom he found killing anything belonging to the farmers. This satisfied the old gent and he went off. When he had gone the Capt. turned to the men and remarked that it was rather rough on the old man, but so long as he did not see it done it was all right.

A. Bellard, at the defense of Washington, end of November 1862, in Gone for a Soldier.

A little excitement was caused in the camp on the 19th by the actions of one of our captains. For some cause or other Captain Gould of Co. E had two of his men tied up by their thumbs to trees, so that their toes would just touch the ground. As the captain was noted as a tyrant, and not liked by any of the Regt. some of the boys untied them. This brought out the noble capt. who cut one of the boys over the head with his sword. He had no sooner done so, when the rest of the Regt. turned out and there was every appearance of a riot. The guard was turned out and ordered to quell the disturbance, but just then Col. Sewell arrived on the scene and demanded the reason for the row. When he was told he ordered the men to their quarters, and as we knew that he would do what was proper in the case . . . we retired.

A. Bellard, after the Battle of Fredericksburg, December 19, 1862, in Gone for a Soldier.

How should General Hooker cure homesickness which had become a disease? Officers and men alike had an intense longing for home. When he took command of the army, desertions were at the rate of two hundred a day. 2922 officers and 82000 men were reported absent, with or without leave! We are not to think that they all were deserters. By far the larger number were absent on leave, but, once home, had not returned.

Charles C. Coffin, the situation at the end of January, 1863, in My Days and Nights on the Battle-Field.

A comrade . . . afterwards related the following: "I was among the wounded . . . Using my musket for a crutch, I began to turn away the burning brushwood, and got some of them out. I tell you, it was hot! Them pines was full of pitch and rosin, and made the fire as hot as a furnace. I was working away, pulling out Johnnies and Yanks, when one of the wounded Johnnies . . . toddled up and began to help . . . The underbrush crackled and roared, and the poor devils howled and shrieked when the fire got at them. By and by another reb—I guess he was a straggler—came up and began to help, too . . . We were trying to rescue a young fellow in gray. The fire was all around him. The last of that fellow I saw was his face . . . I heard him scream "o, mother! o, God!" It left me trembling all over like a leaf.—After it was over, my hands were blistered and burned so I could not open or shut them; but me and them rebs tried to shake hands . . .

Warren Lee Goss, Chancellorsville, May 3, 1863, in Recollections of a Private.

It was reported on the 12th that Richmond had been taken, but as dame rumor was always prolific with reports, no particular notice was taken of it. The wounded were still coming in from the late battle fields, some of them having lain there where they fell for 11 days, without medical aid and very little to eat. Amongst was Lieut. Lawyer, who had been shot through the lungs, by one of his own regt. at about the same time I was. After laying on the field for 3 days, he was picked up by the rebel surgeons and cared for as well as their limited medicine chest would allow.

A. Bellard, at a Washington hospital, May of 1863, in Gone for a Soldier.

The 15th was a very great day for the colored people, as the 1st Regt. Col. Volls [Virginia Colored Volunteers] passed through the city. They marched through the principal streets and made a very good appearance. They had a band of four pieces and were officered by white men. They marched without colors. The sidewalks were lined with "cullud pussons" [colored persons] who were laughing, chatting and shaking hands with their military friends.

A. Bellard, in Washington, June 1863, in
Gone for a Soldier.

Once let the black man get upon his person the brass letters, U.S.; let him get an eagle on his button, and a musket on his shoulder and bullets in his pocket, and there is no power on earth which can deny that he has earned the right to citizenship.

Frederick Douglass in his Monthly, *August 1863.*

He [the hospital's ward master] went with me, and upon reporting myself to him [the doctor], was ordered to the guard house for the night. I was introduced to a cell about four by six, after which the door was double locked and barred. For light and air, there was one small opening near the ceiling, about six inches wide by about a foot in height. While the furniture consisted of a single spittoon, neither a chair nor a bench being provided, so that had either to stand up or lay on the floor. As I could not stand up all night, I lay down on the floor with the spittoon for my pillow, and slept till morning . . . When I had demolished my grub, I was ushered into the presence of the court to be tried, said court being composed of the head doctor and him only . . . I was declared guilty, and sentenced to three weeks in the prisoners' squad for punishment. [Bellard had overstayed his furlough by 2 weeks.]

A. Bellard, September of 1863. Gone for a Soldier.

As soon as a new lot of prisoners made their appearance the old hands would yel [sic] out "Fresh fish." At this signal the new ones were surrounded and a demand made for money or tobacco. If they were so unfortunate as to have neither, a blanket was soon procured, the new arrival was thrown in and tossed up to the ceiling, making him look more like a frog than anything else with his arms and legs spread out trying to catch the air . . . the next toss he got was an extra one that sent him flying against the ceiling . . . He fell back into the blanket unconscious. The boys, thinking perhaps that the man was badly stunned, took him out of the blanket and taking him over to the water troughs . . . threw him

in bodily clothes and all. The guard who stood at the door took no notice of it whatever, being I suppose used to it.

A. Bellard, in the Veteran Reserve Corps, on guard duty, November 1863. Gone for a Soldier.

At the Old Capitol prison [at one time the capitol of the U.S.] rebel soldiers were confined and also a female spy, who I believe was the notorious Belle Boyd. As this female had free use of the jail corridor, the officers of the guard had quite a flirtation with her, and she could be seen walking up and down the corridor with them any day.

A. Bellard, on guard duty at Carroll prison, an annex to the Old Capitol, November 1863. Gone for a Soldier.

If, as is stated, a million of dollars' worth of diamonds were worn at the Russian ball, a million of dollars might be procured by such a Diamond Ball as we suggest—enough money to secure every comfort required by our wounded soldiers, and probably to save hundreds of lives which are now sacrificed for want of suitable attendance, clothing and food. Could the jewels be put to a nobler use?

Harper's Weekly, *November 21, 1863.*

As my three years of service had expired I reported the fact to the Capt. who . . . asked me if I would not re-enlist. I told him I would not, and he made out my papers at once. Getting them into my hands I was once more a citizen, and going over to the Treasury building, I drew my bounty of one hundred dollars and seventy-three dollars monthly, clothing and transportation money. With this in my pocket I felt quite rich.

A. Bellard, discharged in Washington, August of 1864. Gone for a Soldier.

They [the blacks in Gettysburg] regarded the Rebels as having an especial hatred toward them and believed that if they fell into their hands annihilation was sure . . . I can see them yet: men and women with bundles as large as old-fashioned feather ticks slung across their backs. Children, also carrying their bundles, and striving in vain to keep up with their seniors . . . Mothers, anxious for their offspring, would stop for a moment to hurry them up, saying: "Fo' de Lod's sake, you chillen, cum right long quick! If dem Rebs dun kotch you, day tear you all up."

These terrible warnings were sure to have the desired effect; for, with their eyes open wider than ever, they were not long in hastening their steps.

Tillie Pierce, a young [white] citizen of Gettysburg, on Gettysburg in the middle of June 1863, as quoted in R. Wheeler's Voices of the Civil War.

The Irish Brigade, with their emerald flag and the insignia of Erin in golden characters upon it waving above them, was advancing to go into battle in the region of the Devil's Den [west of Little Round Top]. Before they ventured into actual battle they halted. The priest who was their chaplain stood on a high rock above the field . . . and, with bullets flying about him and with the awful battle raging in his front, he pronounced absolution in behalf of his kneeling constituents. For a moment they bowed there while the priest commended their souls to the mercy of God, and then, with a united and terrible shout they dashed forward into the bloody field . . .

Jesse B. Young, Gettysburg, What a Boy Saw in the Army, *July 2, 1863.*

The most friendly relations seemed to exist between the pickets of the two armies. At one place there was a tree which had fallen across the stream, and which was used by the soldiers of both armies in drawing water for their camps. General Longstreet's corps was stationed there . . . and wore blue of a little different shade from our uniform. Seeing a soldier in blue on this log, I rode up to him, commenced conversing with him and asked whose corps he belonged to. He was very polite, and, touching his hat to me, said he belonged to General Longstreet's corps. I asked him a few questions—but not with a view of gaining any particular information—all of which he answered, and I rode off.

Grant, late October 1863 in Chattanooga, Personal Memoirs.

It was a very interesting and a very touching sight to see the first colored regiment from this city march down the street for the front. They were a fine body of men and had a look of satisfaction in their faces, as though they felt they had gained a right to be more respected. Many old, respectable darkies stood at the street corners, men and women with tears in their eyes as if they saw the redemption of their race afar off but still the beginning of a better state of

affairs for them. Though I am very little Negrophilish . . . still I could not but feel moved.

Maria L. Daly, March 12, 1864, Diary.

One veteran told the story of the burning of some of Union soldiers who were wounded during Hooker's fight the battle of Chancellorsville [May 1863] . . . as they lay helpless in the woods. It was a ghastly and awe-inspiring tale. As we sat silently smoking and listening . . . an infantry soldier who had, unobserved by us, been prying into the shallow grave he sat on with his bayonet, suddenly rolled a skull on the ground before us and said in a deep, low voice; "That is what you are all coming to, and some of you will start toward it tomorrow!"

Union Private Frank Wilkeson, May 4, 1864, Recollections of a Private Soldier *(1887).*

On the night of the 10th, Sam Nunnelly came to me and said we would get over in front of our works that night and plunder the dead . . . as we knew there were plenty of them there that had never been searched. I told I would not do it, as we would be in danger of being shot by our own men as well as the enemy. But he said he would go by himself and crawl around . . . So he went and was gone all night, coming back at daylight. He got three watches, some money, knives and other things. He would risk his life any time for plunder.

John O. Casler, after Spotsylvania, May 10, 1864, Four Years in the Stonewall Brigade *(1906).*

Our army, operating in hostile territory, was like a swarm of locusts . . . Where each man of an army takes a little, not much remains. I don't think we were very hard with these people, yet their fences fast melted away into campfires, and their chickens and turkeys and geese into goodly messes . . .

Warren Lee Goss on the fighting, end of May, 1864 on Recollections of a Private.

The colored people whom we met . . . greedily gathered scraps of fat and beef thrown away around our camps, yet their faces were the most contented ones we saw in this country. Discontent and sullen anger, ill concealed, were written all over many of the white countenances. The few darkies whom I talked with in most instances informed us that young "massa" was in the rebel army, and that the younger male servants were either beyond Richmond (presumably to keep them from falling into Union hands) or had been engaged in digging fortifications around it . . .

Warren Lee Goss at the end of May 1864 on the Union army in Virginia in Recollections of a Private.

. . . the South stands today quite as much indebted for a successful prolongation of this struggle to her women as to her generals and soldiers in the field. Fully, fiercely, terribly, malignantly have they entered into this conflict. In many localities I am fully persuaded that neither friend, relative nor neighbor capable of bearing arms, would be allowed to remain at home. The female in their zeal would find some means to drive him away into military service . . .

Chaplain A. M. Stewart on the Union army in Virginia, June 1864 in Camp, March and Battlefield (1865).

The skill and success of the men in collecting forage was one of the features of the march. Each brigade commander had authority to detail a company of foragers, usually about fifty men, with one or two commissioned officers selected for their boldness and enterprise. This party would be dispatched before daylight . . . would proceed on foot five or six miles from the route traveled by their brigade, and then visit every plantation or farm within range. They would usually procure a wagon or family carriage, load it with bacon, corn-meal, turkeys, chickens . . . and would then regain the main road, usually in advance of their [brigade's baggage] train.

Sherman, November 1864, Memoirs (1875).

As rumors of the approach of our army reached the frightened inhabitants, frantic efforts were made to conceal not only their valuable personal effects, plate, jewelry . . . but also articles of food, such as hams, sugar, flour, etc. A large part of these supplies were carried to the neighboring swamps; but the favorite method of concealment was the burial of the treasures in the pathways and gardens adjoining the dwelling-houses. Sometimes, also the graveyards were selected as the best place of security from the "vandal hands of the invaders" . . . Wherever the army halted almost every inch of ground in the vicinity of the dwellings was poked by ramrods, pierced by sabres or upturned with spades . . . Nothing escaped the observation of these sharp-witted soldiers.

A woman standing upon the porch of the house . . . watching the proceedings, instantly became an object of suspicion, and she was watched until some movement betrayed a place of concealment . . . It was all fair spoil of war . . .

George W. Nichols, November 1864, The Story of the Great March (1865).

. . . it is curious to observe the attention bestowed by our soldiers upon camp pets. With a care which almost deserves the name of tenderness, the men gather helpless dumb animals around them; sometimes an innocent kid . . . and again a racoon, a little donkey, a dog or a cat . . . The favorite pet of the camp, however, is the hero of the barnyard. There is not a regiment nor a company, not a teamster nor a Negro at headquarters, nor an orderly, but has a rooster of one kind or another. When the column is moving, these haughty game-cocks are seen mounted upon the breech of a cannon, tied to the packsaddle of a mule among pots and pans, or carried lovingly in the arms of a mounted orderly . . . They must all fight, however, or be killed and eaten . . . Cock-fighting is not, perhaps, one of the most refined or elevating of pastimes, but it furnishes food for a certain kind of fun in camp; and as it is not carried to the point of cruelty, the soldiers cannot be blamed for liking it.

George W. Nichols, end of November 1864, The Story of the Great March.

Society in the South, and especially in Savannah, had undergone a great change. The extremes of social life were very wide apart before the war. They were no nearer the night before Sherman marched into the city. But the morning after, there was a convulsion, . . . a shaking up and settling down of all the discordant elements. The tread of that army of the West . . . was like a moral earthquake, overturning aristocratic pride, privilege and power. Old houses, with foundations laid deep and strong in the centuries, fortified by wealth, name and influence, went down beneath the shock. The general disruption of the former relations of master and slave, and forced submission to the Union arms, produced a common level . . . One could not ask for more courteous treatment than I received during my stay. I am indebted to many ladies and gentlemen of that city for kind invitations . . . There was no concealment of opinion on either side, but with the utmost good

Lincoln and his cabinet: From the left: Lincoln, Welles, Chase, Blair, Seward, C.B. Smith, Bates and Stanton.

feeling full expression was given to our differing sentiments.

Charles C. Coffin in Savannah, January 1865,
Following the Flag *(1865).*

The Almighty has fixed the distinction of the races; the Almighty has made the black man inferior, and, sir, by no legislation, by no partisan success, by no military power, can you wipe out this distinction. You may make the black man free, but when you have done that what have you done?

Representative Fernando Wood of New York, in the House debate over slavery on January 10, 1865.

Mr. Speaker, we shall never know why slavery dies so hard in this Republic and in this Hall, till we know why sin outlives disaster, and Satan is immortal . . .

Republican representative James A. Garfield of Ohio (the future President) in the House during the abolition debate on January 12, 1865.

They were no respecters of persons. Ornaments were snatched from the persons of delicate females, and woe unto him who displayed a watch, fob or gold chain; as he would be relieved of it in short order. The sacred vessels of the churches were appropriated by the drunken mob . . . Valuable cabinets, elegant pianos, costly paintings—many of them imported from foreign lands, the work of some of the great masters—were ruthlessly smashed to pieces.

J. B. Austin, Sherman in Columbia, S.C., *February 17–18, 1865. The Blue and the Gray (1899).*

The work of destruction [blowing up the ironclad vessels in the James] might well have ended here. But the four principal tobacco warehouses of the city . . . were fired; the flames . . . soon involved a wide and widening area; the conflagration passed rapidly beyond control. And in this mad fire, this wild, unnecessary destruction of their property, the citizens of Richmond had a fitting souvenir of the imprudence and recklessness of the departing Administration . . . Pillagers were busy at their vocation, and in the hot breath of the fire were figures as of demons contending for prey.

E. Pollard, April 3, 1865, in Richmond, The Lost Cause *(1866).*

. . . Men, women and children joined the constantly increasing throng. They came from all the streets, running in breathless haste, shouting and hallooing, and dancing with delight . . . No carriage was to be had, so the President, leading his son, walked to General Weitzel's headquarters—Jeff Davis' mansion . . . The walk was long, and the President halted a moment to rest. "May de good Lord bless you, President Linkum!" said an old Negro, removing his hat and bowing, with tears of joy rolling down his cheeks. The President removed his hat and bowed in silence. It was a bow which upset the forms, laws, customs and ceremonies of centuries of slavery.

Charles C. Coffin, Federal newsman, on Lincoln's visit in Richmond, April 4, 1865.

6. The War at Sea and the Foreign Powers

THE HISTORICAL CONTEXT

Unlike the war on land and in the rivers, the North never had a major setback in the war at sea. The blockade of Southern ports yielded only meager fruits at first but improved slowly but steadily and in the later years of the war seriously handicapped the South, not just because more and more ports were occupied by Union troops, but because more and more blockade runners were caught.

Both sides invested heavily in the blockade and in fighting it. In 1861, the North had about 90 ships and 7,600 personnel; the South, none. Of the Federal ships, 35 were of modern build, but only three were steamships. At the end of the war, the U.S. navy had about 51,000 men on ships and 17,000 in government yards. About 470 ships with 2,450 guns were on blockade duty. The effectiveness of the blockade is still in dispute. There was a coastline of 3,500 miles to watch, and in the beginning, about five of six blockade runners got through, but this changed during the course of the war. In 1861, only one in ten was caught; in 1863, one in four; and in 1865, one in two. About 1,500 blockade runners were captured or destroyed, but about half a million bales of cotton were shipped out and half a million rifles, a thousand tons of gunpowder and several hundred cannon were brought in. In 1863, Jefferson Davis still called the blockade a "monstrous pretension," but many Southerners felt the pinch, with scarcities and costs already increasing in 1862. About 8,000 trips were made through the blockade in the four war years, but about 20,000 had taken place in the four preceding years, and the blockade running ships carried less cargo because they were built for speed rather than capacity. Furthermore, the South's needs for all sorts of supplies increased, of course, during the war. While the blockade alone certainly did not win the war for the North, it was one of the main contributing factors, and the 5% naval personnel of the total Union armed forces certainly contributed much more than this low figure indicates.

137

Life on board a blockade ship was extremely boring—waiting was the main occupation. But the crew was awarded 50% of every prize they captured. In the case of *Aeolus*, a small gunboat that captured two runners late in 1864, the captain earned $40,000; the officers, from $8,000 to $20,000; and each seaman, $3,000. Particularly after the first year of the war, there were even greater potential rewards, and certainly more excitement for a blockade running crew because many of the South's ports had been occupied or sealed off, so that the blockading fleet could concentrate on the few remaining open—Wilmington, N.C., Charleston, Mobile, etc. Both sides had refined their tactics. The South used faster boats, painted them gray for low visibility and learned how to slip through on dark or foggy nights. The North used an inner cordon of smaller boats that would signal the larger warships by rockets when a boat tried to enter or leave the port. In the later part of the war, captains of blockade runners received $5,000 in gold or more per round trip, and even a common seaman would get $250. Under these circumstances, many British captains and sailors left their service and worked for the South. While captured Southerners were treated as prisoners of war by the North, British subjects were usually set free.

Places like Nassau in the Bahamas, Bermuda, Havana and Matamoros in Mexico were used as the principal bases by the blockade runners and became boom towns almost overnight. Wilmington, North Carolina, protected by inlets and hard to navigate shoals and by Fort Fisher became the most important port for blockade runners. It changed from a sleepy, quiet town to a bustling, rowdy and violent one, full of speculators and merchants, as well as sailors who hardly knew how to spend all the money they earned and got into frequent fights with the less fortunate Confederate soldiers.

One controversy between the Union and Britain evolved in April 1862, when the Union began to stop British merchant vessels on the way from England to Bermuda or Nassau, because their cargoes were intended for Confederate ports. The *Bermuda* was not only confiscated on these grounds, but purchased by the U. S. navy and used as a blockade ship. This policy aroused British feelings, but American diplomats cited British precedents that showed that during the Napoleonic wars the British navy had done the same to American ships carrying cargo to neutral ports, justifying the confiscation by stating the cargoes were ultimately destined for a French port. The British therefore could not repudiate their own established policy of "continued voyage."

Both sides depended on overseas trade, but the Northern ports remained virtually unmolested during the war. During the first 15

*"John Bull makes a Discovery,"
cartoon showing the British dilemma to choose between cotton
and the strong anti-slavery feeling in the country.*

months, the United States government purchased about 30,000 rifles
from American manufacturers and more than 700,000 from Europe.
The attitude of European governments and Europe's populace was of
vital importance for both North and South. The latter tried desperately
to win diplomatic recognition in London and Paris, and whenever it
scored military successes, this possibility became a real danger for the
North and a constant worry for the able U. S. ambassador in London,
Charles Francis Adams. The South possessed a mighty weapon, cotton, on which a great part of the British textile industry depended,
and, during the first year of the war, Richmond purposely withheld
cotton, trying thereby to compel the British to recognize the Confederate states. This policy was dropped, however, because it hurt the sup-
plier more than the customer. In Britain, the ruling aristocracy and the
large manufacturers usually sympathized with the South. Also, most
people in England were convinced that the North could never conquer
so large an area and the nine million people in the South; after all, if
their superior armies could not control the 13 states during the War of
Independence, why should the Yankees be able to do better? But in
the eyes of the English middle and lower classes the Union represented democracy, equal rights and the dignity of labor, while the
South seemed to stand for aristocracy, privilege and slavery. The
strong British antislavery faction, represented by Richard Cobden, W.
E. Forster and John Bright, hailed the American North as the "beacon
of freedom" for the working class. On the other hand, the Confederacy had some effective propagandists working in England; in particular Henry Hotze, a Swiss who had settled in Alabama, was sent to Europe in 1861 on a purchasing mission and for three years edited the
London *Index*.

In the London government, Chancellor of the Exchequer William E.
Gladstone, and, for a while also Foreign Minister Lord Russell were

inclined to intervene for the South and break the blockade to help the textile industry. But Prime Minister Lord Palmerston was a realist and wanted no conflict with the Union. In the proclamation of the blockade, Lincoln had called the rebels "insurrectionists," and Seward was enraged when, as a result, Britain and most other European states recognized the Confederacy as a "belligerent" thereafter. In September of 1861, when Seward learned that Russell had met with some Southern commissioners, he sent a blistering dispatch to Adams in London, threatening to break off relations if Britain officially recognized the Confederacy. But Adams smoothed things over, and there was no denying that the North's own blockade declaration had amounted to a virtual recognition of the South as a belligerent. Yet beyond that, Britain continued to interpret its own Foreign Enlistment Act very narrowly, which disallowed the construction and arming of warships for a belligerent. With the help of Southern agent James D. Bulloch, ships for the Confederacy were built in Liverpool and sent to the Bahamas without arms, which then arrived in another vessel. In this way, the C.S.S. *Florida* was launched and managed to destroy 38 Union merchant ships before being captured by Union boats in a Brazilian port in October 1864.

The C.S.S. *Alabama*, commanded by the most renowned commerce raider, Raphael Semmes, was even more successful. Although the U. S. consul at Liverpool, Thomas H. Dudley, had brought evidence of the ship's purpose to the attention of the British authorities, Bulloch succeeded in smuggling the ship out of the harbor and equipping her with guns in the Azores. Semmes sailed from the Atlantic to the China Sea and captured or destroyed 64 merchant ships, as well as the Union gunboat *Hatteras*, which was sunk in a battle in the Gulf of Mexico. When the *Alabama* put into Cherbourg for repairs in June 1864, the U.S.S. *Kearsarge* at last caught up with her and sank her. By their raids, the *Florida* and the *Alabama* managed to divert many Union ships from the blockade and to raise insurance rates for Union vessels to incredible heights. They did not affect the outcome of the war but may have prolonged it, and they contributed largely to reducing the leading position the American merchant marine had occupied before the war.

An incident occurring in November 1861 proved to be even more dangerous to British–U.S. relations. Although Lord Russell had assured Ambassador Adams that he would not receive any Southern commissioners in the future, the Confederate government sent two emissaries, James Mason of Virginia and John Slidell of Louisiana to London and Paris. They reached Havana unmolested, but, after being transferred to the British steamship *Trent*, they were stopped by the U.S.S. *San Jacinto*, under Captain Charles Wilkes, on the high seas, on November 8, 1861. This was a clear breach of international law, and while Wilkes was celebrated as a hero in the North, the British public and government were outraged. Palmerston sent an ultimatum to Washington asking for an apology and immediate release of the emissaries. He even sent troops to Canada, added ships to the British Atlantic fleet and put an embargo on all shipments to the United States. War seemed imminent. Lincoln's reaction to the critical situation was "One war at a time," and Seward hinted to the British that Wilkes had acted without instructions. Mason and Slidell were then released and continued their trip to London and Paris. Public opinion in England changed radically in favor of the Union, and the emissaries never succeeded in achieving the foreign intervention that seemed so close at hand during their detention.

The chances for British intervention diminished further after the Union successes at Gettysburg and Vicksburg in the summer of 1863. But another crisis arose during the same year when the ambitious Southern agent Bulloch had two large ironclads, which were expected to do great damage to the blockaders and even to steam into New York harbor, built by a British firm. Again, the guns were withheld to circumvent British laws, but Ambassador Adams bombarded Russell and Palmerston with strongly worded protests. The British decided to detain the ships, apparently before the protests had reached Palmerston, but because of his steadfast attitude, Adams became a hero at home anyway. After this defeat, Bulloch turned his attention to France.

Even the British aristocrats who had leaned toward the South were less inclined to come out for the Confederacy after Lincoln's Emancipation Proclamation had been put into effect, because of the overwhelming opposition to slavery in the country. When the situation began to look desperate for the South, Duncan Kenner, one of the largest Southern slaveholders, finally persuaded Jefferson Davis to take the ultimate step: He went to London and Paris as the president's special envoy and offered emancipation for recognition. But Louis Napoleon would not act without London, and by the time the proposition was presented to Palmerston in March of 1865, the British government refused to side with an obvious loser. Confederate Secretary of State Benjamin was advised that in British opinion, the Southern states had never achieved actual independence, and that through Sherman's march and other Northern successes, the existing objections had increased rather than diminished.

The French public had less interest in the American conflict than the British, but Louis Napoleon had been toying with recognizing the Confederacy ever since he began his Mexican adventure: A French

Maximilian, Austrian archduke, installed as Emperor of Mexico, and his wife Carlotta.

army had invaded Mexico and captured Mexico City in June of 1863, overthrowing the republican government of Benito Juarez, with whom the U. S. government entertained friendly relations. This act was called an "unfriendly act" by the U. S. Congress, but though Napoleon set out to make Hapsburg Archduke Maximilian the Emperor of Mexico under French suzerainty, Lincoln chose to ignore this violation of the Monroe Doctrine and followed a cautious, if not timid, policy. The result proved him right, for the British withdrew their initial support of Napoleon at an early stage, when the extent of Napoleon's ambitions became visible. Also, when U. S. troops occupied Brownsville, Texas, near the Mexican border, Napoleon took the hint and, in 1864, withdrew his support of Maximilian. He wanted a conflict with the United States no more than Lincoln wanted an additional conflict with France. Without French help, Maximilian's regime soon collapsed, he was taken prisoner and shot on Juarez's orders.

CHRONICLE OF EVENTS

1825:

The now independent South American states invite the United States to a congress at Panama to discuss matters of common interest. President John Quincy Adams accepts, but Congress refuses to send delegates out of fear the plan would endanger the Southern slave states.

1861:

March 18: On Seward's suggestion, Lincoln appoints Charles Francis Adams of the famous Massachusetts family as minister to Britain.

April 1: Seward proposes that the government demand "explanations" from Great Britain, France, Spain and Russia about alleged hemispheric interference and ask Congress to declare war on France and Spain if no satisfactory explanations were received—as this would reunite the nation. Lincoln declines, emphasizing that he, not Seward, is the policy maker.

May 6: Lord Russell announces in the British Parliament that the British government had decided to recognize the Confederate States as belligerents.

May 13: Queen Victoria declares Britain's intention to maintain a strict neutrality and to accord both sides rights as belligerents. Charles Francis Adams, U. S. minister to Britain arrives in London; his mission had been to try to prevent the recognition of the South as a belligerent.

May 21: President Lincoln instructs British Minister Charles Francis Adams to refrain from contacting the British government as long as it continues to talk to the domestic enemies of the Union.

June 17: Spain declares its neutrality, but recognizes the Confederacy as a belligerent.

October 12: The Confederate steamer *Theodora*, carrying emissaries John Slidell and James Mason, evades the blockade and takes them to Cuba. Their mission is to obtain recognition of the Confederacy in Britain and France and to purchase military supplies.

November 8: The U.S.S. *Jacinto* under Captain Charles Wilkes forces the British mail packet *Trent*, bound for Britain from Havana, Cuba, to turn over Southern emissaries James Mason of Virginia and John Slidell of Louisiana.

November 15: Southern emissaries Mason and Slidell arrive as prisoners on the *San Jacinto* in Fort Monroe, Virginia, and are sent to Fort Warren in Boston Harbor.

November 18: The Confederate raider *Nashville* captures and burns the Union clipper *Harvey Birch* in the Atlantic.

November 26: In Boston, a banquet is given in honor of Captain Wilkes of the *San Jacinto*.

November 30: British Foreign Secretary Lord John Russell demands that Southern commissioners Mason and Slidell be turned over to the British with an apology.

December 7: The U.S.S. *Santiago de Cuba* halts the British schooner *Eugenia Smith* near the mouth of the Rio Grande, seizing a Confederate purchasing agent.

December 19: Lord Lyons, British minister to the United States, demands from Secretary of State Seward the release of the two Southern commissioners.

December 23: Third meeting between Lord Lyons and Secretary of State Seward. Senator Sumner of Massachusetts urges the president to give in.

December 26: The U.S. Cabinet finally agrees that the seizure of the two Southern commissioners was illegal and orders their release.

1862:

May 15: At Liverpool, England, a vessel, which is to become a famous Confederate raider, the C.S.S. *Alabama*, is launched.

June 11: In a strongly worded letter, British Prime Minister Lord Palmerston protests the "infamous" measures taken by General Butler against the civilian population in New Orleans. The U. S. ambassador, Charles Francis Adams,

The battle between the CSS Alabama, *and the Union warship* Kearsarge, *June 1854.*

finally smoothes things over with Foreign Secretary Lord Russell.

July 16: Confederate Commissioner Slidell requests recognition of the Confederacy from Emperor Napoleon of France.

August 2: Secretary of State Seward instructs the U. S. minister to Britain not to receive or discuss any British offers of mediation on the civil conflict in the States.

October 30: Emperor Napoleon III of France proposes to Russia and Great Britain a joint mediation effort to end the American civil war.

1863:

February 25: The U.S.S. *Vanderbilt* seizes the British merchantman *Peterhoff* as a blockade runner, off St. Thomas in the West Indies. The British protest.

March 18: A Paris banking house opens a loan of three million pounds at 7% to the Confederacy.

May 18: In the House of Lords, Foreign Secretary Lord Russell declares that the British government has no desire to interfere in the American civil war.

May 22: The British and Foreign Anti-Slavery Society in London express strong support for the Union.

July 16: The U.S.S. *Wyoming,* in pursuit of the Confederate raider *Alabama,* gets into a battle with the Japanese navy at Yokohama and sinks several of its ships.

September 5: The completion of two ironclads known as the "Laird Rams" for the Confederacy is detained by British Foreign Secretary Lord Russell before Union Minister Charles Francis Adams can protest.

September 24: Ambrose Dudley Mann is appointed by the Confederate government as a special agent to the Holy See in Rome.

1864:

April 27: President Davis sends a special commissioner to Canada, apparently to obtain help or to try for a possible truce with the Union.

1871:

May–December: After long negotiations, the question of claims resulting from the actions of Confederate raiders such as the *Alabama,* which were built in Britain, is put before a special tribunal in Geneva, Switzerland.

1872

September: The tribunal awards $15,500,000 to the United States for the depredations caused by these ships.

EYEWITNESS TESTIMONY

The great democracy will come out of the present ordeal, even though civil war should be one of its stages, purified, regenerated and more powerful for the promotion of human freedom than ever.
Reynold's Weekly Newspaper, London, March 1861, as quoted in H. Hyman's Heard Round the World *(1969).*

You cannot be too decided or too explicit in making known to the French government that there is not now, nor has there been, nor will there be any—the least—idea existing in this government of suffering a dissolution of this Union to take place in any way whatever. There will be only one nation and one government, and there will be the same republic and the same Constitutional Union that have already survived a dozen national changes and changes of government in almost every other country.
Secretary of State Seward, instructions to William L. Dayton, Minister to France, May 1861.

I hope that New England and her Mayflower pride may be a little taken down by the actions of her English cousins . . . They evidently do not feel any great sympathy with their American relatives—at least their Northern ones. Perhaps they at present feel more for their South Carolina ones, who would be glad, according to Mr. Russell of the *Times* to have an English prince to reign over them; but that we cannot permit.
Maria L. Daly, June 12, 1861, Diary of a Union Lady (1962).

Without doubt the cause represented by the northern states is the most in conformity to the principles and to the interest of France. French policy is incompatible with the pretensions of the Southern states, pushing their pro-slavery theories to the most barbarous consequences . . . From the double point of view of humanity and French interest we ought to hope that the policy of the North prevails and that the Union be maintained.
Revue des Deux Mondes, Paris, June 1861, as quoted in H. Hyman's Heard Round the World.

It is one thing to drive the rebels from the South bank of the Potomac, or even to occupy Richmond, but another to reduce and hold in permanent subjec-

tion a tract of country nearly as large as Russia in Europe . . . Just as England during the revolution had to give up conquering the colonies so the North will have to give up conquering the South.
London Times, July 18, 1861.

. . . the papers only contain great extracts from Southern and European papers, which are very annoying to Northern readers and show what a pitiful mistake the battle of Bull Run was. We have lost our prestige. The Grand Army of the United States is not the imposing body it was imagined.
Maria L. Daly, September 2, 1861, Diary.

. . . there is no doubt of the friendly feeling of the Prussian Government towards the Government of the United States, and its desire that the rebellion should be subdued, as in every allusion to the pretended seceded States Count Bernstorff [the minister of Foreign Affairs] spoke of them as "rebels", "rebellious province" and "subduing the rebellion", in no instance designating them as a Government.
Dr. Norman Judd, head of the Berlin delegation, in a report to Seward, December 14, 1861, as quoted in H. Hyman's Heard Round the World.

I am so convinced that unless we give our good friends here a good lesson this time, we shall have the same trouble with them again soon . . . Surrender or war will have a very good effect on them.
Lord Lyons, British Minister to the United States, in a letter to Foreign Minister Lord Russell on December 21, 1861, referring to the San Jacinto–Trent affair.

General [Winfield] Scott sent me a most gallant message and declared that he had returned fearing to be caught on the other side and unable to return in the event of a war with England.
Maria L. Daly, December 21, 1861, referring to the Mason–Slidell incident, Diary.

Mason and Slidell are to be given up. It seems the law of the United States, if not their own law, is on the side of the English. Seward . . . obliged us to thus set two traitors to the government at large in order to prevent a great point for which we have been so long contending from being endangered, namely, the inviolability of neutral vessels . . . I am glad war with England is at least put off for a season.
Maria L. Daly, December 31, 1861, Diary.

I will venture to say that the course of events in America during the next six weeks must in great measure determine the future of the Government of the United States. For it is they and they only which can control the manner in which foreign nations will make up their minds hereafter to consider them. And in this sense the absence of action will be almost equally decisive.

Charles Francis Adams, minister to Britain, letter from London to Secretary Seward, January 24, 1862.

Opinion on the Anglo-American Conflict is almost unanimous . . . It is desired that war not break out, and our industrialists foresee that, even in case the blockade of Southern ports should be ended, cotton would still run too many risks of capture for it to reach our markets under acceptable conditions. At no price would one want to make common cause with England to destroy a navy that could someday be her rival, for us an auxiliary.

Procurator in Douai, northern France, in a report to Paris, early 1862, at the time of the Trent *conflict, quoted in H. Hyman's* Heard Round the World.

Whereas we had available for immediate purposes one hundred and forty-nine first-class warships, we have now two, these two being the *Warrior* and her sister *Ironside* [experimental ironclads]. There is not a ship in the English navy apart from these two that it would not be madness to trust to an engagement with that little *Monitor.*

London Times, *March 1862.*

I cannot refrain from taking the liberty of saying to you that it is difficult if not impossible to express adequately the disgust which must be excited in the mind of every honorable man by the general order of General Butler . . . Even when a town is taken by assault it is the practice of the commander of the conquering army to protect to his utmost the inhabitants and especially the female part of them, and I will venture to say that no example can be found in the history of civilized nations, till the publication of this order, of a general guilty in cold blood of so infamous an act as deliberately to hand over the female inhabitants of a conquered city to the unbridled license of an unsoldiery. If the Federal government chooses to be served by men capable of such revolting outrages, they must submit to abide by the

deserved opinion which mankind will form of their conduct.

British Prime Minister Lord Palmerston to U.S. Minister to Britain Charles Francis Adams, June 11, 1862, on General Butler's regime in New Orleans.

Father O'Reilly . . . had been much grieved at the want of sympathy shown in Ireland for the North, and says that although England publicly disclaimed all interest in the South, that still she secretly aids it, that vessels for the Confederates are fitting out in several ports . . . In . . . one of the Cunard line of steamers, one of the officers came up to him, thinking him an Englishman, and . . . said: "Well, now, we will agree that it is not sympathy with either side that moves us, but you know we shall all feel glad to see the Yankee nation go to pieces . . ."

Maria L. Daly, June 19, 1862, Diary.

The American struggle continues and . . . the industrial crisis of which the conflict is . . . the sole cause, is aggravated to the point that one can fear, within a short time, a general stoppage of business . . . The big industrialists and, after them, almost the entire mass of the population, would like to see us intervene in the American conflict; they share the thought that the Union is becoming more and more impossible . . . At Le Havre as at Rouen, all sympathies are for the cause of the South.

Procurator's report to Paris, July 10, 1862, as quoted in H. Hyman's Heard Round the World.

We English have to open our eyes to the fact that the war in America has resolved itself into a war between freedom and slavery . . . There is no "medium" course. Slavery or freedom must prevail . . . Providence declares, as plainly as the handwriting on the wall; "Choose you this day which you will serve."

Anonymous letter to the editor of the London Gazette, *after Lincoln's preliminary proclamation of emancipation, September 23, 1862.*

Mr. Lincoln will, on the 1st of next January, do his best to excite a servile war in the states which he cannot occupy with his armies . . . He will appeal to the black blood of the Africans. He will whisper of the pleasures of spoil and of the gratification of yet fiercer instincts; and when the blood begins to flow and when shrieks come piercing through the

darkness, Mr. Lincoln will wait amid the rising flames, till all is consummated, and then he will rub his hands and think that revenge is sweet . . . Sudden and forcible emancipation resulting from the "efforts the Negroes may make for their actual freedom" can only be effected by massacre and utter destruction.
London Times, *October 7, 1862.*

Where he has no power Mr. Lincoln will set the negroes free; where he retains power he will consider them as slaves. This is more like a Chinaman beating his two swords together to frighten his enemy than like an earnest man pressing forward his cause.
London Times, *October 7, 1862.*

We may have our own opinions about slavery; we may be for or against it; but there is no doubt that Jefferson Davis and other leaders of the South have made an army; they are making, it appears, a navy; and they have made what is more than either—they have made a nation.
William E. Gladstone, liberal English states-man, at Newcastle, England, in October 1862.

Privilege thinks it has a great interest in this con-test, and every morning, with blatant voice, it comes into our streets and curses the American Republic. Privilege . . . has beheld thirty millions of men, happy and prosperous, without emperor, without king, without the surroundings of a court, without nobles except such as are made by eminence, in intellect and virtue . . . without great armies and great navies, without great debt and without great taxes.
John Bright, British statesman and supporter of Gladstone, in the British Parliament, March 26, 1863, as quoted in H. Hyman's Heard Round the World.

. . . the Government of the Federal States has fallen into the hands of the smallest, weakest and meanest set of men who ever presided over the policy of a great nation at the critical epoch of its affairs.
The Economist, *London, April 25, 1863, quoted in H. Hyman's* Heard Round the World.

"At the dinner given by the Viceroy of Egypt . . ." Mr. Thayer [U. S. consul-general at Alexandria] con-tinued, "his [Napoleon III] conversation with me was principally upon America. He thinks President Lin-coln a sagacious and moderate man, and doubts if any man in his position would have done better. The two great men of the government are Messrs. Seward and Chase, and he thinks this is the sentiment of the American people . . . As for Beauregard, he regards him as very pompous, a man of more show than performance. Lee is capable but ambitious. Jackson pleased him greatly in some respects as a brave, disinterested man. He was the only one of the rebel leaders who seemed to regret the rebellion or retain his patriotism in any degree. Some of his remarks, considering his position, were decidedly patriotic."
Maria L. Daly, November 12, 1863, Diary.

Nay . . . better for the cotton trade of this country to perish, and to perish forever, than that its future prosperity should be restored with slavery as its basis and foundation.
G. L. Ashworth, head of the Manchester Union and Emancipation Society, friend of John Bright, in the Rochdale Spectator, *April 2, 1864.*

There is no longer any sort of disguise maintained as to the wishes of the privileged classes. Very little sympathy is entertained for the rebels. The true mo-tive is apparent enough. It is the fear of the spread of democratic feeling at home in the event of our success.
Charles Francis Adams, report to Secretary of State Seward from London, 1864, as quoted in H. Hyman's Heard Round the World.

Mr. Lincoln, by a rare combination of qualities—patience, sagacity and honesty—by a still more rare sympathy . . . and by a moderation rarest of all, had attained such vast moral authority that he could make all the hundred wheels of the Constitution move in one direction without exciting any physical force. . . . That despotism . . . was exercized by a man whose brain was a very great one. We do not know in history . . . such an example of the growth of a ruler in wisdom as was exhibited by Mr. Lincoln.
The Economist, *London, April 29, 1865, quoted in H. Hyman's* Heard Round the World.

The truth is, we have absolutely no idea in England of the wealth of a population whose average means are probably over 100 pounds a year for every family in the land . . . we are yet quite unable to realise the condition of a people, the great masses of whose

labourers are all as comfortable as our best paid operatives in Manchester.
The Economist, *London, November 18, 1865.*

Nobody doubts any more that the Union is a power of the first class, a nation which it is very dangerous to offend and almost impossible to attack.
The Spectator, *London, February 17, 1866, quoted in H. Hyman's* Heard Round the World.

The American Revolution marches fast towards its goal—the change of a Federal Commonwealth into a Democratic Republic, one and indivisible. Congress, which only five years ago was little more powerful than a debating club, . . . has suddenly become the Sovereign power, begins even to be conscious that it is Sovereign.
The Spectator, *London, December 22, 1866, quoted in H. Hyman's* Heard Round the World.

The United States are generally the vile corpus out of which by dint of many an experiment, essay, and strange vagary, the good comes by which we tardily profit. The American loves to dabble in those subjects which are somewhat vaguely known as "Social Science", and we believe that in one state or another of the Union . . . education, criminology, legal reforms, sanitary reforms, and so on, have been further sifted than at home.
Law Magazine and Law Review, *London, 1868, quoted in Harold Hyman's* Heard Round the World.

While it rancours in the minds of both nations . . . there can be no real peace between the two countries. And till there is, the vast monetary transactions which are natural between two such countries . . . will be throughout hampered and in part suspended.
The Economist, *London, May 25, 1872, referring to the unsettled* Alabama disputes.

7. The West Up to the Battle of Chattanooga: November 1863

THE HISTORICAL CONTEXT

After the battle of Shiloh, Grant, the hero of Fort Donelson, suddenly found himself in the role of the scapegoat. Northern papers accused him of having been surprised by Beauregard and even of having been drunk at the battle, none of which was true. Halleck assumed supreme command of the Union forces in the West and assembled around himself an army of more than 100,000 men, including almost all the prominent commanders of the North: Grant, Sherman, Buell, Pope, Sheridan, Rosecrans and others.

But Beauregard, who had proclaimed Shiloh as a great Southern triumph, was also having troubles when it became clear that, in the long run, Shiloh had returned the initiative in the Mississippi Valley to the North. Beauregard considered Corinth, Mississippi, a vital strategic point, but with reserves being brought in from eastern Tennessee and Arkansas, he was unable to hold the disease-ridden town. The Union now controlled the railroad to Memphis. Jefferson Davis replaced Beauregard with Braxton Bragg. Memphis, the South's fifth largest city, was now wide open to attack, but before the overcautious Halleck could move close, her fate had been decided on the Mississippi River. Fort Pillow, 50 miles above Memphis, which harbored a small but aggressive Confederate fleet, was attacked by a superior Union navy unit that included five ironclads and four "rams." Thousands of Memphis residents watched the battle from the bluffs. The Southern fleet was destroyed, Memphis occupied and converted into a Union base. As in the days of the galleys, ramming had once again become an important element of naval warfare. It had been discontinued with the advent of gunpowder and sailboats, which were difficult to maneuver into ramming positions. Now, in the age of steam propulsion, the idea had been revived and sold to Secretary of War Stanton by Charles Ellet, a civil engineer from Pennsylvania, who, ironically was the only Union casualty in this battle.

The Mississippi Valley was now under Union control all the way from the North to below Memphis and all the way from the South up to Baton Rouge, Louisiana, and Natchez, Mississippi—both of which had surrendered to Admiral Farragut's fleet coming up the river from New Orleans. But the long stretch of the river in the state of Mississippi remained under Southern control, and Farragut's attempt to crush the strong Vicksburg defenses at the end of June 1862, proved futile, particularly after the defense of the fortress had been taken over by Earl Van Dorn and when the newly completed Southern ironclad *Arkansas* joined the battle. An attempt to divert the river by digging a canal also failed, and by the end of July 1862, Farragut retreated south, fearing that the low water of the river would ground his fleet. Van Dorn then tried to retake Baton Rouge, but the *Arkansas*'s engines failed, and the ship was blown up by her crew to forestall her capture. In spite of all the Union's recent successes, the South continued to command 200 miles of the Mississippi Valley.

After occupying Corinth, Halleck had divided his huge army and sent Buell with about 40,000 men against Chattanooga. For quite some time, Lincoln had aimed to control eastern Tennessee. But the conservative Buell moved much more slowly than was to the president's liking, and his advance was further handicapped: first, by the daring cavalry raids of Nathan Bedford Forrest, who took Murfreesboro by surprise, captured its garrison and destroyed its railroad line; and shortly thereafter by John Hunt Morgan's raiders, who in the middle of August managed to block the railroad line north of Nashville, cutting off Buell's supplies coming in from Louisville. The North had no comparable cavalry forces in 1862 and was operating in hostile country where access to railroad lines was extremely precarious. Buell was unwilling to let his armies live off the country, and, as a result, his army of 40,000 men was immobilized by the 2,500 men under Forrest and Morgan.

Bragg in Mississippi had, meanwhile, also split his forces and moved toward Chattanooga from where he planned to invade Kentucky. He moved his troops by rail in a roundabout route via Mobile, Alabama and Atlanta, Georgia, in a 776-mile trip—the largest Confederate railroad transaction of the entire war. Edmund Kirby Smith's East Tennessee army, ordered to cooperate with Bragg, moved quickly from Knoxville to Richmond, Kentucky, bypassing the Cumberland Gap recently occupied by Union forces. On August 30, Smith's army defeated the inexperienced Union troops commanded by General William Nelson.

Nathan Bedford Forrest, Confederate cavalry leader.

Both he and Bragg then crossed over into Kentucky. Smith occupied Lexington; Bragg operated about 100 miles farther west. The population of Cincinnati, Ohio, less than 75 miles away, hastily began preparing for the defense of the state of Ohio. Smith even prepared for the inauguration of a Confederate governor in Frankfurt, Kentucky. Buell was forced to interrupt his drive to Chattanooga and to go after Bragg, and the Union forces had to abandon the Cumberland Gap.

But the Confederate drive had reached its zenith. Bragg and Smith never managed to join their units and, separately, were too weak to face Buell. The great uprising of the population in favor of the Confederacy on which the invaders had built their hopes was not forthcoming. Only in Lexington had the Confederate troops received an enthusiastic welcome; the rest of the state remained cool. Smith and Bragg had to spread their troops over a wide area while Buell's army was growing steadily, and, after much urging by Halleck, approaching. A major battle developed at Perryville, in the center of Kentucky, on October 8. Bragg attacked what he believed to be a small part of Buell's army, and the divisions of his General Leonidas Polk routed an inexperienced Union division easily. But then Union cavalry under the up and coming Philip Henry Sheridan routed another Southern division in the streets of Perryville.

Buell was never aware that one part of his army was engaged in battle, but when Bragg realized he was facing an army more than twice the size of his own, he retreated before Buell could muster up his full force. Bragg finally, too late, linked up with Kirby Smith's troops but decided to give up the Kentucky campaign and retreated through the Cumberland Gap and Knoxville to Chattanooga. Buell followed slowly, but, in spite of Halleck's urging to attack the retreating enemy, he set out to reestablish his headquarters in Nashville. This was too much for Lincoln, who replaced him with General William S. Rosecrans, whose action at Corinth just a few days earlier had recommended him to Lincoln. There, in a Confederate offensive coordinated with Bragg's campaign, Van Dorn and Sterling Price had attempted to retake the small but important railroad junction town, but after a sharp battle with high casualities on both sides, they had been repulsed by Rosecrans. This turned out to be the last Southern offensive in the West. Grant, the supreme Union commander of the Western area, was not entirely satisfied with Rosecrans's performance; in Grant's opinion, Rosecrans had let the enemy escape. But he could now concentrate on his campaign against the strongest Confederate fortress, Vicksburg.

Recent setbacks in the West had caused President Davis to reshuffle his generals. Joseph E. Johnston, who had recovered from the wounds received at Seven Pines, was made "plenary commander" of the West, covering the territory between the Appalachians and the Mississippi. Under him was Bragg, who had continuous disagreements with his corps commanders, and also the newly appointed commander at Vicksburg, John C. Pemberton, a native of Philadelphia, who was distrusted by the Mississippians he was assigned to defend. Beauregard took Pemberton's place in Charleston. But dissension among the Confederate generals persisted, and Davis's inspection tour of the Western theaters in December 1862 made matters worse. When he took troops from Bragg's army to reinforce Vicksburg, Johnston protested. Johnston also disapproved of Pemberton's defense arrangements and demanded reinforcement from Arkansas. When the Arkansas commander did not cooperate, Johnston threatened to resign. He was persuaded to stay, but the rift between him and Davis was never healed.

Meanwhile, Grant had moved southward from Corinth in the direction of Vicksburg, reaching Oxford, Mississippi by early December, but he ran into many difficulties. Southern cavalry units under Forrest and Van Dorn destroyed his depots and tore up railroad lines. Besides, Lincoln had authorized an independent Union army to be under the command of John Alexander McClernand, an old political ally of the president who knew little about military campaigns but was good at recruiting. He assembled several regiments in Memphis for an independent drive to Vicksburg. When Grant learned about this, he protested, and Halleck sided with him. McClernand's complaint about this "West Point conspiracy" was of no avail, and when he arrived at Memphis his troops had been taken over by Grant's subordinate Sherman; Grant explained this move by the emergency caused by Forrest's raids, and, in fact, these raids proved so effective that the planned two-pronged Grant–Sherman attack on Vicksburg had to be postponed. With communications cut, Sherman could not be informed of Grant's withdrawal, and when the former had worked his way up the Yazoo River and attacked Confederate installations on the bluffs overlooking Chickasaw Bayou, north of Vicksburg, his troops were thrown back with heavy losses.

Just a few days before Sherman's defeat, Rosecrans's army moved from Nashville to confront Bragg's army. Again, the Union army was plagued by Confederate cavalry raids under Forrest, Morgan and Joseph Wheeler, a 26-year-old West Pointer, born in Georgia. The battle of Murfreesboro (Stone's River) began on the last day of 1862, when Bragg's army started a surprise attack that hurled back the Union troops but then was held up by the stiff resistance of Sheridan's division in the center. Bragg ordered his subcommander John C. Breckinridge, former vice president of the United States, to attack the Yankee's position on the Round Forest. Although this very bloody assault did not succeed, Bragg was convinced he had won the day. Rosecrans, however, did not retreat but instead took a favorable position on a hill east of Stone River. On January 1, Breckinridge was again ordered to attack, over his protests, and within one hour lost 1,500 men to Union artillery. By January 3, Rosecrans was receiving reinforcements, and Bragg began to retreat to the South. The Union Army of the Cumberland had suffered almost one-third casualities and was unable to continue its advance for some months. Bragg was severely criticized by most of his commanders, but when President Davis consulted with Johnston, he was advised to retain him.

During the winter of 1862/63, Grant attempted several approaches toward Vicksburg. He tried once more to dig a canal below the fortress to stay out of the range of Vicksburg's guns, but to no avail. He tried a long, roundabout waterroute starting 50 miles above Vicksburg and leading back to the Mississippi 400 miles below in Louisiana. This and another attempt to sail down the Yazoo River failed because of the tre-

John C. Breckinridge, Confederate general and former U.S. vice president.

mendous obstacles nature put in the way of the fleet; when another flotilla commanded by Grant's Admiral David Dixon Porter personally attempted to cut through the bayou north of Vicksburg, his gunboats were immobilized by the jungle and threatened by approaching Confederate infantry so that he had to ask Sherman to come to his support and extricate his fleet.

Getting nowhere after months of struggle, Grant was once again severely criticized and accused of drunkenness. While he probably had a serious drinking problem, there is no evidence that he was ever drunk during critical operations, and it seems that he managed to stay sober practically all the time during the war. Yet, so much pressure was put on Lincoln that he asked Stanton to send a special agent to the West to investigate. The agent, Charles A. Dana, former managing editor of Horace Greeley's *New York Tribune,* received Grant's full cooperation and, in March 1863, submitted a highly favorable report on Grant to Lincoln, who had always stood by Grant—as did his men. The well-known story that Lincoln told a delegation of complaining Congressmen that he would like to know Grant's brand of whiskey so that he could send the same to his other generals may be just an anecdote, but it illustrates Lincoln's attitude and sense of humor perfectly.

By April 1863, Pemberton was convinced that Grant had given up on Vicksburg, "the Gibraltar of the West," and was ready to send some of his troops to help Bragg. But Grant had now worked out a strategy that would ultimately lead to success. He would march his army down the west bank of the Mississippi and rush his fleet past the Vicksburg batteries. The fleet would carry the army across the river, and Vicksburg could then be attacked from the southeast, on dry ground. Sherman and others opposed the risky plan: The gunboat fleet would be dangerously exposed. Even if it succeeded in breaking through, it would be without a safe base, as it could never move up against the current and the army would be operating in hostile territory without supply lines.

But Grant was right. During two dark nights in the middle of April, Admiral Porter managed to get most of his gunboats and transports past the fortress and make a landing at Hard Times, Mississippi. Admiral's Farragut's fleet, attacking from the south, and especially a cavalry raid under Colonel Benjamin Henry Grierson helped to prevent Pemberton from interfering with the crossing. Grierson's highly successful 800-mile ride from La Grange, Tennessee, to Baton Rouge, Louisiana, cut Pemberton's supply lines and lured Confederate cavalry away from the critical spot—a feat as remarkable as any performed by Forrest or Morgan, since it had to be executed in enemy territory. As a result, Grant could ask Sherman to join him, and, by the beginning of May, he had 40,000 troops across the river, opposed by Pemberton's 30,000.

Grant did not do the obvious—march straight north toward Vicksburg—for he feared an attack by Johnston who was trying to assemble another army at Jackson, Mississippi. So he marched straight east, letting his cut-off army live off the land. Units commanded by Sherman and James Birdseye McPherson drove the Confederates out of Jackson, and the town was thoroughly ransacked and then burnt by Sherman's corps. The two Confederate generals could not agree on the next step. Johnston wanted to join up with Pemberton in order to be strong enough to beat Grant, even at the risk of leaving Vicksburg undefended, while Pemberton insisted on holding the fortress. The decision, however, was made by the fast-moving Union troops. Midway between Jackson and Vicksburg, the Union army, under McPherson and McClernand, attacked Pemberton; and, in the fierce battle of Champion's Hill, the Confederates were thrown back to the Big Black River, 10 miles east of Vicksburg. Two days later, the demoralized

Confederates had to yield their strong positions along the Big Black and retreat into Vicksburg, completely exhausted. When Grant laid siege to Vicksburg, he had behind him a 17-day campaign in which he had beaten separate enemy forces five times.

In the first flush of victory, Grant ordered two all-out attacks on the fortress, but they were repulsed. Yet the fall of Vicksburg was only a question of time. Pemberton's desperate cries for reinforcements brought no relief. Not Bragg or Lee or any other Confederate general could spare any units. Only General Richard Taylor in Louisiana sent three brigades, but their attacks on the Union garrison at Milliken's Bend, north of Vicksburg, were frustrated by the spirited defense of green Union troops, mostly blacks, which helped to change the attitude toward blacks in the Union army considerably. The hopes of the besieged rested now entirely on Johnston who, however, considered his force too weak to attack the Union army. He urged Pemberton to try a breakout, but the Confederate troops were half starved and close to mutiny. The starving population sought shelter in caves as the town was bombarded. Pemberton had no choice but to ask for surrender terms, and Grant, deviating from his "unconditional surrender" policy offered to parole the 29,000 prisoners, in part probably because he did not want to tie up his transportation with moving these masses to prison camps.

Strategically, the fall of Vicksburg was probably the most important Union victory of the war, as it placed the whole Mississippi Valley under Northern control. The only remaining Southern strongpoint, Port Hudson in Louisiana, had been under siege by Union general Nathaniel P. Banks and had withstood several assaults, but when the news of Vicksburg's capture reached the fort, General Franklin surrendered as his position had become hopeless. The Confederacy was now cut in two halves, with Texas, Arkansas and most of Louisiana separated from the rest of the secession states. Johnston, in danger of being trapped by Sherman's forces, had to abandon Jackson.

Despite all the recent setbacks and his constant disagreements with Jefferson Davis, Johnston remained in his present position. But John McClernand, who had participated actively in the Vicksburg campaign, was sent home by Grant to await further orders. He had used the assaults on Vicksburg to seek glory for himself and his corps at the expense of the other commanders, supplying congratulatory orders to his men through the press without going through military channels. He saw little action thereafter.

After the Vicksburg debacle, Davis sent Kirby Smith to command the trans-Mississippi Department, which he turned into a virtually autono-

Confederate fortifications around Vicksburg.

mous region. Sterling Price was sent to Arkansas, but he could not prevent the capture of Little Rock in September 1863, which left three-quarters of the state under Union domination. In Tennessee, Rosecrans had hesitated for a long time, much to Lincoln's displeasure, before he maneuvered Bragg out of middle Tennessee, and then, after some more urging, moved on to cross the Tennessee River south of Chattanooga. Meanwhile, in the North, a Union army under Burnside found little resistance before occupying Knoxville, the heart of Union sympathy in Tennessee. A week later, Bragg abandoned the town of Chattanooga. In this critical hour, President Davis did everything possible to strengthen Bragg's threatened army. Units were detached from Johnston's army in Mississippi. Although Lee, at the Rappahannock, could not be persuaded to take over the command in Tennessee, Davis overruled him by sending two divisions under James Longstreet to the Chattanooga region. These divisions had to take a long detour through the Carolinas because Burnside's forces now occupied eastern Tennessee.

Bragg's augmented army now outnumbered Rosecrans's forces, and the battle of Chickamauga Creek, southwest of Chattanooga, became the bloodiest in the Western theater. Bragg's initial attack was held up by Union cavalry and Polk's slow advance. On the second day, however, Longstreet broke through the Union lines and rolled up Rosencrans's right flank. Only the poor coordination between Bragg and Longstreet and Union General George Thomas's tough stand at Snodgrass Hill prevented a total catastrophe. The whole Union army retreated hastily into Chattanooga. Both Longstreet and Forrest urged Bragg to overrun the city before Rosecrans could organize its defense, but Bragg was too appalled by his terrible losses and decided to lay siege to the town instead, a decision for which he was later much criticized.

Rosecrans, stunned and defeated, let the town be surrounded and his supply lines be cut so that his men had to be reduced to half rations.

George H. Thomas, Union general.

In Washington, Lincoln reluctantly approved Stanton's proposal to send two corps of the Army of the Potomac to help Rosecrans. No fewer than 20,000 men, fully equipped, were sent by rail into the Chattanooga region within 11 days—probably the greatest feat of logistics during the entire war. Lincoln then replaced Rosecrans with George Thomas and put Grant in overall command. One week after Grant's arrival at Chattanooga, a new supply route into the town was opened; and, by the middle of November, strong reinforcements under Sherman and Hooker had arrived.

Bragg's army occupied the strategic positions east and south of the town at Missionary Ridge and Lookout Mountain. But his situation had deteriorated, all the more as there was great dissension in his ranks. Longstreet and Forrest refused to continue serving under him, and a personal visit from Jefferson Davis did little to alleviate the tense atmosphere. Bragg kept his job, but Davis ordered him to send Longstreet to Knoxville where the Union army under Burnside was put under siege. This accomplished nothing, however, and Longstreet's troops were sorely needed when Grant began his all-out attack against

Bragg, on November 23. His plan was to attack both flanks of the Confederate army, keeping his center, under Thomas, relatively inactive. But while Hooker succeeded in overrunning Lookout Mountain in the south with relatively few casualties, Sherman on the left got no further than the northernmost end of Missionary Ridge, all additional advances being repulsed by the "Stonewall of the West," Patrick Cleburne's division. Grant now changed his plans and ordered Thomas to attack Missionary Ridge in a frontal assault, a task that seemed impossible to accomplish. But Thomas's four divisions, anxious to redeem their reputation after the Chickamauga defeat, swept up the high and rugged ridge in a tremendous drive continuing without orders, overrunning line after line of the defenders and reaching the top. The Confederate lines broke and—a rare occurrence—panicked. Only the oncoming darkness and the stubborn rearguard resistance of Cleburne's troops prevented a complete disaster, but the defeated army could regroup only after retreating 30 miles to the southeast, in the direction of Atlanta, Georgia.

Various explanations have been given for the overwhelming success of the Union forces in this battle. The Southern troops were possibly discouraged by being exposed to the sight of the greatly superior Yankee forces spread out in front of their eyes for days. Some contradictory orders had also weakened Southern resistance. And Bragg was probably right when he declared that the fight among the Confederate generals had also demoralized the troops.

A few days after the battle of Chattanooga, Longstreet's attack on Union-held Knoxville was also repulsed. This left Georgia wide open for a Yankee invasion.

CHRONICLE OF EVENTS

1862:

April 11: Huntsville, Alabama, is taken over by the Federals. General Halleck assumes the active field command at Pittsburgh Landing, relegating Grant to second spot.

April 12: The great locomotive chase: Union volunteers, trying to break the vital rail line to Chattanooga, detach a locomotive and three freight cars and head North, but are finally caught by Southern pursuers.

April 14: Fort Pillow, Tennessee, on the Mississippi, is bombarded by U. S. mortar boats.

May 10: A poorly equipped Confederate defense fleet attacks a strong ironclad Federal flotilla north of Fort Pillow on the Mississippi, sinking two ironclads. Confederate Commander Montgomery finally has to withdraw to the fort, then to Memphis. Norfolk and Portsmouth in Virginia, as well as Pensacola in Florida are occupied by Union troops.

May 12: Farragut's flotilla occupies Natchez, Mississippi.

May 30: At Corinth, Mississippi, Halleck's Federal troops take 2,000 prisoners after Beauregard withdraws most of his troops.

June 3: Fort Pillow, Tennessee, rendered defenseless after the fall of Corinth and the cutting of the Memphis and Charleston railroad, is given up by the Confederates.

June 5: Federal gunboats push rapidly down the Mississippi toward Memphis.

June 6: Battle of Memphis, Tennessee: A Federal fleet of five ironclads and four rams attacks eight inferior Confederate vessels. A crowd lines the bluffs of the Mississippi watching the fierce battle. Only one Southern gunboat escapes. The mayor then surrenders the city. The river is now open to the Federals except in the state of Mississippi.

June 7: Federal troops under Major General Ormsby Mitchel shell and attack Chattanooga, but are repulsed. Jackson, Tennessee is taken by Federal troops.

June 17: General John Charles Frémont resigns when ordered to serve under Major General Pope. General Braxton Bragg takes over command of the Western Confederate army from Beauregard.

June 20: A Federal expedition of 3,000 men is under way from Baton Rouge, Louisiana by boat, coming up the Mississippi River and trying to establish a base opposite Vicksburg on the west side of the river.

June 27: At Vicksburg, mortar bombardment from the South begins, and Federal troops attempt to dig a canal to cut off a bend of the Mississippi.

June 28: Farragut's fleet steaming north forces a passage past the powerful Confederate land batteries at Vicksburg.

July 9: Confederate cavalry defeats a Federal unit and occupies Tompkinsville, Kentucky.

July 12: Confederate cavalry under John Hunt Morgan captures Lebanon, Kentucky.

July 13: Confederates under Nathan Bedford Forrest capture Murfreesboro, southeast of Union-held Nashville, Tennessee.

Confederate raiding under Morgan around Cynthiana, Kentucky.

July 15: The newly completed Confederate ironclad *Arkansas* is attacked by Farragut's fleet near Vicksburg, but only slightly damaged.

July 17: Major General Grant takes over command of all forces of the Armies of the Tennessee and the Mississippi.

July 18: Confederate units cross the Ohio River and raid Newburg, Indiana.

July 23: Confederate General Bragg begins to move 31,000 troops from Tupelo, Mississippi via Mobile and Montgomery, Alabama, to Chattanooga, Tennessee by railroad. Tupelo is threatened by General Buell's forces approaching it from the west. Bragg and General Edmund Kirby Smith plan to attack Buell's forces from behind.

August 5: A Confederate force of 2,600 under Major General John C. Breckinridge attacks a Federal unit of 2,500 under Brigadier General Thomas Williams at Baton Rouge, Louisiana.

The Federals counterattack successfully with the aid of gunboats in the Mississippi. Williams is killed. The Confederate ram *Arkansas* arrives too late.

August 6: The Federal ironclad *Essex* and four other vessels attack the *Arkansas* at Baton Rouge. Her engines fail, she is set afire and abandoned. Skirmishes at Malvern Hill and Thornburg, Virginia.

August 11: In a daring raid, Confederate guerrillas capture Independence, Missouri.

August 12: John Hunt Morgan captures Gallatin, Tennessee. Several Confederate vessels are captured or burned near Arkansas Pass and Corpus Christi, Texas.

August 17: Sioux Indians in southwestern Minnesota revolt.

August 19: Union troops conduct extensive raids on the Louisiana and Nashville Railroad.

August 25: Minor fighting along the entire front in Missouri, Louisiana, Kentucky, Mississippi, Alabama, Tennessee and Virginia.

August 30: Confederate General Kirby Smith invades Kentucky and defeats 6,500 Federal troops under General William Nelson at Richmond, Kentucky. Confederates are enthusiastically received in Lexington, Kentucky, but generally Kentuckians side with the Union. The city of Cincinnati, Ohio, is alarmed and prepares a defense but no Confederate troops invade Ohio.

August 31: The Federal transport ship *W. B. Terry* is grounded on the Tennessee River at Duck River Sucks and then forced to surrender to the Confederates.

September 2: In Cincinnati, Ohio, as well as Covington and Newport, Kentucky, citizens learn that Confederate troops are near and hastily start military training. Martial law is declared.

September 5–10: Union expedition from Fort Donelson, Tennessee to Clarksville. General Buell withdraws his Union troops from northern Alabama to Murfreesboro, Tennessee.

September 6: John Pope is assigned to fight the Sioux uprising in the Northwest.

September 7: Clarksville, Tennessee, is retaken by Federal units.

September 13: In western Virginia, the Federals evacuate Charleston.

September 17: In Munfordville, Kentucky, the garrison of 4,000 Union soldiers surrenders to Bragg's Confederates. The Confederate invasion of Kentucky forces Union Brigadier General George W. Morgan to evacuate Cumberland Gap.

September 19: In Mississippi, Federal troops under W. S. Rosecrans advance from Corinth and defeat Confederate troops under Sterling Price at Iuka.

September 25: A Federal army under Buell arrives at Louisville, Kentucky, ahead of Bragg's advancing Confederate troops.

September 27: In New Orleans, the first regiment of free blacks is mustered.

October 1: Major General John C. Pemberton takes over command of the Department of Mississippi and the defense of Vicksburg.

October 3: Battle of Corinth, Mississippi. Confederates under Van Dorn and Price attack Rosecrans's troops, which withdraw closer to Corinth.

October 4: After continued heavy fighting, the Confederates withdraw; they suffer 4,200 casualties out of about 22,000 troops, the Federals about 2,500 out of 23,000 troops.

October 5: Federal naval forces occupy Galveston, Texas, with no resistance. Bragg's Confederates retreat from Bardstown, Kentucky, pursued by Buell.

October 8: Battle of Perryville, or Chaplin Hills, Kentucky. Parts of Buell's Federal army attack units of Bragg's army. The Federals win a partial victory and Bragg withdraws, ending the Confederate invasion of Kentucky, after having suffered 3,400 casualties out of 16,000 troops engaged, compared with Federal losses of 4,200 out of about 37,000 troops.

October 14: The Democrats gain in congressional elections in Pennsylvania, Iowa, Ohio and Indiana.

October 18: Confederate raiders under John

Hunt Morgan defeat a Federal cavalry unit near Lexington, Kentucky, and enter the city, capturing the garrison.

October 19: Bragg's retiring Army of Tennessee arrives at Cumberland Gap, Kentucky.

October 20: Lincoln orders Major General John A. McClernand to prepare an expedition against Vicksburg, which interferes with Grant's command in this area.

October 23: Bragg's Confederate army passes from Kentucky into Tennessee through the Cumberland Gap.

October 24: Because of Bragg's escape, Buell is replaced by Rosecrans as Federal commander in Kentucky and Tennessee.

November 8: Major General Nathaniel P. Banks replaces Major General Ben Butler in the command of the Union Department of the Gulf and in New Orleans.

November 13: Federal units occupy the rail center at Holly Center, Mississippi.

November 24: General Joseph E. Johnston is made major commander of the Confederate troops in the West, which puts him above Bragg in Tennessee and Pemberton at Vicksburg.

December 3: In Mississippi, Grant presses Confederate units along the Yocknapatalfa River.

December 5: Lincoln orders the hanging of 39 Indians who participated in the Sioux uprising in Minnesota; originally, 303 Indians had been condemned to die.

December 7: Battle of Prairie Grove, Arkansas. Confederate troops under Major General Thomas C. Hindman attack Federal units under James Blunt and Francis Herron, but are repulsed as the two Federal groups manage to join just in time. Severe winter weather forces Hindman to withdraw, after suffering over 1,300 casualties. Federal losses are only slightly less.

December 10: The United States House of Representatives passes a bill creating the state of West Virginia.

December 12: On the Yazoo River, north of Vicksburg, the Federal ironclad *Cairo* strikes a mine and sinks.

December 18: Union cavalry at Lexington, Tennessee, is defeated by Confederates under Forrest. Grant's army is reorganized, putting John A. McClernand under his command.

December 20: Confederates under Earl Van Dorn capture Grant's huge supply depot at Holly Springs, Mississippi and take 1,500 prisoners. Grant is forced to withdraw from Oxford, Mississippi to La Grange, Tennessee.

December 26: General Sherman moves his forces down the Mississippi to the Yazoo River, and from there to the bluffs and hills protecting Vicksburg from the North. Rosecrans moves his Federal troops from Nashville, Tennessee toward Bragg's army at Murfreesboro, Tennessee.

December 29: Battle of Chickasaw Bayou, Mississippi. Sherman's advance toward Vicksburg

William Tecumseh Sherman, Union general.

is thrown back by a portion of Pemberton's Confederate troops. He loses almost 1,800 men compared with Confederate losses of 200.

December 31: Battle of Murfreesboro, or Stone's River, Tennessee. The Confederates under Bragg attack with their left flank, keeping the Federals under Rosecrans on the defensive. They are finally forced back against Stone's River, but hold their lines. While the Confederates suffer heavy losses, they gain the upper hand, with their cavalry under General Joseph Wheeler inflicting heavy damage to Federal wagons and supplies. Union losses amount to about 13,000 out of a total of 45,000 troops, Confederate losses to about 10,000.

1863:

January 1: Using troops and gunboats, Confederate General John B. Magruder attacks and captures the Union-held city of Galveston, Texas.

January 2: Continued indecisive fighting at Murfreesboro. During the following night, Bragg's army withdraws south.

January 4: Federal Major General A. McClernand begins an unauthorized move up the Arkansas River toward Fort Hindman.

January 5: Federal troops enter Murfreesboro; Rosecrans receives Lincoln's thanks for his achievements in Tennessee.

January 8: The Federal garrison of Springfield, Missouri repulses an attack of Confederates under John S. Marmaduke.

January 9: The Federal garrison at Hartville, Missouri surrenders to Brigadier General Marmaduke.

January 10: Federal forces under McClernand start to envelop the Confederate Fort Hindman, about 50 miles up the Arkansas River from its junction with the Mississippi.

January 11: After a heavy bombardment and attack by land forces and gunboats, Fort Hindman surrenders to McClernand's troops. Grant orders McClernand to return and join his Vicksburg forces. The highly successful Con-

federate raider *Alabama* sinks the U.S.S. *Hatteras* off Galveston, Texas.

January 15: Federal forces burn Mound City, Arkansas, a center of guerilla activities.

January 22: Grant assumes command of all Union troops in Arkansas, reducing McClernand to corps commander. Grant tries again to cut a canal opposite Vicksburg to enable him to move around the fortress city.

January 29: Federal ships bombard defenses at Galveston, Texas.

February 2: Union ram *Queen of the West* runs past the Vicksburg batteries without being seriously damaged and destroys Confederate supplies below Vicksburg.

February 4: Federal forces drive General Marmaduke's troops out of Batesville, Arkansas.

February 8: Publication of the *Chicago Times* is temporarily suspended because of alleged disloyal statements.

February 14: The Federal *Queen of the West* has steamed up the Red River and captures the Confederate *New Era No. 5.* Soon thereafter the *Queen of the West* runs aground and must be abandoned.

February 17: Having passed Vicksburg batteries, U.S.S. gunboat *Indianola* operates at the mouth of the Red River.

February 19: Skirmishes between Grant's reconnaissance units and Confederates north of Vicksburg; also at Leesburg, Virginia and near Rover, Tennessee.

February 20: In the Dakota Territory, there are fights between Federal troops and Indians.

Febuary 24: Off Vicksburg, the Federal gunboat *Indianola* is attacked by several Confederate vessels, including the captured and repaired *Queen of the West.* The *Indianola* finally surrenders.

February 26: Confederate guerillas capture and burn a Federal freight train near Woodburn, Tennessee.

March 2: An 18-day Federal expedition from New Orleans to the mouth of the Rio Grande begins.

March 7: Federal General Banks moves troops from New Orleans toward Port Hudson in support of Grant's Mississippi operations.

March 19: At Vicksburg, a fake ironclad made of logs drifts down the Mississippi and is fired upon.

March 10: Federal troops, mainly blacks, reoccupy Jacksonville, Florida.

March 11: A Federal force of troops and gunboats moves from Yazoo Pass off the Mississippi, but are stopped by the quickly constructed Confederate Fort Pemberton near Greenwood on the Yazoo. After six days of fighting, the Federals withdraw.

March 14: A Federal fleet under Admiral Farragut moves up the Mississippi past the Confederate batteries of Port Hudson, but several of his ships are badly damaged.

March 20: Two of Admiral Farragut's ships run past the Confederate batteries at Grand Gulf, just below Vicksburg.

March 22: At the beginning of a new campaign, a Confederate cavalry unit under Basil Duke, brother-in-law of Hunt Morgan, captures the Federal garrison at Mount Sterling, Kentucky.

March 23: Admiral Farragut's *Hartford* and *Albatross* attack Confederate batteries below Vicksburg.

March 24: After repeated skirmishes in Steele's Bayou north of Vicksburg, the Federal expedition gives up the plan to reach Vicksburg by inland waterways.

March 25: Two Federal rams attempt to run the Vicksburg batteries from north to south; one is sunk, the other one badly damaged.

March 26: In the newly created state of West Virginia, the voters approve gradual emancipation of slaves.

March 28: Battle between Confederate land troops and Union gunboats at Pattersonville, Louisiana.

March 29: Grant sends McClernand to march south on the west side of Mississippi to New Carthage, below Vicksburg. The attempt to dig another canal west of Vicksburg fails.

March 30: Skirmishes at Dutton's Hill, Ken-

tucky, Zoar Church, Virginia, Point Pleasant, West Virginia, Cross Hollow, Arkansas and other points.

March 31: Farragut moves his three gunboats past the Grand Gulf batteries.

April 10: Confederate forces under Earl Van Dorn attack Union units at Franklin, Tennessee but are repulsed in a counterattack.

April 14: Fort Bisland, Louisiana is evacuated by the Confederates after a heavy attack. The former Federal, now Confederate, gunboat *Queen of the West* is destroyed by Federal naval fire.

April 16: Twelve vessels under Federal Admiral David D. Porter, moving downstream, manage to pass the Confederate batteries concentrated on the Vicksburg bluffs, landing at Hard Times, on the west side of the Mississippi.

April 17: Beginning of a prolonged cavalry raid under Federal Colonel B. H. Grierson from La Grange, Tennessee, into Mississippi. Similarly, Confederate Brigadier General John S. Marmaduke starts a raid from Arkansas into Missouri.

April 20: Federal troops in Louisiana occupy Opelousas and Washington.

April 22: Another Federal flotilla attempts to pass the Vicksburg batteries; six of the 12 barges and one of the six transports are sunk.

April 30: Grant's forces have crossed the Mississippi south of Vicksburg.

May 1: South of Vicksburg, McClernand moves toward Port Gibson, which Major General John S. Bowen is forced to evacuate. Grant's bridgehead east of the river is now secured.

May 3: Grand Gulf on the Mississippi is evacuated by the Confederates as Grant's forces spread over the state of Mississippi.

May 5: On the Red River in Louisiana, a Federal flotilla occupies Alexandria. Confederate Major General Earl Van Dorn is assassinated, apparently for private reasons.

May 9: Grant's troops advance fighting skirmishes and approach Utica, Mississippi.

May 11: Federal cavalry raids the New Orleans and Jackson Railroad near Crystal Springs, Mississippi.

May 12: Battle of Raymond, Mississippi. Grant's forces are attacked by a Confederate brigade under Brigadier General John Gregg, about 15 miles south of Jackson. The outnumbered Confederates are repulsed, each side suffering about 500 casualties.

May 13: Grant moves two corps toward Jackson, while McClernand moves north to Clinton.

May 14: Grant's two corps overcome two Confederate brigades and occupy Jackson, the capital of Mississippi. McClernand's forces control the Jackson–Vicksburg rail line. From Alexandria, Louisiana, General Banks starts operations against Confederate Port Hudson.

May 16: Battle of Champion's Hill, Mississippi. Confederate General Pemberton tries to join up with J. E. Johnston's forces, but is blocked at Champion's Hill. In fierce fighting, the hill changes hands three times, and Pemberton finally withdraws toward Vickburg. Of the 29,000 Federals, about 2,400 are casualties; the Confederates, only about 20,000 men, suffer 3,850 casualties.

May 18: Grant's army crosses the Big Black River, takes Haynes' Bluff and begins the siege of Vicksburg.

May 19: First assaults on Vicksburg are repulsed.

May 21: The siege of the Confederates only other Mississippi fortress, Port Hudson, begins, with Banks's troops approaching from the west.

May 22: Grant risks an all-out attack on Vicksburg, but makes no progress, suffering more than 3,000 casualties.

May 26: Federal forces under General Banks set up siege operations around Port Hudson, Louisiana.

May 27: First assault on Port Hudson by about 13,000 Union troops, which include some black units. The attacks fail along the entire lines, with about 2,000 casualties. Sherman's attempt to take Confederate strong point Fort Hill on the Mississippi ends with his gunboat *Cincinnati* sunk.

May 31: President Davis complains to Lee that Johnston did not attack Grant in Mississippi promptly.

June 6: Skirmishes at Berryville, Virginia, near Richmond, Louisiana, on Shelbyville Pike, Tennessee and at Shawneetown, Kansas.

June 7: Confederates attack the Federal garrison at Milliken's Bend, Louisiana, but withdraw when two Federal gunboats join the battle.

June 18: At Vicksburg, Grant relieves Major General John A. McClernand, whom he considers insubordinate and self-seeking, of his command. He is replaced by Major General E. O. C. Ord.

June 22: Federal General Rosecrans moves from Murfreesboro towards Bragg's troops at Tullahoma, Tennessee, outflanking and forcing him to fall back behind the Tennessee River, thus preventing Confederate reinforcing Vicksburg. About 1,000 Federals surrender at Brashear City, Louisiana, after a Confederate attack.

July 1: The Missouri State Convention declares that slavery would cease as of July 4, 1870.

July 2: In Kentucky, the Cumberland River is crossed by 2,500 Confederate cavalry under John Hunt Morgan.

July 3: Pemberton and Grant confer about the surrender of Vicksburg. Morgan continues his cavalry foray into Kentucky.

July 4: Vicksburg formally surrenders to Grant's Federals. About 29,000 Confederates lay down their arms, after a seven-week siege. In Kentucky, Morgan's raiders take Lebanon and Bardstown after some skirmishing.

July 6: In Mississippi, Sherman is pressing toward Jackson to catch up with Joseph E. Johnston's army.

July 8: At Port Hudson, Louisiana, Confederate General Franklin Gardner unconditionally surrenders to General Banks—after Vicksburg's fall his position is hopeless. About 7,000 prisoners are taken.

The whole length of the Mississippi is now open to Union steamers. Morgan's raiders cross into Indiana.

July 13: Morgan crosses into Ohio. Martial law is declared in Cincinnati.

July 15: Morgan's raiders move east of Cincinnati toward the Ohio River. Joseph E. Johnston abandons Jackson, Mississippi, to Sherman.

July 17: At Elk Creek in Indian territory, Union General James G. Blunt attacks Confederate Brigadier General Douglas H. Cooper's troops and forces them to withdraw. In this engagement, Federal black soldiers were fighting Confederate Indians.

July 19: At Buffington Island on the Ohio, Morgan's raiders are almost annihilated by Federal troops; 700 prisoners are taken.

July 26: John Hunt Morgan and his remaining 364 exhausted men have been harassed by Federal troops and finally surrender at Salineville, Ohio. He and his main officers are sent to the Ohio State Penitentiary in Columbus. John J. Crittenden, originator of the Compromises of 1860 and 1861 named after him, dies in Frankfort, Kentucky.

August 10: Federal troops under General F. Steele move toward Little Rock, Arkansas.

August 12: Lincoln refuses to give a new command to General McClernand.

August 16: Rosecrans and the Army of the Cumberland start moving toward the Tennessee River and Chattanooga. Burnside, starting from Camp Nelson, Kentucky, also heads for the Tennessee River, which he reaches on August 20. This is the beginning of the Chickamauga Campaign.

August 18: In Trans-Mississippi Territory, Federal troops engage in a skirmish with Pueblo Indians, at Pueblo, Colorado.

August 21: Four hundred and fifty Confederate and Missouri guerillas under William C. Quantrill sack and burn Lawrence, Kansas, killing about 150 men and boys.

August 25: In retaliation for the Lawrence, Kansas, massacre of civilians perpetrated by Confederate terrorist Quantrill, Brigadier General Thomas Ewing forces people in four Missouri counties to leave their homes.

August 27: Skirmishes in Arkansas, Mississippi, Kentucky, West Virginia and Maryland.

August 29: Rosecrans moves below Chattanooga, flanking the city.

September 1: On the western border of Arkansas, Fort Smith falls to Union forces.

September 2: Union forces under A. E. Burnside enter Knoxville, Tennessee. The Alabama legislature approves the use of slaves in Confederate armies.

September 4: Grant is seriously hurt when his horse shies and falls on him.

September 6: Beauregard evacuates Battery Wagner and Battery Gregg after after a two months' siege and bombardment. Fort Sumter and Charleston still hold out.

September 8: Federal gunboats and transports move up into Sabine Pass on the Louisiana–Texas border, for a drive on Beaumont and Houston but are defeated and driven back by a small Confederate force under Lieutenant Dick Dowling.

September 9: Chattanooga, Tennessee, almost surrounded by Rosecrans's forces, is abandoned by Bragg who moves south into Georgia. Longstreet's corps is sent from northern Virginia to aid Bragg.

September 10: Confederates under Sterling Price evacuate Little Rock, Arkansas.

September 12: Skirmishing and reconnaissance activities continue on the long front south of Chattanooga.

September 16: Rosecrans concentrates his scattered Army of the Cumberland on Chickamauga Creek, Georgia, 12 miles south of Chattanooga, as both sides prepare for a major battle.

September 19: Battle of Chickamauga, first day. Heavy fighting on the north flank of the Federal army, with heavy losses but negligible results.

September 20: After further heavy fighting, Longstreet finds an opening in the Federal lines, attacks and divides them in two. Union troops retreat in disorder toward Chattanooga, only General George Henry Thomas's corps holds out around Snodgrass Hill. The Confederates win the battle, but suffer the greater losses, about 18,500 compared with 16,000 Federals.

September 22: Rosecrans's army occupies a strong position at Chattanooga, but needs reinforcements, which are being sent from Vicksburg.

September 23: In an extremely quick and efficient action, Stanton moves two corps of the Potomac Army to Alabama to support Rosecrans.

September 26: The Lincoln government is distressed to learn that the *New York Post* revealed the troop movements west to Rosecrans.

September 27: Lincoln again urges Burnside to send more help to Rosecrans.

September 30: Confederate cavalry under Major General Joseph Wheeler begins the raiding of communications of Rosecrans's army.

October 2: Rosecrans's army is besieged in Chattanooga, its food supplies dwindle.

October 3: Federal troops under Major General William B. Franklin move westward in another attempt to gain a foothold in Texas, but never reach the Sabine River that forms the border. Confederate General Bragg is criticized for his failure to exploit the victory at Chickamauga. Confederate cavalry raids near Readyville, Tennessee, also at Stockton and Greenfield, Missouri and at Green Well Springs Road, Louisiana.

October 11: Boonville, Missouri, is captured by Joseph Shelby's Confederates. Continued raids by Confederate troops in Alabama, Missouri and Mississippi.

October 13: Republican candidates for governor are successful in Indiana, Iowa and Ohio, where the exiled "copperhead" Vallandigham is beaten by War Democrat John Brough.

October 16: Grant is made commander of the combined department of the Ohio, Cumberland and Tennessee.

October 17: Rosecrans is relieved and George H. Thomas takes over the Army of the Cumberland, and at Chattanooga.

October 23: President Davis relieves General Leonidas Polk, corps commander of the Army of Tennessee. Grant arrives at Chattanooga and confers with General Thomas. A new supply line into Chattanooga is opened.

October 25: Confederates under John S. Marmaduke partially occupy Pine Bluff, Arkansas, but then must withdraw.

October 27: A pontoon bridge is thrown across the Tennessee River at Brown's Ferry, and Hooker's troops advance from the west. By opening this new "cracker line," Chattanooga is relieved.

October 28: Longstreet's Confederates attack Hooker's forces, but fail to interrupt the new supply line.

October 30: Skirmishes at Fourteen Mile Creek in Indian Territory, near Opelousa, Louisiana, at Ford's Mill, North Carolina, Catlett's Station, Virginia and Salyersville, Kentucky.

November 3: In the Bourbeau and Carrion Crow Bayous of Louisiana, Confederates drive back Federal troops who, however, regain their positions when reinforcements arrive. Federal losses are more then 600, while the Confederate casualties amount to only 181.

November 4: In an effort to retrieve the Knoxville area, Bragg sends Longstreet's corps from the Chattanooga area to east Tennessee against Burnside's troops.

November 6: Federal forces under Brigadier General William W. Averell attack Confederates blocking the road at Droop Mountain, West Virginia. The Confederates, attacked from the rear and the front, are forced to retreat. The Federals proceed to Lewisburg, West Virginia, cleaning out remnants of opposition in the area.

November 9: Major General John C. Breckinridge, former vice president and presidential candidate in 1860, supersedes Lieutenant General D. H. Hill as commander of Bragg's Second Corps.

November 12: Skirmishes at Cumberland Gap, Tennessee, Corinth, Mississippi, Roseville, Arkansas and other places.

November 15: In west Tennessee and north Mississippi, Federal authorities tighten prohibitions against trading with the enemy or war profiteers.

November 16: Longstreet's troops are approaching Knoxville, Tennessee, while Burnside withdraws to Knoxville. Federal units under Banks enter Corpus Christi, Texas.

November 17: Knoxville is practically under siege.

November 22: Bragg, unaware of Grant's imminent attack, detaches troops to reinforce Longstreet at Knoxville.

November 23: Grant's all-out attack on Bragg's Army of the Tennessee begins. Orchard Knob is taken. Sherman attacks the Confederate's right flank.

November 24: Further west, Hooker's three divisions attack and take Lookout Mountain, as the Confederates withdraw to Missionary Ridge further east.

November 25: Missionary Ridge is attacked by Sherman from the north, Hooker from the south and Thomas at the center. After heavy fighting, the Confederate lines are broken in several places. Bragg's army flees, there is even a panic among the Southern veterans, but Bragg rescues most of his troops. Of 56,000 Federal troops engaged in the battle, 5,800 are casualties; of around 46,000 Confederates more than 6,600 are casualties. The road into Georgia is partially opened for the Union.

November 26: Generals Sherman and Thomas pursue Bragg.

November 29: Longstreet's attack on Knoxville fails.

Eyewitness Testimony

A short time before leaving Corinth I rode . . . to General Halleck's headquarters . . . when he mentioned to me casually that General Grant was going away the next morning. I inquired the cause and he said that he did not know, but that Grant had applied for a thirty days' leave . . . Of course we all knew that he was chafing under the slights of his anomalous position . . . I found him seated on a campstool . . . he seemed to be assorting letters . . . I then inquired the reason, and he said: "Sherman, you know. You know that I am in the way here. I have stood it as long as I can, and can endure it no longer." I then begged him to stay. I argued with him that . . . if he remained, some happy accident might restore him to favor and his true place . . . Very soon after this . . . I received a note from him, saying that he had reconsidered his intention, and would remain.

General William T. Sherman, in his Memoirs
(1875) about the situation in April of 1862

I have now attained what I have been looking for all my life—a flag—and having attained it all that is necessary to complete the scene is a victory. If I die in the attempt it will be only what every officer has to expect. He who dies in doing his duty to his country, and at peace with his God, has played out the drama of life to the best advantage.

Admiral Farragut, letter to his wife before the assault on New Orleans, end of April 1862.

The Mississippi is the backbone of the rebellion; it is the key to the whole situation. But we must have troops enough not only to hold New Orleans, but to proceed at once towards Vicksburg, which is the key to all that country watered by the Mississippi and its tributaries. If the Confederates once fortify the neighboring hills, they will be able to hold that point for a indefinite time . . .

Lincoln, after the capture of New Orleans, end of April 1862. Quoted in General J. Marshall-Cornwall's Grant as Military Commander *(1970).*

I had taught myself to believe you could not be hurt, danger had so often surrounded you, your high rank in a measure protected you. The first awakening from this hope was the death of [A.S.] Johnston—

his rank was higher—his poor wife had probably thought the same with me . . .

Elise Bragg, letter to her husband, General Braxton Bragg, spring of 1862.

As the officers and soldiers of the United States have been subject to repeated insults from the women (calling themselves ladies) of New Orleans in return for the most scrupulous non-interference and courtesy on our part, it is ordered that hereafter when any female shall by word, gesture or movement insult or show contempt for any officer or soldier of the United States she shall be regarded and held liable to be treated as a woman of the town plying her avocation.

Major General Benjamin F. Butler's proclamation at New Orleans, May 15, 1862.

On the 17th [June] I received a letter from General Sherman and one on the 18th from General McPherson, saying that their respective commands had complained to them of a fulsome, congratulatory order published by General McClernand to the 13th corps, which did great injustice to the other corps engaged in the campaign. This order had been sent north and published, and now papers containing it had reached our camps . . . I at once wrote to McClernand, directing him to send me a copy of this order. He did so, and I at once relieved him from the command . . . and ordered him back to Springfield, Illinois. The publication of his order in the press was in violation of War Department orders and also of mine.

Grant about the aftermath of the battle at Champion's hill, May 16, 1863, in his Personal Memoirs (1885–86).

The Judge was relating some interesting things about the taking of New Orleans . . . The French and English Admirals said it would not be possible for the fleet to pass those forts. They said it would be madness to attempt it, but our commanders say there was not a captain or lieutenant or hardly a sailor who was not determined to do it . . .

Maria L. Daly, May 16, 1862, Diary of a Union Lady (1962).

If the country be satisfied to have me laid on the shelf by a man who is either demented or a traitor to his high trust—well, let it be so . . . As to my reputation, if it can suffer by anything that living specimen of gall & hatred can do—why is it not then worth preserving . . . My consolation is, that the difference between "that individual" and myself is—that if he were to die today, the whole country would rejoice at it—whereas, I believe, if the same thing were to happen to me, they would regret it.

General Beauregard, letter of July 12, 1862, to his aide, General Thomas Jordan, after President Davis had removed him from command.

Has the bill for execution of abolition prisoners after 1st of January next passed? Do it, and England will be stirred into action. It is high time to proclaim the black flag for that period. Let the execution be by the Garrote.

General Beauregard, in a letter to Porcher Miles, chairman of the committee of military affairs, after Lincoln's Preliminary Proclamation, end of September 1862.

This battle was recognized by me as being a decided victory, though not as complete as I had hoped for, nor nearly so complete as I now think was within the easy grasp of the commanding officer at Corinth [Rosecrans]. Since the war it is known that the result, as it was, was a crushing blow to the enemy, and felt by him much more than it was appreciated by the North.

Grant, about the battle of Corinth, October 3–4, 1862, in his Personal Memoirs.

In Tennessee and Mississippi the disparity between our armies and those of the enemy is so great as to fill me with apprehension.

President Jefferson Davis in a letter to Robert E. Lee, December 8, 1862.

The Jews, as a class violating every regulation of trade established by the Treasure Department and also department orders, are hereby expelled from the department within twenty-four hours from the receipt of this order.

General Grant, General Order #11, issued at Holly Springs, Mississippi, on December 17, 1862. The order was rescinded by Halleck and Lincoln three weeks later.

The general [Rosecrans] . . . galloped into the field, followed by his staff and escort . . . Moving down to the extreme left, he was discovered by the enemy, and a full battery opened upon him. Solid shot and shell stormed about us furiously. The general himself was unmoved, but his staff generally

were more sensitive. The inclination to dodge was irresistible.

Correspondent of the Cincinnati Commercial on the battle of Murfreesboro, December 31, 1862.

I heard an insinuating thud! and saw a poor orderly within sabre-distance topple from his saddle and tumble headlong to mother earth. One convulsive shudder, and he was no more. His bridle-hand clutched the reins in death. A comrade loosened his grasp and his faithful gray stood quietly . . . Another bullet went through the jaw of Lieutenant Benton's beautiful chestnut. Smarting with pain, he struck violently with his hoofs at the invisible tormentor . . . The rattle of musketry and roar of artillery was deafening. Still the general charged through it as if it had been harmless rain . . . It was wonderful that he escaped . . . Pushing out to the cedar forest . . . trusty Sheridan was met, bringing out (and falling back with) his tried division in superb order . . . The enemy was dreadfully punished. Still they came on like famished wolves, in columns, by divisions . . .

Correspondent of the Cincinnati Commercial on the battle of Murfreesboro, December 31, 1862.

The enemy . . . turned his guns upon it [Rosecrans's staff], and his accurate aim was soon rewarded, for a solid shot carried away the head of Colonel Garesche, the chief-of-staff, and killed or wounded two or three more orderlies. Garesche's appalling death stunned us all, and a momentary expression of horror spread over Rosecrans' face; but at such time the importance of self-control was vital, and he pursued his course with an appearance of indifference . . .

William T. Sheridan on the battle of Murfreesbord in his Memoirs(1875).

. . . the victory was glorious and complete as far as it went, but it was not consummate. We thought at one time, that the Yankees were as good as routed, but it appears they were not. We thought they would skedaddle that night, but they did not.

Correspondent of the Chattanooga Daily Rebel, on the outcome of the battle of Murfreesboro January 1863.

Though our victory was dearly bought, yet the importance of gaining the day at any price was very great . . . Nashville was firmly established as a base for future operations, Kentucky was safe from the possibility of being overrun; and Bragg, thrown on the defensive, was compelled to give his thoughts to the protection of the interior of the Confederacy and the security of Chattanooga, rather than indulge in schemes of conquest . . .

General P. H. Sheridan, Personal Memoirs (1888).

The long, dreary and—for heavy and continuous rains and high water—unprecedented winter was one of great hardship to all engaged about Vicksburg . . . Troops could scarcely find dry ground on which to pitch their tents. Malaria fevers broke out among the men. Measles and smallpox also attacked them . . .

Grant about the winter 1862/63 around Vicksburg in his Personal Memoirs.

The eyes and hopes of the whole country are now directed to your army. In my opinion, the opening of the Mississippi River will be to us of more advantage than the capture of forty Richmonds.

General Henry W. Halleck, dispatch to Grant on March 20, 1863.

Visitors to the camps went home with dismal stories to relate . . . Because I would not divulge my ultimate plans to visitors, they pronounced me idle, incompetent and unfit to command men in an emergency, and clamored for my removal. They were not to be satisfied, many of them, with my simple removal, but named who my successor should be. McClernand, Frémont, Hunter and McClellan were all mentioned . . . With all the pressure brought to bear upon them, both President Lincoln and General Halleck stood by me to the end of the campaign. I had never met Mr. Lincoln, but his support was constant.

Grant about the situation before Vicksburg, spring of 1863, in Personal Memoirs.

Admiral Porter proceeded with the preparation of the steamers for their hazardous passage of the enemy's batteries. The great essential was to protect the boilers from the enemy's shot, and to conceal the fire under the boilers from view. This he accomplished by loading the steamers . . . with bales of hay and cotton . . . By the 16th of April Porter was ready to start on his perilous trip.

Grant early April 1863 at Vicksburg in Personal Memoirs.

Lights twinkled busily from the Vicksburg hillsides until about ten o'clock, when they disappeared. And about the same moment song and laughter on our side were hushed, as a shapeless mass of what looked like a great great fragment of darkness was discerned floating noiselessly down the river. It was the *Benton* [Porter's flagship]. It passed and disappeared in the night, and was succeeded by another bank of darkness—the *Lafayette* . . . Ten noiseless shapes revealed themselves and disappeared, and then we knew that all the actors in the play had given us the first scene of the first act.

Correspondent of the New York Times Porter's fleet on the way to pass Vicksburg, April 16, 1863.

There were in all perhaps thirty boats . . . each of which was black with spectators, of whom not a few were ladies. These, and the stars, were the witnesses . . . I am bound to say that the stars were the more serious and quiet portion of the gathering. The balance passed the hours of waiting in jokes, laughter, choruses, and love-making—which, together with a running fusillade of champagne corks, indicated anything but an appreciation of the fact that the drama about to open was a tragedy instead of a roaring farce.

Correspondent of the New York Times, April 16, 1863.

The movement of the boats was soon discovered by the Confederate picket who nightly controlled the river in small boats. They immediately crossed the river and fired several houses in the village of De-Soto, so as to illuminate the river.

Confederate officer S. H. Lockett, chief engineer of the Vicksburg defences, as quoted in R. Wheeler's Voices of the Civil War (1976).

. . . the Mississippi bank was ablaze. Our ironclads promptly replied with their heaviest guns, while the transports, hugging the Louisiana shore, ran by as fast as possible. The . . . burned houses made the night as light as day. Again and again the transports were struck . . . but the men stood gallantly at their posts.

Federal newsman Albert Richardson, A Personal History of Ulysses S. Grant (1868).

On the gunboats not a man was killed, and only eight were wounded. On the steamers and barges nobody was even hit. Before daylight the entire fleet,

save the ill-fated *Henry Clay*, was received at New Carthage by Grant's infantry with shouts of delight. To the soliders who had run the steamers on his daring race, the general promptly gave furloughs for forty days and transportation to and from home.
A. Richardson, Personal History (1868).

The affair of Big Black bridge was one which an ex-Confederate participant naturally dislikes to record . . . After the stampede . . . orders were issued for the army to fall back to Vicksburg . . . General Pemberton rode on himself . . . He was very much depressed . . . and for some time rode in silence. He finally said: "Just thirty years ago I began my military career . . . and today—the same date—that career is ended in disaster and disgrace." I strove to encourage him, urging that things were not as bad as they seemd to be . . . that Vicksburg was strong and could not be carried by assault; and that Mr. Davis had telegraphed him "to hold Vicksburg at all hazard," adding that "if besieged he would be relieved." To all of which General Pemberton replied that my youth and hopes were the parents of my judgment . . .
S. H. Lockett, May 18, 1863, as quoted in R. Wheeler's Voices of the Civil War.

Good news from the Mississippi. General Grant has gained several victories and Vicksburg must soon fall . . . I wish something might soon occur, for everything is so expensive. Coal is at eight dollars per ton, and other things are in proportion. Yet there is no increase of salary . . .
Maria L. Daly, May 26, 1863, Diary.

Just across the Mississippi, . . . mortars were put in position and trained directly on the homes of the people . . . Twenty-four hours of each day these preachers of the Union made their touching remarks to the town . . . the women and children of Vicksburg took calmly and bravely the iron storm . . . They became at last such an ordinary occurence of daily life that I have seen ladies walk quietly along the streets while the shells burst above them, their heads protected meanwhile by a parasol held between them and the sun . . . Vicksburg hangs on the side of a hill whose name is poetical—the Sky Parlor . . . Its soil was light and friable, and yet sufficiently stiff to answer the purpose of excavation. Wherever the passage of a street left the face of the hill exposed, into it and under it the people bur-

rowed, making long ranges and systems of chambers within which the women and young took shelter. In them all the offices of life had to be discharged . . . It was rather a point of honor among men not to hide in these places . . .
Edward S. Gregory, Vicksburg resident, Vicksburg besieged and shelled, June 1863, R. Wheeler's Voices of the Civil War.

Our sap [mining trench] ran close up to the outside of the enemy's parapet . . . The soldiers of the two sides occasionally conversed pleasantly across this barrier. Sometimes they exchanged the hard bread of the Union soldiers for the tobacco of the Confederates. At other times the enemy threw over hand grenades and often our men, catching them in their hands, returned them.
Grant, the siege of Vicksburg, June 1863 in Personal Memoirs.

At length all was in readiness; the fuse train was fired, and it went fizzing and popping through the zigzag line of trenches until . . . it vanished. Its disappearance was quickly succeeded by the explosion. . . . So terrible a spectacle is seldom witnessed. Dust, dirt, smoke . . . everything connected with the fort—rose hundreds of feet into the air, as if vomited forth from a volcano. Some who were close spectators even say that they saw bodies of the poor wretches who a moment before had lined the ramparts . . .
James C. Fitzpatrick, Union correspondent, June 25, 1863 at Vicksburg.

I remember one colored man . . . who was thrown to our side. He was not hurt much, but terribly frightened. Someone asked him how high he had gone up. "Dunno, massa, but t'ink 'bout t'ree mile," was his reply.
Grant, June 25, 1863, Personal Memoirs.

Our rations have been cut down to one biscuit and a small bit of bacon per day, not enough scarcely to keep body and soul together, much less to stand the hardships we are called upon to stand. If you can't feed us, you had better surrender us, horrible as the idea is . . . The army is ripe to mutiny unless it can be fed.
"Many soldiers," their communication, received by General Pemberton in Vicksburg, June 28, 1863.

. . . So far as the siege of this place goes, I presume that people at home, in their easy chairs, think it ought to have been finished long since . . . To such let me say, could they be present here . . . and see the configuration of the country, its broken topography, its high and abrupt hills, deep gullies, gorges and dilapidated roads, they would then realize the difficulties of the work. Then there is a large army to feed, great materiel to be brought into position, all of which demands large transportation and the united efforts of thousands of men.—General Grant acts independently of opinions of the public. He fully realizes the responsibility of his position and . . . he is determined to accomplish this work with as great an economy of human life as possible. He feels now that the prize is within his grasp . . .

Charles H. Farrell, in the New York Herald
end of June, 1863.

The great Ulysses—the Yankee generalissimo surnamed Grant—has expressed his intention of dining in Vicksburg on . . . the Fourth of July . . . Ulysses must get into the city before he dines in it. The way to cook a rabbitt is "first catch the rabbitt."

The Daily Citizen, *Vicksburg (printed on wallpaper), on July 2, 1863.*

. . . we were so shorthanded that no man within the lines had ever been off duty more than a small part of each day . . . Our lines were badly battered . . . and the Federal forces were within less than a minute of our defences, so that a single dash could have precipitated them upon us in overwhelming numbers. All of these facts were brought out in the council of war . . . General Pemberton said he had lost all hopes of being relieved by General Johnston . . . He then asked each officer present to give his vote on the question *surrender or not?* Beginning with the junior officer present, all voted to surrender but two . . .

S. H. Lockett, as quoted in R. Wheeler's
Voices of the Civil War.

A few minutes after the Federal soldiers marched in, the soldiers of the two armies were fraternizing and swapping yarns over the incidents of the long siege . . . A hearty cheer was given by one Federal division "for the gallant defenders of Vicksburg!"

Confederate officer S. H. Lockett, as quoted in
R. Wheeler's Voices of the Civil War.

Vicksburg was at last surrendered on the fourth, on which day Meade likewise defeated Lee, so that there has never been a Fourth of July kept before so grandly by the nation. God seems to have at last sent us a leader. General Meade is a native of Spain, but his parents were Americans. Now if Lincoln had but the sense to publish a general amnesty and annul his emancipation act, we might once more be a united nation . . . This last battle has never been surpassed in history. The North and South will now have learned to respect each other.

Maria L. Daly, July 12, 1863, Diary.

I do not remember that you and I ever met personally. I write this now as a grateful acknowledgment for the almost inestimable service you have done the country . . . I thought you should go down the river and join Gen. Banks; and when you turned northward East of the Big Black, I feared it was a mistake. I now wish to make the personal acknowledgment that you were right, and I was wrong.

Lincoln, in a letter to Grant after the Vicksburg campaign, July 13, 1863.

Our division, in advancing, passes the spot where Gen. Bragg is seated upon his horse . . . He looks pale and careworn . . . The enemy seems to be fighting in detached bodies. Longstreet discovers, with his soldiers eye, a gap in their already confused lines . . . The men rush over the hastily constructed breastworks with the old-time familiar rebel yell; and, wheeling then to the right, the column sweeps the enemy before it, and pushes along the Chattanooga road towards Missionary Ridge in pursuit. It is glorious!

Confederate Major William Miller Owen on the battle of Chickamauga, September 19, 1863, In Camp and Battle with the Washington Artillery *(1885).*

We are sadly disappointed in the want of action by our friends in Kentucky. We have so far received no accession to this army . . . Enthusiasm runs high but exhausts itself in words . . . The people here have too many fat cattle and are too well off to fight . . . Unless a change occurs soon we must abandon the garden spot of Kentucky to its own cupidity.

General Braxton Bragg, letter to the Confederate War Department, around September 20, 1862, as quoted by Bruce Catton's Terrible Swift Sword *(1985).*

. . . Thomas had . . . so to speak, placed himself with his back against a rock, and refused to be driven from the field. Here he stayed, despite the fierce and prolonged assaults of the enemy, repulsing every attack. And when the sun went down, he was still there. Well was he called the "Rock of Chickamauga".

Henry M. Cist, Federal staff officer, the battle of Chickamauga, September 20, 1863, The Army of the Cumberland *(1882).*

. . . he [Johnnie Clem of Newark, Ohio, Union soldier] was a fair and beautiful child . . . about twelve years old, but very small of his age . . . only about thirty inches high and weighed about sixty pounds . . . His brigade being partly surrounded by rebels, was retreating, when he, being unable to fall back as fast as the rest of the line, was singled out by a rebel colonel who rode up to him with the summons: "Scoundrel halt! Surrender, you damned little Yankee!" Johnnie halted and brought his gun into position as though he was about to surrender, thus throwing the colonel off his guard. In another moment the gun was cocked, fired, and the colonel fell dead from his horse. His regiment was pursued, and a volley was fired at that moment, and Johnnie fell as though he had been killed, and lay there on the field until . . . [he was able] to slip away unnoticed.

Annie Wittenmyer, Federal nurse, the battle of Chickamauga, September 20, 1863, Under the Guns: A Woman's Reminiscences of the Civil War *(1895).*

After Bragg had given Rosecrans two or three days to collect, reorganize and reanimate his forces, strengthen and man his fortifications, he moved on Chattanooga, closed up about as close around as he could safely get, and went to digging and fortifying . . . We were very scarce of rations, and for a day or two skirmished pretty lively with our Yankee neighbors over a cornfield to see who should have the most corn to parch. I believe we got the most.

Confederate Colonel William C. Oates, after the battle of Chickamauga, The War between the Union and the Confederacy *(1905).*

Every fresh bulletin from the battlefield of Chickamauga, during my three weeks' stay in Cincinnati, brought a long list of the dead and wounded of the Western army, many of whom, of the officers, belonged to the best families of the place. Yet the signs of mourning were hardly anywhere perceptible; the noisy gaiety of the town was not abated one jot.

William H. Russell, British journalist, in the London Times, *September 1863.*

If there was little of beauty or elegance in the place when our troops retreated into it from Chickamauga, there was a great deal less a fortnight subsequently . . . General Saint Clair Morton, the chief of Rosecrans' engineers, had no mercy . . . Residences were turned into blockhouses; black bastions sprang up in former vineyards; rifle pits were run through the graveyards . . . Life in Chattanooga . . . was dreary enough . . . The enemy daily threw a few shells from the top of Lookout Mountain into our camps, but they were too wise to attack with infantry the works which . . . encircled the city. Bragg preferred to rely for the final reduction of the garrison upon his ally Famine—and a very formidable antagonist did our men find him . . . Bragg held the railroad line from Bridgeport [a depot 20 miles to the southwest] . . . thereby compelling Rosecrans to haul his provisions in wagon trains . . . across the Cumberland Mountains.

W. F. G. Shanks, Federal war correspondent in Chattanooga, the Union army report of late September 1863.

The hundreds of citizens who were confined in the town . . . suffered even more than the men. They were forced to huddle together in the centre of the town as best they could; and many of the houses occupied by them during the siege surpassed in filth, point of numbers of occupants and general destitution, the worst tenement-house in New York City.

W. F. G. Shanks, war correspondent in Chattanooga, early October of 1863.

The opposition to you both in the army and out of it has been a public calamity in so far that it impairs your capacity for usefulness . . .

President Davis, letter to General Bragg, dated October 3, 1863, referring to the controversy between Bragg and Polk.

Nothing can prevent the retreat of the army within a fortnight . . . General Rosecrans seems to be insensible to the impending danger, and dawdles with trifles in a manner which can scarcely be imagined . . . All this precious time is lost because our dazed and lazy commander cannot perceive the catastrophe that is close upon us, nor fix his mind upon means of preventing it. I never saw anything that seemed so lamentable and hopeless.

War Department representative, report from Rosecrans's headquarters at Chattanooga, October 16, 1863, as quoted in General Marshall-Cornwall's Grant as Military Commander.

On the 19th of October, after turning the command over to Thomas, General Rosecrans quietly slipped away from the army. He submitted uncomplainingly to his removal, and modestly left us without fuss or demonstration—ever maintaining, though, that the Battle of Chickamauga was in effect a victory, as it had ensured us . . . the retention of Chattanooga . . .

General William T. Sheridan, Personal Memoirs.

At first, with good glasses, we could plainly see Hooker's troops driving the Confederates up the face of the [Lookout] mountain. All were soon lost to view in the dense timber, but emerged again on the open ground, across which the Confederates retreated at a lively pace, followed by the pursuing line which was led by a color-bearer, who, far in advance, was bravely waving on his comrades. The gallantry of the man elicited much enthusiasm among all of us, but as he was a considerable distance ahead of his comrades I expected to see his rashness punished at any moment by death or capture. He finally got quite near the retreating Confederates when suddenly they made a dash at him; but he was fully alive to such a move, and ran back, apparently uninjured, to his friends.

General P. H. Sheridan, the battle of Chattanooga, November 23, 1863 in Personal Memoirs.

They [the attacking Union troops] kept climbing and pulling and scratching until I was in touching distance of the . . . breastwork right on the very apex of Missionary Ridge. I made one jump, and I heard Captain Turner . . . who had four Napoleon guns . . . hallo out [the order to fire], and then a roar. The next order was: "Limber to the rear!" . . . I saw one brigade thrown down their guns and break like quarter horses. Bragg was trying to rally them. I

heard him say: "Here is your commander", and the soldiers halloed back "Here is your mule."

Confederate Private Sam Watkins at Missionary Ridge, as quoted in R. Wheeler's Voices of the Civil War.

Regiments were captured almost entire: battery after battery along the ridge was taken. In some cases the rebels were bayonetted at their guns, and the cannon that but a moment before was firing on our troops were by them captured, turned and used against the rebels as they were driven in masses to the rear.

Union staff officer Henry M. Cist, the storming of Missionary Ridge, November 25, 1863 in The Army of the Cumberland.

. . . These rifle pits were reached nearly simultaneously by several commands, when the troops, in compliance with their instructions, laid down at the foot of the [Missionary] ridge, awaiting further orders. Here they were under hot, plunging, galling fire from the enemy in their work on the crest of the ridge. Without further awaiting and under no orders from their officers, first one regiment, then another started with its colors up the ascent, until with loud hurrahs the entire line . . . advanced over and around rocks, under and over fallen timber, charged up the ridge . . .

Henry M. Cist, November 25, 1863, The Army of the Cumberland.

The strength of the rebellion in the [South's] center is broken. Burnside is relieved from danger in East Tennessee . . . Georgia and the Southeast are threatened in the rear. And another victory is added to the chapter of "Unconditional Surrender Grant."

M. C. Meigs, Grant's quartermaster-master general. Report to Secretary Stanton on the outcome of the battle of Chattanooga, November 25, 1863.

Lincoln is reported to have said when he heard of his [Grant's] failing, "I would like to know what the brand of whiskey he drinks is, to send it to the other Union generals." It is lamentable that drunkenness is so common among our officers.

Maria L. Daly, November 24, 1863, Diary.

8. Closing the Ring: The East: November 1863– March 1865

THE HISTORICAL CONTEXT

When, a few days after the battle of Antietam, Lincoln read his Emancipation Proclamation to his cabinet, he proposed to act under his war powers to seize enemy resources. The emancipation, therefore, could only apply to states in rebellion, not to slavery in states loyal to the Union. Nevertheless, the proclamation had a tremendous effect, because from now on the Union armies would act as armies of liberation and would encourage the slaves to help the Union side. There was, of course, strong opposition among the Democrats and even in the army to such an extent that McClellan thought it necessary to issue an order to his officers emphasizing that the military had to subordinate itself to the civil authorities. In the following elections of November 1862, the Democrats gained considerably, but in December the House rejected a Democratic proposal to condemn the Emancipation Proclamation as a "high crime against the Constitution." Any speculation that the results of the elections might induce the president to refrain from putting the Proclamation into effect was dispelled on January 1, 1863, when Lincoln signed the final Proclamation, which sanctioned the enlisting of black soldiers into the Union armed forces.

In the meantime, the Army of the Potomac was under a new commander. After Antietam, Lincoln had expected McClellan to pursue the retreating Lee, but McClellan crossed the Potomac only on October 26 and then resorted to dilatory tactics. Jeb Stuart's calvary managed to ride completely around the Army of the Potomac for the second time, and Longstreet's corps had time to move between McClellan and Richmond. So Lincoln finally relieved McClellan, replacing him with General Ambrose Everett Burnside, who was reluctant to accept the high command but felt he had to obey orders. He quickly moved his army to Falmouth, opposite Fredericksburg on the Rappahannock, al-

179

Lincoln writing the Emancipation Proclamation, lithograph of 1863.

lowing Lee's subcommanders Longstreet and Jackson to entrench themselves on the heights south of the river. When Burnside's left wing under General William B. Franklin crossed the river and attacked on December 13, it found a breach in Jackson's position on Prospect Hill but failed to exploit it. When the Confederates counterattacked, Franklin's troops were driven back with terrible losses, and, further north, Burnside's assaults from the town of Fredericksburg against Marye's Heights were thrown back time and again with even more severe losses. The battle of Fredericksburg ended as one of the worst defeats for the Union army. The desperate Burnside wanted to lead another charge the next day with his own corps but was talked out of it and recrossed the river two days later.

This disaster led to a Cabinet crisis in Washington. Salmon Chase organized a drive to remove Seward, who was said to have an undue influence on the president. Lincoln stood up for Seward, after which both Seward and Chase offered to resign. Both offers were refused.

Opposition of the generals against Burnside rose after Fredericksburg, particularly after he had tried to cross the Rappahannock to get on Lee's flank. This campaign turned into a miserable "mud march" when torrential rains turned the roads into swamps where men and equipment sank in deep. After several days of hopeless struggle, Burnside gave up, Lincoln gave in to the demands of Franklin, Hooker and the other generals and replaced Burnside with Joseph Hooker, known as "fighting Joe," a man of questionable character, much criticized for his dissipations and his scheming against other generals. But he was successful in improving conditions in his army and lifting the sunken morale of his men. He also reorganized his cavalry, which for the first time became a match for Jeb Stuart's brigade.

Jeb Stuart, Southern cavalry leader.

With his greatly superior army, Hooker again crossed the Rappahannock near Chancellorsville and threatened Lee's left flank, while another large Union contingent under John Sedgwick advanced on Lee's entrenchments at Fredericksburg, nine miles to the west. Apparently Hooker expected Lee to withdraw from this uncomfortable position, but when he did not, Hooker, inexplicably and against the advice of his commanders, moved into defensive positions around Chancellorsville. Lee sensed that the main threat came from there, rather than from Fredericksburg, and sent Stonewall Jackson on a daring route through the wilderness around Hooker's right flank, facing Hooker's main forces with only 15,000 men, while Jubal Early at Fredericksburg was outnumbered almost three to one by Sedgwick. This daring maneuver succeeded. Jackson's surprise attack on May 2 rolled up the Union flank. The fighting continued long into the night, with Lee's divisions joining in. In the confusion, Jackson was wounded by his own men—fatally, as it turned out. On the following day, Sedgwick's troops succeeded where Burnside had failed four and one-half months earlier and finally took Marye's Heights, routing Early's inferior forces in a fierce bayonet charge. But around Chancellorsville, Hooker remained strangely passive and ordered a withdrawal when Stuart, who had taken Jackson's place, and Lee launched an all-out attack. When he heard of Sedgwick's success in the east, Lee did not hesitate to deprive his forces to meet this threat, and again Hooker did not take advantage of the situation, where Stuart's 25,000 troops now faced his own 75,000. Sedgwick held his ground but pulled back on May 4 after learning that Hooker had given up. Hooker overruled all suggestions of a counterattack on May 5 but managed to retreat across the river the following night before Lee could renew his assault. Once again, Lee had achieved an outstanding victory over greatly superior forces, and once again Northern morale reached a new low.

The South, too, faced grave problems. The Union armies were applying increasing pressure in Virginia, Tennessee and Mississippi, and a counterstroke was needed to relieve it. Plans to reinforce Bragg in Tennessee or Pemberton in Mississippi were discussed in Richmond, but the bold proposal of Robert E. Lee prevailed: to invade Pennsylvania. This would lessen the threat at the Rappahannock, would let Confederate armies for once live off the land of the enemy, have desirable political consequences and, by assisting the "Copperheads" in the North, possibly even achieve foreign recognition.

Lee's Army of Northern Virginia, which invaded the Shenandoah Valley in early June 1863, was well rested, had higher morale and was better equipped than the one that had come this way in September 1862. The most severe cavalry fight developed at the very beginning of the campaign when a reconnoitering cavalry force under Union General Alfred Pleasanton clashed with Jeb Stuart's forces at Brandy Station near the Rappahannock. The improved Union cavalry held its own against Stuart's raiders. Later in the month Stuart lost contact with Lee's main forces, leaving the latter in the dark about Hooker's countermoves. Yet Lee managed to advance through the Shenandoah Valley and to cross the Potomac about 80 miles northwest of Washington without encountering any serious obstacles. When his army entered Pennsylvania, he forbade plundering of private property, but this order was not always remembered by his troops. Along the invasion route, the country was stripped of all food and clothing by the Southern soldiers and much property was destroyed, including Thaddeus Stevens's iron forge near Chambersburg. Southern troops began to give Confederate IOUs to merchants in return for the merchandise they had requisitioned. Many blacks were picked up by the troops and sent south to be sold as slaves. Both Davis and Lee felt the time had come for some cautious peace feelers, and, in early July, Alexander Hamilton Stephens, Confederate vice president and an old friend of Lincoln's, set out to meet with Union officials to negotiate prisoner exchanges and possibly advance peace proposals. But just then, one of the decisive battles of the war began.

Lincoln had become greatly dissatisfied with Hooker's reaction to the invasion. Hooker first wanted to march toward Richmond rather then to follow Lee, and Lincoln finally got the impression that Hooker, after Chancellorsville, was afraid to fight Lee. When Hooker, following McClellan's example, continued complaining that he was outnumbered by the enemy, Lincoln removed and replaced him with George Gordon Meade, who had fought well at Antietam, Fredericksburg and Chancellorsville but was relatively unknown outside his own corps. No doubt the troops would have preferred to get McClellan back. The new commander had less than three days to prepare himself for the battle that developed around Gettysburg where Lee intended to concentrate his scattered forces. Confederate General A. P. Hill's advance to the town was held up by Union troops under John Buford and John Reynolds. General fighting had developed earlier than had been intended by either supreme commander. North of the town, Richard S. Ewell's troops attacked Oliver Howard's Union units, which had had to take over after Reynolds had been killed by a sharpshooter. Howard's 11th Union Corps, consisting mostly of Germans, was beaten and retreated toward Cemetery Hill, east of the town, while Lee's main forces had settled on Seminary Ridge, southwest of the town. Lee wanted Ewell to attack this ridge as soon as possible—before the main part of the Union army arrived—but Ewell found the enemy position too strong.

On July 2, Lee wanted Longstreet to attack the ridge, but Longstreet instead suggested going around the southern end of the Union position, thereby getting between them and Washington. Lee reluctantly agreed, but Longstreet, who was much criticized after the battle, was slow in moving his troops around the Yankees' left flank, and, when he did, he found Little Round Top, at the southern end of Cemetery Ridge, occupied by the 3rd Union Corps under Dan Sickles. Meade had not authorized this move, which left Sickles separated from the Union line. However, it did spoil Lee's plans. A desperate struggle for Little Round Top ensued when Longstreet attacked. Sickles was wounded, Meade rushed reinforcements to the hill, and A. P. Hill came up to support Longstreet's attack. Just when an Alabamian brigade was about to storm the top of the hill on which there was only a signal station, Union General Gouverneur K. Warren noticed the danger, raced down and gathered troops and a battery that reached the crest just in time to save this vital position for the Union army. Throughout July 2, the Confederates kept on attacking, but they were uncoordinated, and the Union lines held. Temporary gains on Culp's Hill in the north were lost again when the Yankees counterattacked. At the end of the day, the casualty count for both sides was 35,000.

Lee had come to the conclusion that just one more push was needed to break through the Union lines. Again he rejected Longstreet's suggestion to go around the southern end of the Union position, believing that the fighting on both ends had weakened the Yankee middle. This led to the famous, desperate, all-out assault led by George E. Pickett, Isaac R. Trimble and James J. Pettigrew. A two-hour artillery duel with almost 300 guns preceded the charge. But the Union artillery under Henry J. Hunt had not been knocked out. The general had ordered a cease-fire only to deceive the enemy. The 14,000 Confederates advancing uphill were received by so murderous a fire from the front, right and left that the few hundred Virginians and Tennesseeans who reached the top and broke into the first Union lines were much too weak to hold their positions. After half an hour of fierce fighting, the Confederates moved back, losing half of their men. Pickett's own division lost two-thirds of its men.

Lee expected Meade's counterattack, but it never came. Meade did not know that the Confederate army was badly hurt and short of ammunition, nor that Jeb Stuart, who was riding in his rear, had been stopped by a Union contingent. Apparently he found it hard to believe that he, only three days in command, had beaten the invincible Lee.

The Union had 23,000 casualties, more than a quarter of the troops; the Confederates, 28,000 casualties, more than one-third of their total number. Twenty-seven-thousand muzzle-loading muskets were recovered from the battlefield, of which 24,000 were found loaded. One tree in the line of fire had been hit by 250 bullets.

After World War II, Dwight D. Eisenhower and his British counterpart, Bernard L. Montgomery, visited the Gettysburg battlefield and analyzed the strategies employed by both sides. They came to the conclusion that both Lee and Meade should have lost their jobs. Actually, both offered to resign, and both were refused.

When Lee retreated, Lincoln expected Meade to pursue and destroy the beaten Confederate army before it could cross the Potomac. But Meade seemed content with having driven the invaders from Union soil. He gave Lee a two-day head start, and when he was ready to move in on the enemy at Williamsport, Lee had just managed to slip across the river on a patched-up bridge. During the following months, Lee kept on retreating slowly, to the old battlefield of Manassas, to the Rappahannock and then to the Rapidan River. By the end of November, Meade had crossed the Rapidan in order to attack Lee's flank but was outmaneuvered by Lee and had to retreat across the river. Around the same time, the continuous attempts to bombard Fort Sumter and Charleston into submission reached their climax. The attacks of Union ironclads on Sumter had shown that they could stand a lot of punishment but do only limited damage. The attempts of Union army units to reach Charleston through the coastal swamps and by way of the coastal island also came to nought.

The great setbacks for the South—Vicksburg and Gettysburg—had their repercussions, in particular in North Carolina, where William W. Holden, editor of the *North Carolina Standard*, proposed peace negotiations because compared to the present "military despotism" of Davis and the economic disaster of the war, reunion with the North would be the lesser evil. Although he was beaten for the governorship of the state by his former friend and ally, Governor Zebulon Vance, the peace movement continued in the state and encouraged Lincoln, in December 1863, to announce a plan for amnesty and reconstruction that would allow people in the seceded states to take over the government if they took an oath of allegiance and accepted all Union laws including those on slavery. This corresponded to his theory that secession was illegal and that therefore no state had legally left the Union. It ran contrary, however, to the conviction of the radical Republicans, led by Thaddeus Stevens, that the rebel states had in fact removed themselves from the Union and should be treated as "conquered provinces," in which case Congress, not the president, would have to formulate the terms of their readmission. While Lincoln's plan excluded the top leaders of the South from the amnesty, the radical Republicans still feared that it would keep the old Southern aristocratic ruling class, whom they distrusted, in power. Their demand to revolutionize Southern institutions and manners foreshadowed the Reconstruction program instituted by the Northern Republicans after victory had been won, while Lincoln's ideas of changing as little as possible in civil affairs came close to what Andrew Johnson tried and failed to achieve as president.

Louisiana, of which only the eastern half was occupied by Union forces, became the proving ground for Lincoln's moderate restoration program. He engaged the help of Nathaniel Banks, successor of Benjamin Butler as commander of the Louisiana occupation forces. But no consensus could be reached within the state on the main question— black suffrage.

In March of 1864, General Banks started on a campaign up the Red River, west of the Mississippi. The goal was Shreveport, Louisiana, from where Texas could be overrun, after which troops could be massed along the Mexican border to discourage French imperial forces under Austrian Archduke Maximilian from intervening on behalf of the South. Halleck had approved the plan and Grant had opposed it; but Grant, as the new supreme commander of all Union forces, did not countermand the Red River expedition. This campaign turned into a disaster. Banks's 40,000 men were badly beaten at Sabine Crossroads by inferior Confederate forces under Major General Richard Taylor; and his gunboat fleet was stranded up the river in rapids and shallow water and managed to retreat downriver only after a young Wisconsin engineer, Colonel Joseph Bailey, raised the river level by building a system of dams. The greater part of the supplies of cotton that the fleet had hoped to capture for the Union was instead burned by Confederate General Kirby Smith. The expedition was called off and Banks relieved of his command.

By the beginning of May 1864, when the main campaigns of the year got under way, a number of changes in military command had taken place. In making Grant general in chief, Congress had revived the rank of lieutenant general, which had been last held by George Washington. Halleck resigned as chief of staff, and Grant appointed Sherman as his successor in command of the Western armies, making his own headquarters with the Army of the Potomac. Meade remained in charge of this army, under Grant, and Phil Sheridan came east to command the cavalry. On the Confederate side, Joseph E. Johnston had incurred the displeasure of President Davis because of his feeble support of Pemberton at Vicksburg but was nevertheless appointed successor of Bragg after the latter's disastrous defeat at Chattanooga. He was to oppose Sherman who, on May 7, started out from Chattanooga on his famous march to Atlanta.

While the North had made very substantial gains in 1863, its numerical superiority had been reduced by the necessity of policing about 100,000 square miles of occupied territory and of guarding its long supply lines against cavalry and guerilla raids. In Sherman's case, he found that in advancing toward Atlanta he needed almost as many troops to protect his communication lines, which ran all the way back to Louisville, as he needed at the front. Many Union soldiers were due to be dismissed as their three-year enlistments were up in May or June of 1864. Congress tried to induce soldiers to reenlist by providing special bonuses, chevrons and other privileges, and while about 135,000 men followed, about 100,000 did not. Many of the new conscripts were regarded with contempt by the veteran officers and soldiers, and many deserted at the first opportunity. Thus, much of the North's numerical superiority disappeared during 1864. The South was aware of this and also set its hopes on the forthcoming presidential campaign, expecting a change in policy when the "tyrant in Washington" had been voted out of office.

But Grant had no intention in letting the war drag on until November. In his overall plan, Meade was to move against Lee and Sherman against Johnston to get into the interior of Georgia, while outside the main theaters Banks was supposed to capture Mobile, Sigel in West Virginia was to threaten Richmond from the south, and Benjamin Butler on the Peninsula was to cut Lee's communication line between Petersburg and Richmond. The plan pleased Lincoln, but the three "peripheral" generals were not up to their tasks. Banks campaigned up the Red River instead, suffering defeat; Butler delayed making a surprise attack on virtually undefended Richmond until Beauregard had brought up reinforcements and drove him back at Drewry's Bluff, eight miles south of Richmond; and Sigel in the Shenandoah Valley was attacked and beaten back by John C. Breckinridge's forces at New Market, a battle that became famous because of the participation of 247 teenage cadets of the Virginia Military Institute who fought bravely and became part of the Southern legend. This defeat marked the end of Sigel's career.

Meanwhile, Meade had crossed the Rapidan River and marched through the Wilderness, west of the battlefield of Chancellorsville. The first clash with Lee's forces occurred on May 5. The numerical superiority of the Union troops could not be exploited in the dense woods. After many hours of fierce, confused fighting, in which the underbrush was often set on fire by exploding shells, the Union forces, though unfamiliar with the terrain, gained a position from which to attack Lee's right flank. This was done at dawn on the following day, and the Yankees came close to overruning Lee's headquarters, inducing Lee to lead a counterattack in person. When Longstreet's forces joined his drive, the Confederates gained the initiative.

Longstreet was wounded in the shoulder by his own men, but the assault continued, and both of Grant's flanks suffered heavy losses. He nevertheless decided to continue the fight and marched in the direction of Richmond to the village of Spotsylvania. Sheridan's cavalry, 10,000 men strong, moved even to the outskirts of Richmond. At Yellow Tavern, six miles north of the capital, Jeb Stuart, with only half his men, confronted him. The superior Union cavalry, equipped with rapid-fire carbines, beat the Confederates, and Stuart was mortally wounded; but Sheridan was finally forced to retreat from the area. At Spotsylvania, Lee had anticipated Grant's move, entrenched and withstood all attacks on May 11 and 12, although at one point his army appeared to be split in half. The battle raged for two days, particularly around the "bloody Angle" of Spotsylvania where along a few hundred yards hand-to-hand fighting raged for 18 hours. During the night of the 12th, Lee's forces retreated slightly, but in spite of great expectations in Washington, it became clear soon enough that his lines had not been broken. Casualties on both sides were frightful, but Grant kept on maneuvering, trying in vain to unhinge Lee's position at Spotsylvania. When this failed, he twice decided to push ahead toward Richmond, first to North Anna, then to the Topopotemy Creek still farther south, but Lee again anticipated his moves.

While fighting almost without interruption, both armies then moved farther south to a crossroad called Cold Harbor, east of Richmond, which had been seized by Sheridan's riders on May 31 and was so close to the capital that Union soldiers could hear its church bells. By now, Federal casualties amounted to 44,000, Confederate casualties to about 25,000. Again, Lee got ahead of Grant's army. Outnumbered with his 50,000 against 109,000 Union men, he again entrenched and dared Grant to attack. Grant, who thought the Confederates near collapse and had sworn to fight it out if it took all summer, decided to attack on June 3. The result was a shattering defeat, after the first trenches had been penetrated by Winfield Scott Hancock's corps, which also had fought bravely at the bloody Angle of Spotsylvania—after which the Yankee troops were repulsed with staggering losses.

Grant freely admitted that he had committed a grave error. However, he continued his campaign by disengaging and this time deceiving Lee and crossing the James River for an assault on Petersburg. At the same time, he mobilized Union troops in the Shenandoah Valley, now led by David Hunter and supported by Sheridan's cavalry, to move south toward Lynchburg and then east in the direction of Richmond. But Hunter was plagued by guerillas, in particular a guerilla squad led by John Singleton Mosby, a disciple of Stuart who, supported by the population, constantly cut into Hunter's supply lines. At Lynchburg, Hunter's 15,000 men met with Jubal Early's corps of 10,000 men and decided to retreat to West Virginia, leaving the Valley to the Confederates, while Sheridan's corps fought a bloody battle with a Southern cavalry detachment under Wade Hampton near Tervilian Station. Some of the hardest fighting in this bloody engagement was done by a Michigan brigade under General George Armstrong Custer. The battle was a draw, but Sheridan had to give up his plans to join up with Hunter.

Shortly after this, Grant's forward units were close to the poorly defended Petersburg, but his subcommander William F. Smith failed to realize his great chance. Beauregard, desperately holding on with but 2,500 troops, withdrew almost to the outskirts of the town. After the debacle of Cold Harbor, Union commanders were reluctant to attack entrenched positions, and when Lee rushed in reinforcements, Meade and Grant decided to abandon the attack on Petersburg and to lay siege to it. At the end of this extended and extremely bloody campaign, Northern troops were decimated and dispirited, and many were unwilling to risk their lives as their three-year enlistments were about to expire. In Washington, Democrats began to call Grant a "butcher," but Lincoln continued to defend him stoutly.

By this time, Sherman's army had advanced 80 miles into Georgia. He had divided his forces into three armies, with the bulk at the center commanded by George Thomas, the left wing by John M. Schofield and the right one by Sherman's young protege James B. McPherson. Johnston's opposing force, 50,000 men strong and soon to be increased to 65,000, fought a defensive battle all the way. Sherman, in spite of his reputation as an attacker, did not move against Johnston's fortified positions at Dug Gap and Resaca but let McPherson move around them. At Resaca, only McPherson's overcautiousness prevented Sherman from trapping the defenders, but Johnston decided again to retreat farther, always destroying the single-tracked railroad line from Chattanooga to Atlanta, which was just as quickly restored by Union engineers. At Cassville on May 19, Johnston was ready to strike, but by this time his subcommander and severest critic, John Bell Hood, became overcautious himself, so that Johnston had to retreat farther to Allatoona Pass, southeast of Cassville. Sherman, however, moved his army around the Confederate army straight south in the direction of Dallas, only about 25 miles from Atlanta. Here, Johnston moved in from the east and stalled Sherman at New Hope Church, then farther east at Marietta and Kennesaw Mountain. Sherman, all the while, had to worry about Bedford Forrest's raiders in Mississippi who were interfering with his long supply lines and who had administered a humiliating defeat to a numerically superior Union force at Brice's Crossroads on June 10. Finally, in the middle of July, a larger Union detachment out of Memphis caught up with Forrest at Tupelo, Mississippi, defeated his brigade and wounded Forrest. By this time, Sherman had attacked at Kennesaw Mountain but was repulsed. In spite of his constant retreats, Johnston's standing with his own troops was as high as ever.

Sherman continued to move south, and when he managed to cross the Chattahoochee River, which Johnston had promised to hold, Jefferson Davis grew anxious—as Atlanta was now in immediate danger—and sent Braxton Bragg to Georgia. Bragg sided with the aggressive Hood and against the advice of Lee—who called Hood "all lion and none of the fox." Davis relieved Johnston, with whom he had never been on good terms and replaced him with Hood. Sherman was pleased when he heard this, and most analysts believe that this move may have been Davis's biggest mistake.

Hood immediately went on the attack, trying to catch Thomas's forces separately, but, in the bloodiest fighting so far, he was thrown back into the defense lines surrounding Atlanta. On July 22, he tried again, attacking McPherson's army, but after the initial surprise, he was repulsed with heavy losses. McPherson, however, returning from Sherman's headquarters during the battle, ran into a squad of enemy skirmishers and was shot down. In a few days, Hood had suffered close to 15,000 casualties against Sherman's 6,000, but the advance on Atlanta had been stopped for the time being, and a Union attempt to liberate the notorious prisoner-of-war camp at Andersonville, south of the city, failed. As there were many military targets in the city, Sherman had it shelled, and civilians left in ever increasing numbers.

But Sherman appeared to be stalled and so was Grant at Petersburg. The latter had to deal with an emergency in early July when Jubal Early, with 15,000 Confederates, had appeared east of Frederick, Maryland, and marched toward Washington, appearing in front of Washington's defenses on July 11, just five miles north of the White House. Grant had used the garrison for his Virginia campaign and now rushed the 6th Corps into the defenses. Early now decided to return to Virginia, but only after his troops had pillaged, burned and forced towns like Frederick and Hagerstown, Maryland, to pay large amounts of money. Chambersburg in southern Pennsylvania, which had refused a $100,000 indemnity in gold, was burnt down.

By the end of July, Grant had suffered another setback in the so-called battle of the crater. A long tunnel dug by Union troops under the eastern Petersburg defenses was exploded and buried a Southern regiment and battery in a hole 170 feet long and 30 feet deep, but the following attack, commanded by Union General James H. Ledlie, who remained in his bomb-proof shelter drinking rum, was completely mismanaged and ended in dismal defeat and 4,000 Union casualties. Northern morale was once again at a low point, the only bright spot being Admiral Farragut's victory at Mobile Bay where he destroyed a Confederate flotilla led by the large ironclad *Tennessee,* closing this important Southern port.

By the end of August 1864, things suddenly looked much brighter for the North in general and Lincoln in particular. Sherman had withdrawn from the Atlanta trenches but only in order to march south. He cut off the city in the South and defeated Hood's two corps at Jonesboro, after which Hood had to evacuate in order not to be trapped. On September 2, Sherman's troops occupied the city, and the news of the Union triumph completely changed the mood in Washington and all over the North. Secretary of State Seward remarked that Sherman and Farragut had knocked the bottom out of the Democratic platform denouncing the war. Further good news was received when Sheridan, sent by Grant to destroy Jubal Early, attacked him at Winchester and with his greatly superior troops forced him to retreat to Fisher's Hill, and, after another reverse, to Brown's Gap, Virginia. Once in control of the valley, Sheridan proceeded, according to Grant's instructions, to destroy all crops, barns, cattle and other supplies the Confederates had used to support their armies throughout the war.

But Early had not given up. Reinforced, he launched a surprise attack at Cedar Creek, 15 miles south of Winchester while Sheridan attended a strategy conference in Washington. The Union soldiers panicked and ran, losing 1,300 prisoners, and Early was sure he had won a great victory. Yet Sheridan returned just in the nick of time to organize and personally lead a sweeping counterattack that disintegrated Early's army and ended in a decisive Union victory. Sheridan, together with Sherman and Grant, was now one of the Union's heroes.

Atlanta had fallen, but Hood's army was intact, and Jefferson Davis predicted that Napoleon's fate in Russia would befall Sherman who, cut off from all support and harassed by Southern troops and a hostile population, would end in disgraceful defeat. Indeed, Sherman did find it frustrating to pursue the retreating Hood all the way into Alabama without achieving any tangible results. He therefore suggested to Grant that he ignore Hood and march through Georgia to the coast, abandoning his supply lines and living off the land. The psychological effect of such a move would be tremendous, the North would remain on the offensive and his army would eventually wind up at Lee's back. Getting Grant and then Lincoln to agree to this dangerous strategy took time; when they did, Sherman's famous march to the sea began on November 15 while Hood, now stationed at the Tennessee River in Alabama, marched north into Tennessee, heading for Nashville and eventually Kentucky where he hoped to pick up new recruits. But Sherman had left 60,000 men under Thomas and Schofield to deal with Hood, whose attempts to attack Schofield were frustrated at Pulaski and at the Duck River. A major battle developed at Franklin, Tennessee, 15 miles south of Nashville where Hood ordered a head-on assault on Schofield's lines. After fierce fighting, Schofield broke off and headed north toward Nashville, but the Confederate losses had been so high that Hood's army would never be the same again. Thomas, at Nashville, was unaware of the miserable condition of his adversary and hesitated to attack, though he was urged to do so by Grant and Stanton. When he did attack, on December 15, he crushed Hood's weakened army in two days of heavy fighting, aided by the fact that Forrest's cavalry was too far away to help. Only half of

Hood's army managed to reach Tupelo, Mississippi, by the end of the year. Two weeks later, Hood resigned his command.

Except for a few thousand Georgia militia and some cavalry, Sherman encountered no opposition on his 285-mile march. After he left Atlanta, people in the North heard of him only through Southern newspapers. For the first time, the war had been carried to the heart of the South which until then had remained almost untouched, the border states having borne the brunt of the war. It was Sherman's declared policy to destroy the capacity of the Southern population to sustain the war. His army moved on a front between 25 and 60 miles wide, advancing about 12 miles per day. His foraging parties, called "bummers," joined by Confederate deserters, stragglers, liberated slaves and Georgia unionists, ransacked the countryside. When Milledgeville, capital of Georgia, was occupied, a Yankee Thanksgiving celebration was joined by some haggard, half-starved Union soldiers who had escaped from Andersonville, the notorious Confederate prisoner-of-war camp, a sight that infuriated their luckier comrades. By mid-December, Sherman was closing in on Savannah, which was successfully evacuated by Confederate General William J. Hardee and presented to Lincoln by Sherman "as a Christmas present."

By January of 1865, the only effective military force of the Confederacy left was Robert E. Lee's Army of Northern Virginia which drew most of its supplies from the Carolinas. The next logical move by the North was therefore against Fort Fisher, which guarded the port of Wilmington, North Carolina. The first assaults in December of 1864 by a combined navy and army force had failed, which gave Lincoln an excuse to remove the army commander, the controversial Benjamin Butler, who was replaced by young General Alfred Terry. The assault of his 8,000 men and the largest fleet assembled during the war, led by Admiral David D. Porter, resulted in the capture of the heavily fortified stronghold on January 15. Wilmington was now cut off and fell soon after. The Southern mood turned desperate, hundreds of deserters left Lee's army night after night, and there was talk in Richmond of making Davis step down and making Lee a dictator.

On January 19, Sherman began his campaign from Savannah into South Carolina. Many of his soldiers considered South Carolina as the main culprit responsible for the war and acted accordingly. The countryside was even more savagely pillaged and burned than in Georgia. The army crossed the swamps of the Salkehatchie River, thought to be impassable, by building miles of bridges. Columbia, the capital, was reached on February 17, and within a day the city was in ruins and burning. It is uncertain if the fires were started by Union soldiers, retreating Confederates, blacks or escaped Union prisoners—probably all contributed to the devastating destruction. Charleston was evacuated by the Confederates around the same time. By March, Sherman was in North Carolina, where the looting stopped, and he headed for Fayetteville and Goldsboro.

The rapid decline of Southern fortunes had its repercussions in Richmond. Davis appointed Robert E. Lee supreme commander of the Confederate forces, and Lee's first act was to appoint Johnston to the thankless job of heading all forces to oppose Sherman in the Carolinas. Davis also gave in to the peace party and sent a three-man commission headed by Vice President Stephens to Hampton Roads to negotiate peace terms. Lincoln sent Seward, and the discussions almost broke off prematurely because the Confederates were talking of "two nations" while Seward emphasized "our one common country." Then Lincoln decided to join the conference, which took place on the Union steamer *River Queen* on February 3. Stephens attempted to interest his old friend Lincoln in a joint campaign to get the French army out of Mexico, a project originally launched by the Republican politician Francis Preston Blair. But Lincoln would have none of it. He insisted on a firm stand on the slavery question and that surrender was the only way of stopping the war. The Southern delegates left in a state of dejection, and Davis declared that the South would never surrender to "his Majesty Abraham the First."

Even dyed-in-the-wool Southerners could see by now that the days of slavery were numbered. In January, the constitutional conventions in Tennessee and Missouri had adopted amendments abolishing slavery, and, at the end of the month, the House of Representatives had approved by a two-thirds majority the 13th amendment to the Constitution, which abolished slavery. Many Democrats began to blame their defeat in the November elections on the party's holding on to slavery. Lincoln, at his inaugural reception on March 4, made a special point in welcoming Frederick Douglass, the black abolitionist and advocate, for setting up black regiments, and on the day the 13th amendment was passed in the House, Charles Sumner introduced black Boston lawyer John Rock for admission to the bar at the Supreme Court. Rock was sworn in by the new Chief Justice Salmon P. Chase, who had succeeded Roger B. Taney of Dred Scott fame. The switch from the proslavery Taney to the radical antislavery Chase was typical of the reconstruction of the court that had taken place during Lincoln's administration. On the previous day, before adjourning, Congress had created the so-called Freedmen's Bureau. Its main responsiblity was to provide work and aid the recently freed black population. By February, the question of arming blacks to save the Confederacy was openly discussed. Davis declared that one had to choose "whether the ne-groes shall fight for or against us." After the talks at Hampton Roads had broken down and after Robert E. Lee had come out for arming the blacks, remarking that it would be neither just nor wise to require them to serve in the army as slaves, the Southern House passed a bill that would provide a quota of black soldiers in each state—but the Southern Senate rejected it. The state of Virginia, however, finally pushed through the bill, acted on its own and managed to organize two companies of blacks without giving them freedom. They never saw action.

While Sherman had little trouble in fighting off Confederate attacks at Kinston, Averasborough and Bentonville, North Carolina, the armies around Petersburg and Richmond remained deadlocked. Preparing for a final assault on Petersburg, Grant had moved on to Boydton Plank Road, southeast of the town, on February 5, but after three days of fighting had only succeeded in reaching Hatchers Run at the Vaughn Road crossing. At the end of the month, Sheridan had moved south from the Shenandoah Valley toward Lynchburg and engaged the rem-nants of Early's corps at Mount Crawford and Waynesborough. Early's forces were completely scattered; only he, his staff and a few of his soldiers managed to escape to Richmond. This Valley campaign marked the end of the Shenandoah fighting. Sheridan then moved on to join Grant's army around Petersburg. But Grant himself had made no further progress at Petersburg during the month. A letter he re-ceived from Lee suggesting that they should hold a military conven-tion in order to reach "a satisfactory adjustment of the present un-happy difficulties" came to nought as Grant received instructions from the president to have no conference with Lee except to accept surren-der or on "some minor or purely military matter."

It was Lee who again seized the initiative. Convinced that in the long run his position at Petersburg would become untenable, he launched a surprise attack led by General John B. Gordon (whose division overran Union-held Fort Stedman, east of the city) on March 25. But after some heavy fighting, the Union counterattack retook all lost positions, and in the end, Lee's losses were more than double Grant's.

CHRONICLE OF EVENTS

1862:

September 22: Lincoln announces his Preliminary Emancipation Proclamation.

Federal units reoccupy Harper's Ferry, which had been evacuated by the Confederates.

September 24: In a second proclamation, Lincoln suspends the privilege of the writ of *habeas corpus* and provides military trial of all rebels and insurgents resisting military drafts or guilty of any disloyal practice.

September 27: The Confederate Congress authorizes President Davis to call out men between the ages of 30 and 45.

October 1: Skirmishes along the Potomac near Sharpsburg, Maryland, Sheperdtown and Martinsburg, western Virginia, and Leesburg, Virginia.

October 4: Lincoln, who has visited McClellan at his headquarters, returns to Washington.

October 6: Lincoln orders McClellan to cross the Potomac and attack the enemy.

October 9: Daring raid of "Jeb" Stuart's Confederate cavalry across the Potomac into Chambersburg and Cashtown. They withdraw to Virginia on October 12.

October 13: Lincoln again urges McClellan to take the initiative against the enemy.

October 16: McClellan launches two reconnaissance expeditions from Sharpsburg, Maryland and Harper's Ferry.

October 26: The Army of the Potomac crosses the Potomac into Virginia.

Samuel Heintzelman succeeds Banks as commander of Washington's defenses.

November 3: A Confederate Corps under Longstreet arrives at Culpeper Court House, Virginia, blocking McClellan's slow advance.

November 4: In congressional elections, Democrats gain considerably, especially in New York, New Jersey, Illinois and Wisconsin. The Republican party keeps control of the House of Representatives, however.

November 5: Lincoln relieves McClellan of his command of the Army of the Potomac, replacing him with Major General Burnside. General Fitz-John Porter is replaced by Joseph Hooker.

November 9: Federal cavalry under Ulric Dahlgren undertakes a bold raid into Fredericksburg, Virginia.

November 15: General Burnside begins to move his army from Warrenton, Virginia, toward Fredericksburg.

November 20: Both sides build up their positions near Fredericksburg.

November 21: Jefferson Davis appoints James A. Seddon as secretary of war after George W. Randolph resigns.

November 22: Federal Secretary of War Stanton discharges most political prisoners held by the military.

November 26: Lincoln has a conference with General Burnside at his headquarters and suggests a three-prolonged attack, while Burnside insists on direct assault on Lee at Fredericksburg.

December 1: Lincoln's State of the Union message to the 37th Congress proposes compensation for all states that will abolish slavery before 1900.

Stonewall Jackson moves into position at the right of Lee's army at Fredericksburg.

December 11: Federal troops under Burnside manage to cross the Rappahannock on pontoon bridges and in boats, in spite of Confederate sharpshooters. By nightfall, Fredericksburg is occupied by E. V. Sumner's troops.

December 13: Battle of Fredericksburg, Virginia. Federal troops under Burnside undertake a direct assault against the Confederates entrenched in the hills, but the Confederates under Jackson and Lee repulse all attacks. The Army of the Potomac, about 114,000 men, suffers 12,600 casualties, the Confederates about 5,300 casualties of a total of 72,500 troops. The Federals remain in the city, the Confederates on the hills.

December 15: The defeated Army of the Potomac retreats across the Rappahannock.

Ambrose Burnside, Union general.

December 17: Secretary of State William H. Seward, because of constant disputes with Secretary of the Treasury, Salmon P. Chase, offers his resignation to Lincoln, who does not accept it.

December 20: Treasury Secretary Chase's offer of resignation is refused by Lincoln, who then settles the Cabinet crisis.

December 22: Lincoln congratulates the Army of the Potomac on its bravery at Fredericksburg and calls the defeat "an accident."

December 30: The U.S.S. *Monitor* founders off Cape Hatteras in heavy seas and is towed to the Carolina coast. The greater part of her crew is rescued.

1863:

January 1: Lincoln's final Emancipation Proclamation, pertaining, however, only to areas where people were in rebellion against the United States. Slaves freed by the advancing U. S. armies are to be received into the armed services of the nation. At Murfreesboro, the two armies stay in position.

General Burnside offers his resignation, which Lincoln does not accept.

January 7: Halleck supports Burnside's proposal to attack the Confederates across the Rappahannock.

January 17: Lincoln signs a Congressional resolution providing for the immediate payment of the armed forces and asks for currency reforms.

January 21: Winter rains bog down Burnside's advance across the Rappahannock in Virginia.

Lincoln has Major General Fitz-John Porter cashiered and dismissed from the service of the nation for his part in the second Manassas battle. This decision was reviewed in Porter's favor in 1879.

January 22: The whole Army of the Potomac is stalled in the mud, its advance definitely stopped.

January 24: The dispirited Army of the Potomac settles back into winter quarters across from Fredericksburg, while Burnside proposes the removal of Hooker, Franklin and other commanders.

January 25: Lincoln relieves Burnside and replaces him with Joseph Hooker. Commanders Franklin and Sumner are relieved of their duties.

January 27: The U. S. monitor *Montauk* leads an attack of Federal naval forces against Fort McAllister on the Ogeechee River south of Savannah, Ga., but withdraws after several hours of bombardment.

January 29: The Confederate Congress authorizes borrowing of $15,000,000 through a French financier.

January 31: Two Southern gunboats slip out of Charleston Harbor and raid Federal blockaders, damaging several Union vessels.

February 1: Another successful attack by Federal naval forces on Fort McAllister, Georgia.

February 5: Hooker reorganizes the grand divisions of the Army of the Potomac.

February 16: The U. S. Senate passes the Conscription Act.

February 28: The Federal monitor *Montauk* moves up the Ogeechee River south of Savannah and destroys the C.S.S. *Nashville* near Fort McAllister.

John Singleton Mosby, Confederate raider.

March 2: The Federal Congress appoints four majors and nine brigadier generals for the regular army, and 40 majors and 200 brigadier generals for the volunteer army.

March 3: Lincoln signs the Federal Draft Act, affecting all male citizens between the ages of 20 and 45. A drafted man can hire a substitute or purchase his way out.

A loan to the Federal government of $300,000,000 for 1863 and $600,000,000 for 1864 is also approved.

A third Federal attack on Fort McAllister in Georgia also fails.

March 8: In a daring guerilla raid, Confederate Captain John S. Mosby and 29 men enter Fairfax County Court House, Virginia, and capture Brigadier General E. H. Stoughton and 32 other Union soldiers, as well as 58 horses.

March 17: A Federal cavalry unit under William Woods Averell crosses the Rappahannock at Kelly's Ford, Virginia, but has to withdraw after a hard-fought battle against Confederate units.

April 2: Bread riots in Richmond, with widespread plundering. The crowd is finally dispersed without bloodshed.

Earlier exceptions are revoked, and trade with insurgent states is again restricted to that permitted by the secretary of the treasury.

April 4: Union forces fail in their attempt to capture a Confederate battery at Rodman's Point, near Washington, North Carolina.

April 7: Nine Federal ironclads under Samuel Du Pont enter Charleston Harbor and attack Fort Sumter. More than 2,000 shells are fired at the vessels. Five are disabled, the rest withdraw.

April 11: Blockade runner *Stonewall Jackson* is forced ashore off Charleston, South Carolina by half a dozen Federal blockaders.

April 13: Lincoln orders Admiral Farragut to maintain his position inside Charleston Harbor.

April 15: Confederates withdraw from their siege of Washington, North Carolina.

April 18: The Confederate Congress authorizes the creation of a volunteer navy.

April 24: The Confederate Congress levies a "tax kind" of one of all produce of the land.

Federal raiders, led by General Grenville Dodge, capture Tuscumbia, Alabama.

April 27: The Northern Army of the Potomac begins to move up the Rappahannock, crossing the river on the following day above Fredericksburg, in the Wilderness area.

April 30: Hooker's Army of the Potomac settles around Chancellorsville in the Wilderness area.

May 1: Beginning of the battle of Chancellorsville, Virginia. After initial advances, Hooker withdraws while Lee moves forward cautiously. He and Jackson decide to divide their forces, with Jackson to attack Hooker's right flank.

May 2: Jackson's forces launch a successful surprise attack, but in the darkness he is wounded by one of his own men.

The last meeting of Lee and Jackson, 1869 painting by E.B.D. Julio.

May 3: At Chancellorsville, Lee's troops continue their attack. Hooker is temporarily disabled by a fallen brick. Lee occupies Chancellorsville and turns back counter-attacks.

May 4: At Chancellorsville, Federal Major General John Sedgwick advances near Salem Church, but is threatened from three sides and withdraws across the Rappahannock. Of about 134,000 men, the Federals suffer more than 17,000 casualties. The victorious Confederates, with only 60,000 men have about 12,700 casualties

May 5: The defeated Army of the Potomac recrosses the Rappahannock.

The leader of the Northern Peace Democrats ("Copperheads"), Congressman Clement L. Vallandigham, is arrested in Dayton, Ohio and convicted by a military commission of treasonable sympathies.

May 8: Lincoln declares that aliens who wish to become citizens are not exempt from military service.

May 10: General Stonewall Jackson dies of complications, following amputation of his arm.

May 11: Federal Secretary of the Treasury Salmon P. Chase again tenders his resignation, which Lincoln turns down.

May 13: North Carolina's governor Z. B. Vance complains to President Davis about the growing number of desertions in the Confederate army.

May 29: General Burnside protests the conviction and banishment of "Copperhead" Vallandigham and offers his resignation, which is refused by Lincoln.

June 1: Burnside suppresses the *Chicago Times* because of disloyalty.

June 3: Lee's Army of Northern Virginia, about 75,000 men, begins its drive north.

June 4: At Lincoln's suggestion, Secretary of War Stanton revokes the suspension of the *Chicago Times.*

June 8: Lee's troops arrive at Culpeper Court House, Virginia. Jeb Stuart holds a review of his cavalry.

June 9: The greatest cavalry battle on American soil takes place at Brandy Station on the Rappahannock, between Jeb Stuart's troops and Federal cavalry under Alfred Pleasanton. The Confederates hold the field, but have, for the first time, met a match. About 10,000 men were engaged on either side, the 850 Federal casualties outnumber the 500 Confederates dead.

June 10: Confederate troops under Jackson's successor, General Richard S. Ewell, leave Culpeper and move northwest.

June 12: Ewell crosses the Blue Ridge Mountains into the Shenandoah Valley, engaging in several skirmishes. Off Cape Hatteras, the C.S.S. *Clarence* captures the Union bark *Tacony,* transfers the crew on the *Tacony*, and continues to raid.

June 13: Hooker begins to move northward while Ewell's forces drive near Winchester, Virginia.

June 14: Battle of Second Winchester. The Federal garrison forces at Winchester under Major General R. H. Milroy are forced to withdraw, while Confederates under Robert E. Rodes capture Martinsburg, taking 700 prisoners.

At Port Hudson, Louisiana, Banks launches another assault against the Confederate fortress, but to no avail.

June 15: Milroy's retreat is stopped by Confederate Edward Johnson's division, four miles north of Winchester. Some Federal units manage to escape toward Harper's Ferry, after heavy losses. Excitement in Baltimore and other parts of Maryland because of the threatened invasion, which Hooker declares he is unable to prevent.

In Washington, Lincoln calls for 100,000 militia from Pennsylvania, Maryland, Ohio and West Virginia.

June 17: At the mouth of the Wilmington River, two Federal ironclads battle the Confederate *Atlanta*, which is damaged and surrenders.

June 19: Ewell moves north of the Potomac toward Pennsylvania.

June 20: In Baltimore, breastworks are erected against possible Confederate raids.

June 21: Heavy skirmishing along the fringes of Lee's northward advance.

June 24: Longstreet's and A. P. Hill's corps cross the Potomac to join Ewell in Maryland and to invade Pennsylvania.

June 25: Jeb Stuart's cavalry leaves from Salem Depot, Virginia, to join the Confederates north of the Potomac. His following excursion takes him away from the Gettysburg battlefield.

June 26: Confederates under General Early enter Gettysburg, Pennsylvania and march on toward York.

The Confederate schooner *Archer* under Lieutenant Charles W. ("Savez") Read enters

Portland, Maine, harbor and seizes the Federal *Caleb Cushing*, but is then forced to surrender.

June 27: Lincoln relieves Major General Hooker and appoints Major General George Gordon Meade commander of the Army of the Potomac. Hooker had advised the evacuation of Harper's Ferry.

The Confederate forces in Pennsylvania under Lee, Hill, and Longstreet are almost unopposed and occupy Chambersburg and York and are approaching Harrisburg, the state capital.

Confederates attack Donaldsonville, Louisiana, but are repulsed.

June 29: Meade moves rapidly forward in Maryland. Both armies are moving in the general direction of Gettysburg.

June 30: Meade orders General Reynolds to occupy Gettysburg, on which several Confederate drives are converging.

July 1: Beginning of the three-day battle of Gettysburg. First clash four miles west of the town. Federal cavalry under John Buford and John F. Reynolds's infantry corps fight Confederate units along Willoughby Run, McPherson's Ridge and Herr Ridge. General Reynolds is killed, but the Federals hold. The Federals under O. O. Howard are attacked by Ewell's corps and withdraw through the town to Cemetery Hill and Cemetery Ridge. The town is held by the Confederates. Lee arrives, but against his wishes Cemetery Hill is not attacked. Federal reinforcements arrive, General Meade about midnight. The Confederates have formed a long line south of the town along the ridge.

July 2: The Battle of Gettysburg. The Confederate army concentrates on the somewhat lower Seminary Ridge, west of Cemetery Ridge. Major General G. K. Warren occupies Little Round Top, south of Cemetery Ridge. The Confederates attempt to take Little Round and Big Round Top, further south, and almost succeed, but after very heavy fighting the Federals hold both Tops. General Sickles's corps is attacked from the west by Confederate troops at Peach Orchard and Wheatfield and has to fall back to Cemetery Ridge. Major General Edward Johnson's division attacks Culp's Hill, but neither his nor Ewell's attack of Cemetery Hill, in the northeast of the Ridge, achieve decisive advantages for the Confederates.

President Davis, through Vice President Alexander Stephens and in a direct letter to Lincoln suggests negotiations for the exchange of prisoners and discussions to end the war. Lincoln declines.

July 3: End of the Battle of Gettysburg. Union troops fortify Cemetery Ridge, east of which an artillery duel develops at Culp's Hill and Spangler's Spring. Union forces throw back Confederates at Spangler's Spring. Since Confederate attacks on both flanks have failed, Lee decides to attack the center. At noon, a two-hour artillery duel precedes the all-out attack: Pickett's charge. After desperate fighting, the attackers come close to taking the Ridge, but are finally thrown back, suffering terrible losses. Stuart's cavalry, arriving too late, appears at the rear of Meade's forces and is repulsed by Union cavalry after three hours of fighting. The victorious Union army of more than 85,000 men suffers 23,000 casualties; the Confederates, 65,000 strong, about 20,500 casualties.

In Virginia, Federal units retreat from Suffolk to Norfolk.

July 4: Meade, despite urgings from Washington, does not immediately pursue the retreating Confederate army.

July 6: Lee withdraws toward Hagerstown and Williamsport, still unpursued by Meade.

July 10: The Federal siege of Battery Wagner (South Carolina) in Charleston Harbor, begins, as Union troops land on Morris Island.

Lee concentrates his forces in the Williamsport, Maryland area; skirmishes with the pursuing Union troops develop.

July 11: The first Union assault on Battery Wagner, is beaten back.

July 13: As the first names of the new Federal draft are drawn, riots break out in New York. Draft headquarters are stormed, businesses looted. Fires break out, blacks and Federal officials are the main victims of the mob. Order is restored when troops return from Gettysburg. One thousand people may have been killed, property losses amounted to $1.5 million. Lesser riots occur in Boston, Portsmouth, New Hampshire, Troy, New York and other towns.

The waters of the Potomac have been falling, and Lee manages to cross the river into Virginia.

July 18: A fierce second attack on Battery Wagner in Charleston Harbor is finally beaten back, with frightful losses for the Federals, who lose more than 25% of their troops.

July 19: Meade's army crosses the Potomac at Harper's Ferry and Berlin (now Brunswick).

July 21: Federal units try to gain control of the passes into the Shenandoah Valley to check Lee's movements.

July 22: The New York Chamber of Commerce estimates that Confederate raiders have taken 150 Union merchant vessels valued at over $12 million.

July 23: Federal troops push through Manassas Gap, but are too slow to prevent Lee's army from moving to safety through the Luray Valley of the Shenandoah.

July 24: Union warships again bombard Battery Wagner in Charleston Harbor.

August 1: President Lincoln grants pardon to all soldiers absent without leave if they report back within 20 days.

August 3: Governor Horatio Seymour of New York asks Lincoln to suspend the draft in his state.

August 5: Near Dutch Gap, Virginia, an electric torpedo damages the U.S.S. *Commodore Barney.*

August 7: Lincoln declines to suspend the draft in New York.

August 8: Robert E. Lee offers his resignation to President Davis because of his failure at Gettysburg. Davis rejects it.

August 11: Confederate guns at Battery Wagner, Fort Sumter and James Island pound at

Federal entrenchments at Morris Island.

August 12: From Morris Island, Federal troops return the fire with heavy Parrott rifles, which cause considerable damage at Battery Wagner and Fort Sumter.

August 17: Federal batteries on Morris Island start a major bombardment of Fort Sumter.

August 18: Lincoln tests the new Spencer rifle in Treasury Park, Washington.

August 22: After six days of heavy bombardment, Fort Sumter's defenses are severely damaged, but it does not surrender. The heaviest gun of the Federals, the "Swamp Angel," which fired 200 pound shots, explodes.

August 23: After more than 5000 rounds have been fired into Fort Sumter, it is reduced to a mass of rubble, with only one gun still operating.

August 26: Federal troops capture the Confederate rifle pits in front of Battery Wagner on Morris Island.

August 27: Firing is all but suspended in Charleston Harbor.

August 29: In Charleston Harbor, the Confederate submarine *H. L. Hunley* sinks with five men lost.

August 30: Additional heavy damage is done to Fort Sumter by shelling.

September 9: A naval assault on Fort Sumter is frustrated. The Federals suffer 125 casualties.

September 13: Meade's Army of the Potomac occupies Culpeper Court House from which Lee has withdrawn. Washington urges Grant to send troops east to aid Rosecrans.

September 14: Federal troops push toward the Rapidan River against Lee.

October 3: Another six-day bombardment of Fort Sumter from Morris Island ends.

The Federal War Department orders the enlistment of black troops in the slave states of Maryland, Tennessee and Missouri.

October 5: In Charleston Harbor, the large Federal ironclad *New Ironsides* is severely damaged by a new weapon—a torpedo—fired by the tiny Confederate torpedo boat *David*.

October 9: Lee's army crosses the Rapidan and moves west and north against Meade's right flank.

October 11: Heavy skirmishing between the Rapidan and the Rappahannock in Virginia, as Lee's move gains momentum.

October 13: Lee's army moves toward Manassas and Washington.

Andrew Curtin, staunch supporter of Lincoln, is reelected governor of Pennsylvania.

October 14: Lee's advance corps under A. P. Hill attacks retreating rear units of Meade's army, but as Lee cannot disrupt the Federal army, no third battle of Manassas develops.

October 17: Lincoln asks for 300,000 more volunteers. Lee begins to pull back from Bull Run.

October 19: Jeb Stuart and his "Southern Horse" defeat General Kilpatrick at Buckland Mills, Virginia.

October 26: New bombardment of Charleston.

October 28: After another two-day heavy bombardment, Fort Sumter still holds out.

October 31: Three more days of heavy firing into Fort Sumter.

November 6: President Davis visits Wilmington, North Carolina, the only Southern harbor really open for trade, although it is strongly blockaded.

November 7: Meade's Army of the Potomac crosses the Rappahannock and engages Lee's forces at Rappahannock Station and Kelly's Ford. Lee withdraws to the Rapidan.

November 11: Major General Ben Butler, formerly Federal commander in New Orleans, assumes command in the Department of Virginia and North Carolina.

November 12: Another four-day bombardment of Fort Sumter begins.

November 15: Federal authorities tighten prohibitions against trading with the enemy and with war profiteers.

November 19: At the dedication ceremony of the military cemetery in Gettysburg, Lincoln delivers his famous "Gettysburg Address."

November 20: Further heavy firing into Charleston.

November 26: The Army of the Potomac crosses the Rapidan in an attempt to turn Lee's right flank.

November 27: Lee moves back to block Meade's advance.

John Hunt Morgan and several of his officers escape from the Ohio State Penitentiary.

Sherman and other troops are ordered to rush to the aid of Burnside at Knoxville.

November 28: Lee halts Meade's offensive before it got under way.

The bombardment of Sumter and batteries around Charleston continues.

November 29: Longstreet undertakes an attack on Forts Sanders and Loudon near Knoxville but is eventually forced to withdraw.

President Lincoln is recovering from a mild attack of smallpox.

November 30: Federal troops move into Fort Esperanza in Matagorda Bay, Texas.

General Bragg's request to be relieved is granted by President Davis. Bragg is succeeded by Lieutenant General Hardee.

December 2: Meade's Army of the Potomac completes its withdrawal to north of the Rapidan, abandoning its short-lived "Mine Run" campaign.

December 3: Longstreet begins to move his troops from Knoxville into winter quarters.

December 4: At Charleston, another seven days of bombardment come to an end.

December 6: General William T. Sherman and his staff enter Knoxville, Tennessee, ending the siege of Burnside's army.

December 8: In Washington, at the opening of the 38th Congress, Lincoln issues his Proclamation of Amnesty and Reconstruction, pardoning those who participated in the rebellion if they take an oath to the Union. In any seceded state, the state government would be recognized if at least one tenth of the voters so wished, provided an oath to the union was taken and slavery barred.

December 9: Major General Burnside is replaced by Major General John G. Foster in command

Lincoln and his commanders: To his left, admirals Porter and Farragut, to his right generals Sherman, Thomas, Grant and Sheridan.

of the Department of the Ohio. Burnside was criticized for his insufficient support of Rosecrans at Chickamauga.

A mutiny of black troops at Fort Jackson, Louisiana, is put down.

December 10: Several skirmishes occur in eastern Tennessee.

December 11: During another bombardment of Fort Sumter, a magazine explodes.

December 14: General Longstreet attacks Federal forces at Bean's Station, Tennessee. After some sharp fighting, the Federals withdraw the next day.

December 16: General Joseph E. Johnston succeeds Lieutenant General Hardee in command of the Confederate Army of Tennessee.

December 19: Federal raids on railroads connecting southwest Virginia and West Virginia.

December 23: Fighting at Jacksonport, Arkansas, Culpeper Court House, Virginia, Corinth, Mississippi, Mulberry Village, Tennessee and Centreville, Missouri.

December 25: Confederate guns damage the U.S.S. *Marblehead* in the Stone River, South Carolina. Shore batteries duel with U.S.S. *Pawnee* at John's Island, near Charleston.

December 27: Lincoln and his secretary of war visit Confederate prisoners at Point Lookout, Maryland.

December 28: Confederate legislature abolishes substitution for military service.

December 29: Skirmishes at Waldron, Arkansas, Coldwater, Mississippi, and several places in Tennessee.

December 31: Fighting at Searcy County, Arkansas.

1864:

January 3: Union cavalry drives Confederate troops out of Jonesville in southwestern Virginia.

January 5: Confederate troops return to Jonesville. After sharp fighting, the Federals surrender more than 200 men.

January 8: David O. Dodd, 17 years old, is hanged as a Confederate spy in Little Rock, Arkansas.

January 10: Blockading U.S.S. *Iron Age* is destroyed by bombardment after it gets aground off Lockword's Folly Inlet, South Carolina.

January 15: Skirmish near Petersburg, West Virginia.

January 16: In a cavalry engagement near Dandridge, Tennessee, the Federals have to withdraw.

January 19: The pro-Union Arkansas constitutional convention adopts an antislavery measure.

January 20: At the mouth of Mobile Bay, Federal naval vessels make a reconnaissance of Forts Morgan and Gaines.

January 21: Pro-Union citizens of Tennessee meet at Nashville and propose a constitutional convention to abolish slavery.

Beginning of a five-day reconnaissance by Federal troops on the Matagorda Peninsula, Texas.

January 22: Major General Rosecrans is appointed commander of the Federal Department of the Missouri.

January 23: A policy whereby plantation owners would recognize the freedom of their former slaves and hire them by fair contracts is approved by Lincoln.

January 25: Union forces evacuate Corinth, Mississippi. Firing on Fort Sumter is resumed.

January 29: Confederate troops attack the steamer *Sir William Wallace* on the Mississippi.

Bombardment of Charleston is intensified.

The Confederates add a new ironclad, *Charleston*, to their fleet.

January 30: Major General Frederick Steele assumes command of the Department of Arkansas.

February 1: By order of President Lincoln, 500,000 men are to be drafted on March 10 to serve for three years or the duration of the war.

The U. S. House revives the rank of lieutenant general, with General Grant in mind.

February 2: Small Confederate boats capture the U. S. gunboat *Underwriter* near New Berne, North Carolina, but are forced to flee after setting her on fire.

In Chattanooga, 129 Confederate deserters take an oath of allegiance to the U. S.

February 3: Sherman leaves Vicksburg with 26,000 men to attack Meridian, Mississippi.

President Davis recommends suspension of the writ of habeas corpus to combat spying, desertion and disloyal activities at home.

February 4: In Arkansas, a five day Federal expedition moves from Helena up the White River.

February 5: After a skirmish, Sherman's troops march into Jackson, Mississippi.

February 6: Federal troops cross the Rapidan River at Morton's Ford, Virginia, but have to withdraw. The Confederate Congress bans the import of luxuries and the circulation of U. S. paper money.

February 7: Federal troops occupy Jacksonville, Florida.

February 9: One hundred and nine Federal officers tunnel their way out of Libby Prison in Richmond. Fifty-nine will reach Federal lines.

Union troops occupy John's Island near Charleston, but have to withdraw two days later.

February 10: From Jacksonville, the Federal expedition advances to Lake City.

February 11: Confederate raiders attack the Baltimore and Ohio Railroad, throwing a train off the tracks near Kearneysville, West Virginia.

February 12: Sherman's Meridian, Mississippi, campaign results in several skirmishes.

February 14: Sherman's troops enter Meridian. Confederates under General Polk continue to fall back. Railroads and supplies in the area are destroyed.

In Florida, the Federal expedition captures Gainesville.

February 17: The C.S.S. *Hunley*, a Confederate "semisubmersible" sinks the U.S.S. sloop *Housatonic* with a torpedo. Both crews perish. An act of the Confederate Congress authorizes the use of blacks, free or slave, as laborers (but not yet as soldiers).

February 20: About 5,000 Confederates attack 5,500 Union troops advancing toward Lake City, Florida and force them back to Jacksonville, after heavy losses.

Sherman withdraws from Meridian toward Vicksburg.

February 22: U. S. Secretary of the Treasury Chase offers his resignation, after having been proposed by radical abolitionists as presidential candidate against Lincoln. Lincoln refuses the resignation.

A Federal force under William Sooy Smith, which had supported Sherman's campaign in Mississippi, is attacked by Forrest's Southern cavalry near Okolona, Mississippi. Although greatly outnumbered, the Confederates defeat the Union troops and force them to retreat to Memphis.

February 24: General Braxton Bragg becomes chief of operations in the Confederate armies.

February 25: A Federal detachment of the Army of the Cumberland under Major General J. M. Palmer attacks Confederate positions at Dalton, Georgia but withdraws the following day.

February 26: Lincoln confirms his confidence in the controversial General Benjamin Butler. He also orders that the death sentences of all deserters be commuted to imprisonment during the war.

February 29: A Federal cavalry force of 3,500 men under Judson Kilpatrick pushes south from the Rapidan toward Richmond.

March 1: Kilpatrick, within a few miles of Richmond, decides not to attack and turns east instead.

March 2: The U. S. Senate confirms the nomination of Ulysses S. Grant as lieutenant general.

Part of Kilpatrick's force under Colonel Ulric Dahlgren falls into an ambush at Mantapike Hill and is killed. Papers are found on him indicating a plot to assassinate President Davis.

March 4: Andrew Johnson is confirmed by the U. S. Senate as federal military governor of Tennessee.

March 5: The Confederate government orders every vessel to give one half of its capacity to government shipments.

March 6: Union forces are attacked and pull out of Yazoo City, Mississippi.

March 8: Lieutenant General Grant and Lincoln meet for the first time.

March 10: Major General Franz Sigel, former German revolutionary, takes over the command of the Federal Department of West Virginia.

March 12: General Banks, with troops and gunboats, starts from the Mississippi up the Red River into Louisiana. Grant does not approve of this campaign.

March 14: In the Red River expedition, Fort De Russy, Louisiana, is captured by the Federals.

March 16: Federal troops occupy Alexandria, Louisiana.

March 20: Several skirmishes take place in Arkansas and Missouri.

The C.S.S. *Alabama* arrives at Capetown, South Africa.

March 21: Lincoln approves an act of the

U. S. Congress enabling the territories of Nevada and Colorado to become states.

March 23: Federal troops under Frederick Steele move from Little Rock, Arkansas to join Banks's expedition up the Red River.

March 24: In a raid, Nathan Bedford Forrest and his men penetrate Tennessee and capture Union-held Union City.

March 25: Confederate cavalry attacks Paducah, Kentucky, but has to withdraw.

March 28: Antiwar outbreak in Charleston, Illinois, is ended by troop reinforcements.

March 29: Lincoln dissuades General Meade from requesting a court of inquiry in regard to the battle of Gettysburg.

March 31: In the Red River campaign, skirmishes occur in Natchitoches, Louisiana.

Various skirmishes in Arkansas, Florida and east Kentucky.

April 1: The U. S. transport *Maple Leaf* sinks in St. John's River, Florida, through a mine or a torpedo.

April 4: General Philip Sheridan becomes the cavalry commander of the Army of the Potomac.

The Convention of Louisiana meets at New Orleans and adopts a new state constitution abolishing slavery.

April 5: Battle of Sabine Crossroads, Louisiana. Confederate forces under General Richard Taylor attack Banks's troops. Low water has made the Union gunboats useless. The Federals are beaten and have to withdraw to Pleasant Hill, suffering more than 2,200 casualties.

April 7: The Red River expedition has advanced to Mansfield, Louisiana and heads for Shreveport.

April 9: The Confederates attack again at Pleasant Hill, but are beaten back by the Union forces.

April 11: A pro-Union state government is inaugurated in Arkansas.

April 12: Confederate cavalry under Forrest assaults and captures Fort Pillow, Tennessee; of the 557 Federal defenders, 231 are killed, espe-

cially blacks, allegedly after they had surrendered.

April 13: Federal gunboats on the Red River retreat to Ecore, Louisiana. Banks's Red River Army has also withdrawn to this point.

April 15: Governor Andrew Johnson of Tennessee supports emancipation in a large pro-Union meeting.

April 17: General Grant stops any further exchange of prisoners until the Confederates have balanced Federal releases. He announces that no distinction between white and black prisoners will be made. Confederate forces begin an attack on Plymouth, North Carolina.

April 18: At Poison Springs, Arkansas, a Federal foraging train with 198 wagons is abandoned by the Federals after a fierce attack by Confederates under Sterling Price.

April 19: At Plymouth, North Carolina, the C.S.S. *Albemarle* sinks the U.S.S. *Smithfield*.

April 20: Plymouth is captured by the Confederates under Brigadier General R. F. Hoke. The Federals lose about 2,800 men and large quantities of supplies.

April 21: Federals under General Banks withdraw from Grand Ecore, Louisiana to Alexandria.

April 26: Federal troops begin to evacuate Washington, North Carolina.

Skirmishes around Alexandria, Louisiana.

April 29: The U. S. Congress raises all duties by 50%.

May 1: Skirmishes in Louisiana and Arkansas.

May 3: Grant orders Meade to let the Army of the Potomac cross the Rapidan again and head toward Richmond.

May 5: The Battle of the Wilderness begins. Meade's army, about 110,000 strong, faces Lee's Army of Northern Virginia, about 62,000 men. From the South, General Butler's army is aiming at Richmond via Petersburg.

In North Carolina, Confederate attempts to retake New Berne are defeated. C.S.S. *Albemarle* damages U.S.S. *Sassacus* on the Roanoke River.

May 6: Severe fighting in the Wilderness. General Longstreet is severely wounded by his own men. Union troops suffer very heavy losses, but hold their ground.

Butler's troops come within a few miles of Petersburg, but are stopped.

U.S.S. *Granite City* is captured at Calcasieu Pass, Louisiana.

U.S.S. *Commodore Jones* is sunk by a torpedo in the James River, Virginia.

May 7: In spite of staggering losses (more than 17,000 men), Grant advances toward Spotsylvania, but is anticipated by Lee who blocks him.

Sherman, with a force of almost 100,000 men, starts on his march on Atlanta. At Dalton, Georgia, Confederate General J. E. Johnston's troops are firmly entrenched. In Virginia, Sheridan launches a raid around the Confederate army toward Richmond.

May 8: In Georgia, Sherman has divided his army in two, with McPherson's forces heading for Snake Creek Gap, trying to bypass Johnston's army.

May 9: McPherson's advance is halted. Near Alexandria, Louisiana, Union troops are building dams on the Red River to raise the water level so that their gunboats can retreat downriver.

May 10: Three corps of the Army of the Potomac attack at Spotsylvania, but are finally repulsed after denting Confederate lines.

Sheridan's raiders fight skirmishes with Stuart's cavalry.

May 11: Jeb Stuart's men confront Sheridan's raiders in defense of Richmond. Stuart is mortally wounded, but Sheridan finally has to retreat.

May 12: The Battle of Spotsylvania is renewed. After a day's fierce fighting, very little ground has changed hands, but both sides sustain staggering losses.

In Georgia, Johnston's position is threatened from the rear, so he retreats from Dalton to Resaca.

May 13: Sheridan's cavalry leaves the Richmond area.

Stuart's last attack, at Yellow Tavern.

Federal guns begin a new, four-day bombardment of Fort Sumter.

May 14: The battle for Resaca, Georgia begins. Grant postpones a new attack in Virginia.

May 15: Six thousand five hundred Union troops under Franz Sigel move south in the Shenandoah Valley and are defeated by Major General Breckinridge's troops, who are reinforced by cadets of the Virginia Military Institute at Lexington, Virginia.

Fighting at Resaca. The Confederates withdraw during the night.

May 16: In the Drewry's Bluff area, south of Richmond, General Butler's forces are attacked by General Beauregard's Confederate brigades. The Union troops are defeated and retreat, after suffering more than 4,000 casualties.

May 18: Sherman's armies follow Johnston's withdrawing troops toward Kingston, Georgia.

Union attacks on Lee's position at Spotsylvania fail.

May 19: In the last attack at Spotsylvania, Confederate General Ewell's troops have to pull back.

In Georgia, Johnston orders a counterattack on Sherman's divided forces, but fails and has to retreat to a strong position at Allatoona Pass.

May 20: Grant's army is moving east and south.

May 22: Lee moves fast and beats Grant into position near the North Anna River, Virginia.

May 23: Fighting at the North Anna River begins. In Georgia, Sherman's army heads from the Cassville area toward Dallas, Georgia.

In Florida, Confederate troops capture the U.S.S. *Columbine.*

May 24: Grant crosses the North Anna River, now reinforced by Sheridan's cavalry.

May 25: Around New Hope, Georgia, Sherman's attacks are repulsed.

May 26: The Army of the Potomac recrosses the North Anna River, but swings east and crosses the Pamunkey, going around Lee's right.

General McPherson, under Sherman, reaches Dallas, Georgia.

May 27: Sheridan's cavalry occupies Hanovertown, Virginia, and Grant continues his advances, fighting several skirmishes.

May 28: Lee again moves in front of Grant's army. Near Dallas, Georgia, Confederates under General Hardee make a reconnaissance in force against McPherson, but are repulsed.

In Missouri, Confederates sack Lamar, and skirmishes break out at Warrensburg and Pleasant Hill.

May 30: Grant's troops arrive along the Totopotomy River.

May 31: Grant shifts toward Cold Harbor.

In Cleveland, a group of radical Republicans meet to nominate General John Charles Frémont for president.

June 1: Beginning of the battle of Cold Harbor, Virginia. Lee is well entrenched and has received some reinforcements.

June 3: Grant starts his all-out attack at 4:30 A.M. After suffering terrible losses, he calls it off around noon. He had suffered about 7,000 dead and wounded within one hour. He later regretted this attack. In Georgia, Johnston is forced to withdraw from the New Hope area.

June 5: In the Shenandoah Valley, Confederate troops under W. E. Jones try to stop General Hunter's raid, but are routed. Jones is killed.

June 8: On the second day at the National Union Party convention, Lincoln is nominated for president almost unanimously. Andrew Johnson is nominated for vice president. In Kentucky, John Hunt Morgan and his raiders capture Mount Sterling. His men rob a bank of $18,000.

June 9: Lincoln proposes a constitutional amendment prohibiting slavery.

Morgan's men are driven out of Mount Sterling, Kentucky. General Benjamin Butler sends an expedition to capture Petersburg, but is stopped by Beauregard's forces.

June 10: Battle of Brice's Crossroads, Mississippi. General Samuel D. Sturgis's Federals face Nathan Bedford Forrest's raiders south of Corinth. Sturgis's greatly superior forces are defeated and retreat in panic.

June 11: In Virginia, Sheridan's cavalry tries to join up with David Hunter's raiders, and fights Confederate forces at Trevilian Station. Hunter's men enter Lexington, Virginia and burn the Virginia Military Institute.

June 12: Grant and Meade begin to move the Army of the Potomac across James River.

June 14: In crossing the James River, Grant keeps Lee guessing as to his plan of approach.

In Georgia, Confederate General Leonidas Polk is killed by a shell.

June 15: As Lee still believes Grant's army to be north of the James, Petersburg is exposed to Federal attack, but the chance is not exploited, because of poor organization.

June 16: Beauregard concentrates all available forces to defend Petersburg and stops Federal attacks. In Georgia, Johnston retreats to a new line near Mud Creek.

June 17: Assaults against Petersburg continue.

In the Valley of Virginia, Confederate troops under Breckinridge and Early defend Lynchburg against Hunter's Federals.

Sherman's troops attack along Mud Creek, Georgia.

June 18: As Lee's main force arrives for the defense of Petersburg, Grant decides to besiege it.

June 19: The highly successful Confederate raider C.S.S. *Alabama* is cornered off Cherbourg, France, by the Federal navy, and sunk in a duel with U.S.S. *Kearsarge.*

June 20: Sherman's forces in Georgia move up to Johnston's new defense line along the Kennesaw mountains.

June 21: Grant and Meade move to extend the siege south and west of Petersburg, but their drive on the Weldon Railroad and Petersburg is halted.

June 23: Confederate troops under Jubal Early advance from Lynchburg toward the Shenandoah from which Hunter's troops have withdrawn.

June 24: The constitutional convention of Maryland votes to abolish slavery.

June 27: Sherman's head-on assault against Johnston's strong Kennesaw defense lines is repulsed with heavy losses (more than 2,000 casualties).

June 30: Salmon P. Chase, secretary of the U. S. Treasury, who had hoped to become a presidential candidate, resigns. This time Lincoln accepts. His successor is William Pitt Fessenden.

July 2: Johnston evacuates his Kennesaw position and moves to a prepared line below Marietta, Georgia.

July 3: Confederate troops under Jubal Early move once again into the Harper's Ferry area.

New Federal attacks in the Charleston Harbor.

July 4: Lincoln refuses to sign the radical anti-South reconstruction bill suggested by Congress. His own reconstruction policy, as shown in Louisiana and Arkansas, is much more lenient.

In Georgia, Federal General McPherson's units are now closer to Atlanta than Johnston.

July 5: Jubal Early's troops cross the Potomac into Maryland, without trying to take Harper's Ferry.

Sherman's forces press Johnston's along the Chattahoochee River.

July 6: Hagerstown, Maryland, is occupied by the Confederates.

July 7: In Charleston Harbor, Federal troops are driven from James Island. A new bombardment of Fort Sumter begins.

July 8: Sherman's left wing, under John McAllister Schofield, crosses the Chattahoochee, forcing Johnston to retreat again.

July 9: Battle of Monocacy, Maryland. A federal army of 6,000 men tries to block Early's advance on Washington, but is defeated, suffering 2,000 casualties.

July 11: Confederate soldiers enter Washington suburbs. Federal troops are moving into the capital's fortifications.

July 12: Early abandons plans to assault Washington, and begins retreat in direction of Leesburg, pursued by Federal units under Major General Horatio Wright.

July 14: At Harrisburg, Mississippi, Confederates under Stephen D. Lee and Nathan Bedford Forrest attack Federal troops under A. J. Smith, but are repulsed.

Early's troops cross the Potomac and withdraw to Leesburg, Virginia.

July 17: President Davis relieves General Joseph E. Johnston of his command in Georgia; he is succeeded by General John Bell Hood, a much more impetuous fighter.

Early's Confederates move into the Shenandoah again.

July 18: Lincoln issues a call for 500,000 volunteers.

Vague peace overtures, pursued by editor Horace Greeley, come to nothing as spokesmen for President Davis demand independence for the Confederacy.

July 19: Early's forces are attacked by Federals in skirmishes at Berry's Ford and Ashby's Gap, Virginia. Early retreats toward Winchester.

July 20: In Georgia, General Hood attacks the Federal armies approaching Atlanta, but is repulsed with heavy losses.

July 21: Sherman's armies are closing in on Atlanta. Hood's further attacks are also unsuccessful.

July 22: In heavy fighting near Atlanta, Confederate General W. H. T. Walker and Federal General James B. McPherson are killed. The Confederates suffer much higher losses than the Union troops.

July 24: In the second Battle of Kernstown, Virginia, Federal forces under George Crook are defeated by Early's army and retreat to Bunker Hill, West Virginia.

July 27: Sherman decides to lay at least partial siege to Atlanta.

July 28: Battle of Ezra Church, Georgia. Confederate attacks on Federal positions fail. They withdraw into the fortifications of Atlanta, after suffering about 5,000 casualties.

July 29: Units of Early's cavalry cross the Potomac near Cave Spring and enter Maryland and Pennsylvania. Panic erupts among Northerners.

July 30: A huge mine in the 586-foot-long tunnel dug on the eastern side of the Petersburg defenses is exploded. The Union troops attack, but after heavy fighting are repulsed with great losses.

Chambersburg, Pennsylvania, is entered by Early's troops and burnt because the demanded ransom of $500,000 cannot be paid by the town.

July 31: Federal troops under William W. Averell pursue Early's cavalry and drive them back at Hancock, Maryland.

August 3: Federal forces land on Dauphin Island and surround Fort Gaines at the entrance of Mobile Bay, Alabama, but cannot take the fort.

Early's troops retreat from Maryland to West Virginia.

August 5: Admiral Farragut and his fleet of 18 ships, after a fierce battle against Confederate forts and ships, succeed in closing Mobile as a Confederate port.

The radical Republicans in the U.S. Congress open a campaign against Lincoln.

August 6: The C.S.S. *Tallahassee* leaves Wilmington, North Carolina and starts on a cruise during which she will take more than 30 vessels.

Philip Henry Sheridan, Union general, at Cedar Creek.

August 7: Fort Gaines in Mobile Bay surrenders to the Federal army.

Major General Philip H. Sheridan is made commander of the new Army of the Shenandoah, formed to fight Early's Confederate forces.

August 11: Early retreats from Sheridan's advancing Federal troops, heading south toward Cedar Creek, Virginia.

August 15: Skirmishing at Cedar Creek between Sheridan's and Early's troops. Sheridan withdraws toward Winchester, Virginia. Early's troops follow.

In Georgia, Sherman's troops advance slowly southwest of Atlanta.

August 18: The battle of Weldon Railroad develops as the Federal Fifth Corps under G. K. Warren gets hold of the vital railroad and then turns north toward Petersburg, before being stopped.

August 19: After a heavy Confederate counter-attack, Warren's corps has to retreat, but still holds the railroad.

August 21: In a daring raid, about 2,000 men under Nathan Bedford Forrest occupy Memphis, and then operate against Sherman's supply lines. Further Confederate attacks on Weldon Railroad fail.

August 23: Fort Morgan, the last Confederate bastion in Mobile Bay, falls to the Federals after heavy bombardment.

August 25: Confederate units under A. P. Hill attack Union troops destroying the Weldon Railroad, south of Petersburg, Virginia. The Federals suffer heavy losses, but hold the line.

Early threatens another invasion of Maryland and Pennsylvania.

August 26: Sherman moves to cut off Atlanta completely.

August 28: All of Sherman's units move closer to Atlanta.

August 29: The Democratic national convention meets in Chicago.

August 30: Confederate General Hood tries to attack the Federal flank at Jonesborough, south of Atlanta. There is also fighting at East Point and Flint Ridge.

August 31: At the Democratic convention, Major General George B. McClellan is nominated for president.

Confederate attacks at Jonesborough, Georgia are repulsed with heavy losses.

September 1: Continued heavy fighting at Jonesborough, while Hood begins to evacuate the city.

Skirmishing between Sheridan and Early near Winchester, Virginia.

September 2: Atlanta occupied by Sherman's army. Hood's forces have retreated to Lovejoy's Station.

September 3: In the Shenandoah, Sheridan starts his reinforced army toward Berryville, Virginia, and Early's diminished forces. Skirmish at Berryville.

September 4: In Greeneville, Tennessee, Confederate raider John Hunt Morgan is killed by a Federal raiding party.

At Charleston, another three-day bombardment of Fort Sumter ends, with more than 14,000 rounds fired.

September 5: New skirmishes between Sheridan's and Early's units along the Opequon on the Shenandoah River.

September 7: Sherman orders the population of Atlanta to leave. About 1,600 people leave their homes and all their possessions.

September 8: George McClellan accepts the Democratic nomination, disavowing the "peace plank" in the Democratic platform by declaring that the Union is the one condition of peace.

September 12: Both Lincoln and Grant are worried about "the dead lock" in the Shenandoah Valley.

September 14: R. H. Anderson's corps leaves Early's force to reinforce Lee at Petersburg.

September 16: Forrest's group of 4,500 men begins operating against Sherman's communication lines in Tennessee and northern Alabama.

Wade Hampton's Confederate cavalry defeats Federal soldier-herders at Coggins' Point, Virginia, and takes 2,400 cattle sorely needed in Petersburg, plus 300 prisoners.

September 17: John C. Frémont informs the radical Republicans that he is withdrawing from the election contest.

Early, by now badly outnumbered, nevertheless advances toward Martinsburg, north of Winchester.

September 19: Sheridan attacks Early's spread forces north and east of Winchester and forces him to retreat up the Valley Pike. Each side loses about 4000 men.

Last major trans-Mississippi invasion of the Confederates. A Union train of 202 wagons at Cabin Creek in northeastern Indian Territory is captured.

On Lake Erie, Confederate agents capture the steamer *Philo Parsons,* trying to free Confederate prisoners near Johnson's Island, but are frustrated by the U.S.S. *Michigan.*

September 20: Early escapes the pursuing Sheridan and makes a stand at Fisher's Hill, Virginia.

Large scale Confederate raiding in Missouri.

September 22: Sheridan attacks and defeats Early at Fisher's Hill.

September 24: Forrest's troops capture Athens, Alabama, after some fighting.

In Missouri, Price's troops attack Fayette.

In the Shenandoah, Early retires south, while Sheridan's pursuing troops begin burning barns and crops, according to Grant's orders, so that the Valley may no longer serve as a granary and sanctuary for the Confederates.

September 26: Clash between Sheridan's and Early's cavalry at Brown's Gap, Virginia.

September 29: A two-pronged Federal drive on the Petersburg–Richmond front. Fort Harrison, a major Confederate bastion, is taken by Federals. Attacks on Fort Gilmer in the North fail.

Early's and Sheridan's troops fight at Waynesborough, Virginia.

September 30: Confederate counterattacks on Fort Harrison fail.

Heavy fighting at Peebles Farm, southwest of Petersburg. The Federals extend their siege lines.

October 1: Forrest's men skirmish with Union garrisons at Athens and Huntsville, Alabama, while Price fights Union forces at Union, Franklin and Lake Springs, Missouri.

British blockade-runner *Condor*, pursued by U.S.S. *Niphon*, runs aground near Port Fisher, North Carolina. Confederate spy Rose O'Neal Greenhow, trying to escape in a small boat, drowns.

October 2: Confederate General Hood's men break the Federal supply line between Atlanta and the Chattanooga at Kennesaw Water Tank.

Price's Confederate raiders occupy Washington, Missouri, on the Missouri River.

October 3: Sherman sends General Thomas against Hood's invasion, which is becoming a threat to Sherman's operations.

October 4: The new U. S. Postmaster General William Dennison joins the Cabinet, replacing General Montgomery Blair.

October 5: Battle between Sherman's troops and Confederate troops at Allatoona, northwest of Atlanta.

October 10: Hood's men skirmish around Sherman's supply line near Rome, Georgia.

October 11: Elections in Pennsylvania, Ohio and Indiana show Lincoln supporters stronger than expected.

October 12: Chief Justice Roger Brooke Taney dies in Washington.

Skirmishes between Hood's and Sherman's units at Resaca and other sites north of Atlanta.

October 13: In a very close vote, Marylanders adopt new constitution that abolishes slavery.

Sherman's troops hold Resaca, but Hood's troops seize the railroad line north to Tunnel Hill.

Mosby's men wreck a train near Kearneysville on the Baltimore and Ohio.

Lincoln, in an election estimate, gives the ''supposed copperhead vote'' 114, his own Union vote only 120 electoral votes.

October 15: Price's troops attack Sedalia, and occupy Paris, Missouri.

October 17: Hood's Tennessee Army gives up harassing Sherman's Chattanooga–Atlanta line and moves west into Alabama.

October 19: Early's surprise attack on Federal encampments at Cedar Creek, or Belle Grove, Virginia. Sheridan, returning hastily from Washington, counterattacks and defeats the Confederates. Federal casualties amount to 5,600, Confederate to about 3,000 men. From now on, the Shenandoah Valley is under Federal control.

A small Confederate detachment, operating from Canada, raids St. Albans, Vt.

Price's men occupy Lexington, Mo.

October 21: Sherman holds his pursuit of Hood's army at Gaylesville, Ala.

October 23: In the largest engagement west of

the Mississippi, Price attacks Federals under Samuel Ryan Curtis at Westport, Mo., but is beaten back and forced to withdraw to the Missouri-Kansas State line. Casualties were about 1500 on either side. This is the last Confederate effort west of the Mississippi.

October 25: South of Westport, Missouri, Price's units are again attacked and beaten by Federal troops.

October 27: South of Petersburg, Virginia, Federal troops try to move west to seize the South Side Railroad, but their advance is halted. The Federals also attack east of Richmond at Fair Oaks.

At Plymouth, North Carolina, the Confederate ironclad *Albemarle* is sunk by a torpedo fired by a tiny Federal boat on the Roanoke River.

Sherman, learning that Hood was moving from Gadsden to Decatur, Alabama, decides to start his march from Atlanta to the coast.

October 31: Nevada enters the Union as the 36th state by proclamation of the president.

November 1: Forrest heads south, up the Tennessee River, with a "navy" of two captured vessels. One of them, *Venus,* is driven ashore by Federal gunboats below Johnsonville, Tennessee.

November 4: Forrest's batteries cause great damage to Federal installations at Johnsonville.

November 5: Minor skirmishes at Forts Haskell and Morton, Virginia.

November 7: The Congress of the Confederate States meets in Richmond for the second session of the Second Congress, its last. President Davis announces that the Confederacy favors a negotiated peace, but only with independence.

November 8: Lincoln is reelected president of the United States, with Andrew Johnson of Tennessee as vice president. He receives 2,330,552 votes as against 1,835,985 for Democrat George B. McClellan, who carries only Delaware, New Jersey and Kentucky. In the military vote, Lincoln has a huge majority. The Republicans now have a majority of more than

two-thirds in the House and a heavy plurality in the Senate.

November 12: Sherman readies his force of 60,000 infantry and 5,500 artillery for his march south, despite being detached and cut off from all communications from the rear.

November 13: A large part of Early's force is detached to reinforce the Confederates at Richmond.

November 14: Lincoln accepts the resignation of Major General George B. McClellan.

November 16: Sherman leaves Atlanta, leaving behind him a smoking city and a desolated population.

November 19: Governor Joe Brown of Georgia calls for all men between the ages of 16 and 55 to oppose Sherman, but finds little response.

November 20: Sherman's advancing army skirmishes at Walnut Creek, East Macon and Griswoldville, Georgia.

November 21: Hood's army moves from Florence, Alabama, toward Tennessee.

November 22: General Slocum's wing of Sherman's army occupies Georgia's state capital of Milledgeville. The state legislature passes a levy en masse and flees. Widespread foraging, looting and burning takes place along the path of the advancing army.

November 24: John McAllister Schofield's Union force drives away Forrest's cavalry at Pulaski, Tennessee, and takes a strong position south of the Duck River.

November 25: Confederate agents, operating from Canada, set fire to at least 10 New York hotels.

November 26: Skirmishes between Sherman's troops and Confederate cavalry at Sandersville, Georgia.

November 29: Schofield, threatened by Hood's Confederate army and Forrest's cavalry manages to pull out without being attacked.

At Sand Creek, Colorado Territory, a Federal force attacks an Indian camp of five hundred Arapaho and Cheyenne, killing 500–600 warriors, women and children. The government

The Confederates burn their navy yard at Savannah.

later condemned the massacre.

November 30: Battle at Franklin, Tennessee. In a bloody battle, Hood attacks Schofield's forces, but cannot defeat them. The Confederates suffer more than 6,000 casualties, the Federals significantly fewer.

December 1: Schofield's Federal troops take positions near Nashville, Tennessee.

December 3: Sherman's army reaches Millen, Georgia.

Union and Confederate armies dig in south of Nashville.

December 5: The Congress of the United States meets for the second session of the 38th Congress.

Forrest's cavalry moves up to Murfreesboro, Tennessee, but cannot take the town.

December 6: Lincoln names former Secretary of the Treasury Salmon P. Chase as chief justice.

Lincoln sends his annual message to Congress.

Grant orders General Thomas at Nashville to attack Hood at once, but Thomas hesitates,

waiting for his cavalry. Grant is ready to remove him.

December 9: U.S.S. *Otsego* and a tug are sunk by Confederate torpedoes on the Roanoke River near Jamesville, North Carolina.

December 10: Sherman's army arrives in front of Savannah and decides to surround it, rather than assault it.

December 12: Federals capture the C.S.S. *Resolute* on Savannah River.

December 13: Federal troops attack Fort McAllister on the Ogeechee River below Savannah and capture it.

Contact is established between the Union fleet and Sherman's army, solving the latter's supply problems.

December 15: The battle of Nashville begins. General George H. Thomas's Army of the Cumberland attacks General John Bell Hood's Confederate Army of Tennessee and drives it back to a new position.

December 16: In a renewed massive assault, the Confederate lines are finally broken. The Federal army of about 50,000 men suffer about 3,000 casualties, the Confederates, with fewer than 30,000 men, lose about 6,000.

December 17: Hood's rear guard stands firm and allows the rest of the Confederate army to retreat.

December 18: At Savannah, General Hardee refuses Sherman's surrender demand.

Lincoln calls for 300,000 more volunteers to replace casualties.

December 20: General William Joseph Hardee, urged by Beauregard and others, successfully moves his 10,000 men out of Savannah.

December 21: Federal units occupy Savannah.

December 23: A Federal fleet arrives from Fort Monroe, Virginia to attack Fort Fisher near Wilmington, North Carolina.

General Benjamin F. Butler commands the Federal land forces.

December 24: Naval bombardment of Fort Fisher begins, with almost 60 warships participating.

December 25: Federal landings at Fort Fisher fail.

December 26: Hood's Confederate Army of Tennessee crosses the Tennessee River at Bainbridge, Tennessee, thus ending the campaign. Hood is heading toward Tupelo, Mississippi.

December 28: Grant admits to Lincoln that the Wilmington expedition was a gross failure.

December 30: At a Cabinet meeting, Lincoln indicates that General Butler will be removed from his command of the Army of the James.

1865:

January 2: Federal troops operating against the Mobile and Ohio Railroad fight Confederate units at Franklin and Lexington, Mississippi.

January 4: A new Federal attempt is made against Fort Fisher, North Carolina, with troops under Major General Alfred H. Terry and a huge fleet approaching the fort.

January 6: Republicans in the House of Representatives, led by J. M. Ashley of Ohio, again push the proposal of the 13th Amendment, which abolishes slavery.

January 7: Major General Benjamin F. Butler is

removed from the command of the Department of Virginia and North Carolina, and replaced by General E. C. Ord.

January 9: The constitutional convention of Tennessee adopts an amendment abolishing slavery.

January 11: The constitutional convention of Missouri adopts an ordinance abolishing slavery.

Confederate raiders under Thomas Lafayette Rosser fall on Beverly, West Virginia, capturing 580 Federals.

January 13: A powerful Federal fleet under Admiral Porter begins bombarding Fort Fisher, North Carolina while 8,000 Union soldiers are put ashore above the fort.

John Bell Hood resigns as commander of the Confederate Army of Tennessee. Lieutenant General Richard Taylor succeeds him.

January 14: Bombardment of Fort Fisher continues, while Union troops under General Terry hold off Confederate units under General Bragg.

January 15: In a two-pronged assault, Federal troops penetrate Confederate defenses on the west side of the fort and by late evening have taken the entire fort and captures its garrison. Wilmington, North Carolina, the last major access point for the South, is thereby cut off as a blockade-running port. Federal losses amount to about 1,300 men.

January 16: Francis Preston Blair, Republican political leader, shows Lincoln a letter in which Jefferson Davis talks of negotiations "between the two nations."

January 18: Lincoln gives Blair a letter declaring that he is ready to negotiate peace to the people "of our one common country."

January 19: Sherman begins his march from Savannah northward into South Carolina.

January 21: Sherman moves his entire headquarters to Beaufort, South Carolina.

January 23: A fleet of 11 Confederate vessels tries to head downriver below Richmond on the James, but fails as four of the vessels go aground.

January 24: Grant approves an exchange of prisoners between Confederates and Federals.

January 27: President Davis names three commissioners to start informal talks with Federal authorities, as a result of Francis Preston Blair's visit.

January 29: Skirmishes at Robertsville, South Carolina, Harrodsburg and Danville, Kentucky.

January 31: The U. S. House of Representatives passes the 13th Amendment of the Constitution, abolishing slavery, by a two-thirds majority. It had long since been approved by the Senate.

General Robert E. Lee is appointed general-in-chief of the Confederate armies.

February 1: Sherman begins his march into the heart of South Carolina, from Savannah and Beaufort, South Carolina.

Confederate Secretary of War James A. Seddon resigns.

February 3: At Hampton Roads, offshore from Fort Monroe, Virginia, Lincoln and Secretary of State Seward meet Confederate Vice President Alexander H. Stephens and two other Southern delegates to discuss the fate of the United States and the Confederate States and the possibility of a truce. The discussions end in a deadlock.

February 5: Grant attacks southwest of Petersburg and reaches the Boydton Plank Road to extend his lines. (Battle of Hatcher's Run.)

February 6: President Davis names Major General John C. Breckinridge as Confederate secretary of war.

February 7: Battle of Hatcher's Run ends as Federals give up Boydton Plank Road, but fortify their lines below Burgess's Mill.

In South Carolina, Sherman's troops take Edisto River Bridge.

February 8: Lincoln signs a resolution of the U. S. House of Representatives declaring that the 11 seceded states are not entitled to representation in the electoral college.

February 11: Skirmishes at Aiken, Johnson's Station and Battery Simkins, South Carolina.

Ruins of Charleston, S.C.

February 14: Sherman's troops cross the Congaree River and turn toward Columbia, South Carolina.

February 16: Union shells are fired into Columbia.

February 17: Columbia, capital of South Carolina, surrenders to the Union troops. At night, large fires break out. A great part of the city is destroyed.

Charleston, South Carolina, is evacuated by the Confederates.

The U. S. Senate votes to repudiate all debts of Confederate governments.

February 18: Federal units under Brigadier General Alexander Schimmelfennig enter Charleston.

Fort Anderson, North Carolina, is bombarded by Federal naval units.

February 19: Confederate troops pull out of Fort Anderson.

At Columbia, South Carolina, Sherman's men destroy foundries, railroad lines, machine shops and the arsenal.

February 21: Confederate General Braxton Bragg arrives at Wilmington, North Carolina, and orders evacuation to save his troops.

February 22: Federal troops enter Wilmington without opposition.

Lee appoints General Joseph E. Johnston commander of the Departments of South Carolina, Georgia and Florida, placing Beauregard under his command.

Sherman's troops reach Rocky Mount, South Carolina.

February 26: Sherman's troops reach Hanging Rock, South Carolina, while other movements are slowed down by heavy rain.

February 27: In the Shenandoah Valley, Sheridan's force of 10,000 cavalry men start moving south toward Lynchburg.

March 2: At Waynesborough, Virginia, Sheridan's forces attack the remains of Jubal Early's Confederate army and disperse them. Early and a few followers retreat to Richmond. Sheridan turns toward Charlottesville, Virginia.

Lee asks Grant for a conference, but Grant replies that he has no authority for such a meeting.

March 3: In the last regular session of the 38th Congress of the United States, a Bureau for the Relief of Freedmen and Refugees is established.

Sherman's troops enter Cheraw, South Carolina, while the Confederates pull back across the Pee Dee River.

Lincoln instructs Grant not to discuss any political questions with Lee.

March 4: In Washington, the second inauguration of Abraham Lincoln as president and the inauguration of the new Vice President Andrew Johnson, whose incoherent, rambling speech shocks many members of the audience.

Sherman's troops march to Florence, South Carolina.

March 7: Federal troops enter North Carolina, with skirmishing southwest of Fayetteville.

New Berne, North Carolina, is made a Federal supply base.

March 8: Confederates under Bragg attack Federals moving out from New Berne. In the battle of Kinston, Bragg's attacks are repulsed after three days fighting.

The Confederate Senate approves the use of blacks as soldiers, with a vote of 9 to 8.

March 11: Fayetteville, North Carolina, is occupied by Sherman's forces.

Lincoln proclaims pardon for all deserters who will return within 60 days.

March 13: The Confederate Congress authorizes the president to call upon owners to volunteer their slaves. It is implied that such slaves would be made free by action of the states.

March 14: Federal troops under General Cox take Kinston, North Carolina.

March 16: Battle of Averasborough, North Carolina. Sherman's left flank, under General Henry W. Slocum, attacks Confederates under General William Joseph Hardee, who block their advance toward Goldsborough. Hardee finally retreats.

March 19: Battle of Bentonville, North Carolina, begins. Three assaults by the Confederates south of Bentonville are beaten off.

March 20: Sherman's right wing under General Oliver Otis Howard arrives at Bentonville to relieve Sherman's left wing under Slocum.

March 21: Sherman's right wing moves around the Confederate's left and finally forces a retreat. Federal casualties at Bentonville amount to about 1,500, Confederate casualties to about 2,600 men.

March 22: Union forces under James Harrison Wilson strike toward Selma, Alabama.

March 25: In a surprise move, Confederates under Major General John B. Gordon attack Fort Stedman east of Petersburg and take the fort, but have to withdraw under heavy counterattacks of superior Federal forces, incurring about 4,000 casualties.

The siege of Mobile, Alabama, by Federal forces under General Canby begins.

Lincoln visits Grant at City Point, Virginia.

March 26: Sheridan's forces cross the James River to join up with Grant at Petersburg.

March 27: Lincoln, Grant and Sherman meet at City Point, aboard the *River Queen.*

Eyewitness Testimony

I have insisted that Stanton shall be removed & that Halleck shall give way to me as Comdr. in Chief. I will not serve under him—for he is an incompetent fool—in no way fit for the important place he holds . . . The only safety for the country and for me is to get rid of lots of them . . . I feel that I have done all that can be asked in twice saving the country . . . You should see my soldiers now! You never saw anything like their enthusiasm. It surpasses anything you ever imagined.

McClellan to his wife, September 20, 1862.

The proclamation of the President, which gives in a certain contingency—almost sure to occur—freedom to four millions of men, is one of those stupendous facts in human history which marks not only an era in the progress of a nation, but an epoch in the history of the world. Shall we recognize and use it wisely, or shall we, blindly and foolishly, refuse to see that we have now our future in our hands . . . Let the President know that everywhere throughout the land he is hailed as Wisest and Best and that by this great deed . . . he recreates a nation.

. . . By a single blow he has palsied the right arm of rebellion.

New York Tribune, September 24, 1862.

. . . in the face of all this, yesterday the President issued a proclamation freeing all slaves in those states which shall be in rebellion on the first of January next. Better wait until we have the power to perform than utter these weak threats.

Maria L. Daly, September 24, 1862, Diary of a Union Lady (1962).

The war is going against us heavily. The Revolution is raging at all points while the folly, weakness and criminality of our heads is becoming more decidedly manifest . . . The people are strong and willing, but "there is no king in Israel." Abraham Lincoln has neither sense nor principle. The man of the day has not yet come.

David Strother, former Harper correspondent, after Lincoln's Preliminary Emancipation Declaration, September 1862.

I would not hesitate to make it even with our diminished numbers, did the army exhibit its former temper and condition; but, as far as I am able to judge, the hazard would be great and a reverse disastrous. I am therefore led to pause.

Lee to President Davis, September 25, 1862.

There is no law but the despotic will of poor Abe Lincoln, who is worse than a knave because he is the cover for every knave and fanatic who has the address to use him. Therefore we have not one devil, but many to contend with. Yet he only stands between us and internal revolution. It is terrible. God help our unhappy country!

Maria L. Daly, September 28, 1862, Diary.

Another winter campaign before us and its load of debt. As for property, it has no value. I do not feel that banknotes are safe day by day. As for gold and silver, one never sees such a thing any longer.

Maria L. Daly, September 28, 1862, Diary.

It is a dash of the pen to destroy four thousand millions of our property, and it is as much a bid for the slaves to rise in insurrection, with the assurance of aid from the whole military and naval power of the United States.

The Whig, Richmond, commenting on Lincoln's Emancipation Proclamation, October 1, 1862.

McClellan, Pierrepont says, is popular because he keeps his soldiers out of harm's way as much as possible. "I think, too," he said, "there were 34,000 on furlough at the last battle." No wonder he says McClellan is popular—with 18,000 stragglers! The rebels shoot their stragglers, so they have none. We talked despondently enough of the state of the country. Both of the gentlemen seemed to feel that it would be utterly broken up into four parts at least. New York would be a free city, perhaps, like Hamberg [Hamburg].

Maria L. Daly, October 4, 1862, Diary.

You remember my speaking to you of what I called your overcautiousness? Are you not over-cautious when you assume that you cannot do what the enemy is constantly doing? Should you not claim to be at least his equal in prowess, and act upon the claim?

Lincoln, letter to General McClellan, October 13, 1862.

The whole North seems to be going for the Democrats. What a revolution of public opinion since Lincoln's election. I almost feel sorry for the Republicans, struggling 20 years for power and losing it after one year's possession . . .
Maria L. Daly, October 23, 1862, Diary.

I am sick, tired and disgusted with the condition of military affairs here in the east and I wish myself back in the western army. With all my efforts I can get nothing done. There is an immobility here that exceeds all that any man can conceive of. It requires the lever of Archimedes to move this inert mass. I have tried my best, but without success.
General Henry W. Halleck, letter to Governor H. R. Gamble of Missouri, end of October 1862.

This town is filled with littleness. There is not a man destined to endurance. This great Republic, late the wonder and envy of the nations, is crumbling into blood-stained fragments because there is no head and hand to guide and light it through the peril . . . There's no human granite nowadays. It's all clay.
Federal Colonel James A. Mulligan, observations on Washington in his journal entry of October 31, 1862.

Late at night I was sitting alone in my tent, writing to my wife. All the staff were asleep. Suddenly someone knocked upon the tentpole, and, upon my invitation to enter, there appeared Burnside and Buckingham [of the War Department], both looking very solemn . . . After a few moments, Buckingham said to Burnside: "Well, general, we had better tell General McClellan the object of our visit." I very pleasantly said that I should be glad to learn it. Whereupon Buckingham handed me the . . . orders of which he was the bearer . . . I saw that both—especially Buckingham—were watching me most intently . . . I read the papers with a smile, immediately turned to Burnside and said: "Well, Burnside, I turn the command over to you." They soon retired.
George B. McClellan on his dismissal on November 5, 1862 in McClellan's Own Story (1887).

The sole defeat of General McClellan has been that he lacked motive power . . . That overcautious disposition was noticed long ago, but there was a fond hope that experience would cure it . . . It has been demonstrated to be an inseparable part of General McClellan's nature. It is the presence of this fatal quality alone . . . that reconciles us . . . to the displacement of a commander otherwise so competent.
Editorialist of the New York Times, *after McClellan's dismissal.*

Those whom the gods wish to destroy, they first make mad. Lincoln has removed McClellan and appointed Secretary [Caleb B.] Smith of the Interior, a poor country lawyer, Judge of the Supreme Court. Burnside succeeds McClellan. I trust he will not allow himself to be goaded on by the public clamor to do anything rash with the new levies.
Maria L. Daly, November 9, 1862, Diary.

As our case is new, so we must think anew, and act anew. We must disenthrall ourselves, and then we shall save our country. Fellow-citizens, we cannot escape history . . . In giving freedom to the slave, we assure Freedom to the free—honorable alike in what we give, and what we preserve. We shall nobly save, or meanly lose, the last best hope on earth.
Lincoln, State of the Union message of December 1, 1862.

I never saw a more pitiful procession than they made trudging through the deep snow . . . little children tugging along with their doll babies . . . women so old and feeble that they could carry nothing . . . Some had a Bible and a toothbrush in one hand, a picked chicken and a bag of flour in the other. Most of them had to cross a creek swollen with winter rains, and deadly cold with winter ice and snow. We took the battery horses down and ferried them over . . . Where they were going we could not tell, and I doubt if they could.
Robert Stiles, on the evacuation of Fredericksburg, December 1862, in Four Years under Marse Robert *(1903).*

Jackson . . . appeared that day in a bright new uniform which replaced his former dingy suit, having actually exchanged his faded old cap for another which was resplendent in gold lace . . . his men did not like it, fearing, as some of them said, that "Old Jack would be afraid of soiling his clothes and would not get down to his work."
Fitzhugh Lee, before the battle of Fredericksburg in General Lee of the Confederate Army *(1895).*

I was near my colors. A twelve-pounder shell . . . burst right in front of me. One fragment struck me just below the heart, making a bad wound. Another blew off my hat. Another small bit entered my mouth and broke out three of my best jaw-teeth, while the gravel, bits of . . . earth and minute fragments of shell covered my face with bruises. I fell insensible, and lay so for some time, when another fragment of shell, striking me on the left leg, below the knee, brought me to my senses. My mouth was full of blood, fragments of teeth and gravel . . .

Colonel Edward E. Cross of New Hampshire, during the battle of Fredericksburg, as quoted in R. Wheeler's Voices of the Civil War *(1976).*

The Confederates had had a day of such savage pleasure as seldom falls to the lot of soldiers, a day on which they saw their opponents doing just what they wished them to do . . .

Francis W. Palfrey, Union officer, summarizing the battle of Fredericksburg in Antietam and Fredericksburg *(1882).*

Gone are the proud hopes, the high aspirations that swelled our bosoms a few days ago. Once more unsuccessful, and only a bloody record to show our men were brave . . . [The army] has strong limbs to march and meet the foe, stout arms to strike heavy blows, brave hearts to dare—but the brains, the brains! Have we no brains to use arms and limbs and eager hearts with cunning? Perhaps Old Abe has some funny stories to tell appropriate to the occasion.

William Thompson Lusk, after the battle of Fredericksburg in War Letters *(1911).*

The narrow river brought the outposts of the armies within speaking distance; and conversations, jokes, newspapers and tobacco were exchanged by the pickets . . . until prohibited. The Confederate pickets are said to have repeatedly remarked, "Before you'un Yanks can get to Richmond you'uns will have to get up Early, go up a Longstreet, get over the Lee of a Stonewall, and climb two Hills."

Unnamed Union soldier, report on the line-up before Fredericksburg, December 1862, as quoted in R. Wheeler's Voices of the Civil War.

I have no heart to write. Since I opened my diary last, the battle of Fredericksburg occurred and our repulse with the loss of 14,000 killed, wounded and missing. Burnside hoped to surprise the enemy, but our dilatory government officials kept his bridges and supplies so long behindhand they had two weeks to fortify themselves. Poor Burnside will therefore have to suffer.

Maria L. Daly, December 20, 1862, Diary.

"Our failure was an accident, was it, Mr. President? The Lord deliver us from any more of such accidents! The worst accident that has befallen us is to have a commander at our head who is not able to lead us to victory. Little Mac [McClellan] would never have dreamed of hurling men against such a stronghold when nothing was to be gained by it but certain defeat."

Union officer, comments on Lincoln's message to the army after Fredericksburg, December 22, 1862, quoted by Jesse Bowman Young in his What a Boy Saw in the Army, *(1894).*

Today unbind thy captive,/ So only are unbound;/ Lift up the people from the dust,/ Trump of their rescue, sound!/Pay ransom to the owner,/ And fill the bag to the brim./Who is the owner? The slave is the owner/ And ever was. Pay him./ O North! give him beauty for rags,/ And honor, O South! for his shame; Nevada! coin thy golden crags/ With Freedom's image and name!

Ralph Waldo Emerson "Boston Hymn" (January 1, 1863).

The Confederacy is the last hope for the perpetuation of that system of government which our forefathers founded—the asylum of the oppressed and the home of true representative liberty . . . Every crime which could characterize the course of demons has marked the course of the invader.

Jefferson Davis, speech in Richmond on January 5, 1863.

The Emancipation Proclamation is . . . the most startling political crime, the most stupid political blunder yet known in American history . . . Southern people have now only to choose between victory and death.

The Richmond Enquirer *on January 7, 1863.*

General Wadsworth's daughter . . . declared herself a dreadful abolitionist, Republican, and all that, and in the same breath wished we had a monarchy, hated the blacks . . . But, she said, Lincoln is a miserable creature whose inordinate conceit and vanity make his stupidity and vulgarity unendurable.

Maria L. Daly, January 9, 1863, Diary.

A great many men from different regts. took advantage of this mud march to desert or to attempt to do so, for they were nearly all brought back by the cavalry scouts, who caught them making their way to the Potomac River. The woods were full of them. The mud I suppose sickened them. Hundreds of horses and mules were also lost.

Alfred Bellard on the "mud march" at the Rappahannock, January 1863 in Gone for a Soldier *(1975).*

. . . it was dreadful work. The roads, under the influence of the rain, were becoming shocking. And by daylights, when the boats should have been on the banks, ready to slide down into the water, but fifteen had been gotten up—not enough for one bridge, and five were wanted! . . . Night arrived, but the pontoons could not be got up. The rebels had discovered what was up, and the pickets on the opposite bank called over to ours that they "would come over tomorrow and help us build the bridge." . . . An indescribable chaos of pontoons, wagons and artillery encumbered the road down to the river—supply wagons upset by the roadside, artillery stalled in the mud . . .

It was no longer a question of how to go on; it was a question of how to get back. That night . . . the three days' cooked rations which the men had taken in their haversacks . . . would give out; and the other six days' provisions were in the supply trains which stuck fast in the mud miles behind . . .

William Swinton, then correspondent of the New York Times, *on Burnside's attempt to cross the Rappahannock, January 22, 1863.*

. . . the next morning the army wretchedly began its return to camp. Some ironically offered to get into the boats and row them to camp through the mud . . . Finally the army began to corduroy the road (i.e., cover the worst spots with logs . . .), and with laughter and jest, and oath and execration, it floundered back into its camps; but not until the enemy had facetiously put up a big placard on the opposite shore which read: BURNSIDE STUCK IN THE MUD.

Warren Lee Goss on Burnside's retreat, January 24, 1863, in Recollections of a Private *(1890).*

There are some things in regard to which I am not quite satisfied with you. I believe you to be a brave and skilful soldier, which, of course, I like. I also believe you do not mix politics with your profession, in which you are right. You have confidence in yourself which is valuable, if not an indispensable quality. You are ambitious which, within reasonable bounds, does good rather than harm. But I think that during Gen. Burnside's command of the Army, you have taken counsel of your ambition and thwarted him as much as you could, in which you did a great wrong to the country and to a most meritorious and honorable brother officer. I have heard, in such a way as to believe it, of your recently saying that both the Army and the Government needed a Dictator. Of course it was not *for* this, but in spite of it that I given you the command. Only those generals who gain successes can set up dictators. What I now ask of you is military success, and I will risk the dictatorship.

Lincoln, in a letter to Major General Joseph Hooker, after he made him commander of the Army of the Potomac, January 26, 1863.

The storm has culminated here in deep snow which does not improve our comfort. I came particularly hard on some of our troops whom I was obliged to send some eleven miles up the Rappahannock to meet a recent move of General Burnside. Their bivouac in the rain and snow was less comfortable than at their former stations . . . General Burnside's designs have apparently been frustrated, either by the storm or by other causes; and on last Saturday he took a special steamer to Washington to consult with military oracles at the Federal seat of Government. Saturday I heard of his being closeted with President Lincoln, Secretary Stanton and General Halleck. I suppose we shall have a new programme next week.

General Robert E. Lee, letter to his wife, January 29, 1863.

Although so many were absent, the first order which General Hooker issued provided that one brigade commander, one field officer of a regiment, and two men out of every hundred might be absent at one time, not exceeding ten days to the near States and fifteen days for the States farther away . . . The soldiers were informed that if they did not return on the day fixed they would be court-martialed. If they did not return, their regiment could have no more furloughs. It touched their honor.

Charles C. Coffin, end of January 1863 in My Days and Nights on the Battlefield *(1863).*

I am told that several regiments in the Army of the Potomac declare that they will never fire another shot, that the government can draft men but cannot make them fight, that they will no longer be butchered for political generals, etc. Two regiments at Baton Rouge have likewise laid down their arms on account of having Negro regiments raised.

Maria L. Daly, February 13, 1863, Diary.

. . . let all your efforts be directed to the prompt supply of these [food] articles in the districts where our armies are operating . . . Alone, unaided, we have met and overthrown the most formidable combination of naval and military armaments that the lust of conquest ever gathered together for the subjugation of a free people . . . We must not forget; however, that the war is not yet ended and that we are still confronted by powerful armies and threatened by numerous fleets; and that the Government which controls these fleets and armies is driven to the most desperate efforts to effect the unholy purposes in which it has thus far been defeated.

Jefferson Davis, in a Proclamation of April 10, 1863.

At last the whole army stood in line of battle—General Hooker with the President and other noted visitors . . . in the midst of a brilliantly dressed body of officers . . . When the troops had presented arms, and the banners had drooped, and the bands had united in a piercing blast of music, the commanding general and troops passed in review, proud, hopeful, exultant, confident in their leader, and believing in their beloved President, "Father Abraham." During that visit the President had made a hasty visit to many of the camps . . . galloping from one encampment to another, greeted with hearty cheers, showing his long, ungainly figure to poor advantage on horseback, making a very brief address now and then to the boys, and leaving his image—the picture of patience, fidelity, political shrewdness and indomitable gentleness and human kindness—indelibly printed in their hearts.

Jesse Bowman Young, Hooker's grand review at Falmouth, early April 1863, in What a Boy Saw in the Army.

The enemy must either ingloriously fly or come out from behind his defences and give us battle upon our own ground, where certain destruction awaits him.

General Hooker, proclamation to his army before the battle of Chancellorsville, end of April 1863.

As soon as Jackson was en route [around Hooker's right flank], Lee began to demonstrate against our centre and left, to make Hooker believe the main attack was to be there, and to prevent him from observing the turning column in its progress toward our right. . . . It is always pleasant to think your adversary is beaten, and Hooker thought . . . Jackson might be retreating on Gordonsville. It was evident enough that he was either doing that or making a circuit to attack [our right] . . .

Union General Abner Doubleday on the battle of Chancellorsville, May 1, 1863 in Chancellorsville and Gettysburg *(1882).*

About sundown the soldiers of the Eleventh Corps, with stacked arms, were boiling their coffee, smoking their pipes . . . and playing cards among the baggage waggons . . . Some were chasing rabbits with shouts of laughter, and all were unprepared, when a few shots were heard . . . and Jackson's men . . . burst upon them like a clap of thunder from a cloudless sky . . . Everything was in confusion. No change of front was possible, and the officers, isolated from the rank-and-file, could not rally them. The impetuosity of Jackson's attack was terrible . . .

Warren Lee Goss, on the battle of Chancellorsville, in Recollections of a Private.

We ran through the enemy's camps . . . Tents were standing and camp-kettles were on fire, full of meat. I saw a big Newfoundland dog lying in one tent as quietly as if nothing had happened. We had a nice chance to plunder their camps and search the dead, but the men were afraid to stop, as they had to keep with the artillery, and were near a good many officers who might whack them over the heads with their swords if they saw them plundering.

John O. Casler, Chancellorsville, May 2, 1863, in Four Years on the Stonewall Brigade *(1906).*

. . . the skirmishers had no sooner fallen back than the whole line was engaged. Before long a regt. of Red Legged Zouaves who were on the left of the first line broke, and running past our Regt. their officers called upon us to fire into them. We did not obey the order. The Red Leggs started to rest, and soon after all the troops on our left had fallen back thus leaving us in a bad position. The bullets were now flying round us like hail . . .

Alfred Bellard, the battle of Chancellorsville in Gone for a Soldier.

Lee's attack at Chancellorsville.

The rebels soon made their appearance again, advancing in a solid body about twelve deep and not a musket to be seen. One of our officers told us not to fire as they were comming [sic] in to surrender. No notice was taken of such orders, however, and we blazed away until they were close to us. All at once their guns came from behind their backs . . . This was too hot for us, and we had to fall back under heavy fire. The rebels came up to our works and poured lead into us like hail, but came no further.
Alfred Bellard, at Chancellorsville in Gone for a Soldier.

Soon after we left the works I received a wound in the legg [sic] that prevented me from keeping up with the Regt. and I had to paddle my own canoe . . . My leg had now got so stiff that when I got up after laying down a short time it was like getting up on a wooden leg . . . In the afternoon I went over to the corps field hospital, where the doctors were busy in probing for balls, binding up wounds and in cutting off arms and legs, a pile of which lay under the table.
Bellard, at Chancellorsville in Gone for a Soldier.

Upon the South porch of [the Chancellor House], General Hooker stood leaning against one of its pillars, observing the fighting, looking anxious and much careworn . . . I doubt if any orders were given by him to the commanders on the field, unless, perhaps, to "retire when out of ammunition."
Darius Couch, Hooker's second-in-command, at Chancellorsville, May 3, 1863, as quoted in R. Wheeler's Voices of the Civil War.

. . . the enemy had so strengthened his position near Chancellorsville, that it was deemed inexpedient to assault it with less than our whole force, which could not be concentrated until we were relieved from the danger that menaced our rear [from Sedgwick's Corps]. It was accordingly resolved still further to reinforce the troops in front of General Sedgwick, in order, if possible, to drive him across the Rappahannock . . . The next morning, it was found that General Sedgwick had made good his escape and removed his bridges . . .

Robert E. Lee, May 4, 1863 at Chancellorsville
in Recollections and Letters.

As to the charge that the battle was lost because the general was intoxicated . . . he probably abstained from the use of ardent spirits when it would have been far better for him to have continued in his usual habit in that respect . . . In looking for the causes of the loss at Chancellorsville, the primary ones were that Hooker expected Lee to fall back without risking a battle. Finding himself mistaken, he assumed the defensive and was outgeneraled and became demoralized by the superior tactical boldness of the enemy.

Darius Couch, Hooker's second-in-command, as quoted in R. Wheeler's Voices of the Civil War.

While the great victory . . . was causing joy and congratulation throughout the Confederacy, Gen. Stonewall Jackson lay dying at a small farmhouse a few miles from where he had led his last and most famous attack. No one had supposed his wounds would prove mortal . . . But an attack of pneumonia . . . supervened.

Edward A. Pollard, The Lost Cause *(1866).*

About half-past one he [Stonewall Jackson] was told that he had but two hours to live, and answered again, feebly but firmly, "Very good; it is all right." A few moments before he died he cried out in his delirium, "Order A. P. Hill to prepare for action! Pass the infantry to the front rapidly. Tell Major Hawks—" then stopped . . . Presently a smile . . . spread itself over his pale face, and he said quietly, and with an expression as if of relief, "Let us cross over the river and rest under the shade of the trees."

Dr. Hunter McGuire, Jackson's medical director, as quoted in R. Wheeler's Voices of the Civil War.

Hooker has crossed the Rappahannock, but been obliged to retreat with the loss of ten thousand men which, after his boastful proclamations and arrogant criticisms of other generals, must be to him a great mortification. He was so sure of victory that he declared that Lee's army was now the legitimate property of the Army of the Potomac, but on going to take possession, he found that nine points of the law, namely possession, were all in their favor . . .

Maria L. Daly, May 10, 1863, Diary.

The [overseas] agents of the Confederate Government stated in their official dispatches that if General Lee could establish his army firmly on Northern soil England would at once acknowledge the independence of the South . . . While thus elated by hopes of foreign intervention, the Confederate spies and sympathizers who thronged the North greatly encouraged the Davis Government by their glowing accounts of the disaffection there, in consequence of the heavy taxation rendered necessary by the war, and by the unpopularity of the draft which soon would have to be enforced as a defensive measure. They overrated the influence of the Copperhead, or anti-war party, and prophesied that a rebel invasion would be followed by outbreaks in the principal cities which would paralyze every effort to reinforce the Federal forces in the field.

General Abner Doubleday on the situation end of May, 1863 in Chancellorsville and Gettysburg.

Must I shoot the simple-minded soldier boy who deserts, while I must not touch a hair of a wily agitator who induces him to desert? . . . I think that in such a case to silence the agitator and save the boy is not only constitutional, but, withal, a great mercy.

Lincoln, justifying C. L. Vallandigham's conviction by a military court, in May of 1863. Quoted in N. W. Stephenson's Abraham Lincoln and the Union *(1918).*

If the head of Lee's army is at Martinsburg and the tail of it on the Plank road between Fredericksburg and Chancellorsville, the animal must be very slim somewhere. Could you not break him?

Lincoln, telegram to General Hooker when Lee's invasion into Maryland began, June 9, 1863.

The present movement of General Lee . . . will be of infinite value as disclosing the . . . easy susceptibility of the North to invasion . . . Not even the Chinese are less prepared by previous habits of life and education for martial resistance than the Yankees . . . We can . . . carry our armies far into the enemy's country, exacting peace by blows leveled at his vitals.

Richmond Examiner, July 7, 1863, three days after the battle of Gettysburg.

Hastening to Pennsylvania, I became an observer of the great events which followed . . . Harrisburg was a bedlam when I entered it . . . The railroad stations were crowded with an excited people—with trunks, boxes and bundles . . . tumbling it into the cars, rushing here and there in a frantic manner; shouting, screaming as if the Rebels were about to dash into the town and lay it in ashes . . .

Charles C. Coffin, June 15, 1863, at the beginning of Lee's Gettysburg campaign in Following the Flag *(1865).*

Another rebel raid into Pennsylvania by Lee has been more successful than the last. Our wretched Administration have allowed all the three-year's men to return without making any provision whatever to replace them. Truly God has a controversy with this people . . . There is not one honest, clever man left; at least such are not permitted to have influence. One would not admit the men who rule us in Washington, with the exception of Chase and Seward, even into the drawing room.

Maria L. Daly, June 18, 1863, Diary.

[Southern General] Jenkins was at the head of 2,000 cavalry, and soon became a terror to the farmers in that vicinity [the Cumberland Valley] by his heavy exactions, in the way of horses, cattle, grain etc. It must be confessed he paid for what he took in Confederate scrip, but as this paper money was not worth ten cents a bushel, there was very little consolation in receiving it . . . Having had some horses stolen, he sternly called on the [Chambersburg] authorities to pay him their full value. They did so without a murmur—in Confederate money. He pocketed it with a grim smile, evidently appreciating the joke.—He boasted greatly of his humanity . . . but if the local papers are to be believed, it must be chronicled . . . that he seized a great many Negroes who were tied and sent south as slaves.

General Abner Doubleday, June 1863, Chancellorsville and Gettysburg.

The hearty greeting given to the soldiers [in Maryland] . . . gladdened the army. In Virginia, the Army of the Potomac was considered a ruthless invader . . . now, however, the atmosphere rang with cheers; the Stars and Stripes were everywhere floating in the breeze; men, women and children vied with each other in their exhibitions of loyalty and zeal . . .

Jesse Bowman Young: The Army of the Potomac marches north to meet Lee's invasion, June 1863, in What A Boy Saw in the Army.

General Hooker asked [Washington] that the troops at Harper's Ferry might be placed under his command . . . This was refused, whereupon he informed the War Department that . . . he wished to be relieved of the command of the army . . . General Meade was placed in command; and what was denied to General Hooker was substantially granted to General Meade—that he was to use his best judgment in holding or evacuating Harper's Ferry!

Charles C. Coffin, June 27, 1863, Following the Flag.

It was a dismal day at Frederick when the news was promulgated that General Hooker was relieved . . . Notwithstanding the result of Chancellorsville, the soldiers had a good degree of confidence in him. General Meade was unknown except to his own corps . . . I saw him soon after he was informed that the army was under his command . . . It was in the hotel at Frederick. He stood silent and thoughtful, by himself. Few of all the noisy crowd around new of the change . . . The correspondents of the press knew it long before the corps commanders were informed . . .

Charles C. Coffin, 1863, Following the Flag.

. . . people began to feel that the boast of the Georgia Senator Toombs, that he would call the roll of his slaves at the foot of Bunker Hill monument, might soon be realized.

General Abner Doubleday, after Lee's invasion of Pennsylvania, late June of 1863 in Chancellorsville and Gettysburg.

The Valley of Pennsylvania . . . was delightful to look upon . . . Its broad grain fields, clad in golden garb, were waving their welcome to the reapers and binders . . . It was a type of the fair and fertile Valley of Virginia at its best, before it became the highway of the armies and the ravages of war had left it wasted and bare. This melancholy contrast . . .

brought to our Southern sensibilities a touch of sadness.

John B. Gordon, Reminiscences of the Civil
War *(1904).*

. . . the orders from General Lee for the protection of private property and persons were of the most stringent character . . . Going into camp in an open country and after dark, it was ascertained that there was no wood to be had for even the limited amount of necessary cooking, and I was appealed to by the men for permission to use a few rails from an old-fashioned fence near the camp. I agreed that they might take the top layer of rails, as the fence would still be high enough to answer the farmer's purpose.—When morning came, the fence had nearly all disappeared, and each man declared that he had taken only the top rail! . . . there was no alternative except good-naturedly to admit that my men had gotten the better of me that time.

*John B. Gordon, on Lee in Pennsylvania, end of
June, 1863 in* Reminiscences of the Civil
War.

I assured these ladies [in York, Pennsylvania] that the troops behind me, though ill-clad and travel-stained, were good men and brave; that beneath their rough exteriors were hearts as loyal to women as ever beat in the breasts of honorable men; that their own experience and the experience of their mothers, wives and sisters at home had taught them how painful must be the sight of a hostile army in their town . . .

*John B. Gordon in York, Pennsylvania, June
28, 1863 in* Reminiscences of the Civil War.

All Sunday the army [Meade's] was passing through Frederick. It was a strange sight. The churches were open, and some officers and soldiers attended service . . . The stores were also open, and the town was cleaned of goods—boots, shoes, needles, pins, tobacco, pipes, paper, pencils . . . The lines of march were like the sticks of a fan, Frederick being the point of divergence.

Charles C. Coffin, June 28, 1863, Following
the Flag.

One of the brigades . . . under command of Colonel Roy Stone, had been assigned a position where it came under a heavy artillery fire; and as the troops took their posts Colonel Stone remarked: "We have come to stay." This went quickly through the brigade, the men adopted it as a watchword . . . And a very large part of them never left that ground.

William Swinton of the New York Times. The
Battle of Gettysburg, *fighting at McPherson's
Barn, July 1, 1863.*

. . . for seven or eight minutes ensued probably the most desperate fight ever waged between artillery and infantry at close range, without a particle of cover on either side. They gave us volley after volley . . . and we gave them double-canister as fast as we could load . . . How peerless these cannoners sprang to work! . . . The very guns became things of life . . . Every man was doing the work of two or three . . . Up and down the line, men reeling and falling; splinters flying from wheels and axles where bullets had hit; in the rear horses tearing and plunging . . . drivers yelling, shells bursting, shot shrieking overhead—wreck and carnage indescribable . . .

Every man's shirt soaked with sweat, and many of them sopped with blood from wounds not severe enough to make such bulldogs let go . . . For a few moments the whole Rebel line seemed to waver . . . but their second line came steadily on . . .

*Union cannoneer Augustus Buell, the Confederate attack on Seminary Ridge, July 1, 1863,
quoted in Wheeler's* Voices of the Civil War.

. . . General [Richard S.] Ewell and I were riding through the streets of Gettysburg. In a previous battle he had lost one of his legs, but prided himself on the efficiency of the wooden one which he used in its place. As we rode together, a body of Union soldiers, posted behind some buildings and fences on the outskirts of the town, suddenly opened a brisk fire. A number of Confederates were killed or wounded, and I heard the ominous sound of a Minie ball [actually a conical bullet] as it struck General Ewell, at my side. I quickly asked: "Are you hurt, sir?" "No, no," he replied, "I am not hurt . . . It don't hurt a bit to be shot in a wooden leg."

John B. Gordon, the Confederates in Gettysburg, July 1, 1863 in Reminiscences.

The look of earnestness which gathers on soldiers' faces before a battle was, perhaps, now deepened by the thought that the impending battle was to be fought on our own soil and of the consequences if we met defeat . . . The general feeling was well expressed by a sergeant of a Pennsylvania regiment

who said: "We've got to fight our best today or have these rebs for our masters!"
Warren Lee Goss, Recollections of a Private.

The steadfastness and valor displayed on both sides made the result for some few minutes doubtful; but a struggle so desperate and bloody could not be a long one. The enemy fell back. A short lull was succeeded by another onslaught which was again repelled . . . Of our regiment, eighty-five enlisted men and six officers had been wounded. Beside these, twenty-six . . . had fallen dead . . . O'Rorke was among the dead. Shot through the neck, he had fallen without a groan, and we may hope without a pang.
Captain Porter Farley, the fight for Little Round Top, as quoted in Wheeler's Voices of the Civil War.

He [General Gouverneur K. Warren] came from the direction of the hilltop [Little Round Top, south of the Federal positions]. His speed and manner indicated unusual excitement. Before he reached us he called out to [Colonel] O'Rorke to lead his regiment that way, up the hill. O'Rorke answered him that General Weed had gone ahead and expected this regiment to follow him. "Never mind that" answered Warren, "I'll take the responsibility . . . O'Rorke turned the head of the regiment to the left . . . and led it diagonally up the eastern slope of Little Round Top. Warren rode off evidently bent upon securing other troops.
Captain Porter Farley, of Colonel Patrick H. O'Rorke's regiment, Union troops occupy the vital Little Round Top, July 2, 1863 as quoted in Wheeler's Voices of the Civil War.

The day was not lost, after all! . . . Hancock the Magnificent [General Winfield Scott Hancock, senior corps commander], one of the most inspiring figures that ever aroused and led men on any battlefield, was to seen riding up and down the field, planting batteries, marshalling the reinforcements as they arrived . . . [The enemy's] line, it is true, was thin by this time and was not well reinforced; but it made up in courage and spirit what it lacked in weight . . .
Jesse B. Young, the Confederate onslaught is stopped by Federal reinforcements in the evening of July 2, 1863 in What a Boy Saw in the Army.

. . . I believed that Providence was indeed "taking the proper view" and that the war was nearly over.

Every battery was limbered to the front . . . An artillerist's heaven is to follow the routed enemy, after a tough resistance, and throw shells and canister into his disorganized and fleeing masses . . . There is no excitement on earth like it . . . Now we saw our heaven just in front and were already breathing the very air of victory . . . But we only had a moderately good time with Sickles' retreating corps after all. They fell back upon fresh troops . . .
Confederate officer E. Porter Alexander, Longstreet's chief of artillery, the evening of July 2, 1863 at Gettysburg, as quoted in Wheeler's Voices of the Civil War.

On . . . opposite hills, Lee and Meade, surrounded by staff and couriers and with glasses in hand, are surveying the intervening space. Over it the flying shells are plunging, shrieking, bursting. The battered Confederate line staggers, reels and is bent back before the furious blast. The alert Federals . . . rush through this thin and wavering line. Instantly, from the opposite direction, with deafening yells, come the Confederates in countercharge, and the brave Federals are pressed back . . .
John B. Gordon, on the fighting south of Gettysburg, on July 2, 1863 in Reminiscences of the Civil War.

Right, left and rear of us, caissons were exploded; scudding fragments of wheels . . . were sent into the air a hundred feet high, like the eruption of a volcano . . . When a caisson was exploded, yells of exultation were heard along the whole rebel lines . . . If a constellation of meteoric worlds had exploded above our heads, it would have been scarcely more terrible than this iron rain of death . . . Cemetery Hill and Ridge were ploughed and furrowed . . . The flowers upon the graves at the Cemetery were shot away. Tombs and monuments were knocked to pieces, and ordinary gravestones shattered in rows.
Warren Lee Goss on the great Confederate cannonade on July 3, 1863 in Recollections of a Private.

The temper of his [Lee's] army was such, and it's confidence in its ability to defeat the Yankees at all times and under all circumstances so great, that Lee himself, with all his equipoise of character, caught something of this overconfidence.
Warren Lee Goss, July 2 at Gettysburg in Recollections of a Private.

. . . [The Confederates] came on in magnificent order, with the step of men who believed themselves invincible . . . A light wind sprang up, and the smoke of their guns drifted over the valley towards the cemetery. For a moment it threatened to obscure the charging columns from the sight of those who were about to encounter them in the grapple of death . . . It was but for a moment. The smoke drifted lazily away to the westward, revealing to us the gray lines steadily advancing . . . shells burst upon their compact masses. Their shattered lines do not waver, but steadily closing up the gaps of death, come on in magnificent order. With banners waving, with steady step, they sweep on like an irrestible wave of fate . . . Now they are at musket range, and from behind the stone wall a wave of flame, perceivable even in this noonday light, springs from the muzzles of the line of Union muskets. Volley after volley is poured in with deadly effect upon them.

Warren Lee Goss, Pickett's charge, July 3, 1863
in Recollections of a Private.

The heroic rebel, General [Lewis A.] Armistead, determined to conquer or die, waving his hat on the point of his sword, jumps the wall, followed by his men, rushes forward and seizes a Union battery. Troops are now rushing in upon them from every side . . . Armistead falls mortally wounded among the artillery he has captured . . . Groups of Federals are surrounded by Confederates—Confederates surrounded by Federals. Shots, shrieks, imprecations, shouts and yells; fierce calls for surrender, with defiant answers; all mingle together in a devilish uproar of sounds.

W. L. Goss, the Confederates' farthest advance
on Cemetery Hill in Recollections of a Private.

The lines waver. The soldiers of the front rank look round for their supports. They are gone—fleeing over the field, broken, shattered, thrown into confusion by the remorseless fire . . . Thousands of rebels throw down their arms and give themselves up as prisoners. How inspiring the moment! . . . It is the high-water mark of the Rebellion—a turning point of history and of human destiny.

Charles C. Coffin, the end of Pickett's charge,
July 3, 1863 in Following the Flag.

General Lee came up as our troops were falling back and encouraged them as well as he could; begged

them to re-form their ranks and reorganize their forces . . . it was then that he used the expression that has been mentioned so often; "It was all my fault; get together and let us do the best we can toward saving that which is left us."

Confederate General James Longstreet on the
end of the battle of Gettysburg, quoted in
Wheeler's Voices of the Civil War.

The battle was now over, but nobody knew it . . . Thousands of men were lying unattended, scattered over the field, mingled with . . . hundreds of dead and dying horses . . . It was possible, as night came on, to make a bit of a fire here and there in the rear . . . "Listen, boys!" was the shout of one of the men, as they lay on the ground . . . "The fight must be over. Listen! There is a band in the rear beginning to tune up . . ." It was a sight and situation long to be remembered. The field was covered with the slain; the full moon looked down with softened luster on the field . . . trodden down for miles by the two great armies; surgeons were cutting off limbs, administering whisky, chloroform, and morphine to deaden pain . . . when suddenly a band of music began to play in the rear of the Union line of battle, down somewhere on the Taneytown road . . . "Home—Sweet, Sweet Home" was the tender air . . .

Jesse Bowman Young, What a Boy Saw in
the Army.

The next morning was the Fourth of July, but it seemed at the time to those who were at Gettysburg a somber and terrible national holiday, with the indescribable horrors of the field . . . The army did not know the extent of the victory; the nation did not realize as yet what had been done. The armies were still watching each other, although the Confederates had withdrawn from the town of Gettysburg and concentrated their troops on Seminary Ridge.— The people in the village came out of their cellars . . . they cherished new hopes, for they could see no rebel soldiers . . .

Jesse B. Young, July 4, 1863, What a Boy
Saw in the Army.

. . . the dead bodies of men and horses had lain there putrefying under the summer sun for three days . . . I recall . . . the shocking distension and protrusion of the eyeballs of dead men and dead horses. Several human and inhuman corpses sat upright against a fence, with arms extended in the air, and faces hideous with something very like a fixed leer, as if taking a fiendish pleasure in showing us what we essentially were and might at any moment become.

Robert Stiles, July 4, 1863 at Gettysburg in
Four Years under Marse Robert.

If I had had Stonewall Jackson at Gettysburg, I would have won that fight; and a complete victory there would have given us Washington and Baltimore, if not Philadelphia, and would have established the independence of the Confederacy.

Lee, his reputed words after the battle, quoted
in Wheeler's Voices of the Civil War.

After a long period of gloom and discouragement, we can again congratulate our readers upon good news. On 3rd July, at five p.m., the broken masses of Lee's rebel army, recoiling from the shock of Meade's veterans, were flying to the mountains, throwing aside their guns and cartridge boxes, and strewing the plains of Southern Pennsylvania with the materials of war . . . Within twelve hours after the defeat of the rebels under Lee the garrison of Vicksburg surrendered to General Grant . . . It is assumed by some of our papers and many of our people that the defeat of Lee's army and the fall of Vicksburg involve the collapse of the rebellion . . . The capture of Vicksburg . . . bisects the rebel country, and leaves General Grant's army free to operate . . . against Mobile or . . . against Chattanooga—the geographical and strategical centre of the Confederacy. . . . But it will probably be a mistake to expect the actual surrender of the rebels, so long as Bragg, Beauregard and Johnston have armies under their control.

Harper's Weekly, *July 18, 1863.*

The draft began on Saturday, very foolishly ordered by the government who supposed that these Union victories would make the people willing to submit . . . All day yesterday there were dreadful scenes enacted in the city. The police were successfully opposed; many were killed, many houses were gutted and burned; the colored asylum was burned and all the furniture was carried off by *women*; Negroes were hung in the streets! All last night the fire-bells rang, but at last, in God's good mercy, the rain came down in torrents and scattered the crowds, giving the city authorities time to organize . . . I ordered the doors to be shut and no gas to be lighted

in front of the house . . . I did not wonder at the spirit in which the poor resented the three-hundred-dollar clause.

Maria L. Daly, July 14, 1863, Diary.

At the time the riots took place in New York, all the boys in the hospital who could walk, volunteered to form a company or regt. and proceed to New York, but were not allowed to do so by the doctors. The verdict of the soldiers were that whenever one of them was caught, to string him up at once and be done with it.

Alfred Bellard, at a Washington hospital,
around July 15, 1863 in Gone for a Soldier.

. . . Mr. Bowsie's brother was seized by a rioter who asked him if he had $300. "No" said he. "Then come along with us" said the rioter and they kept him for two hours. Mrs. Hilton said she never saw such creatures, such gaunt-looking savage men and women and even little children armed with brickbats, stones, pokers, shovels and tongs, coal-scuttles and even tin pans and bits of iron. They passed her house about four o'clock on Monday morning and continued on in a constant stream until nine o'clock . . . Among those killed and wounded have been found men with delicate hands and feet, and under their outward laborer's clothes were fine cambric shirts and costly underclothing. . . . I hope it will give the Negroes a lesson, for since the war commenced, they have been so insolent as to be unbearable. I cannot endure free blacks. They are immoral, with all their piety.

Maria L. Daly, July 23, 1863, Diary.

It was not in order to avoid the draft that the colored orphan asylum was burned, that private house were sacked; that inoffensive colored persons were beaten, mutilated and murdered; that Brooks's clothing establishment and a score of smaller stores were pillaged. . . . For these outrages the draft was merely the pretext; the cause was the natural turbulence of a heterogeneous populace, aggravated by the base teachings of despicable politicians and their newspaper organs.

Harper's Weekly *August 1, 1863.*

It is important that this riot should teach us something more useful than a revival of Know-Nothing prejudices. We ought to learn from it . . . that riots are the natural and inevitable diseases of great cities, epidemics, like smallpox and cholera, which must be treated scientifically, upon logical principles, and with the light of large experience . . . while the baton is the proper weapon of the policeman in times of peace and order, the rifle and howitzer are the only merciful weapons in times of riot.

Harper's Weekly, August 1, 1863.

The President and the Cabinet were there, with famous soldiers and civilians. The oration by Mr. Everett was smooth and cold. Delivered, doubtless, with his accustomed graces, it yet wanted one stirring thought, one vivid picture, one stirring appeal. The few words of the President were from the heart to the heart. They cannot be read, even, without kindling emotion . . . It was as simple and felicitous and earnest a word as was ever spoken.

Harper's Weekly, on Lincoln's Gettysburg address, December 5, 1863.

As Congress was in session I paid several visits to the Capitol when off duty, to hear our law makers debate on a bill that was before them, to increase the soldiers pay 50 pr. ct. The bill was not passed, but was amended so as to give us 16 instead of 13 dollars per month. It was however good wages for a soldier . . .

Alfred Bellard, in Washington, November of 1863 in Gone for a Soldier.

. . . Nor has less unrelenting warfare been waged by these pretended friends of human rights and liberties against the unfortunate negroes . . . The hope last year entertained of an early termination of the war has not been realized . . . The patriotism of the people has proved equal to every sacrifice demanded by their country's need.

President Jefferson Davis, message to the fourth session of the First Confederate Congress, December 7, 1863.

. . . Mr. Lincoln recognized the general at once from the pictures he had seen from him. With a face radiant with delight, he advanced rapidly . . . and cried out: "Why, here is General Grant! Well, this is a great pleasure, I assure you," at the same time seizing him by the hand . . . and then the President presented his distinguished guest to Mr. Seward. The Secretary of State was very demonstrative in his welcome . . . Mrs. Lincoln . . . and the general chatted together very pleasantly for some minutes. The visitors had by this time become so curious to

catch a sight of the general that . . . they became altogether unmanageable . . . Seward, after some persuasion, induced the general to stand upon a sofa, thinking the visitors would be satisfied with a view of him, and retire; but . . . their shouts were renewed and a rush was made to shake his hands.

Horace Porter, Grant at the White House, early March of 1864. Campaigning with Grant.

In my first interview with Mr. Lincoln alone he stated to me that he had never professed to be a military man or to know how campaigns should be conducted, and never wanted to interfere in them; but that procrastination on the part of commanders, and the pressure from the people at the North and Congress, *which was always with him*, forced him into issuing his series of "Military Orders" . . . All he wanted or had ever wanted was someone who would take the responsibility and act, and call on him for all assistance needed.

Grant, about his first conversation, after being made supreme commander, in March of 1864, in Personal Memoirs *(1885–86).*

While in Washington, General Grant had been so much an object of curiosity, and had been so continually followed by admiring crowds when he appeared in the streets, and even in his hotel, that it had become very irksome to him . . . The President had given him a cordial invitation to dine that evening at the White House, but he begged to be excused for the reason that he would lose a whole day, which he could not afford at that critical period. "Besides" he added, "I have become very tired of this show business."

General Horace Porter, March 1864 in Campaigning with Grant.

. . . She [Mrs. Julia Ward Howe, author and reformer, who won fame by her "Battle Hymn of the Republic"] was talking to Charles Sumner about some individual cases of misfortune and distress. After a pause, he said: "I have concluded no longer to think of individuals; I can now only consider mankind in masses." Mrs. Howe wrote it in her diary, adding: "I believe the Almighty has not yet come to this conclusion."

Maria L. Daly, March 11, 1864, Diary.

Property is the fruit of labor—property is desirable—is a positive good in the world. That some should be rich, shows that others may become rich,

Cartoon by Thomas Nast, assailing the 1864 Democratic Convention advocating the end of the war.

and hence is just encouragement to industry and enterprise. Let not him who is houseless pull down the house of another.

Lincoln, in a speech to the New York Working-men's Democratic Republican Association, on March 21, 1864.

We children of fortune lose much of what is noble and true by being so shielded. The working classes are the best classes among us in this country. They are the most appreciative, the most intelligent, patriotic, and disinterested. What are called our better class is only the richer and better clothed.

Maria L. Daly, March 22, 1864, Diary.

Baron Gerolt [the Prussian minister] . . . predicts a terrible financial crisis and anarchy so soon as the war ceases, and he is very far-sighted. He says the members of Congress are a disgrace to the nation, they are so ignorant and corrupt. Mr. Chase is so little a minister of finance that he allows himself to

be governed by the gold-brokers of New York. Instead of regulating the gold market, he makes a pact with them.

Maria L. Daly, April 3, 1864, Diary.

Lincoln alone harmonizes in himself all those qualities which are essential to a representation of average Yankeeism. He has no education beyond that of common schools and the attorney's office, and is rich in moral and immoral features which distinguish the genuine son of the Puritan from the rest of mankind. He is shrewd, energetic, shallow, cunning, selfish, egotistical, hard-hearted, vulgar, hypocritical and fanatical . . . We shall be greatly mistaken if he is not the reelected candidate for the Presidency.

Richmond Dispatch, April 7, 1864.

All foreigners look at us with astonishment (I should think too with disgust) to see how little we as a people seem to feel the dreadful state of the country

. . . When I hear sensible men say that it will be better to have Lincoln again than change, it gives me indeed a feeling of despair . . . It seems to me we have no moral conscientiousness. The emigrants who come over here without our education soon lose their virtue and adopt our vices. This on top of their ignorance makes them worse than ourselves.
Maria L. Daly, April 17, 1864, Diary.

The quick, elastic step and easy, swinging gait of the men, the cheery look upon their faces, and the lusty shouts which with they greeted their new commander as he passed, gave proof of the . . . superb spirit which animated their hearts.—If the general's nature had been as emotional as that of Napoleon, he might have been moved to utter the words of the French emperor as his troops filed past him in moving to the field of Waterloo: "Magnificent, magnificent!" But as General Grant was neither demonstrative nor communicative, he gave no expression whatever to his feelings.
General Horace Porter, moving toward the Rapidan, May 4, 1864 in Campaigning with Grant.

This advance by General Grant inaugurated the seventh act in the "On to Richmond" drama played by the armies of the Union. The first advance, led by General McDowell, had been repelled by Beauregard and Johnston at Bull Run; the next five, under the leadership respectively of McClellan, Pope, Burnside, Hooker and Meade, had been repelled by Lee.
John B. Gordon, Confederate general, before the battle of the Wilderness, May 1864, in Reminiscences of the Civil War.

Whether you shall remain at the head of the Treasury Department is a question which I do not allow myself to consider from any standpoint other than my judgment of the public service, and, in that view, I do not perceive occasion for change.
Lincoln to Secretary Salmon P. Chase who had appeared as a potential rival candidate for the presidency, spring of 1864, quoted in N. W. Stephenson's Abraham Lincoln and the Union.

. . . we reached Chancellorsville and bivouacked near the blackened ruins of the old Chancellor House. Weather-stained remnants of clothing, rusty gun barrels and bayonets, tarnished brasses and equipments, with bleaching bones and grinning skulls, marked

Lincoln at Hampton Roads, cartoon of 1865.

this memorable field. In the cavity of one of these skulls was a nest with three speckeled eggs of a field bird. In yet another was a wasp nest. Life in embryo in the skull of death!
Warren Lee Goss, May 4, 1864 in Recollections of a Private.

. . . if one army outnumbers another more than two to one, and the larger one can be indefinitely reinforced and the smaller not at all, then if the stronger side will but make up its mind to stand all the killing the weaker can do, and will keep it so made up, there can be but one result. Billy [Stiles's friend] says the realization of this new order of things did not affect the resolution of the men, but that it did affect their spirits. I can only say I believe he is exactly correct.
Robert Stiles, Confederate artillery adjutant. In the Wilderness, May 4, 1864, Four Years under Marse Robert.

As for the Wilderness, it was uneven, with woods, thickets, and ravines right and left. Tangles thickets of pine, scrub-oak, and cedar prevented our seeing the enemy, and prevented anyone in command of a large force from determining accurately the position of the troops he was ordering to and fro. The appalling rattle of the musketry, the yells of the enemy, and the cheers of our own men were constantly in our ears. At times, our lines, while firing could not see the array of the enemy, not fifty yards distant.

Brigade Commander Alexander Stewart Webb, on the battle of the Wilderness, May 5, 1864. Quoted in Battles and Leaders of the Civil War *(1884–88).*

. . . we were awake at an early hour . . . Some [of the men] were laughing and cracking their jokes about hunting for the Johnnies through the forest, of the grand times we should have marching down to Richmond . . . how when the war was over "we would hang Jeff Davis to the sour apple tree" . . . Another class, more thoughtful, were lying on the ground, silent, alone . . . with compressed lips, seeming not to notice what was transpiring around them. They were thinking of wives and little ones far away . . . Others were leaning against the trees, writing letters . . .

Theodore Gerrish, Union private, May 5, 1864 in Army Life *(1882).*

Cavalry men soon came back with the thrilling intelligence that General Lee's army in great force was rapidly advancing. There was no time to lose . . . The rebels evidently knew but little of our force, position and intention, and it is safe to say that we knew less of theirs . . . The rebels fought like demons . . . trees were completely riddled with bullets in a moment's time; blood ran in torrents . . . and men for a time seemed transformed to beings that had no fear . . . The rifle barrels touched, as from their muzzles they poured death into each other's faces . . .

Theodore Gerrish, May 5, 1864, Army Life.

What awful, what sickening scenes! No, we have ceased to get sick at such sights. Here a friend struck dead by a ball through the head or heart! . . . Another dropping his gun, quickly clapping his hand upon his breast, stomach or bowels, through which a Minnie has passed, and walking slowly to the rear to lie down and die . . . many more, with bullet holes, from which the blood is freely flowing, walking back and remarking, with a laugh somewhat distorted with pain, "See, the rascals have hit me!"

Chaplain A. M. Stewart, the Wilderness Battle, May 5, 1864. Camp, March and Battlefield *(1865).*

Aides came galloping in from the right, laboring under intense excitement, talking wildly, and giving the most exaggerated reports of the engagement. Some declared that a large force had broken and scattered Sedgwick's entire corps . . . It was asserted at one time that both Sedgwick and Wright had been captured. Such tales of disaster would have been enough to inspire serious apprehension . . . But it was in just such sudden emergencies that General Grant was always at his best. Without the change of a muscle of his face, or the slightest alteration in the tone of his voice, he quietly interrogated the officers . . . Reinforcements were hurried to the point attacked, and preparations made for Sedgwick's corps to take up a new line . . . General Grant soon walked over to his camp, seated himself on a stool in front of his tent, lighted a fresh cigar, and then continued to receive further advices from the right.

General H. Porter about the battle of the Wilderness, May 6, 1864 in his Campaigning with Grant.

It may not have been generally observed that Jackson and Longstreet were both struck down in the Wilderness, just one year apart . . . each by the fire of his own men . . . I observed an excited gathering some distance back of the lines, and pressing toward it I heard that General Longstreet had just been shot down . . . I could not learn anything definite as to the character of his wound, but only that it was serious . . . When the ambulance moved off, I followed it a little way . . . The members of the staff surrounded the vehicle . . . They were literally bowed down with grief . . . I rode up to the ambulance and looked in . . . The blood had paled out of his face . . . I noticed how white and dome-like his great forehead looked . . . how spotless white his socks and his fine gauze undervest, save where the black-red gore from his breast and shoulder had stained it . . . and then he very quietly moved his unwounded arm and . . . carefully lifted the saturated undershirt from his chest, and heaved a deep sigh. He is not

dead, I said to myself, and he is calm and entirely master of the situation . . .
Robert Stiles, May 6, in the Wilderness, in
Four Years under Marse Robert.

Flames sprang up in the woods in our front . . . with crackling roar it came down upon the Union line. The wind drove the blinding smoke and heat into our faces . . . At last, they gave way and fell back to the second line of log entrenchments. With a shout the rebel column approached . . . and attempted to seize the abandoned position. The impartial flames in turn drove them back . . . The fire swept on and reached our second line of intrenchments. Finally, blistered, blinded and suffocating, they gave way. The enemy yelled with exultation. They rushed forward . . . The fire was the most enemy our men met that day . . . It is estimated that two hundred of our wounded men were consumed . . . After sundown the Confederates made an attack on the right . . . creating considerable confusion. The night prevented them from following up their success. Thus ended this terrible battle, the full details of which were hid in the tangled woods and darkling forests, where its mysteries will never be disclosed. It was a drawn battle.
Warren Lee Goss, the battle of the Wilderness,
May 6, 1864, in Recollections of a Private.

The ground fought over had varied in width, but averaged three-quarters of a mile. The killed, and many of the wounded of both armies, lay within this belt where it was impossible to reach them. The woods were set on fire by the bursting shells, and the conflagration raged. The wounded who had not strength to move themselves were either suffocated or burned to death. Finally the fire communicated with our breastworks in places. Being constructed of wood, they burned with great fury.
Grant on the battle of the Wilderness in his
Personal Memoirs.

[General Meade]: "This is a crisis that cannot be looked upon too seriously. I know Lee's methods well by past experience; he will throw his whole army between us and the Rapidan, and cut us off completely from our communications." The general [Grant] rose to his feet, took his cigar out of his mouth, turned to the officer and replied, with a degree of animation which he seldom manifested:

George Meade, Union general.

"Oh, I am heartily tired of hearing about what Lee is going to do . . . Go back to your command, and try to think what we are going to do ourselves, instead of what Lee is going to do."
Horace Porter on the battle of the Wilderness in
Campaigning with Grant.

He [Lee] discussed the dominant characteristics of his great antagonist: his indomitable will and untiring persistency; his direct method of waging war by delivering constant and heavy blows upon the enemy's front rather than by seeking advantage through strategic manoeuvre. General Lee also said that General Grant held so completely and firmly the confidence of the Government that he could command to any extent its limitless resources in men and materials . . . He, however, hoped—perhaps I may say he was almost convinced—that if we could keep the Confederate army between General Grant and Richmond, checking him for a few months longer . . . some crisis in public affairs or change in public opinion at the North might induce the authorities at Washington to let the Southern States go, rather than force their retention in the Union at so heavy a cost.

Confederate General John B. Gordon, Lee on May 7, 1864, in Reminiscences of the Civil War.

Reports had reached me to the effect that General Grant's army was retreating or preparing to retreat, and I called General Lee's attention to these rumors. He had heard them, but they had not made the slightest impression upon his mind . . . Indeed, he said in so many words: "General Grant is not going to retreat. He will move his army to Spotsylvania . . . Spotsylvania is now General Grant's best strategic point . . . I have already made arrangements to march by the shortest practicable route, that we may meet him there."

John B. Gordon, May 7, 1864, Reminiscences of the Civil War.

Grant's military standing with the enlisted men this day hung on the direction we turned to the Chancellorsville House. If to the left [northward, in retreat], he was to be rated with Meade and Hooker and Burnside and Pope . . . At the Chancellorsville House we turned to the right [toward Spotsylvania] . . . Our spirits rose . . . The enlisted men understood the flanking movement. That night we were happy.

Frank Wilkeson, Union soldier, evening of May 7, 1864 in Recollections of a Private Soldier in the Army of the Potomac *(1887).*

The battle . . . was probably the most desperate engagement in the history of modern warfare . . . It was chiefly a savage hand-to-hand fight across the breastworks. Rank after rank was riddled by shot and shell and bayonet thrusts, and finally sank, a mass of torn and mutilated corpses; then fresh troops rushed madly forward . . . The opposing flags were in places thrust against each other, and muskets were fired with muzzle against muzzle. Skulls were crushed with clubbed muskets, and men stabbed to death with swords and bayonets between the logs in the parapet which separated the combatants. Wild cheers, savage yells and frantic shrieks rose above the sighing of the wind . . . Even the darkness of the night

and the pitiless storm failed to stop the fierce contest . . .

Horace Porter, the renewed battle of Spotsylvania on May 12, 1864 in Campaigning with Grant.

From where I stood, and in front of a rebel rifle pit, lay stretched in all positions over fifty of our unburied soldiers, and within the pit and lying across each other, perhaps as many rebel dead. It seems almost incredible what a change a little less than a week had wrought, by exposure to sun and hot air. The hair and skin had fallen from the head, and the flesh from the bones—all alive with disgusting maggots. Many of the soldiers stuffed their nostrils with green leaves. Such a scene does seem too revolting to record. Yet, how else convey any just conception of what is done and suffered here?

Chaplain A. M. Stewart, May 18th at Spotsylvania in Camp, March and Battlefield.

Through the masterly tactics of Grant and the unparalleled struggles of our soldiers, Lee has . . . fallen back . . . from post to post [toward Richmond]; yet has each one of these recedings rendered our work of finally beating them more difficult; carrying us still farther from our base of operations . . . Everyone with half a military idea will readily believe that our losses . . . were much greater than the rebels'. How could it be otherwise? Almost invariably we had to make the assaults upon Lee's veteran army, posted in rifle pits, behind breastworks, and in hiding places, where one soldier is equal to two making the attack. These things are not written under any feeling of discouragement, must less to discourage others. We were never more hopeful.

Chaplain A. M. Stewart at Hanover Court House, May 28, 1864, Camp, March and Battlefield.

Your order for an attack is received. I have endeavored to represent to you my condition. In the present position of my line an attack by me would be simply preposterous—not only that, but an attack on the part of the enemy of any vigor would probably carry my lines more than half their length. I have called on General Wright for about 100,000 rounds of ammunition . . .

General W. F. Smith, to Meade, at the battle of Cold Harbor, June 2, 1864, quoted by General James Marshall-Cornwall, in Grant as Military Commander *(1970).*

[I noticed] that the men were calmly writing their names and home addresses on slips of paper, and pinning them on the backs of their coats, so that their dead bodies might be recognized upon the field, and their fate made known to their families at home . . . Such courage is more than heroic—it is sublime.

General Horace Porter, aide to Grant, on the battle at Cold Harbor, in his Campaigning with Grant.

[Grant] was determined to fight the decisive battle of the war and massed his troops and rushed them on our works amidst a storm of shot and shell that it seemed no man could stand; but they were repulsed with great slaughter. The battle (at least the main part of it) did not last more than an hour. It was the most destructive that had been fought during the war, considering the length of time the engagement lasted.

John O. Casler, the Battle of Cold Harbor, June 3, 1864 in Four Years in the Stonewall Brigade.

The opinion of corps commanders not being sanguine of success, you may direct a suspension of farther advance for the present. Hold our most advanced positions and strengthen them . . . It is necessary that we should detain all the army now with Lee . . . To do this effectually it will be better to keep the enemy out of the entrenchments of Richmond than to have them go back there.

Grant to Meade, on June 3, 1864, at Cold Harbor, as quoted by General J. Marshall-Cornwall in Grant as Military Commander.

In the opinion of a majority of its survivors, the battle of Cold Harbor should never have been fought. There was no military reason to justify it. It was the dreary, dismal, bloody, ineffective close of the Lieutenant-General's first campaign with the Army of the Potomac, and corresponded in all its essential features with what had preceded it.

Lieutenant Colonel McMahon, on the battle of Cold Harbor, June 1–3, 1864, quoted in Battles and Leaders of the Civil War.

We were nor [after Cold Harbor] in the position from which General McClellan had been driven two years before. It was a fortunate thing . . . that we had at the head of the army a man who knew nothing of the word defeat—one who was equal to the emergency. Undoubtedly General Grant was disap-

pointed, . . . but he well understood that General Lee had lost heavily in the campaign . . . and so he conceived the idea of throwing his army across the James River . . . with intent to capture Petersburg . . .

Theodore Gerrish, June 12, 1864, Army Life.

He showed himself the personification of earnest, vigorous action in rousing his subordinate commanders to superior exertions. Even his fits of anger and his resort to intemperate language stood him at times in good stead in spurring on every one upon that active field. He sent ringing despatches to all points of the lines, and paced up and down upon the field in his nervous, restless manner . . . and made running comments on the actions of his subordinates . . . He had much to try him on this occasion, and if he was severe in his reprimands and showed faults of temper, he certainly displayed no faults as a commander.

General H. Porter, about Meade during the battle for Petersburg, June 14–18, 1864 in Campaigning with Grant.

I do not allow myself to suppose that either the Convention or the League have concluded to decide that I am either the greatest or the best man in America, but rather they have concluded it is not best to swap horses while crossing the river, and have further concluded that I am not so poor a horse that they might not make a botch of it in trying to swap.

Lincoln, addressing a delegation of the National Union League, after his renomination at Baltimore, June 1964.

When we waked up on the morning of the 13th and found no enemy in our front we realized that a new element had entered into this move—the element of uncertainty . . . Even Marse Robert who knew everything knowable, did not appear to know what his old enemy proposed to do or where he would be most likely to find him . . . We did not cross the James River . . . until the night of the 17th; but from that time everything seemed to have waked up, and though we saw no enemy, yet we knew where he was and that Petersburg was his immediate objective . . . We . . . arrived in Petersburg in the early morning, our division and our battalion being among the first of Lee's troops to arrive. We were just in time . . . The whole population of the city appeared to be in the streets and thoroughly alive to the narrow escape they had made . . . Ladies old and young met us at their front gates . . . and did not at all shrink from grasping our rough and dirty hands.

Confederate Adjutant Robert Stiles, June 17–18, 1864, in Petersburg, Virginia. Four Years under Marse Robert.

Of Abraham Lincoln we have nothing to change in the views often expressed in these columns. That he unites perfect patriotism and great sagacity to profound conviction and patient tenacity, and that his conduct of our affairs has been, upon the whole, most admirable and wise, we are more than ever convinced. And that no public man in our history since Washington has inspired a deeper popular confidence we have no doubt whatever that the result of the election will establish. Of Andrew Johnson it is enough to say that there is no man in the country, unless it be Mr. Lincoln himself, whom the rebels more cordially hate.

Harper's Weekly, *June 23, 1864, after the Republican Convention in Baltimore.*

Here is the Potomac army at a seemingly dead stand. No more flank movements practicable. Richmond not yet captured, nor soon likely to be . . . General Grant finds it a far different matter pushing aside Western armies and capturing Vicksburg to conquering Lee and entering Richmond.

Chaplain A. M. Stewart, July 1, 1864 in Camp, March and Battlefield.

General Halleck will not give orders except as he receive them; the President will give none, and until you positively and explicitly direct what is to be done, everything will go on in the deplorable and fatal way in which it has gone for the past week.

Charles Anderson Dana, assistant secretary of war, to Grant on July 12, 1864, after Early's retreat from Washington, as quoted in General James Marshall-Cornwall's Grant as Military Commander.

. . . forming the brigade on Pen. Ave. we marched through Georgetown . . . with bands playing and colors flying. The streets being thronged with people to see us off. Reaching Fort Reno soon after . . . orders were given to keep awake and have an eye on the supposed rebels in front . . . Had the rebels made an attempt on Was[hington] that night, nothing could have saved it, as there was no troops round

the city but our brigade, and we were supposed to be unfit for active service. The morning of the 11th guns were heard in our front, and long lines of dust could be seen rising above the tree tops showing that large bodies of troops were on the march. Re-enforcements now commenced to arrive . . . both white and black . . . Several large houses that stood in our front, and would have afforded protection to rebel sharp shooters, were burnt down.

Alfred Bellard, defending Washington against Early's approaching army, July 1864 in Gone for a Soldier.

It was the saddest affair I have witnessed in the war. Such opportunity for carrying fortifications I have never seen and do not expect again to have.

Grant, on the great mine explosion east of Petersburg, on July 30, 1864. Reported in Lieutenant-Colonel J. B. Mitchell's Decisive Battles of the Civil War (1955).

Except for what Farragut had already accomplished on the Mississippi, it would have been considered a foolhardy experiment for wooden vessels to attempt to pass so close to one of the strongest forts [Morgan] on the coast; but when to the forts were added the knowledge of the strength of the ram and the supposedly deadly character of the torpedoes, it may be imagined that the coming event impressed the person taking his first glimpse of naval warfare as decidedly hazardous and unpleasant . . .

John C. Kinney, assistant to Admiral Farragut, before his attack at Mobile Bay, Alabama, August 4, 1864, as quoted in R. Wheeler Voices of the Civil War.

Thus the [Federal] monitor *Tecumseh*, at the commencement of the fight . . . went to her fate at the bottom of the Gulf . . . The pilot with whom I sometime afterwards conversed at Pensacola . . . told me that the vessel careened so that the water began to run into the mouth of the turret, he and Captain [of the *Tecumseh*] Craven were on the ladder together, the captain on the top step, with the way open for his easy and honorable escape. The pilot said: "Go ahead, captain!" "No, sir!" replied Captain Craven. "After you, pilot. I leave my ship last!" Upon this the pilot sprung up, and the gallant Craven went down, sucked under by the vortex . . .

Southern observer D. B. Conrad, about the naval battle in Mobile Bay, August 5, 1864, as quoted in Wheeler's Voices of the Civil War.

But at this supreme moment . . . Admiral Farragut's flagship, the *Hartford*, forged ahead; and Farragut, showing the nerve and determination of the officer and the man, gave the order: "Damn the torpedoes! Go ahead!" And away he went, crashing through their bed to victory and renown. Some of the officers told me afterwards that they could hear the [torpedo primers] snapping under the bottoms of their ships, and that they expected every moment to be blown into high air (providentially, the torpedoes had been rendered ineffective by their long exposure to the water) The slightest delay at that time on the part of Farragut, subjected as he was to the terrible fire of the fort and fleet, would have been disaster, defeat and the probable loss of his entire squadron; but he proved to be the man for the emergency . . . Farragut had already won half the battle. He had passed the fort and fleet and had his wooden vessels and three monitors left in good fighting trim.

Southern observer D. B. Conrad, at Mobile Bay, August 5, 1864, as quoted in Wheeler's Voices of the Civil War.

The [Federal] *Monongahela*, going at full speed, struck the *Tennessee* [the Confederate flagship] amidships, a blow that would have sunk almost any vessel of the Union navy, but which inflicted not the slightest damage on the solid iron hull of the ram . . . The two flagships approached each other, bow to bow, iron against oak (the *Hartford*) . . . The other vessels of the fleet were unable to do anything for the defense of the admiral . . . It was a thrilling moment for the fleet, for it was evident that if the ram could strike the *Hartford* the latter must sink. But for the two vessels to strike fairly, bows on, would probably have involved the destruction of both . . . the *Tennessee* slightly changed her course; the port bow of the *Hartford* met the port bow of the ram and the ships grated against each other . . . The *Hartford* poured her whole port broadside against the ram, but the solid shot merely dented the side and bounded into the air . . .

John C. Kinney, Farragut's assistant, Mobile Bay, August 5, 1864, as quoted in Wheeler's Voices of the Civil War.

The *Tennessee* now became the target for the whole fleet, all the vessels of which were making toward her, pounding her with shot and trying to run her down. As the *Hartford* turned to make for her again,

we ran in front of the [Federal] *Lackawanna* which . . . was moving under full headway with the same object. She struck us on our starboard side, amidships, crushing halfway through . . . For a time it was thought that we must sink, and the cry rang out over the deck, "Save the Admiral! Save the Admiral!" The port boats were ordered lowered, and in their haste some of the sailors cut the falls, and two of the cutters dropped into the water wrong side up, and floated astern. But the admiral . . . looked over the side of the ship, and finding there were still a few inches to spare above the water's edge, instantly ordered the ship ahead again at full speed, after the ram.

John C. Kinney, Farragut's assistant, Mobile Bay, August 5, 1864, as quoted in Wheeler's Voices of the Civil War.

Realizing the impossibility of directing the firing of the guns without the use of the rudder, and that the ship [the Confederate *Tennessee*] had been rendered utterly helpless, I went to the lower deck and informed the [wounded] Admiral [Buchanan] of her condition, and that I had not been able to bring a gun to bear upon any of our antagonists for nearly half an hour, to which he replied: "Well, Johnston, if you cannot do them any further damage you had better surrender."

Captain James D. Johnston, second-in-command at the Tennessee, *as quoted in Wheeler's* Voice of the Civil War.

The unfortunate *Lackawanna* . . . again came up on our starboard side and, singularly enough, another collision seemed imminent. And now the admiral became a trifle excited. He had no idea of whipping the rebels to be himself sunk by a friend . . . he inquired: "Can you say 'For God's sake' by signal?"—"Then say to the *Lackawanna*: 'For God's sake get out of the way and anchor!' " . . . the fault was equally divided, each ship being too eager to reach the enemy.

John C. Kinney, Farragut's assistant, as quoted in Wheeler's Voices of the Civil War.

It is suggested that the Constitution does not authorize the President to make any condition such as the abandonment of slavery . . . Those who say so are honestly mistaken . . . The government of the United States is bound by every consideration to secure peace; and peace is impossible while the active

cause for war remains, watching for its opportunity. The cry that the President cannot constitutionally require the destruction of this cause . . . is but another effort of the enemies of the country to prolong the war indefinitely.
Harper's Weekly, August 6, 1864.

This morning, as for some days past, it seems exceedingly probable that this Administration will not be re-elected. Then it will be my duty to so co-operate with the President elect, as to save the Union between the election and the inauguration; as he will have secured his election on such grounds that he can not possibly save it afterwards.
Lincoln, memo presented at the Cabinet meeting on August 23, 1864, which he asked the members to sign.

Our ranks are constantly diminished by battle and disease, and few recruits are received; the consequences are inevitable . . .
General Robert E. Lee in a letter to President Davis, September 2, 1864.

The events of the last month had satisfied me that the commander opposed to me was without enterprise, and possessed an excessive caution which amounted to timidity . . . When I look back to this battle, I can contribute my escape from utter annihilation to the incapacity of my opponent.
Confederate General Jubal Early, about Sheridan at the Opequon Creek and Winchester, August and September 1864. Quoted in Battles and Leaders of the Civil War.

My own judgment is that Johnston acted very wisely: he husbanded his men and saved as much of his territory as he could, without fighting decisive battles in which all might be lost . . . Hood was unquestionably a brave, gallant soldier and not destitute of ability; but unfortunately his policy was to fight the enemy whereever he saw him, without thinking much of the consequences of defeat.
Grant, about the fall of Atlanta, September 2, 1864, in his Personal Memoirs.

I assert that our military plans make it necessary for the inhabitants [of Atlanta] to go away, and I can only renew my offer of services to make their exodus in any direction as easy and comfortable as possible.—You cannot qualify war in harsher terms than I will. War is cruelty, and you cannot refine it. And

those who brought war into our country deserve all the curses and maledictions a people can pour out. I know I had no hand in making this war, and I know I will make more sacrifices today than any of you to secure peace. But you cannot have peace and a division of our country . . . You might as well appeal against a thunderstorm as against these terrible hardships of war . . . We don't want your Negroes or your horses or your houses or your lands . . . But we do want, and will have, a just obedience to the laws of the United States . . . and if it involves the destruction of your improvements, we cannot help it . . .
General Sherman, reply to the protest of the citizens of Atlanta, Georgia, against his evacuation orders, September 1864.

By order, the Chief Engineer has destroyed by powder and fire all the store-houses, depot-buildings and machine-shops. The heaven is one expanse of lurid fire; the air is filled with flying, burning cinders; buildings covering two hundred acres are in ruins or in flames; every instant there is the sharp detonation . . . of exploding shells or powder concealed in the buildings . . . These are the machine-shops where have been forged and cast the Rebel cannon, shot and shell that have carried death to many a brave defender of our nation's honor. The warehouses have been the receptacles of munitions of war, stored to be used for our destruction. The city which, next to Richmond, has furnished more material for prosecuting the war than any other in the South, exists no more as a means for injury to be used by the enemies of the Union.
Major George Ward Nichols, aide-de-camp to Sherman, on the burning of Atlanta, September 1864 in The Story of the Great March *(1865).*

The platform of the Chicago [Democratic] Convention will satisfy every foreign and domestic enemy of American Union and Liberty. It declares that the government of the United States is guilty of resisting rebellion, and that the American people cannot maintain the authority of their laws. It has no word of righteous wrath against the recreant citizens who have plunged the country in the blood of civil war, but lavishes its fury upon the constituted authorities which have steadily defended the Union . . . And this at a moment when stout old Farragut is thundering at Mobile; when the inexorable Grant clutches at the Weldon Road . . . when Early's Shenandoah invasion is too late for success; when Sherman is closing around Atlanta; when State after State is supplying its quota of fresh soldiers; when gold steadily declines; when a universal public confidence is awakening . . .

Harper's Weekly, September 10, 1864.

With respectable talents, a pure character, and patriotic purposes, he is wanting in that high moral sense that perceives the truest truth, and that high moral courage that does and dares in its behalf. He waits, he hesitates in the presence of great opportunities; he compromises with time and with truth, and he is no fit man to deal with the sharp exigencies and the sublime occasions of this hour.

Springfield Republican, September 18, 1864, on the Democratic candidate for president, General McClellan.

. . . the Judge brought home a clever caricature of McClellan [the Democratic presidential candidate] in the character of Hamlet, the gravedigger a jolly Irish soldier. Hamlet holds Lincoln's head in his hand and says "A fellow of infinite jests, where be thy jibes now?"

Maria L. Daly, September 19, 1864, Diary.

Mr. Sermon . . . has been all through Illinois and tells us that Lincoln's partner has made three million dollars, having had permits for buying cotton, sugar, tobacco etc. and that it is well understood that Lincoln goes shares . . . The set of china bought for the White House from a china merchant in the city, for 1,500 dollars, appeared in the bill as costing 3,000 dollars. Mrs. Lincoln pocketing one thousand five hundred dollars . . . Lincoln is a clever hypocrite under the mask of honest boorishness . . .

Maria L. Daly, September 25, 1864, Diary.

His eye is now fixed upon a point far beyond that where he was assailed by the enemy . . . And if but a half, nay, one-fourth, of the men to whom the service has a right, will give him their strength, I see no chance for Sherman to escape from a defeat or a disgraceful retreat.

President Davis, about General John Bell Hood, in a speech at Columbia, South Carolina, on October 3, 1864.

Never before was I so confident that energy, harmony and determination would rid the country of its enemy and give to the women of the land that peace their good deeds have so well deserved . . . We must beat Sherman, we must march into Tennessee . . . We must push the enemy back to the banks of the Ohio.

President Davis, in a speech at Augusta, Georgia, on October 5, 1864.

The question of making soldiers of negroes, of regularly enlisting them, for their own safety as well as our own, must have presented itself to every reflecting mind. Because the Yankees have not been able to make soldiers out of their drafted negroes, it does not follow that we cannot train our slaves to make very efficient troops. We believe that they can be, by drill and discipline, moulded into steady and reliable soldiers.

Richmond Inquirer, October 6, 1864.

I wish all men to be free. I wish the material prosperity of the already free which I feel sure the extinction of slavery would bring. I wish to see, in process of disappearing, the only thing which ever could bring this nation to civil war.

Lincoln, in a letter to Henry W. Hoffman, Maryland political leader, on October 10, 1864.

Andy Johnson who boasts that he was taught to read by his wife, is to be Vice President. It seems that statesmanship is much less of a trade than rail-splitting, shoe-making or tailoring. The last two can be learned by practice only, but statesmanship comes by itself.

Maria L. Daly, October 30, 1864, Diary.

Tomorrow is election day and all good citizens must wish it over. To the great discontent of the public, General [Benjamin F.] Butler has been put in command here and no one can tell what may not be done to secure Lincoln's election. Republicans are now most unscrupulous. I shall order my doors shut . . .

Maria L. Daly, November 7, 1864, Diary.

It has long been a grave question whether any Government, not too strong for the liberties of its people, can be strong enough to maintain its own existence, in great emergencies . . . We cannot have free government without elections; and if the rebellion would force us to forego, or postpone a national election, it might fairly claim to have already conquered and ruined us.

Lincoln, in a victory speech right after his re-election, on November 10, 1864.

With the force, however, you have left with General Thomas, he must be able to take care of Hood and destroy him. I really do not see that you can withdraw from where you are to follow Hood without giving up all we gained in Territory. I say, then, go as you propose.

Great fortune attend you. I believe you will be eminently successful, and at worst can only make a march less fruitful of results than is hoped for.

Grant, last messages to Sherman, November 2 and 7, 1864, before the latter's march to the sea, when the communications were cut. Quoted in General J. Marshall-Cornwall's Grant as Military Commander.

Lincoln has been reelected. Vox populi, vox Dei. So it must be for the best . . . It is well that Lincoln has so large a majority, as now there will be no one to lay the blame upon . . . Poor McClellan! What a lesson he has had on the instability of popular favor and of fair-weather friends. None of his old companions-in-arms, hardly, voted for him, and the reason is clear—it would not be the way to promotion.

Maria L. Daly, November 15, 1864, Diary.

The Republicans may deny it as they may, but the soldiers were not allowed to vote for McClellan . . . In the meanwhile, our real blockade runners are staying at our hotels, and one of them confessed that he got off by paying $15,000. The details I hear of the corruption of our office-holders and others are so shameful that I cannot bear to record them.

Maria L. Daly, November 17, 1864, Diary.

. . . Even the common soldiers caught the inspiration, and many a group called out to me as I worked my way past them, "Uncle Billy, I guess Grant is waiting for us at Richmond!" There was a devil-may-care feeling pervading officers and men that made me feel the full load of responsibility; for success would be accepted as a matter of course, whereas, should we fail, this march would be adjudged the wild adventure of a crazy fool. I had no

purpose to march direct to Richmond . . . but always designed to reach the seacoast first.

William T. Sherman, moving out of Atlanta, November 1864 in Memoirs *(1875).*

General Sherman is at the executive mansion [of Milledgeville, Georgia], its former occupant having, with extremely bad grace, fled from his distinguished visitor, taking with him the entire furniture of the building. As General Sherman travels with a . . . roll of blankets and a haversack full of hard-tack . . . which is as complete for a life in the open air as in a palace, this discourtesy . . . was not a serious inconvenience.

George W. Nichols, November 24, 1864, The Story of the Great March.

. . . Howard, with the 15th and 17th Corps, arrived at Gordon and began the destruction of the Georgia Central Railroad. It was here that the most serious fight of the campaign has occurred up to this date . . . The enemy, about five thousand strong, advanced upon our troops who had thrown up temporary breastworks . . . The Rebels were chiefly composed of militia . . . With the ignorance of danger common to new troops, the Rebels rushed upon our veterans with the greatest fury. They were received with grape-shot and musketry at point-blank range . . . The Rebels . . . were soon in full flight . . .

G. W. Nichols, November 24, 1864 in The Story of the Great March.

The daily skirmishing . . . had no more effect than a fly would have on the back of a sea turtle. Sherman moved on without any interruption, leaving a black and smoldering trail of ruin behind him. Thousands of Negroes, with their plunder, flocked to the Federal Army as it passed through the country. When the crowd became too burdensome, the Federals would take up their bridges at the crossing of some river and leave the poor, deluded followers on the opposite bank to ponder over the mutability of human plans and to cast a longing look at the receding forms of their supposed deliverers.

Confederate Officer J. P. Austin in The Blue and the Gray *(1899).*

I feel how weak and fruitless must be any words of mine which should attempt to beguile you from the grief of a loss so overwhelming. But I cannot refrain from tendering you the consolation that may

Destruction of Southern RR lines.

be found in the thanks of the Republic they died to save . . . I pray that our Heavenly Father may assuage the anguish of your bereavement, and leave you only the cherished memory of the loved and lost, and the solemn pride that must be yours, to have laid so costly a sacrifice upon the altar of Freedom.

Lincoln, in a letter to Mrs. Lydia Bixby, dated November 21, 1864. (Actually, of her five sons, only two had fallen in battle, two had apparently deserted and the fifth was dishonorably discharged.)

On Friday last I saw Edwin Booth and his two brothers [Junius Brutus and John Wilkes] in *Julius Caesar* . . . In the midst of the performance, there was a cry of fire. Fortunately, we did not know the extent of the danger. The performance was inter-rupted, but the tumult was soon appeased. When we read the papers the next day, we read of the plot to burn the city, and of the many fires which have been discovered . . . This [is the] work, it is suspected, of rebel emissaries, alas, some of those, perhaps, whose houses have been burnt in the Shenandoah Valley or in Georgia. War! How horrible are its consequences, how brutalizing its effects!

Maria L. Daly, November 28, 1864, Diary.

Went on Monday night to . . . a party given in honor of Goldwin Smith [an Oxford professor who supported the North] . . . We heard Miss Read sing Mrs. Howe's battlesong to the tune of "John Brown" . . . it was no place to sing the "Battle Hymn" and bring John Brown, the source of all our woe, in a mixed company . . .

Maria L. Daly, December 6, 1864, Diary.

Ruins of the Nashville and Chattanooga Railroad bridge.

I had nearly completed my preparations to attack the enemy tomorrow, but a terrible storm of freezing rain has come on today, which will make it impossible for our men to fight to any advantage. I am therefore compelled to wait . . . Major-General Halleck informs me that you are very dissatisfied with my delay in attacking. I can only say I have done all in my power to prepare, and if you deem it necessary to relieve me I shall submit without a murmur.

General G. H. Thomas to Grant, on December 9, 1864, before the battle of Nashville. Quoted in Gen. J. Marshall-Cornwall's Grant as Military Commander.

If you delay attack longer the mortifying spectacle will be witnessed of a rebel army moving for the Ohio River, and you will be forced to act, accepting such weather as you find. Let there be no further delay . . . I am in hopes of receiving a dispatch from you today that you have moved. Delay no longer for weather or reinforcements.

Grant, telegram to Thomas on December 11, 1864. Quoted in Gen. J. Marshall-Cornwall's Grant. (Thomas attacked at Nashville only on December 15).

. . . on the 15th and 16th of December were fought, in front of Nashville, the great battles in which General Thomas so nobly fulfilled his promise to ruin [Confederate General John Bell] Hood . . . Rumors of these great victories reached us . . . by piecemeal, but his official report came in on the 24th . . . I wrote at once through my chief of staff . . . to General Thomas, complimenting him in the highest

terms. His brilliant victory at Nashville was necessary to mine at Savannah to make a complete whole . . .
Sherman, December 1864 in Georgia, Memoirs.

Oh, proud was our army that morning,/ That stood where the pine darkly towers,/ When Sherman said "Boys, you are weary,/But today fair Savannah is ours!"/Then sang we the song of our chieftain,/ That echoes o'er river and lea,/ And the stars in our banner shone brighter/ When Sherman marched down to the sea.
Samuel H. M. Byers, "Sherman's March to the Sea" (December 1864).

I beg to present to you, as a Christmas gift, the city of Savannah, with 150 heavy guns and plenty of ammunition, and also about 25,000 bales of cotton.
General Grant's message to President Lincoln on December 22, 1864.

Like the tribes of Israel/ Fed on quails and manna,/ Sherman and his glorious band/Journeyed through the rebel land,/Fed from Heaven's all-bounteous hand,/ Marching on Savannah!
Oliver Wendell Holmes, "Sherman's in Savannah" (December 22, 1864).

The cruelties practiced on this campaign towards citizens have been enough to blast a more sacred cause than ours. We hardly deserve success.
A Yankee corporal in Savannah, Georgia, end of December 1864, letter quoted by Robert Penn Warren in The Legacy of the Civil War *(1961).*

As the division of Major General John W. Geary, of the twentieth Corps, was the first to enter Savannah, that officer was appointed to command the place, or to act as a sort of governor. He very soon established a good police, maintained admirable order; and I doubt if Savannah, either before or since, has had a better government than during our stay.
Sherman, Savannah, end of December 1864 in his Memoirs.

The fire of Secession had died out . . . At a meeting of the citizens [of Savannah], resolutions expressive of gratitude for the charity bestowed by Boston, New York and Philadelphia were passed, also of a desire for future fellowship and amity.—A store at the corner of Bay and Barnard Streets was taken for a depot, the city canvassed and a registry made of

all who were in want. I passed a morning among the people who came for food . . . well-dressed women wearing crape for their husbands and sons who had fallen while fighting against the old flag—all stood patiently waiting their turn to enter the building, where through the open doors they could see barrels of flour, pork, beans, and piles of bacon, hogsheads of sugar, molasses and vinegar.
Charles C. Coffin, aid from the North arrives in Savannah, end of December 1864, Following the Flag.

You howled when Butler went to New Orleans. Others howled when he was removed from that command. Somebody has been howling ever since at his assignment to military command. How long will it be before you, who are howling for his assignment to rule Kentucky, will be howling to me to remove him?
Lincoln, to a group of Kentuckians who wanted the controversial General Benjamin Butler assigned to their state, on January 2, 1865.

Colonel Badeau [military secretary to Grant] dined with us . . . he said that Grant was one of the purest and most disinterested natures he had ever met with— social, unostentatious, affable and fatherly with the officers of his staff . . . having no jealousy of the fame of others; taking no credit to himself for every movement ever planned by him; and unwilling to be praised or flattered . . . Sherman is perhaps more brilliant than Grant, Badeau said, but has not his moral courage in emergencies or in assuming responsibility.
Maria L. Daly, January 19, 1865, Diary.

Somehow our men had got the idea that South Carolina was the cause of all our troubles. Her people were the first to fire on Fort Sumter, had been in a great hurry to precipitate the country into civil war; and therefore on them should fall the scourge of war in its worst form.
Sherman, the invasion of South Carolina, February 1, 1865, in his Memoirs.

. . . desolation marked one of those splendid South Carolina estates where the proprietors formerly had dispensed a hospitality that distinguished the old regime of that proud state. I slept on the floor of the house, but the night was so bitter cold that I got up by the fire several times; and when it burned low, I rekindled it with an old mantle-clock and the wreck

of a bedstead which stood in the corner of the room—the only act of vandalism that I recall done by myself personally during the war.
Sherman, early February 1865 in South Carolina, Memoirs.

The small force in Sherman's front offered but slight resistance to his advance. He swept on with his army of sixty thousand men, like a full developed cyclone, leaving behind him a track of desolation and ashes fifty miles wide . . . Bummers and foragers swarmed on his flanks, who plundered and robbed everyone who was so unfortunate as to be within their reach . . . Poor, bleeding, suffering South Carolina! Up to that time, she had felt but slightly—away from the coast [where the Federals had been operating since 1861]—the devastating effects of the war; but her time had come; the protestations of her old men and the pleadings of her noble women had no effect in staying the ravages of sword, flame and pillage.—Columbia's fate could readily be foretold from the destruction along Sherman's line of march after he left Savannah. Beautiful homes, with their tropical gardens, which had been the pride of their owners for generations, were left in ruins . . .
Confederate officer J. P. Austin, February 1865. The Blue and the Gray.

We captured twenty-five cannon . . . These guns . . . will be carried as trophies. General Mowrer fired them today in a salute in honor of the inauguration of Mr. Lincoln for his second term. Our honored President would have been as glad and proud as we, could he have heard the roaring of our cannon and our shouts of joy and victory.
George W. Nichols, the Union troops in Cheraw, near the North Carolina border, March 3, 1865, in The Story of the Great March.

In spite of the timidity and faithlessness of many who should give to me the popular feeling and hope to the popular heart, I am satisfied that it is in the power of the good men and true patriots of the country to reanimate the wearied spirit of our people . . . I expect the hour of deliverance.
Jefferson Davis, letter to a Confederate congressman, March 3, 1865.

We read this morning the account of Andy Johnson's drunken speech in the Senate on taking the oath of office. He walked up and down saying that he was a plebeian; our President was a plebeian; the people were all [plebeians]. ''You owe everything to the plebeians'' etc. etc., trusting out his fist almost into the faces of the diplomatic corps. It will be a great scandal; perhaps it may cause a reaction. The inauguration ball was likewise more like an orgy than anything else. Lincoln's inauguration address was like a sermon . . .
Maria L. Daly, March 7, 1865, Diary.

[General Joseph E. Johnston's] force had dwindled down to the veriest skeleton of an army. But he gathered its scattered fragments together and once more threw himself in front of Sherman's advancing columns . . . A fierce engagement took place at Bentonville, N.C. It was maintained with the same old-time vigor for several hours . . . [Two days later] Johnston was forced to give way to a vastly superior force and fall back in the direction of Raleigh. This was the last battle fought by General Johnston.
J. P. Austin, the battle of Bentonville, March 19–21, 1865, in The Blue and the Gray.

There was scarcely a home within its [Petersburg's] corporate limits that was not open to the sick and wounded . . . Its women, who were noted for culture and refinement, became nurses, as consecrated as Florence Nightingale . . .
Confederate General John B. Gordon, Petersburg, Virginia in March of 1865. Reminiscences of the Civil War.

As the solitary signal shot rang out in the stillness, my alert pickets who had crept close to the Union sentinels, sprang like sinewy Ajaxes upon them and prevented the discharge of a single alarm shot . . . Simultaneously my stalwart axemen leaped over our breastworks, closely followed by the selected 300 and the packed column of infantry . . . soon was heard the thud of heavy axes as my brave fellows slashed down the Federal obstructions. The next moment the infantry sprang upon the Union breastworks and into the fort, overpowering the gunners . . . They turned this captured artillery upon the flanking lines on each side of the fort, clearing the Union breastworks of their defenders for some distance in both directions. Up to this point, the success had exceeded my most sanguine expectations. We had taken Fort Stedman and a long line of breastworks . . . We had captured nine heavy cannon, eleven mortars, nearly 1,000 prisoners, including General McLaughlen, with a loss of less than half a dozen men . . .

General John B. Gordon, the surprise attack on Union Fort Stedman, east of Petersburg, March 25, 1865. Reminiscences of the Civil War.

Events seem hastening on to end this rebellion. Victories every day, and all our neutral friends are coming to shake hands with us on our success. How much the Union men at the South have suffered!

Maria L. Daly, March 26, 1865, Diary.

The full light of the morning revealed the gathering forces of Grant and the great preponderance of his numbers. It was impossible for me to make further headway with my isolated corps, and General Lee directed me to withdraw . . . This last supreme effort to break the hold of General Grant upon Petersburg and Richmond was the expiring struggle of the Confederate giant, whose strength was nearly exhausted . . .

John B. Gordon, March 26, 1865, at Fort Stedman in Reminiscences of the Civil War.

9. The End of the War: April 1865

THE HISTORICAL CONTEXT

After the failure at Fort Stedman, Lee's army amounted to no more than 50,000 men and was diminished daily by numerous desertions. His thinning ranks around Richmond and Petersburg were stretched to the breaking point. Grant began his great drive by sending Sheridan against the Confederate right flank, and although Gouverneur K. Warren's corps was slow in supporting Sheridan at Five Forks, the Confederates led by Pickett collapsed under the onslaught. On the 2nd of April, Grant attacked on all fronts, and Sheridan cut off the last railroad line leading into Petersburg. Lee knew that he had to withdraw, his only slim chance being a retreat to the southwest enabling him to link up with Johnston. That, of course, meant giving up Petersburg and Richmond. When Lee's message to this effect reached Jefferson Davis in Richmond, the great exodus from the city was begun by everybody who could manage it. Great amounts of military and industrial material were destroyed, and when the army left, mobs swarmed over the city. There was more destruction at Richmond by Southerners than there had been at Atlanta or Columbia by Northerners.

Lincoln had been at Grant's headquarters since the Fort Stedman attack was being repulsed, and on April 3 both entered the Confederate capital. While Grant immediately proceeded west to pursue Lee, Lincoln, with a small escort, went through the streets, enthusiastically greeted by huge masses of liberated blacks. Lee's army, by now down to 35,000 men, marched west to Amelia Courthouse but was unable to proceed to Danville because Sheridan had cut him off. He then led his exhausted army straight west toward Lynchburg, but a quarter of his troops were cut off and captured at Sayler's Creek on April 7. He made a last attempt to break through on April 9, against Sheridan's units again blocking his way, but by this time he was practically surrounded. Some of his generals suggested dispersing the troops and starting a guerilla warfare, which would indeed have been very difficult for the Union army to stamp out. But Lee realized this would lead to prolonged bitterness and prevent any reconciliation. During the last two days, the two army commanders had exchanged feelers about sur-

George Pickett, Confederate general.

render terms, and Grant had suggested the same terms as at Vicksburg: parole until exchanged. Now, on April 9, they met at Appomattox Court House. The famous scene has been described by many witnesses, and most agree that, judging by appearances, no one could have guessed that Grant was the victor and Lee the loser. Grant, following Lincoln's orders, confined himself strictly to military matters, but his terms were generous. He let Confederate officers and enlisted men take home their horses and, hearing that Lee's army was half-starved, sent 25,000 day rations to the surrendering army. Three days later, the Confederates stacked their arms and surrendered their flags, with both armies giving each other the salute of honor. By this gentlemen's agreement, Grant forestalled any future punitive action against Lee or any of his officers.

The surrender of the remaining Confederate armies was now only a question of time, but the next surrender, of Johnston's army, did not come off as smoothly. Sherman, even less politically minded than

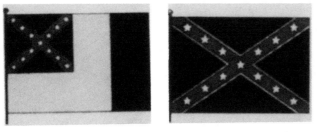

Confederate flags.

Grant, had apparently misunderstood Lincoln at their last meeting at the *River Queen* and not only went far beyond mere political matters but also had granted such generous terms to Johnston and the Confederate secretary of war, General Breckinridge, that Washington could not possibly be expected to ratify them. No one would have been punished; all political rights and rights of person and property were to be respected—which could have even revived slavery. Washington responded by canceling the armistice and ordering Sherman to resume hostilities. There was, in fact, no more fighting, and Johnston surrendered on the same terms as Lee. Sherman, after a campaign that had made him a great hero of the North, was infuriated, not so much because his treaty had been canceled but because, in announcing this, Secretary of War Stanton had hinted that Sherman must have been out of his mind—or disloyal. Such an accusation was incredible considering that Sherman, next to Grant, had contributed more to the military victory of the North than anyone else. Stanton and Sherman remained enemies for the rest of their lives.

How Lincoln would have handled the immense task of bringing the Southern states back into the Union is impossible to say. No doubt his position had shifted somewhat toward the radical Republicans in the course of the war, from no emancipation to emancipation with colonization to general emancipation with limited suffrage. No doubt he intended to act alone in reuniting the nation on a basis acceptable to the majority of the people, and he had half a year to work this out, for Congress would not reconvene until late in the fall.

But the one man who had the prestige, the foresight and the political skill to accomplish this immense task was assassinated on April 14. The actor John Wilkes Booth, brother of the great Edwin Booth, was, in contrast to the rest of his family, an ardent Confederate sympathizer. He had been with the Virginia militia that captured John Brown in 1859, but he had never taken up arms for the South during the war. Instead, for six months he had conspired to abduct Lincoln on March 20, 1865, and take him to Richmond. When this failed and Richmond surrendered, he and seven persons of dubious character plotted to kill Lincoln, Grant, Seward and Vice President Johnson. Nothing worked

John Wilkes Booth, Lincoln's assassin.

properly: The plans to kill Grant and Johnson fell afoul; Seward, on his sickbed from an accident, was severely wounded but not killed. Only Lincoln was assassinated. He and his party had attended a performance of a comedy, *Our American Cousin*, at Ford's Theater in Washington on Good Friday, April 14. When his guard left him for a few minutes to have a beer across the street, Booth entered the president's box and shot Lincoln in the back of the head, fatally wounding him. Lincoln died the following day without regaining consciousness. Booth, who had illusions of becoming the hero of the South, vaulted to the stage, breaking his leg in the process, shouted *"Sic semper tyrannis! The South is avenged!"* and escaped, but was discovered in a barn near Bowling Green, Virginia, on April 26. The barn was set afire by his pursuers, and either they killed him or he shot himself.

Booth did not live enough to realize that his deed had done more harm to the South than the whole of Sherman's army. For, with Lincoln, the first American president to be assassinated and the last martyr of the war, any hope for a magnanimous reconciliation, based on a wider vision, had been destroyed once and for all. The wave of shock and indignation that swept the whole North left the radical Republi-

Lincoln's assassination at Ford's Theater.

cans who wanted to punish the South in control of the federal government. Secretary of War Edwin M. Stanton made himself something like a dictator for the first two weeks after the assassination. A man of great ability and energy, but by nature extremely suspicious, Stanton was quick to announce to the nation that Lincoln had been the victim of Jefferson Davis's agents, although no evidence was ever produced. He and the other leading radicals also made sure that Lincoln's body, after lying in state beneath the Capitol dome, was taken around the country by special train via New York, Chicago and many other cities before reaching Springfield, Illinois, thus making sure that millions saw the open casket, so that the murder of the beloved president, committed by the South, would be well-remembered.

Andrew Johnson, sworn in as the 17th president on April 15, had started out as a tailor in eastern Tennessee and worked his way up to mayor of Greeneville, state representative and senator, U. S. congressman, governor of Tennessee and U. S. senator. A Democrat, he remained in the Senate as the only Southerner after his state seceded. Lincoln, whom he supported vigorously, made him military governor of Tennessee and, in 1864, his running mate. As a Union and prowar Democrat, he was ideally suited to balance Lincoln's ticket. But Johnson's idea of Reconstruction was based on the idea that the South had never been out of the Union and therefore did not have to be readmitted. He also was not inclined to grant equal civil rights to the blacks, and this, too, was certain to get him into conflict with the new Congress, in which the Republicans had a vast majority.

During the month of May, the remaining Confederate armies had surrendered, the last one being that of the Trans-Mississippi Department under Edmund Kirby Smith whose activity during the last months had consisted mainly of small raids and guerilla warfare. Many Union prisoners of war had been released from Southern and Western Confederate encampments before that date and were on their way home. One great tragedy occurred on April 27, when the steampowered riverboat *Sultana* caught fire and exploded on the Mississippi, with more than 2,000 passengers on board, most of them liberated Federal soldiers. More than 1,200 men perished in the greatest catastrophe on the Mississippi. The casualty number came close to that of the *Titanic* half a century later.

Jefferson Davis and the remnants of his government had fled south. He was captured by a Michigan cavalry unit on May 10 near Irwinville, Georgia, together with his wife, his postmaster and secretary. Arriving at Fort Monroe, Virginia, he was put in chains and locked up. He was never brought to trial and was released on bail two years later. Lee had encouraged Southern leaders to request pardons as soon as possible, and Vice President Stephens and other members of Davis's Cabinet were granted such pardons. Lee himself, though supported by Grant's recommendation, received his pardon only on Christmas Day of 1868.

All seceded states were occupied by Federal troops. They found a country cruelly devastated by years of invasion and fighting. Virginia, Tennessee, Georgia and South Carolina had suffered most. The new industries that had grown in wartime were destroyed for the most part. Of the white men of military age, one-fourth had been killed. Two-fifths of the livestock, half of the farm machinery, in all, two-thirds of accumulated Southern wealth disappeared during the war years. Many thousands of plantations and farms were ruined and deserted. The balance between the Northern and Southern economies had changed radically: Between 1860 and 1870, Southern manufacturing and agricultural capital, not counting slaves, declined by almost 50%, while that in the North grew by the same percentage. In 1870, the South held no more than 12% of the total national wealth, compared with 30% in 1860, and Southern per capita income, which, including slaves, had been two-thirds of the Northern average, dropped to less than two-fifths during that same decade and stayed at that level for several decades.

The plight of white Southerners was worsened by wild fears of a great uprising of the freed black population. This nightmare had existed before the war. What had happened in Haiti at the end of the 18th century could happen in the deep South, and now, with almost four million blacks in the South who did not quite know what to do with their newly acquired freedom, this possibility had become a certainty in the minds of many former slave-owners. They even predicted the date of this uprising: New Year's Day, 1866. Nothing of the sort, of course, materialized, but the nightmare persisted and hamstrung energies so badly needed for Southern reconstruction.

The war had come to an end, and the questions about the strengths and weaknesses of either side and the inevitability of the outcome have been discussed ever since. In retrospect, we feel that the North was bound to win because of her great superiority in resources and manpower. But there have been enough examples in history of smaller states holding their own against the attack of larger ones. Historians have pointed at the examples of Paraguay, which fought Brazil, Argentina and Uruguay for six years (1865–71) before succumbing; of Frederick II of Prussia who held his own against Austria, France and Russia in the war of seven years (1756–63); and the American colonies in 1776 against England. One could also add that the inferiority in numbers was offset by the fact that almost all of the fighting occurred on Southern soil, where the population sided with and aided the defending armies and made things as difficult as possible for the invaders.

Some have claimed that Southern leadership was superior. It is true that Davis had better military training than Lincoln and that, at least during the first two years of the war, the Southern armies were generally led by better generals. But Lincoln turned out to be a far better war leader than Davis, not only politically but also in his overall military concept of the situation. His idea, often opposed by his generals, that Northern strategy should be to exploit the numerical superiority by simultaneously attacking on several fronts proved correct. The poor generals were about equally divided between North and South: McClellan, Burnside, Hooker and Pope in the North; Pemberton, Bragg, Hood and others in the South. Also, in Grant, Sherman, Sheridan, Rosecrans, Farragut and others, the Union had leaders who could stand up to Lee, Jackson, J. E. Johnston, Beauregard, and Stuart. Administratively, Lincoln, with Stanton, Chase and Charles F. Adams, probably had the better team to work with, but Davis had Josiah Gorgas as chief ordnance officer and many other capable aides.

There is also an "internal strife theory" that maintains that Davis had to fight his Southern opponents almost as much as the Union invaders. It is correct that he was opposed not only by Southern Unionists, former Whigs and Constitutional Unionists but also by his own Vice President Stephens and many Southern state governors. Also in the course of the war, most of the nonslaveowners in the South became less than enthusiastic about a war that, in their estimate, was fought to preserve slavery. But the North had the same, if not even graver, internal problems. The prowar Democrats were constantly critical of the administration, while the sympathies of peace-Democrats were often on the side of the South. Lincoln himself was opposed not only by the peace parties but also by the impatient abolitionists, and many men and women of the old Eastern establishment looked down on the "railsplitter." Even the most enlightened Republicans were reluctant to accept blacks as their equals or even as their brothers in arms, and the draft laws of 1863 produced the worst race riots and massacres this country has ever known. So, here, too, the odds were about even.

One should not forget that only in retrospect does the victory of the North seem to be a foregone conclusion. Right after the first battle of Bull Run and then again before Gettysburg in 1863, the occupation of Washington by the Confederate armies seemed a distinct possibility, and again in the summer of 1864, the North, after terrible losses in Virginia, seemed ready for peace negotiations and for the election of a Democratic president. Almost miraculously, Sherman and Sheridan's successes at Atlanta and in the Shenandoah Valley changed the outlook just at the right time.

One hundred and twenty-five years after the end of the war, it seems clear that the South was destined to be overwhelmed, particularly after her entire coastline was cut off by the North. And also clear that she was indeed fighting for a lost cause. It is hard to imagine how slavery could have lived on much longer after it had ceased to exist anywhere else in the world, and some historians are of the opinion that the North did the South a favor by forcing her to abandon it. The miracle is, rather, that the South not only held out for so long, but also, after her final defeat and 10 years of occupation, managed to emerge socially almost intact—except, of course, for the institution of slavery. The North probably overestimated the military strength of the South but underestimated the depth of the Southern tradition in the United States, which before the war had dominated political life out of all proportion to the South's population. During the first 70 years of the Union, two-thirds of the presidents and the speakers of the house had come from Southern states, and the Supreme Court had always been dominated by Southern justices.

CHRONICLE OF EVENTS

1865:

March 29: Beginning of the Appomattox Campaign: The Union Armies of the Potomac and of the James move against Lee at Petersburg and Richmond, numbering about 125,000 men. Lee has less than half that number at his disposal.

March 30: Sheridan assembles his troops at Dinwiddie Court House, southwest of Petersburg.

April 1: Sheridan and Warren's Fifth Corps attack at Five Forks, north of Dinwiddie, splitting General Pickett's troops from the rest of the Confederate army. Sheridan removes Warren as commander of the Fifth Corps because of disobedience. Petersburg is now almost encircled.

April 2: As the Federal armies advance along the whole line, Lee advises President Davis that Richmond must be abandoned. Resistance at Forts Gregg and Baldwin allows the Confederates to regroup, but their overstretched lines are too weak to halt the Federal attacks. Davis and his Cabinet leave the capital for Danville, Virginia. General disorder and looting start in Richmond. Selma, Alabama, is attacked and taken by the Federals under General James Harrison Wilson. Confederate General Forrest's attempts to relieve the city fail. General Ambrose P. Hill is killed. Fort Blakely near Mobile, Alabama, is besieged by Union troops.

April 3: Petersburg and Richmond surrender to the Union armies. Lee's army struggles westward, pursued by Grant.

April 4: President Lincoln visits Richmond. Lee's army, arriving at Amelia Court House, Virginia, does not find the expected supplies there.

April 5: U. S. Secretary of State Seward is critically injured in a carriage accident in Washington.

April 6: Lee's army, attempting to cross the Appomattox River at Farmville and High

Fortifications at Petersburg.

Union mortar.

Bridge, is split up at Sayler's Creek. Ewell's troops are forced to surrender. Gordon's troops must also surrender to the Federals. Lee has lost about one-third of his remaining forces.

April 7: Sheridan's cavalry, supported by infantry, moves west and north to block Lee at Appomattox Station and Court House.

Grant opens correspondence with Lee, proposing surrender of the Army of Northern Virginia. Lee asks for the terms.

April 9: Lee's last council of war, near Appomattox. At dawn, Confederates attack, trying to force a passage through the Federal lines in front of them, but fail. In the early afternoon, Lee meets Grant, Sheridan and other Federal commanders at Appomattox Court-House. Lee accepts Grant's terms of surrender.

In Alabama, Spanish Fort is evacuated by the Confederates after heavy bombardment and attack.

At Mobile, Alabama, Confederate Fort Blakeley is stormed by the Federals.

April 10: Victory celebrations in the Northern cities.

Continued bombardment of forts around Mobile, Alabama.

April 11: Sherman's forces continue to advance toward Goldsborough, North Carolina.

The Confederate government train arrives at Greensborough, North Carolina.

April 12: Mobile, Alabama, has been evacuated

George Armstrong Custer, Union general who led the final cavalry charge at Appomattox Court House.

and is entered by Federal troops under General E. R. S. Canby.

Montgomery, Alabama is occupied by James H. Wilson's cavalry. Salisbury, North Carolina is also taken by the Federals, with 1,300 Confederate prisoners taken.

In a formal ceremony at Appomattox Court House, the Confederate army lay down their arms and battle flags.

April 13: Sherman's troops enter Raleigh, North Carolina and are heading toward Greensborough.

U. S. Secretary of War Stanton orders the draft halted.

April 14: Shortly after 10 P.M., President Lincoln is shot by John Wilkes Booth during a performance of a comedy, *Our American Cousin*, at Ford's Theatre in Washington. The bullet goes through the back of his head and stops near the right eye. The assassin escapes from the theater with his right leg injured when he leaped to the stage. Secretary of State Seward, recovering from his accident, is stabbed in his bed by an accomplice of Booth, Lewis Payne.

At Fort Sumter, Robert Anderson, now a general, hoists the same Federal flag he had lowered four years earlier.

In Raleigh, North Carolina, Sherman agrees to confer with Confederate General E. T. Johnston on suspension of operations.

April 15: President Lincoln dies at 7:22 A.M. At 11 A.M., Chief Justice Salmon P. Chase administers the oath of office to Vice President Andrew Johnson who, in taking over the presidency, asks the Cabinet to remain with him.

April 17: Sherman and Johnston meet at the Bennett House, near Durham Station, North Carolina.

John Wilkes Booth and his helper David Herold hide south of Port Tobacco, Maryland, awaiting transportation across the Potomac.

April 18: At Durham Station, Sherman and Johnston sign a "Memorandum or basis of agreement," calling for an armistice by all armies in the field. They further agree on far-reaching political terms which go far beyond their authority.

April 19: Funeral services for President Lincoln in Washington. His body is taken back to Springfield, Ill.

Major General Pope suggests the surrender of all Confederate troops west of the Mississippi.

April 20: Federal troops occupy Macon, Georgia. Skirmishes are still going on in Georgia and Alabama. Lee recommends suspension of all hostilities.

April 21: Union expedition from Donaldsonville to Bayou Goula, Louisiana.

April 22: Booth and accomplice David E. Herold escape to Virginia.

April 24: Grant arrives at Raleigh and advises Sherman that his agreement with Johnston had been disapproved by the President. Hostilities are to be resumed if there is no surrender.

Andrew Johnson.

Sherman is infuriated by Stanton's hint of disloyalty.

April 26: Federal troops surround the barn of Richard H. Garrett, between Port Conway and Bowling Green, Va., where Booth and Herold are hiding. Herold surrenders, Booth is mortally wounded, probably by one of the soldiers, Boston Corbett.

At a second meeting of Sherman and Johnston, an armistice is arranged, following Grant's formula at Appomattox.

April 27: North of Memphis on the Mississippi, the steamer *Sultana* explodes, carrying hundreds of Federal soldiers released from Confederate prison camps. At least 1,238 die, probably more.

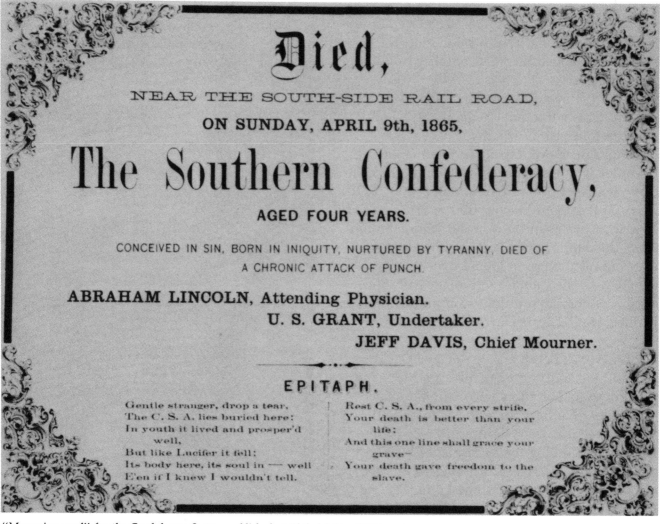

"Mourning card" for the Confederate States, published at Philadelphia, 1865.

May 1: President Johnson orders the naming of nine army officers to try eight Lincoln assassination conspirators.

May 2: President Johnson, in a proclamation, accuses President Davis and others of inciting the murder of Lincoln. A $100,000 reward is offered for the arrest of Davis.

May 3: Jefferson Davis and the remainder of his cabinet move to Washington, Georgia.

The Lincoln funeral train reaches Springfield, Illinois.

Skirmishes are still going on in Boonville and Pleasant Hill, Missouri.

May 4: In Alabama, Confederate Lieutenant

General Richard Taylor surrenders his forces, the last Confederate forces east of the Mississippi, to Union Major General E. R. S. Canby.

May 10: President Davis, his wife and members of his cabinet are surprised by Union troops near Irwinville, Georgia, and taken into custody. The Confederate government has come to an end.

In a proclamation, President Johnson declares that armed resistance may be regarded as virtually at an end.

May 12: The last land engagement takes place at Palmito Ranch on the Rio Grande in Texas.

May 17: Major General Philip H. Sheridan is

named Federal commander west of the Mississippi.

May 23: The Grand Armies of the Republic pass in last review in Washington.

May 24: Sherman's army parades in Washington.

May 25: Twenty tons of captured Confederate powder explode in Mobile, Alabama, setting off numerous other explosions.

May 26: The Confederate Army of Trans-Mississippi formally surrenders at New Orleans.

EYEWITNESS TESTIMONY

Our line is now unbroken from the Appomattox to Dinwiddie . . . I now feel like ending the matter . . . In the morning, push around the enemy, if you can, and get on to his right rear. The movements of the enemy's cavalry, may of course modify your action. We will act all together as one army here, until it is seen what can be done with the enemy.

Grant to Sheridan at the beginning of the Appomattox Campaign, March 29, 1865. Quoted in General James Marshall-Cornwall in Grant as Military Commander *(1970).*

Generals were writing dispatches and telegraphing from dark to daylight. Staff-officers were rushing from one headquarters to another, wading through swamps, penetrating forests and galloping over corduroy roads, carrying instructions, getting information and making extraordinary efforts to hurry up the movements of the troops.

General Horace Porter, aide to Grant, about the night of March 31 during the Appomattox Campaign, in his Campaigning with Grant *(1897).*

In the first encounter General Sheridan's forces were repelled . . . But soon the devoted little band of gray was torn by artillery, harried by cavalry, and assaulted by infantry on every side; and the Confederate flags went down . . . Five Forks fell, with the loss of large numbers of Confederates killed, wounded, and prisoners . . . As General Lee rode back toward Petersburg from Five Forks . . . he said to one of his aides: "This is bad business, colonel." In a few minutes he added: "It has happened as I told them in Richmond it would happen. The line has been stretched until it is broken."

John B. Gordon, the battle of Five Forks, April 1, 1865, in his Reminiscences of the Civil War *(1904).*

The blue masses poured into the works. There were high parapets and deep ditches; but . . . it was only a matter of physical agility to climb over them. Only small garrisons were in the forts, and very few men in the connecting lines . . . Lee's troops were forced back to an inner line . . . and there resisted all further attempts to break through them. Before 10 A.M. Lee knew he could only hope to cling to his trenches until night, and that a longer defense of Richmond and Petersburg was not possible. All his skill would be required to extricate his army . . . from the lines. In the midst of the turmoil, excitement and danger, Lee was as calm and collected as ever.

Confederate General Fitzhugh Lee, April 2, 1865. General Lee of the Confederate Army *(1895).*

We are now up and have a continuous line of troops, and in a few hours will be entrenched from the Appomatox below Petersburg to the river above . . . The whole captures since the army started out gunning will amount to no less than twelve thousand men . . . I think the President might come out and pay us a visit tomorrow.

Grant, telegram to Lincoln after the victory at Appomatox, April 2, 1865. Quoted in General James Marchall-Cornwall, Grant as Military Commander.

The report of a great misfortune soon traverses a city without the aid of printed bulletins. But that of the evacuation of Richmond fell upon many incredulous ears . . . There were but few people in the streets; no vehicles disturbed the quiet of the Sabbath; the sound of the church-going bells rose into the cloudless sky . . . How was it possible to imagine that in the next twenty-four hours . . . this peaceful city, a secure possession for four years, was at last to succumb? . . . The disorder increased each hour. The streets were thronged with fugitives making their way to the railroad depots; pale women and shoeless children struggled in the crowd; oaths and blasphemous shouts smote the ear . . . In the afternoon a special train . . . [was prepared to carry] from Richmond President Davis and some of his Cabinet . . . it was proposed to maintain order . . . by two regiments of militia; to destroy every drop of liquor in the warehouses and to establish a patrol through the night. But the militia ran through the fingers of their officers . . . and in a short while the whole city was plunged into mad confusion and indescribable horrors . . .

Edward A. Pollard, correspondent of the Examiner, *April 2, 1865 in Richmond.* The Lost Cause. *(1866).*

As the cry "Yankees!" was raised, this motley crowd tore up the street, cursing, screaming, trampling upon each other . . . Presently . . . following up the tangled mass of plunderers, but not pressing

Ruins of Richmond, with the undamaged Capitol building.

or interfering with them, was seen a small body of Federal cavalry, riding steadily along . . . At the corner of Eleventh Street they broke into a trot for the public square, and in a few moments their guidons were planted on the Capitol and fluttered there, a strange spectacle in the early morning light. A few hours thereafter, and [General Godfrey] Weitzel's troops were pouring through the streets of the city.
E. Pollard, April 3, in Richmond, The Lost
Cause.

Stretching from the Exchange Hotel to the slopes of Church Hill . . . was the array, with its unbroken line of blue, fringed with bright bayonets. Strains of martial music, flushed countenances, waving swords betokened the victorious army. As the line turned at

the Exchange Hotel . . . the movement was the signal for a wild burst of cheers from each regiment. Shouts from a few Negroes were the only response. Through throngs of sullen spectators . . . through curtains of smoke; through the . . . commotion of frightful sounds, moved the garish procession of the grand army . . . A regiment of Negro cavalry swept by the hotel. As they turned the street corner they drew their sabres with savage shouts, and the blood mounted even in my woman's heart with quick throbs of defiance.
A Richmond lady spectator, report of April 3, 1865, quoted by E. Pollard in The Lost
Cause.

Many of the citizens, panic-stricken, had escaped with the army. Most of the whites who remained stayed indoors. A few groups of Negroes gave cheers; but the scene generally was one of complete desertion. Grant rode quietly until he came to a comfortable-looking brick house . . . and here he and the staff dismounted . . . The general was anxious to move westward at once with the leading infantry columns, but he prolonged his stay until the President came up. Mr. Lincoln soon arrived, accompanied by Robert [his eldest son] . . . and his little son, "Tad", and Admiral Porter. He dismounted in the street and came in through the front gate with long and rapid strides, his face beaming with delight. He seized General Grant's hand as the general stepped forward to greet him, and stood shaking it for some time and pouring out his thanks and congratulations . . . I doubt whether Mr. Lincoln ever experienced a happier moment in his life.

Horace Porter, April 3 in Petersburg, Virginia,
Campaigning with Grant.

It would be unwise, even if it were possible, to conceal the great moral, as well as material injury to our cause that must result from the occupation of Richmond by the enemy. It is equally unwise and unworthy of us, as patriots engaged in a most sacred cause, to allow our energies to falter, our spirits to grow faint, or our efforts to become relaxed, under reverses however calamitous.

Jefferson Davis, proclamation from Danville,
Virginia, on April 4, 1865.

Relieved from the necessity of guarding cities . . . with our army free to move from point to point . . . and where the foe will be far removed from his base . . . nothing is now needed to render our triumph certain but . . . our own unquenchable resolve.

Lee, proclamation of April 4, 1865, as quoted
by James M. McPherson in Battle Cry of
Freedom *(1988).*

Richmond is ours! Lee is retreating! . . . It was entered on Sunday last, the 2nd, by General Weitzel, whose command is mostly Negro troops . . . The streets are brilliant with flags. On Saturday when the news came, there was an impromptu meeting in Wall Street. All business adjourned, a few speeches, and then the multitude sang the Doxology [hymn of praise] and the 100th Psalm in Wall Street, the seat of the money-changers; it was a good augury.

Maria L. Daly, April 5, 1865, Diary of a
Union Lady *(1962).*

I had left behind me in that city [Petersburg] of gloom the wife who had followed me during the entire war. She was ill. But . . . I found comfort in the hope that some chivalric soldier of the Union army would learn of her presence and guard her home against all intruders. My confidence in American manhood was not misplaced.—To bring up the rear and adequately protect the retreating army was an impossible task. With characteristic vigor, General Grant pressed the pursuit. Soon began the continuous and final battle . . . General Lee was riding everywhere and watching everything, encouraging his brave men by his calm and cheerful bearing. He was often exposed to great danger from shells and bullets . . . On that doleful retreat . . . it was impossible for us to bury our dead or carry with us the disabled wounded. There was no longer any room in the crowded ambulances which had escaped capture.

General John B. Gordon, on the retreating Confederates, April 5–7, 1865 in Reminiscences
of the Civil War.

The result of the last week must convince you of the hopelessness of further resistance on the part of the Army of Northern Virginia in this struggle. I feel that it is so, and regard it as my duty to shift from myself the responsibility of any further effusion of blood, by asking of you the surrender of that portion of the C.S. Army known as the Army of Northern Virginia.

Grant, letter to Lee, on April 7, 1865.

On the evening of April 8th, [Lee's] little army, with its ammunition nearly exhausted, was confronted by the forces of Grant, which had been thrown across our line of retreat at Appomattox. Then came the last sad Confederate council of war. It was called by Lee to meet at night. It met in the woods at his headquarters, and by a low-burning bivouac fire. There was no tent there, no table, no chairs and no camp-stools. On blankets spread upon the ground or on saddles at the roots of trees, we sat around the great commander . . . no tongue or pen will ever be able to describe the unutterable anguish of Lee's commanders as they looked into the clouded face of their beloved leader and sought to draw from it some ray of hope . . . It was finally determined that with Fitz Lee's cavalry, my infantry and Long's artillery . . . we should attempt at daylight the next morning

to cut through Grant's lines . . . The utmost that could be hoped for was that we might reach the mountains of Virginia and Tennessee . . . and ultimately join General Johnston . . .
General John B. Gordon, April 8 at Appomattox. Reminiscences of the Civil War.

The Confederate battle lines were still advancing when I discovered a heavy column of Union infantry coming from the right and upon my rear . . . Longstreet was assailed by other portions of the Federal army. He was so hardly pressed that he could not join, as contemplated, in the effort to break the cordon . . . around us . . . Such was the situation when I received a significant inquiry from General Lee . . . The Commander wished me to report . . . what progress I was making . . . I said: "Tell General Lee that my command has been fought to a frazzle, and unless Longstreet can unite in the movement . . . I cannot long go forward." . . . when General Lee received my message, he said: "There is nothing left me but to go and see General Grant, and I had rather die a thousand deaths."—My troops were still fighting . . . when the final note from General Lee reached me. It notified me that there was a flag of truce between General Grant and himself, stopping hostilities . . .
General John B. Gordon, April 9, 1865. Reminiscences of the Civil War.

When I went into the [Appomattox Court-] house I found General Lee. We greeted each other, and after shaking hands took our seats. I had my staff with me, a good portion of whom were in the room during the whole of the interview.—What General Lee's feelings were I do not know. As he was a man with much dignity, with an impassable face . . . his feelings were entirely concealed from my observation; but my own feelings . . . were sad and depressed. I felt like anything rather than rejoicing at the downfall of a foe who had fought so long and valiantly and had suffered so much . . . General Lee was dressed in full uniform which was entirely new, and was wearing a sword of considerable value . . . In my rough traveling suit . . . I must have contrasted very strangely with a man so handsomely dressed, six feet high and of faultless form . . .
U. S. Grant, Appomattox Court House, afternoon of April 9, 1865, in Personal Memoirs (1885–86).

As I wrote [the surrender terms] . . . the thought occurred to me that the officers had their own private horses and effects, which were important to them but of no value to us; also that it would be an unnecessary humiliation to call upon them to deliver their side arms . . . When he read over that part of the terms . . . he remarked . . . that this would have a happy effect upon his army.—General Lee, after all was completed and before taking his leave, remarked that his army was in very bad condition for want of food, and they were without forage; that his men had been living for some days on parched corn exclusively, and that he would have to ask me for ration and forage. I told him, "Certainly." Lee and I separated as cordially as we had met . . . When the news of the surrender first reached our lines, our men commenced firing a salute of a hundred guns in honor of the victory. I at once sent word, however, to have it stopped. The Confederates were now our prisoners, and we did not want to exult over their downfall.
Grant, April 9, 1865, Personal Memoirs.

The arms, artillery and public property to be parked and stacked, and turned over to the officers appointed by me to receive them. This will not embrace the side-arms of the officers, nor their private horses or baggage. This done, each officer and man will be allowed to return to his home, not to be disturbed by the United States authority so long as they observe their paroles and the laws in force where they may reside.
Grant's final conditions of surrender, written out and given to Lee at Appomattox Court House on April 9, 1865.

I have done for you all that was in my power to do. You have done all your duty. Leave the result to God. Go to your homes and resume your occupations. Obey the laws and become as good citizens as you were soldiers.
Robert E. Lee, addressing his soldiers after the surrender at Appomattox, April 9, 1865.

I have forgotten to mention a visit we paid to Ward Beecher . . . we waited until he came from church, which he did, opening the door with a "Hurrah, hurrah", flinging down his hat, rushing at his little baby grandson, not knowing any stranger was in the house. Truly muscular Christianity! Beecher is no

hypocrite; thoroughly wise, however, in his own conceit and confident of his own ability to direct the universe.
Maria L. Daly, April 9, 1865, Diary.

After four years of arduous service, marked by unsurpassed courage and fortitude, the Army of Northern Virginia has been compelled to yield to overwhelming numbers and resources . . . By the terms of the agreement officers and men can return to their homes and remain until exchanged. You will take with you the satisfaction that proceeds from the consciousness of duty faithfully performed, and I earnestly pray that a Merciful God will extend to you his blessing and protection. With an increasing admiration of your constancy and devotion to your country, and a grateful remembrance of your kind and generous considerations for myself I bid you an affectionate farewell.
General Robert E. Lee, last general order, on April 10, 1865.

. . . whole lines of men rushed down to the roadside and crowded around him [Lee] to shake his hands. All tried to show him the veneration and esteem in which they held him . . . it was no shame on our manhood "that something upon the soldier's cheek washed off the stains of powder" . . . and that we could only grasp the hand of "Uncle Robert" and pray "God help you, General!"
William Miller Owen, Lee returning after the surrender. In Camp and Battle with the Washington Artillery (1885).

Three days after the surrender, the Confederates marched by division to a designated spot in the neighborhood of Appomattox Court-House, and there the troops stacked their arms and deposited their accoutrements. Less than eight thousand presented themselves with muskets in their hands; but the capitulation included, in addition, about eighteen thousand unarmed. Paroles were then distributed to the men, and the Army of Northern Virginia passed out of existence.
William Swinton, war correspondent, April 12, 1865. Campaigns of the Army of the Potomac *(1882).*

Lee has surrendered to Grant . . . I hope the animosity that has so long reigned will now pass away. May God comfort and change the hearts of our so long vindictive foes! They will have much to suffer for their folly and ambition.
Maria L. Daly, April, 1865, Diary.

What visions thronged as we looked into each other's eyes! Here pass the men of Antietam, the Bloody Lane, the Sunken Road, the Cornfield, the Burnside Bridge . . . Here come Cobb's Georgia Legion which held the Stonewall at Marye's Heights at Fredericksburg, close before which we piled our dead for breastworks . . . Now the sad great pageant— Longstreet and his men! What shall we give them for greeting that has not already been spoken . . . Ah, is this Pickett's Division? this little group left of those who on the lurid last day of Gettysburg breasted level cross-fire and thunderbolts of storm, to be strewn back drifting wrecks, where after that awful, futile, pitiful charge we buried them in graves a furlong wide . . . How could we help falling on our knees, all of us together, and praying God to pity and forgive us all?
Joshua L. Chamberlain, Union General who commanded the troops that formally accepted the surrender of the Confederate army, as quoted in Jeremy Barnes in The Pictorial History of the Civil War *(1988).*

. . . I will not take any part in hanging or killing those men [the Southern leaders], even the worst of them. Frighten them out of the country, open the gates, let down the bars, scare them off. Enough lives have been sacrificed; we must extinguish our resentments if we expect harmony and union.
Lincoln, at his last Cabinet meeting, April 14, 1865, reported by Secretary Welles.

The most startling incident in the life of Mr. Lincoln was a dream he had only a few days before his assassination . . . "About ten days ago" said he, "I retired very late. I had been waiting for important dispatches from the front. I could not have been long in bed when I fell into a slumber . . . I soon began to dream. There seemed to be a death-like stillness about me. Then I heard subdued sobs, as if a number of people were weeping . . . I went from room to room; no living person was in sight, but the same mournful sounds met me as I passed along . . . I kept on until I arrived at the East Room which I entered. There I met with a sickening surprise. Before me was a catafalque, on which rested a corpse wrapped in funeral vestments. Around it were stationed soldiers who were acting as guards; and there was a throng of people . . . weeping pitifully. "Who is dead in the White House?" I demanded of one of the soldiers. "The President" was his answer "he was killed by an assassin!" Then came a loud burst of grief from the crowd which awoke me . . . and although it was only a dream, I have been strangely annoyed by it ever since."

Ward Hill Lamon, former partner and frequent bodyguard of Lincoln's in Recollections of Abraham Lincoln *(1895).*

It was the custom for the guard who accompanied the President to the theater to remain in the little passageway outside the box . . . Whether Parker occupied it at all I do not know. If he did, he left almost immediately; for he confessed to me the next day that he went to a seat in the front of the first gallery, so that he could see the play. The door of the President's box was shut. Probably Mr. Lincoln never knew that the guard had left his post. And to think that in that one moment of test one of us should have utterly failed in his duty! He looked like a convicted criminal the next day.

William H. Crook, one of Lincoln's personal guards about the evening of the assassination. Quoted in R. Borreson's When Lincoln Died, *(1966).*

When the second scene of the third act was being performed, and this deponent was intently observing the proceedings upon the stage, with his back toward the door, he heard the discharge of a pistol behind him, and looking around, saw through the smoke a man between the door and the President. At the same time deponent heard him shout some word which deponent thinks was "Freedom!" The deponent instantly sprang toward him and seized him, he wrested himself from the grasp and made a violent thrust at the breast of deponent with a large knife. Deponent parried the blow by striking it up and received a wound several inches deep in his left arm between the elbow and the shoulder. The man rushed to the front of the box and deponent endeavored to seize him again, but only caught his clothes as he was leaping over the railing of the box. As he went over upon the stage deponent cried out with a loud voice: "Stop that man!"

Major Henry R. Rathbone who accompanied Lincoln and his wife to the theater on April 14. Quoted in R. Borreson's When Lincoln Died.

Lincoln's funeral cortege in Washington.

The giant sufferer lay extended diagonally across the bed which was not long enough for him . . . His features were calm and striking. I had never seen them appear to better advantage, than for the first hour I was there. The room was small and over-crowded. The surgeons and members of the Cabinet were as many as should have been on the room, but there were many more, and the hall and other rooms in front were full . . . A little before seven I went into the room where the dying President was rapidly drawing near the closing moments. The death strug-gle had begun.

Gideon Welles, secretary of the navy, as quoted in Borreson's When Lincoln Died.

What dreadful news! President Lincoln assassi-nated; Secretary Seward's throat cut! Just as we were rejoicing over the return of peace, everything once again in confusion. Poor Lincoln! . . . The Secretary is old already, weakened from having broken his arm; he will scarcely survive. God save us all. What may not a day bring forth!

Maria L. Daly, April 15, 1865, Diary.

The poor rail-splitter, who in these four years of severe schooling had at least learned that only a

military man could carry on military operations; whose vanity and self-sufficiency have lost us Chancellorsville and Fredericksburg . . . whose indecent speeches and stories made him and the nation a byword; whose weakness allowed unlimited plunder by those around him, even members of his own family; whose undignified haste in going to Richmond in the rear of a conquering army and placing himself in the seat, still warm, of Jefferson Davis, sending for Mrs. Lincoln and receiving the visits of all his rebellious subjects, was the regret of all noble-minded people! All this will be forgotten in this shameful, cowardly act of his assassination, whilst his heart was full of forgiveness of his enemies, and whilst he was planning for the good of all . . . For it was the rejection of Douglas by the Charleston Convention four years ago that elected Abraham Lincoln and Jefferson Davis, and it was not any fault in Abraham Lincoln. Nor can we blame him that when elected by a legal majority, he accepted the Presidency. Every American feels competent for any place.
Maria L. Daly, April 19, 1865, Diary.

Thy task is done; the bond are free:/We bear thee to an honored grave,/whose proudest moment shall be/The broken fetters of the slave./

Pure was thy life; its bloody close/Hath placed thee with the sons of light/Among the noble host of those/Who perished in the cause of right.
*William Cullen Bryant, "The Death of Lincoln,"
in the* New York Evening Post, *April 20,
1865.*

None of the artists or pictures has caught the deep though subtle and indirect expression of this man's face. There is something else there. One of the great portrait painters of two or three centuries ago is needed.
*Walt Whitman, "Of Lincoln" (August 12,
1863) in* Specimen Days *(1882/3).*

Today President Lincoln's funeral procession passes through the city . . . I shall not go to see the show . . . I will let the servants go instead; I am sick of pageants. Both yesterday and today all business has been suspended . . . Poor Mrs. Lincoln! . . . A house nearer Fifth Avenue opposite to us, having not been put in mourning, was tarred, and for two days men have been at work at it. Tomorrow the theaters will reopen, and then, I suppose, all will be over.
Maria L. Daly, April 25, 1865, Diary.

Mrs. Young tells me that we have no idea of the destitution of the South; that most of the men (even the Union men) were driven into the Confederate Army because their families would else have starved, and told me several heart-rending examples . . .
Maria L. Daly, April 25, 1865, Diary.

I did go yesterday to see the [Lincoln funeral] procession, and it was most imposing . . . how little did the friends of McClellan dream that they should ever have felt so much interest in him and mourn his untimely and cruel death . . . Very fine dirge music, and fifty thousand men of different societies, clubs etc., and a few colored soldiers with "Abraham Lincoln, Our Liberator" etc. on their breasts, guarded by a police force [because the City Council opposed their joining the procession], marched. It was very, very sorrowful.
Maria L. Daly, April 26, 1865, Diary.

All day long and through the night a stream of people filed reverently by the catafalque. Some of them were his colleagues at the bar; some his old friends from New Salem; some crippled soldiers fresh from the battlefield of the war; some were little children who, scarce realizing the impressiveness of the scene, were destined to live and tell their children yet to be born the sad story of Lincoln's death.
*William H. Herndon, Lincoln's former law
partner, on Lincoln's coffin at Springfield, Illinois, as quoted in Borreson's* When Lincoln
Died *(1965).*

O Captain! my Captain! our fearful trip is done,/ The ship has weathered every rack, the prize we sought is won./The port is near, the bells I hear, the people all exulting,/While follow eyes the steady keel the vessel grim and daring,/

But O heart! heart! heart!/O the bleeding drops of red, Where on the deck my Captain lies,/Fallen cold and dead.
*Walt Whitman, "In Memory of Lincoln"
(1865).*

Poor Edwin Booth is ruined by his brother's act. His engagement of marriage is broken, his future as an actor blasted. Many go as far as to declare he should never appear again . . . The melancholy Dane: he will look and act more naturally than ever! This blow has fallen upon him in the height of his fame.
Maria L. Daly, April 30, 1865, Diary.

He [Judge Daly] has had a most interesting visit to Richmond . . . He feels that these people have still to be taught humility. They must be convinced that they have been guilty of a crime and not be allowed to feel that they are heroes and martyrs. He said the Confederate parole officers of Lee's army thronged the Spottswood house in their Confederate uniforms as haughty as though they had not been worsted, and that our men almost felt that they were the intruders.

Maria L. Daly, April 30, 1865, Diary.

10. Reconstruction and Outlook: May 1865–May 1868

THE HISTORICAL CONTEXT

Before the Union soldiers went home, there was a Grand Review in Washington on May 23–24 when the Army of the Potomac and Sherman's troops marched down Pennsylvania Avenue with the crowd and the soldiers joining in "John Brown's Body." The demobilization thereafter was completed very effectively, and within two months more than 600,000 men had been discharged. A little more than a year later, the army of the United States was down to 65,000 men, after reaching a high of more than a million in May of 1865. Thus, the army did not develop into a permanent power in the United States. The number of warships was reduced from more than 500 to 117 by the end of 1865. Most of the mustered out soldiers and sailors seem to have readjusted readily to civilian life (more readily than the soldiers returning from the two World Wars and Vietnam).

Still, life after the war was profoundly different from what it had been before, and would never be the same again. Aside from the horrible human cost, which left almost every Southern and Northern family in mourning, and the dismal impoverishment of the South, the centralization of the government that had happened during the war years changed the fabric of society. Until 1860, the only direct contact with the federal government the average citizen had was the postal service. Now, the War Department controlled state militias; many direct taxes were imposed, a Federal Bureau of Internal Revenue was in place, national banking system had been instituted and federal money had been printed.

The most radical changes, of course, took place in the South. All seceded states were put under martial law, and an occupation force of 200,000 men was to maintain law and order. There were four million blacks who, at this point, were neither slaves nor citizens. The newly created Freedmen's Bureau was to regulate their relations, with their

269

former masters. It also issued thousands of daily rations to needy whites and blacks and so did the occupation army. The North imposed no organized vengeance, no Confederates were tried for treason—the only Southern war criminal punished by the courts was Henry Wirz, the former commander of the Andersonville prison camp where thousands of Union soldiers had died of starvation and exposure. He was hanged in Washington in November 1865. On the other hand, a Washington military court gave short shrift to the apprehended conspirators of the Lincoln assassination. Four were hanged at the Old Penitentiary on July 7, including Mrs. Mary Surratt, in whose boarding house much of the planning had taken place and whose guilt has been in dispute ever since. Other convicted conspirators were imprisoned in Florida.

Since Congress would not convene till November, the problem of how to deal with the South depended on the new president. Andrew Johnson retained Lincoln's Cabinet, an indication that he would not radically change the policy set by his predecessor. He was proud of his humble origins, considered himself a champion of the common people and, during the first months of his administration, seemed bent on punishing the Southern aristocrats as traitors and on confiscating their property. This conformed with the ideas of the radical Republicans who intended to overthrow the Southern ruling class, to confiscate their land, to enfranchise the liberated slaves and to give them confiscated land. On the other end of the scale, Democrats in the North envisioned prompt Southern self-reconstruction that would have required only that Southern state governments declare their loyalty to the Union and the exercise of control in the election of Congressmen, after which states would be allowed to stay in power. This course would have endangered the blacks and Southern Unionists and even jeopardized the ratification of the 13th amendment. In between these extreme views there were many compromise positions advocating either full or gradual enfranchisement of the freedmen and various sorts of economic assistance to them and also various kinds of disenfranchisement of leading Southerners.

It turned out soon enough that the president's ideas differed much more widely from that of the radical Republicans than had first appeared. He was suspicious of corporations, banks and New England bondholders, as his paragon, Andrew Jackson had been, and he had a conception of white supremacy that could not be reconciled with the ideals so many Northerners had been fighting for. He also insisted that the Southern states had not left the Union and that, therefore, there was no reconstruction, only "restoration." His first two proclamations, on May 29, 1865, showed the direction in which he planned to proceed. The first granted a general amnesty and restitution of all

property except slaves to all those who took the oath of allegiance—
but with exceptions. Not included were high Confederate army officers and officials, men who had resigned as judges, officers or congressmen to join the rebellion, or who had mistreated war prisoners or
committed other war crimes, and all people with property valued at
more than $20,000. Those exempted from the amnesty could ask for
individual pardons. In the second proclamation, he appointed a provisional governor for North Carolina who was to call in delegates to
draft a new state constitution. During the next few weeks, he did the
same for six other states. All appointed governors had come out
against secession in 1861.

His state proclamations were criticized immediately by radical Republicans like Charles Sumner and Thaddeus Stevens, particularly because
Johnson wanted only white men as delegates. In response to such criticism, Johnson then suggested to the provisional governor of Mississippi to enfranchise literate blacks and those who possessed property
worth $250 or more—hardly more than 10% of the black state popula-
tion.

However, none of the Southern state conventions would accept this
meager compromise. None permitted any black suffrage in the proposed constitutions, and, by the fall of 1865, it was clear that even in
the North black enfranchisement could not count on popular majorities. Votes taken on constitutional amendments for Connecticut, Wisconsin and Minnesota all showed a majority against the proposals.
This may have been one reason why Johnson completely changed his
course. He now hoped for a coalition of conservative Republicans,
Northern Democrats and Southern aristocrats and Unionists who
would restore Southern states' rights, and he talked less of the traitors
in the South and more of reconciliation and forgiving. He even supported Governor Sharkey of Mississippi who pleaded for an armed
state militia, which no doubt sooner or later would have clashed with
the occupation army, part of which consisted of blacks. He also
granted pardons to thousands of prominent Confederates who had
been exempted from the general amnesty, and all signs pointed to
their early return to power. This development aroused even the conservative Republicans.

Conflicts arose everywhere. The Freedmen's Bureau had granted abandoned plantation lands to freedmen, a policy originated in January
1865 by Sherman in Georgia. Now thousands of pardoned planters returned and claimed their land. The Bureau sided with the freedmen
but was overruled by the president, and many blacks felt betrayed.
Even after Congress convened in December, the redistribution of
Southern plantation land demanded by Thaddeus Stevens and other

radicals was considered unethical and illegal by the Republican majority, and within a year almost all arable land controlled by the Freedman's Bureau was again in the possession of its former Confederate owners.

Southern landowners could never agree to the argument of Northern idealists that blacks had earned the land by a lifetime of toil. They were convinced that blacks would never work unless they were forced to and became exasperated when freedmen would accept work from their former masters for wages, but then quite as soon as they had earned enough to live, though their work was sorely needed at harvest time. When, to protect the ignorant blacks from exploitation, the Bureau supervised contracts proposed by the landowners, it was denounced as a vicious institution. The general complaint was that the Bureau's local agents, mostly middle-class Northerners, were unable to understand the difference between a black freedman and a white Northern laborer. Actually, the Bureau helped both sides by getting blacks back to work. Since Southern courts were usually prejudiced against the blacks, Congress instituted, over Johnson's veto, a Freedmen's U.S. Court, which existed between 1866 and 1868. Despite Southern resistance, this Court helped many freedmen in the disputes with their employers. The Bureau also fought against the more offensive so-called black codes introduced by Southern states, which excluded blacks from jury duty, prohibited intermarriage and required segregation in public accommodations. The Republican Congress was of little help in these matters because such codes also existed in many Northern states.

Congress convened in December, and the moderate Republican senator from Maine, William Pitt Fessenden, became the chairman of the Joint Committee for Reconstruction. Lyman Trumbull of Illinois was chosen chairman of the Judiciary Committee. But legislation introduced by the latter, which was to strengthen the Bureau and protect the rights of the freedmen, was vetoed by Johnson, who declared that the Constitution did not favor a "system for the support of the indigent." When he was serenaded by the jubilant Democrats on February 22, 1866, in his reply he called the radicals traitors and compared himself to Christ. Congress still wished to avoid a break with the president and presented him, in March, with a Civil Rights Bill that referred to blacks as U. S. citizens and guaranteed their right to own property, to engage in contracts and to sue in court. The bill had the overwhelming support of both houses but was vetoed by Johnson on March 27 as unconstitutional because it "discriminated against whites."

By now he had practically all Republicans solidly against him, and both the Civil Rights bill and a revised Freedmen's Bureau bill were passed over his veto in April and July 1866. The Republicans also proposed an amendment—the Fourteenth—to the Constitution, defining all natives or naturalized persons as citizens (thereby finally terminating the Dred Scott decision) and prohibiting states from infringing on privileges and immunities of citizens and from denying to anyone the equal protection of the law. It also proposed reduced representation in Congress for any state withholding suffrage to any section of its citizens and excluded any person from holding office who had broken his oath to support the Constitution by participating in rebellion. Although the abolitionists were not satisfied with the way the amendment evaded the direct enfranchisement of the freedmen, they gave in and the amendment was passed in Congress—and promptly vetoed by the president who declared that it was illegal in that it had been passed by a Congress from which the Southern states were still excluded.

In the election campaign of 1866, Johnson sided with the Democrats while all but a few conservative Republicans stood against him. The Johnson–Democratic coalition, calling itself "National Union," demanded immediate readmission of the Southern states and the discontinuation of the Freedmen's Bureau. But most voters distrusted the Democrats, and the outbreaks of violence in Memphis and New Orleans, in which many blacks were killed, discredited the National Union's claim that the Southern states were ready to peacefully obey all U. S. laws. Johnson's undignified campaign speeches during which he exchanged insults with hecklers and hostile crowds, or again compared himself to Jesus, did the rest. In the elections, the Republicans kept their three-to-one majority in both houses and controlled all Northern states as well as Tennessee, Missouri and West Virginia.

In spite of their overwhelming victory, the Republicans could not get the 14th amendment ratified because it required the cooperation of at least four of the Southern states. Their stubborn resistance was supported by the president, whereupon the Republicans, after months of debate, passed a Reconstruction Act that, though it contained some concessions to the moderates, unmistakably bore the stamp of Thaddeus Stevens. It stated that no legal governments now existed in the Southern states and divided the "rebel country" into five military districts whose commanding generals were in charge of protecting persons in their rights and property, of maintaining order and of punishing all criminals, if necessary, without permitting the participation of civil officials. New state constitutions were to be framed by conventions for which, in practice, only three groups of people qualified as delegates: blacks, Northerners now residing in the South and natives able to show that they had not participated officially in the war—about 700,000 out of a population of four million. When this act was passed

Edwin Stanton, Secretary of War.

in Congress, the Republicans did not fear a presidential veto, which they could easily override; however, the president could, as commander in chief, direct the district commanders, so Congress quickly moved to curtail his military powers. At Secretary of War Stanton's suggestion, all presidential orders and instructions to the military must now be issued through the general of the army, Ulysses S. Grant, who, from here on, could not be removed without the Senate's consent. Grant, the most popular man in the country, had originally favored a more moderate reconstruction policy not so different from Johnson's. But Johnson had never established a good relationship with Grant, and the outbreak of violence in New Orleans and other Southern places had convinced Grant that stronger measures were needed.

Also, in March of 1867, the 40th Congress passed the Tenure of Office Act, which provided that any officer, including cabinet members, appointed with the approval of the Senate could only be removed with its consent. Finally, since Southern whites had been reluctant to cooperate in establishing new constitutions, a second Reconstruction Act, passed on March 23, was designed to put the machinery in motion to have state conventions elected. The occupation army was to register voters, which would be mostly freedmen, "carpetbaggers" from the North, and "scalawags," Southern white Unionists.

The Johnson/Stanton contro-versy. The cartoon, after Shake-speare's Romeo and Juliet, *shows Johnson stabbed by Stan-ton.*

With these measures, the president had been reduced to a mere fig-urehead and a purely parliamentary form of government established. Only the Supreme Court, which, in April of 1866, had come out against martial rule in peacetime, could, theoretically, now subject all Reconstruction Acts to judicial review. But when the House passed a bill requiring a two-thirds majority of justices for declaring an act of Congress unconstitutional and, early in 1868, deprived the Court of appellate jurisdiction, the Court cooperated and let Congress have its way.

The president and his cabinet were now isolated. The only cabinet member who supported the reconstruction program was Stanton, but Johnson hesitated to get rid of him. In August 1867, Johnson sus-pended Stanton, since, according to the Tenure of Office Act, he could no longer dismiss him outright. He persuaded Grant to act as interim secretary of war, putting Grant in an awkward position because he did not agree with Johnson's policies. He acted as go-between and advised Johnson not to remove General Sheridan, new commander of the Lou-isiana–Texas district and Daniel Sickles, commander of the Carolina district who had strictly enforced the Reconstruction laws. Johnson re-moved them nevertheless, and this action further embittered the Re-publican radicals. In the elections of 1867 when the question of black suffrage in the Northern states was finally put to a vote and defeated in Minnesota, Ohio and Kansas, they felt their whole reconstruction program to be endangered. Things came to a head when the Senate overruled Stanton's suspension and Grant willingly vacated his office. Johnson, furious at Grant, removed Stanton on February 21, 1868—a clear violation of the Tenure of Office Act—and nominated General Lorenzo Thomas to replace him—after Sherman had declined the of-fice. Stanton refused to yield and barricaded himself in his office, and three days later, the House moved to impeach the president, with a vote along party lines, 126 to 47.

"Carpetbaggers," contemporary cartoon showing Carl Schurz, who was actually opposed to radical reconstruction policies.

Radicals in Congress had asked for Johnson's impeachment as early as January 1867. Their opinion was that impeachment as provided by the Constitution did not require criminal acts but only grave misuse of power. But the Judiciary Committee was controlled by moderates who had maintained that Johnson had not committed actual crimes. Now the mood changed, and the committee appointed to draw up charges included some of the leading radicals like Thaddeus Stevens, Benjamin Butler and John Logan. The first eight articles of impeachment dealt with Johnson's removal of Stanton and appointment of Thomas, the 9th with his attempt to persuade one of the district army commanders to take orders directly from him instead of through the general of the army, the 10th, drafted by Benjamin Butler, accused him of exciting the people of the United States against Congress, and the 11th summarized all previous charges.

The trial before the Senate, with Chief Justice Salmon P. Chase presiding, lasted from March 5 to May 26. Johnson was ably defended (by Benjamin R. Curtis, Jeremiah Black, William M. Evarts, and T. A. R. Nelson) and showed restraint during the trial. He promised to enforce the Reconstruction Acts and appointed a new secretary of war, General John M. Schofield, who was agreeable to all factions. Although great pressure was applied to those senators who seemed inclined to vote against impeachment, the first vote, on article 11, showed 35 for and 19 against impeachment, with seven Republican senators siding with the 12 Democrats. Since a two-thirds majority was required, this meant that the impeachment had been rejected by just one vote. The votes on the other articles were identical. In retrospect, it appears that the arguments for impeachment stood on rather shaky ground and that the whole procedure was simply a power struggle between the president and Congress. A conviction could have upset the balance of power provided by the Constitution. The seven "recusant" Republicans were bitterly denounced, but in view of the coming presidential election, the Republicans closed ranks soon thereafter.

A few days before the final vote in Congress, the Republicans nominated Ulysses S. Grant as presidential candidate. Grant had been a Democrat all his life and went over to the radical Republicans only after Johnson had called him a liar over the Stanton incident. On the Democratic side, Johnson had become a liability and was dropped, and the former governor of New York, Horatio Seymour, was nominated. Seymour lost, partly because his running mate, Francis P. Blair of Missouri, was too extreme for Northern Democrats. Although Grant carried 26 states to Seymour's eight, Seymour obtained more white votes than Grant, who had been elected by the 700,000 blacks voting for the first time in a presidential election. To keep the radicals in power, a 15th amendment was drafted that would ensure black majorities in the South and also give the ballot to blacks in a number of Northern states.

The state conventions, which had started in the winter of 1867–68, were much ridiculed by Southern whites as "Black and Tan" conventions, but they did a creditable job and produced some very progressive constitutions. By the time Grant took over the presidency, only Virginia, Texas, Mississippi and Georgia were still unrepresented in Congress. The delay in the first three was caused by interparty strife among the Republicans and the stringent disenfranchisement provisions in the new constitutions; but by 1869, all three had been readmitted. Georgia had been restored in June 1868, but the state legislature then expelled its 27 black members, claiming that the Constitution did not give blacks the right to hold office. Consequently, the state was returned to military control and the military commander purged the legislature drastically, reseated the black members and had the 14th and 15th amendments ratified. Georgia was readmitted in July 1870. The strategy of the radicals, who wanted to secure the supremacy in the South with the help of the blacks and the exclusion of the old white establishment, had been successful, at least temporarily. With the ratification of the 15th amendment, Reconstruction seemed to be completed, and the country could finally pay attention to other problems. Important developments had taken place during the last few years, like the purchase of Alaska, the completion of the first transcontinental railroad and the laying of the first transatlantic submarine cable. All of these events pointed to a brighter future, but during the never-ending fight over Reconstruction, little attention had been paid to them.

Under the new president, Ulysses S. Grant, however, peace and harmony did not return to the United States. He carried more goodwill and a higher reputation than most other presidents when he assumed office, but his political inexperience and unfortunate choice of associates turned his administration into a period of unprecedented corruption. Even worse, Reconstruction proved to be not just unfinished but apparently presented unsolvable problems. In the long run, the Southern Republican party, which never had any roots in the region and consisted mainly of poor, illiterate blacks, was no match for the well-educated and financed whites who were bent on restoring the old traditions, and, step-by-step, they regained their former power. The shameless exploitation exercised by the "carpetbaggers" and other Northern white politicians had discredited the Republican efforts. When finally, in 1876, as a part of a political deal following the contested presidential election, the Northern occupation troops were withdrawn from the South, an era of fighting for liberty and equality came to an end.

As a result of a compromise between Northern radicals and Southern exslaveholders, the Southern black was abandoned by the Republican Party and was gradually pushed out of any administrative and government positions. From about 1880 on, white supremacy had successfully reestablished itself in the South. Blacks were excluded from voting by education requirements and poll taxes. In spite of the three great constitutional amendments, strict segregation ruled everywhere and Ku Klux Klan terror intimidated blacks from making further efforts to improve their situation. Although in 1776 the Declaration of Independence had stated unequivocally that all men were created equal, the fact was that no one in the South and few in the North were really ready to accept blacks as their equals. The ideal of equality between the races for which so many in the past decades had fought was once again pushed to the background. Even the Supreme Court soon accepted partial segregation in the South in its formula of "separate but equal." The emphasis, from here on, would be on economic expansion and prosperity. The new age of industrial capitalism, steam engines and electricity called for individual initiative and freedom.

Fifteen years of civil war and Reconstruction had changed the country radically. The prosperous North felt redeemed by history and developed a degree of self-righteousness that supported the tendency to tell other nations what to do. The impoverished South was inclined to self-pity and blamed the prevailing illiteracy, the excesses of the Ku Klux Klan, the lynchings and other shortcomings on her defeat. All Americans agreed that slavery was gone forever, and the unity of the nation was never again to come into question. Americans, as soldiers, had seen other parts of their country and continued to travel more extensively. Much of the large-scale planning of the post-Reconstruction period was based on wartime experience, as, for instance, the ready-made clothing industry was an offshoot of the mass-produced blue uniforms. On the other hand, the disillusionment with the corruption of the Grant years and the breakdown of the ideals so many thousands had died for led to a distrust of politics, and in particular of mere logic in politics. The ideologies of the political parties became vaguer than ever. Still, some real heroes had emerged and would stay engraved in the public memory; these men, in contrast to the earlier heroes of the War of Independence, were not simple, clear-cut personalities but had inner conflicts: for the North, Lincoln, Grant, Sherman, Sheridan; for the South, Lee, Jackson and, after some years, Jefferson Davis. When Ulysses S. Grant died, in 1885, shortly after completing his memoirs, a number of former Southern generals served as pallbearers in their gray uniforms, signifying the end of the most dramatic era in American history.

CHRONICLE OF EVENTS

1865:

May 29: President Johnson grants amnesty and pardon to all persons who participated in the "existing rebellion," with a few exceptions.

June 3: Southern naval forces on the Red River surrender.

June 6: In Missouri, the new state constitution abolishing slavery is ratified.

Confederate prisoners willing to take the oath of allegiance are declared released by President Johnson, with the exception of higher officers.

June 13–21: President Johnson appoints provisional governors in Mississippi, Georgia, Texas and Alabama.

June 23: President Johnson declares the Federal blockade of the Southern states at an end. At Doaksville, Indian Territory, Cherokee leader Stand Watie surrenders the Indian battalion to Federal Lieutenant Colonel Mathews.

June 28: The C.S.S. *Shenandoah* under Lieutenant Waddell, unaware that the war is over, has captured numerous whalers in the Bering Sea.

June 30: All eight conspirators accused of the Lincoln assassination are found guilty by the military commission. Four, including one woman, are sentenced to be hanged. The executions are carried out on July 7.

August: Confederate General Jo Shelby refuses to surrender and leads a force of about 1,000 men to Mexico City. His offer to form a "foreign legion" is turned down by Emperor Maximilian, who, however, provides the men with a large tract of land near Vera Cruz.

Confederate raider *Shenandoah* is informed that the war has ended.

September 14: At Fort Smith, Arkansas, representatives of nine Indian tribes sign a treaty of loyalty with the United States and renounce all Confederate agreements.

October 11: President Johnson paroles Confederate Vice President Alexander H. Stephens and several Confederate Cabinet members.

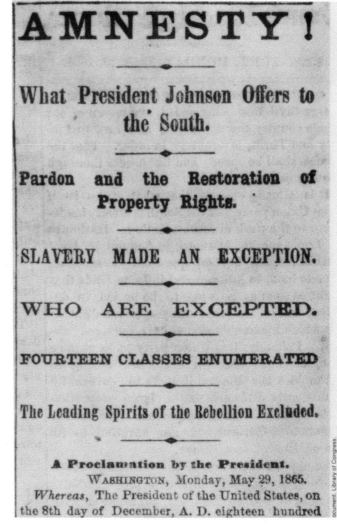

Johnson's Amnesty Proclamation.

November 6: C.S.S. *Shenandoah* surrenders to British officials at Liverpool.

November 10: Captain Henry Wirz, commander of the notorious Andersonville, Georgia, Confederate prison is convicted of cruelty by a military commission and hanged.

November 13: The 13th Amendment is ratified by the state of South Carolina.

December 1: The suspension of the privilege of the writ of habeas corpus is revoked, except for former Confederate states.

December 18: The 13th Amendment to the U. S. Constitution abolishing slavery is declared in effect by Secretary Seward after approval by 27 states.

1866:

February: Congress broadens the authority of the Freedmen's Bureau, introducing a provision that anyone accused of interfering with the civil rights of a freed person will be tried by a military court. President Johnson's veto is overridden. Nevertheless, the Southern states begin to enact discriminatory black codes, to keep former slaves from participating in a free society.

April 2: President Johnson declares the insurrection in all Southern states to be at an end, except for Texas, which has not yet formed a government.

April 9: Over President Johnson's veto, Congress adopts the Civil Rights Act, which guarantees citizenship to all native-born individuals, except the untaxed Indians.

April 30–May 2: Race riots in Memphis, Tennessee. Forty-six blacks are killed, more than 80 wounded. One white man is injured.

May: In Pulaski, Tennessee, an informal organization, called the Ku Klux Klan, is started, and several vigilante groups, which are determined to prevent blacks from making use of their new rights, are formed.

June: Congress adopts the 14th Amendment to the Constitution, extending all laws on citizenship to all blacks. Former office holders who engaged in insurrection or rebellion are barred from holding any office, unless specifically authorized by Congress by a two-thirds vote. This provision seeks to prevent the return of Southern Democrats into state and federal governments.

July 16: The Supplementary Freedmen's Bureau Act is passed by Congress over the president's veto.

July 24: Tennessee is restored to the Union.

July 29: The first trans-Atlantic submarine cable is laid between Ireland and Newfoundland.

July 30: Race riot in New Orleans. Thirty-four blacks are killed, more than 200 injured. Four whites are killed, 10 policemen injured.

August 20: The National Labor Union is organized by William H. Sylvis. It advocates equal

Blacks vote for the first time in 1868, engraving in Harper's Weekly.

rights for all, including women and blacks, also the eight-hour day and the elimination of monopoly.

August: President Johnson declares the insurrection in Texas at an end, thereby marking the official end of the Civil War.

November: In the Congressional elections, the Republicans, who have portrayed the president as sympathetic to the Southern cause, strengthen their hold on the national government.

1867:

January 7: Congressional investigation of President Johnson.

January 8: Blacks in District of Columbia are enfranchised.

March: Congress passes the first Reconstruction Act, which divides the South into five military districts headed by governors who take their orders from the Supreme Commander of the Army, General Grant. The governors are to supervise elections of state conventions to draft new state constitutions. Many white Southerners boycott these elections.

March 2: Congress passes the Tenure of Office Act, requiring the president to get approval from the Senate before removing any officials whose appointment originally required Senate approval. Johnson vetoes this as an infringement on the balance of powers, but his veto is overridden.

The Command of the Army Act, which limits the military powers of the president, is passed.

March 23: The Second Reconstruction Act becomes law.

March 30: Alaska is purchased from Russia for $7,200,000.

April–May: In two decisions, the Supreme Court rules that it has no jurisdiction to stop the enforcements of Reconstruction legislation passed by Congress.

May: In Nashville, Tennessee, the Ku Klux Klan is organized as the "invisible empire of the South." Former Confederate General Nathan Bedford Forrest accepts the post of grand wizard. The Klan will fight the freed blacks and the "carpetbaggers"—Northerners who are coming South to enrich themselves.

Jefferson Davis has served two years at Fort Monroe and is released on bail.

August: President Johnson asks Secretary of War Edwin Stanton, who has been working against Johnson, to resign. Stanton refuses, invoking the Tenure of Office Act, and the president suspends him.

1868:

February: President Johnson, determined to test the constitutionality of the Tenure of Office Act, dismisses Stanton, whereupon the House of Representatives impeaches Johnson for "high crimes and misdemeanor." Stanton declares he will continue in his office until forcibly expelled.

March 5: The U. S. Senate convenes as a court

of impeachment. Chief Justice Salmon Chase presides.

May 16: In the Senate vote on the Articles of Impeachment, 35 votes are for conviction, 19 are against, including those of seven Republicans. Since a two-thirds majority is required, the president is acquitted by one vote. Stanton resigns.

The radical Republicans, still in full control of the party, nominate General Ulysses Simpson Grant as their presidential candidate.

June: Seven former Confederate states have reorganized their government under the Reconstruction Act and are readmitted to the Union by Congress.

June 22: Arkansas is readmitted to the Union.

June 25: Omnibus bill readmits North Carolina, South Carolina, Louisiana, Alabama and Florida to the Union.

July 28: The 14th Amendment, giving citizenship to all blacks, becomes part of the Constitution.

July: The Democratic Party drops Johnson and nominates Horatio Seymour, governor of New York, for president.

The 14th Amendment comes into force.

August: Thaddeus Stevens, leader of the radical Republicans, dies.

September: In Georgia, the legislature expels its black members. Military government is reimposed. More blacks are now being elected to state and local offices in the South.

November: Ulysses S. Grant is elected president.

December: "Lame-duck" President Johnson proclaims the pardon of all former Southerners, except for some 300 leaders, but Congress counteracts much of the executive clemency.

1869:

January: General Forrest tries, in vain, to dissolve the Ku Klux Klan and resigns as grand wizard.

February: Congress passes the 15th Amendment, guaranteeing the right to vote to every male citizen.

Three imprisoned Ku Klux Klansmen, 1869.

March: Ulysses S. Grant is inaugurated president of the United States. His more moderate policy toward the South results in the reestablishment of many Southerners who are inclined to deny the blacks their new rights.

September 24: "Black Friday" on the New York stock exchange.

October 4 and 5: Conservatives win control in Tennessee and Virginia.

1870:

January–March: The 15th Amendment, granting voting rights to all citizens, including blacks, is passed after Virginia, Mississippi and Texas have ratified it.

Free education is being established in the South, but black children are forced into segregated schools.

The troubled Grant administration, contemporary cartoon.

May: Congress passes an anti-Ku Klux Klan Act.

May 10: The first continental railroad is completed.

July: Georgia ratifies the 15th Amendment and is readmitted to the Union, the last of the former Confederate states.

December: In the third session of the 41st Congress, representatives from all states are present for the first time since 1860.

1871:

April: Another anti-Ku Klux Klan Act is passed by Congress, which declares that acts by armed groups may be treated as rebellion.

December: Union claims against Britain on damages suffered from raids by Confederate boats built in Britain during the war are put before a special tribunal in Geneva.

1872:

June: In spite of many scandals revealed during his administration, Grant is renominated by the Republicans. He is opposed by Horace Greeley, editor of the *New York Tribune,* candidate of the Democrats and a group called the "Liberal Republicans."

November: Grant wins the election easily, and the devastated Greeley goes insane and dies at the end of the month.

1874:

November: Democrats gain a majority in the House of Representatives.

1876:

November: Samuel J. Tilden, Democratic governor of New York, wins the popular vote in the presidential election over the Republican Rutherford B. Hayes, governor of Ohio, but disputes arise over the voting in South Carolina, Oregon, Florida and Louisiana.

1877:

March: The Electoral Commission set up by Congress declares Hayes the winner. In a secret deal, Democrats had agreed to this outcome against the promise of withdrawal of all federal garrisons from the former rebel states.

April: The last Federal troops are removed from Louisiana.

EYEWITNESS TESTIMONY

I say the traitor has ceased to be a citizen, and in joining the rebellion has become a public enemy. He forfeited the right to vote with loyal men when he renounced his citizenship and sought to destroy our Government. . . . Treason must be made odious, and traitors must be punished and impoverished. Their great plantations must be seized and divided into small farms, and sold to honest, industrious men.

Andrew Johnson, in a speech in Nashville, Tennessee, June 9, 1864.

In the North no person can step into a railroad car but the rapid change which is going on will be apparent on him. Many are travelling who never travelled before on cars or steamboats, so that the character of the travelling masses is quite different from what it used to be. Formerly only merchants and professional men and persons of wealth and leisure travelled, but now the whole country, as soldiers, fathers, brothers, sister, mothers of soldiers are passing to and fro in every train.

Philadelphia Public Ledger, *November 7, 1864.*

What the effect of the war will be on the South eventually, who shall predict? But the masses of the poor white will be much enlightened by all they have passed through, and by their contact with Northern minds. They will be no longer controlled by a few wealthy leaders. Northern energy and intelligence will be diffused in various ways throughout those Southern sections whose fertility is incalculable. When the present rebellion is put down the progress of the country as a whole will probably be much more rapid than at any former period, and the history of a new life will begin from the present war.

Philadelphia Public Ledger, *November 7, 1864.*

I shall go to my grave with the firm belief that Davis, Cobb, Toombs and a few others of the arch-conspirators and traitors should have been tried, convicted, and hanged for treason . . . If it was the last act of my life I'd hang Jeff Davis as an example. I'd show coming generations that, while rebellion was too popular a revolt to punish many who partic-

ipated in it, treason should be made odious and archtraitors should be punished.

Andrew Johnson in 1865, as quoted by Avery Craven in Reconstruction, the Ending of the Civil War *(1969).*

There is one, and only one, sure and safe policy for the immediate future, namely: the North must remain the absolute Dictator of the Republic until the spirit of the North shall become the spirit of the whole country . . . The South is still unpurged of her treason. Prostrate in the dust she is no less a traitor at this hour than when her head was erect . . . They cannot be trusted with authority over their former slaves . . . The only hope for the South is to give the ballot to the Negro and in denying it to the rebels.

The Independent, *radical Republican publication, May 5, 1865.*

Just say to the people: "organize your state governments: I will aid you by enrollment of loyal citizens; you will not expect me to discriminate among people equally loyal; once enrolled vote for delegates to the Convention to reform your State Constitution; I will aid you in collecting and declaring their suffrages; your Convention and yourselves must do the rest; but you may count on the support of the National Government in all things constitutionally expedient". This will terminate all discussion.

Chief Justice Chase to President Johnson, May 7, 1865, as quoted in Walter L. Fleming's Documentary History of Reconstruction *(1966).*

Yesterday came the news of the capture of Jefferson Davis. He was surprised and first attempted to escape in one of his wife's dresses to the woods . . . Poor wretch! I have no sympathy with his cause nor his ambition, but I cannot but feel sorry for him. What torture of mind he will suffer until his end comes! The death of a traitor, though it may not be proven that he sanctioned the death of poor President Lincoln.

Maria L. Daly, May 15, 1865, Diary of a Union Lady *(1962).*

At about three o'clock yesterday all that is mortal of Jeff'n Davis, late so-called President of the alleged Confederate States, was duly, but quietly and effectively, committed to that living tomb prepared within

the impregnable walls of Fortress Monroe . . . No more will Jeff'n Davis be known among the masses of men . . . he is buried alive.
New York Herald, *May 23, 1865.*

Washington is full of Southern people, and the President is occupied half the time in receiving delegations from Dixie. The effect of this is an increasingly evident leaning toward a more conservative policy.
Henry D. Cooke, letter to Senator John Sherman of Ohio, July 1865, quoted in Kenneth M. Stampp's The Era of Reconstruction *(1972).*

He [Judge Daly] made the acquaintance of General Sherman and General Phil Sheridan, both, like Grant, men of great simplicity and sincerity. Sheridan has a splendid face and Sherman looks like a man who did not easily forget; he has a strong fighting face.
Maria L. Daly, June 2, 1865, Diary.

There was a brutal scene at the hotel where a drunken sergeant, with a pair of tailor's shears, insisted on cutting the buttons from the uniform of a gray-headed old Brigadier, who had just come in from Johnston's army; but he bore himself modestly and very handsomely through it. His staff was composed of fine-looking, stalwart fellows, evidently gentlemen, who appeared intensely mortified at such treatment . . . They had no clothes save their Rebel uniforms . . .
Whitelaw Reid, Ohio journalist, after the war, 1865, quoted in Walter L. Fleming's Documentary History of Reconstruction.

Much ill-feeling had been kept alive by the United States Treasury agents, searching the country for Confederate cotton and branded mules and horses. Many of these agents . . . were more rogues and fortune-hunters. They would propose to seize a man's property in the name of the United States, but abandon the claim on the payment of heavy bribes, which of course went into their own pockets . . . Such practices had a pernicious effect, engendering a contempt for the government, and a murderous ill-will which too commonly vented itself upon soldiers and negroes.
J. T. Trowbridge, New England author who traveled through most Southern states in 1865, The South *(1865). Quoted in Walter L. Fleming's* Documentary History of Reconstruction.

I cannot help but remark that it must be a matter of gratitude as well as surprise, for our people to see a Government which was lately fighting us with fire and sword and shell, now generously feeding our poor and distressed . . . Again, the Confederate soldier, with one leg or one arm, the crippled maimed and broken, and the worn and destitute men who fought bravely their enemies then, their benefactors now, have their sacks filled and are fed.
A Southern reporter's account, 1865, in Annual Cyclopedia, *quoted in Walter L. Fleming's* Documentary History of Reconstruction.

For miles, the countryside looked like a broad black streak of ruin and desolation—the fences all gone; lonesome smoke stacks, surrounded by dark heaps of ashes and cinders, marking the spots where human habitations had stood; the fields along the road wildly overgrown by weeds, with here and there a sickly patch of cotton or corn cultivated by Negro squatters.
Carl Schurz traveling through South Carolina in the summer of 1865 in his Memoirs *(1907/ 08).*

The confusion and disorder of the transition period would have been infinitely greater had no agency interfered which possessed the confidence of the emancipated slaves; which could disabuse them of any extravagant notions . . . which could administer to them good advice and be voluntarily obeyed. No other agency, except one placed there by the national government, could have wielded that moral power whose interposition was so necessary to prevent the southern society from falling at once into the chaos of a general collision between its different elements.
Carl Schurz, report to Johnson on the Freedmen's Bureau, summer of 1865.

The predominant feeling of those lately in rebellion is that of deep-seated hatred, amounting in many cases to a spirit of revenge towards the white Unionists of the State, and a haughty contempt for the negro, whom they cannot treat as a freeman. The hatred for the white loyalists is intensified by the accusation that he deserted the South in her extremity and is, therefore, a traitor . . .
Joint Committee on Reconstruction, report of 1865, as quoted in Walter L. Fleming's Documentary History of Reconstruction.

I am satisfied that the mass of the thinking men of the South accept the present situation of affairs in good faith . . . I was pleased to learn from the leading men whom I met, that they not only accepted the decision arrived at as final . . . but as a fortunate one for the whole country.

Ulysses S. Grant, Report to President Johnson,
summer of 1865, quoted in Avery Craven's Reconstruction, the Ending of the Civil War.

Of the splendidly equipped road . . . of the 49 locomotives, 37 passenger cars (many of which had never been used) and 550 freight, baggage and gravel cars, there remained fit for use, though in damaged condition, between Jackson and Canton, 1 locomotive, 2 second class passenger cars, 1 first class passenger car, 1 baggage car, 1 provision car, 2 stock and 2 flat cars.

House of Representatives, report on the rail-
ways in Mississippi 1865, as quoted in Walter
F. Fleming's Documentary History of Reconstruction.

The state of affairs which led to the massacre [of New Orleans] is believed to be the legitimate result of the reconstruction policy of Andrew Johnson. There can be no safety for the country against the fell spirit of Slavery . . . unless the Government shall confer on every citizen in the States we represent the American birthright of impartial suffrage, and equality before the law. It is a policy which will finally regenerate the South itself.

Governor H. C. Warmoth of Louisiana, at the
"Southern Loyalist" convention in Philadelphia,
September 3, 1865. Quoted in Richard N. Cur-
rent's Those Terrible Carpetbaggers (1988).

East Tennesseeans, though opposed to slavery and secession, do not like niggers. There is at this day more prejudice against color among the middle and poorer classes—the "Union" men, of the South, who owned few or no slaves—than among the planters who owned them by the scores and hundreds . . .

J. T. Trowbridge, New England author, The
South *as quoted in Walter L. Fleming's* Documentary History of Reconstruction.

At Bladen Springs . . . a freedman was chained to a pinetree and burned to death. About two weeks after, and fifteen miles from Bladen, another freedman was burned to death. In the latter part of May, fifteen miles South of Bladen, a freedman was shot outside the planter's premises and the body dragged

into the stable, to make it appear he had shot him in the act of stealing . . . About the first of June, six miles west of Bladen, a freedman was hung. His body is still hanging. About the last of May, three freedmen were coming down the Bigbee river in a skiff, when two of them were shot; the other escaped to the other shore . . . A preacher (near Bladen Springs) states in the pulpit that the roads in Choctaw county stunk with the dead bodies of servants that had fled from their masters . . .

Freedman's Bureau, report on atrocities in Ala-
bama, July 20, 1865, as quoted in Walter L.
Fleming's Documentary History of Reconstruction.

I see the president is precipitating things. I fear before Congress meets he will have so be-deviled matters as to render them incurable. I almost despair of resisting Executive influence . . . Is it possible to devise any plan to arrest the government in its ruinous course?

Thaddeus Stevens, letter to Charles Sumner,
September 1865, quoted in Avery Craven's Reconstruction, the Ending of the Civil War.

The future condition of the conquered power depends on the will of the conqueror. They must come in as new states or remain as conquered provinces . . . Congress must create states and declare when they are entitled to be represented . . . We have turned, or are about to turn, loose four million slaves without a hut to shelter them or a cent in their pockets. The infernal laws of slavery have prevented them from acquiring an education . . . This Congress is bound to provide for them until they can take care of themselves. If we do not furnish them with homesteads . . . if we leave them to the legislation of their late masters, we had better had left them in bondage.

Thaddeus Stevens in Congress, September 18,
1865.

The loyal men of the nation . . . regard his [Johnson's] actions and his speeches with almost sickening anxiety, and many of them are apt to fear that the immense pressure brought to bear upon him, acting on habits of thoughts and prejudices almost unavoidable under the circumstances of his Southern birth and breeding, may work mischiefs which even the power of Congress may find hard to mend.

The Independent, *radical Republican publica-*
tion, September 21, 1865.

It would not do to let the negro have universal suffrage now; it would breed a war of races. There was a time in the Southern states when the slaves of large owners looked down on non-slave owners because they did not own slaves . . . The outrages are mostly from non-slave holding whites against the negro, and from the negro upon the non-slave holding whites. The negro will vote with the late master whom he does not hate, rather than the non-slave-holding white whom he does hate. Universal suffrage will create another war, not against us, but a war of races.

Andrew Johnson, in an interview October 3, 1865, as quoted in Walter L. Fleming's Documentary History of Reconstruction.

There is among the plantation negroes a widely spread idea that land is to be given them by the Government, and this idea is at the bottom of much idleness and discontent. At Orangeburg and at Columbia, country negroes with whom I have conversed asked me "When is de land goin' fur to be dewided?" . . . There is also a widely spread idea that the whites are to be driven out of the lower section of the State, and that the negroes are there to live by themselves. That so absurd ideas could exist I could not believe till I found them myself.

Sidney Andrews, travelling correspondent for the Boston Advertiser, *on the South since the war, October 1865.*

The war has decided first: That . . . the States of the Federal Union have not the right . . . to secede therefrom. The doctrine of secession . . . is now exploded for any practical purpose. The theory of absolute sovereignty of a State . . . must also be materially modified to conform to this . . . decision . . . The God of Battles has pronounced an irreversible judgment, after a long, desperate and sanguinary struggle, and it would be neither politic nor patriotic to invoke a new trial of the fearful issue.

Governor J. L. Orr, Address to the South Carolina legislature, October 1865, quoted in Walter L. Fleming's Documentary History of Reconstruction.

It is difficult to measure the mischief which has already ensued from the "experiment" which has been made . . . Looking at the distress which it has caused among loyal people by the revival of the rebel spirit, it is heart-rending. Looking at it anyway, it is

a terrible failure. It will be for Congress to apply the remedy . . .

Charles Sumner, in a letter published in The Independent, *November 2, 1865.*

It shall be unlawful for any officer, station agent, collector or employee on any railroad in this State, to allow any freedman, negro or mulatto, to ride in any first class passenger cars, set apart or used by and for white persons; and any person offending against the provisions of this section, shall be deemed guilty of a misdemeanor . . .

Mississippi law, November 21, 1865 ("Jim Crow" Law), quoted in Walter L. Fleming's Documentary History of Reconstruction.

Went last night to the Fifth Avenue hotel to the reception to General Grant . . . the music struck up "The Conquering Hero Comes". The crowd was dreadful . . . I nearly had my bouquet dragged out of my hand and my lace torn . . . General Grant, after his health was drunk, thanked the ladies most heartfully for the very great compliments they had paid him in a few very sincere words . . . It was interesting to watch the shade of *shy* embarrassment which crossed General Grant's face when any direct praise was given him.

Maria L. Daly, November 21, 1865, Diary.

I cannot begin to attempt to unfold the policy of that man in whom people confided as a true patriot, and whom we have now found to be worse than the man who is now incarcerated in Fortress Monroe . . . We have been oppressed with taxes, and debts, and he [the Lord] has sent us more than lice, and has afflicted us with Andrew Johnson.

Thaddeus Stevens, in reaction to Johnson's message to Congress, November 1865.

Make all men peers before the law,/Take hands from off the negro's throat,/Give black and white an equal vote.
Keep all your forfeit lives and lands,/But give the common redress/To labor's utter nakedness.
Then shall the Union's mother-heart/Her lost and wandering ones recall/Forgiving and restoring all.

John Greenleaf Whittier, "To the Thirtyninth Congress" (December 1865).

Strike at the Black Codes as you have already struck at the Slave Codes. There is nothing to choose between them. Strike at once; strike hard. You have already proclaimed Emancipation; proclaim Enforcement also.

Charles Sumner, as reported by the New York Times *December 7, 1865.*

I have never desired bloody punishments to any great extent. But . . . there are punishments quite as appalling, and longer remembered than death. They are more advisable, because they would reach a greater number. Strip a proud nobility of their bloated estates; reduce them to a level with plain republicans; send them forth to labor, and teach their children to enter the workshops or handle the plow, and you will thus humble the proud traitors. Teach his posterity to respect labor and eschew treason. Conspirators are bred among the rich and vain . . .

Thaddeus Stevens in Congress, March 1866, as quoted in Walter L. Fleming's Documentary History of Reconstruction.

The whole work of reorganizing the South and restoring its relations with the Union is the most important kind of work upon which a government can enter . . . In a free country it is the legislature only which is capable of it. In this country the performance of it is expressly forbidden to anybody but the legislature. The phrase "the President's policy", which is now heard so often, is a solecism of which no American who knows the nature of his own institutions ought to be guilty. The President has *opinions;* he ought not to have a policy. It is for Congress to frame a policy; it is for him to carry it out.

The Nation, *April 5, 1866.*

From the time these Confederate States withdrew their representation in Congress and levied war against the United States, the great mass of the people became and were insurgents, rebels, traitors, and all of them assumed and occupied the political, legal and practical relation of enemies of the United States . . . their people reduced to the condition of enemies, conquered in war, entitled only by public law to such rights . . . as might be vouchsafed by the conqueror . . .

Joint Committee on Reconstruction, report acted on by Congress, June 20, 1866.

I think there is a kindly feeling on the part of the planters towards the freedmen. They are not held at

all responsible for anything that has happened . . . The Freedmen's Bureau, or any agency to interfere between the freedman and his former master, is only productive of mischief . . . It has a tendency to create dissatisfaction and disaffection on the part of the laborer . . .

J. D. B. De Bow, editor of De Bow's Review, *statement in Report of Joint Committee on Reconstruction, 1866, quoted in Walter L. Fleming's* Documentary History of Reconstruction.

If any white person and any negro, or the descendant of any negro, to the third generation inclusive, though one ancestor of each generation be a white person, intermarry, or live in adultery or fornication with each other, each of them must, on conviction, be imprisoned in the penitentiary, for not less than two, not more than seven years . . .

Penal Code of Alabama, 1866, quoted by Walter L. Fleming in Documentary History of Reconstruction.

People are thinking about their private business; they want to go to work to repair their losses; they do not wish any more war, domestic or foreign . . . They are an afflicted people, terribly afflicted . . . From Harper's Ferry to New Market, which is about eighty miles . . . the country was almost a desert. There were no fences. Speaking of the condition of the valley after General Sheridan retired, I described wheatfields growing without any enclosure; someone asked me whether the stock would not destroy the wheat. I said "Certainly, if General Sheridan had not taken the precaution of removing all the stock".

A native of Virginia, in the Report of Joint Committee on Reconstruction, 1866, quoted in Walter F. Fleming's Documentary History of Reconstruction.

The first feelings [after the defeat] were those of baffled rage. Men who had fought four years for an idea smarted with actual anguish under the stroke which showed their utter failure. Then followed a sense of bewilderment and helplessness . . . the National Government could at the time have prescribed no condition for the return of the Rebel States which they would not have promptly accepted. They expected nothing; were prepared for the worst; would have been thankful for anything.

Whitelaw Reid, Ohio journalist, in After the War (1866).

The rebels . . . think they have power again, and it emboldens them . . . They say that they will have a united south, and with the democratic party in the north, and the President to help them, they will soon have the control of the whole country again.

William H. Smith, deserter from the Confederacy, 1866, statement in the Report of Joint Committee on Reconstruction.

The negroes here spend their time going to "funerals", religious howlings, promiscuous sexual intercourse, thieving and "conjuring". At the "funerals" they bellow like cattle when one of their number is slaughtered . . . The stupendous wrong and folly consists in taking a poor, ignorant, childlike race from under the fostering care of a patriarchal government and withdrawing from it the protection of interest . . .

Transactions of the Alabama Historical Society vol IV (1866) as quoted in Walter L. Fleming's Documentary History of Reconstruction.

I can tell you from what I know and have seen myself, and also from what negroes have told me, that they have been promised lands and mules— forty acres and a mule—on divers occasions . . . At a barbecue there I saw a man who was making a speech to the negroes, telling them what good he had done for them; that he had been to Washington City and procured from one of the Departments here certain pegs . . . there were painted red and blue. He said that those pegs had been obtained . . . at a great expense to himself; that they had been made by the Government for the purpose of staking out the negroes' forty acres. He told the negroes that all he wanted was to have the expenses paid back to him, which was about a dollar a peg . . . and he would advise them, in selecting the forty acres, to take half woodland and half clear; that nobody would dare to interfere with those pegs.

John G. Pierce, statement in Ku Klux Report, Alabama Testimony, around 1866, quoted in Walter L. Fleming's Documentary History of Reconstruction.

The whole machinery of this bureau has been used by the basest men, for the purpose of swindling the negro, plundering the white man and defrauding the Government. There may be an honest man connected with the Bureau, but I fear that the commissioners sent by your Excellency to probe the rottenness of this cancer will find their search for such as fruitless as that of the cynic of old—

Wade Hampton, report to Johnson, 1866, on the Freedmen's Bureau, quoted in Walter L. Fleming's Documentary History of Reconstruction.

For lo! the fall of Ocean's wall/Space mocked and time outrun;/And round the world the thought of all/ Is as the thought of one!
The poles unite, the zones agrees,/The tongues of striving cease;/As on the sea of Galilee,/The Christ is whispering: Peace!

John Greenleaf Whittier, "The Cable Hymn," when the first submarine trans-ocean cable was laid (July 29, 1866).

Why don't you hang Thad Stevens and Wendell Phillips? I can tell you, my countrymen, I have been fighting traitors in the South, and . . . I am prepared to fight traitors in the North, God being willing with your help.

President Johnson in Cleveland, in early September 1866, when urged by the audience to hang Jefferson Davis. Quoted by Kenneth M. Stampp in The Era of Reconstruction *(1972).*

I would rather be elected by loyal negroes than by disloyal white men. I would rather associate with loyal negroes than with disloyal white men. I would rather be buried in a Negro than in a rebel graveyard. And after death, I would sooner go to a Negro heaven than a white rebel's hell.

Governor William G. Brownlow of Tennessee, at the "Southern Loyalist" Convention, September 1866. Quoted in Robert Selph Henry's The Story of Reconstruction *(1963).*

Every nonregenerate rebel . . . every deserter, every sneak who ran away from the draft calls himself a Democrat. Every man who labored for the rebellion in the field, who murdered Union prisoners by cruelty and starvation . . . calls himself a Democrat. Every wolf in sheep's clothing who pretends to preach the gospel but proclaims the righteousness of man-selling and slavery; everyone who shoots down negroes in the streets . . . calls himself a Democrat.

Governor Oliver P. Morton of Indiana, during the election campaign of 1866, quoted in Kenneth N. Stampp's The Era of Reconstruction.

The one thing which is now plain is that the Northern people are determined that there shall be no longer any such thing as political equality on American soil . . . About the cause of the determination and about its wisdom and about the mean used to carry it out, there may be a good deal of difference of opinion; about its existence we believe there is none.

The Nation, Jan. 17, 1867, quoted in Avery Craven's Reconstruction, the Ending of the Civil War.

The South is making a great effort to control the negro vote. It will, for the present, be successful to some extent. In large cities and towns, on public thoroughfares, where the negro is more intelligent and is in constant communication with the outside world, he will generally vote right. But in the interior and out-of-the-way places, they vote generally as their old masters direct. Indeed, the latter do not hesitate to boast of the reckless course they intend to pursue to control the negro vote in their respective communities.

John Lynch of Ohio, operator of a large plantation in northeast Louisiana, in a letter to Senator John Sherman of Ohio, April 20, 1867, as quoted in Richard N. Current's Those Terrible Carpetbaggers.

No one more gladly welcomes the Northern man who comes in all sincerety to make a home here and to become one of our people, than I, but for the adventurer and office-seeker who comes among us with one dirty shirt and a pair of dirty socks in a rusty old carpetbag, and before his washing is done becomes a candidate for office, I have no welcome.

A. J. Fletcher, Reconstruction secretary of state in Tennessee, 1867, quoted in Robert Selph Henry's The Story of Reconstruction. (This is believed to be the origin of the term "carpetbagger.")

Military Posts were established at intervals of 20 or 30 miles. There was one at Greensboro, Ala., and the negroes grew, under its influence, impudent beyond endurance. One day a young man, Mr. Tom Cowan, resented an insolent remark made to him by a negro passing on the street. Immediately, a Yankee officer stepped up to Mr. Cowan and slapped him in the face. The young man drew his pistol and killed the officer and . . . hid in a little, dark closet . . .

In less than 30 minutes the street was filled with a black, surging mass of howling negroes, led by the Yankee soldiers, searching for the young man . . .

Mrs. T. L. Kennedy, 1867, quoted in Walter L. Fleming's Documentary History of Reconstruction.

This is one of the last great battles with slavery. Driven from these legislative chambers, driven from the field of war, this monstrous power has found a refuge in the Executive Mansion, where in utter disregard of the Constitution and laws, it seeks to exercise its ancient far-reaching sway. Andrew Johnson is the impersonation of the tyrannical slave power. He is the lineal successor of John C. Calhoun and Jefferson Davis . . .

Charles Sumner, during the impeachment trial of President Johnson, March 1868, as quoted in Avery Craven's Reconstruction, the Ending of the Civil War.

Order No. K. K. Clansmen—Meet at the Trysting Spot when Orion kisses the Zenith. The doom of treason is death. *Dies irae.* The wolf is on his walk— the serpent coils to strike. Action! Action! Action! By midnight and the Tomb; by Sword and Torch and the Sacred Oath at Forrester's Altar, I bid you come! The clansmen of Glen Iran and Alpine will greet you at the new-made grave. *Remember the Ides of April.—* By command of the Grand D. I. H. Cheg. V.

Ku Klux Klan circular in Montgomery, Alabama, April 1868, quoted in Walter L. Fleming's The Sequel of Appomattox (1919).

Can any party afford to treat its leading men as a part of the Republican press has been treating leading Republicans during the last few weeks? . . . We have heard language applied to the Mr. Fessenden and Mr. Trumbull . . . which was fit only for a compound of Benedict Arnold and John Morissey.

The Nation, May 14, 1868. The mentioned two senators had voted against impeachment.

The Republican party may fairly claim the credit of the most signal impartiality in the conclusion of the impeachment trial . . . The Republicans in the Senate were numerous enough to convict him. The country generally desired to see him ousted. It was felt that it would bring peace where there was now doubt and discord, and that it would tend powerfully to the speedy restoration of the Union and the revival of industry and business. We may even say that the

world expected his conviction . . . Notwithstanding all this, the trial ended in acquittal . . . In spite of party feeling and party pressure, there are seven Republican Senators who have said on their oaths that the evidence and the law would not justify his conviction. It is creditable to these senators that they have had the firmness thus to decide . . . This is the highest instance of impartiality and honesty in all political history. It is a glory to the institutions of the republic.
New York Sun, *May 19, 1868.*

News of the failure to convict Johnson will be like Greek fire through out the entire South. The eyes of rebels sparkle like those of the fiery serpent. They hope they have found their "Lost Cause" . . .
Daniel Rochards, letters of May 18 and July 19, 1868 to Elihu B. Washburne, congressman from Illinois, quoted in Richard N. Current's Those Terrible Carpetbaggers.

What effect a verdict of acquittal will have on Mr. Johnson during the brief period that he will occupy the White House, it is impossible to say. For the past two years his course has been more damaging to his supporters than to his opponents. Men who feel a stain as wound would not regard a vote of thirty-five ayes to nineteen nays, on a charge of high crimes and misdemeanors in office, as a cause for self-gratulation. But the President is happily organized to meet this exigency; his sensibilities are not keen, and his cuticle is thick; and if his vanity and self-confidence shall impel him to continue to hurl defiance in the face of Congress, he will harm that body and the Republican Party much less than he will himself and his friends. If, on the other hand, he shall pursue the even tenor of his way, while Congress devotes itself to legitimate legislation, and the people plunge enthusiastically into the Presidential

canvass, Mr. Johnson will soon lapse into obscurity and be forgotten.
New York Sun, *May 23, 1868.*

The Freedmen's Bureau, an institution devised by Congress under the influence of the very best people . . . intended as a means of protection for the freedmen . . . in the hands of bad men proved, instead of a blessing, to be the worst curse of the race, as under it he was misled, debased and betrayed.
John Wallace, a black man, Carpet Bag Rule in Florida *(1868,) quoted in Walter L. Fleming's* Documentary History of Reconstruction.

When in a few weeks, his [Johnson's] term shall end, and he shall go back to lead in person the Ku Klux Klan in Tennessee, he will be found by his old neighbors to be a more rusted, corroded, and mildewed thing than the ancient sign in Greeneville which still says "A. Johnson, Tailor"! The sight of that rusty sign will perhaps make him wish that he had never laid aside his needle and thread, and he will then be, for the first time in three years, of the same opinion with his fellow countrymen.
The Independent *December 17, 1868.*

Did Texas [during the war] cease to be a state? Or, if not, did the State cease to be a member of the Union? . . . The Union of the United States never was a purely artificial and arbitrary relation . . . Not only, therefore, can there be no loss of separate and independent autonomy to the States through their union under the Constitution, but it may be not unreasonably said that the preservation of the States, and the maintenance of their governments, are as much within the design and care of the Constitution as the preservation of the Union . . .
Chief Justice Chase, opinion in Texas vs. White, *1869, quoted in Walter L. Fleming's* Documentary History of Reconstruction.

Appendix A
List of Documents

1. The Kansas–Nebraska Act, May 30, 1854
2. Lincoln's "House Divided" Speech, June 17, 1858
3. The Lincoln–Douglas Debate, Freeport, August 27, 1858
4. John Brown's Last Speech, November 2, 1859
5. President Buchanan on Secession, December 3, 1860
6. South Carolina Ordinance of Secession, December 20, 1860
7. South Carolina Declaration of Causes of Secession, December 24, 1860
8. The Constitution of the Confederate States of America, March 14, 1861
9. Lincoln's First Inaugural Address, March 4, 1861
10. Seward's Plan to Avert Civil War, and Lincoln's Reply, April 1, 1861
11. Frémont's Proclamation on Slaves, August 30, 1861
12. Homestead Act, May 20, 1862
13. Horace Greeley, Letter to Lincoln, in the *New York Tribune*, August 20, 1862
14. Lincoln's Reply to Greeley, August 22, 1862
15. From Lincoln's Preliminary Emancipation Proclamation, September 22, 1862
16. Address to President Lincoln by Working-Men of Manchester, England, December 31, 1862
17. Lincoln's Reply to the Working-Men of Manchester, England, January 19, 1863
18. The Emancipation Proclamation, January 1, 1863
19. The French in Mexico, Mr. Seward's letter to Minister Charles Francis Adams March 3, 1862
20. Lincoln's Letter to Governor Johnson on the Reconstruction of Tennessee, September 11, 1863
21. The Gettysburg Address, November 19, 1863
22. Lincoln's Proclamation on Amnesty and Reconstruction, December 8, 1863
23. The Thirteenth Amendment, January 31, 1865
24. Lincoln's Second Inaugural Address, March 4, 1865
25. Jefferson Davis's Last Message to the People of the Confederacy, April 4, 1865

1. The Kansas–Nebraska Act
May 30, 1854

An Act to Organize the Territories of Nebraska and Kansas.

Be it enacted . . . , That all that part of the territory of the United States included within the following limits, except such portions thereof as are hereinafter expressly exempted from the operations of this act, to wit: beginning at a point in the Missouri River where the fortieth parallel of north latitude crosses the same; thence west on said parallel to the east boundary of the Territory of Utah, on the summit of the Rocky Mountains; thence on said summit northward to the forty-ninth parallel of north latitude; thence east on said parallel to the western boundary of the territory of Minnesota; thence southward on said boundary to the Missouri River; thence down the main channel of said river to the place of beginning, be, and the same is hereby, created into a temporary government by the name of the Territory of Nebraska; and when admitted as a State or States, the said Territory, or any portion of the same, shall be received into the Union with or without slavery, as their constitution may prescribe at the time of their admission: . . .

Sec. 14. *And be it further enacted, . . .* That the Constitution, and all laws of the United States which are not locally inapplicable, shall have the same force and effect within the said Territory of Nebraska as elsewhere within the United States, except the eighth section of the act preparatory to the admission of Missouri into the Union, approved March 6, 1820, which, being inconsistent with the principle of nonintervention by Congress with slavery in the States and Territories, as recognized by the legislation of eighteen hundred and fifty, commonly called the Compromise Measures, is hereby declared inoperative and void; it being the true intent and meaning of this act not to legislate slavery into any Territory or State, nor to exclude it therefrom, but to leave the people thereof perfectly free to form and regulate their domestic institutions in their own way, subject only to the Constitution of the United States: *Provided,* That nothing herein contained shall be construed to revive or put in force any law or regulation which may have existed prior to the act of March 6, 1820, either protecting, establishing, prohibiting, or abolishing slavery. . . .

Sec. 19. *And be it further enacted,* That all that part of the Territory of the United States included within the following limits, except such portions thereof as are hereinafter expressly exempted from the operations of this act, to wit, beginning at a point on the western boundary of the State of Missouri, where the thirty-seventh parallel of north latitude crosses the same; thence west on said parallel to the eastern boundary of New Mexico; thence north on said boundary to latitude thirty-eight; thence following said boundary westward to the east boundary of the Territory of Utah, on the summit of the Rocky Mountains; thence northward on said summit to the fortieth parallel of latitude; thence east on said parallel to the western boundary of the State of Missouri; thence south with the western boundary of said State to the place of beginning, be, and the same is hereby, created into a temporary government by the name of the Territory of Kansas; and when admitted as a State or States, the said Territory, or any portion of the same, shall be received into the Union with or without slavery, as their constitution may prescribe at the time of their admission: . . .

2. Lincoln's House Divided Speech
June 17, 1858

MR. PRESIDENT AND GENTLEMEN OF THE CONVENTION: If we could first know where we are, and whither we are tending, we could better judge what to do, and how to do it. We are now far into the fifth year since a policy was initiated with the avowed object and confident promise of putting an end to slavery agitation. Under the operation of that policy, that agitation has not only not ceased, but has constantly augmented. In my opinion, it will not cease until a crisis shall have been reached and passed. "A house divided against itself cannot stand." I believe this government cannot endure permanently half slave and half free. I do not expect the Union to be dissolved; I do not expect the house to fall; but I do expect it will cease to be divided. It will become all one thing, or all the other. Either the opponents of slavery will arrest the further spread of it, and place it where the public mind shall rest in the belief that it is in the course of ultimate extinction, or its advocates will push it forward till it shall become alike lawful in all the States, old as well as new, North as well as South.

Have we no tendency to the latter condition?

Let any one who doubts, carefully contemplate that now almost complete legal combination—piece of machinery, so to speak—compounded of the Nebraska doctrine and the Dred Scott decision. Let him consider not only what work the machinery is adapted to do, and how well adapted, but also let him study the history of its construction, and trace, if he can, or rather fail, if he can, to trace the evidences of design, and concert of action, among its chief architects, from the beginning.

The new year of 1854 found slavery excluded from more than half the States by State Constitutions, and from most of the National territory by Congressional prohibition. Four days later, commenced the struggle which ended in repealing that Congressional prohibition. This opened all the National territory to slavery, and was the first point gained. . . .

While the Nebraska Bill was passing through Congress, a *law case*, involving the question of a negro's freedom, by reason of his owner having voluntarily taken him first into a free State, and then into a territory covered by the Congressional prohibition, and held him as a slave for a long time in each, was passing through the United States Circuit Court for the District of Missouri; and both Nebraska Bill and lawsuit were brought to a decision in the same month of May, 1854. The negro's name was "Dred Scott," which name now designates the decision finally made in the case. Before the then next Presidential election, the law case came to, and was argued in, the Supreme Court of the United States; but the decision of it was deferred until after the election. Still, before the election, Senator Trumbull, on the floor of the Senate, requested the leading advocate of the Nebraska Bill to state *his opinion* whether the people of a Territory can constitutionally exclude slavery from their limits; and the latter answers: "That is a question for the Supreme Court."

The election came. Mr. Buchanan was elected, and the indorsement, such as it was, secured. That was the second point gained. . . . The Presidential inauguration came, and still no decision of the court; but the incoming President, in his inaugural address, fervently exhorted the people to abide by the forthcoming decision, whatever it might be. Then in a few days, came the decision.

The reputed author of the Nebraska Bill finds an early occasion to make a speech at this capital indorsing the Dred Scott decision, and vehemently denouncing all opposition to it. The new President, too, seizes the early occasion of the Silliman letter to indorse and strongly construe that decision, and to express his astonishment that any different view had ever been entertained!

At length a squabble springs up between the President and the author of the Nebraska Bill, on the mere question of *fact*, whether the Lecompton Constitution was or was not in any just sense made by the people of Kansas; and in that quarrel the latter declares that all he wants is a fair vote for the people, and that he cares not whether slavery be voted *down* or voted *up*. I do not understand his declaration, that he cares not whether slavery be voted down or voted up, to be intended by him other than as an apt definition of the policy he would impress upon the public mind. . . . That principle is the only shred left of his original Nebraska doctrine. Under the Dred Scott decision "squatter sovereignty" squatted out of existence, tumbled down like temporary scaffolding; like the mould at the foundry, served through one blast, and fell back into loose sand; helped to carry an election, and then was kicked to the winds. His late joint struggle with the Republicans, against the Lecompton Constitution, involves nothing of the original Nebraska doctrine. That struggle was made on a point—the right of a people to make their own constitution—upon which he and the Republicans have never differed.

The several points of the Dred Scott decision, in connection with Senator Douglas's "care not" policy, constitute the piece of machinery, in its present state of advancement. This was the third point gained. The working points of that machinery are:

Firstly, That no negro slave, imported as such from Africa, and no descendant of such slave, can ever be a citizen of any State, in the sense of that term as used in the Constitution of the United States. This point is made in order to deprive the negro, in every possible event, of the benefit of that provision of the United States Constitution which declares that "The citizens of each State shall be entitled to all privileges and immunities of citizens in the several States."

Secondly, That, "subject to the Constitution of the United States," neither Congress nor a Territorial Legislature can exclude slavery from any United States Territory. This point is made in order that individual men may fill up the Territories with slaves, without danger of losing them as property, and thus to enhance the chances of permanency to the institution through all the future.

Thirdly, That whether the holding a negro in actual slavery in a free State makes him free, as against the holder, the United States courts will not decide, but will leave to be decided by the courts of any slave State the negro may be forced into by the master. This point is made, not to be pressed immediately; but, if acquiesced in for a while, and apparently indorsed by the people at an election, then to sustain the logical conclusion that what Dred Scott's master might lawfully do with Dred Scott, in the free State of Illinois, every other master may lawfully do with any other one, or one thousand slaves, in Illinois, or in any other free State.

Auxilliary to all this, and working hand in hand with it, the Nebraska doctrine, or what is left of it, is to educate and mould public opinion, at least Northern public opinion, not to care whether slavery is voted down or voted up. This shows exactly where we now are; and partially, also, whither we are tending. . . .

Why was the amendment, expressly declaring the right of the people, voted down? Plainly enough now,—the adoption of it would have spoiled the niche for the Dred Scott decision. Why was the court decision held up? Why even a Senator's individual opinion withheld, till after the Presidential election? Plainly enough now,—the speaking out then would have damaged the "perfectly free" argument upon which the election was to be carried. Why the outgoing President's felicitation on the indorsement? Why the delay of a reargument? Why the incoming President's advance exhortation in favor of the decision? These things look like the cautious patting and petting of a spirited horse preparatory to mounting him, when it is dreaded that he may give the rider a fall. And why the hasty after-indorsement of the decision by the President and others?

We cannot absolutely know that all these exact adaptations are the result of preconcert. But when we see a lot of framed timbers, different portions of which we know have been gotten out at different times and places and by different workmen,—Stephen, Franklin, Roger, and James, for instance,—and when we see these timbers joined together, and see they exactly make the frame of a house or a mill, all the tenons and mortises exactly fitting, and all the lengths and proportions of the different pieces exactly adapted to their respective places, and not a piece too many or too few,—not omitting even scaffolding,—or, if a single piece be lacking, we see the place in the frame exactly fitted and prepared yet to bring such piece in,—in such a case, we find it impossible not to believe that Stephen and Franklin and Roger and James all understood one another from the beginning, and all worked upon a common plan or draft drawn up before the first blow was struck. . . .

3. The Lincoln–Douglas Debate Freeport, August 27, 1858

LINCOLN'S OPENING SPEECH AND DOUGLAS'S REPLY

Mr. Lincoln's Speech

. . . I now proceed to propound to the Judge the interrogatories, so far as I have framed them. I will bring forward a new installment when I get them ready. I will bring them forward now only reaching to number four.

The first one is:

Question 1.—If the people of Kansas shall, by means entirely unobjectionable in all other respects, adopt a State constitution, and ask admission into the Union under it, *before* they have the requisite number of inhabitants according to the English bill,—some ninety-three thousand,—will you vote to admit them?

Q. 2. Can the people of a United States Territory, in any lawful way, against the wish of any citizen of the United States, exclude slavery from its limits prior to the formation of a State constitution?

Q. 3. If the Supreme Court of the United States shall decide that States cannot exclude slavery from their limits, are you in favor of acquiescing in, adopting, and following such decision as a rule of political action?

Q. 4. Are you in favor of acquiring additional territory, in disregard of how such acquisition may affect the nation on the slavery question? . . .

Senator Douglas's Reply

First, he desires to know if the people of Kansas shall form a constitution by means entirely proper and unobjectionable, and ask admission into the Union as a State, before they have the requisite population for a member of Congress, whether I will vote for that admission. . . . I will answer his question. In reference to Kansas, it is my opinion that as she has population enough to constitute a slave State, she has people enough for a free State. I will not make Kansas an exceptional case to the other States of the Union. I hold it to be a sound rule, of universal application, to require a Territory to contain the requisite population for a member of Congress before it is admitted as a State into the Union. I made that proposition in the Senate in 1856, and I renewed it during the last session, in a bill providing that no Territory of the United States should form a constitution and apply for admission until it had the requisite population. On another occasion I proposed that neither Kansas nor any other Territory should be admitted until it had the requisite population. Congress did not adopt any of my propositions containing this general rule, but did make an exception of Kansas. I will stand by that exception. Either Kansas must come in as a free State, with whatever population she may have, or the rule must be applied to all the other Territories alike. I therefore answer at once, that, it having been decided that Kansas has people enough for a slave State, I hold that she has enough for a free State. I hope Mr. Lincoln is satisfied with my answer; . . .

The next question propounded to me by Mr. Lincoln is, Can the people of a Territory in any lawful way, against the wishes of any citizen of the United States, exclude slavery from their limits prior to the formation of a State constitution? I answer emphatically, as Mr. Lincoln has heard me answer a hundred times from every stump in Illinois, that in my opinion the people of a Territory can, by lawful means, exclude slavery from their limits prior to the formation of a State constitution. Mr. Lincoln knew that I had answered that question over and over again. He heard me argue the Nebraska Bill on that principle all over the State in 1854, in 1855, and in 1856, and he has no excuse for pretending to be in doubt as to my position on that question. It matters not what way the Supreme Court may hereafter decide as to the abstract question whether slavery may or may not go into a Territory under the Constitution, the people have the lawful means to introduce it or exclude it as they please, for the reason that slavery cannot exist a day or an hour anywhere, unless it is supported by local police regulations. Those police regulations can only be established by the local legislature; and if the people are opposed to slavery, they will elect representatives to that body who will by unfriendly legislation effectually prevent the introduction of it into their midst. If, on the contrary, they are for it, their legislation will favor its extension. Hence, no matter what the decision of the Supreme Court may be on that abstract question, still the right of the people to make a slave Territory or a free Territory is perfect and complete under the Nebraska Bill. I hope Mr. Lincoln deems my answer satisfactory on that point. . . .

. . . The third question which Mr. Lincoln presented is, if the Supreme Court of the United States shall decide that a State of this Union cannot exclude slavery from its own limits, will I submit to it? . . . He casts an imputation upon the Supreme Court of the United States, by supposing that they would violate the Constitution of the United States. I tell him that such a thing is not possible. It would be an act of moral treason that no man on the bench could ever descend to. Mr. Lincoln himself would never in his partisan feelings so far forget what was right as to be guilty of such an act.

The fourth question of Mr. Lincoln is, Are you in favor of acquiring additional territory, in disregard as to how such acquisition may affect the Union on the slavery question? This question is very ingeniously and cunningly put.

The Black Republican creed lays it down expressly that under no circumstances shall we acquire any more territory, unless slavery is first prohibited in the country. . . . I answer that whenever it becomes necessary, in our growth and progress, to acquire more territory, that I am in favor of it, without reference to the question of slavery; and when we have acquired it, I will leave the people free to do as they please, either to make it slave or free territory, as they prefer. It is idle to tell me or you that we have territory enough. . . . I tell you, increase, and multiply, and expand, is the law of this nation's existence. You cannot limit this great Republic by mere boundary lines, saying, "Thus far shalt thou go, and no farther." Any one of you gentlemen might as well say to a son twelve years old that he is big enough, and must not grow any larger; and in order to prevent his growth, put a hoop around him to keep him to his present size. What would be the result? Either the hoop must burst and be rent asunder, or the child must die. So it would be with this great nation. With our natural increase, growing with a rapidity unknown in any part of the globe, with the tide of emigration that is fleeing from despotism in the Old World to seek refuge in our own, there is a constant torrent pouring into this country that requires more land, more territory upon which to settle; and just as fast as our interests and our destiny require additional territory in the North, in the South, or on the islands of the ocean, I am for it; and when we acquire it, will leave the people, according to the Nebraska Bill, free to do as they please on the subject of slavery and every other question. . . .

4. John Brown's Last Speech
November 2, 1859

I have, may it please the Court, a few words to say.

In the first place, I deny everything but what I have all along admitted,—the design on my part to free the slaves. I intended certainly to have made a clean thing of that matter, as I did last winter, when I went into Missouri and there took slaves without the snapping of a gun on either side, moved them through the country, and finally left them in Canada. I designed to have done the same thing again, on a larger scale. That was all I intended. I never did intend murder, or treason, or the destruction of property, or to excite or incite slaves to rebellion, or to make insurrection.

I have another objection; and that is, it is unjust that I should suffer such a penalty. Had I interfered in the manner which I admit, and which I admit has been fairly proved (for I admire the truthfulness and candor of the greater portion of the witnesses who have testified in this case),—had I so interfered in behalf of the rich, the powerful, the intelligent, the so-called great, or in behalf of any of their friends,—either father, mother, brother, sister, wife, or children, or any of that class,—and suffered and sacrificed what I have in this interference, it would have been all right; and every man in this court would have deemed it an act worthy of reward rather than punishment.

This court acknowledges, as I suppose, the validity of the law of God. I see a book kissed here which I suppose to be the Bible, or at least the New Testament. That teaches me that all things whatsoever I would that men should do to me, I should do even so to them. It teaches me, further, to "remember them that are in bonds, as bound with them." I endeavored to act up to that instruction. I say, I am yet too young to understand that God is any respecter of persons. I believe that to have interfered as I have done—as I have always freely admitted I have done—in behalf of His despised poor, was not wrong, but right. Now, if it is deemed necessary that I should forfeit my life for the furtherance of the ends of justice, and mingle my blood further with the blood of my children and with the blood of millions in this slave country whose rights are disregarded by wicked, cruel, and unjust enactments,—I submit; so let it be done!

Let me say one word further.

I feel entirely satisfied with the treatment I have received on my trial. Considering all the circumstances, it has been more generous than I expected. But I feel no consciousness of guilt. I have stated from the first what was my intention, and what was not. I never had any design against the life of any person, nor any disposition to commit treason, or excite slaves to rebel, or make any general insurrection. I never encouraged any man to do so, but always discouraged any idea of that kind.

Let me say, also, a word in regard to the statements made by some of those connected with me. I hear it has been stated by some of them that I have induced them to join me. But the contrary is true. I do not say this to injure them, but as regretting their weakness. There is not one of them but joined me of his own accord, and the greater part of them at their own expense. A number of them I never saw, and never had a word of conversation with, till the day they came to me; and that was for the purpose I have stated.

Now I have done.

5. President Buchanan on Secession
Extract from the Fourth Annual Message to Congress December 3, 1860

. . . The long-continued and intemperate interference of the Northern people with the question of slavery in the Southern States has at length produced its natural effects. The different sections of the Union are now arrayed against each other, and the time has arrived, so much dreaded by the Father of his Country, when hostile geographical parties have been formed. . . .

It can not be denied that for five and twenty years the agitation at the North against slavery has been incessant. In 1835 pictorial handbills and inflammatory appeals were circulated extensively throughout the South of a character to excite the passions of the slaves, and, in the language of General Jackson, "to stimulate them to insurrection and produce all the horrors of a servile war." This agitation has ever since been continued by the public press, by the proceedings of State and county conventions and by abolition sermons and lectures. The time of Congress has been occupied in violent speeches on this never-ending subject, and appeals, in pamphlet and other forms, indorsed by distinguished names, have been sent forth from this central point and spread broadcast over the Union.

How easy would it be for the American people to settle the slavery question forever and to restore peace and harmony to this distracted country! They, and they alone, can do it. All that is necessary to accomplish the object, and all for which the slave States have ever contended, is to be let alone and permitted to manage their domestic institutions in their own way. As sovereign States, they, and they alone, are responsible before God and the world for the slavery existing among them. For this the people of the North are not more responsible and have no more right to interfere than with similar institutions in Russia or in Brazil.

Upon their good sense and patriotic forbearance I confess I still greatly rely. Without their aid it is beyond the power of any President, no matter what may be his own political proclivities, to restore peace and harmony among the States. Wisely limited and restrained as is his power under our Constitution and laws, he alone can accomplish but little for good or for evil on such a momentous question.

And this brings me to observe that the election of any one of our fellow-citizens to the office of President does not of itself afford just cause for dissolving the Union. This is more especially true if his election has been effected by a mere plurality, and not a majority of the people, and has resulted from transient and temporary causes, which may probably never again occur. . .

After all, he is no more than the chief executive officer of the Government. His province is not to make but to execute the laws. And it is a remarkable fact in our history that, notwithstanding the repeated efforts of the antislavery party, no single act has ever passed Congress, unless we may possibly except the Missouri compromise, impairing in the slightest degree the rights of the South to their property in slaves; and it may also be observed, judging from present indications, that no probability exists of the passage of such an act by a majority of both Houses, either in the present or the next Congress. . . .

I have purposely confined my remarks to revolutionary resistance, because it has been claimed within the last few years that any State, whenever this shall be its sovereign will and pleasure, may secede from the Union in accordance with the Constitution and without any violation of the constitutional rights of the other members of the Confederacy; that as each became parties to the Union by the vote of its own people assembled in convention, so any one of them may retire from the Union in a similar manner by the vote of such a convention.

In order to justify secession as a constitutional remedy, it must be on the principle that the Federal Government is a mere voluntary association of States, to be dissolved at pleasure by any one of the contracting parties. If this be so, the Confederacy is a rope of sand, to be penetrated and dissolved by the first adverse wave of public opinion in any of the States.

Such a principle is wholly inconsistent with the history as well as the character of the Federal Constitution. . . .

It was intended to be perpetual, and not to be annulled at the pleasure of any one of the contracting parties. . . .

It may be asked, then, Are the people of the States without redress against the tyranny and oppression of the Federal Government? By no means. The right of resistance on the part of the governed against the oppression of their governments can not be denied. It exists independently of all constitutions, and has been exercised at all periods of the world's history. Under it old governments have been destroyed and new ones have taken their place. It is embodied in strong and express language in our own Declaration of Independence. But the distinction must ever be observed that this is revolution against an established government, and not a voluntary secession from it by virtue of an inherent constitutional right. In short, let us look the danger fairly in the face. Secession is neither more nor less than revolution. It may or it may not be a justifiable revolution, but still it is revolution.

What, in the meantime, is the responsibility and true position of the Executive? He is bound by solemn oath, before God and the country, "to take care that the laws be faithfully executed," and from this obligation he can not be absolved by any human power. But what if the performance of this duty, in whole or in part, has been rendered impracticable by events over which he could have exercised no control? Such at the present moment is the case throughout the State of South Carolina so far as the laws of the United States to secure the administration of justice by means of the Federal judiciary are concerned. All the Federal officers within its limits through whose agency alone these laws can be carried into execution have already resigned. We no longer have a district judge, a district attorney, or a marshal in South Carolina. In fact, the whole machinery of the Federal Government necessary for the distribution of remedial justice among the people has been demolished, and it would be difficult, if not impossible, to replace it.

The only acts of Congress on the statute book bearing upon this subject are those of February 28, 1795, and March 3, 1807. These authorize the President, after he shall have ascertained that the marshal, with his *posse comitatus*, is unable to execute civil or criminal process in any particular case, to call forth the militia and employ the Army and Navy to aid him in performing this service, having first by proclamation commanded the insurgents "to disperse and retire peaceably to their respective abodes within a limited time." This duty can not by possibility be performed in a State where no judicial authority exists to issue process, and where there is no marshal to execute it, and where, even if there were such an officer, the entire population would constitute one solid combination to resist him.

The bare enumeration of these provisions proves how inadequate they are without further legislation to overcome a united opposition in a single State, not to speak of other States who may place themselves in a similar attitude. Congress alone has power to decide whether the present laws can or can not be amended so as to carry out more effectually the objects of the Constitution. . . .

Apart from the execution of the laws, so far as this may be practical, the Executive has no authority to decide what shall be the relations between the Federal Government and South Carolina. He has been invested with no such discretion. He possesses no power to change the relations heretofore existing between them, much less to acknowledge the independence of that State. This would be to invest a mere executive officer with the power of recognizing the dissolution of the confederacy among our thirty-three sovereign States. It bears no resemblance to the recognition of a foreign *de facto* government, involving no such responsibility. Any attempt to do this would, on his part, be a naked act of usurpation. It is therefore my duty to submit to Congress the whole question in all its bearings. The course of events is so rapidly hastening forward that the emergency may soon arise when you may be called upon to decide the momentous questions whether you possess the power by force of arms to compel a State to remain in the Union. I should feel myself recreant to my duty were I not to express an opinion on this important subject.

The question fairly stated is, Has the Constitution delegated to Congress the power to coerce a State into submission which is attempting to withdraw or has actually withdrawn from the Confederacy? If answered in the affirmative, it must be on the principle that the power has been conferred upon Congress to declare and to make war against a State. After much serious reflection I have arrived at the conclusion that no such power has been delegated to Congress or to any other department of the Federal Government. It is manifest upon an inspection of the Constitution that this is not among the specific and enumerated powers granted to Congress, and it is equally apparent that its exercise is not "necessary and proper for carrying into execution" any one of these powers. So far from this power having been delegated to Congress, it was expressly refused by the Convention which framed the Constitution. . . .

But if we possessed this power, would it be wise to exercise it under existing circumstances? The object would doubtless be to preserve the Union. War would not only present the most effectual means of destroying it, but would vanish all hope of its peaceable reconstruction. Besides, in the fraternal conflict a vast amount of blood and treasure would be expended, render-

ing future reconciliation between the States impossible. In the meantime, who can foretell what would be the sufferings and privations of the people during its existence?

The fact is that our Union rests upon public opinion, and can never be cemented by the blood of its citizens shed in civil war. If it can not live in the affections of the people, it must one day perish. Congress possesses many means of preserving it by conciliation, but the sword was not placed in their hand to preserve it by force. . . .

6. South Carolina Ordinance of Secession
December 20, 1860

We, the people of the State of South Carolina, in Convention assembled, do declare and ordain, and it is hereby declared and ordained, that the ordinance adopted by us in Convention, on the 23d day of May, in the year of our Lord 1788, whereby the Constitution of the United States of America was ratified, and also all Acts and parts of Acts of the General Assembly of this State ratifying the amendments of the said Constitution, are hereby repealed, and that the union now subsisting between South Carolina and other States under the name of the United States of America is hereby dissolved.

7. South Carolina Declaration of Causes of Secession
December 24, 1860

The people of the State of South Carolina in Convention assembled, on the 2d day of April, A.D. 1852, declared that the frequent violations of the Constitution of the United States by the Federal Government, and its encroachments upon the reserved rights of the States, fully justified this State in their withdrawal from the Federal Union; but in deference to the opinions and wishes of the other Slaveholding States, she forbore at that time to exercise this right. Since that time these encroachments have continued to increase, and further forbearance ceases to be a virtue.

And now the State of South Carolina having resumed her separate and equal place among nations, deems it due to herself, to the remaining United States of America, and to the nations of the world, that she should declare the immediate causes which have led to this act.

In 1787, Deputies were appointed by the States to revise the articles of Confederation; and on 17th September, 1787, these Deputies recommended, for the adoption of the States, the Articles of Union, known as the Constitution of the United States.

. . . Thus was established by compact between the States, a Government with defined objects and powers, limited to the express words of the grant. . . . We hold that the Government thus established is subject to the two great principles asserted in the Declaration of Independence; and we hold further, that the mode of its formation subjects it to a third fundamental principle, namely, the law of compact. We maintain that in every compact between two or more parties, the obligation is mutual; that the failure of one of the contracting parties to perform a material part of the agreement, entirely releases the obligation of the other; and that, where no arbiter is provided, each party is remitted to his own judgment to determine the fact of failure, with all its consequences.

In the present case, that fact is established with certainty. We assert that fourteen of the States have deliberately refused for years past to fulfil their constitutional obligations, and we refer to their own statutes for the proof.

The Constitution of the United States, in its fourth Article, provides as follows:

"No person held to service or labor in one State under the laws thereof, escaping into another, shall, in consequence of any law or regulation therein, be discharged from such service or labor, but shall be delivered up, on claim of the party to whom such service or labor may be due."

This stipulation was so material to the compact that without it that compact would not have been made. The greater number of the contracting parties held slaves, and they had previously evinced their estimate of the value of such a stipulation by making it a condition in the Ordinance for the government of the territory ceded by Virginia, which obligations, and the laws of the General Government, have ceased to effect the objects of the Constitution. The States of Maine, New Hampshire, Vermont, Massachusetts, Connecticut, Rhode Island, New York, Pennsylvania, Illinois, Indiana, Michigan, Wisconsin and Iowa, have enacted laws which either nullify the acts of Congress, or render useless any attempt to execute them. In many of these States the fugitive is discharged from the service of labor claimed, and in none of them has the State Government complied with the stipulation made in the Constitution. The State of New Jersey, at an early day, passed a law in conformity with her constitutional obligation; but the current of Anti-Slavery feeling has led her more recently to enact laws which render inoperative the remedies provided by her own laws and by the laws of Congress. In the State of New York even the right of transit for a slave has been denied by her tribunals; and the States of Ohio and Iowa have refused to surrender to justice fugitives charged with murder, and with inciting servile insurrection in the State of Virginia. Thus the constitutional compact has been deliberately broken and disregarded by the non-slaveholding States; and the consequence follows that South Carolina is released from her obligation. . . .

We affirm that these ends for which this Government was instituted have been defeated, and the Government itself has been destructive of them by the action of the nonslaveholding States. Those States have assumed the right of deciding upon the propriety of our domestic institutions; and have denied the rights of property established in fifteen of the States and recognized by the Constitution; they have denounced as sinful the institution of Slavery; they have permitted the open establishment among them of societies, whose avowed object is to disturb the peace of and eloin the property of the citizens of other States. They have encouraged and assisted thousands of our slaves to leave their homes; and those who remain, have been incited by emissaries, books, and pictures, to servile insurrection.

For twenty-five years this agitation has been steadily increasing, until it has now secured to its aid the power of the common Government. Observing the *forms* of the Constitution, a sectional party has found within that article establishing the Executive Department, the means of subverting the Constitution itself. A geographical line has been drawn across the Union, and all the States north of that line have united in the election of a man to the high office of President of the United States whose opinions and purposes are hostile to Slavery. He is to be intrusted with the administration of the common Government, because he has declared that "Government cannot endure permanently half slave, half free," and that the public mind must rest in the belief that Slavery is in the course of ultimate extinction.

This sectional combination for the subversion of the Constitution has been aided, in some of the States, by elevating to citizenship persons who, by the supreme law of the land, are incapable of becoming citizens; and their votes have been used to inaugurate a new policy, hostile to the South, and destructive of its peace and safety.

On the 4th of March next this party will take possession of the Government. It has announced that the South shall be excluded from the common territory, that the Judicial tribunal shall be made sectional, and that a war must be waged against Slavery until it shall cease throughout the United States.

The guarantees of the Constitution will then no longer exist; the equal rights of the States will be lost. The Slaveholding States will no longer have the power of self-government, or self-protection, and the Federal Government will have become their enemy.

Sectional interest and animosity will deepen the irritation; and all hope of remedy is rendered vain, by the fact that the public opinion at the North has invested a great political error with the sanctions of a more erroneous religious belief.

We, therefore, the people of South Carolina, by our delegates in Convention assembled, appealing to the Supreme Judge of the world for the rectitude of our intentions, have solemnly declared that the Union heretofore existing between this State and the other States of North America is dissolved, and that the State of South Carolina has resumed her position among the nations of the world, as a separate and independent state, with full power to levy war, conclude peace, contract alliances, establish commerce, and to do all other acts and things which independent States may of right do.

8. The Constitution of the Confederate States of America
March 11, 1861

WE, the people of the Confederate States, each State acting in its sovereign and independent character, in order to form a permanent federal government, establish justice, insure domestic tranquillity, and secure the blessings of liberty to ourselves and our posterity—invoking the favor and guidance of Almighty God—do ordain and establish this Constitution for the Confederate States of America.

ART. I.

SEC. 1.—All legislative powers herein delegated shall be vested in a Congress of the Confederate States, which shall consist of a Senate and House of Representatives.

SEC. 2. (1) The House of Representatives shall be chosen every second year by the people of the several States; and the electors in each State shall be citizens of the Confederate States, and have the qualifications requisite for electors of the most numerous branch of the State Legislature; but no person of foreign birth, not a citizen of the Confederate States, shall be allowed to vote for any officer, civil or political, State or Federal.

(2) No person shall be a Representative who shall not have attained the age of twenty-five years, and be a citizen of the Confederate States, and who shall not, when elected, be an inhabitant of that State in which he shall be chosen.

(3) Representatives and direct taxes shall be apportioned among the several States which may be included within this Confederacy, according to their respective numbers, which shall be determined by adding to the whole number of free persons, including those bound to service for a term of years, and excluding Indians not taxed, three-fifths of all slaves. The actual enumeration shall be made within three years after the first meeting of the Congress of the Confederate States, and within every subsequent term of ten years, in such manner as they shall by law direct. The number of Representatives shall not exceed one for every fifty thousand, but each State shall have at least one Representative; and until such enumeration shall be made, the State of South Carolina shall be entitled to choose six; the State of Georgia ten; the State of Alabama nine; the State of Florida two; the State of Mississippi seven; the State of Louisiana six; and the State of Texas six.

(4) When vacancies happen in the representation of any State, the Executive authority thereof shall issue writs of election to fill such vacancies.

(5) The House of Representatives shall choose their Speaker and other officers; and shall have the sole power of impeachment; except that any judicial or other federal officer resident and acting solely within the limits of any State, may be impeached by a vote of two-thirds of both branches of the Legislature thereof.

SEC. 3. (1) The Senate of the Confederate States shall be composed of two Senators from each State, chosen for six years by the Legislature thereof, at the regular session next immediately preceding the commencement of the term of service; and each Senator shall have one vote.

(2) Immediately after they shall be assembled, in consequence of the first election, they shall be divided as equally as may be into three classes. The seats of the Senators of the first class shall be vacated at the expiration of the second year; of the second class at the expiration of the fourth year; and of the third class at the expiration of the sixth year; so that one-third may be chosen every second year; and if vacancies happen by resignation or otherwise during the recess of the Legislature of any State, the Executive thereof may make temporary appointments until the next meeting of the Legislature, which shall then fill such vacancies.

(3) No person shall be a Senator, who shall not have attained the age of thirty years, and be a citizen of the Confederate States: and who shall not, when elected, be an inhabitant of the State for which he shall be chosen.

(4) The Vice-President of the Confederate States shall be President of the Senate, but shall have no vote, unless they be equally divided.

(5) The Senate shall choose their other officers, and also a President *pro tempore*, in the absence of the Vice-President, or when he shall exercise the office of President of the Confederate States.

(6) The Senate shall have sole power to try all impeachments. When sitting for that purpose they shall be on oath or affirmation. When the President of the Confederate States is tried, the Chief-Justice shall preside; and no person shall be convicted without the concurrence of two-thirds of the members present.

(7) Judgment in cases of impeachment shall not extend further than removal from office, and disqualification to hold and enjoy any office of honor, trust, or profit, under the Confederate States; but the party convicted shall, neverthe-

less, be liable to and subject to indictment, trial, judgment, and punishment according to law.

Sec. 4. (1) The times, places, and manner of holding elections for Senators and Representatives, shall be prescribed in each State by the Legislature thereof, subject to the provisions of this Constitution; but the Congress may, at any time, by law, make or alter such regulations, except as to the times and places of choosing Senators.

(2) The Congress shall assemble at least once in every year; and such meeting shall be on the first Monday in December, unless they shall, by law, appoint a different day.

Sec. 5. (1) Each House shall be the judge of the elections, returns, and qualifications of its own members, and a majority of each shall constitute a quorum to do business; but a smaller number may adjourn from day to day, and may be authorized to compel the attendance of absent members, in such manner and under such penalties as each House may provide.

(2) Each House may determine the rules of its proceedings, punish its members for disorderly behavior, and, with the concurrence of two-thirds of the whole number, expel a member.

(3) Each House shall keep a journal of its proceedings, and from time to time publish the same, excepting such part as may in its judgment require secrecy, and the ayes and nays of the members of either House, on any question, shall, at the desire of one-fifth of those present, be entered on the journal.

(4) Neither House, during the session of Congress, shall, without the consent of the other, adjourn for more than three days, nor to any other place than that in which the two Houses shall be sitting.

Sec. 6. (1) The Senators and Representatives shall receive a compensation for their services, to be ascertained by law, and paid out of the Treasury of the Confederate States. They shall, in all cases except treason and breach of the peace, be privileged from arrest during their attendance at the session of their respective Houses, and in going to and returning from the same; and for any speech or debate in either House, they shall not be questioned in any other place.

(2) No Senator or Representative shall, during the time for which he was elected, be appointed to any civil office under the authority of the Confederate States, which shall have been created, or the emoluments whereof shall have been increased during such time; and no person holding any office under the Confederate States shall be a member of either House during his continuance in office. But Congress may, by law, grant to the principal officer in each of the Executive Departments a seat upon the floor of either House, with the privilege of discussing any measure appertaining to his department.

Sec. 7. (1) All bills for raising revenue shall originate in the House of Representatives; but the Senate may propose or concur with amendments as on other bills.

(2) Every bill which shall have passed both Houses shall, before it becomes a law, be presented to the President of the Confederate States; if he approve he shall sign it; but if not, he shall return it with his objections to that House in which it shall have originated, who shall enter the objections at large on their journal, and proceed to reconsider it. If, after such reconsideration, two-thirds of that House shall agree to pass the bill, it shall be sent, together with the objections, to the other House, by which it shall likewise be reconsidered, and if approved by two-thirds of that House, it shall become a law. But in all such cases, the votes of both Houses shall be determined by yeas and nays, and the names of the persons voting for and against the bill shall be entered on the journal of each House respectively. If any bill shall not be returned by the President within ten days (Sundays excepted) after it shall have been presented to him, the same shall be a law, in like manner as if he had signed it, unless the Congress, by their adjournment, prevent its return; in which case it shall not be a law. The President may approve any appropriation and disapprove any other appropriation in the same bill. In such

case he shall, in signing the bill, designate the appropriations disapproved; and shall return a copy of such appropriations, with his objections, to the House in which the bill shall have originated; and the same proceedings shall then be had as in case of other bills disapproved by the President.

(3) Every order, resolution, or vote, to which the concurrence of both Houses may be necessary (except on questions of adjournment) shall be presented to the President of the Confederate States; and before the same shall take effect shall be approved by him; or being disapproved by him, may be repassed by two-thirds of both Houses, according to the rules and limitations prescribed in case of a bill.

SEC. 8.—The Congress shall have power—

(1) To lay and collect taxes, duties, imposts, and excises, for revenue necessary to pay the debts, provide for the common defence, and carry on the Government of the Confederate States; but no bounties shall be granted from the treasury; nor shall any duties or taxes on importations from foreign nations be laid to promote or foster any branch of industry; and all duties, imposts, and excises shall be uniform throughout the Confederate States.

(2) To borrow money on the credit of the Confederate States.

(3) To regulate commerce with foreign nations, and among the several States, and with the Indian tribes; but neither this, nor any other clause contained in the Constitution shall be construed to delegate the power to Congress to appropriate money for any internal improvement intended to facilitate commerce; except for the purpose of furnishing lights, beacons, and buoys, and other aids to navigation upon the coasts, and the improvement of harbors, and the removing of obstructions in river navigation, in all which cases, such duties shall be laid on the navigation facilitated thereby, as may be necessary to pay the costs and expenses thereof.

(4) To establish uniform laws of naturalization, and uniform laws on the subject of bankruptcies throughout the Confederate States, but no law of Congress shall discharge any debt contracted before the passage of the same.

(5) To coin money, regulate the value thereof, and of foreign coin, and fix the standard of weights and measures.

(6) To provide for the punishment of counterfeiting the securities and current coin of the confederate States.

(7) To establish post-offices and post-routes; but the expenses of the Post-office Department, after the first day of March, in the year of our Lord eighteen hundred and sixty-three, shall be paid out of its own revenues.

(8) To promote the progress of science and useful arts, by securing for limited times to authors and inventors the exclusive right to their respective writings and discoveries.

(9) To constitute tribunals inferior to the Supreme Court.

(10) To define and punish piracies and felonies committed on the high seas, and offences against the law of nations.

(11) To declare war, grant letters of marque and reprisal, and make rules concerning captures on land and water.

(12) To raise and support armies; but no appropriation of money to that use shall be for a longer term than two years.

(13) To provide and maintain a navy.

(14) To make rules for government and regulation of the land and naval forces.

(15) To provide for calling forth the militia to execute the laws of the Confederate States; suppress insurrections, and repel invasions.

(16) To provide for organizing, arming, and disciplining the militia, and for governing such part of them as may be employed in the service of the Confederate States; reserving to the States, respectively, the appointment of the officers, and the authority of training the militia according to the discipline prescribed by Congress.

(17) To exercise exclusive legislation, in all cases whatsoever, over such district (not exceeding ten miles square) as may, by cession of one or more States, and the acceptance of Congress, become the seat of the government of the Con-

federate States; and to exercise a like authority over all places purchased by the consent of the Legislature of the State in which the same shall be, for the erection of forts, magazines, arsenals, dock-yards, and other needful buildings, and

(18) To make all laws which shall be necessary and proper for carrying into execution the fore-going powers, and all other powers vested by this Constitution in the Government of the Con-federate States, or in any department or officer thereof.

SEC. 9. (1) The importation of negroes of the African race, from any foreign country, other than the slaveholding States or Territories of the United States of America, is hereby forbidden; and Congress is required to pass such laws as shall effectually prevent the same.

(2) Congress shall also have power to prohibit the introduction of slaves from any State not a member of, or Territory not belonging to, this Confederacy.

(3) The privilege of the writ of *habeas corpus* shall not be suspended, unless when in cases of rebellion or invasion the public safety may re-quire it.

(4) No bill of attainder, or *ex post facto* law, or law denying or impairing the right of property in negro slaves shall be passed.

(5) No capitation or other direct tax shall be laid unless in proportion to the census or enu-meration hereinbefore directed to be taken.

(6) No tax or duty shall be laid on articles exported from any State, except by a vote of two-thirds of both Houses.

(7) No preference shall be given by any reg-ulation of commerce or revenue to the ports of one State over those of another.

(8) No money shall be drawn from the trea-sury but in consequence of appropriations made by law; and a regular statement and account of the receipts and expenditures of all public money shall be published from time to time.

(9) Congress shall appropriate no money from the treasury except by a vote of two-thirds of both Houses, taken by yeas and nays, unless it be asked and estimated for by someone of the heads of departments, and submitted to Con-gress by the President; or for the purpose of paying its own expenses and contingencies; or for the payment of claims against the Confed-erate States, the justice of which shall have been judicially declared by a tribunal for the investi-gation of claims against the Government, which it is hereby made the duty of congress to estab-lish.

(10) All bills appropriating money shall specify in federal currency the exact amount of each appropriation and the purposes for which it is made; and Congress shall grant no extra com-pensation to any public contractor, officer, agent, or servant, after such contract shall have been made or such service rendered.

(11) No title of nobility shall be granted by the Confederate States; and no person holding any office of profit or trust under them shall, without the consent of the Congress, accept of any pre-sent, emoluments, office, or title of any kind whatever, from any king, prince, or foreign state.

(12) Congress shall make no law respecting an establishment of religion, or prohibiting the free exercise thereof; or abridging the freedom of speech or of the press; or the right of the people peaceably to assemble and petition the Government for a redress of grievances.

(13) A well-regulated militia being necessary to the security of a free State, the right of the people to keep and bear arms shall not be in-fringed.

(14) No soldier shall, in time of peace, be quartered in any house without the consent of the owner; nor in time of war, but in a manner prescribed by law.

(15) The right of the people to be secure in their persons, houses, papers, and against un-reasonable searches and seizures, shall not be violated; and no warrant shall issue but upon probable cause, supported by oath or affirma-tion, and particularly describing the place to be searched, and the person or things to be seized.

(16) No person shall be held to answer for a capital or otherwise infamous crime, unless on a presentment or indictment of a grand jury,

except in cases arising in the land or naval forces, or in the militia, when in actual service, in time of war, or public danger; nor shall any person be subject for the same offence to be twice put in jeopardy of life or limb; nor be compelled in any criminal case to be a witness against himself; nor be deprived of life, liberty, or property, without due process of law; nor shall any private property be taken for public use without just compensation.

(17) In all criminal prosecutions the accused shall enjoy the right to a speedy and public trial, by an impartial jury of the State and district wherein the crime shall have been committed, which district shall have been previously ascertained by law, and to be informed of the nature and cause of the accusation; to be confronted with the witnesses against him; to have compulsory process for obtaining witnesses in his favor; and to have the assistance of counsel for his defence.

(18) In suits at common law, where the value in controversy shall exceed twenty dollars, the right of trial by jury shall be preserved; and no fact so tried by a jury shall be otherwise reexamined in any court of the Confederacy, than according to the rules of the common law.

(19) Excessive bail shall not be required, nor excessive fines imposed, nor cruel or unusual punishment inflicted.

(20) Every law, or resolution having the force of law, shall relate to but one subject, and that shall be expressed in the title.

SEC. 10. (1) No State shall enter into any treaty, alliance, or confederation; grant letters of marque and reprisals; coin money; make any thing but gold and silver coin a tender in payment of debts; pass any bill of attainder, or *ex post facto* law, or law impairing the obligation of contracts; or grant any title of nobility.

(2) No State shall, without the consent of Congress, lay any imposts or duties on imports or exports, except what may be absolutely necessary for executing its inspection laws; and the net produce of all duties and imposts, laid by any State on imports or exports, shall be for the use of the Treasury of the Confederate States; and all such laws shall be subject to the revision and control of Congress.

(3) No State shall, without the consent of Congress, lay any duty of tonnage, except on sea-going vessels, for the improvement of its rivers and harbors navigated by the said vessels; but such duties shall not conflict with any treaties of the Confederate States with foreign nations; and any surplus of revenue, thus derived, shall, after making such improvement, be paid into the common treasury; nor shall any State keep troops or ships of war in time of peace, enter into any agreement or compact with another State, or with a foreign power, or engage in war, unless actually invaded, or in such imminent danger as will not admit of delay. But when any river divides or flows through two or more States, they may enter into compacts with each other to improve the navigation thereof.

ART. II.

SEC. 1. (1) The Executive power shall be vested in a President of the Confederate States of America. He and the Vice-President shall hold their offices for the term of six years; but the President shall not be reëligible. The President and Vice-President shall be elected as follows:

(2) Each State shall appoint, in such manner as the Legislature thereof may direct, a number of electors equal to the whole number of Senators and Representatives to which the State may be entitled in Congress; but no Senator or Representative, or person holding an office of trust or profit under the Confederate States, shall be appointed an elector.

(3) The electors shall meet in their respective States and vote by ballot for President and Vice-President, one of whom, at least, shall not be an inhabitant of the same State with themselves; they shall name in their ballots the person voted for as President, and in distinct ballots the person voted for as Vice-President, and they shall make distinct lists of all persons voted for as President, and of all persons voted for as Vice-President, and of the number of votes for each;

which list they shall sign, and certify, and transmit, sealed, to the Government of the Confederate States, directed to the President of the Senate. The President of the Senate shall, in the presence of the Senate and House of Representatives, open all the certificates, and the votes shall then be counted; the person having the greatest number of votes for President shall be the President, if such number be a majority of the whole number of electors appointed; and if no person shall have such a majority, then, from the persons having the highest numbers, not exceeding three, on the list of those voted for as President, the House of Representatives shall choose immediately, by ballot, the President. But, in choosing the President, the votes shall be taken by States, the Representative from each State having one vote; a quorum for this purpose shall consist of a member or members from two-thirds of the States, and a majority of all the States shall be necessary to a choice. And if the House of Representatives shall not choose a President, whenever the right of choice shall devolve upon them, before the fourth day of March next following, then the Vice-President shall act as President, as in case of the death, or other constitutional disability of the President.

(4) The person having the greatest number of votes as Vice-President shall be the Vice-President, if such number be a majority of the whole number of electors appointed; and if no person have a majority, then from the two highest numbers on the list, the Senate shall choose the Vice-President; a quorum for the purpose shall consist of two-thirds of the whole number of Senators, and a majority of the whole number shall be necessary for a choice.

(5) But no person constitutionally ineligible to the office of President shall be eligible to that of Vice-President of the Confederate States.

(6) The Congress may determine the time of choosing the electors, and the day on which they shall give their votes; which day shall be the same throughout the Confederate States.

(7) No person except a natural born citizen of the Confederate States, or a citizen thereof, at the time of the adoption of this Constitution, or a citizen thereof born in the United States prior to the 20th December, 1860, shall be eligible to the office of President; neither shall any person be eligible to that office who shall not have attained the age of thirty-five years, and been fourteen years a resident within the limits of the Confederate States, as they may exist at the time of his election.

(8) In case of the removal of the President from office, or of his death, resignation, or inability to discharge the powers and duties of the said office, the same shall devolve on the Vice-President; and the Congress may, by law, provide for the case of the removal, death, resignation, or inability both of the President and the Vice-President, declaring what officer shall then act as President, and such officer shall then act accordingly until the disability be removed or a President shall be elected.

(9) The President shall, at stated times, receive for his services a compensation, which shall neither be increased nor diminished during the period for which he shall have been elected; and he shall not receive within that period any other emolument from the Confederate States, or any of them.

(10) Before he enters on the execution of the duties of his office, he shall take the following oath or affirmation:

"I do solemnly swear (or affirm) that I will faithfully execute the office of President of the Confederate States, and will, to the best of my ability, preserve, protect, and defend the Constitution thereof."

SEC. 2. (1) The President shall be commander-in-chief of the army and navy of the Confederate States, and of the militia of the several States, when called into the actual service of the Confederate States; he may require the opinion in writing, of the principal officer in each of the Executive Departments, upon any subject relating to the duties of their respective offices; and he shall have power to grant reprieves and pardons for offences against the Confederate States, except in cases of impeachment.

(2) He shall have power, by and with the advice and consent of the Senate, to make treaties, provided two-thirds of the Senators present concur; and he shall nominate, and, by and with the advice and consent of the Senate, shall appoint ambassadors, other public ministers, and consuls, Judges of the Supreme Court, and all other officers of the Confederate States, whose appointments are not herein otherwise provided for, and which shall be established by law; but the Congress may by law vest the appointment of such inferior officers, as they think proper, in the President alone, in the courts of law, or in the heads of departments.

(3) The principal officer in each of the Executive Departments, and all persons connected with the diplomatic service, may be removed from office at the pleasure of the President. All other civil officers of the Executive Department may be removed at any time by the President, or other appointing power, when their services are unnecessary, or for dishonesty, incapacity, inefficiency, misconduct, or neglect of duty; and when so removed, the removal shall be reported to the Senate, together with the reasons therefore.

(4) The President shall have power to fill all vacancies that may happen during the recess of the Senate, by granting commissions which shall expire at the end of the next session; but no person rejected by the Senate shall be reappointed to the same office during their ensuing recess.

Sec. 3. (1) The President shall, from time to time, give to the Congress information of the state of the Confederacy, and recommend to their consideration such measures as he shall judge necessary and expedient; he may, on extraordinary occasions, convene both Houses, or either of them; and, in case of disagreement between them, with respect to the time of adjournment he may adjourn them to such time as he shall think proper; he shall receive ambassadors and other public ministers; he shall take care that the laws be faithfully executed, and

shall commission all the officers of the Confederate States.

Sec. 4. (1) The President and Vice-President, and all civil officers of the Confederate States, shall be removed from office on impeachment for, or conviction of, treason, bribery, or other high crimes and misdemeanors.

ART. III.

Sec. 1. (1) The judicial power of the Confederate States shall be vested in one Superior Court, and in such inferior courts as the Congress may from time to time ordain and establish. The judges, both of the Supreme and inferior courts, shall hold their offices during good behavior, and shall, at stated times, receive for their services a compensation, which shall not be diminished during their continuance in office.

Sec. 2. (1) the judicial power shall extend to all cases arising under the Constitution, the laws of the Confederate States, or treaties made or which shall be made under their authority; to all cases affecting ambassadors, other public ministers, and consuls; to all cases of admiralty or maritime jurisdiction; to controversies to which the Confederate States shall be a party; to controversies between two or more States; between a State and citizens of another State, where the State is plaintiff; between citizens claiming lands under grants of different States, and between a State or the citizens thereof, and foreign States, citizens, or subjects; but no State shall be sued by a citizen or subject of any foreign State.

(2) In all cases affecting ambassadors, other public ministers, and consuls, and those in which a State shall be a party, the Supreme Court shall have original jurisdiction. In all the other cases before mentioned, the Supreme Court shall have appellate jurisdiction, both as to law and fact, with such exceptions, and under such regulations as the Congress shall make.

(3) The trial of all crimes, except in cases of impeachment, shall be by jury, and such trial shall be held in the State where the said crimes shall have been committed; but when not com-

mitted within any State, the trial shall be at such place or places as the Congress may by law have directed.

SEC. 3. (1) Treason against the Confederate States shall consist only in levying war against them, or in adhering to their enemies, giving them aid and comfort. No person shall be convicted of treason unless on the testimony of two witnesses to the same overt act, or on confession in open court.

(2) The Congress shall have power to declare the punishment of treason, but no attainder of treason shall work corruption of blood, or forfeiture, except during the life of the person attainted.

ART. IV.

SEC. 1. (1) Full faith and credit shall be given in each State to the public acts, records, and judicial proceedings of every other State. And the Congress may, by general laws, prescribe the manner in which such acts, records, and proceedings shall be proved, and the effect thereof.

SEC. 2. (1) The citizens of each State shall be entitled to all the privileges and immunities of citizens of the several States, and shall have the right of transit and sojourn in any State of this Confederacy, with their slaves and other property; and the right of property in said slaves shall not be thereby impaired.

(2) A person charged in any State with treason, felony, or other crime against the laws of such State, who shall flee from justice, and be found in another State, shall, on demand of the executive authority of the State from which he fled, be delivered up to be removed to the State having jurisdiction of the crime.

(3) No slave or other person held to service or labor in any State or Territory of the Confederate States, under the laws thereof, escaping or unlawfully carried into another, shall, in consequence of any law or regulation therein, be discharged from such service or labor; but shall be delivered up on claim of the party to whom

such slave belongs, or to whom such service or labor may be due.

SEC. 3. (1) Other States may be admitted into this Confederacy by a vote of two-thirds of the whole House of Representatives, and two-thirds of the Senate, the Senate voting by States; but no new State shall be formed or erected within the jurisdiction of any other State; nor any State be formed by the junction of two or more States, or parts of States, without the consent of the Legislatures of the States concerned as well as of the Congress.

(2) The Congress shall have power to dispose of and make all needful rules and regulations concerning the property of the Confederate States, including the lands thereof.

(3) The Confederate States may acquire new territory; and Congress shall have power to legislate and provide governments for the inhabitants of all territory belonging to the Confederate States, lying without the limits of the several States, and may permit them, at such times, and in such manner as it may by law provide, to form States to be admitted into the Confederacy. In all such territory, the institution of negro slavery, as it now exists in the Confederate States, shall be recognized and protected by Congress and by the territorial government; and the inhabitants of the several Confederate States and Territories shall have the right to take to such territory any slaves lawfully held by them in any of the States or Territories of the Confederate States.

(4) The Confederate States shall guarantee to every State that now is or hereafter may become a member of this Confederacy, a Republican form of Government, and shall protect each of them against invasion; and on application of the Legislature, (or of the Executive when the Legislature is not in session,) against domestic violence.

ART. V.

SEC. 1. (1) Upon the demand of any three States, legally assembled in their several Conventions, the Congress shall summon a Convention of all the States, to take into consideration such amendments to the Constitution as the said States shall concur in suggesting at the time when the said demand is made; and should any of the proposed amendments to the Constitution be agreed on by the said Convention—voting by States—and the same be ratified by the Legislatures of two-thirds of the several States, or by conventions in two-thirds thereof—as the one or the other mode of ratification may be proposed by the general convention—they shall thenceforward form a part of this Constitution. But no State shall, without its consent, be deprived of its equal representation in the Senate.

ART. VI.

1.—The Government established by this Constitution is the successor of the Provisional Government of the Confederate States of America, and all the laws passed by the latter shall continue in force until the same shall be repealed or modified; and all the officers appointed by the same shall remain in office until their successors are appointed and qualified, or the offices abolished.

2. All debts contracted and engagements entered into before the adoption of this Constitution, shall be as valid against the Confederate States under this Constitution as under the Provisional Government.

3. This Constitution, and the laws of the Confederate States, made in pursuance thereof, and all treaties made, or which shall be made, under the authority of the Confederate States, shall be the supreme law of the land; and the judges in every State shall be bound thereby, any thing in the Constitution or laws of any State to the contrary notwithstanding.

4. The Senators and Representatives before mentioned, and the members of the several State Legislatures, and all executive and judicial offices, both of the Confederate States and of the several States, shall be bound, by oath or affirmation, to support this Constitution; but no religious test shall ever be required as a qualification to any office or public trust under the Confederate States.

5. The enumeration, in the Constitution, of certain rights, shall not be construed to deny or disparage others retained by the people of the several States.

6. The powers not delegated to the Confederate States by the Constitution, nor prohibited by it to the States, are reserved to the States, respectively, or to the people thereof.

ART. VII.

1.—The ratification of the conventions of five States shall be sufficient for the establishment of this Constitution between the States so ratifying the same.

2. When five States shall have ratified this Constitution in the manner before specified, the Congress, under the provisional Constitution, shall prescribe the time for holding the election of President and Vice-President, and for the meeting of the electoral college, and for counting the votes and inaugurating the President. They shall also prescribe the time for holding the first election of members of Congress under this Constitution, and the time for assembling the same. Until the assembling of such Congress, the Congress under the provisional Constitution shall continue to exercise the legislative powers granted them; not extending beyond the time limited by the Constitution of the Provisional Government.

Adopted unanimously by the Congress of the Confederate States of South Carolina, Georgia, Florida, Alabama, Mississippi, Louisiana, and Texas, sitting in convention at the capitol, in the city of Montgomery, Ala,., on the eleventh day of March, in the year eighteen hundred and sixty-one.

Howell Cobb
President of the Congress.

[Signatures]

9. Lincoln's First Inaugural Address March 4, 1861

FELLOW-CITIZENS OF THE UNITED STATES:—In compliance with a custom as old as the Government itself, I appear before you to address you briefly, and to take in your presence the oath prescribed by the Constitution of the United States to be taken by the President "before he enters on the execution of his office.". . .

Apprehension seems to exist among the people of the Southern States that by the accession of a Republican administration their property and their peace and personal security are to be endangered. There has never been any reasonable cause for such apprehension. Indeed, the most ample evidence to the contrary has all the while existed and been open to their inspection. It is found in nearly all the published speeches of him who now addresses you. I do but quote from one of those speeches when I declare that "I have no purpose, directly or indirectly, to interfere with the institution of slavery in the States where it exists. I believe I have no lawful right to do so, and I have no inclination to do so.". . .

I now reiterate these sentiments; and, in doing so, I only press upon the public attention the most conclusive evidence of which the case is susceptible, that the property, peace and security of no section are to be in any wise endangered by the now incoming administration. I add, too, that all the protection which, consistently with the Constitution and the laws, can be given, will be cheerfully given to all the States when lawfully demanded, for whatever cause—as cheerfully to one section as to another. . . .

I take the official oath to-day with no mental reservations, and with no purpose to construe the Constitution or laws by any hypercritical rules. And, while I do not choose now to specify particular acts of Congress as proper to be enforced, I do suggest that it will be much safer for all, both in official and private stations, to conform to and abide by all those acts which stand unrepealed, than to violate any of them, trusting to find impunity in having them held to be unconstitutional. . . .

A disruption of the Federal Union, heretofore only menaced, is now formidably attempted.

I hold that, in contemplation of universal law and of the Constitution, the Union of these States is perpetual. Perpetuity is implied, if not expressed, in the fundamental law of all national governments. It is safe to assert that no government proper ever had a provision in its organic law for its own termination. Continue to execute all the express provisions of our national Constitution, and the Union will endure forever—it being impossible to destroy it except by some action not provided for in the instrument itself.

Again, if the United States be not a government proper, but an association of States in the nature of contract merely, can it as a contract be peaceably unmade by less than all the parties who made it? One party to a contract may violate it—break it, so to speak; but does it not require all to lawfully rescind it?

Descending from these general principles, we find the proposition that in legal contemplation the Union is perpetual confirmed by the history of the Union itself. The Union is much older than the Constitution. It was formed, in fact, by the articles of Association in 1774. It was matured and continued by the Declaration of Independence in 1776. It was further matured, and the faith of all the then thirteen States expressly plighted and engaged that it should be perpetual, by the Articles of Confederation in 1778. And, finally, in 1787 one of the declared objects for ordaining and establishing the Constitution was "to form a more perfect Union."

But if the destruction of the Union by one or by a part only of the States be lawfully possible, the Union is less perfect than before the Constitution, having lost the vital element of perpetuity.

It follows from these views that no State upon

its own mere motion can lawfully get out of the Union; that resolves and ordinances to that effect are legally void; and that acts of violence, within any State or States, against the authority of the United States, are insurrectionary or revolutionary, according to circumstances.

I therefore consider that, in view of the Constitution and the laws, the Union is unbroken; and to the extent of my ability I shall take care, as the Constitution itself expressly enjoins upon me, that the laws of the Union be faithfully executed in all the States. Doing this I deem to be only a simple duty on my part; and I shall perform it so far as practicable, unless my rightful masters, the American people, shall withhold the requisite means, or in some authoritative manner direct the contrary. I trust this will not be regarded as a menace, but only as the declared purpose of the Union that it will constitutionally defend and maintain itself.

In doing this there needs to be no bloodshed or violence; and there shall be none, unless it be forced upon the national authority. The power confided to me will be used to hold, occupy, and possess the property and places belonging to the Government, and to collect the duties and imposts; but beyond what may be necessary for these objects, there will be no invasion, no using of force against or among the people anywhere. Where hostility to the United States, in any interior locality, shall be so great and universal as to prevent competent resident citizens from holding the Federal offices, there will be no attempt to force obnoxious strangers among the people for that object. While the strict legal right may exist in the government to enforce the exercise of these offices, the attempt to do so would be so irritating, and so nearly impracticable withal, that I deem it better to forego for the time the uses of such offices.

The mails, unless repelled, will continue to be furnished in all parts of the Union. So far as possible, the people everywhere shall have that sense of perfect security which is most favorable to calm thought and reflection. The course here indicated will be followed unless current events and experience shall show a modification or change to be proper, and in every case and exigency my best discretion will be exercised according to circumstances actually existing, and with a view and a hope of a peaceful solution of the national troubles and the restoration of fraternal sympathies and affections.

That there are persons in one section or another who seek to destroy the Union at all events, and are glad of any pretext to do it, I will neither affirm nor deny; but if there be such, I need address no word to them. To those, however, who really love the Union may I not speak?

Before entering upon so grave a matter as the destruction of our national fabric, with all its benefits, its memories, and its hopes, would it not be wise to ascertain precisely why we do it? Will you hazard so desperate a step while there is any possibility that any portion of the ills you fly from have no real existence? Will you, while the certain ills you fly to are greater than all the real ones you fly from—will you risk the commission of so fearful a mistake?

All profess to be content in the Union if all constitutional rights can be maintained. Is it true, then, that any right, plainly written in the Constitution, has been denied? I think not. Happily the human mind is so constituted that no party can reach to the audacity of doing this. Think, if you can, of a single instance in which a plainly written provision of the Constitution has ever been denied. If by the mere force of numbers a majority should deprive a minority of any clearly written constitutional right, it might, in a moral point of view, justify revolution—certainly would if such a right were a vital one. But such is not our case. All the vital rights of minorities and of individuals are so plainly assured to them by affirmations and negations, guaranties and prohibitions, in the constitution, that controversies never arise concerning them. But no organic law can ever be framed with a provision specifically applicable to every question which may occur in practical administration. No foresight can anticipate, nor any document of reasonable length contain, express provisions for all possible questions. Shall fugitives from labor be surrendered by national or by State authority? The Constitution does not expressly say. *May* Congress prohibit slavery in the Territories? The Constitution does not expressly say. *Must* Congress protect slavery in the Territories? The Constitution does not expressly say.

From questions of this class spring all our constitutional controversies, and we divide upon them into majorities and minorities. If the minority will not acquiesce, the majority must, or the Government must cease. There is no other alternative; for continuing the Government is acquiescence on one side or the other.

If a minority in such case will secede rather than acquiesce, they make a precedent which in turn will divide and ruin them; for a minority of their own will secede from them whenever a majority refuses to be controlled by such minority. For instance, why may not any portion of a new confederacy a year or two hence arbitrarily secede again, precisely as portions of the present Union now claim to secede from it? All who cherish disunion sentiments are now being educated to the exact temper of doing this.

Is there such perfect identity of interests among the States to compose a new Union as to produce harmony only, and prevent renewed secession?

Plainly, the central idea of secession is the essence of anarchy. A majority held in restraint by constitutional checks and limitations, and always changing easily with deliberate changes of popular opinions and sentiments, is the only true sovereign of a free people. Whoever rejects it does, of necessity, fly to anarchy or to despotism. Unanimity is impossible; the rule of a minority, as a permanent arrangement, is wholly inadmissible; so that, rejecting the majority principle, anarchy or despotism in some form is all that is left.

I do not forget the position assumed by some, that constitutional questions are to be decided by the Supreme Court; nor do I deny that such decisions must be binding, in any case, upon the parties to a suit, as to the object of that suit, while they are also entitled to a very high respect and consideration in all parallel cases by all other departments of the government. And, while it is obviously possible that such decision may be erroneous in any given case, still the evil effect following it, being limited to that particular case, with the chance that it may be overruled and never become a precedent for other cases, can better be borne than could the evils of a different practice. At the same time, the candid citizen must confess that if the policy of the government, upon vital questions affecting the whole people, is to be irrevocably fixed by decisions of the Supreme Court, the instant they are made, in ordinary litigation between parties in personal actions, the people will have ceased to be their own rulers, having to that extent practically resigned the government into the hands of that eminent tribunal. Nor is there in this view any assault upon the court or the judges. It is a duty from which they may not shrink to decide cases properly brought before them, and it is no fault of theirs if others seek to turn their decisions to political purposes.

One section of our country believes slavery is right, and ought to be extended, while the other believes it is wrong, and ought not to be extended. This is the only substantial dispute. The fugitive slave clause of the Constitution and the law for the suppression of the foreign slave trade are each as well enforced, perhaps, as any law can ever be in a community where the moral sense of the people imperfectly supports the law itself. The great body of the people abide by the dry legal obligation in both cases, and a few break over in each. This, I think, cannot be perfectly cured; and it would be worse in both cases after the separation of the sections than before. The foreign slave trade, now imperfectly suppressed, would be ultimately revived, without restriction, in one section, while fugitive slaves, now only partially surrendered, would not be surrendered at all by the other.

Physically speaking, we cannot separate. We cannot remove our respective sections from each other, nor build an impassable wall between them. A husband and wife may be divorced and go out of the presence and beyond the reach of each other; but the different parts of our country cannot do this. They cannot but remain face to face, and intercourse, either amicable or hostile, must continue between them. Is it possible, then, to make that intercourse more advantageous or more satisfactory after separation than before? Can aliens make treaties easier than friends can make laws? Can treaties be more faithfully enforced between aliens than laws can among friends? Suppose you go to war, you cannot fight always; and when, after much loss on both sides, and no gain on either, you cease fighting, the identical old questions as to terms of intercourse are again upon you.

This country, with its institutions, belongs to the people who inhabit it. Whenever they shall grow weary of the existing government, they can exercise their constitutional right of amending it, or their revolutionary right to dismember or overthrow it. I cannot be ignorant of the fact that many worthy and patriotic citizens are desirous of having the national Constitution amended. While I make no recommendation of amendments, I fully recognize the rightful authority of the people over the whole subject, to be exercised in either of the modes prescribed in the instrument itself, and I should, under existing circumstances, favor rather than oppose a fair opportunity being afforded the people to act upon it. I will venture to add that to me the convention mode seems preferable, in that it allows amendments to originate with the people themselves, instead of only permitting them to take or reject propositions originated by others not especially chosen for the purpose, and which might not be precisely such as they would wish to either accept or refuse. I understand a proposed amendment to the constitution—which amendment, however, I have not seen—has passed Congress, to the effect that the Federal Government shall never interfere with the domestic institutions of the States, including that of persons held to service. To avoid misconstruc-

tion of what I have said, I depart from my purpose not to speak of particular amendments so far as to say that, holding such a provision to now be implied constitutional law, I have no objection to its being made express and irrevocable. . . .

Why should there not be a patient confidence in the ultimate justice of the people? Is there any better or equal hope in the world? In our present differences is either party without faith of being in the right? If the Almighty Ruler of nations, with his eternal truth and justice, be on your side of the North, or on yours of the South, that truth and that justice will surely prevail by the judgment of this great tribunal of the American people.

By the frame of the government under which we live, this same people have wisely given their public servants but little power for mischief; and have, with equal wisdom, provided for the return of that little to their own hands at very short intervals. While the people retain their virtue and vigilance, no administration, by any extreme of wickedness or folly, can very seriously injure the government in the short space of four years.

My countrymen, one and all, think calmly and well upon this whole subject. Nothing valuable can be lost by taking time. If there be an object to hurry any of you in hot haste to a step which you would never take deliberately, that object will be frustrated by taking time; but no good object can be frustrated by it. Such of you as are now dissatisfied still have the old Constitution unimpaired, and, on the sensitive point, the laws of your own framing under it; while the new administration will have no immediate power, if it would, to change either. If it were admitted that you who are dissatisfied hold the right side in the dispute, there still is no single good reason for precipitate action. Intelligence, patriotism, Christianity, and a firm reliance on Him who has never yet forsaken this favored land, are still competent to adjust in the best way all our present difficulty.

In your hands, my dissatisfied fellow-countrymen, and not in mine, is the momentous issue of civil war. The government will not assail you. You can have no conflict without being yourselves the aggressors. You have no oath registered in heaven to destroy the government, while I shall have the most solemn one to "preserve, protect, and defend" it.

I am loath to close. We are not enemies, but friends. We must not be enemies. Though passion may have strained, it must not break, our bonds of affection. The mystic chords of memory, stretching from every battle-field and patriot grave to every living heart and hearthstone all over this broad land, will yet swell the chorus of the Union when again touched, as surely they will be, by the better angels of our nature.

10. Seward's Plan to Avert Civil War April 1, 1861

Some Thoughts for the President's Consideration, April 1, 1861.

First. We are at the end of a month's administration, and yet without a policy either domestic or foreign.

Second. This, however, is not culpable, and it has even been unavoidable. The presence of the Senate, with the need to meet applications for patronage, have prevented attention to other and more grave matters.

Third. But further delay to adopt and prosecute our policies for both domestic and foreign affairs would not only bring scandal on the administration, but danger upon the country.

Fourth. To do this we must dismiss the applicants for office. But how? I suggest that we make the local appointments forthwith, leaving foreign or general ones for ulterior and occasional action.

Fifth. The policy at home. I am aware that my views are singular, and perhaps not sufficiently explained. My system is built upon this idea as a ruling one, namely, that we must.

CHANGE THE QUESTION BEFORE THE PUBLIC FROM ONE UPON SLAVERY, OR ABOUT SLAVERY, for a question upon UNION OR DISUNION:

In other words, from what would be regarded as a party question, to one of patriotism or union.

The occupation or evacuation of Fort Sumter, although not in fact a slavery or a party question, is so regarded. Witness the temper manifested by the Republicans in the free States, and even by the Union men in the South.

I would therefore terminate it as a safe means for changing the issue. I deem it fortunate that the last administration created the necessity.

For the rest, I would simultaneously defend and reinforce all the ports in the gulf, and have the navy recalled from foreign stations to be prepared for a blockade. Put the island of Key West under martial law.

This will raise distinctly the question of union or disunion. I would maintain every fort and possession in the South.

FOR FOREIGN NATIONS

I would demand explanations from Spain and France, categorically, at once.

I would seek explanations from Great Britain and Russia, and send agents into Canada, Mexico, and Central America to rouse a vigorous continental spirit of independence on this continent against European intervention.

And, if satisfactory explanations are not received from Spain and France,

Would convene Congress and declare war against them.

But whatever policy we adopt, there must be an energetic prosecution of it.

For this purpose it must be somebody's business to pursue and direct it incessantly.

Either the President must do it himself, and be all the while active in it, or

Devolve it on some member of his Cabinet. Once adopted, debates on it must end, and all agree and abide.

It is not in my especial province;

But I neither seek to evade nor assume responsibility.

Reply to Secretary Seward's Memorandum

April 1, 1861.

Hon. W. H. Seward.

My dear Sir:—Since parting with you I have been considering your paper dated this day, and entitled "Some Thoughts for the President's Consideration." The first proposition in it is, "*First*, We are at the end of a month's administration, and yet without a policy either domestic or foreign."

At the beginning of that month, in the inaugural, I said: "The power confided to me will be used to hold, occupy, and possess the property and places belonging to the Government, and to collect the duties and imposts." This had your distinct approval at the time; and, taken in connection with the order I immediately gave General Scott, directing him to employ every means in his power to strengthen and hold the forts, comprises the exact domestic policy you now urge, with the single exception that it does not propose to abandon Fort Sumter.

Again, I do not perceive how the reinforcement of Fort Sumter would be done on a slavery or a party issue, while that of Fort Pickens would be on a more national and patriotic one.

The news received yesterday in regard to St. Domingo certainly brings a new item within the range of our foreign policy; but up to that time we have been preparing circulars and instructions to ministers and the like, all in perfect harmony, without even a suggestion that we had no foreign policy.

Upon your closing propositions—that "whatever policy we adopt, there must be an energetic prosecution of it.

"For this purpose it must be somebody's business to pursue and direct it incessantly.

"Either the President must do it himself, and be all the while active in it, or

"Devolve it on some member of his Cabinet.

Once adopted, debates on it must end, and all agree and abide"—I remark that if this must be done, I must do it. When a general line of policy is adopted, I apprehend there is no danger of its being changed without good reason, or continuing to be a subject of unnecessary debate; still, upon points arising in its progress I wish, and suppose I am entitled to have, the advice of all the Cabinet.

Your obedient servant,

A. Lincoln.

11. Frémont's Proclamation on Slaves
August 30, 1861

Head-quarters Western Department.

St. Louis, Aug, 30, 1861.

Circumstances in my judgment are of sufficient urgency to render it necessary that the commanding General of this department should assume the administrative powers of the State. Its disorganized condition, helplessness of civil authority and the total insecurity of life, and devastation of property by bands of murderers and marauders, who infest nearly every county in the State, and avail themselves of public misfortunes, in the vicinity of a hostile force, to gratify private and neighborhood vengeance, and who find an enemy wherever they find plunder, finally demand the severest measures to repress the daily increasing crimes and outrages, which are driving off the inhabitants and ruining the State.

In this condition, the public safety and success of our arms require unity of purpose, without let or hindrance to the prompt administration of affairs. In order, therefore, to suppress disorders, maintain the public peace, and give security to the persons and property of loyal citizens, I do hereby extend and declare established martial law throughout the State of Missouri. The lines of the army occupation in this State are for the present declared to extend from Leavenworth, by way of posts of Jefferson City, Rolla, and Ironton, to Cape Girardeau on the Mississippi River. All persons who shall be taken with arms in their hands within these lines shall be tried by court-martial, and if found guilty, will be shot. Real and personal property of those who shall take up arms against the United States, or who shall be directly proven to have taken an active part with their enemies in the field, is declared confiscated to public use, and their slaves, if any they have, are hereby declared free men.

All persons who shall be proven to have destroyed, after the publication of this order, railroad tracks, bridges, or telegraph lines, shall suffer the extreme penalty of the law. All persons engaged in treasonable correspondence, in giving or procuring aid to the enemy, in fermenting turmoil, and disturbing public tranquillity, by creating or circulating false reports, or incendiary documents, are warned that they are exposing themselves.

All persons who have been led away from allegiance, are required to return to their homes forthwith. Any such absence without sufficient cause, will be held to be presumptive evidence against them. The object of this declaration is to place in the hands of military authorities power to give instantaneous effect to the existing laws, and supply such deficiencies as the conditions of the war demand; but it is not intended to suspend the ordinary tribunals of the country, where law will be administered by civil officers in the usual manner, and with their customary authority, while the same can be peaceably administered.

The commanding General will labor vigilantly for the public welfare, and, by his efforts for their safety, hopes to obtain not only acquiescence, but the active support of the people of the country.

J. C. FREMONT,
Major-General Commanding.

12. Homestead Act
May 20, 1862

AN ACT to secure homesteads to actual settlers on the public domain.

Be it enacted, That any person who is the head of a family, or who has arrived at the head of a family, or who has arrived at the age of twenty-one years, and is a citizen of the United States, or who shall have filed his declaration of intention to become such, as required by the naturalization laws of the United States, and who has never borne arms against the United States Government or given aid and comfort to its enemies, shall, from and after the first of January, eighteen hundred and sixty-three, be entitled to enter one quarter-section or a less quantity of unappropriated public lands, upon which said person may have filed a pre-emption claim, or which may, at the time the application is made, be subject to pre-emption at one dollar and twenty-five cents, or less, per acre; or eighty acres or less of such unappropriated lands, at two dollars and fifty cents per acre, to be located in a body, in conformity to the legal subdivisions of the public lands, and after the same shall have been surveyed: *Provided,* That any person owning or residing on land may, under the provisions of this act, enter other land lying contiguous to his or her said land, which shall not, with the land so already owned and occupied, exceed in the aggregate one hundred and sixty acres.

Sec. 2. That the person applying for the benefit of this act shall, upon application to the register of the land office in which he or she is about to make such entry, make affidavit before the said register or receiver that he or she is the head of a family, or is twenty-one or more years of age, or shall have performed service in the Army or Navy of the United States, and that he has never borne arms against the Government of the United States or given aid and comfort to its enemies, and that such application is made for his or her exclusive use and benefit, and that said entry is made for the purpose of actual settlement and cultivation, and not, either directly or indirectly, for the use or benefit of any other person or persons whomsoever; and upon filing the said affidavit with the register or receiver, and on payment of ten dollars, he or she shall thereupon be permitted to enter the quantity of land specified: *Provided, however,* That no certificate shall be given or patent issued therefore until the expiration of five years from the date of such entry; and if, at the expiration of such time, or at any time within two years thereafter, the person making such entry—or if he be dead, his widow; or in case of her death, his heirs or devisee; or in case of a widow making such entry, her heirs or devisee, in case of her death—shall prove by two credible witnesses that he, she, or they have resided upon or cultivated the same for the term of five years immediately succeeding the time of filing the affidavit aforesaid, and shall make affidavit that no part of said land has been alienated, and that he has borne true allegiance to the Government of the United States; then, in such case, he, she, or they, if at that time a citizen of the United States, shall be entitled to a patent, as in other cases provided for by law: *And provided, further,* That in case of the death of both father and mother, leaving an infant child or children under twenty-one years of age, the right and fee shall inure to the benefit of said infant child or children; and the executor, administrator, or guardian may, at any time within two years after the death of the surviving parent, and in accordance with the law of the State in which such children for the time being have their domicile, sell said land for the benefit of said infants, but for no other purpose; and the purchaser shall acquire the absolute title by the purchase, and be entitled to a patent from the United States, on payment of the office fees and sum of money herein specified. . . .

13. Horace Greeley, Letter to Lincoln, in the *New York Tribune* August 20, 1862

Dear Sir—I do not intrude to tell you—for you must know already—that a great proportion of those who triumphed in your election, and of all who desire the unqualified suppression of the Rebellion now desolating our country, are sorely disappointed and deeply pained by the policy you seem to be pursuing with regard to the slaves of Rebels . . . The Rebels are everywhere using the late antinegro riots in the North as they have long used your officers' treatment of negroes in the South, to convince the slaves that they have nothing to hope from a Union success—that we mean in that case to sell them into a bitterer bondage to defray the cost of the war. Let them impress this as the truth and the Union will never be restored,—never. We cannot conquer ten millions of people united in solid phalanx against us. We must have scouts, spies, guides . . . from the Blacks of the South, whether we allow them to fight for us or not, or we shall be baffled and repelled.

14. PRESIDENT LINCOLN'S LETTER August 22, 1862

EXECUTIVE MANSION,
Washington

Hon. Horace Greeley:

DEAR SIR: I have just read yours of the nineteenth, addressed to myself through the New-York *Tribune*. If there be in it any statements or assumptions of fact which I may know to be erroneous, I do not now and here controvert them. If there be in it any inferences which I may believe to be falsely drawn, I do not now and here argue against them. If there be perceptible in it an impatient and dictatorial tone, I waive it in deference to an old friend, whose heart I have always supposed to be right.

As to the policy I "seem to be pursuing," as you say, I have not meant to leave any one in doubt.

I would save the Union. I would save it the shortest way under the Constitution. The sooner the National authority can be restored, the nearer the Union will be "the Union as it was." If there be those who would not save the Union unless they could at the same time *save* Slavery, I do not agree with them. If there be those who would not save the Union unless they could at the same time *destroy* Slavery, I do not agree with them. My paramount object in this struggle *is* to save the Union, and is *not* either to save or destroy Slavery. If I could save the Union without freeing *any* slave, I would do it; and if I could save it by freeing *all* the slaves, I would do it; and if I could do it by freeing some and leaving others alone, I would also do that. What I do about Slavery and the colored race, I do because I believe it helps to save this Union; and what I forbear, I forbear because I do *not* believe it would help to save the Union. I shall do *less* whenever I shall believe what I am doing hurts the cause, and I shall do *more* whenever I shall believe doing more will help the cause. I shall try to correct errors when shown to be errors; and I shall adopt new views so fast as they shall appear to be true views. I have here stated my purpose according to my view of *official* duty, and I intend no modification of my oft-expressed *personal* wish that all men, everywhere, could be free.

Yours,
A. LINCOLN.

15. From Lincoln's Preliminary Emancipation Proclamation, Presented to his Cabinet
September 22, 1862

That on the first day of January in the year of our Lord, one thousand eight hundred and sixty three, all persons held as slaves, within any state, or designated part of a state, the people whereof shall then be in rebellion against the United States shall be then, thenceforward, and forever, free.

16. Address to President Lincoln by the Working-Men of Manchester, England
December 31, 1862

To Abraham Lincoln, President of the United States:
As citizens of Manchester, assembled at the Free-Trade Hall, we beg to express our fraternal sentiments toward you and your country. We rejoice in your greatness as an outgrowth of England, whose blood and language you share, whose orderly and legal freedom you have applied to new circumstances, over a region immeasurably greater than our own. We honor your Free States, as a singularly happy abode for the working millions where industry is honored. One thing alone has, in the past, lessened our sympathy with your country and our confidence in it—we mean the ascendency of politicians who not merely maintained negro slavery, but desired to extend and root it more firmly. Since we have discerned, however, that the victory of the free North, in the war which has so sorely distressed us as well as afflicted

you, will strike off the fetters of the slave, you have attracted our warm and earnest sympathy. We joyfully honor you, as the President, and the Congress with you, for many decisive steps toward practically exemplifying your belief in the words of your great founders: "All men are created free and equal." You have procured the liberation of the slaves in the district around Washington, and thereby made the centre of your Federation visibly free. You have enforced the laws against the slave-trade, and kept up your fleet against it, even while every ship was wanted for service in your terrible war. You have nobly decided to receive ambassadors from the negro republics of Hayti and Liberia, thus forever renouncing that unworthy prejudice which refuses the rights of humanity to men and women on account of their color. In order more effectually to stop the slave-trade, you have made with our Queen a treaty, which your Senate has ratified, for the right of mutual search. Your Congress has decreed freedom as the law forever in the vast unoccupied or half unsettled Territories which are directly subject to its legislative power. It has offered pecuniary aid to all States which will enact emancipation locally, and has forbidden your Generals to restore fugitive slaves who seek their protection. You have entreated the slave-masters to accept these moderate offers; and after long and patient waiting, you, as Commander-in-Chief of the Army, have appointed to-morrow, the first of January, 1863, as the day of unconditional freedom for the slaves of the rebel States. Heartily do we congratulate you and your country on this humane and righteous course. We assume that you cannot now stop short of a complete uprooting of slavery. It would not become us to dictate any details, but there are broad principles of humanity which must guide you. If complete emancipation in some States be deferred, though only to a predetermined day, still in the interval, human beings should not be counted chattels. Women must have the rights of chastity and maternity, men the rights of husbands, masters the liberty of manumission. Justice demands for the black, no less than for the white, the protection of law—that his voice be heard in your courts. Nor must any such abomination be tolerated as slave-breeding States, and a slave market—if you are to earn the high reward of all your sacrifices, in the approval of the universal brotherhood and of the Divine Father. It is for your free country to decide whether any thing but immediate and total emancipation can secure the most indispensable rights of humanity against the inveterate wickedness of local laws and local executives. We implore you, for your own honor and welfare, not to faint in your providential mission. While your enthusiasm is aflame, and the tide of events run high, let the work be finished effectually. Leave no root of bitterness to spring up and work fresh misery to your children. It is a mighty task, indeed, to reörganize the industry not only of four millions of the colored race, but of five millions of whites. Nevertheless, the vast progress you have made in the short space of twenty months fills us with hope that every stain on your freedom will shortly be removed, and that the erasure of that foul blot upon civilization and Christianity—chattel slavery—during your Presidency will cause the name of Abraham Lincoln to be honored and revered by posterity. We are certain that such a glorious consummation will cement Great Britain to the United States in close and enduring regards. Our interests, moreover, are identified with yours. We are truly one people, though locally separate. And if you have any ill-wishers here, be assured they are chiefly those who oppose liberty at home, and that they will be powerless to stir up quarrels between us, from the very day in which your country becomes, undeniably and without exception, the home of the free. Accept our high admiration of your firmness in upholding the proclamation of freedom.

17. Lincoln's Reply to the Working-Men of Manchester, England
January 19, 1863

To the Working-Men of Manchester:

I have the honor to acknowledge the receipt of the address and resolutions which you sent me on the eve of the new year. When I came, on the 4th of March, 1861, through a free and constitutional election to preside in the Government of the United States, the country was found at the verge of civil war. Whatever might have been the cause, or whosoever the fault, one duty, paramount to all others, was before me, namely, to maintain and preserve at once the Constitution and the integrity of the Federal Republic. A conscientious purpose to perform this duty is the key to all the measures of administration which have been and to all which will hereafter be pursued. Under our frame of government and my official oath, I could not depart from this purpose if I would. It is not always in the power of governments to enlarge or restrict the scope of moral results which follow the policies that they may deem it necessary for the public safety from time to time to adopt.

I have understood well that the duty of self-preservation rests solely with the American people; but I have at the same time been aware that favor or disfavor of foreign nations might have a material influence in enlarging or prolonging the struggle with disloyal men in which the country is engaged. A fair examination of history has served to authorize a belief that the past actions and influences of the United States were generally regarded as having been beneficial toward mankind. I have, therefore, reckoned upon the forbearance of nations. Circumstances—to some of which you kindly allude—induce me especially to expect that if justice and good faith should be practised by the United States, they would encounter no hostile influence on the part of Great Britain. It is now a pleasant duty to acknowledge the demonstration you have given of your desire that a spirit of amity and peace toward this country may prevail in the councils of your Queen, who is respected and esteemed in your own country only more than she is by the kindred nation which has its home on this side of the Atlantic.

I know and deeply deplore the sufferings which the working-men at Manchester, and in all Europe, are called to endure in this crisis. It has been often and studiously represented that the attempt to overthrow this government, which as built upon the foundation of human rights, and to substitute for it one which should rest exclusively on the basis of human slavery, was likely to obtain the favor of Europe. Through the action of our disloyal citizens, the working-men of Europe have been subjected to severe trials, for the purpose of forcing their sanction to that attempt. Under the circumstances, I cannot but regard your decisive utterances upon the question as an instance of sublime Christian heroism which has not been surpassed in any age or in any country. It is indeed an energetic and reinspiring assurance of the inherent power of truth and of the ultimate and universal triumph of justice, humanity, and freedom. I do not doubt that the sentiments you have expressed will be sustained by your great nation; and, on the other hand, I have no hesitation in assuring you that they will excite admiration, esteem, and the most reciprocal feelings of friendship among the American people. I hail this interchange of sentiment, therefore, as an augury that whatever else may happen, whatever misfortune may befall your country or my own, the peace and friendship which now exist between the two nations will be, as it shall be my desire to make them, perpetual.

Abraham Lincoln.

18. The Emancipation Proclamation
January 1, 1863

BY THE PRESIDENT OF THE UNITED STATES OF AMERICA:

A Proclamation.

Whereas on the 22d day of September, A.D. 1862, a proclamation was issued by the President of the United States, containing, among other things, the following, to wit:

"That on the 1st day of January, A.D. 1863, all persons held as slaves within any State or designated part of a State the people whereof shall then be in rebellion against the United States shall be then, thenceforward, and forever free; and the executive government of the United States, including the military and naval authority thereof, will recognize and maintain the freedom of such persons and will do no act or acts to repress such persons, or any of them, in any efforts they may make for their actual freedom.

"That the executive will on the 1st day of January aforesaid, by proclamation, designate the States and parts of States, if any, in which the people thereof, respectively, shall then be in rebellion against the United States; and the fact that any State or the people thereof shall on that day be in good faith represented in the Congress of the United States by members chosen thereto at elections wherein a majority of the qualified voters of such States shall have participated shall, in the absence of strong countervailing testimony, be deemed conclusive evidence that such State and the people thereof are not then in rebellion against the United States."

Now, therefore, I, Abraham Lincoln, President of the United States, by virtue of the power in me vested as Commander-in-Chief of the Army and Navy of the United States in time of actual armed rebellion against the authority and government of the United States, and as a fit and necessary war measure for suppressing said rebellion, do, on this 1st day of January, A.D. 1863, and in accordance with my purpose so to do, publicly proclaimed for the full period of one hundred days from the first day above mentioned, order and designate as the States and parts of States wherein the people thereof, respectively, are this day in rebellion against the United States the following, to wit:

Arkansas, Texas, Louisiana (except the parishes of St. Bernard, Plaquemines, Jefferson, St. John, St. Charles, St. James, Ascension, Assumption, Terrebonne, Lafourche, St. Mary, St. Martin, and Orleans, including the city of New Orleans), Mississippi, Alabama, Florida, Georgia, South Carolina, North Carolina, and Virginia (except the forty-eight counties designated as West Virginia, and also the counties of Berkeley, Accomac, Northhampton, Elizabeth City, York, Princess Anne, and Norfolk, including the cities of Norfolk and Portsmouth), and which excepted parts are for the present left precisely as if this proclamation were not issued.

And by virtue of the power and for the purpose aforesaid, I do order and declare that all persons held as slaves within said designated States and parts of States are, and henceforward shall be, free; and that the Executive Government of the United States, including military and naval authorities thereof, will recognize and maintain the freedom of said persons.

And I hereby enjoin upon the people so declared to be free to abstain from all violence, unless in necessary self-defense; and I recommend to them that, in all cases when allowed, they labor faithfully for reasonable wages.

And I further declare and make known that such persons of suitable condition will be received into the armed service of the United States to garrison forts, positions, stations, and other places, and to man vessels of all sorts in said service.

And upon this act, sincerely believed to be an act of justice, warranted by the Constitution upon military necessity, I invoke the considerate judgment of mankind and the gracious favor of Almighty God.

19. The French in Mexico
Mr. Seward to Mr. Adams
March 3, 1862

Department of State,
Washington, March 3, 1862.

Sir: We observe indications of a growing opinion in Europe that the demonstrations which are being made by Spanish, French, and British forces against Mexico are likely to be attended with a revolution in that country which will bring in a monarchical government there, in which the crown will be assumed by some foreign prince.

This country is deeply concerned in the peace of nations, and aims to be loyal at the same time in all its relations, as well to the allies as to Mexico. The President has therefore instructed me to submit his views on the new aspect of affairs to the parties concerned. He has relied upon the assurances given to this government by the allies that they were seeking no political objects and only a redress of grievances. He does not doubt the sincerity of the allies, and his confidence in their good faith, if it could be shaken, would be reinspired by explanations apparently made in their behalf that the governments of Spain, France, and Great Britain are not intending to intervene and will not intervene to effect a change of the constitutional form of government now existing in Mexico, or to produce any political change there in opposition to the will of the Mexican people. Indeed, he understands the allies to be unanimous in declaring that the proposed revolution in Mexico is moved only by Mexican citizens now in Europe.

The President, however, deems it his duty to express to the allies, in all candor and frankness, the opinion that no monarchical government which could be founded in Mexico, in the presence of foreign navies and armies in the waters and upon the soil of Mexico, would have any prospect of security or permanency. Secondly, that the instability of such a monarchy there would be enhanced if the throne should be assigned to any person not of Mexican nativity. That under such circumstances the new government must speedily fall unless it could draw into its support European alliances, which, relating back to the present invasion, would, in fact, make it the beginning of a permanent policy of armed European monarchical intervention injurious and practically hostile to the most general system of government on the continent of America, and this would be the beginning rather than the ending of revolution in Mexico.

These views are grounded upon some knowledge of the political sentiments and habits of society in America.

In such a case it is not to be doubted that the permanent interests and sympathies of this country would be with the other American republics. It is not intended on this occasion to predict the course of events which might happen as a consequence of the proceeding contemplated, either on this continent or in Europe. It is sufficient to say that, in the President's opinion, the emancipation of this continent from European control has been the principal feature in its history during the last century. It is not probable that a revolution in the contrary direction would be successful in an immediately succeeding century, while population in America is so rapidly increasing, resources so rapidly developing, and society so steadily forming itself upon principles of democratic American government. Nor is it necessary to suggest to the allies the improbability that European nations could steadily agree upon a policy favorable to such a counter-revolution as one conducive to their own interests, or to suggest that, however studiously the allies may act to avoid lending the aid of their land and naval forces to domestic revolutions in Mexico, the result would nevertheless be traceable to the presence of those forces there, although for a different purpose, since it may be deemed certain that but for their presence there no such revolution could probably have been attempted or even conceived.

The Senate of the United States has not, indeed, given its official sanction to the precise measures which the President has proposed for lending our aid to the existing government in Mexico, with the approval of the allies, to relieve it from its present embarrassments. This, however, is only a question of domestic administration. It would be very erroneous to regard such a disagreement as indicating any serious difference of opinion in this government or among the American people in their cordial good wishes for the safety, welfare, and stability of the republican system of government in that country.

I am, sir, your obedient servant,

William H. Seward.

20. Reconstruction of Tennessee
Lincoln's Letter to Governor Johnson
September 11, 1863

Executive Mansion, Washington,
September 11, 1863.

HON. ANDREW JOHNSON.

My dear sir:—All Tennessee is now clear of armed insurrectionists. You need not to be reminded that it is the nick of time for reinaugurating a loyal State government. Not a moment should be lost. You and the co-operating friends there can better judge of the ways and means that can be judged by any here. I only offer a few suggestions. The reinauguration must not be such as to give control of the State and its representation in Congress to the enemies of the Union, driving its friends there into political exile. The whole struggle for Tennessee will have been profitless to both State and nation if it so ends that Governor Johnson is put down and Governor Harris put up. It must not be so. You must have it otherwise. Let the reconstruction be the work of such men only as can be

trusted for the Union. Exclude all others, and trust that your government so organized will be recognized here as being the one of republican form to be guaranteed to the State, and to be protected against invasion and domestic violence. It is something on the question of time to remember that it cannot be known who is next to occupy the position I now hold, nor what he will do. I see that you have declared in favor of emancipation in Tennessee, for which may God bless you. Get emancipation into your new State government—constitution—and there will be no such word as fail for your case. The raising of colored troops, I think, will greatly help every way.

Yours very truly,
A. Lincoln.

21. The Gettysburg Address
November 19, 1863

Four score and seven years ago our fathers brought forth on this continent, a new nation, conceived in Liberty, and dedicated to the proposition that all men are created equal.

Now we are engaged in a great civil war, testing whether that nation or any nation so conceived and so dedicated, can long endure. We are met on a great battle-field of that war. We have come to dedicate a portion of that field, as a final resting place for those who here gave their lives that that nation might live. It is altogether fitting and proper that we should do this.

But, in a larger sense, we can not dedicate—we can not consecrate—we can not hallow—this ground. The brave men, living and dead, who struggled here, have consecrated it, far above our poor power to add or detract. The world will little note, nor long remember what we say here, but it can never forget what they did here. It is for us the living, rather, to be dedicated here to the unfinished work which they who fought here have thus far so nobly advanced. It is rather for us to be here dedicated to the great task remaining before us—that from these honored dead we take increased devotion to that cause for which they gave the last full measure of devotion—that we here highly resolve that these dead shall not have died in vain—that this nation under God, shall have a new birth of freedom—and that government of the people, by the people, for the people, shall not perish from the earth.

22. Lincoln's Plan of Reconstruction Proclamation of Amnesty and Reconstruction December 8, 1863

A Proclamation

Whereas in and by the Constitution of the United States it is provided that the President "shall have power to grant reprieves and pardons for offenses against the United States, except in cases of impeachment;" and

Whereas a rebellion now exists whereby the loyal State governments of several States have for a long time been subverted, and many persons have committed and are now guilty of treason against the United States; and

Whereas, with reference to said rebellion and treason, laws have been acted by Congress declaring forfeitures and confiscation of property and liberation of slaves, all upon terms and conditions therein stated, and also declaring that the President was thereby authorized at any time thereafter, by proclamation, to extend to persons who may have participated in the existing rebellion in any State or part thereof pardon and amnesty, with such exceptions and at such times and on such conditions as he may deem expedient for the public welfare; and

Whereas the Congressional declaration for limited and conditional pardon accords with well-established judicial exposition of the pardoning power; and

Whereas, with reference to said rebellion, the President of the United States has issued several proclamations with provisions in regard to the liberation of slaves; and

Whereas it is now desired by some persons heretofore engaged in said rebellion to resume their allegiance to the United States and to re-inaugurate loyal State governments within and for their respective States:

Therefore, I, Abraham Lincoln, President of the United States, do proclaim, . . . to all persons who have, directly or by implication, participated in the existing rebellion, except as hereinafter excepted, that a full pardon is hereby granted to them and each of them, with restoration of all rights of property, except as to slaves and in property cases where rights of third parties shall have intervened, and upon the condition that every such person shall take and subscribe an oath and thenceforward keep and maintain said oath inviolate, and which oath shall be registered for permanent preservation and shall be of the tenor and effect following, to wit:

I, ——— ———, do solemnly swear, in presence of Almighty God, that I will henceforth faithfully support, protect, and defend the Constitution of the United States and the Union of the States thereunder; and that I will in like manner abide by and faithfully support all acts of Congress passed during the existing rebellion with reference to slaves, so long and so far as not repealed, modified, or held void by Congress or by decision of the Supreme Court; and that I will in like manner abide by and faithfully support all proclamations of the President made during the existing rebellion having reference to slaves, so long and so far as not modified or declared void by decision of the Supreme Court. So help me God.

The persons excepted from the benefits of the foregoing provisions are all who are or shall have been civil or diplomatic officers or agents of the so-called Confederate Government; all who have left judicial stations under the United

States to aid the rebellion; all who are or shall have been military or naval officers of said so-called Confederate Government above the rank of colonel in the army or of lieutenant in the navy; all who left seats in the United States Congress to aid the rebellion; all who resigned commissions in the Army or Navy of the United States and afterwards aided the rebellion; and all who have engaged in any way in treating colored persons, or white persons in charge of such, otherwise than lawfully as prisoners of war, and which persons may have been found in the United States service as soldiers, seamen, or in any other capacity.

And I do further proclaim, declare, and make known that whenever, in any of the States of Arkansas, Texas, Louisiana, Mississippi, Tennessee, Alabama, Georgia, Florida, South Carolina, and North Carolina, a number of persons, not less than one-tenth in number of the votes cast in such State at the Presidential election of the year A. D. 1860, each having taken oath aforesaid, and not having since violated it, and being a qualified voter by the election law of the State existing immediately before the so-called act of secession, and excluding all others, shall re-establish a State government which shall be republican and in nowise contravening said oath, such shall be recognized as the true government of the State, and the State shall receive thereunder the benefits of the constitutional provision which declares that "the United States shall guarantee to every State in this Union a republican form of government and shall protect each of them against invasion, and, on application of the legislature, or the executive (when the legislature can not be convened), against domestic violence."

And I do further proclaim, declare, and make known that any provision which may be adopted by such State government in relation to the freed people of such State which shall recognize and declare their permanent freedom, provide for their education, and which may yet be consistent as a temporary arrangement with their present condition as a laboring, landless, and homeless class, will not be objected to by the National Executive.

And it is suggested as not improper that in constructing a loyal State government in any State the name of the State, the boundary, the subdivisions, the constitution, and the general code of laws as before the rebellion be maintained, subject only to the modifications made necessary by the conditions hereinbefore stated, and such others, if any, not contravening said conditions and which may be deemed expedient by those framing the new State government.

To avoid misunderstanding, it may be proper to say that this proclamation, so far as it relates to State governments, has no reference to States wherein loyal State governments have all the while been maintained. And for the same reason it may be proper to further say that whether members sent to Congress from any State shall be admitted to seats constitutionally rests exclusively with the respective Houses, and not to any extent with the Executive. And, still further, that this proclamation is intended to present the people of the States wherein the national authority has been suspended and loyal State governments have been subverted a mode in and by which the national authority and loyal State governments may be re-established within said States or in any of them; and while the mode presented is the best the Executive can suggest, with his present impressions, it must not be understood that no other possible mode would be acceptable.

ABRAHAM LINCOLN.

23. The Thirteenth Amendment Passed by the House on January 31, 1865

Sec. 1: Neither slavery nor involuntary servitude, save as a punishment for crime whereof the party shall have been duly convicted, shall exist within the United States, or any place subject to their jurisdiction.

Sec. 2: Congress shall have power to enforce this article by appropriate legislation.

24. Lincoln's Second Inaugural Address March 4, 1865

FELLOW-COUNTRYMEN:—At this second appearing to take the oath of the presidential office there is less occasion for an extended address than there was at the first. Then a statement somewhat in detail of a course to be pursued seemed fitting and proper. Now, at the expiration of four years, during which public declarations have been constantly called forth on every point and phase of the great contest which still absorbs the attention and engrosses the energies of the nation, little that is new could be presented. The progress of our arms, upon which all else chiefly depends, is as well known to the public as to myself, and it is, I trust, reasonably satisfactory and encouraging to all. With high hope for the future, no prediction in regard to it is ventured.

On the occasion corresponding to this four years ago all thoughts were anxiously directed to an impending civil war. All dreaded it, all sought to avert it. While the inaugural address was being delivered from this place, devoted altogether to *saving* the Union without war, insurgent agents were in the city seeking to *destroy* it without war—seeking to dissolve the Union and divide effects by negotiation. Both parties deprecated war, but one of them would *make* war rather than let the nation survive, and the other would *accept* war rather than let it perish, and the war came.

One eighth of the whole population was colored slaves, not distributed generally over the Union, but localized in the southern part of it. These slaves constituted a peculiar and powerful interest. All knew that this interest was somehow the cause of the war. To strengthen, perpetuate, and extend this interest was the object for which the insurgents would rend the Union even by war, while the Government claimed no right to do more than to restrict the territorial enlargement of it. Neither party expected for the war the magnitude or the duration which it has already attained. Neither anticipated that the *cause* of the conflict might cease with or even before the conflict itself should cease. Each looked for an easier triumph, and a result less fundamental and astounding. Both read the same Bible and pray to the same God, and each invokes His aid against the other. It may seem strange that any men should dare to ask a just God's assistance in wringing their bread from the sweat of other men's faces, but let us judge not, that we be not judged. The prayers of both could not be answered. That of neither has been answered fully. The Almighty has His own purposes. "Woe unto the world because of offenses; for it must needs be that offenses come, but woe to that man by whom the offense cometh." If we shall suppose that American slavery is one of those offenses which, in the providence of God, must needs come, but which, having continued through His appointed time, He now wills to remove, and that He gives to both North and South this terrible war as the woe due to those by whom the offense came, shall we discern therein any departure from those divine attributes which the believers in a living God always ascribe to Him? Fondly do we hope, fervently do we pray, that this mighty scourge of war may speedily pass away. Yet, if God wills that it continue until all the wealth piled by the bondsman's two hundred and fifty years of unrequited toil shall be sunk, and until every drop of blood drawn with the lash shall be paid by another drawn with the sword, as was said three thousand years ago, so still it must be said, "The judgments of the Lord are true and righteous altogether."

With malice toward none, with charity for all, with firmness in the right as God gives us to see the right, let us strive on to finish the work we are in, to bind up the nation's wounds, to care for him who shall have borne the battle and for his widow and his orphan, to do all which may achieve and cherish a just and lasting peace among ourselves and with all nations.

25. Jefferson Davis's Last Message to the People of the Confederacy April 4, 1865

Danville, Va. April 4, 1865.
To the People of the Confederate States of America.

The General in Chief of our Army has found it necessary to make such movements of the troops as to uncover the capital and thus involve the withdrawal of the Government from the city of Richmond.

It would be unwise, even were it possible, to conceal the great moral as well as material injury to our cause that must result from the occupation of Richmond by the enemy. It is equally unwise and unworthy of us, as patriots engaged in a most sacred cause, to allow our energies to falter, our spirits to grow faint, or our efforts to become relaxed under reverses, however calamitous. While it has been to us a source of national pride that for four years of unequaled warfare we have been able, in close proximity to the center of the enemy's power, to maintain the seat of our chosen Government free from the pollution of his presence; while the memories of the heroic dead who have freely given their lives to its defense must ever remain enshrined in our hearts; while the preservation of the capital, which is usually regarded as the evidence to mankind of separate national existence, was an object very dear to us, it is also true, and should not be forgotten, that the loss which we have suffered is not without compensation. For

many months the largest and finest army of the Confederacy, under the command of a leader whose presence inspires equal confidence in the troops and the people, has been greatly trammeled by the necessity of keeping constant watch over the approaches to the capital, and has thus been forced to forego more than one opportunity for promising enterprise. The hopes and confidence of the enemy have been constantly excited by the belief that their possession of Richmond would be the signal for our submission to their rule, and relieve them from the burden of war, as their failing resources admonish them it must be abandoned if not speedily brought to a successful close. It is for us, my countrymen, to show by our bearing under reverses how wretched has been the self-deception of those who have believed us less able to endure misfortune with fortitude than to encounter danger with courage. We have now entered upon a new phase of a struggle the memory of which is to endure for all ages and to shed an increasing luster upon our country.

Relieved from the necessity of guarding cities and particular points, important but not vital to our defense, with an army free to move from point to point and strike in detail the detachments and garrisons of the enemy, operating on the interior of our own country, where supplies are more accessible, and where the foe will be far removed from his own base and cut off from all succor in case of reverse, nothing is now needed to render our triumph certain but the exhibition of our own unquenchable resolve. Let us but will it, and we are free; and who, in the light of the past, dare doubt your purpose in the future?

Animated by the confidence in your spirit and fortitude, which never yet has failed me, I announce to you, fellow-countrymen, that it is my purpose to maintain your cause with my whole heart and soul; that I will never consent to abandon to the enemy one foot of the soil of any one of the States of the Confederacy. . . . If by stress of numbers we should ever be compelled to a temporary withdrawal from her limits, or those of any other border State, again and again will we return, until the baffled and exhausted enemy shall abandon in despair his endless and impossible task of making slaves of a people resolved to be free.

Let us not, then, despond, my countrymen; but, relying on the never-failing mercies and protecting care of our God, let us meet the foe with fresh defiance, with unconquered and unconquerable hearts.

Jeff'n Davis.

26. The Burning of Columbia, S. C. Report of General Sherman on the Campaign of the Carolinas April 4, 1865

. . . In anticipation of the occupation of the city, I had made written orders to General Howard touching the conduct of the troops. These were to destroy, absolutely, all arsenals and public property not needed for our own use, as well as all railroads, depots, and machinery useful in war to an enemy, but to spare all dwellings, colleges, schools, asylums, and harmless private property. I was the first to cross the pontoon bridge, and in company with General Howard rode into the city. The day was clear, but a perfect tempest of wind was raging. The brigade of Colonel Stone was already in the city, and was properly posted. Citizens and soldiers were on the streets, and general good order prevailed. General Wade Hampton, who commanded the Confederate rear-guard of cavalry, had, in anticipation of our capture of Columbia, ordered that all cotton, public and private, should be moved into the streets and fired, to prevent our making use of it. Bales were piled everywhere, the rope and bagging cut, and tufts of cotton were blown about in the wind, lodged in the trees and against houses, so as to resemble a snow storm. Some of these piles of cotton were burning, especially one in the very heart of the city, near the Court-house, but the fire was partially subdued by the labor of our soldiers. During the day the Fifteenth corps passed through Columbia and out on the Camden road. The Seventeenth did not enter the town at all; and, as I have before stated, the left wing and cavalry did not come within two miles of the town.

Before one single public building had been fired by order, the smoldering fires, set by Hampton's order, were rekindled by the wind, and communicated to the buildings around. About dark they began to spread, and got beyond the control of the brigade on duty within the city. The whole of Wood's division was brought in, but it was found impossible to check the flames, which, by midnight, had become unmanageable, and raged until about four A.M., when the wind subsiding, they were got under control. I was up nearly all night, and saw Generals Howard, Logan, Woods, and others, laboring to save houses and protect families thus suddenly deprived of shelter, and of bedding and wearing apparel. I disclaim on the part of my army any agency in this fire, but on the contrary, claim that we saved what of Columbia remains unconsumed. And without hesitation, I charge General Wade Hampton with having burned his own city of Columbia, not with a malicious intent, or as the manifestations of a silly "Roman stoicism," but from folly and want of sense, in filling it with lint, cotton, and tinder. Our officers and men on duty worked well to extinguish the flames; but others not on duty, including the officers who had long been imprisoned there, rescued by us, may have assisted in spreading the fire after it had once begun, and may have indulged in unconcealed joy to see the ruin of the capital of South Carolina. During the eighteenth and nineteenth, the arsenal, railroad depots, machine shops, foundries, and other buildings were properly destroyed by detailed working parties, and the railroad track torn up and destroyed down to Kingsville and the Wateree bridge, and up in the direction of Winnsboro. . . .

27. Lincoln's Last Public Address
April 11, 1865

FELLOW-CITIZENS:—We meet this evening not in sorrow, but in gladness of heart. The evacuation of Petersburg and Richmond, and the surrender of the principal insurgent army, give hope of a righteous and speedy peace, whose joyous expression cannot be restrained. In the midst of this, however, He from whom all blessings flow must not be forgotten.

A call for a national thanksgiving is being prepared, and will be duly promulgated. . . . By these recent successes, the reinauguration of the national authority—reconstruction—which has had a large share of thought from the first, is pressed much more closely upon our attention. It is fraught with great difficulty. Unlike a case of war between independent nations, *there is no authorized organ for us to treat with*—no one man has authority to give up the rebellion for any other man. We simply must begin with and mould from disorganized and discordant elements. Nor is it a small additional embarrassment that we, the loyal people, differ among ourselves as to the mode, manner, and measure of reconstruction. As a general rule, I abstain from reading the reports of attacks upon myself, wishing not to be provoked by that to which I cannot properly offer an answer. In spite of this precaution, however, it comes to my knowledge that I am much censured for some supposed agency in setting up and seeking to sustain the new State government of Louisiana. In this I have done just so much and no more than the public knows. In the Annual Message of December, 1863, and the accompanying proclamation, I presented a plan of reconstruction, as the phrase

goes, which I promised, if adopted by any State, would be acceptable to and sustained by the Executive Government of the nation. I distinctly stated that this was not the only plan which might possibly be acceptable, and I also distinctly protested that the Executive claimed no right to say when or whether members should be admitted to seats in Congress from such States. This plan was in advance submitted to the then Cabinet, and approved by every member of it. One of them suggested that I should then and in that connection apply the Emancipation Proclamation to the theretofore excepted parts of Virginia and Louisiana; that I should drop the suggestion about apprenticeship for freed people, and that I should omit the protest against my own power in regard to the admission of members of Congress. But even he approved every part and parcel of the plan which has since been employed or touched by the action of Louisiana. The new constitution of Louisiana, declaring emancipation for the whole State, practically applies the proclamation to the part previously excepted. It does not adopt apprenticeship for freed people, and is silent, as it could not well be otherwise, about the admission of members to Congress. So that, as it applied to Louisiana, every member of the Cabinet fully approved the plan. The message went to Congress, and I received many commendations of the plan, written and verbal, and not a single objection to it from any professed emancipationist came to my knowledge until after the news reached Washington that the people of Louisiana had begun to move in accordance with it. From about July, 1862, I had corresponded with different persons supposed to be interested in seeking a reconstruction of a State government for Louisiana. When the message of 1863, with the plan before mentioned, reached New Orleans, General Banks wrote me that he was confident that the people, with his military co-operation, would reconstruct substantially on that plan. I wrote to him and some of them to try it. They tried it, and the result is known. Such has been my only agency in setting up the

Louisiana government. As to sustaining it my promise is out, as before stated. But, as bad promises are better broken than kept, I shall treat this as a bad promise and break it, whenever I shall be convinced that keeping it is adverse to the public interest; but I have not yet been so convinced. I have been shown a letter on this subject, supposed to be an able one, in which the writer expresses regret that my mind has not seemed to be definitely fixed upon the question whether the seceded States, so called, are in the Union or out of it. It would perhaps add astonishment to his regret were he to learn that since I have found professed Union men endeavoring to answer that question. I have purposely forborne any public expression upon it. As appears to me, that question has not been nor yet is a practically material one, and that any discussion of it, while it thus remains practically immaterial, could have no effect other than the mischievous one of dividing our friends. As yet, whatever it may become, that question is bad as the basis of a controversy, and good for nothing at all—a merely pernicious abstraction. We all agree that the seceded States, so called, are out of their proper practical relation with the Union, and that the sole object of the Government, civil and military, in regard to those States, is to again get them into their proper practical relation. I believe that it is not only possible, but in fact easier, to do this without deciding or even considering whether those States have ever been out of the Union, than with it. Finding themselves safely at home, it would be utterly immaterial whether they had been abroad. Let us all join in doing the acts necessary to restore the proper practical relations between these States and the Union, and each forever after innocently indulge his own opinion whether, in doing the acts he brought the States from without into the Union, or only gave them proper assistance, they never having been out of it. The amount of constituency, so to speak, on which the Louisiana government rests, would be more satisfactory to all if it contained fifty thousand, or thirty thousand, or even twenty thousand, instead of twelve thousand, as it does. It is also unsatisfactory to some that the elective franchise is not given to the colored man. I would myself prefer that it were now conferred on the very intelligent, and on those who serve our cause as soldiers. Still, the question is not whether the Louisiana government, as it stands, is quite all that is desirable. The question is, Will it be wiser to take it as it is and help to improve it, or to reject and disperse? Can Louisiana be brought into proper practical relation with the Union sooner by sustaining or by discarding her new State government? Some twelve thousand voters in the heretofore Slave State of Louisiana have sworn allegiance to the Union, assumed to be the rightful political power of the State, held elections, organized a State government, adopted a Free State constitution, giving the benefit of public schools equally to black and white, and empowering the Legislature to confer the elective franchise upon the colored man. This Legislature has already voted to ratify the Constitutional Amendment recently passed by Congress, abolishing slavery throughout the nation. These twelve thousand persons are thus fully committed to the Union and to perpetuate freedom in the State—committed to the very things, and nearly all things, the nation wants—and they ask the nation's recognition and its assistance to make good this committal. Now, if we reject and spurn them, we do our utmost to disorganize and disperse them. We, in fact, say to the white man: You are worthless or worse; we will neither help you nor be helped by you. To the black we say: This cup of liberty which these, your old masters, held to your lips, we will dash from you, and leave you to the chances of gathering the spilled and scattered contents in some vague and undefined when, where, and how. If this course, discouraging and paralyzing both white and black, has any tendency to bring Louisiana into proper practical relations with the Union, I have so far been unable to perceive it. If, on the contrary, we recognize and sustain the new government of Louisiana, the converse of all this is made true. We encourage the hearts and nerve the arms of twelve thousand to adhere to their work, and argue for it, and proselyte for it, and fight for it, and feed it, and grow it, and ripen it to a complete success. The colored man, too, in seeing all united for him, is inspired with vigilance, and energy, and daring to the same end. Grant that he desires the elective franchise, will he not attain it sooner by saving the already advanced steps towards it, than by running backward over them? Concede that the new government of Louisiana is only to what it should be as the egg is to the fowl, we shall sooner have the fowl by hatching the egg than by smashing it. Again, if we reject Louisiana, we also reject one vote in favor of the proposed amendment to the National Constitution. To meet this proposition, it has been argued that no more than three fourths of those States which have not attempted secession are necessary to validly ratify the amendment. I do not commit myself against this, further than to say that such a ratification would be questionable, and sure to be persistently questioned, while a ratification by three fourths of all the States would be unquestioned and unquestionable. I repeat the question, Can Louisiana be brought into proper practical relation with the Union sooner by sustaining or by discarding her new State government? What has been said of Louisiana will apply to other States. And yet so great peculiarities pertain to each State, and such important and sudden changes occur in the same State, and withal so new and unprecedented is the whole case, that no exclusive and inflexible plan can safely be prescribed as to details and collaterals. Such exclusive and inflexible plan would surely become a new entanglement. Important principles may and must be inflexible. In the present situation as the phrase goes, it may be my duty to make some new announcement to the people of the South. I am considering, and shall not fail to act, when satisfied that action will be proper.

28. The Civil Rights Act
April 9, 1866

An Act to protect all Persons in the United States in their Civil Rights, and furnish the Means of their Vindication.

Be it enacted, That all persons born in the United States and not subject to any foreign power, excluding Indians not taxed, are hereby declared to be citizens of the United States; and such citizens, of every race and color, without regard to any previous condition of slavery or involuntary servitude, except as a punishment for crime whereof the party shall have been duly convicted, shall have the same right, in every State and Territory in the United States, to make and enforce contracts, to sue, be parties, and give evidence, to inherit, purchase, lease, sell, hold, and convey real and personal property, and to full and equal benefit of all laws and proceedings for the security of person and property, as is enjoyed by white citizens, and shall be subject to like punishment, pains, and penalties, and to none other, any law, statute, ordinance, regulation, or custom, to the contrary notwithstanding.

SEC. 2. *And be it further enacted,* That any person who, under color of any law, statute, ordinance, regulation, or custom, shall subject, or cause to be subjected, any inhabitant of any State or Territory to the deprivation of any right secured or protected by this act, or to different punishment, pains, or penalties on account of such person having at any time been held in a condition of slavery or involuntary servitude, except as a punishment for crime whereof the party shall have been duly convicted, or by reason of his color or race, than is prescribed for the punishment of white persons, shall be deemed guilty of a misdemeanor, and, on conviction, shall be punished by fine not exceeding one thousand dollars, or imprisonment not exceeding one year, or both, in the discretion of the court.

Sec. 3. *And be it further enacted*, That the district courts of the United States, . . . shall have, exclusively of the courts of the several States, cognizance of all crimes and offences committed against the provisions of this act, and also, concurrently with the circuit courts of the United States, of all causes, civil and criminal, affecting persons who are denied or cannot enforce in the courts or judicial tribunals of the State or locality where they may be any of the rights secured to them by the first section of this act. . . .

Sec. 4. *And be it further enacted*, That the district attorneys, marshals, and deputy marshals of the United States, the commissioners appointed by the circuit and territorial courts of the United States, with powers of arresting, imprisoning, or bailing offenders against the laws of the United States, the officers and agents of the Freedmen's Bureau, and every other officer who may be specially empowered by the President of the United States, shall be, and they are hereby, specially authorized and required, at the expense of the United States, to institute proceedings against all and every person who shall violate the provisions of this act, and cause him or them to be arrested and imprisoned, or bailed, as the case may be, for trial before such court of the United States or territorial court as by this act has cognizance of the offence. . . .

Sec. 8. *And be it further enacted*, That whenever the President of the United States shall have reason to believe that offences have been or are likely to be committed against the provisions of this act within any judicial district, it shall be lawful for him, in his discretion, to direct the judge, marshal, and district attorney of such district to attend at such place within the district, and for such time as he may designate, for the purpose of the more speedy arrest and trial of persons charged with a violation of this act; and it shall be the duty of every judge or other officer, when any such requisition shall be received by him, to attend at the place and for the time therein designated.

Sec. 9. *And be it further enacted*, That it shall be lawful for the President of the United States,

or such person as he may empower for that purpose, to employ such part of the land or naval forces of the United States, or of the militia, as shall be necessary to prevent the violation and enforce the due execution of this act.

Sec. 10. *And be it further enacted*, That upon all questions of law arising in any cause under the provisions of this act a final appeal may be taken to the Supreme Court of the United States.

29. The First Reconstruction Act **March 2, 1867**

An Act to provide for the more efficient Government of the Rebel States

WHEREAS no legal State governments or adequate protection for life or property now exists in the rebel States of Virginia, North Carolina, South Carolina, Georgia, Mississippi, Alabama, Louisiana, Florida, Texas, and Arkansas; and whereas it is necessary that peace and good order should be enforced in said States until loyal and republican State governments can be legally established: Therefore,

Be it enacted, That said rebel States shall be divided into military districts and made subject to the military authority of the United States as hereinafter prescribed, and for that purpose Virginia shall constitute the first district; North Carolina and South Carolina the second district; Georgia, Alabama, and Florida the third district; Mississippi and Arkansas the fourth district; and Louisiana and Texas the fifth district.

Sec. 2. That it shall be the duty of the President to assign to the command of each of said districts an officer of the army, not below the rank of brigadier-general, and to detail a sufficient military force to enable such officer to perform his duties and enforce his authority within the district to which he is assigned.

Sec. 3. That it shall be the duty of each officer assigned as aforesaid, to protect all persons in their rights of persons and property, to suppress insurrection, disorder, and violence, and to punish, or cause to be punished, all disturbers of the public peace and criminals; and to this end he may allow local civil tribunals to take jurisdiction of and to try offenders, or, when in his judgment it may be necessary for the trial of offenders, he shall have power to organize military commissions or tribunals for that purpose, and all interference under color of State authority with the exercise of military authority under this act, shall be null and void.

Sec. 4. That all persons put under military arrest by virtue of this act shall be tried without unnecessary delay, and no cruel or unusual punishment shall be inflicted, and no sentence of any military commission or tribunal hereby authorized, affecting the life or liberty of any person, shall be executed until it is approved by the officer in command of the district, and the laws and regulations for the government of the army shall not be affected by this act, except in so far as they conflict with its provisions: *Provided*, That no sentence of death under the provisions of this act shall be carried into effect without the approval of the President.

Sec. 5. That when the people of any one of said rebel States shall have formed a constitution of government in conformity with the Constitution of the United States in all respects, framed by a convention of delegates elected by the male citizens of said State, twenty-one years old and upward, of whatever race, color, or previous condition, who have been resident in said State for one year previous to the day of such election, except such as may be disfranchised for participation in the rebellion or for felony at common law, and when such constitution shall provide that the elective franchise shall be enjoyed by all such persons as have the qualifications herein stated for electors of delegates, and when such constitution shall be ratified by a majority of the persons voting on the question of ratification who are qualified as electors for delegates, and when such constitution shall have been submitted to Congress for examination and approval, and Congress shall have approved the same,

and when said State, by a vote of its legislature elected under said constitution, shall have adopted the amendment to the Constitution of the United States, proposed by the Thirty-ninth Congress, and known as article fourteen, and when said article shall have become a part of the Constitution of the United States said State shall be declared entitled to representation in Congress, and senators and representatives shall be admitted therefrom on their taking the oath prescribed by law, and then and thereafter the preceding sections of this act shall be inoperative in said State: *Provided*, That no person excluded from the privilege of holding office by said proposed amendment to the Constitution of the United States, shall be eligible to election as a member of the convention to frame a constitution for any of said rebel States, nor shall any such person vote for members of such convention.

Sec. 6. That, until the people of said rebel States shall be by law admitted to representation in the Congress of the United States, any civil governments which may exist therein shall be deemed provisional only, and in all respects subject to the paramount authority of the United States at any time to abolish, modify, control, or supersede the same; and in all elections to any office under such provisional governments all persons shall be entitled to vote, and none others, who are entitled to vote, under the provisions of the fifth section of this act; and no persons shall be eligible to any office under any such provisional governments who would be disqualified from holding office under the provisions of the third *article* of said constitutional amendment.

30. The Purchase of Alaska
March 30, 1867

Convention for the Cession of the Russian Possessions in North America to the United States

Concluded March 30, 1867. Ratifications exchanged at Washington, June 20, 1867. Proclaimed June 20, 1867.

. . . ART. I. . . . His Majesty the Emperor of all the Russias agrees to cede to the United States, by this Convention, immediately upon the exchange of the ratifications thereof, all the territory and dominion now possessed by his said Majesty on the continent of America and in the adjacent islands, the same being contained within the geographical limits herein set forth, to wit: The eastern limit is the line of demarcation between the Russian and the British possessions in North America, as established by the convention between Russia and Great Britain, of February 28—16, 1825, and described in Articles III. and IV. of said convention, in the following terms: . . .

" 'IV. With reference to the line of demarcation laid down in the preceding article, it is understood—

" '1st. That the island called Prince of Wales Island shall belong wholly to Russia,' . . .

" '2d. That whenever the summit of the mountains which extend in a direction parallel to the coast from the 56th degree of north latitude to the point of intersection of the 141st degree of west longitude shall prove to be at the distance of more than ten marine leagues from the ocean, the limit between the British possessions and the line of coast which is to belong to Russia as above mentioned, (that is to say, the limit to the possessions ceded by this convention,) shall be formed by a line parallel to the winding of the coast, and which shall never exceed the distance of ten marine leagues therefrom.' " . . .

ART. II. . . . In the cession of territory and dominion made by the preceding article are included the right of property in all public lots and squares, vacant lands, and all public buildings, fortifications, barracks, and other edifices which are not private individual property. It is, however, understood and agreed, that the churches which have been built in the ceded territory by the Russian Government, shall remain the property of such members of the Greek Oriental Church resident in the territory as may choose to worship therein. . . .

ART. III. . . . The inhabitants of the ceded territory, according to their choice, reserving their natural allegiance, may return to Russia within three years; but, if they should prefer to remain in the ceded territory, they, with the exception of uncivilized native tribes, shall be admitted to the enjoyment of all the rights, advantages, and immunities of citizens of the United States, and shall be maintained and protected in the free enjoyment of their liberty, property, and religion. The uncivilized tribes will be subject to such laws and regulations as the United States may from time to time adopt in regard to aboriginal tribes of that country. . . .

ART. VI. In consideration of the cession aforesaid, the United States agree to pay at the Treasury in Washington . . . seven million two hundred thousand dollars in gold. . . .

31. The Impeachment of President Johnson
March 2, 1868

IN THE HOUSE OF REPRESENTATIVES, UNITED STATES, *March 2, 1868.*

ARTICLES EXHIBITED BY THE HOUSE OF REPRESENTATIVES OF THE UNITED STATES, IN THE NAME OF THEMSELVES AND ALL THE PEOPLE OF THE UNITED STATES, AGAINST ANDREW JOHNSON, PRESIDENT OF THE UNITED STATES, IN MAINTENANCE AND SUPPORT OF THEIR IMPEACHMENT AGAINST HIM FOR HIGH CRIMES AND MISDEMEANORS IN OFFICE.

ARTICLE I. That said Andrew Johnson, President of the United States, on the 21st day of February, A. D. 1868, at Washington, in the district of Columbia, unmindful of the high duties of his office, of his oath of office, and of the requirement of the Constitution that he should take care that the laws be faithfully executed, did unlawfully and in violation of the Constitution and laws of the United States issue an order in writing for the removal of Edwin M. Stanton from the office of Secretary for the Department of War, said Edwin M. Stanton having been theretofore duly appointed and commissioned, by and with the advice and consent of the Senate of the United States, as such Secretary; and said Andrew Johnson, President of the United States, on the 12th day of August, A. D. 1867, and during the recess of said Senate, having suspended by his order Edwin M. Stanton from said office, and within twenty days after the first day of the next meeting of said Senate—that is to say, on the 12th day of December, in the year last aforesaid—having reported to said Senate such suspension, with the evidence and reasons for his action in the case and the name of the person designated to perform the duties of such office temporarily until the next meeting of the Senate; and said Senate thereafterwards, on the 13th day of January, A. D. 1868, having duly considered the evidence and reasons reported by said Andrew Johnson for said suspension, and having refused to concur in said suspension, whereby and by force of the provisions of an act entitled "An act regulating the tenure of certain civil offices," passed March 2, 1867, said Edwin M. Stanton did forthwith resume the functions of his office, whereof the said Andrew Johnson had then and there due notice; and said Edwin M. Stanton, by reason of the premises, on said 21st day of February, being lawfully entitled to hold said office of Secretary for the Department of War; which said order for the removal of said Edwin M. Stanton is in substance as follows; that is to say:

EXECUTIVE MANSION,
Washington, D. C., February 21, 1868.
HON. EDWIN M. STANTON,
Washington, D. C.
SIR: By virtue of the power and authority vested in me as President by the Constitution and laws of the United States, you are hereby removed from office as Secretary for the Department of War, and your functions as such will terminate upon the receipt of this communication.

You will transfer to Brevet Major-General Lorenzo Thomas, Adjutant-General of the Army, who has this day been authorized and empowered to act as Secretary of War *ad interim*, all records, books, papers, and other public property now in your custody and charge.

Respectfully, yours,
ANDREW JOHNSON.

which order was unlawfully issued with intent then and there to violate the act entitled "An act regulating the tenure of certain civil offices," passed March 2, 1867 . . . whereby said Andrew Johnson, President of the United States, did then and there commit and was guilty of a high misdemeanor in office.

ART. II. That on said 21st day of February, A. D. 1868, at Washington, in the District of Columbia, said Andrew Johnson, President of the United States, . . . did, with intent to violate the Constitution of the United States and the act aforesaid, issue and deliver to one Lorenzo Thomas a letter of authority in substance as follows; that is to say:

EXECUTIVE MANSION,
Washington, D. C., February 21, 1868.
Brevet Major-General LORENZO THOMAS,
Adjutant-General United States Army,
Washington, D. C.
SIR: The Hon. Edwin M. Stanton having been this day removed from office as Secretary for the Department of War, you are hereby authorized and empowered to act as Secretary of War *ad interim*, and will immediately enter upon the discharge of the duties pertaining to that office.

Mr. Stanton has been instructed to transfer to you all the records, books, papers, and other public property now in his custody and charge.

Respectfully yours,
ANDREW JOHNSON.

then and there being no vacancy in said office of Secretary for the Department of War; whereby said Andrew Johnson, President of the United States, did then and there commit and was guilty of a high misdemeanor in office.

ART. III. That said Andrew Johnson, President of the United States, on the 21st day of February, A. D. 1868, at Washington, in the District of Columbia, did commit and was guilty of a high misdemeanor in office in this, that without authority of law, while the Senate of the United States was then and there in session, he did appoint one Lorenzo Thomas to be Secretary for the Department of War *ad interim*, without the advice and consent of the Senate, and with intent to violate the Constitution of the United States, . . .

ART. IV. That said Andrew Johnson, President of the United States, . . . did unlawfully conspire with one Lorenzo Thomas, and with other persons to the House of Representatives unknown, with intent, by intimidation and threats, unlawfully to hinder and prevent Edwin M. Stanton, then and there the Secretary for the Department of War, . . . from holding said office of Secretary for the Department of War, contrary to and in violation of the Constitution of the United States and of the provisions of an act entitled "An act to define and punish certain conspiracies," approved July 31, 1861; . . .

ART. V. That said Andrew Johnson, President of the United States, . . . did unlawfully conspire with one Lorenzo Thomas, and with other persons to the House of Representatives unknown, to prevent and hinder the execution of an act entitled "An act regulating the tenure of certain civil offices," passed March 2, 1867. . . .

ART. VI. That said Andrew Johnson, President of the United States, . . . did unlawfully conspire with one Lorenzo Thomas by force to seize, take, and possess the property of the United States in the Department of War, and then and there in the custody and charge of Edwin M. Stanton, Secretary for said Department, contrary to the provisions of an act entitled "An act to define and punish certain conspiracies," approved July 31, 1861, and with intent to violate and disregard an act entitled

"An act regulating the tenure of certain civil offices," passed March 2, 1867; . . .

ART. VII. That said Andrew Johnson, President of the United States, . . . did unlawfully conspire with one Lorenzo Thomas with intent unlawfully to seize, take, and possess the property of the United States in the Department of War, in the custody and charge of Edwin M. Stanton, Secretary for said Department, with intent to violate and disregard the act entitled "An act regulating the tenure of certain civil offices, passed March 2, 1867; . . .

ART. VIII. That said Andrew Johnson, President of the United States, . . . with intent unlawfully to control the disbursement of the moneys appropriated for the military service and for the Department of War, . . . did unlawfully, and in violation of the Constitution of the United States, and without the advice and consent of the Senate of the United States, . . . there being no vacancy in the office of Secretary for the Department of War, and with intent to violate and disregard the act aforesaid, then and there issue and deliver to one Lorenzo Thomas a letter of authority, . . .

ART. IX. That said Andrew Johnson, President of the United States, on the 22d day of February, A. D. 1868, . . . in disregard of the Constitution and the laws of the United States duly enacted, as Commander in Chief of the Army of the United States, did bring before himself then and there William H. Emory, a major-general by brevet in the Army of the United States, actually in command of the Department of Washington and the military forces thereof, and did then and there, as such Commander in Chief, declare to and instruct said Emory that part of a law of the United States, passed March 2, 1867, entitled "An Act making appropriations for the support of the Army for the year ending June 30, 1868, and for other purposes," especially the second section thereof, which provides, among other things, that "all orders and instructions relating to military operations issued by the President or Secretary of War shall be issued through the General of the Army, and in case of his inability through the next in rank," was unconstitutional . . . with intent thereby to induce said Emory, in his official capacity as commander of the Department of Washington, to violate the provisions of said act and to take and receive, act upon, and obey such orders as he, the said Andrew Johnson, might make and give, and which should not be issued through the General of the Army of the United States, according to the provisions of said act, . . .

March 3, 1868.

The following additional articles of impeachment were agreed to, viz:

ART. X. That said Andrew Johnson, President of the United States, unmindful of the high duties of his office and the dignity and proprieties thereof, and of the harmony and courtesies which ought to exist and be maintained between the executive and legislative branches of the Government of the United States, . . . did attempt to bring into disgrace, ridicule, hatred, contempt, and reproach the Congress of the United States and the several branches thereof, to impair and destroy the regard and respect of all the good people of the United States for the Congress and legislative power thereof (which all officers of the Government ought inviolably to preserve and maintain), and to excite the odium and resentment of all the good people of the United States against Congress and the laws by it duly and constitutionally enacted; and, in pursuance of his said design and intent, openly and publicly, and before divers assemblages of the citizens of the United States, . . . did, on the 18th day of August, A. D. 1866, and on divers other days and times, . . . make and deliver with a loud voice certain intemperate, inflammatory, and scandalous harangues, and did therein utter loud threats and bitter menaces, as well against Congress as the laws of the United States, duly enacted thereby, amid the cries, jeers, and laughter of the multitudes then assembled and in hearing, which are set forth in the several specifications hereinafter written in substance and effect; that is to say:

Specification first.—In this, that at Washington, . . . in the Executive Mansion, to a committee of citizens who called upon the President of the United States, speaking of and concerning the Congress of the United States, said Andrew Johnson, President of the United States, . . . on the 18th day of August, A. D. 1866, did in a loud voice declare in substance and effect, among other things; that is to say: . . .

We have witnessed in one department of the Government every endeavor to prevent the restoration of peace, harmony, and union. We have seen hanging upon the verge of the Government, as it were, a body called, or which assumes to be, the Congress of the United States, while in fact it is a Congress of only a part of the States. We have seen this Congress pretend to be for the Union, when its every step and act tended to perpetuate disunion and make a disruption of the States inevitable. . . . We have seen Congress gradually encroach, step by step, upon constitutional rights, and violate, day after day and month after month, fundamental principles of the Government. We have seen a Congress that seemed to forget that there was a limit to the sphere and scope of legislation. We have seen a Congress in a minority assume to exercise power which, allowed to be consummated, would result in despotism or monarchy itself.

Specification second.—In this, that at Cleveland, in the State of Ohio, . . . on the 3d day of September, A. D. 1866, before a public assemblage of citizens and others, said Andrew Johnson, President of the United States, speaking of and concerning the Congress of the United States, did in a loud voice declare in substance and effect, among other things; that is to say:

I will tell you what I did do. I called upon your Congress that is trying to break up the Government. . . .

In conclusion, besides that, Congress had taken much pains to poison their constituents against him. But what had Congress done? Have they done anything to restore the Union of these

States? No. On the contrary, they have done everything to prevent it. And because he stood now where he did when the rebellion commenced, he had been denounced as a traitor. Who had run greater risks or made greater sacrifices than himself? But Congress, factious and domineering, had undertaken to poison the minds of the American people.

Specification third.—In this, that at St. Louis, in the State of Missouri, . . . on the 8th day of September, A. D. 1866, . . . said Andrew Johnson, President of the United States, speaking of and concerning the Congress of the United States, did in a loud voice declare in substance and effect, among other things; that is to say:

Go on . . . if you will go back and ascertain the cause of the riot at New Orleans, perhaps you will not be so prompt in calling out "New Orleans." If you will take up the riot at New Orleans and trace it back to its source or its immediate cause, you will find out who was responsible for the blood that was shed there. If you will take up the riot at New Orleans and trace it back to the Radical Congress, you will find that the riot at New Orleans was substantially planned. . . . You will also find that that convention did assemble, in violation of law, and the intention of that convention was to supersede the reorganized authorities in the State government of Louisiana, which had been recognized by the Government of the United States; and every man engaged in that rebellion in that convention, with the intention of superseding and upturning the civil government which had been recognized by the Government of the United States, I say that he was a traitor to the Constitution of the United States; and hence you find that another rebellion was commenced, *having its origin in the Radical Congress.* . . .

And I have been traduced, I have been slandered, I have been maligned, I have been called Judas Iscariot and all that. Now, my countrymen, here to-night, it is very easy to indulge in epithets; it is easy to call a man a Judas and cry out "traitor;" but when he is called upon to give arguments and facts he is very often found wanting. Judas Iscariot—Judas. There was a Judas, and he was one of the twelve apostles. Oh, yes; the twelve apostles had a Christ. The twelve apostles had a Christ, and he never could have had a Judas unless he had had twelve apostles. If I have played the Judas, who has been my Christ that I have played the Judas with? Was it Thad. Stevens? Was it Wendell Phillips? Was it Charles Sumner? These are the men that stop and compare themselves with the Savior, and everybody that differs with them in opinion, and to try to stay and arrest their diabolical and nefarious policy, is to be denounced as a Judas. . . .

which said utterances, declarations, threats, and harangues, highly censurable in any, are peculiarly indecent and unbecoming in the Chief Magistrate of the United States, by means whereof said Andrew Johnson has brought the high office of the President of the United States into contempt, ridicule, and disgrace, to the great scandal of all good citizens; whereby said Andrew Johnson, President of the United States, did commit and was then and there guilty of a high misdemeanor in office.

ART. XI. That said Andrew Johnson, President of the United States, . . . did on the 18th day of August, A. D. 1866, at the city of Washington, in the District of Columbia, by public speech, declare and affirm in substance that the Thirty-ninth Congress of the United States was not a Congress of the United States authorized by the Constitution to exercise legislative power under the same, but, on the contrary, was a Congress of only part of the States; thereby denying and intending to deny that the legislation of said Congress was valid or obligatory upon him, the said Andrew Johnson, except in so far as he saw fit to approve the same, . . . in pursuance of said declaration the said Andrew Johnson, President of the United States, . . . on the 21st day of February, A. D. 1868, at the city of Washington, in the District of Columbia, did unlawfully, and in disregard of the requirement of the Constitution that he should take care that the laws be faithfully executed, attempt to prevent the execution of an act entitled "An act regulating the tenure of certain civil offices," passed March 2, 1867, by unlawfully devising and contriving, and attempting to devise and contrive, means by which he should prevent Edwin M. Stanton from forthwith resuming the functions of the office of Secretary for the Department of War, notwithstanding the refusal of the Senate to concur in the suspension theretofore by said Andrew Johnson of said Edwin M. Stanton from said office of Secretary for the Department of War, and also by further unlawfully devising and contriving, and attempting to devise and contrive, means then and there to prevent the execution of an act entitled "An act making appropriations for the support of the Army for the fiscal year ending June 30, 1868, and for other purposes," approved March 2, 1867, and also to prevent the execution of an act entitled "An act to provide for the more efficient government of the rebel States," passed March 2, 1867, whereby the said Andrew Johnson, President of the United States, did then, to wit, on the 21st day of February, A. D. 1868, at the city of Washington, commit and was guilty of a high misdemeanor in office.

May 16–26, 1868
SATURDAY, MAY 16, 1868.
THE UNITED STATES *vs.* ANDREW JOHNSON, PRESIDENT.

The Chief Justice stated that, in pursuance of the order of the Senate, he would first proceed to take judgment of the Senate on the eleventh article. The roll of the Senate was called, with the following result:

The Senators who voted "guilty" are Messrs. Anthony, Cameron, Cattell, Chandler, Cole, Conkling, Conness, Corbett, Cragin, Drake, Edmunds, Ferry, Frelinghuysen, Harlan, Howard, Howe, Morgan, Morrill of Maine, Morrill of Vermont, Morton, Nye, Patterson of New Hamp-

shire, Pomeroy, Ramsey, Sherman, Sprague, Stewart, Sumner, Thayer, Tipton, Wade, Williams, Willey, Wilson, and Yates—35.

The Senators who voted "not guilty" are Messrs. Bayard, Buckalew, Davis, Dixon, Doolittle, Fessenden, Fowler, Grimes, Henderson, Hendricks, Johnson, McCreery, Norton, Patterson of Tennessee, Ross, Saulsbury, Trumbull, Van Winkle, and Vickers—19.

The Chief Justice announced that upon this article thirty-five Senators had voted "guilty" and nineteen Senators "not guilty," and declared that two-thirds of the Senators present not having pronounced him guilty, Andrew Johnson, President of the United States, stood acquitted of the charges contained in the eleventh article of impeachment.

TUESDAY, MAY 26, 1868.
THE UNITED STATES *vs.* ANDREW JOHNSON, PRESIDENT.

The Senate ordered that the vote be taken upon the second article of impeachment. The roll of the Senate was called, with the following result:

The Senators who voted "guilty" are Messrs. Anthony, Cameron, Cattell, Chandler, Cole, Conkling, Conness, Corbett, Cragin, Drake, Edmunds, Ferry, Frelinghuysen, Harlan, Howard, Howe, Morgan, Morrill of Maine, Morrill of Vermont, Morton, Nye, Patterson of New Hampshire, Pomeroy, Ramsey, Sherman, Sprague, Stewart, Sumner, Thayer, Tipton, Wade, Willey, Williams, Wilson, and Yates—35.

The Senators who voted "not guilty" are Messrs. Bayard, Buckalew, Davis, Dixon, Doolittle, Fessenden, Fowler, Grimes, Henderson, Hendricks, Johnson, McCreery, Norton, Patterson of Tennessee, Ross, Saulsbury, Trumbull, Van Winkle, and Vickers—19.

The Chief Justice announced that upon this article thirty-five Senators had voted "guilty" and nineteen Senators had voted "not guilty," and declared that two-thirds of the Senators present not having pronounced him guilty, Andrew Johnson, President of the United States, stood acquitted of the charges contained in the second article of impeachment.

The Senate ordered that the vote be taken upon the third article of impeachment. The roll of the Senate was called, with the following result:

The Senators who voted "guilty" are Messrs. Anthony, Cameron, Cattell, Chandler, Cole, Conkling, Conness, Corbett, Cragin, Drake, Edmunds, Ferry, Frelinghuysen, Harlan, Howard, Howe, Morgan, Morrill of Maine, Morrill of Vermont, Morton, Nye, Patterson of New Hampshire, Pomeroy, Ramsey, Sherman, Sprague, Stewart, Sumner, Thayer, Tipton, Wade, Willey, Williams, Wilson, and Yates—35.

The Senators who voted "not guilty" are Messrs. Bayard, Buckalew, Davis, Dixon, Doolittle, Fessenden, Fowler, Grimes, Henderson, Hendricks, Johnson, McCreery, Norton, Patterson of Tennessee, Ross, Saulsbury, Trumbull, Van Winkle, and Vickers—19.

The Chief Justice announced that upon this article thirty-five Senators had voted "guilty" and nineteen Senators had voted "not guilty," and declared that two-thirds of the Senators present not having pronounced him guilty, Andrew Johnson, President of the United States, stood acquitted of the charges contained in the third article.

No objection being made, the secretary, by direction of the Chief Justice, entered the judgment of the Senate upon the second, third, and eleventh articles, as follows:

The Senate having tried Andrew Johnson, President of the United States, upon articles of impeachment exhibited against him by the House of Representatives, and two-thirds of the Senators present not having found him guilty of the charges contained in the second, third, and eleventh articles of impeachment, it is therefore

Ordered and adjudged, That the said Andrew Johnson, President of the United States, be, and he is, acquitted of the charges in said articles made and set forth.

A motion "that the Senate sitting for the trial of the President upon articles of impeachment do now adjourn without day" was adopted by a vote of 34 yeas to 16 nays.

Those who voted in the affirmative are Messrs. Anthony, Cameron, Cattell, Chandler, Cole, Conkling, Corbett, Cragin, Drake, Edmunds, Ferry, Frelinghuysen, Harlan, Howard, Morgan, Morrill of Maine, Morrill of Vermont, Morton, Nye, Patterson of New Hampshire, Pomeroy, Ramsey, Sherman, Sprague, Stewart, Sumner, Thayer, Tipton, Van Winkle, Wade, Willey, Williams, Wilson, and Yates.

Those who voted in the negative are Messrs. Bayard, Buckalew, Davis, Dixon, Doolittle, Fowler, Henderson, Hendricks, Johnson, McCreery, Norton, Patterson of Tennessee, Ross, Saulsbury, Trumbull, and Vickers.

The Chief Justice declared the Senate sitting as a court of impeachment for the trial of Andrew Johnson, President of the United States, upon articles of impeachment exhibited against him by the House of Representatives, adjourned without day.

32. The Fourteenth Amendment Passed by Congress **June 13, 1866,** Ratified and Proclaimed **July 28, 1868**

Sec. 1: All persons born or naturalized in the United States and subject to the jurisdiction thereof, are citizens of the United States and of the State wherein they reside. No State shall make or enforce any law which shall abridge the privileges or immunities of citizens of the United States; nor shall any State deprive any person of life, liberty or property, without due process of law, nor deny any person within its jurisdiction the equal protection of the laws . . .

33. The Fifteenth Amendment
March 30, 1870

Sec. 1: The right of the citizens of the United States to vote shall not be denied or abridged by the United States or by any State on account of race, color, or previous condition of servitude.

Sec. 2: The Congress shall have power to enforce this article by appropriate legislation.

Appendix B
Major Battles of the Civil War

Name (Locale)	Date	Commanders	Theater of Operations (E-East, W-West)	Winner (N-North, S-South)
Fort Sumter, S. C.	4/12–13/1861	Anderson, Beauregard	E	S
Bull Run I (Manassas), Va.	7/21/61	McDowell, J. E. Johnson	E	S
Wilson's Creek, Mo.	8/10/61	Lyon, Price, McCulloch	W	S
Ball's Bluff (Leesburg), Va.	10/21/61	Stone, Baker, Evans	E	S
Cheat Mountain, W. Va. (McDowell)	12/13/61	Milroy, Jackson	W	Draw
Mills Spring (Logan's Cross-roads), Ky.	1/19/1862	Thomas, Zollicoffer	W	N
Fort Henry, Tenn.	2/6/62	Grant, Tilighman	W	N
Roanoke Island, N. C.	2/8/62	Burnside, Shaw	E	N
Fort Donelson, Tenn.	2/15/62	Grant, Buckner	W	N
Valverde, N. M.	2/21/62	Sibley, Canby	W	S
Pea Ridge, Ark.	3/6/62	Curtis, Van Dorn	W	N
Hampton Roads, Va. (Monitor—Merrimac/Virginia)	3/9/62	Worden, Jones	E	Draw

Name (Locale)	Date	Commanders	Theater of Operations (E-East, W-West)	Winner (N-North, S-South)
Kernstown (I), Va.	3/23/62	Jackson, Shields	E	Draw
Apache Canyon, N. M. (La Glorietta Pass)	3/26–28/62	Slough, Scurry	W	S
Pigeon's Ranch, N. M.	3/28/62	Chivington, Scurry	W	Draw
Shiloh (Pittsburgh Landing), Tenn.	4/6–7/62	Grant, Prentiss J. E. Johnston, Beauregard	W	Draw
Island No. 10, Miss.	4/6–7/62	Pope, Foote	W	N
New Orleans, La.	4/24–25/62	Farragut	W	N
Williamsburg, Va.	5/5/62	McClellan, J. E. Johnston	E	Draw
McDowell, Va.	5/8/62	Jackson, Schenk	E	S
Drewry's Bluff, Va.	5/15/62	Porter, Franklin	E	S
Winchester, Va.	5/25/62	Jackson, Ewell, Banks	E	S
Seven Pines (Fair Oaks), Va.	5/31–6/1/62	J. E. Johnston, McClellan	E	Draw
Memphis, Tenn.	6/6/62	Montgomery, Davis	W	N
Port Republic, Va.	6/8/62	Frémont, Jackson, Ewell	E	S
Secessionville, S. C.	6/16/62	Benham, Evans	E	S
Seven Days, Va. (Oak Grove, Gaines Mills, Malvern Hill etc.)	6/25–7/1/62	McClellan, Lee	E	S
Baton Rouge, La.	8/5/62	Breckinridge, Williams	W	N

Cedar Mountain (Slaughter Mountain), Va.	8/9/62	Jackson, Hill, Pope, Banks	E	Draw
Bull Run II (Manassas II)	8/29–31/62	Jackson, Longstreet, Pope	E	S
Richmond, Ky.	8/30/62	Kirby Smith, Nelson	W	S
Crampton's Gap & South Mountain, Va.	9/14/62	McLaw, Franklin, Pleasonton	E	N
Antietam (Sharpsburg), Md.	9/17/62	McClellan, Burnside, Lee, Hill	E	Draw
Corinth, Miss.	10/3–4/62	Rosecrans, Van Dorn	W	N
Perryville (Chaplin Hills), Ky.	10/8/62	Buell, Bragg	W	N
Fredericksburg, Va.	12/13/62	Burnside, Jackson	E	S
Chickasaw Bayou, Miss.	12/29/62	Sherman, Pemberton	W	S
Murfreesboro (Stone's River), Tenn.	12/31/62	Rosecrans, Bragg	W	S
Chancellorsville, Va.	5/1–4/1863	Hooker, Lee, Jackson	E	S
Champion's Hill (Baker's Creek), Miss.	5/16/63	Grant, McClernand, Pemberton	W	N
Second Winchester, Va.	6/14/63	Ewell, Milroy	E	S
Gettysburg, Va.	7/1–3/63	Meade, Lee	E	N
Vicksburg, Miss.	7/3–4/63	Grant, Pemberton	W	N
Port Hudson, La.	7/8/63	Banks, Gardner	W	N
Chickamauga, Tenn.	9/20/63	Longstreet, Thomas, Rosecrans	W	S
Chattanooga, Tenn.	11/23–24/63	Grant, Sherman, Bragg	W	N
Sabine Crossroads, La.	4/5/1864	Taylor, Banks	W	S

Name (Locale)	Date	Commanders	Theater of Operations (E-East, W-West)	Winner (N-North, S-South)
Wilderness, Va.	5/5–6/64	Meade, Lee	E	Draw
Spotsylvania, Va.	5/10–12 & 5/18–19/64	Grant, Lee	E	Draw
New Market, Va.	5/15/64	Breckinridge, Sigel	E	S
Cold Harbor, Va.	6/1–3/64	Grant, Lee	E	S
Monocacy River, Md.	7/9/64	Early, Wallace	E	S
Kernstown (II), Va.	7/24/64	Early, Crook	E	S
Ezra Church, Ga.	7/28/64	Hood, S. D. Lee	E	N
Winchester (III), Va.	9/19/64	Sheridan, Early	E	N
Cedar Creek, Va.	10/19/64	Sheridan, Early	E	N
Westport, Mo.	10/23/64	Curtis, Price	W	N
Franklin, Tenn.	11/30/64	Hood, Schofield	W	N
Nashville, Tenn.	12/15–16/64	Hood, Thomas	W	N
Port Fischer, N. C.	1/15/1865	Porter, Terry, Bragg	E	N
Boydton Plank Rd. (Hatcher's Run), Va.	2/5/65	Grant, Lee	E	Draw
New Berne, N. C.	3/8–11/65	Bragg, Cox	E	N
Averasborough, N. C.	3/16/65	Slocum, Hardee	E	N
Bentonville, N. C.	3/19–21/65	Sherman, Johnston	E	N
Fort Stedman, Va.	3/25/65	Gordon	E	N
Five Forks, Va.	4/1/65	Lee, Pickett, Sheridan, Warren	E	N

Appendix C
Biographies of Major Personalities

Adams, Charles Francis (1807–1886): Son of President John Quincy Adams, U. S. minister to Great Britain during the civil war and three years thereafter, managed to smooth over many diplomatic crises between the two countries and was a successful watchdog over possible diplomatic violations of neutrality. In the 1870s, he served as arbitrator in the case of the *Alabama* claims.

Anderson, Robert (1805–1871): A proslavery Kentuckian loyal to the Union, commander at Fort Sumter during the crisis of 1860–61. On his own initiative, moved his garrison from indefensible Fort Moultrie to Sumter on December 26, 1860. Avoiding open confrontation as long as possible, he was forced to return fire after bombardment of the fort began on April 12, 1861 and was forced to surrender the following day. Served then as brigadier general in the Department of Kentucky. When his health began to fail, he was relieved from field command. Took part in the reraising of the flag ceremony after Charleston was captured.

Atzerodt, George A. (1835–1865): Lincoln assassination conspirator, assigned to assassinate Vice President Andrew Johnson, but panicked at the last moment. He fled but was captured in Maryland, tried and hanged on July 7, 1865.

Baker, Edward Dickinson (1811–1861): London-born, Illinois politician and friend of Abraham Lincoln, Oregon senator and brigade commander under Charles Pomeroy Stone. In October 1861, he moved his brigade atop Ball's Bluff, where his troops were attacked and driven into the Potomac. Baker was killed.

Banks, Nathaniel Prentiss (1816–1894): Union general defeated by Jackson in the Shenandoah and at Cedar Mountain. Replaced Benjamin F. Butler at New Orleans, then unsuccessfully attacked Port Hudson. Led the disastrous Red River campaign in 1864, thereafter without a command.

Barlow, Francis Channing (1834–1896): Union division commander, wounded at Gettysburg and aided by Confederate General John B. Gordon. The two met many years after the war when both believed the other killed. Barlow later became the founder of the American Bar Association.

Beauregard, Pierre Gustave Toutant (1818–1893): Confederate general, bombarded Fort Sumter in April 1861 and fought at Bull Run I and Shiloh. Evacuated Corinth, later defeated Benjamin F. Butler at Drewry's Bluff, also participated in the defense of Petersburg. Had many conflicts with Jefferson Davis. Was powerless to stop Sherman's march to the sea.

Beecher, Henry Ward (1813–1887): Prominent abolitionist speaker, fought the Fugitive-Slave laws and supported antislavery settlements in Kansas. Critical of Lincoln for delaying emancipation, but favored quick return of the seceded states to the Union after the war. Brother of Harriet Beecher Stowe.

Booth, John Wilkes (1838–1865): Lincoln's assassin. He was an actor, like his more famous brother Edwin Thomas. Unlike the rest of his family, his sympathies were entirely with the South, but he never entered military service. Seems to have planned the kidnapping of President-elect Lincoln in 1861, and later engaged in several plots to capture Lincoln and take him to Richmond. Shot Lincoln in the back of his head on April 14, 1865, at Ford's Theater in Washington; also wounded Major Rathbone, guest in the presidential lodge. Jumping from the box, he broke his leg but managed to escape. Assisted by his fellow conspirator Herold, he entered Virginia and crossed the Rappahannock River, but was trapped by a cavalry detachment near Port Royal, at the farm of Richard H. Garrett. He refused to surrender and the tobacco shed he occupied was set afire. He either shot himself or was killed by Union bullets. The rest of his conspirators failed, except for Lewis T. Powell, who wounded Secretary of State Seward.

Boyd, Belle (1843–1900): Most famous of the Confederate spies, worked for Jackson during the Shenandoah Valley campaign 1862. Arrested in July of that year, then released and again arrested at Martinsburg. Again released because of ill health, she was captured on a blockade runner, and married the prize master, Samuel Hardinge, who allowed her to proceed to Canada and England. In England she had a stage career.

Bragg, Braxton (1817–1876): Confederate general, fought at Shiloh, Perryville and Murfreesboro, won an important victory at Chickamauga, but was constantly engaged in disputes with his subordinates. Laid siege to Chattanooga where he was defeated by Grant. Became advisor to Jefferson Davis, who had staunchly supported him.

Breckinridge, John Cabell (1821–1875): Vice president under Buchanan, fought for the neutrality of his native Kentucky. In 1860, candidate for the Southern faction of the Democratic party. He received 72 votes in the electoral college, continued to work for the neutrality of Kentucky and remained in the Senate until October 1861. He then joined the Confederate army and fought at Fort Donelson, Vicksburg, Murfreesboro and Chattanooga. He was then transferred to Virginia and fought at New Market and, under Lee, at Cold Harbor, also under Early, at Monocacy. Finally he became Jefferson Davis's war secretary.

Bright, John (1811–1889): British statesman and orator, son of a Quaker, fought against the corn laws and against British participation in the Crimean war. Served in Gladstone's cabinet and sympathised with the Union cause.

Brown, John (1800–1859): Abolitionist, born in Connecticut, helped establish a free state settlement at Osawatomie, Kansas, and organized the raid along the Pottawatamie Creek where he murdered five men. In October 1859, he took over the armory at Harper's Ferry. He and his party of 21 men killed six people and seized hostages. His plan was to set up

a free state for slaves in the Virginia and Maryland mountains. A detachment of marines under Robert E. Lee and Jeb Stuart arrived the following day and stormed the armory. Brown's two sons were killed and he was knocked unconscious and taken prisoner. After a trial in Charlestown, Virginia, he was hanged on December 2, 1859, after a spirited defence. He became a myth and a martyr of many abolitionists and blacks.

Brown, Joseph Emerson (1821–1894): Governor of Georgia, extreme states' rights man, violently opposed Jefferson Davis's conscription policy. Davis considered him a major obstacle in the prosecution of the war. In June 1865 he turned Republican, but returned to the Democrats in 1880 and became senator for Georgia.

Buchanan, James (1791–1868): Democratic president of the United States 1857–61, attempted to appease the South by his proslavery leanings. He could not prevent the division of the Democratic Party in 1860, and after Lincoln's election pursued delaying tactics, leaving all major decisions to his successor. He left Major Anderson at Fort Sumter without sufficient instructions and did not reinforce the fort. When war broke out, he sided with the Union.

Buckner, Simon Bolivar (1823–1914): Confederate general, tried to reinforce Fort Donelson and was abandoned there by his superiors Floyd and Pillow. Receiver of Grant's famous demand for "unconditional surrender." Fought under Bragg in Tennessee, then under Longstreet at Knoxville. He was finally ordered to join Kirby Smith's cut-off trans-Mississippi detachment. Served as pallbearer at his old friend Grant's funeral. Became governor of Kentucky, was vice presidential candidate in 1896.

Buell, Don Carlos (1818–1898): Helped organize the Army of the Potomac under his friend McClellan, then commanded in eastern Tennessee and took Nashville. Played a decisive role in the battle of Shiloh. Then moved his troops toward Chattanooga, but was forced back by Bragg's invasion of Kentucky. Participated in the battle of Perryville, but was slow in pursuing the enemy and was relieved in October 1862.

Burnside, Ambrose Everett (1824–1881): Union general, successful at Roanoke Island and New Berne, twice refused the command of the main Union army. Fought at Bull Run II, South Mountain and Antietam. After McClellan's removal, took command of the Army of the Potomac and suffered a severe defeat at

Fredericksburg. After the utter failure of his "Mud-March" in January 1863, he resigned and was given command in the Department of the Ohio. He advanced to Knoxville and was there besieged by Longstreet. Fought also at the Wilderness, Spotsylvania and Cold Harbor; participated in the siege of Petersburg where he failed to follow up on the great mine explosion. Resigned in April 1865 and served as Rhode Island's governor and senator until his death. The term "sideburns," derived from his peculiar whiskers, is his main legacy.

Butler, Benjamin Franklin (1818–1893): Born in New Hampshire, supported Jefferson Davis, then Breckinridge for the presidency in 1860, Then became a War Democrat and helped the Union cause in Maryland, lifting the blockade of Washington right after the outbreak of hostilities. His declaration that escaping slaves were "contraband" became controversial, and even more so his regime in captured New Orleans—in particular his "Woman Order," which was received with great indignation throughout the South and in England. He was removed from his post in December 1862 and branded an outlaw by Jefferson Davis. Unsuccessful as military commander at Petersburg and Fort Fischer, he was removed from command. Became a radical Republican and a leader of the movement to remove Andrew Johnson. Presidential candidate of the Greenback Party in 1884.

Calhoun, John Caldwell (1782–1850): South Carolina lawyer, known as the "father of the secession" and "father of the Confederacy." Vice president under John Quincy Adams and Andrew Jackson, developer of the theory of "nullification," threatened to use force against the North decades before the outbreak of the Civil War. Secretary of state under John Tyler, he remained the most eloquent and determined defender of slavery and the equal rights of the South until his death.

Cameron, Simon (1799–1889): Political boss of Pennsylvania for half a century, Democratic senator in 1845, turned Republican in 1857. At the 1860 convention, he switched his support to Lincoln when the Lincoln's managers promised him a cabinet post. He became Lincoln's first secretary of war, but his administration was full of war contract corruption, and he was forced to resign in January 1862. As minister to Russia he assured that country's support of the Union cause. He supported Lincoln in 1864. He was repeatedly accused of corruption, but managed to serve in the Senate from 1867 to 1877 and even passed

his seat on to his son. His political machine in Pennsylvania survived until 1921.

Chase, Salmon Portland (1808–1873): Born in New Hampshire and raised in Ohio, extreme antislavery political, presidential contender in 1860. Lincoln made him secretary of the treasury in March 1861. He repeatedly came into conflict with Secretary of State Seward. Mentioned as an alternative presidential candidate in 1864. Lincoln finally accepted his offer to resign in June 1864 and made him Chief Justice in December of that year. Strong supporter of the war effort and of radical reconstruction. Presided impartially over the impeachment trial of Andrew Johnson and become a Democrat in 1870. He declared the Legal Tender Act of 1862 unconstitutional, but in 1870 reversed himself. Continued to run for the presidency.

Chesnut, Mary Boykin (1823–1886): Well-known Civil War diarist, was in touch with the inner circles of the Confederacy throughout the war because of her husband's position in the Confederate government. Started her diary in February 1861 and kept it up through the war. She and her husband lost much of their fortune and never got over the defeat of the South.

Clay, Henry (1777–1852): Born in Virginia, became active in Kentucky politics, then in the House and Senate. He pushed the "Missouri Compromise" in 1820, which settled the slavery question for several decades. Disliked Andrew Jackson and became a Whig leader. Helped to promote the Compromise Tariff of 1833. Ran for president against Polk in 1844 and opposed the annexation of Texas. Reentered the Senate in 1849 and once more managed to find a temporary solution of the slavery controversy in the Compromise of 1850. Known as the "Great Compromiser."

Cleburne, Patrick Ronayne (1828–1864): Confederate general, the "Stonewall of the West," born in Ireland, fought at Shiloh, Corinth, Perryville, Murfreesboro, Chickamauga and Chattanooga. In winter of 1864/65, he proposed abolishing slavery in "reasonable time" and recruiting blacks for military service. He fell at the battle of Franklin.

Cobden, Richard (1804–1865): British politician, spokesman for free trade and the Manchester School, fought for the repeal of the corn laws. Like his close associate John Bright, he favored the Union during the Civil War.

Cox, Jacob Dolson (1828–1900): Union general, fought

in Maryland, western Virginia and Tennessee—where he stopped Hood's invasion. Later participated in Sherman's Carolina campaign. Supported Andrew Johnson's Reconstruction policies, but later broke with him and became a Grant partisan. Under Grant, he served as secretary of the interior, but resigned late in 1870.

Crittenden, John Jordan (1787–1863): Kentucky politician who tried to prevent the outbreak of hostilities by proposing a compromise characterized by the extension of the Missouri Compromise. His efforts failed. He also helped to keep Kentucky in the Union.

Curtis, Samuel Ryan (1805–1866): Union general, defeated the Confederates under Van Dorn at Pea Ridge, Arkansas, in March 1862. In 1863, he was removed because conflicts had developed with Governor Gamble of Missouri. In 1864, he participated in the repulse of Price's invasion of Missouri.

Custer, George Armstrong (1839–1876): Union cavalry general, served first under McClellan and fought at Antietam, Chancellorsville and Gettysburg, where he helped to defeat Jeb Stuart's attack. Played a major role at Yellow Tavern, Winchester, Cedar Creek and Five Forks. After the war, he rose to lieutenant colonel, fought the Indians and was killed in the massacre of Little Big Horn in 1876.

Daly, Maria Lydig (1824–1894): Wife of a prominent New York City judge and a pro-Union Democrat, wrote the *Diary of a Union Lady, 1861–1865.* She was an admirer of McClellan and extremely critical of Lincoln. Her diary is of great interest.

Dana, Charles Anderson (1819–1897): Managing editor of Greeley's *New York Tribune*, worked for the War Department and reported criticisms of Rosecrans and Grant. Lincoln made him assistant secretary of war. After the war, he became the publisher and editor of the *New York Sun.*

Davis, Jefferson (1808–1889): Only president of the Confederacy. Born in Kentucky, graduated from West Point. Eloped with the daughter of his commander, Zachary Taylor. Colonel of the 1st Mississippi Rifles during the Mexican War, then member of the House and Senate. Secretary of war under Pierce. Emphatic supporter of the states' rights, he withdrew from the Senate in January 1861 and was elected president of the Confederacy the following month. Throughout the war, he participated actively in all military decisions and irritated many of his supporters by his support of Pemberton and Bragg, and his feuds with Beauregard and J. E. Johnston. Also antagonized

many states' rights defenders by his autocratic ways and attempts to centralize his government. He and his cabinet fled from Richmond when Lee withdrew his troops; he was captured in Georgia on May 10, 1865. He was imprisoned at Fort Monroe and faced charges of treason, but was never brought to trial. Released after two years. In his autobiography, he blamed part of the Southern defeat on Johnston and Beauregard. He never sought to have his citizenship restored, but this was done anyway under President Carter. It seems that he is more popular in the South now than he was during his administration.

DeBow, James Dunwoody Brownson (1820–1867): Editor of *DeBow's Review* (New Orleans) and an ardent secessionist. He supported Breckinridge, then Jefferson Davis, and had considerable influence on forming public opinion in the South. He also served in the Confederate Treasury Department.

Dodd, David Owen (1846–1864): Confederate spy, born in Texas, was caught at the capture of Little Rock with Morse-coded notes on Union troop strength. Sentenced to hang, but was offered his life if he would reveal his helpers. He refused and was hanged in January of 1864, only 17 years old.

Doubleday, Abner (1819–1893): West Pointer and Union career artillerist, served under Anderson at Fort Sumter, firing the first shot against the attacking Confederates. Then fought at Bull Run II, South Mountain, Antietam and Fredericksburg, Chancellorsville and Gettysburg. After the last battle, he was relieved for having moved too slowly. Wrote *Reminiscences* on Fort Sumter and on the battles of Chancellorsville and Gettysburg. He has been incorrectly credited with the invention of baseball.

Douglas, Stephen Arnold (1813–1861): Leading Democratic politician, born in Vermont, but became a prominent representative of Illinois. Originator of the Kansas–Nebraska Act of 1854, which superceded the old Missouri Compromise and left Kansas wide open for civil war. His popular sovereignty theory did not succeed in keeping the Democratic Party together. His public discussions with Lincoln, his contender for the Illinois Senate in 1858, made Lincoln famous although Douglas won the election. Eventually he alienated the Southern Democrats, and, while he attained the Democratic presidential nomination, he was undercut by the Southern proslavery Democrats who nominated Breckinridge, thus paving the way for the Republican Lincoln. He tried to find a compromise until the bombardment of Fort Sumter began, whereafter he strongly supported the administration. He died in June 1861 before major hostilities began.

Douglass, Frederick (1817–1895): Escaped slavery in 1838 and became a day laborer in New Bedford, Massachusetts. William Lloyd Garrison hired him as a speaker for the Anti-Slavery Society. He later broke with Garrison as he did not believe in his nonresistance policy. Founded *The North Star* in 1847. He sympathized with John Brown and fled the country after the raid on Harper's Ferry. After his return, he tried to convince Lincoln to fight openly against slavery and to enlist black men. Sided with the radical Republicans after the war and served under Grant in various capacities, always fighting for improvement of the conditions of freedmen.

Early, Jubal Anderson (1816–1894): Confederate general, fought at Bull Run I, Williamsburg, Malvern Hill, Antietam, Bull Run II, Fredericksburg, Chancellorsville and Gettysburg. He commanded in the Shenandoah Valley in the Winter of 1863–64. Then participated at the battles of the Wilderness, Spotsylvania and Cold Harbor, and invaded the Shenandoah Valley and Maryland once more. Before retreating to Virginia, he burned Chambersburg, Pennsylvania. In September and October of 1864, he was decisively defeated by Sheridan and was recalled by Lee. He refused to return and was removed by Lee when his forces were destroyed at Waynesboro in March 1865. Early fled to Mexico, but soon returned and became president of the Southern Historical Society. He became a defender of Lee and feuded with Longstreet who had turned Republican.

Ellet, Charles (1810–1862): Engineer, sold the idea of unarmed, speedy ram-boats to Secretary Stanton. His flotilla of rams destroyed the Confederate fleet at Memphis on April 28, 1862, with Ellet as the only Union casualty in this encounter; he died of his wounds on June 6 of that year.

Ellsworth, Ephraim Ellmer (1837–1861): Union colonel and close friend of Abraham Lincoln, became the first martyr for the Union. While occupying Alexandra, Virginia, he removed a Confederate flag from the Marshall House and was shot by the proprietor while descending.

Emerson, Ralph Waldo (1803–1882): Essayist, poet and philosopher, born in Boston, became strongly interested in abolitionism during the 1850s and actively supported the North during the war.

Ewell, Richard Stoddert (1817–1872): Confederate general, served under Jackson at Bull Run I, then in the Shenandoah Valley, the Seven Days' battle and at Cedar Mountain. In the beginning of Bull Run II, he lost a leg. After his recovery, he took over Jackson's corps and won a great victory at Winchester, but at Gettysburg failed to exploit the situation on the first evening, finding Lee's instructions too vague. At Spotsylvania he lost one of his divisions and after North Anna relinquished his command. Captured at Sayler's Creek April 6, 1865.

Farragut, David Glasgow (1801–1870): Union Navy commander, became famous by running the batteries below New Orleans and occupying the city. He was made rear admiral and fought at Vicksburg. He captured Galveston, Corpus Christi and Sabine Pass. After the capture of Port Hudson, he received a hero's welcome in New York. At Mobile Bay, he is supposed to have uttered: "Damn the torpedos [mines]—full speed ahead!" One of the first to enter Richmond, and the first to hold the rank of full admiral in the U. S. service.

Fessenden, William Pitt (1806–1869): Maine Republican, resigned his seat in the Senate to become secretary of the treasury, succeeding Salmon P. Chase. Then, as senator again, was member of the Joint Committee on Reconstruction, where he was more conservative than his friends had expected.

Fillmore, Millard (1800–1874): President of the United States 1850–1853, running mate of Whig President Taylor, encouraged the Compromise of 1850 and made Daniel Webster secretary of state. Was not renominated in 1852 and could not stop the disintegration of the Whig Party. Then joined the Know-Nothing Movement, opposed Lincoln and supported Andrew Johnson against the radical reconstructionists.

Foote, Andrew Hull (1806–1863): Union admiral, known as the "Gunboat Commodore," cooperated with Grant in the capture of Forts Henry and Donelson and took part in the operations against Island #10. Died of Bright's Disease in the middle of the war.

Forrest, Nathan Bedford (1821–1877): Tennessee slave trader and plantation owner, raised a mounted battalion at his own expense. Fought at Fort Donelson, Corinth and raised a brigade with which he captured Murfreesboro in 1862. In June 1863, he was wounded by a disgruntled subordinate. His raids in Tennessee proved to be very dangerous for Grant, Sherman and other Union commanders. Forrest had disputes with Bragg and Wheeler. When his forces captured Fort Pillow, he was made responsible for the massacre of black troops taken prisoner there. Helped Hood to invade Tennessee in fall of 1864. After that, his troops began to dwindle away. After the war, he resumed planting and became an early leader of the Ku Klux Klan.

Frémont, John Charles (1813–1890): Western explorer, played a major part in securing California for the United States, but was forced to resign his army commission after disobeying orders of the head of the local government, appointed by Washington. Then made a fortune in gold that was found on his California property. First presidential candidate of the Republicans in 1856, he lost to Buchanan. When war broke out, Lincoln made him commander of the Western Department, where he failed to provide support for his subordinate Lyon. On August 30, 1861, he declared martial law and issued an emancipation declaration that was revoked by Lincoln. Although his wife, Jessie Benton Frémont, argued with Lincoln personally at the White House, Frémont was relieved of his post in November 1861. He was unsuccessful as commander of the Mountain Department and in fighting Jackson in the Shenandoah Valley. He refused to serve under John Pope in the Army of Virginia and was relieved. Mentioned as a Republican candidate for the presidency in 1864, he withdrew in favor of McClellan.

Garfield, James Abram (1831–1881): President of the United States, took part in the actions at Shiloh and Corinth, was also member of the commission which cashiered Fitz-John Porter; then Rosecrans's chief of staff, participated at Chickamauga and Chattanooga. Was highly critical of Rosecrans and resigned his commission at the end of 1863. Then served nine terms in the House and a member of the commission that settled the Tilden-Hayes dispute in 1876. Elected President in 1880; shot by Charles J. Guiteau, a disappointed office seeker, on July 2, 1881. He died 11 weeks later.

Garrison, William Lloyd (1805–1879): Leader of the abolitionist movement for more than three decades. Founded the *Liberator* in 1831 and remained its head until 1866. Also cofounded the American Anti-Slavery Society. Was opposed to any use of violence. Supported the Lincoln administration only after the Emancipation Proclamation. Was also involved in the prohibition and women's suffrage movements.

Gist, States Rights (1831–1864): Confederate general, fought at Fort Sumter, and Bull Run I, also at Vicksburg under J. E. Johnston and at the defense of Jackson, Mississippi. Fought under Bragg at Chickamauga and Chattanooga, and during the Atlanta Campaign against Sherman. He was killed at the assault on Franklin on November 30, 1864.

Gladstone, William Ewart (1809–1898): British statesman, dominant Liberal leader between 1864 and 1894, four times prime minister between 1863 and 1894. During the Civil War, as chancellor of the exchequer, he was more inclined to recognize the independence of the Confederacy than was Prime Minister Palmerston.

Gordon, John Brown (1832–1904): Confederate general, fought at Bull Run I, Williamsburg and through the Seven Days. Wounded at Antietam, fought again at Chancellorsville and Gettysburg. He earned Lee's praise at the battle of the Wilderness and was made major general after Spotsylvania. Saw further action at Cold Harbor, Monocacy and Cedar Creek. Led the last Confederate attack against Fort Stedman in April 1865.

Gorgas, Josiah (1818–1883): Chief ordnance officer of the Confederacy throughout the war. In spite of a dismal lack of materials and the Union blockade, he managed to keep the Confederate armies relatively well supplied. Organized a fleet of blockade runners; J. E. Johnston admired him greatly.

Grant, Ulysses Simpson (1822–1885): Supreme Union commander during the last part of the war. Born near New Richmond, Ohio, originally named Hiram Ulysses Grant. Attended West Point where he excelled in horsemanship. Served under Zachary Taylor and Winfield Scott during the Mexican War. Resigned his captaincy in 1854 amid rumors of heavy drinking and tried several civilian jobs, unsuccessfully. When war broke out, his first applications to the War Department met with no success. Was finally given assignments in Kentucky and Missouri. His first fame came with the capture of Fort Henry and Fort Donelson, where his nickname "Unconditional Surrender" Grant originated. Then got in conflict with his superior, General Halleck. He was surprised by the Confederates at Shiloh, but restored the situation the next day. His advance on Corinth was delayed by Halleck's cautious tactics. Grant's first attempts against Vicksburg failed, but in April 1863 he started a brilliant maneuver by crossing the Mississippi River south of the city and advancing only after having taken Jackson. When Vicksburg fell on

July 4, 1863, he was made major general, then given charge of all the armies in the West. He then saved the situation at Chattanooga and in the winter of 1863/64 was given command of all the Union armies. He engaged in a long campaign against Lee, fighting him at the Wilderness, Spotsylvania and Cold Harbor where he was soundly defeated by Lee. But he turned south and besieged Petersburg and Richmond and took both cities after a 10-month siege. After Lee's surrender at Appomattox and Lincoln's death he became the most popular man in the country. Johnson ordered him to replace Stanton as secretary of war, but Grant resigned readily when Congress reinstated Stanton, which earned him Johnson's wrath. In 1868, he was nominated and elected president, but he appointed many undeserving friends and relatives who exploited their positions for their personal gain. The result was a series of unprecedented scandals; these however, left him personally untainted and did not prevent his reelection in 1872, against Horace Greeley. Under his administration, white suprematists regained full control of the South. His efforts for another nomination failed, as did a number of financial ventures he engaged in after his second term. Wrote his excellent *Memoirs* while dying of cancer of the throat.

Greeley, Horace (1811–1872): Founder of the *New York Tribune*, abolitionist, opposed Lincoln in 1860 but eventually backed him in 1864. Was critical of Johnson's lenient treatment of the South. Criticized corruption under Grant and became the leader of the Liberal Republican movement in 1872, as whose Presidential candidate he was thoroughly beaten by Grant. As a result of this defeat and the death of his wife, he lost his mind and died a few weeks later.

Grierson, Benjamin Henry (1826–1911): Union cavalry commander, famous for his daring, 800-mile ride from La Grange, Tennessee to Baton Rouge, Louisiana, undertaken to distract attention from Grant's crossing the Mississippi south of Vicksburg, in April and May 1863. He conducted a second major Mississippi raid in 1864, and also participated in the attacks on Mobile, Alabama.

Halleck, Henry Wagner (1815–1872): Union army chief of staff, born in New York, West Pointer, resigned his captaincy in 1854 and became a successful San Francisco lawyer after having written several books on military matters. Succeeded Frémont in the West, and, after the fall of Forts Henry and Donelson, was appointed commander of all forces in the West.

He proved too slow, however, as a field commander, allowing the Confederates to escape from Corinth. A good administrator, he then served under Grant as his army staff head. Never popular with his troops, he was head of the occupied Division of the South during the Reconstruction at his death.

Hampton, Wade (1818–1902): One of the largest Southern slave and plantation owners, fought at Bull Run I, Seven Pines and the Seven Days, but became famous as a cavalry raider, participating in Stuart's ride around McClellan's army in Maryland. Wounded in a cavalry fight at Gettysburg, but fought again at the Wilderness. In August 1864, he was given the overall command of the mounted Confederate troops, and managed a raid as late as September 1864 that brought 2,500 cattle to the hungry Confederate soldiers. Then put in charge of all of Johnston's cavalry, he surrendered with Johnston.

Hardee, William Joseph (1815–1873): Born in Georgia, West Pointer, wrote textbooks on rifle and light infantry tactics that became standard and were used by both sides. Joined the Confederacy and was wounded at Shiloh, later served under Bragg and Hood whom he disliked. He succeeded in evacuating Savannah at the last moment. After the war, he became an Alabama plantation owner.

Harrison, Benjamin (1833–1901): Grandson of President William Henry ("Tippecanoe") Harrison, Union general who fought in the Atlanta campaign. During Sherman's march to the sea fought in Nashville, later in the Carolinas. Senator after the war, he was elected as Republican president in 1888, but defeated for reelection by Cleveland in 1892.

Haupt, Herman (1817–1905): Civil engineer and specialist in bridge building and railroads, was most useful to the Union by introducing many innovations for repairing damaged railroads and rebuilding bridges. Lincoln admired his "bean-pole bridges." He never accepted his commission as a brigadier general. Wrote *General Theory of Bridge Construction*, and, after the war, several treatises on railroading.

Heintzelman, Samuel Peter (1805–1880): Native of Pennsylvania and West Pointer, wounded at Bull Run I, and overly cautious at Yorktown during McClellan's Peninsula Campaign, but successful at Seven Pines. Also fought at Seven Days and Bull Run II. Was then put in charge of the Washington fortifications.

Herold, David E. (1842–1865): Unemployed druggist's clerk, involved in Booth's plan to kidnap Lincoln, helped Booth to escape and to reach Virginia after the assassination. When surrounded by Union cavalry, together with Booth, he surrendered, cursed by Booth. Herold was tried by a military court and hanged in Washington, July 7, 1865.

Hill, Ambrose Powell (1825–1865): Confederate general, directed the fight at Hanover Court House during Bull Run I, also fought as division commander at Cedar Mountain, Bull Run II and at the capture of Harper's Ferry. Participated in Jackson's march around the Union flank and was wounded carrying the wounded Jackson to the rear. He performed poorly at Gettysburg and at the Wilderness, but returned for the fighting at North Anna and Cold Harbor. During the last days of the war, he was killed at the siege of Petersburg.

Holden, William Woods (1812–1892): North Carolina journalist and politician, switched his allegiance from Douglas to Breckinridge, inbetween was a Union delegate, then got in opposition to the Davis administration and favored peace. In 1864, he lost his bid for governor of North Carolina to Zebulon Vance. In May 1865, Andrew Johnson appointed him provisional governor of North Carolina, but he was then defeated for a regular term. His editorials in the *North Carolina Standard* then took on a Radical Republican slant. He was elected as Republican governor in 1868. His term was marked by corruption.

Holmes, Oliver Wendell (1841–1935): Son of the writer Oliver Wendell Holmes and future Supreme Court Justice, fought with the Union army and was wounded at Ball's Bluff and Antietam, also fought at Fredericksburg. Mustered out as captain. He is reported to have warned Lincoln at Fort Stevens, near Washington, in unmistakable terms not to raise his head above the breastworks.

Hood, John Bell (1831–1879): Born in Kentucky, West Pointer, joined the South and fought at Seven Pines, Seven Days and Bull Run II. Wounded in the arm at Gettysburg and lost his leg at Chickamauga. In the Atlanta campaign, he disagreed with Hardee and Johnston, whom he finally replaced. His attacks on Sherman's army proved disastrous, and he was equally unsuccessful at Franklin and Nashville. After the war, he became a prosperous merchant.

Hooker, Joseph (1814–1879): Fought under McClellan at the Peninsula, also at Williamsburg and Malvern Hill, then under Pope at Bull Run II. After Burnside's "Mud March," Lincoln made Hooker commander of the Army of the Potomac, although

Lincoln was aware of his poor reputation and his constant fights with his superiors. He proved an utter failure at the Wilderness. In the Gettysburg campaign, he resigned a few days before the battle. He participated in battles around Chattanooga, but resigned when he was not appointed successor to McPherson.

Jackson, Andrew (1767–1845): President of the United States 1829–1837, started as politician and judge in Tennessee, then as military commander against the Indians and then against the British in the battle of New Orleans, 1812. Became a national hero and head of a popular movement that advocated greater participation of the common man in government, fighting all privileges and monopolies. After his election as president, he introduced the "spoils system" by which party members were awarded government posts. He coerced South Carolina and his Vice President Calhoun to accept the federal tariff. He fought against the Bank of the United States, and beat Clay in the election campaign of 1832. Highly controversial, despised by his adversaries as a high-handed dictator and admired by his friends as a frontiersman and forceful Democratic leader, he is considered the real founder of the Democratic Party, while his enemies united in the Whig Party. Neither party ever took a clear stand in the question of slavery.

Jackson, Thomas Jonathan ("Stonewall") (1824–1863): After Lee the most revered of the Confederate commanders. Born in Clarksburg, western Virginia, went to West Point and served in the Mexican War. He earned his nickname at Bull Run I. In March 1862, he was defeated at Kernstown in the Shenandoah, but in May defeated Frémont at McDowell and launched his brilliant campaign through the valley, but showed little vigor in support of Lee during the Seven Days battle. He brought about the victory at Bull Run II, captured Harper's Ferry and distinguished himself at Antietam. He also won at Fredericksburg. His greatest victory was at Chancellorsville where he was mortally wounded by his own troops. His arm was amputated and he died a week later. Lee is supposed to have said that, had Jackson been alive, the battle of Gettysburg would not have been lost.

Johnson, Andrew (1808–1875): President of the United States, 1865–1869. Born in North Carolina, started as a tailor, and is supposed to have learnt how to read and write from his wife. Started in politics as a Jacksonian Democrat, first in the state house, then as a congressman, then governor of Tennessee 1853–1857. He was an opponent to the slaveowners' power, but no abolitionist. Lincoln made him military governor of Tennessee (1862–65), and chose him as running mate in 1864. Sworn in as president on April 15, 1865, he tried to follow Lincoln's reconstruction ideas. He granted many pardons and reestablished Southern state governments, but got in conflict with the Republican-dominated Congress as soon as it reconvened. He opposed its much stricter reconstruction policy and refused to sign the laws passed by Congress, while Congress curtailed his powers more and more. When he suspended Secretary of War Stanton, he was impeached by the House and was acquitted in the Senate by 35 votes for conviction and 19 against (a two-thirds majority was required). He remained powerless until his term expired, failed to be elected into the Senate in 1871 and 1873, but succeeded in 1875. He died shortly thereafter.

Johnston, Albert Sidney (1803–1862): Born in Kentucky, went to West Point, and commanded the 1st Texas Rifles in the Mexican War. Joined the Confederate army and was given the command of the western theater. He had to abandon Kentucky and most of Tennessee, but succeeded in surprising Grant in the battle of Shiloh. There he was wounded in the leg and bled to death. Considered one of the best soldiers, North or South.

Johnston, Joseph Eggleston (1807–1891): Native of Virginia and West Pointer, had a distinguished career including service in the Mexican war before he resigned his commission after Virginia seceded. Managed to fool the Union general in the Shenandoah by detaching himself and participating in Bull Run I. Although he was made full general after this, he was displeased by being ranked only number four out of five. This, coupled with Johnston's withdrawing from Manassas Junction, angered Jefferson Davis. In May 1862, he launched an attack south of the Chickahominy River and fought the battle of Fair Oaks, where McClellan was beaten. He was then given the command of the West, but too few troops to prevent Sherman's and Grant's advance to Jackson, Mississippi and Vicksburg. He was then put in charge of Bragg's army, beaten at Chattanooga and operated skillfully against the advancing Sherman. But Jefferson Davis was displeased with his constant withdrawals and relieved him. The Confederate Congress insisted on his reappointment, but by this time his

troops were too weak to stop Sherman's advance. He was one of the most effective Confederate commanders. In his *Narrative of Military Operations*, he was highly critical of Davis. He died from a cold caught at the funeral of his main opponent, Sherman.

Juarez, Benito (1806–1872): One of Mexico's great leaders, a Zapotec Indian, governor of Oaxaca, then president of Mexico, was confronted with a military invasion of the British, Spanish and French. Only the French remained; they placed Archduke Maximilian on an imperial throne. Juarez received aid from the United States, which did not wish French intervention in favor of the Confederacy. At the end of the civil war, the French withdrew their troops, and Maximilian was overthrown by Juarez, who had him shot in 1867.

Kennedy, Robert Cobb (1835–1865): Tried to burn down New York City. Born in Georgia, he fought as a captain at Shiloh, was later captured and escaped to Canada in October 1864. He and seven others then went to New York to set the city aflame, but the fires set in several hotels and in Barnum's Museum proved ineffective. In December 1864, he tried to return to the Confederacy, but was captured near Detroit and was sentenced to hang as a spy by a New York military commission.

Laird, John (1805–1874): English engineer, constructed iron ships equipped with guns. His company, led by his sons, constructed the *Alabama* for the Confederacy. Two further "rams" were contracted by the South, but seized by British authorities.

Lamon, Ward Hill (1828–1893): Law partner and frequent bodyguard of Abraham Lincoln. He took part in altering the president-elect's route to Washington when a conspiracy to assassinate him was suspected. During the war, he was marshal of the District of Columbia. Extremely loyal to Lincoln, he was nevertheless often attacked in the Senate for his antiabolitionist views. He was in Richmond when Lincoln was assassinated.

Lee, Robert Edward (1807–1870): Most successful and popular general and leader of the South, born at Stratford, Virginia, graduated from West Point in 1829 and was posted to the engineers. Fought in the Mexican War, then headed West Point in 1852. Led a force of marines against John Brown's men at Harper's Ferry. Winfield Scott tried to keep him in the Union army, but Lee joined the Confederacy after Virginia seceded. His first campaign in western Virginia's Cheat Mountains was unsuccessful. Jefferson

Davis made him his military advisor. After Seven Pines, Lee took over the Army of Northern Virginia. In the Seven Days' battle managed to remove McClellan's army from the gates of Richmond. Thereafter, he was affectionately known as "Marse Robert." He won decisive battles at Bull Run II, Fredericksburg and Chancellorsville, but after a desperate fight lost at Gettysburg, from where, however, he retreated brilliantly. Fought a retiring campaign from the Wilderness to Petersburg against Grant, and held out at Petersburg and Richmond for almost 10 months against overwhelming odds. In January 1865 he had been made commander in chief of all the Confederate armies. He surrendered to Grant at Appomattox in April 1865. After the war, he became president of Washington College in Lexington, Virginia.

Lincoln, Abraham (1809–1865): President of the United States during the Civil War. Born in a log cabin in backwoods Hardin County, Kentucky, grew up in newly broken pioneer farms in frontier country. His school attendance in Kentucky and Indiana amounted to less than a year. Worked in stores, mills, post offices, also as railsplitter and was chosen captain of a volunteer company in the Black Hawk War of 1832, but saw no action. Studied law on his own and was elected to the Illinois state legislature in 1834, achieving some prominence as a Whig. Obtained his license as an attorney and moved to Springfield, Illinois in 1837. Served one term in the U. S. House of Representatives and worked for Zachary Taylor for president. He then retired from politics until 1854 when he came out fighting Douglas's Kansas–Nebraska Act. His attempts for senatorship in 1855 failed, and in 1856 he joined the new Republican Party, and was mentioned as a vice presidential possibility in the same year. Instead, he became famous in his senatorial race against Douglas in 1858. Although he lost, he had by now a large following in the Republican Party, yet his nomination for president in 1860 was as much attributable to the opposition to the frontrunner Seward as to anything else. Because of the split among the Democrats, he was elected, but with a minority of the popular vote. Seven states had already seceded before his inauguration, and the outbreak of hostilities as well as the secession of four more states could not be prevented. During the war, Lincoln's foremost aim was the preservation of the Union, and he resisted the call for the emancipation of the slaves for a long time.

His originally rather conservative ideas did turn more radical during the war years, however. He had to overcome not only the difficulties of the war, but dissension among the men on his side and within his cabinet, but through patience and steadiness he succeeded in alienating as few people as possible and, in spite of some dictatorial measures he felt compelled to take (suspension of the writ of *habeas corpus*), acquired a great moral authority and popularity. Although seriously challenged by the Democrats as well as within his own party, he won reelection in 1864 in the wake of Grant's and Sherman's military successes. When he was assassinated, a few days after military victory had been won, he was recognized at home and abroad as a great moral and political leader of noble vision and deep humanity. His legend soon began to grow, and he is still seen today as one of the foremost symbols of American democracy.

Lincoln, Mary Todd (1818–1882): Married Abraham Lincoln in 1842. One son died before the war, and another son and her brother-in-law during the war. After her husband's assassination, she was deeply disturbed and also beset by money problems. In 1871, her third son died, and, in 1875, her only remaining son had her committed as insane. She recovered from a suicide attempt, was released in the following year and spent her final years at the home of her sister.

Livermore, Mary Ashton Rice (1820–1905): Cofounder of the U.S. Sanitary Commission and active in various reform movements, editor of the *New Covenant*, Chicago. Wrote an interesting account of her war experiences.

Longstreet, James (1821–1904): Confederate general, fought at Bull Run I, the Peninsula Campaign, Williamsburg, Seven Pines and the Seven Days, also assisted Lee at Bull Run II, South Mountain, Antietam and Fredericksburg. At Gettysburg, he opposed Lee's plans, probably correctly. After Chickamauga, he criticized Bragg, was then sent to east Tennessee, but rejoined Lee at the Wilderness where he was wounded. Finally participated in the Petersburg operations. After the war, he became a Republican minister to Turkey.

Lovejoy, Elijah Parish (1802–1837): Early abolitionist, worked for his cause in Philadelphia, St. Louis and Alton, Illinois. He was repeatedly attacked by hostile mobs and finally killed when an attacking crowd destroyed his press and burned down the building on November 7, 1837. His work was continued by his brother Owen, who as Congressman was given the honor by Lincoln of introducing the bill abolishing slavery in the territories.

Lyon, Nathaniel (1818–1861): Commander of the St. Louis arsenal during the peak of the secessionist agitation in Missouri, tried in vain to come to an understanding with pro-Confederate Governor Claiborne Jackson and Sterling Price. Took charge of the Army of Southwest Missouri, attacked at Wilson's Creek, and was killed. It was widely believed that he had been abandoned by his department Commander John C. Frémont.

McClellan, George Brinton (1826–1885): Union commander, fought in the Mexican War and studied European army tactics during the Crimean War, then became chief engineer and vice president of the Illinois Central. After some minor successes in western Virginia, he was called to take charge in Washington, and hailed as the "young Napoleon." He skillfully reorganized the Army of the Potomac, but was extremely reluctant to advance against the enemy, always overestimating the enemy's strength. His Peninsula campaign began promisingly, but stopped within the sight of Richmond. He began to blame Lincoln and Stanton for his repeated setbacks, and most of his troops were put under Pope's command. After Pope's defeat at Bull Run II, McClellan was restored to active command, but failed to exploit his advantageous position at Antietam. Further frustrated by Jeb Stuart's raids around the Army of the Potomac, he was relieved of his command in November 1862. Ever popular with his troops, he ran for president as a Democrat in 1864, but did not support the party's plank for ending the war at all costs. Grant's and Sherman's successes assured his defeat in the election where he carried only three states. Later, he served as governor of New Jersey.

McClernand, John Alexander (1812–1900): Illinois politician, supported by Lincoln. With little military experience, he participated in Grant's operations against Forts Henry and Donelson, was then highly successful in raising troops in Illinois, Indiana and Iowa. Planned his own campaign against Vicksburg from Memphis but was forestalled by Grant and Sherman. After the final assault on Vicksburg, he claimed all the credit for himself and his troops, disparaging the achievements of all others, and was relieved by Grant.

McCulloch, Ben (1811–1862): Confederate general, fought in the War for Texas Independence, the Mexican War and under Earl Van Dorn at Pea Ridge where he was killed on March 7, 1862.

McDowell, Irvin (1818–1885): Commander of the Union troops around the capital when war broke out. Political pressure made him advance on Manassas, but in the battle of Bull Run I, his troops were too inexperienced to carry out his plans. Four days after the Union defeat he was replaced by McClellan. Then fought at Cedar Mountain and Bull Run II where he was blamed for the Union defeat, but eventually cleared.

McPherson, James Birdseye (1828–1864): Union general, served first under Halleck and Grant, fought at Vicksburg, then in Tennessee. In Sherman's Atlanta campaign, he moved too slowly against Johnston at Snake Creek. He was killed at the outskirts of Atlanta when, returning from Sherman's headquarters, he ran into a squad of enemy skirmishers.

Mason, James Murray (1798–1871): Virginia lawyer, legislator and supporter of Calhoun, sent by Jefferson Davis on a diplomatic mission to Britain. The British mail-steamer *Trent* was intercepted by the U.S.S. *San Jacinto*, Mason was taken prisoner and moved to Boston. He was eventually released by the Union government, but his efforts in Britain in behalf of the Confederacy achieved nothing.

Maximilian of Austria, Archduke of Austria (1832–1867): Brother of Emperor Francis Joseph, was made emperor of Mexico when a French army sent by Napoleon III invaded Mexico and occupied Mexico City. He never became popular with the native population and, when Napoleon withdrew his troops, he was easily overthrown by his archenemy Benito Juarez, captured and shot. Because of the French presence in Mexico and the possibility of French intervention in the Civil War, Grant postponed his move on Mobile, so that a campaign, if necessary, could be started into Texas. After the Civil War, Sheridan guarded the line of the Rio Grande until the French withdrew.

Meade, George Gordon (1815–1872): Union general, the victor at Gettysburg. Was wounded at the Seven Days' battle, and fought again at South Mountain and Antietam, also at Fredericksburg and Chancellorsville where he was frustrated by Hooker's timidity. When Lee invaded Pennsylvania, Meade was given the command against him three days before the battle of Gettysburg where he maneuvered well, but was afterwards blamed for letting Lee escape. He then served with Grant in the Overland, Petersburg and Appomattox campaigns, but often felt slighted because all the credit was given to Grant and Sheridan.

Morgan, John Hunt (1825–1864): One of the leading Confederate raiders, fought at Shiloh and Corinth, and, in July 1862, conducted a raid through Kentucky that hampered the advance of Buell on Chattanooga. In December 1862, he raided Rosecrans's supply lines. Against Bragg's instructions, he crossed into Indiana and Ohio in July 1863, where he was taken prisoner and confined in the Ohio state penitentiary. He escaped in November, but his force was surprised at Greeneville, Tennessee, where he was killed.

Mosby, John Singleton (1833–1916): Confederate raider, joined Jeb Stuart's staff as a scout. Later, he and his regiment wreaked havoc on Union supply lines. At Fairfax County House, he captured the sleeping Union General Stoughton and came close to capturing a train in which Grant was traveling. Custer executed some of his men as guerrillas, and Mosby retaliated in kind. He disbanded his command on April 20, 1865.

Napoleon, Louis (1808–1873): French Emperor (1852–70), nephew of Napoleon I. Was inclined to recognize the Confederacy early in the war, but did not get Britain and Russia's support. His expedition into Mexico violated the Monroe Doctrine and ended in utter failure.

Opdyke, George (1805–1880): Mayor of New York City during the draft riots. He gained the state commission's cooperation and the aid of federal troops to restore order. He continued to support the draft energetically.

Palmerston, Henry John Temple, 3rd Viscount (1784–1865): British prime minister throughout the Civil War. He personally tended to favor the South, but strictly enforced Queen Victoria's neutrality proclamations. His hostile attitude during the *Trent* crisis was softened somewhat by Victoria's husband, Prince Albert. He is supposed to have discussed joint military operations with Confederate delegates at one point, but returned to strict impartiality once the *Trent* dispute was settled.

Patterson, Robert (1792–1881): Union general, was directed to occupy Johnston's forces in the Shenandoah Valley to prevent him from reinforcing Beauregard at Bull Run, but was completely outmaneuvered by Johnston who detached his troops and contributed to the South's first great victory at Manassas.

Patton, George Smith (1833–1864): Grandfather of the famous World War II general, Confederate commander, fought in western Virginia, the Shenandoah, New Market and Cold Harbor. He faced Sheridan's advance on Winchester, was wounded in the leg and died from loss of blood.

Pemberton, John Clifford (1814–1881): Confederate general. Fought at Norfolk, sent to Mississippi in October 1862 to guard Vicksburg and Port Hudson. After Grant had crossed the river below Vicksburg, Pemberton was forced back into the Vicksburg defenses. After the fortress was besieged and had to surrender, he was no longer acceptable to the soldiers and offered to serve as a private. However, Jefferson Davis gave him the command of the artillery defenses of Richmond.

Pickens, Francis Wilkinson (1805–1869): Governor of South Carolina at the time of her secession in December 1860. A believer in Calhoun's nullification theories, he did all in his power to force the capitulation of Fort Sumter. He then organized the state forces. No military expert, he was nevertheless critical of Southern generals for their lack of dash.

Pickett, George Edward (1825–1875): Leader of the famous last charge at Gettysburg, Confederate general, fought Indians and Mexicans, fought at Williamsburg, Seven Pines, Gaines Mill and Antietam, then in Longstreet's campaign in southeastern Virginia. At Gettysburg, he was in charge of only one-third of the troops engaged in the last, desperate attack. He fought again at Drewry's Bluff and Cold Harbor. His division was all but destroyed at Five Forks and Sayler's Creek.

Pierce, Franklin (1804–1869): President of the United States 1853–1857, a Jacksonian Democrat who favored the 1850 Compromise, had Southern leanings and defeated the Whig candidate Winfield Scott for the presidency. His policies were vigorously expansionist, but failed mostly, except in Commodore Perry's Japanese expedition. His support of the Kansas–Nebraska Act enraged many northern Democrats, and he was, therefore, not renominated in 1854. Spoke out vigorously against the Civil War and the Republican government.

Pinkerton, Allan (1819–1884): Native of Scotland, founder of the famous detective agency, an abolitionist who worked for the "Underground Railroad" of fugitive slaves. Escorted Lincoln on his way to Washington and helped to foil the kidnapping plot—which may never have existed. Gathered information for

McClellan, but consistently overestimated the Confederate strength, sometimes by 200% or 300%. After McClellan's removal, he returned to his Chicago Agency. In the South he was hated for his killing of the Jesse James family, in the North for his union-busting activities.

Polk, Leonidas (1806–1864): Native of North Carolina, West Pointer, then bishop of Louisiana. Joined the Confederate Army in 1861, fought in the Mississippi Valley, at Shiloh and Perryville, then at Murfreesboro and Chickamauga where he was severely criticized by Bragg, whose removal Polk demanded from his old friend Jefferson Davis. Bragg ordered a court martial, but Davis sent him to Mississippi. He was killed by an artillery round in June 1864, while consulting with Johnston at Pine Mountain.

Pope, John (1822–1892): Union general, successful at Island #10 and Memphis, but unable to contain Stonewall Jackson in the Shenandoah Valley. After he was named commander of the newly formed Army of Virginia, he antagonized his troops by comparing them unfavorably to his former western troops. His troops were defeated at Cedar Mountain and Bull Run II after which he charged Fitz-John Porter with disobedience. Since most of his officers were McClellan supporters, Lincoln removed Pope and reinstated McClellan when the Confederates invaded Maryland. Pope thereafter fought the Sioux in the Northwest.

Porter, Davis Dixon (1813–1891): Union naval officer, participated in the operations against New Orleans and bombarded Vicksburg. In January 1863, he ran his command past the Vicksburg batteries and took part in the attacks on Fort Fisher. After the war he became commandant at Annapolis.

Porter, Fitz-John (1822–1901): Union general who fought at Yorktown, Beaver Dam Creek and Malvern Hill. At Bull Run II, he was ordered to attack but failed to do so because the order was based on incorrect information. Pope, supported by Stanton, had him relieved, and his friend McClellan did not come to his rescue. His name was cleared in 1878.

Powell, Lewis Thornton (1844–1865): Conspirator with John Wilkes Booth, forced his way into Seward's home where the secretary of war lay ill. He wounded him severely around face and neck, and Seward was first thought to be dead, but his neck brace saved him. Powell fled but lost his way and was arrested at Surratt's boardinghouse. He was tried, found guilty and hanged on July 7, 1865.

Price, Sterling (1809–1867): Leader of the Confederate forces in Missouri at the outbreak of the hostilities. He fought at Wilson's Creek and captured the Union garrison at Lexington. He never cooperated with McCulloch, but fought under Van Dorn at Pea Ridge. His force arrived too late for Shiloh, but he fought at Corinth. Led a large force of cavalry into Missouri in summer and fall of 1864 and was finally defeated at Westport. He then retreated into Arkansas and achieved little during the concluding months of the war.

Quantrill, William Clarke (1837–1865): Guerrilla leader on the Confederate side, outlawed by the Union authorities. His band attracted some notorious names in Missouri's civil war. In 1862, he took Independence, and, in 1863, Lawrence, Kansas, killing all male inhabitants. In 1864, he headed a smaller band that included Jesse James and continued pillaging in Kentucky. In May 1865, he was hit and paralyzed by a Union bullet and died in prison in June 1865.

Rathbone, Henry Reed (?–1911): Union officer on administrative duty in Washington in 1865. He and his fiancee Clara Harris were invited by Lincoln to accompany the presidential couple to Ford's theater on April 14. Rathbone lunged for Booth and was wounded in his forearm. He married Clara Harris, moved to Germany, went insane and murdered her. He died in an insane asylum.

Rhett, Robert Barnwell (1800–1876): One of the first secession advocates in South Carolina, called the "Father of Secession." He drafted his state's Ordinance of Secession, and owned and edited the *Charleston Mercury,* in which he criticized the Davis administration severely. After the war he refused to apply for a pardon.

Rosecrans, William Starke (1819–1898): Union general, took part in McClellan's early campaigning in western Virginia, then served under Pope in the advance on Corinth. He succeeded Buell as commander of the Army of the Ohio, renamed Army of the Cumberland. He defeated Bragg at Murfreesboro and then maneuvered the Confederates out of middle Tennessee. He was beaten by Longstreet at Chickamauga and sent to the Department of the Missouri, but relieved from this post in December of 1864. In 1867, he became chairman of the Military Affairs Committee in the House of Representatives.

Russell, Lord John (1792–1878): British foreign secretary during the Civil War, granted the belligerent status to the Confederacy but no recognition as an independent state. Clashed with the Union on the question of the rights of neutrals, and failed to stop the sailing of the Confederate raider *Alabama* built in Britain for which his country later paid £3 million in settlements. After the war, he succeeded Palmerston as prime minister.

Schimmelfennig, Alexander (1824–1865): A veteran Prussian engineering officer who fled after the revolution of 1848/49 and joined the War Department in 1853. He saw action at Bull Run II, Chancellorsville and Gettysburg where he was hit by a rifle butt, forcing him to hide in a pigsty until the Confederates left the town. For the rest of his career he was plagued by illness. He died in September 1865.

Schurz, Carl (1829–1906): German 1848 liberal who fled after the revolution and settled in Wisconsin. First a backer of Frémont, but by 1860 an ardent Lincoln supporter; Lincoln made him first minister to Spain, then a brigadier general. He fought under Frémont in the Shenandoah Valley, then at Bull Run II and Chancellorsville and Gettysburg. Also led a division at Chattanooga but got into conflict with Hooker, was relegated to a rear echelon and resigned his command early in 1864. After the war, he reported to Andrew Johnson on the conditions in the defeated South, then became Washington correspondent of the *New York Tribune* and edited various other journals and papers. U.S. senator 1869–1875 for Missouri, he opposed the radical reconstruction program under Grant, but became President Hayes's secretary of the interior. In 1884 he led the "Mugwump Party," then supported Grover Cleveland for president.

Scott, Dred (c. 1800–1858): Born into slavery in Virginia, moved with his owner to Alabama and Missouri and was sold to an army surgeon from Pennsylvania who took him into free areas in Illinois, Iowa and Minnesota. After returning to Missouri, he sought his freedom in the courts, on account of his family's travels in free territory. The Supreme Court decided against him in a famous, widely criticized decision. Scott was freed one year later through a private manumission, but died shortly thereafter.

Scott, Winfield (1786–1866): Virginian by birth, fought in various Indian Wars and in the War of 1812. Commander in chief of the army since 1841. At the outbreak of the Civil War, he offered his command to Lee, who declined. He was criticized for the defeat at Bull Run I, and pushed aside by McClellan. He retired on November 1, 1861. His "Anaconda"

plan, though at first rejected in Washington, did provide the major aspects of the eventual Union victory.

Semmes, Raphael (1809–1877): Famous Confederate commerce raider, fought in the Mexican War, where his brig *Somers* sank off Vera Cruz. Commanded the *Havana*, renamed *Sumter* in June 1861, in many successful raids. Finally, his boat was blockaded at Gibraltar by the U.S.S. *Kearsarge*. From September 1862 to June 1864, he commanded the most successful raider, the *Alabama* which was also blockaded and sunk by the *Kearsarge*. He surrendered with Johnston's army and was imprisoned for four months in 1865–66.

Seward, William Henry (1801–1872): Lincoln's secretary of state. Started out as a New York lawyer and Whig politician and served as state governor from 1839–42. Joined the Republican party in 1856 and became one of its leaders and forerunner for the presidential nomination in 1860, but his extreme opposition to slavery and the rise of the more moderate Lincoln were his undoing. Lincoln made him his secretary of state, and as such he attempted to dominate his boss, but his maneuverings were skillfully deflected by Lincoln. He then became a very effective foreign secretary. While convalescing from a carriage accident, he was attacked and wounded by Lewis Powell on the night of Lincoln's assassination. He advocated mild treatment of the South and supported Andrew Johnson throughout his term, leaving the state department when Grant was inaugurated. One of his great achievements was the purchase of Alaska in 1867, for a long time known as "Seward's Folly."

Seymour, Horatio (1810–1886): Democratic governor of New York 1852–54 and again in 1862. He opposed conscription, but declared New York City in a state of insurrection during the draft riots in July 1863 and called for a return to order. Democratic nominee for president in 1868, defeated by Grant.

Sheridan, Philip Henry (1831–1888): Next to Grant and Sherman the most famous Union commander. Fought as cavalry officer at Perryville and Murfreesboro, was beaten at Chickamauga but successful at Missionary Ridge in the battle of Chattanooga. Fought against Jeb Stuart in the Overland campaign with varying success until Stuart was killed at Yellow Tavern. He then managed to clear the Shenandoah Valley of Early's army, turning a defeat into a spectacular victory at Cedar Creek. He systematically devastated the Valley to prevent its further use by the Confederates. In March 1865, he destroyed the rest of Early's forces at Waynesboro and by breaking through the Confederate lines at Five Forks assured their retreat from Petersburg and Richmond. After the war, he headed a Texas force to hold Maximilian of Austria in place, and headed the Reconstruction governments of Texas and Louisiana.

Sherman, William Tecumseh (1820–1891): After Grant, the best known Union commander. West Pointer, fought in the Mexican War, then failed in a banking and a law career. Fought at Bull Run I, then succeeded Robert Anderson in Kentucky, but failed there as well as subsequently in Missouri under Halleck. Then served under Grant at Shiloh where he was unprepared for the Confederate attack, but put up a stiff fight. He also mediated between Grant and Halleck. Participated in the fights around Vicksburg. At Chattanooga, his assault at Tunnel Hill failed. He succeeded Grant in overall command in the West. He started his Atlanta campaign in May 1864 and forced Johnston, then Hood all the way back to Atlanta and then to Savannah, devastating the land around him. His subsequent drive through South Carolina was even more destructive. He accepted Johnston's surrender at Durham Station on April 18, 1865, but his liberal terms were rejected by Secretary of War Stanton, which led to a feud between the two. After the war, he replaced Grant as commander in chief and refused to get involved in politics.

Sickles, Daniel Edgar (1819–1914): Controversial Union general. A New York lawyer and Democratic congressman, he shot down Philip Barton Key, son of the composer of the "Star Spangled Banner" near the White House in 1859. Key had had an affair with Sickles's wife. He was acquitted on grounds of temporary insanity. The defense attorney who gained this innovative verdict was Edwin M. Stanton. Sickles fought in the Peninsular campaign, at Fredericksburg and Chancellorsville. His headquarters had a very poor reputation. On the second day of Gettysburg, he decided to make an unauthorized advance to the Peach Orchard, which may or may not have frustrated Longstreet's assault. Sickles lost a leg in this battle. After the war he was minister to Spain, held various political offices in New York and again served in Congress 1893–95.

Sigel, Franz (1824–1902): Born in Baden, Germany, a major figure in the 1848–49 revolution, fled to the United States and became a teacher in St. Louis. He served under Lyon at Camp Jackson and Wilson's

Creek, later at Pea Ridge, in the Shenandoah, Bull Run II and Fredericksburg. In 1863, he led another expedition into the Shenandoah and was thoroughly beaten by Breckinridge at New Market. He was then removed from his post, and held no further commands.

Slidell, John (1793–1871): Lawyer in New York, and in New Orleans, then congressman and senator, finally appointed ambassador to France by the Confederacy. Together with James M. Mason, he was captured on the *Trent* and became the center of an international incident. He was eventually released, but met with no success in Paris.

Smith, Edmund Kirby (1824–1893): Confederate general, fought in the Mexican War, and against Indians in Texas. Served as J. E. Johnston's staff head and fought at Bull Run I where he was wounded. In 1862, he cooperated with Bragg in the invasion of Kentucky and fought for the rest of the war in trans-Mississippi, being cut off from the eastern Confederacy since the fall of Vicksburg; in this capacity, he often exceeded his authority. He defeated Banks in his Red River campaign. Later he confined himself to small raids and guerrilla activity and was the last Confederate general to surrender, on May 26, 1865.

Stanley, Henry Morton (1841–1904): Originally John Rowlands, Confederate officer and famous explorer, was captured on the second day of Shiloh, then joined the Union army and was sent to Harper's Ferry with an artillery unit. He fell ill and was discharged, but later joined the U. S. navy and ended his career by deserting in Portsmouth, New Hampshire. He was probably the only man to serve in both armies and the Union navy. Later gained fame as a journalist and explorer in Africa, in particular his meeting with David Livingstone on Lake Tanganyika.

Stanton, Edwin McMasters (1814–1869): Lincoln's secretary of war since January 1862. Born in Ohio, he was a successful lawyer in Pittsburgh and Washington and served as Buchanan's attorney general. He accepted the Dred Scott decision and in 1860 supported Breckinridge for president. Nominally a Democrat, he was first extremely critical of Lincoln's policies, but then became his secretary of war after Simon Cameron resigned. Although he had no military experience, he was highly effective in his job, being an excellent organizer and able administrator. Friend of McClellan, but instrumental in his removal when he proved to be inadequate. Rumors that he was in any way connected with the Lincoln assassination were entirely unfounded. He cooperated with the Radical Republicans after the war and soon got into conflict with Andrew Johnson who, in 1868, tried to remove him from office. This triggered the impeachment movement against Johnson. He resigned in May 1868 and was appointed to the Supreme Court by Grant, but died before being sworn in.

Stephens, Alexander Hamilton (1812–1883): Vice president of the Confederacy. Georgia lawyer, then leader of the Whigs in the House, supported Douglas in 1860. Vice president under Jefferson Davis with whom he was in constant friction because he objected to conscription and the suspension of *habeas corpus*. He also came out for early peace negotiations, but his participation in peace missions in July 1863 and again in February 1865 came to naught, though he had always entertained friendly relations with Lincoln. After the war, he was imprisoned in Boston's Fort Warren for five months. Elected to the U. S. Senate in 1866, he was denied the right to sit there, but he returned to the House in 1873.

Stevens, Thaddeus (1792–1868): Radical Republican and champion of the equality of man. Born in Vermont, as lawyer in Gettysburg defended runaway slaves. Entered Congress as a Whig in 1848, supported Lincoln in 1860 but was a severe critic of his moderate policy toward the South. He favored a policy of abolishing the old state lines in the South and recolonizing the whole region. Chairman of the Committee on Reconstruction, introduced the 14th Amendment and was the main instigator of the impeachment proceedings against Andrew Johnson. He died a few months after Johnson's acquittal.

Stone, Charles Pomeroy (1824–1887): Union general, fought in the Mexican War and served with Patterson in the Shenandoah in 1861. When his subordinate Edward Baker was defeated and killed at Ball's Bluff, Stone became the scapegoat. He was arrested without charges and held in confinement for 189 days, never charged and never cleared. Served later as Banks's chief of staff and took part in the Petersburg operations. After the war, he served in Egypt for 13 years and was the engineer who laid the foundation of the Statue of Liberty in New York Harbor.

Stowe, Harriet Beecher (1811–1896): American novelist and humanitarian. Her novel *Uncle Tom's Cabin* (1852), first published in the abolitionist paper *National Era*, was not intended as abolitionist propaganda, but had a tremendous effect in the North. More than 300,000 copies were sold in one year. Her other novel on slavery, *Dred*, and her many other novels were less successful. She worked energetically for the antislavery movement, but never associated herself with the abolitionists. All through her life, she was harassed by financial worries. Sister of Henry Ward Beecher.

Stuart, James Ewell Brown ("Jeb") (1833–1864): Famous cavalry leader of the Confederates, West Pointer and Indian fighter, participated in the crushing of John Brown's raid on Harper's Ferry, fought at Bull Run I. As leader of a cavalry brigade fought at Seven Days, Bull Run II, Antietam, Fredericksburg, Chancellorsville, Gettysburg and the battle of the Wilderness. At the Peninsula campaign and again after Antietam, he led his command around McClellan's army. Led many cavalry raids in 1862 and 1863, including the largest one, at Brandy Station in June 1863. At Gettysburg, he arrived too late to attack the Union's rear flank and was defeated by Custer and Gregg. He stopped Sheridan's cavalry at Yellow Tavern on May 11, 1864, but was mortally wounded in the battle.

Sumner, Charles (1811–1874): Abolitionist Republican senator from Massachusetts, hated by all Southerners. He was attacked and severely injured by Preston S. Brooks, nephew of Senator Andrew Pickens Butler of South Carolina whom he had severely verbally attacked in May 1856. He returned to the Senate in December 1859. Together with Thaddeus Stevens led the radical Reconstruction program and the impeachment proceedings against President Johnson. Later got into conflict with President Grant and helped organize the short-lived Liberal Republican Party.

Surratt, Mary E. (1820–1865): Ran a boarding house in Washington where much of the planning for Lincoln's assassination was done. It has never been decided whether she knew about the plot, but she was convicted by the military commission and hanged on July 7, 1865. Her son John, an active member of the plot, fled to Canada and was apprehended in Egypt in 1867 but released after a trial.

Taney, Roger Brooke (1777–1864): Supreme Court chief justice from 1836 to 1864. Supporter of Andrew Jackson who made him successor to Chief Justice

John Marshall. His ruling in the Dred Scott case stirred up heated controversies all through the country in 1857. Clashed with Lincoln on the question of suspension of the *habeas corpus*. Lincoln considered him an archfoe, but today he is seen by many as a great jurist.

Taylor, Zachary (1784–1850): President of the United States 1849–1850, won the decisive battle of the Mexican War, became a popular hero and was elected president on a Whig ticket. He supported the Wilmot Proviso but opposed the measures that led to the Compromise of 1850. Charges of corruption were lodged against members of his cabinet until his death from cholera in July 1850 prevented his taking any action.

Terry, Alfred Howe (1827–1890): Union general, fought at Port Royal and Fort Pulaski, as well as Charleston and Petersburg. After Butler's failure to take Fort Fisher, North Carolina, he led a second attempt on January 15, 1865 and succeeded. After the war he served on the frontier and was George A. Custer's superior when Custer was killed at Little Big Horn in 1876.

Thomas, George Henry (1816–1870): Union general, veteran of the Seminole and Mexican Wars, commanded the Army of the Tennessee after Shiloh, fought at Perryville and Stones River, and bravely held his position on Snodgrass Hill at Chickamauga. Put in command at Chattanooga by Grant, his troops broke the Confederate lines in the assault on Missionary Ridge. Then was sent against Hood's army in Tennessee, which threatened Sherman's rear, and finally defeated the Confederates at Nashville.

Tilden, Samuel Jones (1814–1886): New York lawyer and moderate Democrat. Supported Andrew Johnson and broke up the infamous Tweed Ring in New York. In 1876, he ran for president and beat Hayes in the popular vote, but a snag developed in the Electoral College. A special commission struck a secret deal with the Southern states and decided in favor of Hayes, who then removed the Union occupation forces from the South.

Toombs, Robert Augustus (1810–1885): Born in Georgia, Southern secessionist leader. Failing to gain the Confederate presidency, he joined the army and fought at Seven Days and Malvern Hill, also at Bull Run II and Antietam—where he was wounded. Fled the country after the end of the war, later returned and resumed his law practice.

Trollope, Anthony (1815–1882): English novelist, famous for his "Barsetshire Chronicles," traveled extensively and wrote an account of his visit to the United States.

Turner, Nat (1800–1831): Slave in Virginia, led a revolt in August 1831. Fifty-five whites were killed in Southampton County, Virginia. A reign of terror spread by militia and federal troops followed during which 100–200 blacks were killed. Turner and 16 other blacks were captured two months later and hanged.

Vallandigham, Clement Laird (1820–1871): Prominent Democratic politician in Ohio and unofficial leader of the "Copperheads," the Northern peace democrats. Supported Douglas in 1860, then became a severe critic of Lincoln whose administration he attacked so violently that the commander of the Department of the Ohio, General Burnside, ordered his arrest. He was convicted, but Lincoln commuted his prison sentence to expulsion to the Confederates, who, however, did not want him. From Canada, he ran for governor of Ohio but was defeated. In 1864, he slipped back into Ohio and was tolerated by the authorities.

Vance, Zebulon Baird (1830–1894): North Carolina politician, supported Unionist John Bell for the presidency in 1860, then joined the Confederate army and fought at New Bern and the Seven Days. Elected governor in 1862, engaged in blockade-running. He opposed a separate surrender by the state, was re-elected in 1864 and imprisoned from May till July 1865. Again governor in the late 1870s.

Van Dorn, Earl (1820–1863): Confederate general, fought in Mexico and Indian Territory, and assumed command in Arkansas early in 1862. He managed to coordinate the movements of McCulloch and Price, but was beaten at Pea Ridge. Participated in the fighting around Corinth, defended Vicksburg, but failed in his attack on Baton Rouge and in his attempts to retake Corinth in October 1862. Then commanded the mounted troops under Pemberton and raided Holly Springs, Miss. On May 7, 1863 he was killed by Dr. George B. Peters for attentions he had paid to Peters' wife.

Victoria (1819–1901): Queen of England, Monarch of the United Kingdom and Ireland. During the Civil War, issued a proclamation of neutrality on May 13, 1861. Outraged by the *Trent* incident, she nevertheless let her husband, Prince Albert, modify the ultimatum to Washington. Opposed all efforts to get her country involved in the conflict, although her prime minister, Lord Palmerston, was sympathetic to the Southern cause.

Wade, Benjamin Franklin (1800–1878): Radical Republican senator from Ohio 1851–1869, denounced the fugitive laws and the Kansas–Nebraska Act and became the chairman of the Joint Committee on the Conduct of the War, which often interfered with Lincoln's and his generals' policies. In response to Lincoln's tentative Reconstruction plans, he, in cooperation with Henry W. Davis, introduced the Wade–Davis Bill in 1864, which proposed a harsher treatment of the South. Lincoln vetoed it and was denounced in the Wade–Davis manifesto. He fought Andrew Johnson whom, as president pro tempore of the Senate, he would have succeeded in case of impeachment. Defeated for the Senate in 1869, he resumed his law practice.

Walker, William (1824–1860): Native of Nashville, led a freebooting expedition in Mexico in 1853 and installed himself in Nicaragua as leader of the government. He was compelled to quit in 1857, and then tried to reintroduce slavery in Central America. In 1860, he tried to enter Honduras but was caught by the British who handed him over to the local authorities who had him shot.

Wallace, Lewis (1827–1905): Union general and author, fought in Virginia and at Fort Donelson, but arrived late at the battlefield of Shiloh and was blamed for the defeat on the first day of the battle. Later successfully defended Cincinnati during Kirby Smith's invasion of Kentucky. Defending Maryland in early 1864, he delayed Early's drive at Monocacy River. Sat on the courts martial that tried the Lincoln conspirators and the one condemning Henry Wirz. His Mexican venture to aid Juarez against Maximilian collapsed. Later governor of New Mexico Territory and diplomat in Turkey, and finally a prolific writer, best remembered for *Ben Hur*.

Warren, Gouverneur Kemble (1830–1882): Union general, West Pointer, wounded at Gaines' Mill, then engaged at Bull Run II, Antietam and Fredericksburg. Frustrated at Chancellorsville, he played a decisive role at Gettysburg by saving Little Round Top for the Union army by his initiative. Fought at the Wilderness, Spotsylvania and Cold Harbor. Had disagreements with Meade and Sheridan. The latter accused him of attacking too late and in a disorganized way at Five Forks and removed him from command.

Warren spent years attempting to have this decision corrected, which was done in 1882, a few months after his death.

Webster, Daniel (1782–1852): Native of New Hampshire, senator since 1827, engaged in a famous debate with Robert Hayne from South Carolina in January 1830, on slavery, tariff and western expansion. Eloquent defender of a consolidated national government and supporter of the Wilmot Proviso. He split with the abolitionists and supported Clay's Compromise of 1850 to preserve the unity of the nation. Lost his bid for the Whig nomination for president in 1852 to Winfield Scott and died before the election. One of the greatest orators of his time.

Weed, Thurlow (1797–1882): New York state legislator and leading Whig politician, backed the nomination of Clay and Taylor, turned Republican in 1855 and became a Seward follower, but failed to secure his nomination for president in 1860. Then supported the Lincoln administration, went on special diplomatic missions to France and England. Supported Reconstruction policy of Andrew Johnson, after whose fall he lost all influence.

Weitzel, Godfrey (1835–1884): Union general, fought at Port Hudson, Petersburg and Richmond. In December 1864, he was put in charge of the newly created 25th Corps, the only all-black corps in American history. Participated in Butler's unsuccessful attack on Fort Fisher and was given the honor to command the first troops to enter Richmond in April 1865. Later served under Sheridan along the Texas–Mexico border.

Welles, Gideon (1802–1878): Lincoln's secretary of the navy, one of two cabinet members to serve throughout his presidency (the other was William H. Seward). Started as a Connecticut journalist and legislator. Effectively converted the peacetime navy into a modern fighting force. Often moderated tensions within the cabinet, particularly among Stanton, Chase and Seward. Stayed in Johnson's cabinet and left office only when Grant was inaugurated.

Whitman, Walt (1819–1892): American poet, sang the praises of freedom and dignity of the individual and celebrated democracy and the brotherhood of man. Supported the abolitionist and free soil movements and was a passionate admirer of Lincoln, whom he celebrated in his war time poems published under the title of *Drum-Taps*. One of his early discoverers was Ralph Waldo Emerson.

Whittier, John Greenleaf (1807–1892): American

Quaker poet and reformer, wrote many idyllic poems but was at the same time a fiery abolitionist and a cofounder of the Republican party. Wrote for many abolitionist publications. His famous civil war poem "Barbara Frietchie" is not based on fact.

Wilmot, David (1814–1868): Congressman from Pennsylvania and Jacksonian Democrat, famous for his "Proviso" (1846) that proposed to eliminate slavery in all lands gained from Mexico. It failed in Congress because of vehement Southern opposition. Helped organize the new Republican party and was temporary chairman at the convention that nominated Lincoln in 1860. Took Simon Cameron's Senate seat in 1861.

Wirz, Henry (1823–1865): Confederate general, severely wounded at Seven Pines, took command of the Andersonville prison, Georgia, in March 1864. Twelve thousand Union soldiers died there. He was at first given safe conduct, but then sent to Washington for trial by a military tribunal. He was convicted of having had a part in killing prisoners on contradictory evidence. Clearly, he had never tried to improve the horrible conditions in the camp. He was hanged in November 1865, the only individual executed for war crimes.

Wise, John (c. 1808–1879): Tried repeatedly to introduce balloon observation service in the Union army, but with little success. He later raised a cavalry company. After the war, he resumed ballooning and was lost with his passengers over Lake Michigan in 1879.

Wood, Fernando (1812–1881): Born in Philadelphia. Became a New York politician and mayor of the city 1855–58 and 1861–62. A harsh critic of the Lincoln administration, recommended mercy for John Brown and at one time suggested that New York City leave the state and the Union. Throughout the war, he was a leading peace Democrat.

Wood, John Taylor (1830–1904): Grandson of President Zachary Taylor, Confederate naval commander, commander of the C.S.S. *Virginia (Merrimac)* at Hampton Roads. After his vessel was scuttled, he commanded a company of sharpshooters at Drewry's Bluff, then became a commando-style raider against the Union fleet. In 1864, he commanded the highly successful *Tallahassee*. Captured with Jefferson Davis, but then escaped to Cuba and settled in Nova Scotia.

Worden, John Lorimer (1818–1897): Union navy commander, served at Pensacola Harbor, Florida, in March 1861, was seized and held by the Confederates but exchanged in October 1861. He then was offered command of the *Monitor*, Ericsson's experimental armored craft. He arrived too late at Hampton Roads to prevent the destruction of the *Cumberland* and *Congress*, but fought the *Virginia (Merrimac)* successfully, getting wounded in the face during the battle. Thereafter he commanded the U.S.S. *Montauk* in the South Atlantic Blockading Squadron and sank the Confederate steamer *Nashville*. Finally supervised the construction of improved ships of the *Monitor* type.

Yancey, William Lowndes (1814–1863): Extreme states' rights advocate, worked as journalist, then congressman, proposed a Southern Confederacy as early as 1858 and played a leading part in the splitting of the Democratic Party in 1860. Tried to gain recognition for the Confederacy in England and France, then served in the Confederate Senate. Opposed Jefferson Davis's ideas of a strong central government, he always tried to limit the president's powers.

Zeppelin, Ferdinand von (c. 1839–1917): German aviation engineer, became an observer of the Civil War in 1863. He ascended in a balloon at St. Paul in August 1863, then returned to Germany and participated in the Franco–Prussian War of 1870–71. Later developed the dirigible and the technique of aerial bombardment, but vehemently denied his willingness to bomb his American friends when war threatened between the two countries in 1917. He died before war broke out between Germany and the U.S.

Zollicoffer, Felix Kirk (1812–1862): Confederate general, in charge of the Tennessee forces after the fall of Fort Sumter, then commander in Kentucky. At Mill Springs, he was killed at the very beginning of the battle, because he had ridden up to a Federal unit, too nearsighted to realize it was not his own.

Appendix D

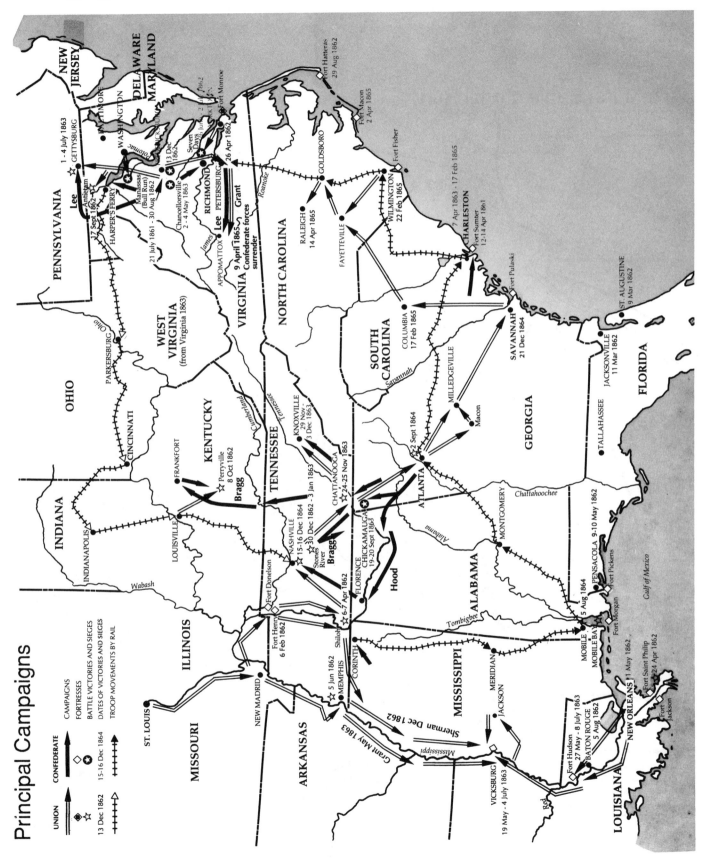

371

The First Battle of Bull Run

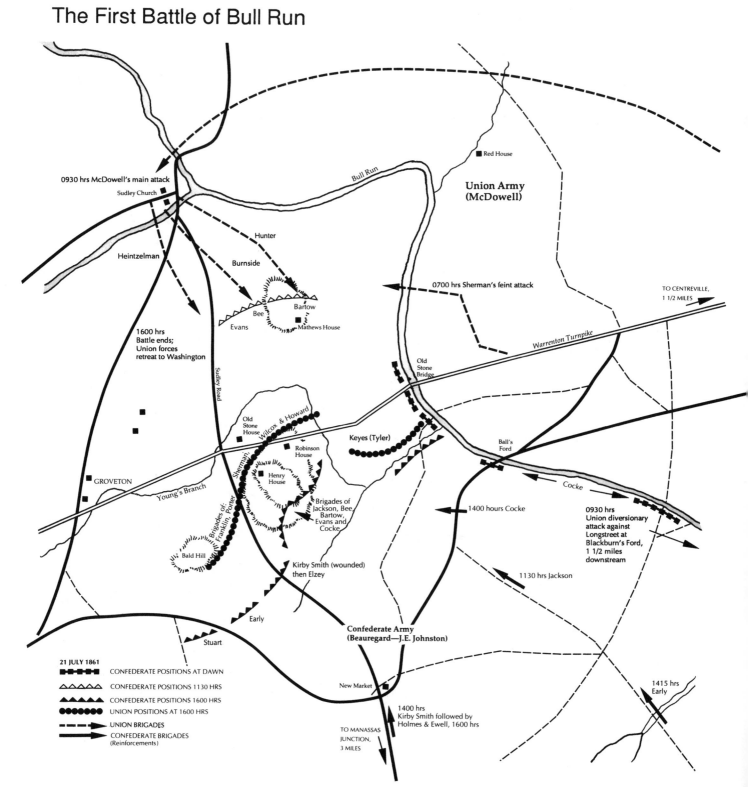

0930 hrs McDowell's main attack

Sudley Church

Heintzelman

Hunter

Burnside

Bee

Bartow

Evans

Mathews House

1600 hrs
Battle ends;
Union forces
retreat to Washington

Sudley Road

Old
Stone
House

Wilcox & Howard

Robinson
House

GROVETON

Young's Branch

Henry
House

Sherman

Brigades of: Franklin Porter

Brigades of
Jackson, Bee,
Bartow,
Evans and
Cocke

Bald Hill

Kirby Smith (wounded)
then Elzey

Early

Stuart

Red House

Bull Run

**Union Army
(McDowell)**

0700 hrs Sherman's feint attack

TO CENTREVILLE,
1 1/2 MILES

Warrenton Turnpike

Old
Stone
Bridge

Keyes (Tyler)

Ball's
Ford

Cocke

1400 hours Cocke

0930 hrs
Union diversionary
attack against
Longstreet at
Blackburn's Ford,
1 1/2 miles
downstream

1130 hrs Jackson

**Confederate Army
(Beauregard—J.E. Johnston)**

1415 hrs
Early

New Market

1400 hrs
Kirby Smith followed by
Holmes & Ewell, 1600 hrs

TO MANASSAS
JUNCTION,
3 MILES

21 JULY 1861

CONFEDERATE POSITIONS AT DAWN

CONFEDERATE POSITIONS 1130 HRS

CONFEDERATE POSITIONS 1600 HRS

UNION POSITIONS AT 1600 HRS

UNION BRIGADES

CONFEDERATE BRIGADES
(Reinforcements)

372

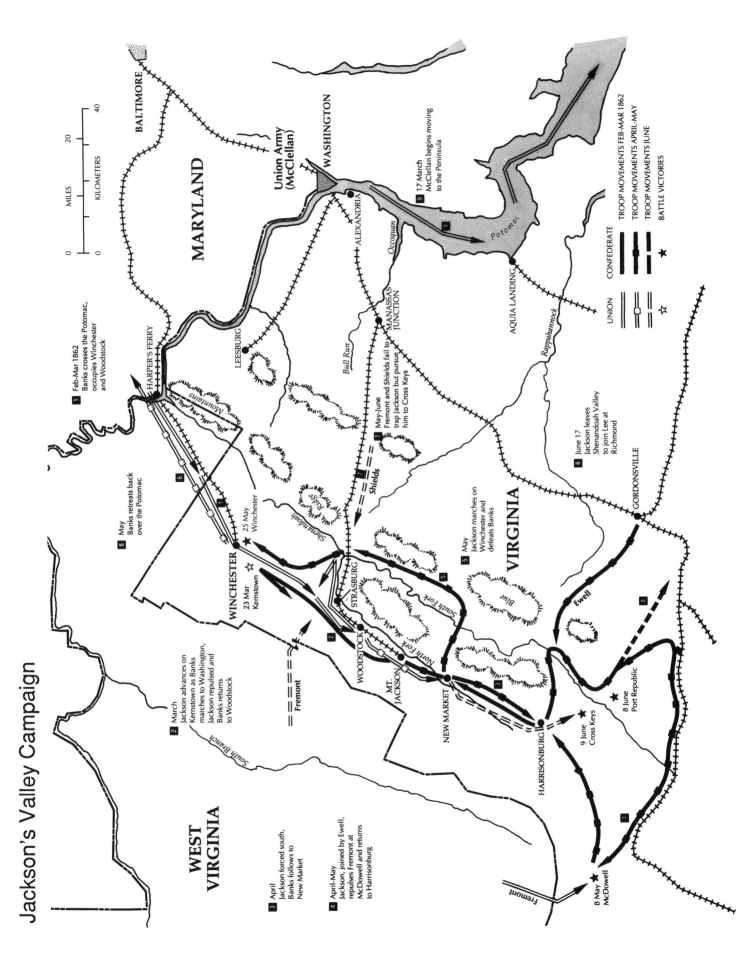

Jackson's Valley Campaign

MARYLAND

BALTIMORE

MILES
KILOMETERS
0   20   40

WEST VIRGINIA

WASHINGTON

Union Army
(McClellan)

ALEXANDRIA

Occoquan

MANASSAS
JUNCTION

Bull Run

AQUIA LANDING

Rappahannock

HARPER'S FERRY

LEESBURG

Mountains

Shenandoah

Ridge

Blue Ridge

WINCHESTER

25 May
Winchester

23 Mar Kernstown

STRASBURG

South Fork

North Fork

WOODSTOCK

MT. JACKSON

NEW MARKET

HARRISONBURG

Fremont

Shields

Ewell

GORDONSVILLE

South Branch

VIRGINIA

9 June
Cross Keys

8 June
Port Republic

8 May
McDowell

Fremont

1 Feb-Mar 1862
Banks crosses the Potomac,
occupies Winchester
and Woodstock

2 March
Jackson advances on
Kernstown as Banks
marches to Washington,
Jackson repulsed and
Banks returns
to Woodstock

3 April
Jackson forced south,
Banks follows to
New Market

4 April-May
Jackson, joined by Ewell,
repulses Fremont at
McDowell and returns
to Harrisonburg

5 May
Jackson marches on
Winchester and
defeats Banks

6 May
Banks retreats back
over the Potomac

7 May-June
Fremont and Shields fail to
trap Jackson but pursue
him to Cross Keys

8 June 17
Jackson leaves
Shenandoah Valley
to join Lee at
Richmond

9 17 March
McClellan begins moving
to the Peninsula

Potomac

TROOP MOVEMENTS FEB-MAR 1862
TROOP MOVEMENTS APRIL-MAY
TROOP MOVEMENTS JUNE
BATTLE VICTORIES

UNION   CONFEDERATE

373

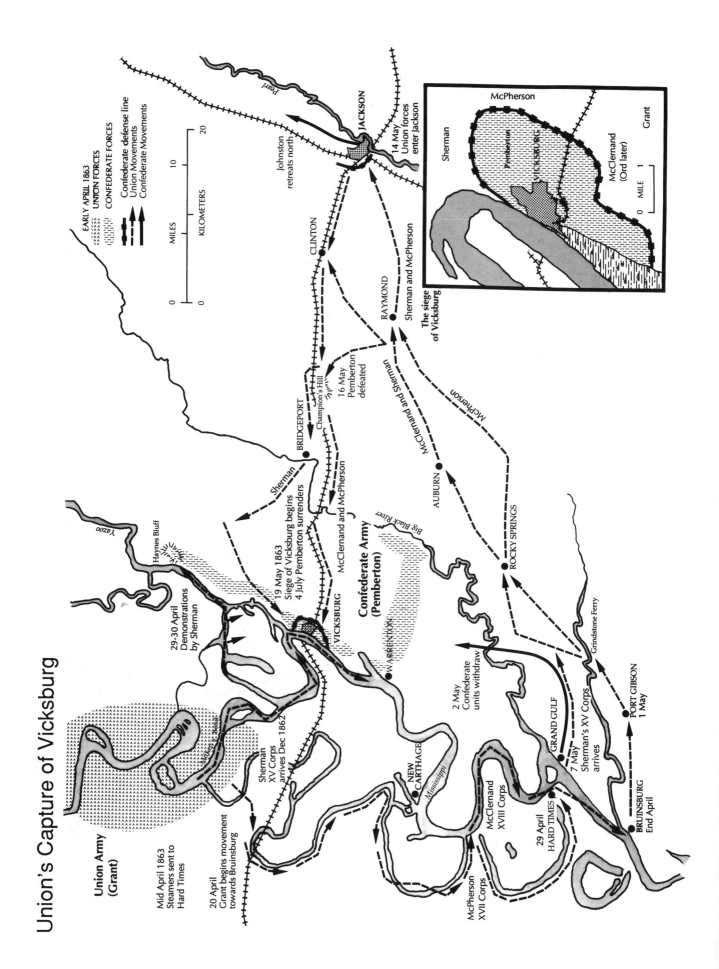

Union's Capture of Vicksburg

Union Army (Grant)

Mid April 1863
Steamers sent to
Hard Times

20 April
Grant begins movement
towards Bruinsburg

29–30 April
Demonstrations
by Sherman

Haynes Bluff

Yazoo

Sherman
XV Corps
arrives Dec 1862

19 May 1863
Siege of Vicksburg begins
4 July Pemberton surrenders

VICKSBURG

WARRENTON

2 May Confederate
units withdraw

Confederate Army (Pemberton)

Big Black River

NEW CARTHAGE

Mississippi

McClernand
XVIII Corps

29 April
HARD TIMES

McPherson
XVII Corps

7 May Sherman's XV Corps
arrives

GRAND GULF

Grindstone Ferry

BRUINSBURG
End April

PORT GIBSON
1 May

ROCKY SPRINGS

AUBURN

McClernand and Sherman

McPherson

RAYMOND

Sherman and McPherson

McClernand and McPherson

Champion's Hill

16 May
Pemberton defeated

BRIDGEPORT

Sherman

CLINTON

Johnston retreats north

JACKSON

14 May Union forces enter Jackson

Pearl

EARLY APRIL 1863
UNION FORCES
CONFEDERATE FORCES

Confederate defense line
Union Movements
Confederate Movements

MILES
KILOMETERS
0   10   20

The siege of Vicksburg

McPherson

Sherman

Pemberton

VICKSBURG

Grant

McClernand
(Ord later)

0   MILE   1

374

Battle of Gettysburg

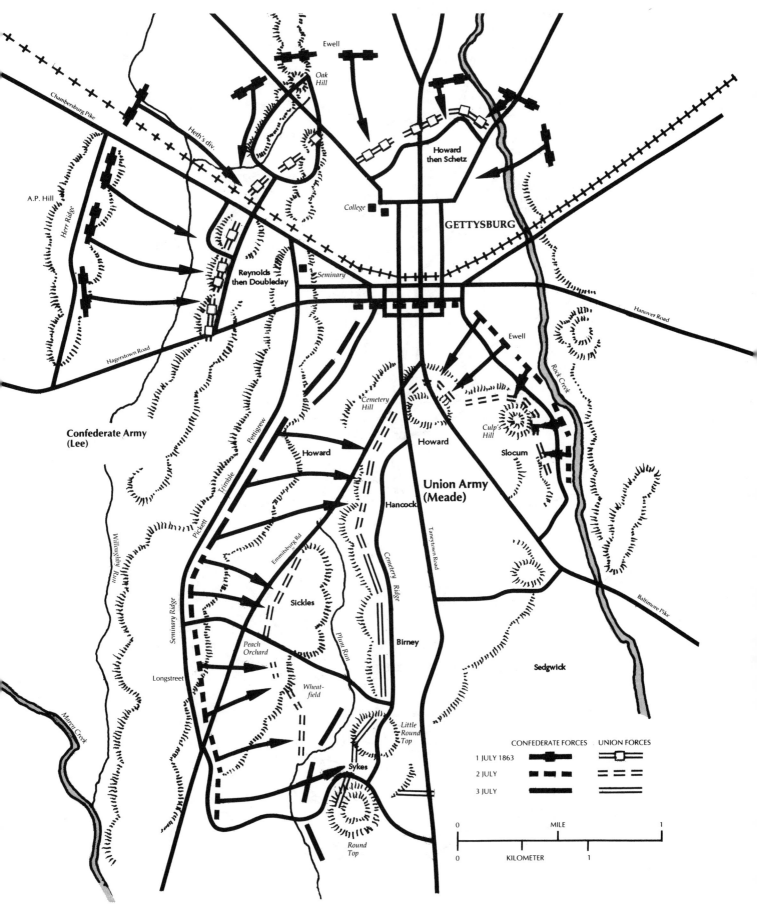

A.P. Hill

Herr Ridge

Chambersburg Pike

Heth's div.

Ewell

Oak Hill

Howard
then Schetz

College

GETTYSBURG

Seminary

Reynolds
then Doubleday

Hagerstown Road

Hanover Road

Ewell

Rock Creek

Cemetery
Hill

Culp's
Hill

Howard

Slocum

**Confederate Army
(Lee)**

Pettigrew

Trimble

Howard

Hancock

**Union Army
(Meade)**

Pickett

Willoughby Run

Seminary Ridge

Emmitsburg Rd

Sickles

Plum Run

Cemetery Ridge

Taneytown Road

Birney

Sedgwick

Baltimore Pike

Peach
Orchard

Longstreet

Wheat-
field

Little
Round
Top

Marsh Creek

Sykes

Round
Top

CONFEDERATE FORCES	UNION FORCES
1 JULY 1863	
2 JULY	
3 JULY	

0   MILE   1

0   KILOMETER   1

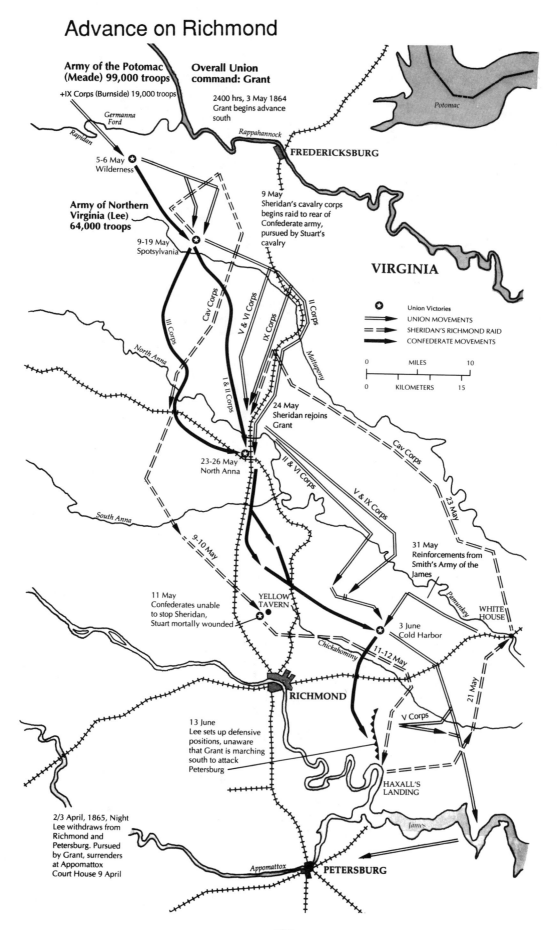

Advance on Richmond

Army of the Potomac
(Meade) 99,000 troops

+IX Corps (Burnside) 19,000 troops

Germanna Ford

Rapidan

5-6 May
Wilderness

Army of Northern
Virginia (Lee)
64,000 troops

9-19 May
Spotsylvania

Overall Union
command: Grant

2400 hrs, 3 May 1864
Grant begins advance
south

Rappahannock

FREDERICKSBURG

9 May
Sheridan's cavalry corps
begins raid to rear of
Confederate army,
pursued by Stuart's
cavalry

Potomac

VIRGINIA

⊛ Union Victories

⟹ UNION MOVEMENTS

⇢ SHERIDAN'S RICHMOND RAID

➡ CONFEDERATE MOVEMENTS

0 — MILES — 10

0 — KILOMETERS — 15

North Anna

Cav Corps

III Corps

V & VI Corps

IX Corps

II Corps

1 & II Corps

Mattapony

24 May
Sheridan rejoins
Grant

Cav Corps

23 May

23-26 May
North Anna

South Anna

II & VI Corps

V & IX Corps

31 May
Reinforcements from
Smith's Army of the
James

Pamunkey

WHITE
HOUSE

9-10 May

11 May
Confederates unable
to stop Sheridan,
Stuart mortally wounded

YELLOW
TAVERN

3 June
Cold Harbor

Chickahominy

11-12 May

21 May

RICHMOND

13 June
Lee sets up defensive
positions, unaware
that Grant is marching
south to attack
Petersburg

V Corps

2/3 April, 1865, Night
Lee withdraws from
Richmond and
Petersburg. Pursued
by Grant, surrenders
at Appomattox
Court House 9 April

HAXALL'S
LANDING

James

Appomattox

PETERSBURG

376

Bibliography

Adams, F. Colburn, *The Story of a Trooper*. New York: Dick & Fitzgerald, 1865.

Adams, James Truslow (ed.), *Album of American History*, vol. III. New York: Scribner's, 1969.

Austin, J. B., *The Blue and the Gray*. Atlanta: The Franklin Printing and Publishing Co., 1899.

Barnes, Jeremy, *The Pictorial History of the Civil War*. New York: Gallery Books, 1988.

Beale, Howard K., "What Historians Have Said about the Causes of the Civil War." Social Science Research Council, Bull. #54, 1946.

Beard, Charles and Mary R., *A Basic History of the United States*. Philadelphia: New Home Library, 1944.

Bellard, Alfred, *Gone for a Soldier*, ed. D. H. Donald. Boston: Little, Brown & Co., 1975.

Borreson, R., *When Lincoln Died*. New York: Appleton, 1966.

Botts, John Minor, *The Great Rebellion*. New York: Harper, 1866.

Bowman, John S. (ed.), *The Civil War Almanac*. New York: World Alm. Publ. (Bison), 1985.

Browne, Junius Henri, *Four Years in Secessia*. Hartford: O. D. Case & Co., 1865.

Casler, John O., *Four Years in the Stonewall Brigade*, ed. J. I. Robertson Jr. Dayton, Ohio: Morningside Bookshop, 1906 (facs. 1971).

Catton, Bruce, *The Civil War*. New York: American Heritage Press, 1971.

———, *The Coming Fury*. New York: Washington Square Press, 1961.

————, *Reflections on the Civil War*, ed. J. Leekley. Garden City, N.Y.: Doubleday, 1981.

————, *A Stillness at Appomattox*. New York: Washington Square Press, 1965.

————, *Terrible Swift Sword*. New York: Washington Square Press, 1963.

Catton, William and Bruce, *Two Roads to Sumter*. New York: McGraw Hill, 1963.

Chesnut, Mary Boykin, *A Diary from Dixie*. New York: D. Appleton & Co., 1929.

Cirker, H. & B. (eds.), *Dictionary of American Portraits*. New York: Dover, 1967.

Cist, Henry M., *The Army of the Cumberland*, vol. 7 of *Campaigns of the Civil War*. New York: Scribner's Sons, 1882.

Coffin, Charles Carlton, *The Boys of '61*. Boston: Estes & Lauriat, 1884.

————, *My Days and Nights on the Battlefield*. Boston: Ticknor, 1863.

————, *Following the Flag*. Boston: Estes & Lauriat, 1865.

Commager, Henry Steele, *Documents of American History*. New York: Appleton-Century, 1962.

Cox, Jacob D., *Atlanta*, vol. 9 of *Campaigns of the Civil War*. New York: Scribner's, 1882.

Craven, Avery, *Reconstruction, The Ending of the Civil War*. New York: Holt, Rinehart & Winston, 1969.

Current, Richard N., *Those Terrible Carpetbaggers*. New York: Oxford Univ. Press, 1988.

Daly, Maria L., *Diary of a Union Lady*, ed. H. E. Hammond. New York: Funk & Wagnall, 1962.

Doubleday, Abner, *Chancellorsville and Gettysburg*, vol. 6 of *Campaigns of the Civil War*. New York: Scribner's, 1882.

———, *Reminiscences of Fort Sumter and Moultrie, 1860–61*. New York: Harper, 1876.

Farragut, Loyall, *The Life of David Glasgow Farragut*. New York: Appleton, 1879.

Fleming, Walter L., *Documentary History of Reconstruction*, 2 vols. New York: McGraw Hill, 1907–66.

———, *The Sequel of Appomattox*. New Haven: Yale Univ. Press, 1919.

Force, M. F., *From Fort Henry to Corinth*, vol. 2 of *Campaigns of the Civil War*. New York: Scribner's Sons, 1881.

Franklin, John Hope, *Reconstruction after the Civil War*. Chicago: Univ. of Chicago Press, 1961.

Gerrish, Theodore, *Army Life. A Private's Reminiscences of the Civil War*. Portland, Me., Hoyt, Fogg and Donham, 1882.

Goddard, Samuel, *Letters on the American Rebellion*. Boston: Nichols & Noyes, 1870.

Gordon, John B., *Reminiscences of the Civil War*. New York: Scribner's, 1904.

Goss, Warren Lee, *Recollections of a Private*. New York: Thomas E. Crowell & Co., 1890.

Grant, Ulysses S., *Personal Memoirs*, 2 vols. New York: Sampson, Low, Marston, 1885–86.

Greene, Francis Vinson, *The Mississippi*, vol. 8 of *Campaigns of the Civil War*. New York: Scribner's Sons, 1882.

Handlin, Oscar, *Readings in American History*. New York: Knopf, 1957.

Headley, J. T., *The Great Rebellion*, 2 vols. Hartford: Hurlbut, Williams & Co., 1863–66.

Henry, Robert Selph, *The Story of Reconstruction*. Indianapolis: Bobbs Merrill, 1938.

Hunter, Alexander, *Johnny Reb and Billy Yank*. New York: The Neale Publ. Co., 1904.

Hyman, Harold (ed.), *Heard Round the World*. New York: Knopf, 1969.

Johnson, R., Johnson, Buel and Clough, Clarence, *Battles and Leaders of the Civil War*, 4 vols. New York: Century Press, 1884–88.

Lee, Fitzhugh, *General Lee of the Confederate Army*. London: Chapman and Hall, 1895.

Lee, Captain Robert E., *Recollections and Letters of General Robert E. Lee*. New York: Doubleday, Page and Co., 1904.

The Life History of the United States, vol. 5 (1849–65). New York: Time Inc., 1963.

Livermore, Mary A., *My Story of the War*. Hartford: A. D. Worthington & Co., 1889.

Long, E. B. and Barbara, *The Civil War Day by Day*. Garden City, N.Y.: Doubleday, 1971.

Lusk, William Thompson, *War Letters*. Privately printed, 1911.

McClellan, George B., *McClellan's Own Story*. New York: Charles L. Webster, 1887.

McPherson, James M., *Battle Cry of Freedom*. New York: Oxford Univ. Press, 1988.

———, *Ordeal by Fire: The Civil War and Reconstruction*. New York: Knopf, 1982.

Marshall-Cornwall, General Sir James, *Grant as Military Commander*. New York: Van Nostrand Reinhold Co., 1970.

Mitchell, Lt. Col. Joseph B., *Decisive Battles of the Civil War*. New York: Putnam, 1955.

Nevins, Allan, *American Press Opinion, from Washington to Coolidge*. Washington, D.C.: Kennikat, 1969.

Nichols, George Ward, *The Story of the Great March*. New York: Harper & Brothers, 1865.

Nicolay, John G., *The Outbreak of the Rebellion*, vol. 1 of *Campaigns of the Civil War*. New York: Ch. Scribner's Sons, 1881.

Oates, William C., *The War Between the Union and the Confederacy*. New York: The Neale Publ. Co., 1905.

Owen, William Miller, *In Camp and Battle with the Washington Artillery*. 2nd ed. New Orleans: Pelican Publ. Co., 1964.

Palfrey, Francis Winthrop, *Antietam and Fredericksburg*, vol. 5 of *Campaigns of the Civil War*. New York: Ch. Scribner's Sons, 1882.

Pollard, Edward A., *The Lost Cause*. New York: E. B. Treat and Co., 1866.

Porter, Horace, *Campaigning with Grant*. New York: The Century Co., 1897.

Pressly, Thomas J., *Americans Interpret their Civil War*. Princeton, N.J.: Princeton University Press, 1954.

Richardson, Albert D., *A Personal History of Ulysses S. Grant*. Hartford: Amer. Publ. Co., 1868.

Sandburg, Carl, *Storm over the Land*. New York: Harcourt, 1942.

Sheridan, P. H., *Personal Memoirs*, 2 vols. New York: Charles L. Webster & Co., 1888.

Sherman, William Tecumseh, *Memoirs*, 2 vols. New York: C. L. Webster & Co., 1875.

Sifakis, Stewart, *Who Was Who in the Civil War*. New York: Facts On File, 1988.

Stampp, Kenneth M., *The Era of Reconstruction*. New York: Knopf, 1972.

Stanley, Dorothy (ed.), *The Autobiography of Sir Henry Morton Stanley*. Boston & New York: Houghton, Mifflin, 1909.

Stephenson, Nathaniel W., *Abraham Lincoln and the Union*. New York: United States Publ. Assoc., 1918.

Stevenson, Burton Egbert (ed.), *Poems of American History*. Freeport, N.Y.: Books of Libraries Press, 1922.

Stewart, A. M., *Camp, March and Battlefield*. Philadelphia: J. B. Rodgers, 1865.

Stiles, Robert, *Four Years under Marse Robert*. New York & Washington: The Neale Publ. Co., 1903.

Stillwell, Leander, *The Story of a Common Soldier, or, Army Life in the Civil War*. Kansas City, Mo.: Franklin Hudson Publ. Co., 1920.

Swinton, William, *Campaigns of the Army of the Potomac*. New York: Ch. Scribner's Sons, 1882.

Symonds, Craig L., *The Battlefield Atlas of the Civil War*. Baltimore: Nautical and Aviation Publ. Co., 1983.

Trollope, Anthony, *North America*, 2 vols. New York: Chapman and Hall, 1862.

Urban, John W., *Battlefield and Prison Pen*. Philadelphia: Hubbard Bros., 1882.

Warren, Robert Penn, *The Legacy of the Civil War*. New York: Random House, 1961.

Wheeler, Richard, *Voices of the Civil War*. New York: Thomas Y. Crowell Co., 1976.

Wilkeson, Frank, *Recollections of a Private Soldier in the Army of the Potomac*. New York: G. B. Putnam's Sons, 1887.

Wittenmeyer, Annie, *Under the Guns: A Woman's Reminiscences of the Civil War*. Boston: E. B. Stillings & Co., 1895.

Young, Jesse Bowman, *What a Boy Saw in the Army*. New York: Hunt & Eaton, 1894.

INDEX